R. Gupta's®

POPULAR MASTER GUIDE

DMRC

DELHI METRO RAIL CORPORATION

Junior Engineer

MECHANICAL

Recruitment Exam

by

RPH Editorial Board

RAMESH PUBLISHING HOUSE, NEW DELHI

Published by

O.P. Gupta *for* Ramesh Publishing House

Admin. Office

12-H, New Daryaganj Road, Opp. Officers' Mess,
New Delhi-110002 ☏ 23275224, 23245124

E-mail: info@rameshpublishinghouse.com
For Online Shopping: www.rameshpublishinghouse.com

Showroom

• Balaji Market, Nai Sarak, Delhi-6 ☏ 23253720, 23282525
• 4457, Nai Sarak, Delhi-6, ☏ 23918938

Book Code: R-1789

ISBN: 978-93-5012-719-3

Price: ₹ 330

Printed at: Deepak Offset, Delhi

CONTENTS

PAPER-I

KNOWLEDGE OF DISCIPLINE/TRADE

GENERAL INTELLIGENCE & REASONING, QUANTITATIVE APTITUDE & GENERAL AWARENESS

PAPER-II

SELECTION PROCESS

Scheme of Computer Based Test (CBT)

- The CBT will consist of two papers (Paper-I and Paper-II), to be held on the same day at the same centre.
- Paper-I will consist of multiple-choice objective type questions, bilingual (Hindi/English), on **General Awareness, General Intelligence & Reasoning, Quantitative Aptitude** and **Knowledge of the discipline/trade.**
- In Paper-I, There will be a total of 120 questions, each carrying equal marks. There will be negative marking. For every wrong answer 1/3 marks will be deducted. The Paper-I shall be of 1.5 hours' duration.
- Paper-II will consist of objective type questions on **General English** to judge the knowledge of **English language.** There will be a total of 60 questions, each carrying equal marks. There will be negative marking. For every wrong answer 1/3 marks will be deducted. The Paper-II shall be of 45 minutes' duration.

Previous Paper (Solved)

DMRC–Junior Engineer (Mechanical) Online Exam-2018*

PAPER-I

Knowledge of Discipline / Trade (Mechanical Engineering)

1. Heat is added in the Otto cycle during the:
A. Isentropic process
B. Reversible constant volume process
C. Reversible constant temperature process
D. Reversible constant pressure process

2. Alloy steel containing 23 to 30% chromium with carbon less than 0.35% is known as ______.
A. shock-resistance steel
B. heat-resistance steel
C. magnet steel
D. stainless steel

3. Alloy atoms can form a compound with base metal atoms that forms:
A. Soluble metal
B. Solid solution
C. Intermetallic compound
D. Mechanical mixture

4. The function of a casing in a centrifugal pump is to ______.
A. increase the velocity
B. decrease the pressure
C. decrease the velocity
D. increase the pressure

5. The polar modulus of a shaft is given by:
A. Polar moment of inertia of the shaft/(maximum radius)^3
B. Polar moment of inertia of the shaft/(maximum radius)^2
C. (maximum radius)^2/Polar moment of inertia of the shaft
D. Polar moment of inertia of the shaft/(maximum radius)

6. The load carrying capacity of a bearing can be increased by ______.
A. increasing the speed
B. increasing the Sommerfeld number
C. increasing the minimum film thickness
D. decreasing the velocity

7. In the electronics industry, which welding process is used to connect the leads on small electronic components and in integrated circuitary?
A. Laser beam welding
B. Forge welding
C. Thermite welding
D. Electron beam welding

8. Coefficient of performance (COP) of Carnot heat pump is given by:

[when H $\rightarrow$ High temperature energy reservoir; L $\rightarrow$ Low temperature energy reservoir; T $\rightarrow$ Absolute temperature]

A. $\frac{1}{T_H - T_L}$ B. $1-\frac{T_L}{T_H}$

C. $\frac{T_H}{T_H - T_L}$ D. $\frac{T_L}{T_H - T_L}$

9. Which type of pattern is used to produce a small casting in large quantities in moulding machines?
A. Split pattern
B. Solid pattern
C. Gated pattern
D. Match plate pattern

* Exam Held on 17-04-2018.

10. Continuity equation is given as ______.

A. Q = PV B. $Q = \frac{V}{T}$

C. $Q = \frac{A}{V}$ D. Q = AV

11. Which process is also known as 'lost wax process'?

A. Shell moulding process
B. Centrifugal casting
C. Investment casting
D. Continuous casting

12. Compared to a vapour compression refrigeration system, a vapour absorption system requires ______ effort to compress the fluid refrigerant.

A. less B. either more or less
C. more D. unpredictable

13. For the same temperature of source and sink, the thermal efficiency of Carnot cycle:

A. is less than that of Stirling cycle.
B. is greater than that of Stirling cycle.
C. may be greater or less than that of Stirling cycle depending upon the working substance.
D. is equal to thermal efficiency of Stirling cycle.

14. Thermal efficiency of ideal Otto cycle is given by:

[r = Compression ratio; γ = Adiabatic exponent]

A. $\frac{1}{r^{\gamma-1}}$ B. $1-\frac{1}{r^{\gamma-1}}$

C. $1-\frac{1}{r^{\gamma}}$ D. $r^{\gamma-1}$

15. Entropy:

A. is a point function
B. in a reversible adiabatic process always increases
C. is a path function
D. has the unit of kJ/kg

16. Carnot cycle consists of:

A. Two reversible constant volume and two reversible isentropic process.
B. Two reversible isobaric and two reversible isentropic process.
C. Two reversible isothermal and two reversible isobaric process.
D. Two reversible isothermal and two reversible isentropic process.

17. An Electrolux refrigerator has which of the following working substance(s)?

A. Ammonia, water and hydrogen
B. Ammonia and hydrogen
C. Hydrogen
D. Ammonia and water

18. The cause of friction between two surfaces is ______.

A. load
B. the material & roughness
C. the material
D. roughness

19. What should be the angle between the axes of a two-cylinder V-engine to balance the primary forces completely?

A. 45° B. 60°
C. 30° D. 90°

20. The Francis Turbine consists of _____ blades.

A. 6 to 8 B. 12 to 14
C. 2 to 4 D. 16 to 24

21. In oxyacetylene welding the approximate flame temperature of oxygen and various fuel gas combinations is ______.

A. 3,200°C B. 3,500°C
C. 2,500°C D. 2,100°C

22. Molybdenum high speed steel contains:

A. 6% vanadium, 2% chromium and 4% tungsten
B. 2% vanadium, 4% chromium and 6% tungsten
C. 4% vanadium, 6% chromium and 2% tungsten
D. 2% vanadium, 6% chromium and 4% tungsten

23. Which flame occurs when the oxygen to acetylene ratio is 1.1 to 1?
A. Neutral flame B. Oxydising flame
C. Acetylene flame D. Reducing flame

24. The value of specific speed of turbine is equal to:
A. $\frac{N}{\sqrt{H}}$ B. P
C. $\frac{P}{H}$ D. $\frac{N}{H}$

25. If the air screw of an aeroplane rotates clockwise when viewed from the rear and the aeroplane takes a right turn, the gyroscopic effect will:
A. tend to raise the nose and depress the tail.
B. tend to raise the tail and depress the nose.
C. tilt the aeroplane about spin axis.
D. tilt the aeroplane about neutral axis.

26. Newton's Second Law of Motion gives a relation between force, mass and ______.
A. velocity B. displacement
C. acceleration D. time

27. For complete dynamic balance, at least _____ masses are necessary.
A. three B. one
C. two D. four

28. The casting method which is only adopted for bushings, gun barrels and CI pipes is _____.
A. investment casting
B. slush casting
C. centrifugal casting
D. die casting

29. One of the Tds equation has the form:
A. Tds = dh + pdv B. Tds = dh + vdp
C. Tds = dh – vdp D. Tds = du – pdv

30. The property of a liquid which offers resistance to the movement of fluid is called:
A. elasticity B. volume
C. viscosity D. density

31. The velocity through a pitot tube is given by______.
A. $V = Cvh$ B. $V=\sqrt{2gp}$
C. $V = 2gh$ D. $V=Cv\sqrt{2gh}$

32. A drum weighing 60 N and holding 40 kgf of water is raised from a well by means of a wheel and axle with an effort of 120 N. Its mechanical advantage (MA) will be _____.
A. 0.83 B. 4.5
C. 3.77 D. 3

33. For a cantilever beam of length L carrying a uniform distribution load W over the whole length, what will be the value of the maximum bending moment?
A. $\frac{WL}{2}$ B. $\frac{WL^2}{4}$
C. $\frac{WL^2}{2}$ D. $\frac{-WL^2}{2}$

34. If a simple screw jack has a thread of 10 mm, pitch and length of the handle is 400 mm, then its velocity ratio (V.R.) will be ____.
A. 0.62 B. 125.6
C. 80 D. 25.13

35. The unit of specific heat is _____.
A. KJ/Kg°K B. KJ/Kg
C. KJ/°K D. KJ-Kg

36. The zeroth law of thermodynamics defines _______.
A. temperature
B. pressure
C. internal energy
D. enthalpy

37. The ratio of the polar moment of inertia of the shaft section to the maximum radius is called _______.
A. moment of resistance
B. modulus of rigidity of shaft
C. polar modulus
D. sectional modulus

38. The relationship between the coefficient of performance of refrigerator ($[COP]_R$) and coefficient of performance of heat pump ($[COP]_{HP}$) is given as:
A. $[COP]_R = 2[COP]_{HP}$
B. $[COP]_{HP} = [COP]_R$
C. $[COP]_R = [COP]_{HP} - 1$
D. $[COP]_R = [COP]_{HP} + 1$

39. A system is said to be in equilibrium when the resultant of all forces acting on it is ______.
A. negative B. infinity
C. zero D. one

40. The magnitude of the gyroscopic couple applied to a disc of moment of inertia I, spinning with angular velocity *w* and having an angular velocity of precision w_p is ______.
A. Iww_p B. I^2ww_p
C. Iww_p^2 D. Iw^2w_p

41. Priming is required for a _____ pump.
A. submersible B. gear
C. reciprocating D. centrifugal

42. In Otto cycle, if the pressure at the beginning of the compression is 1 bar and at the end of the compression is 10 bar, then the compression ratio will be given as:
[$\gamma = 1.4$]
A. $(10)^{1.4}$ B. 10
C. $\frac{1}{10}$ D. $(10)^{1/1.4}$

43. Heat is rejected in the diesel cycle:
A. during the reversible constant pressure process
B. during the reversible isothermal process
C. during the isentropic process
D. during the reversible constant volume process

44. If the distance moved by a load is 5 mm and the distance moved by effort is 250 mm, then the velocity ratio of a simple machine will be ______.
A. 30 B. 0.02
C. 50 D. 40

45. When stress (σ) and elasticity (E) remain constant, the energy absorbing capacity of dynamic forces, is a function of its _____.
A. width
B. length
C. cross-section
D. volume

46. The function of boiler in the Rankine power cycle is:
A. The addition of heat at constant pressure
B. The addition of heat at constant temperature
C. The addition of heat at constant entropy
D. The addition of heat at constant volume

47. The design of the Pelton wheel is NOT based on the:
A. diameter of the jet.
B. diameter of the wheel.
C. number of buckets.
D. length of the wheel.

48. 1 Pascal is equal to ______ .
A. 1 MN/m^2 B. 1 KN/m^2
C. 1 GN/m^2 D. 1 N/m^2

49. A venturimeter is used for the measurement of ______.
A. pressure B. discharge
C. volume D. velocity

50. In case of impulse turbine, the pressure of steam as it passes on the moving blades from entry to the exit _____.
A. initially increases and then decrease
B. increases
C. remains constant
D. decreases

51. Good moulding sand contains _____ per cent of silica sand (SiO_2).
A. 80.8 B. 1.5
C. 14.9 D. 2.5

52. Austenitic stainless steel contains ______.
A. 8% chromium and 18% nickel
B. 18% chromium and 18% nickel
C. 18% chromium and 8% nickel
D. 8% chromium and 8% nickel

53. An impulse turbine is used for ______.
A. medium head B. low head
C. zero head D. high head

54. The axis of spin, the axis of precision and the axis of gyroscopic torque are in _____.
A. three perpendicular planes
B. three parallel planes
C. two perpendicular planes
D. two parallel planes

55. For a simply supported beam carrying a uniformly distributed load (W) over full length (*l*) of beam, what will be the value of the maximum bending moment?

A. $\frac{Wl^2}{2}$ B. $\frac{Wl}{4}$

C. $\frac{Wl^2}{8}$ D. $\frac{Wl^2}{4}$

56. The specific weight (*w*) of a fluid is given by the equation ______.

A. $w = \frac{\rho}{g}$ B. $w = \rho^2 \times g$

C. $w = \rho \times g/2$ D. $w = \rho \times g$

57. The friction of a body is high when the coefficient of friction is ______.
A. low B. average
C. high D. zero

58. According to _____ law, the intensity of pressure at any point in a fluid at rest is the same in all directions.
A. Newton's B. Boyle's
C. Bernaulli's D. Pascal's

59. In a stress-strain curve of brittle materials, the ultimate stress point and break point are ______.
A. the same B. not the same
C. maximum D. minimum

60. In a simple machine, if the mechanical advantage is 40 and the velocity ratio is 50, then its efficiency is ______.
A. 80% B. 70%
C. 75% D. 85%

61. Manometers are used for the measurement of ______.
A. velocity B. pressure
C. volume D. temperature

62. A standard or double housing planer of size 750 mm × 350 mm × 2.5 mm means that a planer can machine a work of:
A. width 750, height 350 and length 2.5.
B. height 750, length 350 and width 2.5.
C. length 750, width 350 and height 2.5.
D. height 750, width 350 and length 2.5.

63. Vickers hardness test is calculated by the formula ______.
A. VHN = 1.845 P/D^2
B. VHN = 1.845 D/P^2
C. VHN = 1.854 D/P^2
D. VHN = 1.854 P/D^2

64. The maximum stress which a material can withstand before it fractures is called ______.
A. yield point stress
B. allowable stress
C. breaking stress
D. ultimate stress

65. Clausius' inequality is given by:
[Q = Heat transferred, T = Temperature of boundary]

A. $\oint \frac{\delta Q}{T} \geq 0$ B. $\oint \frac{\delta Q}{T} = 0$

C. $\oint \frac{\delta Q}{T} \leq 0$ D. $\oint \frac{\delta T}{T} \leq 0$

66. A swab is used in casting for:
A. repairing and finishing the pattern
B. cleaning mould sand
C. moistening the sand around the edge before a moving pattern
D. reinforcement of sand in the top part of a moulding box

67. The Poisson's ratio of cast iron is ______.
A. 0.27 B. 0.30
C. 0.29 D. 0.28

68. The load at which the column member just buckles is called _____.

A. breaking load B. point load
C. crippling load D. design load

69. 1 poise is equal to _______.

A. 0.8 N.sec/m^2 B. 2 N.sec/m^2
C. 1/10 N.sec/m^2 D. 1/20 N.sec/m^2

70. The relation F = $m \times a$ is based on ______.

A. Newton's third law of motion
B. D'Alembert's principle
C. Newton's first law of motion
D. Newton's second law of motion

71. The ratio of transverse displacement to the distance from the lower face is called _________.

A. shear strain B. longitudinal strain
C. lateral strain D. tensile strain

72. The velocity ratio of a simple screw jack is given by ——.

A. $\frac{2\pi}{p}$ B. $\frac{\pi l}{p}$

C. $\frac{2l}{p}$ D. $\frac{2\pi l}{p}$

73. The ratio of the brake power output to the fuel energy input per unit time is called ______.

A. relative efficiency
B. thermal efficiency
C. volumetric efficiency
D. mechanical efficiency

74. If the function angle (ϕ) is 30° for the forward moving object on a rough horizontal surface, then the friction multiple (μ) will be ____.

A. 0.422
B. 0.211
C. 0.877
D. 0.577

75. In which way the efficiency of the Rankine cycle expressed?

[w_{net} = Net work output of the cycle (kJ/kg)

q_{in} = Heat given in cycle (kJ/kg)

q_{out} = Heat liberated from cycle (kJ/kg)]

A. $\frac{q_{out}}{q_{in}}$ B. $1-\frac{w_{net}}{q_{out}}$

C. $\frac{w_{net}}{q_{in}}$ D. $1-\frac{w_{net}}{q_{in}}$

General Awareness, General Intelligence & Reasoning and Quantitative Aptitude

76. The Doklam Standoff is a border dispute between which of the following two countries?

A. India and Bangladesh
B. India and China
C. India and Nepal
D. India and Pakistan

77. Who won the Man Booker Prize for Fiction for 2017?

A. Haun Kong
B. Marlon James
C. George Saunders
D. Arundhati Roy

78. For framing the Indian Constitution, Dr. B.R. Ambedkar was the chairman of which of the following committees?

A. Drafting committee
B. Rules of precedure committee
C. Provincial constitution committee
D. Union powers committee

79. Which Act was passed in India in 1976 to prohibit the smuggling of human organs and the activity of forced labour?

A. Labour Eradication Act
B. Juvenile Labour Eradication Act
C. Bonded Labour System Eradication Act
D. Unlawful Labour Eradication Act

80. Which of the following rivers is the only river found in Indian desert?

A. Ravi B. Tapi
C. Looni D. Vyas (Byas)

81. Which global credit rating agency has a significant stake in the Indian credit rating agency ICRA?

A. Moody's Investors Service
B. Fitch Ratings
C. Standard and Poor's
D. Morningstar, Inc.

82. Budget 2018 set emoluments to the President at ₹ _____ lakh.

A. 10 B. 2.5
C. 5 D. 7

83. Purana Quila in Delhi was built by _____.

A. Firoze Shah Tughlaq
B. Bahlol Lodi and Ibrahim Lodi
C. Humayun and Sher Shah
D. Babur and Humayun

84. Kohima is the capital of which state of India?

A. Manipur B. Nagaland
C. Mizoram D. Meghalaya

85. Siliguri is located in _____ .

A. Assam B. West Bengal
C. Bhutan D. Nepal

86. The paintings at the famous Ajanta Caves (and not Ellora) are devoted to _____.

A. Christianity B. Buddhism
C. Jainism D. Hinduism

87. Which player has been selected by the Badminton Association of India (BAI) for its first Lifetime Achievement Award?

A. Pullela Gopichand
B. SM Arif
C. Chetan Anand
D. Prakash Padukone

88. Muhammad Quli Qutub Shah founded the city of _____.

A. Aurangabad
B. Hyderabad
C. Ahmedabad
D. Golconda

89. As on February 2018, the fiscal deficit for 2017-18 was _____.

A. 3.50%
B. 4.20%
C. 5.60%
D. 7.80%

90. Mahatma Gandhi led the famous Dandi March (Salt Satyagraha) in March _____.

A. 1934
B. 1932
C. 1931
D. 1930

91. 5 gm of a mixed metal contains $3\frac{3}{4}$ gm copper and the rest gold. Find the ratio of the weight of Gold and Copper.

A. 3 : 4 B. 1 : 3
C. 4 : 3 D. 3 : 1

92. The numbers X, Y, Z are in Arithmetic series. If X + Y + Z = 27 and XYZ = 648. Then X ÷ Y × Z = _____.

A. 8 B. 4
C. 12 D. 6

93. The average temperature of Monday, Tuesday, Wednesday and Thursday was 48° while on Tuesday, Wednesday, Thursday and Friday it was 46°. If the temperature on Monday was 46° then find the temperature on Friday.

A. 35 B. 34
C. 38 D. 39

94. An observer of height 1.8 km is standing 20.5 in away from a tower of 22.3 m height. What is the angle of elevation from the eye of the observer to the top of the tower?

A. 75° B. 45°
C. 60° D. 30°

95. If the cost price of an item is 75% of its selling price, find the percentage of profit.

A. $33\frac{1}{3}\%$ B. $33\frac{2}{3}\%$
C. 33% D. 25%

96. The efficiency of A is double that of B. If they can complete a job in 20 hours by working together, then how many days will A take to complete the same job working alone?

A. 30 B. 40
C. 60 D. 50

97. If the angle B in a right-angle triangle ABC is the right-angle, Base AB = 2 cm and Altitude BC = 3 cm, then $\sin^2 A$ = ?

A. $\frac{9}{\sqrt{13}}$ B. $\frac{9}{13}$
C. $\frac{3}{\sqrt{13}}$ D. $\frac{13}{9}$

98. Three friends go together for a walk. The lengths of their paces are 36 cm, 80 cm and 90 cm respectively. What is the maximum distance each friend may cover if he covers it with the whole number of his full paces?

A. 2 m 40 cm B. 7 m 20 cm
C. 7 m 80 cm D. 2 cm

99. Which of the following is a pair of co-indivisible number?

A. 2, 24 B. 3, 15
C. 25, 65 D. 8, 27

100. If $\frac{1}{2}$ is a root of the equation $x^2 + kx - \frac{5}{4} = 0$, then k = ______.

A. –2 B. –4
C. 2 D. 4

101. The HCF of $xy + y^2$, $xy - y^2$ and $x^2y^2 - y^2$ is:

A. $y(x - y)$ B. $y(x + y)$
C. y D. $y^2(x + y)(x - y)$

102. There is spirit and water in a utensil in the ratio of 3 : 5. How much water should be added to 800 ml of this solution to make the ratio of spirit and water 12 : 25?

A. 130 ml
B. 125 ml
C. 120 ml
D. 100 ml

103. P and Q borrowed ₹ 22,400 and ₹ X at the rate of 12% per annum compound interest for 2 and 3 years respectively. If the maturity value of both the loans is the same, then X = ?

A. ₹ 20,400 B. ₹ 20,000
C. ₹ 20.800 D. ₹ 21,200

104. A person is running on a circular track at the speed of 18 km/hr. If he completes a round in 2.2 minute, then what is the radius of the track?

A. 105 m B. 110 m
C. 115 m D. 95 m

105. A person sold an item at a loss of 30%. Had he charged ₹ 900 more for it, he would have earned a profit of 15%. Find the cost-price of the item.

A. ₹ 2,200 B. ₹ 3,000
C. ₹ 2,000 D. ₹ 1,800

106. Few equations are solved on the basis of a set pattern. Select the appropriate option out of the four for the unsolved equation on the basis of the same.

16 + 25 = 9, 36 + 9 = 9, 49 + 16 = ?

A. 11 B. 65
C. –11 D. 13

107. In a code language, GEAR is written as 2143, TAN as 546 and STAR as 7543, then how will NEAT be written in the same code language?

A. 6234
B. 5431
C. 2361
D. 6145

108. Shivam walks on foot from his home to temple. First, he walks 2 km towards the East, then turns to left and walks 3 km. In the end, he turns right and walks 2 km to reach the temple. In which direction is the temple situated in respect of Shivam's house?

A. South-West
B. South-East
C. North-West
D. North-East

109. Six friends P, Q, R, S, T and U are sitting in a circle facing each other. Each person is sitting exactly opposite to the other. R is not sitting adjacent to T or U. S is sitting adjacent to Q on the right side. Q is sitting exactly opposite P. U is sitting adjacent to T on the left side. Neither P nor S is sitting opposite R. Who is sitting opposite U?

A. S B. R
C. P D. Q

110. Which word CANNOT be formed using letters of the given word not more than the number of times each letter appears in the given word?
DIRECTION

A. INCITE B. DOCTOR
C. EDITION D. DOCTRINE

111. Select the option that is related to the third term in the same manner as second term is related to the first term.

4 : 80 : 7 : ?

A. 216 B. 392
C. 343 D. 49

112. If '÷' sign and '–' sign are interchanged and number '5' and number '3' are interchanged them. What will be the value of the given expression?

(60 – 3) ÷ 5 = ?

A. 9 B. 25
C. 4 D. 15

113. In a code language ENUMERATE is written as MUNEETAR. How will DOMINATED be written in the same code language?

A. MODINTEDA
B. IMODNDETA
C. TEDANMODI
D. ATEDNIMOD

114. Select the option that is related to the third term in the same manner as second term is related to the first term.

1 : 1 : : 3 : ?

A. 15 B. 30
C. 6 D. 27

115. Select the option that is related to the third term in the same way as the second term is related to the first term.

Major : Minor : : Shallow : ?

A. Brim
B. Water
C. Surface
D. Deep

116. If FROG is called SNAKE; SNAKE is called DUCK; DUCK is called SPARROW; and SPARROW is called DOG, which of the following animals will be a reptile?

A. FROG B. DOG
C. SPARROW D. DUCK

117. Select the most appropriate option to fill in the blank.

0, 20, 50, 90, 140, 200, _____

A. 300 B. 260
C. 270 D. 250

118. In a bicycle race, Leela finished the race before Bela. Veena finished before Sheena and Sasha finished before Asha. If Bela finished the race before Sasha and Leela finished after Sheena, then who among the friends finished the race at the record place?

A. Leela B. Asha
C. Sheena D. Veena

119. Select the most appropriate option to fill in the blank.

$4, 2, 1, \frac{1}{2}, \frac{1}{4},$ _____

A. $\frac{1}{7}$ B. $\frac{1}{8}$

C. $\frac{1}{6}$ D. $\frac{1}{5}$

120. Brajesh is the only son of father in law of Pallavi's husband. Brajesh has a son named Ajeet. How is Pallavi related to Ajeet?

A. Niece
B. Aunt
C. Mother-in-law
D. Mother

ANSWERS

1	2	3	4	5	6	7	8	9	10
B	B	C	D	D	A	A	C	D	D
11	**12**	**13**	**14**	**15**	**16**	**17**	**18**	**19**	**20**
C	A	D	B	A	D	A	B	D	D
21	**22**	**23**	**24**	**25**	**26**	**27**	**28**	**29**	**30**
A	B	A	A	B	C	C	C	C	C
31	**32**	**33**	**34**	**35**	**36**	**37**	**38**	**39**	**40**
D	C	D	D	A	A	C	C	C	A
41	**42**	**43**	**44**	**45**	**46**	**47**	**48**	**49**	**50**
D	D	D	C	D	A	D	D	B	C
51	**52**	**53**	**54**	**55**	**56**	**57**	**58**	**59**	**60**
A	C	D	A	B	D	C	D	A	A
61	**62**	**63**	**64**	**65**	**66**	**67**	**68**	**69**	**70**
B	A	D	D	C	C	A	C	C	D
71	**72**	**73**	**74**	**75**	**76**	**77**	**78**	**79**	**80**
A	D	B	D	C	B	C	A	C	C
81	**82**	**83**	**84**	**85**	**86**	**87**	**88**	**89**	**90**
A	C	C	B	B	B	D	B	A	D
91	**92**	**93**	**94**	**95**	**96**	**97**	**98**	**99**	**100**
B	A	C	B	A	A	B	B	D	C
101	**102**	**103**	**104**	**105**	**106**	**107**	**108**	**109**	**110**
C	B	B	A	C	A	D	D	A	B
111	**112**	**113**	**114**	**115**	**116**	**117**	**118**	**119**	**120**
B	A	B	D	D	D	C	C	B	B

PAPER-II

GENERAL ENGLISH

Directions (Q. Nos. 1-5): *Read the following passage and answer the questions below.*

There are many ways of communicating without using speech. Signals, signs, symbols and gestures may be found in every known culture. The basic function of a signal is to impinge upon the environment in such a way that it attracts attention, as for example, the dots and dashes of a telegraph circuit, Coded to refer to speech, the potential for communication is very great. While less adaptable to the codification of words, signs contain greater meaning in and of themselves. A stop sign or a petrol bunk sign conveys meaning quickly and conveniently. Symbols are more difficult to understand than either signals or signs because of their *intricate* relationship with the receiver's cultural perceptions. In some cultures, applauding in a theatre provides performers with an auditory symbol of approval. Gestures such as waving and shaking hands also communicate certain cultural messages.

1. The word 'intricate' as found in the passage means _____.
   A. difficult
   B. complex
   C. interior
   D. complicated

2. When does the author consider the potential for communication to be high?
   A. When speech is not used.
   B. When the communication becomes a symbol of approval.
   C. When signals are coded to refer to speech.
   D. When meanings are conveyed quickly.

3. It can be inferred that the passage talks about different aspects of _____.
   A. written language
   B. oral language
   C. non-verbal language
   D. verbal language

4. A sign may be defined as something that is
   A. less able to be adapted to refer to speech.
   B. an interruption in the environment.
   C. more difficult to describe than other forms of communication.
   D. a gesture.

5. What is an example of a sign as found in the passage?
   A. An applauding sign
   B. The dots and dashes sign
   C. A petrol bunk sign
   D. A telegraphic circuit sign

6. The antonym of youthful is _____.
   A. active B. young
   C. elderly D. tiresome

7. Identify the error in the sentence given:
   The drank men have been causing problems at the traffic junction since late afternoon.
   A. at the traffic junction
   B. The drank men
   C. since late afternoon
   D. have been causing problems

8. Identify which type of noun the underlined word is:
   Would you like to have some <u>cheese</u>?
   A. Proper Noun B. Common Noun
   C. Abstract Noun D. Collective

9. Identify which type of adverb the underlined word:
   It is surprising that both the horses galloped <u>away</u>.
   A. Adverb of place B. Adverb of reason
   C. Adverb of manner D. Adverb of degree

10. Fill in the blanks with appropriate preposition:
    What time does this train get _____ Chennai?
    A. to B. at
    C. in D. until

11. The synonym of rubble is ______.
A. stubble B. rabble
C. debris D. confuse

12. Transform the sentences into indirect speech:
The teacher said, "Have you done your homework, Vishal?"
A. The teacher asked Vishal if he did his homework.
B. The teacher asked Vishal if he has done his homework.
C. The teacher asked Vishal if he had done his homework.
D. The teacher asked if Vishal done his homework.

13. The word 'perpetual' can be used as a synonym for ______.
A. viewpoint B. position
C. unending D. final

14. Fill in the blanks with appropriate preposition:
The actor got ____ the car and drove away.
A. after B. where
C. into D. till

15. Identify the error in the sentence given:
The two tenants staying on the first floor yell loudly early in the morning.
A. yell loudly
B. The two tenants
C. early in the morning
D. staying on the first floor

16. Identify the underlined conjunction:
You must either follow my instructions or resign
A. Phrase conjunction
B. Co-ordinating conjunction
C. Subordinating conjunction
D. Correlative conjunction

17. Change the voice of the sentence:
Several innovations have been introduced by us in the field of medical technology.
A. We had introduced several innovations in the field of medical technology.
B. We introduced several innovations in the field of medical technology.
C. We have introduced several innovations in the field of medical technology.
D. We shall introduce several innovations in the field of medical technology.

18. The antonym of dependent is ______.
A. dependable B. autonomous
C. diverse D. ample

19. Identify the error in the sentence given:
Sam wishes to tell everyone about the books that has changed his life.
A. about the books
B. that has changed his life.
C. everyone
D. Sam wishes to tell

20. Change the voice of the sentence:
This picture was painted by Satish Mathur
A. Satish Mathur had painted this picture.
B. Satish Mathur paints this picture.
C. Satish Mathur has painted this picture.
D. Satish Mathur painted this picture.

21. _____ is a synonym of secret.
A. Cryptic B. Overt
C. Cryogenic D. Synchronic

22. The word 'achievement' is a synonym of ___.
A. feat B. effort
C. successful D. exert

23. Identify the error in the sentence given:
I've heard that both Nirmala and her friend has been preparing hard for the entrance exam.
A. both Nirmala and her friend
B. has been preparing hard
C. for the entrance exam
D. I've heard that

24. Identify the error in the sentence given:
Where have you been? Run fastly and try to board the bus.
A. and try to board
B. Where have you bean?
C. the bus
D. Run fastly

25. Rash is the antonym of _____.
A. careful B. irritation
C. reckless D. reaction

26. Transform the sentences into indirect speech: The manager said to the employees, "I shall pay your wages tomorrow."

A. The manager told the employees that he shall pay their wages tomorrow.

B. The manager told the employees that he shall pay their wages the next day.

C. The manager told the employees that he may pay their wages the next day.

D. The manager told the employees that he shall pay the wages the next day.

27. Transform the sentences into indirect speech: "Please take me to your officer," said the visitor to the constables.

A. The visitor demanded that the constables to take him to their officer.

B. The visitor told the constables to take him to their officer.

C. The visitor demanded the constables to take him to their officer.

D. The visitor requested the constables to take him to their officer.

28. Identify the error in the sentence given: After the meeting was over, I returned back to Delhi.

A. I returned back   B. was over

C. to Delhi   D. After the meeting

29. Identify the error in the sentence given: My proposal for introducing diploma courses have been submitted to the management for approval.

A. My proposal for

B. introducing diploma courses

C. have been submitted

D. to the management for approval.

30. The synonym of Persistent is ______.

A. attempt   B. continual

C. intermittent   D. sporadic

31. Change the voice of the sentence: A possible connection between cancer and smoking has been shown by research.

A. Research is shown a possible connection between cancer and smoking.

B. Research had shown a possible connection between cancer and smoking.

C. Research has shown a possible connection between cancer and smoking.

D. Research has showed a possible connection between cancer and smoking.

32. Change the voice of the sentence: Many people believe that a knowledge of English is indispensable.

A. It was believed by many people that knowledge of English is indispensable.

B. It is being believed by many people that knowledge of English is indispensable.

C. It is believed by many people that knowledge of English is indispensable.

D. Many people have a belief that knowledge of English is indispensable.

33. Identify which type of adverb is the underlined word: Both the boys arrived early for the interview.

A. Adverb of degree

B. Adverb of manner

C. Adverb of time

D. Adverb of frequency

34. Transform the sentences into indirect speech: The nurse said, "Alas! The poor woman died yesterday."

A. The nurse exclaimed in sorrow that the poor woman had died the yesterday.

B. The nurse exclaimed in sorrow that the poor woman had died the previous day.

C. The nurse exclaimed that the poor woman had died yesterday.

D. The nurse said that the poor woman had died the previous day.

35. Change the voice of the sentence: It is reported that the museum has been badly damaged by the fire.

A. The museum is reported to be badly damaged by the fire.

B. The museum is reported to have badly damaged by the fire.

C. The museum is being reported to have bee damaged by the fire.

D. The museum is reported to have been badly damaged by the fire.

36. Choose the correct meaning of the underlined words/phrases:
Our Maths professor is <u>every inch</u> a true gentleman.
A. fabulously B. mercifully
C. completely D. benevolently

37. Identify which type of adverb is the underlined word:
Let's not go to the beach today. The sea appears <u>very</u> stormy.
A. Adverb of place B. Adverb of manner
C. Adverb of degree D. Adverb of reason

38. Identify the underlined part of speech in the given sentence:
<u>Ouch</u>! That was a sharp prick on the finger.
A. Conjunction B. Interjection
C. Adjective D. Adverb

39. Transform the sentences into indirect speech:
Sita said, "Mother, I am hungry."
A. Sita told her mother that she was hungry.
B. Sita told her mother that she is hungry.
C. Sita told her mother that I am hungry.
D. Sita told her mother that I was hungry.

40. Choose the correct meanings of the underlined words/phrases:
Many leaders have found the issue of unemployment <u>a tough nut to crack</u>.
A. cracking the issue
B. a difficult problem to solve
C. tougher than expected
D. problematic to open

41. The word 'vociferous' is an antonym of ____.
A. unnatural B. powerful
C. quiet D. harmless

42. Enlarge is a synonym of ______.
A. magnify B. shorten
C. condense D. cover

43. The synonym of confer is ______.
A. accept B. grant
C. coniferous D. refuse

44. Identify which type of adverb is the underlined word:
You have repeated this error <u>thrice</u>.
A. Adverb of manner
B. Adverb of time
C. Adverb of degree
D. Adverb of frequency

45. Choose the correct meanings of the underlined words/phrases:
I heard that Mr. Sunil Kumar, our physics teacher is leaving school <u>for good.</u>
A. temporarily B. permanently
C. at last D. in a good manner

46. Identify which type of pronoun the underlined word is:
I don't eat tomatoes as I'm allergic to <u>them.</u>
A. reflexive B. possessive
C. relative D. personal

47. Identify the error in the sentence given:
In the past, young boys had been enjoying to play football. But now they are too studious.
A. young boys had been enjoying to play football
B. they are too studious
C. In the past
D. But now

48. Identify the underlined part of speech in the given sentence:
Sunil is a millionaire. He has <u>enough</u> money.
A. Interjection B. Noun
C. Adjective D. Adverb

49. Choose the correct meanings of the underlined words/phrases:
The employees sometimes have to work ten hours <u>at a stretch.</u>
A. patiently B. continuously
C. moderately D. deliberately

50. Identify the underlined part of speech in the given sentence:
Sorry Sir. I could not get <u>any</u> sugar from the shop.
A. Conjunction B. Verb
C. Adverb D. Adjective

51. Identify which type of adverb is the underlined word:
Sachin played <u>fabulously</u> to score a double century.
A. Adverb of manner

B. Adverb of frequency
C. Adverb of reason
D. Adverb of negation

52. Fill in the blanks with appropriate preposition:
The monkey climbed ______ our house through the window.
A. into   B. to
C. in   D. at

53. Fill in the blanks with appropriate preposition:
The teacher explained that water boils _____ 100 degree celsius.
A. on   B. until
C. at   D. in

54. Fill in the blanks with appropriate preposition:
The workers have gone _____ strike demanding better pay.
A. for   B. in
C. on   D. into

55. Identify the error in the sentence given:
The engineer and his assistant, though working closely for long hours, does not like each other.
A. does not like each other
B. The engineer and his assistant
C. though working closely
D. for long hours

56. Kindle is an antonym of _____ .
A. dwindle   B. ignite
C. arouse   D. extinguish

57. Identify which type of noun the underlined word is:
<u>Shimla</u> is one of the most beautiful places I've seen.
A. Common   B. Proper
C. Material   D. Collective

58. Identify which type of pronoun the underlined word is:
I went to the zoo with a friend of <u>mine.</u>
A. possessive   B. personal
C. relative   D. reflexive

59. Identify the error in the sentence given:
In spite of the medication Ramesh is been having, he continues to be in a critical condition.
A. Ramesh is been having
B. he continues to be
C. In spite of the medication
D. in a critical condition

60. The synonym of meticulous is:
A. delicious   B. thorough
C. careless   D. through

ANSWERS

1	2	3	4	5	6	7	8	9	10
B	C	C	A	C	C	B	B	A	A
11	**12**	**13**	**14**	**15**	**16**	**17**	**18**	**19**	**20**
C	C	C	C	A	D	C	B	B	D
21	**22**	**23**	**24**	**25**	**26**	**27**	**28**	**29**	**30**
A	A	B	D	A	B	D	A	C	B
31	**32**	**33**	**34**	**35**	**36**	**37**	**38**	**39**	**40**
C	C	C	B	D	C	C	B	A	B
41	**42**	**43**	**44**	**45**	**46**	**47**	**48**	**49**	**50**
C	A	B	D	B	D	A	C	B	D
51	**52**	**53**	**54**	**55**	**56**	**57**	**58**	**59**	**60**
A	A	C	C	A	D	B	A	A	B

Previous Paper (Solved)

DMRC–Junior Engineer (Mechanical) Online Exam-2017*

PAPER-I

Knowledge of Discipline / Trade (Mechanical Engineering)

1. Orifice meter is the application of:
A. Pitot tube
B. Bourdon's tube
C. Venturimeter
D. Bernoulli's theorem

2. Any point on a link connecting double slider crank chain will trace a:
A. Hyperbola B. Parabola
C. Ellipse D. Circle

3. Grey cast iron has:
A. Low compressive strength
B. Carbon in the form of free graphite
C. High tensile strength
D. High stiffness

4. Which of the following is related to Age hardening?
A. Duralumin B. Brass
C. Copper D. Silver

5. 1 TON of Refrigeration is:
A. 10.258 kW B. 96.8 kW
C. 3.518 kW D. 1.38 kW

6. If all variables of a steam are independent of time, it is said to be in:
A. Unsteady flow B. Uniform flow
C. Closed flow D. Steady flow

7. Orifice meter is the application of:
A. Bernoulli's equation
B. Continuity equation
C. Pascal's law
D. Newton's law

8. The cupola furnace is used to manufacture:
A. Wrought iron B. Pig iron
C. Steel D. Cast iron

9. Useful power available at crankshaft is known as:
A. Friction power B. Indicated power
C. Thermal power D. Brake power

10. Which of the below are applications of inversions of the slider crank mechanisms?
1. Oscillating cylinder engine mechanism
2. Toggle mechanism
3. Indexing mechanisms
4. Whitworth quick return mechanism
A. 2 and 3 B. 3 and 4
C. 1 and 2 D. 1 and 4

11. When two non-intersecting and non-coplanar shafts are connected by gears, the arrangement is known as:
A. bevel gearing B. helical gearing
C. spiral gearing D. spur gearing

12. A pulley and belt in a belt drive forms:
A. rolling pair B. sliding pair
C. turning pair D. cylindrical pair

13. A pitot tube directed into a water stream having a velocity 2.5 m/sec. It has a gauge difference of 20 cm on mercury water manometer, then coefficient of velocity is equal to:
A. 2.22 B. 1.26
C. 1.12 D. 3.33

* Exam Held on 18-02-2017.

14. What is property of a sand due to which it evolves a great amount of steam and other gases?
A. Permeability B. Adhesiveness
C. Cohesiveness D. Collapsibility

15. The machining of copper will be improved by addition of:
A. Sulphur B. Zinc
C. Tin D. Vanadium

16. What is the process for improving fatigue resistance of the metal by setting of compressive stresses in its surface?
A. Hot piercing B. Extrusion
C. Cold peening D. Cold heading

17. Which test can be considered only for multi-cylinder engine?
A. Motoring test
B. Morse test
C. Brake test
D. Frictional power test

18. Which cycle is most preferred in gas turbine?
A. Otto cycle B. Dual cycle
C. Brayton cycle D. Diesel cycle

19. The stiffness is the ability of the material to resist:
A. Deformation within plastic limit
B. Deflection under stress
C. Externally applied force with breakdown or yielding
D. Fracture due to high impact loads

20. Internal energy of ideal gas is a function of:
A. Temperature alone
B. Pressure and temperature
C. Temperature and volume
D. Pressure and volume

21. A combination of simple machines is known as ______.
A. A machine
B. Work
C. A simple machine
D. A compound machine

22. Which is the latest law passed by Indian government against pollution?
A. BS V B. BS IV
C. BS I D. BS II

23. The type of bearing used in crankshaft is:
A. Ball bearing B. Plain bearing
C. Magnetic bearing D. Roller bearing

24. Which load acts on bearing in its plane of rotation?
A. thrust load B. axial load
C. point load D. radial load

25. The moment due to friction, in a flat collar pivot bearing is proportional to:
A. $\frac{(r_1^3 - r_2^3)}{(r_1 - r_2)}$ B. $\frac{(r_1^2 - r_2^2)}{(r_1 + r_2)}$
C. $\frac{(r_1^2 - r_2^2)}{(r_1 - r_2)}$ D. $\frac{(r_1^3 - r_2^3)}{(r_1^2 - r_2^2)}$

26. Variation of bending moment due to concentrated loads will be:
A. circular B. parabolic
C. cubical D. linear

27. The intensity of pressure in KPa of oil with specific gravity 0.8 equivalent to 40 m of water is:
A. 313.9 KPa B. 313920 KPa
C. 320 KPa D. 311.5 KPa

28. The equation PV = mRT holds good for which gas?
A. Monoatomic gas B. Diatomic gas
C. Real gas D. Ideal gas

29. To drain out the floody water which pump is used?
A. Gear pump
B. Vane pump
C. Centrifugal pump
D. Reciprocating pump

30. The maximum fluctuating energy for a flywheel is given by _____ (with usual notations)
A. 2 ECs B. 2 ECs^2
C. ECs/2 D. 2 E^2Cs

31. The process in which temperature remains constant is known as:
A. Isochoric B. Isentropic
C. Isobaric D. Isothermal

32. NPSH is required for:
A. Turbine B. Centrifugal pump
C. Motor D. Gear pump

33. The recrystallization temperature of steel is:
A. 800°C B. 900°C
C. 600°C D. 400°C

34. How much per cent of inhalation of CO causes human death?
A. 0% B. 0.3%
C. 0.9% D. 1%

35. In the study of hydraulic pump, NPSH stands for:
A. Net Positive Suction Head
B. New Positive Suction Head
C. Net Pressure Suction Head
D. Net Positive Small Head

36. Work place centre in centerless grinding will be:
A. Above the line joining the two wheel centers
B. On the line joining the two wheel centers
C. At the intersection of the line joining the wheel centers with the work place plane
D. Below the line joining the two wheel centers

37. The working principle of hydraulic trubine is:
A. Newtons law
B. Bernaullis principle
C. Mass inertia
D. Impulse momentum

38. The Calorific value in S.I. engine is:
A. Very low B. Medium
C. Low D. High

39. Which sliding bearing operates without any lubrication?
A. hydrostatic lubricated bearing
B. hydro-dynamic lubricated bearing
C. boundary lubricated bearing
D. zero film bearing

40. CNG cylinder Engine is known as:
A. S.E. B. C.E.
C. C.I. D. S.I.

41. Working principle of planer is:
A. Tool moves over stationary work
B. Tool is stationary and work reciprocates
C. Tool moves over reciprocating work
D. Work is stationary and tool reciprocates

42. According to Joule's law, the internal energy of a perfect gas is the function of absolute:
A. density B. temperature
C. volume D. pressure

43. What does steel contain?
A. 50% or more iron
B. Elements like phosphorus. sulphur and silicon in varying quantities
C. Alloying elements like chromium, tungsten nickel and copper
D. Less than 50% iron

44. The chip space between the back of one tooth and the face of the next tooth, in a plane million cutter is called:
A. Gash B. Fillet
C. Land D. Face

45. At the point of contra flexure, the bending moment is:
A. bending moment is zero or changes sign
B. bending moment is maximum
C. bending moment is minimum
D. shearing force is maximum

46. Total number of pitches in a riveted joint are:
A. Two B. Five
C. Four D. Three

47. What are the units of moment of inertia of an area?
A. kg/m^2 B. m^3
C. m^4 D. $kg\text{-}m^2$

48. The Ideal cycle is also known as:
A. Brayton cycle B. Otto cycle
C. Dual cycle D. Carnot cycle

49. The coefficient of friction depends upon:
A. Area of contact
B. Nature of surface
C. Strength of surface
D. Shape of surface

50. Unit of specific volume is:
A. Kg/m^3 B. N/m^2
C. m^3/kg D. N/m^3

51. The filling of suction pipe up to valve of delivery pipe is known as:
A. Priming B. Installing
C. Capillary action D. Surface tension

52. For Ovens and dryers, the following material is used to make bearings:
A. Bronze B. Graphite alloy
C. Babbitt D. Cast iron

53. If the fixed link in a four chain mechanism is changed, then the relative motion of other links:
A. Will change
B. Could change or remain unaltered depending on which link is fixed
C. Will not occur
D. Will remain same

54. A cycle consisting of one isobar, one isochore and two isentropic processes is known as:
A. Carnot cycle B. Stirling cycle
C. Otto cycle D. Diesel cycle

55. Joules cycle is also known as:
A. Constant pressure
B. Constant entropy
C. Constant temperature
D. Constant volume

56. The fluid which has no motion and forces, is known as:
A. Kinematic B. Kinetic
C. Static D. Dynamic

57. A fixed gear having 200 teeth is in mesh with another gear having 50 teeth. The two gears are connected by an arm. How many number of turns should be made by the smaller gear for one revolution of arm about the center of bigger gear?
A. 5 B. 3
C. 4 D. 2

58. Ball bearing are, usually made from:
A. High carbon steel
B. Low carbon steel
C. Chrome steel
D. Medium carbon steel

59. What is lower critical point for all steel?
A. 700°C B. 723°C
C. 913°C D. 600°C

60. Which method is used to produce cast iron and steel pipe?
A. Investment casting
B. Ttue Centrifugal casting
C. Die casting
D. Slush casting

61. The simple gas turbine cycle has ___ efficiency and work ratio.
A. very low B. high
C. very high D. low

62. The following is known as positive clutch:
A. Single plate clutch B. Cone clutch
C. Centrifugal clutch D. Dog clutch

63. For an incompressible fluid, which property does not change:
A. Density B. Mass
C. Weight D. Viscosity

64. Which of the following is an extensive property?
A. Volume B. Pressure
C. Density D. Viscosity

65. The nozzles are used in Turbine to increase the:
A. Temperature B. Pressure
C. Volume D. Velocity

66. For the equilibrium, two non collinear forces acting at a joint along straight line:
A. forces must be equal and of the same sign
B. forces must be equal in magnitude but opposite in sign
C. each force must be zero
D. one of the forces must be zero

67. A self-excited vibration of the journal is called:
A. Shaft whirl B. Journal whirl
C. Bearing whirl D. Oil whirl

68. The sand used for making core is:
A. Green sand B. Dry sand
C. Oil sand D. Loam sand

69. Specific weight of pure water at standard temperature and pressure in terms of N/m^3 is equal to:
A. 9810 B. 1
C. 9.810 D. 1000

70. An isobaric process, has constant:
A. temperature B. pressure
C. density D. volume

71. In this milling machine, the table can be tilted in a vertical plane by providing a swivel arrangement at the knee:
A. Hand milling machine
B. Universal milling machine
C. Plain milling machine
D. Vertical milling machine

72. _____ is an inversion of Double slider crank chain.
A. Scotch yoke mechanism
B. Reciprocating engine
C. Coupling rod of a locomotive
D. Hand pump

73. What is used to produce uniform packing of sand in a mould?
A. Stripper plate machine
B. Squeezing machine
C. Sand slinger
D. Jolt machine

74. What is the general use of metal extrusion process?
A. Uniform hollow section
B. Uniform solid section
C. Varying solid & hollow section
D. Uniform solid & hollow section

75. The tool life is affected by:
A. Cutting speed B. Feed
C. Depth of cut D. All of these

General Awareness, General Intelligence & Reasoning and Quantitative Aptitude

76. The Montague-Chelmsford report formed the basis for which of the following Acts?
A. Rowlatt Act 1920
B. Government of India Act 1919
C. Indian Councils Act 1909
D. Indian Councils Act 1861

77. Where were the 35th National Games held in India?
A. New Delhi B. Jharkhand
C. Kerala D. Rajasthan

78. In which year was the ₹ 1000 coin first introduced in India?
A. 2000 B. 1996
C. 1964 D. 1954

79. Who is the Minister of State for External Affairs in the cabinet of Narendra Modi?
A. Rajen Guhain B. Krishnan Pal
C. Jual Oram D. M.J. Akbar

80. Which article of the Indian constitution provides procedure for impeachment of the President?
A. Article 61 B. Article 31
C. Article 91 D. Article 41

81. With which country has ISRO signed a MoU to use Land Remote Sensing Satellite data in December 2016?
A. Russia B. USA
C. New Zealand D. Germany

82. Where is the famous monumental tomb 'Bibi Ka Maqbara' located?
A. Agra B. Hyderabad
C. Jaipur D. Aurangabad

83. Who is the current Chief Minister for state of Chattisgarh?
A. Raman Singh
B. Shivraj Singh Chouhan
C. Ajit Jogi
D. Babulal Gaur

84. What are the second highly imported products by India?
A. Agricultural products
B. Petroleum products

C. Electronic goods
D. Automobiles

85. Where is the National Institute of Rural Development (NIRD) located?
A. Pune B. Hyderabad
C. Bangalore D. Chennai

86. Who was the first ruler of Maratha Empire?
A. Sambhaji B. Rajaramji
C. Sahuji D. Shivaji

87. On which river is the Tehri Hydroelectric Project constructed in India?
A. Sutlej B. Bhagirathi
C. Narmada D. Krishna

88. Who dethroned the last Nanda Ruler and occupied Pataliputra in 321 BC?
A. Ashoka B. Kautilya
C. Bindusara D. Chandragupta

89. In which year were the states in India recognized largely on linguistic basis?
A. 1949 B. 1950
C. 1936 D. 1956

90. Which Indian city is known as 'Zero Mile Center'?
A. Bhopal B. Mumbai
C. Surat D. Nagpur

91. If α and β are the roots of $x^2 - 2x - 3 = 0$, then find the value of $\alpha^2 + \beta^2$.
A. 10 B. 1
C. 0 D. 9

92. A shopkeeper sells an item at ₹ 36 and incurs a loss of 10%. At what price should the shopkeeper sell it to gain 30%?
A. ₹ 58.5 B. ₹ 45.5
C. ₹ 52 D. ₹ 65

93. Two bicycle riders Anna and Bhan are cycling in a circular track of 150 m length at 10 m/s and 15 m/s respectively. How much time it will take them to meet to the first time at the starting point?
A. 60 seconds
B. 30 seconds
C. 40 seconds
D. 20 seconds

94. What is the sum of the first 75 terms of the arrangement 150 × 2 + 148 × 4 + 146 × 6 + ______ ?
A. 292600 B. 273950
C. 252850 D. 284050

95. If $\frac{1}{2.017} = 0.4957$, then what is the value of $\frac{1}{0.0002017} = ?$
A. 49.57 B. 495.7
C. 4957 D. 4.957

96. Find the value of $\tan^2 75° - \sec^2 75° + 1 - \frac{1}{2}$.
A. 0 B. –1
C. 1 D. $-\frac{1}{2}$

97. The sum of the present ages of A, B and C is 90 years. Six years ago, their ages were in the ratio of 1 : 2 : 3. What is the present age of C?
A. 42 years B. 48 years
C. 43 years D. 46 years

98. Find the HCF of 2867 and 5002.
A. 59 B. 60
C. 61 D. 62

99. What is mean proportional of 0.32 and 0.02?
A. 0.8 B. 0.08
C. 0.56 D. 0.96

100. Arrange $\frac{12}{7}, \frac{13}{9}$ and $\frac{7}{5}$ in descending order.
A. $\frac{7}{5}, \frac{13}{9}, \frac{12}{7}$ B. $\frac{12}{7}, \frac{13}{9}, \frac{7}{5}$
C. $\frac{13}{9}, \frac{7}{5}, \frac{12}{7}$ D. $\frac{7}{5}, \frac{12}{7}, \frac{13}{9}$

101. X and Y drink milk daily. X can drink 4 litres of milk in 3 days while Y can drink 8 litres of milk in 7 days. In how many days can the two persons together consume 52 litres of milk. If each of them drinks the same quantity of milk every day?
A. 39 days B. 42 days
C. 21 days D. 35 days

102. If the angle of elevation at a point 500 m away from the foot of the tower is 30° then find the height of the tower.

A. $\frac{500}{\sqrt{3}}$ metre B. $500\sqrt{3}$ metre

C. $\sqrt{3}$ metre D. 500 metre

103. The average of indefinite (n) numbers is 41. If two-third numbers are increased by 9 and remaining numbers are decreased by 6 then find the new average.

A. 39 B. 45
C. 42 D. 36

104. Rajni borrowed a loan for 7 years at 9% simple interest per annum. After 7 years she paid ₹ 13,040 to repay the loan. What was the loan amount?

A. ₹ 8,000 B. ₹ 8,400
C. ₹ 7,600 D. ₹ 8,500

105. One litre is taken out of 10 litre milk and one litre water is added to the remaining milk. Again one litre of the mixture is taken out and one litre of water is added to the remaining mixture. What will be the quantity of milk in the mixture?

A. 9 litre B. 810 mililitre
C. 7.21 litre D. 8.1 litre

106. One morning after the Sunrise, Ram and Krishan were talking to each other face-to-face. If the shadow of Krishan was exactly on the right of Ram then in which direction Krishan was standing?

A. East B. South
C. North D. West

107. Complete the series:
R, O, L, I, F, ?

A. C B. G
C. H D. D

108. Identify the word which is in the same analogy?
Milk : Emulsion : : Butter : ?

A. Suspension B. Gel
C. Solution D. Aerosol

109. If 3 = 10, 5 = 27, 7 = 52, then 9 = ?

A. 85 B. 95
C. 105 D. 75

110. Complete the series:
CVD, EUF, GTH, ?

A. SJS B. JSS
C. SSJ D. ISJ

111. If Parul & Quilon means Parul is brother of Quilon. Parul ≠ Quilon means Parul is mother of Quilon and Parul > Quilon means Parul is daughter of Quilon, then who is the father in 'X ≠ Y & W > Z'?

A. Y B. Z
C. X D. W

112. What will be remainder when 1803 × 392 is divided by 29?

A. 24 B. 17
C. 5 D. 12

113. In a certain code, RUNNER is written as TWPPGT. How is MOUSE written in that code?

A. OQWUG B. OUGQW
C. QOWUF D. UGOQC

114. Complete the series:
2, 7, 28, 63, 126, ?

A. 215 B. 217
C. 252 D. 216

115.

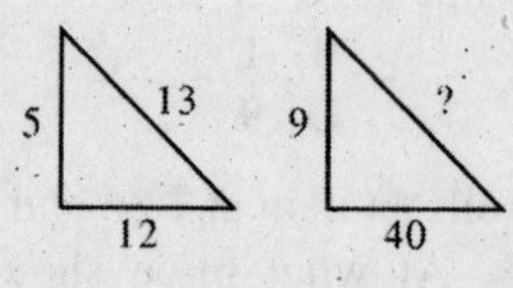

Look at the picture above. Each of them follows a trend. Identify and pick the correct number for the question mark.

A. 52 B. 39
C. 41 D. 26

116. Five coloured balls are arranged in a line. Red is on the left of blue and on right of green. Yellow is on the right of blue. Orange is between blue and yellow. Which ball is on exactly left of the orange ball?

A. Yellow B. Blue
C. Red D. Green

117. Complete the series:
5, 10, 40, 80, 320, 640, ?
A. 120 B. 2560
C. 480 D. 12803

118. Friends A, B, C, D, E, F and G are sitting in a line facing north on a bench to get photographed:
- F is exactly on right of E
- E is fourth on the right of G
- C is the neighbour of B and D
- the one who is third on the left of D, is in the end

then who are sitting on the right of C?
A. D, E, F and A B. G, B and C
C. Only B D. G and B

119. Identify the number that fits into the Analogy:
81 : 3 : : 16 : ?
A. 2 B. 4
C. 9 D. 8

120.

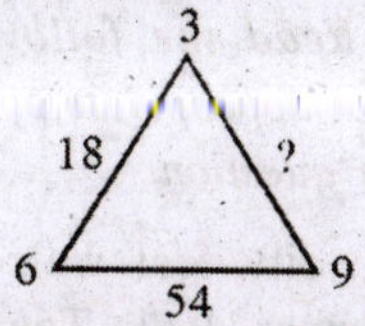

Look at the picture above. It follows a trend. Identify and pick the correct number for the question mark.
A. 36 B. 27
C. 9 D. 54

ANSWERS

1	2	3	4	5	6	7	8	9	10
D	C	B	A	C	D	A	D	D	D
11	**12**	**13**	**14**	**15**	**16**	**17**	**18**	**19**	**20**
C	C	B	A	A	C	B	C	B	A
21	**22**	**23**	**24**	**25**	**26**	**27**	**28**	**29**	**30**
D	B	B	D	D	D	A	C	C	A
31	**32**	**33**	**34**	**35**	**36**	**37**	**38**	**39**	**40**
D	B	A	B	A	A	D	D	D	D
41	**42**	**43**	**44**	**45**	**46**	**47**	**48**	**49**	**50**
B	B	A	A	A	B	C	D	B	C
51	**52**	**53**	**54**	**55**	**56**	**57**	**58**	**59**	**60**
A	B	D	D	A	C	C	C	B	B
61	**62**	**63**	**64**	**65**	**66**	**67**	**68**	**69**	**70**
A	D	A	A	D	C	D	C	A	B
71	**72**	**73**	**74**	**75**	**76**	**77**	**78**	**79**	**80**
B	A	C	D	D	B	C	D	D	A
81	**82**	**83**	**84**	**85**	**86**	**87**	**88**	**89**	**90**
B	D	A	C	B	D	B	D	D	D
91	**92**	**93**	**94**	**95**	**96**	**97**	**98**	**99**	**100**
A	C	B	A	C	D	A	C	B	B
101	**102**	**103**	**104**	**105**	**106**	**107**	**108**	**109**	**110**
C	A	B	A	D	C	A	B	A	D
111	**112**	**113**	**114**	**115**	**116**	**117**	**118**	**119**	**120**
B	B	A	A	C	B	B	D	A	B

PAPER-II

GENERAL ENGLISH

Directions (Q. Nos. 1-5): *Read the following paragraph and choose the most appropriate option from those given under each question.*

To make visitors to the city feel welcome during the Commonwealth Games. India Tourism Development Corporation (ITDC) is set to train taxi and auto drivers. CISF personnel posted at monuments, dhaba owners, hotel staff etc. Participants will be taught English as well as courtesy and ways to communicate with tourists. At present, there is a shortage of trained guides in the city and with Commonwealth Games drawing close; the issue has to be addressed promptly. With hundreds of historical sites to visit and each monument boasting its own unique history, foreign nationals are often left to fend for themselves and depend on tourist books and brochures for information. Language is another problem. Quite a contrast to facilities offered in tourist sites in western countries, where trained guides-proficient in several languages-are easily available to aid visitors apart from group-guided trips at regular intervals. Although the Archeological Survey of India (ASI) plans to introduce audio guide services in five languages at some world heritage sites our experts point that not a single monument or tourist place in the city has an interpretation center where tourists can come and get all information pertaining to a particular site. ASI is also in the process of bringing out more brochures and guides for foreign visitors in the city. Experts say such facilities are crucial if the government wants to promote Delhi as a 'heritage city'. Various agencies like INTACH are also involved in the plans.

1. This passage is regarding ____
- A. The majesty of the histolical sites of India.
- B. Shortage of English learned dhaba owners.
- C. Launching of new facilities in the country.
- D. The preparations by the Government and ASI for commonwealth games.

2. To portray Delhi as 'Heritage City' the government must _____
- A. Discourage English among the locals.
- B. Encourage Hindi among the locals.
- C. Charge for better sanitary and health facilities to the visitors.
- D. Make sure that the tourists are provided an interpretation center and multilingual guides at heritage places.

3. 'Fend for themselves' in the passage means.
- A. To follow the rules and regulations.
- B. To lookout for the safety of one's self.
- C. To be vigilant about the one's mistakes.
- D. To take care of and provide for yourself, without depending on anyone else.

4. It can be said from the passage that.
- A. At many heritage places the government seems less equipped and sluggish to provide basic facilities.
- B. The heritage places are well equipped.
- C. New schemes and ideas ought to be used for smooth travel experience of the travellers.
- D. Government is equipped for the tourists who are coming for visits.

5. ______ are to be provided to residents who offer place to tourists under ITDC's plan.
- A. Visits to the Ganges Ghats and local cities
- B. Better tourist guides and interpretation centers
- C. Relaxed stay, friendly and hospitable treatment
- D. Etiquette training and hospitality treatment

6. There are no passengers on the railway platform. I think the train ______.
A. must had left
B. have left
C. must have left
D. must has left

7. What is a synonym of the word 'banish'?
A. disgust B. clean
C. fade D. exile

8. Unlike most monarchs in that ______ age. Ashok believed in religious tolerance.
A. dogmatic B. feudal
C. primeval D. historical

9. Ajay is a very unlikeable person; ______, most people seem to like him.
A. much B. otherwise
C. still D. subsequently

10. Identify the underlined part of speech in the given sentence:
Only noble people can form great nations.
A. preposition B. adverb
C. adjective D. conjunction

11. "I will avenge your murder." Asha cried over her daughter's corpse. (Change the narration of the sentence)
A. Asha decided to avenge her murder.
B. Asha cried over her daughter's corpse that she would avenge her murder.
C. Asha cried over her daughter's corpse that she would revenge her murder.
D. Asha decided to avenge her daughter's death.

12. Jaycee is a miss know-it-all. She's the kind of girl who thinks she knows everything ______ everyone.
A. through B. about
C. without D. within

13. She said to me, "I don't trust you." (Change the narration of the sentence.)
A. "I don't trust you" she said.
B. She said me I do not trust you.
C. She told me that she didn't trust me.
D. She decided not to trust me.

14. We need to brush our teeth twice a day. (Choose the most appropriate one which best expresses the given sentence in passive voice.)
A. Our teeth were needed to brush twice a day.
B. Our teeth are needed to brush twice a day.
C. Our teeth need to be brushed twice a day.
D. Our teeth are needed by us to brush twice a day.

15. What is an antonym of the word 'paucity'?
A. certainty B. excess
C. timidity D. beauty

16. Her interest and concentration in the study of human psychology is indeed very ______.
A. broad B. strong
C. large D. deep

17. We got back to church late at night but we didn't go to sleep immediately. We were very hungry.
In the above sentence "but" stands as:
A. pronoun B. conjunction
C. adverb D. adjective

18. What is a synonym of the word 'generic'?
A. general B. specific
C. precise D. fresh

19. It is impossible to achieve anything without ______ a certain amount of pain while making an effort.
A. sacrificing B. imbibing
C. getting D. enduring

20. What is a synonym of the word 'indifferent'?
A. unresponsive B. unkind
C. mean D. expensive

21. The problems of teenager ______ to the children by psychiatrists yesterday.
A. had explained B. was explained
C. were explained D. are explained

22. The pancakes are delicious and light. I really love their taste.
Which Part of speech is "light"?
A. adverb B. noun
C. adjective D. verb

23. "Excuse the mess." The house ______.
A. is painting B. is being painted
C. has painted D. has been painted

24. The Taj Mahal is the _____ constructed monument of love in the world but is taken care by the authorities rather poorly.
A. most brilliantly B. mere brilliant
C. too brilliant D. much brilliantly

25. What is an antonym of the word 'abolish'?
A. avoid B. chastise
C. establish D. choose

26. Do you emulate others?
(Choose the most appropriate one which best expresses the given sentence in passive voice.)
A. Are others imitated by you?
B. Are others being imitated by you?
C. Have others being imitated by you?
D. Were others being imitated by you?

27. Although Donald Trump was the dark horse in the race for the white house but he was giving his speech to the audience ______.
A. confidently B. inconsiderably
C. instantly D. expensively

28. The government applied the fix pay rule to recruit new candidates for jobs. They thought it was a good idea.
Which Part of speech is "thought"?
A. adverb B. adjective
C. noun D. verb

29. You can buy your bus passes _____ the ticket counter of any bus station of Gujarat state.
A. through B. at
C. in D. from

30. What is an antonym of the word 'forsake'?
A. embrace B. abandon
C. reject D. craft

31. I like Bollywood films and watch them with much excitement. But I also watch films of Hollywood ______.
A. basically B. sadly
C. nearly D. occasionally

32. Being a doctor is hard work, especially if you're ______ call all the time.
A. while B. on
C. in D. with

33. Ravi had difficulties climbing back up to the tree house because he had injured his ankle as he was climbing ______ .
A. down to B. out of
C. down D. into

34. "Don't touch the electric-wire," the mechanic siad to us. The mechanic _______ us not to touch the electric-wire.
A. ordered B. recommended
C. warned D. threatened

35. Although we can use an elevator to reach the top of the Eiffel Tower, we decided to walk. I was exhausted by the time we got _____ to the top.
A. up B. in to
C. up to D. in

36. Mr. Sharma requested Ms. Sharma to go with him.
(Change the narration of the sentence.)
A. Mr. Sharma says, "Let Ms. Sharma come with me."
B. Mr. Sharma says to Ms. Sharma, "Please come with me."
C. Mr. Sharma said to Ms. Sharma, "Please, come with me."
D. Mr. Sharma said Ms. Sharma, "You have to come with me."

37. It is an established fact now that English is the most _____ spoken language in the globe today.
A. beautifully B. greatly
C. broadly D. widely

38. What is an antonym of the word 'abound'?
A. discourage B. dwindle
C. rest D. bless

39. What is an antonym of the word 'colossal'?
A. simple B. little
C. roof D. lovely

40. What is an antonym of the word 'zenith'?

A. bottom B. pit
C. apex D. past

41. "Yes, I'll give you my car for a week", he said to Narendra. He ______ to give Narendra his car for a week.

A. granted D. confessed
C. promised D. requested

42. What is an antonym of the word 'restrain'?

A. release B. silence
C. thrive D. disregard

43. There has been a ______ lack of effectiveness in all the crucial areas of the working of Public Sector Undertakings.

A. surprising B. simulative
C. positive D. conspicuous

44. Jeson finished his degree at Cambridge University, ______, he settled in London and took up a job with a large international bank.

A. instead B. subsequently
C. definitely D. still

45. Rahul went _____ the store, but I don't think he found what he was looking for because he came back out almost immediately.

A. up to B. in
C. out D. into

46. I didn't go to the very formal banquet because you never came back from the drycleaners with my favourite suit.
Which Part of speech is "favourite"?

A. pronoun B. adverb
C. adjective D. noun

47. Francis didn't give his sisters presents: _____ he gave each of them an envelope with $50.

A. also B. still
C. subsequently D. instead

48. Our customer service center will help you resolve that problem. Just walk _____ the hall and take the elevator up to the third floor.

A. in B. down to
C. into D. down

49. The cricket player was rejected because he had done something that was ___ the rules.

A. without B. against
C. around D. outside

50. This mail was _____ yesterday, but the clerk forgot to do that.

A. being posted
B. to be posted
C. had been posted
D. posted

51. A small snail climbed over the slippery log and inched slowly toward the nearby fields. Which Part of speech is "slippery"?

A. adjective B. conjunction
C. adverb D. verb

52. "She never buys me flowers!" he said. She _____ that he never bought her flowers.

A. explained B. complained
C. warned D. accused

53. Which type of adverb is used in the following sentence?
"John is moving somewhere from to Berlin to Bonn with his friends in a train."

A. time B. place
C. manner D. frequency

54. "Let's go for a walk" she said. She—to go for a walk.

A. requested B. recommended
C. proposed D. offered

55. Donald is said to be very powerful.
(Choose the most appropriate one which best expresses the given sentence in active voice.)

A. People say he is very rich.
B. Donald said he is very rich.
C. Donald said I am very rich.
D. People say Donald is very rich.

56. The weather was quite warm, so we walked lazily along the shady path near an old cemetery in the countryside.
Which part of speech is "weather"?

A. adverb B. adjective
C. pronoun D. noun

57. There was a squeaking sound that I had heard. There was a mouse underneath the piano.
Which Part of speech is "underneath"?
A. adjective B. preposition
C. verb D. adverb

58. I ______ him ten thousand pounds last year.
A. lend B. lent
C. was lent D. lended

59. "I assure I'll write to you", she said to him. She ______ to write to him.
A. agreed
B. granted
C. promised
D. accused

60. What is an antonym of the word 'heedless'?
A. speedy B. mindful
C. unaware D. heartless

ANSWERS

1	2	3	4	5	6	7	8	9	10
D	D	D	A	D	C	D	D	C	C
11	**12**	**13**	**14**	**15**	**16**	**17**	**18**	**19**	**20**
B	B	C	C	B	D	B	A	D	A
21	**22**	**23**	**24**	**25**	**26**	**27**	**28**	**29**	**30**
C	C	B	A	C	A	A	D	B	A
31	**32**	**33**	**34**	**35**	**36**	**37**	**38**	**39**	**40**
D	B	C	C	C	C	D	B	B	A
41	**42**	**43**	**44**	**45**	**46**	**47**	**48**	**49**	**50**
C	A	D	B	D	C	D	D	B	B
51	**52**	**53**	**54**	**55**	**56**	**57**	**58**	**59**	**60**
A	B	B	C	D	D	B	B	C	B

Previous Paper (Solved)

DMRC–Junior Engineer (Mechanical) Exam-2016*

PAPER-I

LOGICAL ABILITY, QUANTITATIVE APTITUDE & GENERAL AWARENESS

Directions (Qs. No. 1 & 2) : *The questions are based on the following information.*

Out of the total 390 students studying in a college of Arts and Science, boys and girls are in the ratio of 7 : 6 respectively and the number of students studying Arts and Science are in the ratio of 3 : 7 respectively. The boys and girls studying Arts are in the ratio of 4 : 5 respectively.

1. How many boys are studying Science?
A. 155 B. 156
C. 158 D. None of these

2. What is the ratio between the girls studying Arts and Science respectively?
A. 8 : 13 B. 13 : 23
C. 23 : 36 D. None of these

3. "SAWEN" is a regional international government body:
A. In combating wildlife crime in the region
B. In combating regional terrorism
C. For health & welfare programs
D. For poverty alleviation in region

4. World's first white tiger safari was recently opened in the state of:
A. Gujarat B. Maharashtra
C. Madhya Pradesh D. Assam

5. India's first indigenous rotavirus vaccine named rotavac:
A. Is to combat infant mortality due to jaundice
B. Is to combat infant mortality due to diarrhea
C. Is to combat adult Japanese encephalitis
D. Is inactivated polio vaccine

6. Who was recently conferred with Skoch Lifetime Achievement award?
A. Sushma Swaraj
B. Suresh Manohar Parrikar
C. Suresh Prabhu
D. M. Venkaiah Naidu

7. 2015–2016 Irani cup cricket title was won by
A. Rest of India
B. Mumbai
C. Delhi
D. Karnataka

Directions (Qs. No. 8) : *The following question is followed by two statements I and II. Select the choice as follows.*

(*a*) If statement I alone is sufficient to answer the question.
(*b*) If statement II alone is sufficient to answer the question.
(*c*) If statement I and II are both required to answer the question.
(*d*) If both statements I and II are insufficient to answer the question and more data is required.

8. Can Mohan be considered a successful mountaineer:
I. Mohan has taken part in seven mountaineering expeditions in the last ten years.
II. The norm for a mountaineer to be considered successful is being a member of expeditions 4 to 5 times in fifteen years.
A. (*a*) B. (*b*)
C. (*c*) D. (*d*)

* Exam Held on 17-04-2016.

Directions (Qs. No. 9) : *The following are the statistics of some matches of a cricket team bowlers and the wickets taken. A, B, C & D are the fast bowlers of the team.*

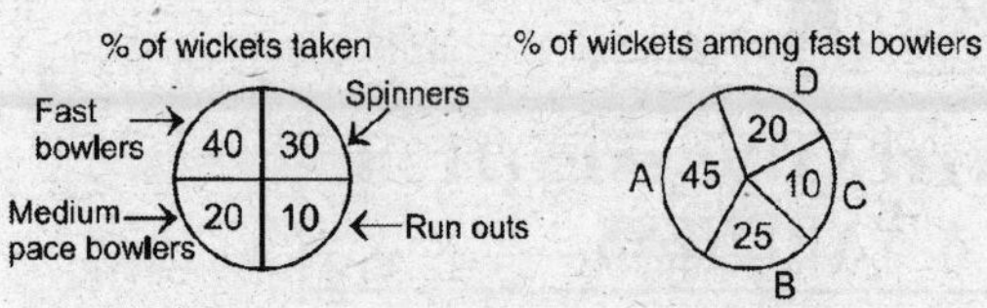

9. If the inter-se wicket taking ratio between bowler groups remains the same and the run out are limited to 2 only, how many more wickets would spinners take, based on the original presumption that spinners took 15 wickets earlier:

A. 1 B. 2
C. 3 D. 0

10. Which actor has been selected for the prestigious 47th Dadasaheb Phalke Award for the year 2015?

A. Dilip Kumar
B. Amitabh Bachchan
C. Satrughan Sinha
D. Manoj Kumar

11. Union Government recently gave nod for issuance of UDAY bonds to four states of India initially. One of the states is not included in this?

A. Uttar Pradesh B. Bihar
C. Rajasthan D. Chattishgarh

12. Which more suitable for crops like cashew nut?

A. Red laterite soil
B. Black soil
C. Alluvial soil
D. Arid soil

13. Two equal glasses filled with alchohol & water in the proportion 2 : 1 and 3 : 2 are emptied into a third glass. The proportion of alchohol and water in the third glass will be:

A. 13 : 17 B. 19 : 7
C. 13 : 11 D. 19 : 11

Directions (Qs. No. 14) : *Study the information given in this question to answer them.*

Number of the voters registered and voted from different constituency

Constituency	*Number of voters in thousands*	
	Registered	*Voted*
I	180	105
II	250	150
III	290	170
IV	320	200
V	200	110

14. Which constituency had the lowest percentage of polling?

A. I B. V
C. III D. IV

15. The least number of complete years, in which a sum of money put out at 20% compound interest compounded annually will be more than double, is:

A. 3 B. 4
C. 5 D. 6

Directions (Qs. No. 16 to 20) : *Answer the questions on the basis of information given below.*

A tournament is organized among five teams Ahmedabad, Bombay, Calcutta, Delhi and England. This is a round robin league tournament where each team has to play every other team exactly once. For any team, three points are awarded for a win, one point for a draw and no point for a loss.

The following table is incomplete even after the end of the tournament.

TEAM	W	D	L	P (Total Point)
Ahmedabad				7
Bombay				2
Calcutta				1
Delhi				10
England				7

Where
W = Number of matches won
L = Number of matches lost
D = Number of matches drawn
P = Total Points

16. Which team/s did Ahmedabad beat?
A. Only Delhi and England
B. Only Delhi
C. Only Bombay and Calcutta
D. Only Bombay and England

17. Which team/s drew the match with Bombay?
A. Only Ahmedabad
B. Only Calcutta and Delhi
C. Only Delhi and England
D. Only England

18. Which team had the highest number of draw?
A. Bombay B. Ahmedabad
C. Calcutta D. Delhi

19. Which of the following team/s did team England beat?
A. Only Delhi
B. Only Bombay and Calcutta
C. Only Ahmedabad and Delhi
D. Only Ahmedabad and Bombay

20. Team England drew match with:
A. Only Calcutta and Delhi
B. Only Ahmedabad
C. Only Bombay
D. Only Bombay and Calcutta

21. S is the mid-point of the side QR of the triangle PQR and T is the mid point of QS. If O is the mid point of PT, then area of Δ QOT is equal to:
A. 1/2 area of Δ PQR
B. 1/4 area of Δ PQR
C. 1/6 area of Δ PQR
D. 1/8 area of Δ PQR

22. The positive square root of $\left(\sqrt{48}-\sqrt{45}\right)$ is:
A. $\frac{\sqrt[4]{3}}{2}\left(\sqrt{5}-\sqrt{3}\right)$ B. $\frac{\sqrt[4]{3}}{\sqrt{2}}\left(\sqrt{5}-\sqrt{3}\right)$
C. $\frac{\sqrt{2}}{\sqrt[4]{3}}\left(\sqrt{5}-\sqrt{3}\right)$ D. $\frac{\sqrt{2}}{\sqrt[4]{3}}\left(\sqrt{5}+\sqrt{3}\right)$

23. Which of the following was used as a chemical weapon in the First World War?
A. Mustard gas B. Water gas
C. Hydrogen cyanide D. Carbon monoxide

24. What is the full form of the term 'NPA' as used in banking environment?
A. Not Profitable Assets
B. Net Performing Assets
C. Non Performing Assets
D. New Potential Accounts

25. The expected energy of electrons at absolute zero is called:
A. Work function B. Potential energy
C. Emission energy D. Fermi energy

26. One Kilo byte represents:
A. 1024 bytes B. 1000 bytes
C. 100 bytes D. 1064 bytes

27. Creation of MUDRA bank was proposed in the recent budget proposal of the Government of India. MUDRA stands for:
A. Monetary Union Development Repay agency
B. Medium Units Development & Reconstruction Agency
C. Micro Units Development Refinance Agency
D. Multipurpose Undertakings Development Refinance Agency

28. The position of how many letters in the word BRAKES remains unchanged when they are arranged in alphabetical order?
A. 1 B. 3
C. 2 D. None of these

29. In a row of 16 boys, when Ashish was shifted two places towards the left, he became 7th from left end. What was his earlier position from the right end of the row?
A. 10th B. 12th
C. 9th D. 8th

30. A metallic sphere is melted and is cast into a solid cylinder. If the radius of the base of the cylinder is equal to the radius of the sphere, then the ratio of the surface area of the sphere to the total surface area of the cylinder is?
A. 1 : 1 B. 7 : 8
C. 6 : 7 D. 7 : 5

31. The total cost price of two items is ₹ 10,200 and their selling prices are equal. If one of the two items is sold at a loss of 12% and another is sold at a loss of 18%, then the cost price of the item which is sold at a loss of 18% is:

A. ₹ 5280 B. ₹ 4920
C. ₹ 5820 D. None of these

32. A petrol tank at a filling station has a capacity of 400 litres. The attendant sells 40 litres of petrol from the tank to one customer and then replenishes it with kerosene oil. This process is repeated with six customers. What quantity of pure petrol will the seventh customer get when he purchases 40 litres of petrol?

A. 20.50 litres B. 20.25 litres
C. 21.25 litres D. None of these

33. A and B are two alloys of gold and copper prepared by mixing metals in the ratios 5 : 3 and 5 : 11 respectively. Equal quantities of these alloys are melted to form a third alloy C. The ratio of gold and copper in the alloy C is:

A. 33 : 25 B. 25 : 33
C. 17 : 15 D. 15 : 17

34. The formula for the number of diagonals in a polygon of n sides is $d = \frac{1}{2}[n(n-3)]$. If the number of diagonals in a polygon is twice as many as the number of sides, what is the number of sides:

A. 3 B. 5
C. 7 D. None of these

35. Peeyush walked 8 kms. west and turned right and walked 3 kms. Then again he turned right and walked 12 kms. How far is he from the starting point?

A. 5 kms. B. 7 kms.
C. 9 kms. D. None of these

36. Which one of the following statements correctly describes the Fourth Schedule of the Constitution of India?

A. It contains the scheme of the distribution of powers between the union and states
B. It allocates seats in the council of states
C. It contains the languages listed in the constitution
D. It contains the provisions regarding the administration of tribal areas

Directions (Qs. No. 37) : *In the following question two statements are followed by two possible inferences. Point out which of the following answer choice applies. Assume statements to be correct even if they very from facts.*

(*a*) Only inference I follows
(*b*) Only inference II follows
(*c*) Both inferences I and II follow
(*d*) Neither inferences I nor II follow

37. All fish are tortoise, no tortoise is a crocodile:

I. No crocodile is a fish.
II. No fish is a crocodile.

A. (*a*) B. (*b*)
C. (*c*) D. (*d*)

38. When three coins are tossed together, the probability that all coins have the same face is:

A. 1/4 B. 1/6
C. 1/3 D. None of these

39. A man walked diagonally across a square plot. What was the percent saved by not walking along edges?

A. 20% B. 30%
C. 40% D. 50%

Directions (Qs. No. 40) : *In the following question a number series is given. After the series a number is given followed by (a), (b), (c), (d) and (e). You have to complete the series starting with the number given following the sequence of the given series and answer the question given below the series.*

40.

6	10	7	12	8	14
4	(*a*)	(*b*)	(*c*)	(*d*)	(*e*)

What will come in place of (*d*)

A. 6 B. 5
C. 8 D. 9

41. If 1 is coded as R, 2 as T, 3 as Z, 4 as B, 5 as O, 6 as L, 7 as C, 8 as J, 9 as V, which of the following is the coded form of 28147962?

A. TRJBCVLT B. TJRBCVLT
C. TJRCBVLT D. None of these

42. Five girls are sitting on a bench to be photographed. Sejal is to the left of Rashmi and to the right of Binni. Mamta is to the left of Rashmi. Ragini is between Rashmi and Mamta. Who is sitting immediately right to Ragini?

A. Rashmi B. Mamta
C. Binni D. Sejal

43. Amar can complete a work in 3 days, Bobby in 4 days and Cheenu in 5 days. If they complete the same work together and get ₹ 14,100 as remuneration, then the share of Cheenu in rupees will be:

A. ₹ 2800 B. ₹ 3000
C. ₹ 3200 D. ₹ 3600

44. The work done by a woman in 8 hours is equal to the work done by a man in 6 hours and by a boy in 12 hours. If working 6 hours per day 9 men can complete a work in 6 days, then how many days can 12 men, 12 women and 12 boys together finish the same work working 8 hours per day?

A. $1\frac{1}{3}$ days B. $3\frac{2}{3}$ days
C. $1\frac{1}{2}$ days D. None of these

45. Who among the following is well known as an exponent of flute?

A. Madhup Mudgal B. Shafaat Ahmad
C. Ronu Mazumdar D. Debu Choudhari

KNOWLEDGE OF DISCIPLINE / TRADE

46. Match list-I with List-II and select the correct answer using the codes given below the list:

List-I (Material properties)	***List-II (Test to determine properties)***
(*a*) Ductility	1. Impact test
(*b*) Toughness	2. Fatigue test
(*c*) Endurance limit	3. Tension test
(*d*) Resistance to penetration	4. Hardness test

Codes:

A. (*a*)-3, (*b*)-2, (*c*)-1, (*d*)-4
B. (*a*)-4, (*b*)-2, (*c*)-1, (*d*)-3
C. (*a*)-3, (*b*)-1, (*c*)-2, (*d*)-4
D. (*a*)-4, (*b*)-1, (*c*)-2, (*d*)-3

47. Concurrent force system is the system when:

A. Lines of action of all forces pass through a point
B. Lines of action of all forces are parallel to each other
C. Lines of action of all forces lie along same line
D. Lines of action of all forces are not parallel to each other

48. A couple is formed when:

A. Two unequal and unlike parallel force acting on a body
B. Two unequal and like parallel force acting on a body
C. Two equal and unlike parallel force acting on a body
D. Two equal and like parallel force acting on a body

49. The total area under the stress-strain curve of a mild steel specimen tested up to failure under tension is a measure of its:

A. Breaking strength B. Toughness
C. Hardness D. Stiffness

50. Which material has highest value of poission's ratio?

A. Elastic Rubber B. Wood
C. Copper D. Steel

51. The motion transmitted between teeth of two spur gears is generally:

A. Sliding
B. Rolling
C. Rotary
D. Partly sliding and partly rolling

52. The static deflection of a shaft under a flywheel is 4 mm. What is the critical speed in rad/sec if g = 10 m/s^2?

A. 50 B. 20
C. 10 D. None of these

53. According to Indian Standard specifications $50H_7g_6$ means that:

1. Actual size is 50 mm
2. Tolerance grade for hole is 7
3. Tolerance grade for shaft is 6

Which of the statements made above are correct?

A. 1 and 2 B. 1, 2 and 3
C. 2 and 3 D. None of these

54. A wooden block rests on a horizontal force as shown in figure. The force (P) acting on it at an angle of 25° with horizontal. Assume the mass of block to be 8 kg and coefficient of friction is 0.45.

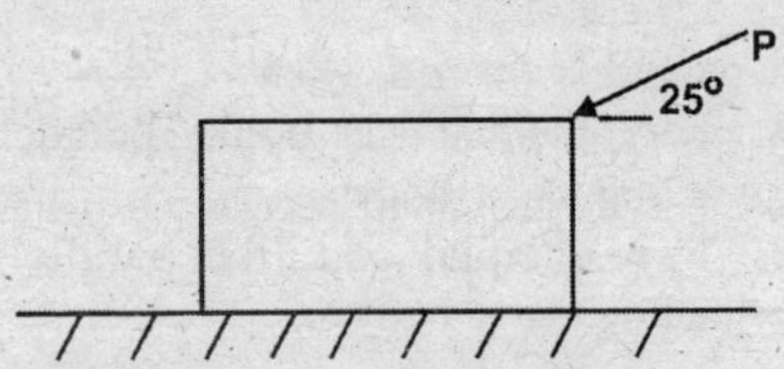

The force (P) is:

A. 42.45 N B. 49.31 N
C. 52.21 N D. None of these

55. The maximum distortion energy theory of failure is suitable to predict the failure of which one of the following type of materials?

A. Brittle B. Ductile
C. Composite D. Plastics

56. Consider two rods A, B of the same material and subjected to equal axial load. The rod A is of uniform cross-section with diameter d, and the rod B taper uniformly from diameter d at one end to diameter $d/2$ at other end. The ratio of elongation of rod A to elongation of rod B will be:

A. 1 : 1 B. 1 : 2
C. 1 : 3 D. 1 : 4

57. A Hook's joint is used to connect:

A. Two parallel shafts
B. Two intersecting shafts
C. Two non parallel intersecting shafts
D. Two non parallel non-intersecting shafts

58. A truss is said to be perfect when it satisfies the following conditions:

A. $m = 2j + 3$ B. $m = 3j - 2$
C. $m = 2j - 3$ D. $m = 3j + 2$

59. Enlarging an existing circular hole with a rotating single point tool is called:

A. Boring B. Drilling
C. Reaming D. Internal turning

60. Plug gauge is used to measure:

A. Shaft size
B. Hole size
C. Wire thickness
D. Depth of threads

61. In order to have interference fit, it is essential that the lower limit of the shaft should be:

A. Greater than upper limit of the hole
B. Lesser than upper limit of the hole
C. Greater than lower limit of the hole
D. Lesser than lower limit of the hole

62. A steel plate of thermal conductivity 50 W/mK and thickness 10 cm passes a heat flux by conduction of 25 kW/m^2. If the temperature of hot surface of the plate is 100°C, then what is the temperature of cooler surface of the plate?

A. 30°C B. 40°C
C. 50°C D. None of these

63. Gears are manufactured in mass production by:

A. Milling B. Shaping
C. Hobbing D. Forming

64. In blanking and piercing operation, clearance between die and punch depends on:

A. Diameter of hole required
B. Thickness of sheet material
C. Number of pieces to be made
D. Capacity and types of press

65. Gate is provided in moulds to:
A. Give passage to gases
B. Compensate for shrinkage
C. Feed the casting at a constant rate
D. Avoids cavities

66. The electric resistance welding operates with:
A. Low current and high voltage
B. High current and low voltage
C. Low current and low voltage
D. High current and high voltage

67. An orthogonal cutting operation is being carried out under the following conditions
Cutting speed (V) = 2m/s,
depth of cut = 0.5 mm,
chip thickness = 0.6 mm
Then chip velocity is:
A. 2 m/s B. 1.66 m/s
C. 1 m/s D. None of these

68. The rake angle of a cutting tool is 15°, the shear angle is 45° and the cutting velocity is 35 m/min. What is the velocity of chip along the tool face?
A. 28.5 m/s B. 27.3 m/s
C. 25.3 m/s D. None of these

69. A 40 mm diameter rod is to be turned on a lathe at a cutting speed of 30 m/min. The required spindle speed should be approximately:
A. 120 rpm B. 180 rpm
C. 240 rpm D. None of these

70. A tank containing air is stirred by a paddle wheel. The work input to the paddle wheel is 9000 kJ and heat transferred to the surroundings from the tank is 3000 kJ. The external work done by the system is:
A. Zero B. 3000 kJ
C. 6000 kJ D. None of these

71. If the thermal efficiency of a Carnot heat engine is 40%, then Co-efficient of performance of a refrigerator working within same temperature limits would be:
A. 4.5 B. 3.5
C. 1.5 D. None of these

72. A heat engine is supplied with 280 kJ/s of heat at a constant fixed temperature of 520 K and heat rejection takes place at 260 K temperature. If the engine is reversible, the heat rejected would be approximately equal to:
A. 85 kJ/s B. 110 kJ/s
C. 140 kJ/s D. None of these

73. An engine operate between temperature limits of 900 K and T_2, and an other engine operates between T_2 and 400 K. For both engines to be equally efficient, T_2 should be equal to:
A. 600 K B. 625 K
C. 650 K D. None of these

74. Two cars A and B move at 54 km/hr in the same direction and the car B is 300 m ahead of car A. If the car A is accelerated at $6 m/s^2$ while car B continue to move with the same velocity, calculate the time taken by car A to overtake car B:
A. 10 s B. 20 s
C. 15 s D. None of these

75. Draft is provided in pattern so that:
A. It can be easily withdrawn from mould cavity
B. Sand can be filled easily
C. Compression can be done effectively
D. Casting can be solidifying easily

76. Arc blow is:
A. A casting defect B. A welding defect
C. A forging defect D. A fitting defect

77. A simply supported beam of span l and carrying uniform distributed load W per unit length, then maximum bending moment is given by:
A. $Wl^2/2$ B. $Wl^2/4$
C. $Wl^2/8$ D. $Wl^2/16$

78. In an arc welding:
A. Flux is coated on the surface to be welded
B. Flux is poured on the surface in the form of powder
C. Flux is coated on the electrode
D. No flux is used

79. The point of contraflexture in a loaded beam refers to the section where:
A. Bending moment is maximum
B. Shear force is maximum
C. Shear force is zero
D. Bending moment change sign

80. Which of the following fitting is a boiler mounting?
A. Superheater
B. Economizer
C. Feed check valve
D. Blow down cock

81. Which is not a part of petrol engine?
A. Valve mechanism B. Fuel injector
C. Induction coil D. Air filter

82. The moment of Inertia of an area is always least with respect to:
A. Vertical axis
B. Radius of gyration
C. Centroidal axis
D. None of these

83. During metal cutting operation, it was observed that the chip thickness is 2 mm and the shear angle is 30°. The corresponding length of shear plane is:
A. 1 mm B. 2 mm
C. 3 mm D. 4 mm

84. If the principle stresses on a plane stress problem are S_1 = 100 MPa and S_2 = 40 MPa, then the magnitude of shear stress (MPa) will be:
A. 60 B. 50
C. 30 D. None of these

85. A body moves with a speed of 10 m/s in the curved path of 25 m radius of curvature. If the tangential acceleration is 3 m/s^2, then total acceleration for the body will be:
A. 3.3 m/s^2 B. 4 m/s^2
C. 5 m/s^2 D. None of these

86. A Kaplan turbine is suitable for:
A. Low head and low discharge
B. Low head and high discharge
C. High head and low discharge
D. High head and high discharge

87. Cavitation in centrifugal pumps can be reduced by:
A. Reducing the discharge
B. Reducing the suction head
C. Throttling the discharge
D. Increasing the flow velocity

88. Polar moment of inertia of a hollow shaft having D and *d* as outer and inner diameters, is given by:

A. $\frac{\pi}{8}\left(D^4 - d^4\right)$ B. $\frac{\pi}{32}\left(D^4 - d^4\right)$

C. $\frac{\pi}{64}\left(D^4 - d^4\right)$ D. $\frac{\pi}{12}\left(D^4 - d^4\right)$

89. Two block of weight 50 N and 30 N respectively are connected by a light string passing over a smooth frictionless pulley. The acceleration with which the weights move:
A. 2.25 m/s^2 B. 2.45 m/s^2
C. 3.05 m/s^2 D. None of these

90. Two shafts whose axes are not in the same straight line and are not parallel but intersect each other. Which of the following couplings can be used for this type of shafts?
A. Flexible coupling
B. Universal coupling
C. Oldham's coupling
D. Rigid coupling

91. A bench vice is provided with which type of threads:
A. V-Threads
B. BSW Threads
C. Buttress Threads
D. Acme Threads

92. The 'Crowning' of the flat pulley is generally done:
A. To reduce the belt friction
B. To prevent the belt joint from damaging the belt surface
C. To prevent the belt from running off the pulley
D. In case of cross belt drive only

93. The thickness of a gear tooth is measured:
A. Along the pitch circle
B. Along the root circle
C. Along the outer circle
D. Average of the profile

94. The cycle generally used for petrol engine is:
A. Otto cycle B. Dual cycle
C. Carnot cycle D. Brayton cycle

95. The power transmitted by a circular shaft rotating at N rpm under action of torque T is:
A. $\frac{2\pi NT}{75}$ B. $\frac{2\pi NT}{4500}$
C. $\frac{2\pi NT}{650}$ D. None of these

96. A belt pulley of 200 mm diameter such that the ratio of tension in tight side and slack side is 1.2. The maximum tension in the belt not to exceed 240 kN. Speed of the pulley is 60 rpm. Find the safe power that can be transmitted by the pulley:
A. 25.13 W B. 26.41 W
C. 24.2 W D. None of these

97. The resultant upward pressure of a fluid on a floating body is equal to the weight of the fluid displaced by the body. This is known as:
A. Pascal law
B. Buoyancy force
C. Specific gravity of liquid
D. Viscosity of liquid

98. A point 20 mm below HP and 30 mm behind VP, Its top view will be:
A. 20 mm below XY
B. 30 mm below XY
C. 20 mm above XY
D. 30 mm above XY

99. Which of the following welding method uses a pool of molten metal?
A. Carbon arc welding
B. Submerged arc welding
C. TIG arc welding
D. MIG arc welding

100. A hacksaw blade cuts on the:
A. Forward stroke
B. Return stroke
C. Both forward and return stroke
D. None of these

101. Sand acquires a predetermined shape under pressure and retains the same when pressure is removed. This is due to the property of sand known as:
A. Plasticity
B. Cohesiveness
C. Refractoriness
D. Adhesiveness

102. The size of the lathe is expressed as:
A. Gross weight of the lathe
B. Diameter of the chuck
C. Maximum speed of the chuck
D. Swing of the lathe

103. The resistance per unit area, offered by a body against deformation is known as:
A. Load B. Pressure
C. Stress D. Strain

104. The heat engine that operates the most efficiently between a high-temperature reservoir and a low-temperature reservoir is the:
A. Carnot Engine
B. C.I. Engine
C. S.I. Engine
D. Gas Turbine Engine

105. The cycle generally used for gas turbines is:
A. Otto cycle
B. Brayton cycle
C. Carnot cycle
D. Dual cycle

106. Relation between number of links (I) and number of pairs (P) is:
A. I = 2P – 2 B. I = 2P – 3
C. I = 2P – 4 D. None of these

107. In centre less grinding, work piece is clamped in:
A. Bed B. Vice
C. Chuck D. Collet

108. Which of the following measuring device is used for measuring the rate of flow of a fluid flowing through a pipe:
A. Venturi meter
B. Orifice meter
C. Pitot tube
D. All of these

109. In a refrigeration cycle the heat is absorbed by refrigerant at:
A. Evaporator
B. Condenser
C. Expansion valve
D. Compressor

110. Effort required at the circumference of the screw jack to lift the load (W) is given by:
A. W tan $(\alpha - \varphi)$
B. W tan $(\varphi - \alpha)$
C. W tan $(\alpha + \varphi)$
D. None of these

111. On a ladder resting on a smooth ground and leaning against vertical wall, the force of friction will be:
A. Away from the wall at its upper end
B. Towards the wall at its upper end
C. Upwards at its upper end
D. Downwards at its upper end

112. For a given steam temperature of 850°C and vacuum of 0.1 kg/cm^2 absolute, the Rankine cycle efficiency will be maximum when steam pressure is:
A. 100 kg/cm^2
B. 200 kg/cm^2
C. Critical pressure (225.4 kg/cm^2)
D. 350 kg/cm^2

113. In a two-fluid heat exchanger, the inlet and outlet temperature of the hot fluid are 65°C and 40°C respectively. For the cold fluid, these are 15°C and 42°C. The heat exchanger is a:
A. Parallel flow heat exchanger
B. Counter flow heat exchanger
C. Heat exchange device where both parallel flow and counter flow operations are possible
D. None of the above

114. The conditions for the stable equilibrium of a floating body are:
A. The meta-centre should lie above the centre of gravity
B. The centre of buoyancy and the centre of gravity must lie on the same vertical line
C. A righting couple should be formed
D. All the above are correct

115. Generally least count of the commonly used vernier is:
A. 0.1 mm
B. 0.01 mm
C. 0.02 mm
D. 0.2 mm

116. If a ball which is dropped from a height of 2.25 m on a smooth floor attains the height of bounce equal to 1.00 m, the coefficient of the restitution between the ball and the floor is equal to:
A. 0.25
B. 0.50
C. 0.67
D. 0.33

117. A spherical vessel with an inside diameter of 2 m is made of material having an allowable stress in tension of 500 kg/cm^2. The thickness of a shell to withstand a pressure of 25 kg/cm^2 should be:
A. 5 cm
B. 10 cm
C. 2.5 cm
D. 1.25 cm

118. Choose the correct statement:
A. An adiabatic process is always reversible
B. An isentropic process is never reversible
C. An adiabatic process is always isentropic
D. A frictionless adiabatic process is always isentropic

119. A pump delivers water at a rate of 0.025 m^3/s against a head of 30 m. If the overall efficiency of the pump is 75%, the power required by the pump is:
A. 1 kW
B. 4.9 kW
C. 7.8 kW
D. 9.8 kW

120. Morse test is carried out to determine ..... of an engine:
A. I.H.P.
B. F.H.P.
C. B.H.P.
D. Efficiency

ANSWERS

1	2	3	4	5	6	7	8	9	10
C	B	A	C	B	D	A	C	A	D
11	**12**	**13**	**14**	**15**	**16**	**17**	**18**	**19**	**20**
B	A	D	B	B	C	B	A	B	B
21	**22**	**23**	**24**	**25**	**26**	**27**	**28**	**29**	**30**
D	B	A	C	D	A	C	C	D	C
31	**32**	**33**	**34**	**35**	**36**	**37**	**38**	**39**	**40**
A	C	D	C	A	B	C	A	B	A
41	**42**	**43**	**44**	**45**	**46**	**47**	**48**	**49**	**50**
B	A	D	C	C	C	A	C	D	A
51	**52**	**53**	**54**	**55**	**56**	**57**	**58**	**59**	**60**
D	A	C	B	B	B	C	C	A	B
61	**62**	**63**	**64**	**65**	**66**	**67**	**68**	**69**	**70**
A	C	C	B	C	B	B	A	C	A
71	**72**	**73**	**74**	**75**	**76**	**77**	**78**	**79**	**80**
C	C	A	A	A	B	C	C	D	C
81	**82**	**83**	**84**	**85**	**86**	**87**	**88**	**89**	**90**
B	C	D	C	C	B	B	B	B	B
91	**92**	**93**	**94**	**95**	**96**	**97**	**98**	**99**	**100**
D	C	A	A	B	A	B	D	B	A
101	**102**	**103**	**104**	**105**	**106**	**107**	**108**	**109**	**110**
A	D	C	A	B	C	D	D	A	C
111	**112**	**113**	**114**	**115**	**116**	**117**	**118**	**119**	**120**
C	D	B	D	C	C	C	D	D	A

PAPER-II

GENERAL ENGLISH

Directions (Qs. No. 1-3) : *In the following questions, Choose the word opposite in meaning to the given word as your answer:*

1. Equilibrium :
A. Work out B. Disturb
C. Imbalance D. Unevenness

2. Superfluous :
A. Essential B. Excess
C. Unwanted D. Urgent

3. Veteran :
A. Activist B. Enthusiast
C. Novice D. Master

Directions (Qs. No. 4) : *In the following question, a sentence has been given in active/passive voice. Out of the four alternatives suggested, select the one which best expresses the same sentence in passive / active voice.*

4. Open the door.
A. Let the door shall be opened.
B. The door shall be opened.
C. The door was opened.
D. Let the door be opened.

Directions (Qs. No. 5-6) : *In the following questions, a sentence has been given in direct / indirect. Out of the four alternatives suggested, select the one which best expresses the same sentence in Direct/ Indirect and mark your answer.*

5. My friend requested me to bring him a sandwich.
A. He said, "My friend, please bring me a sandwich."
B. My friend said, "Will you bring me a sandwich"
C. "Please bring me a sandwich", said my friend.
D. "Please bring my friend a sandwich," said he

6. Ram said, "If I had the tools I could mend the car"
A. Ram told that he had the tools for mending the car.
B. Ram said that if he had the tools he could mend the car.
C. Ram said I could mend the car if I have the tools.
D. Ram told that he could mend the car if he had the tools.

Directions (Qs. No. 7-10) : *In these questions, a sentence has been given in active/passive voice. Out of the four alternatives suggested below, select the one which best expresses the same sentence in passive/ active voice.*

7. The vintage cars hold a special place in the hearts of their owners.
A. A special place in the hearts of the vintage car owners is held by them.
B. A special place was held by the vintage cars in the heart of their owners.
C. A special place is held by the vintage cars in the hearts of their owners.
D. A special place is being held by vintage cars in the hearts of their owners.

8. Quinine tastes bitter.
A. Quinine is bitter when it is tasted.
B. Quinine is bitter tasted
C. The taste of quinine is bitter.
D. Quinine is tasted bitter

9. The gardener ought to water the plants daily.
A. The plants have been watered daily by the gardener.
B. The plants ought to water daily by the gardener.
C. The plants are ought to water daily by the gardener
D. The plants ought to be watered daily by the gardener.

10. What amused you?
    A. What you are made to amuse by?
    B. By what are you being amused?
    C. By what were you amused?
    D. By what have you been amused?

Directions (Qs. No. 11-15) : *In these questions, sentences are given with blanks to be filled in with an appropriate and suitable word. Four alternatives are suggested for each question. Choose the correct alternative out of the four.*

11. She feared that she .... :
    A. will fail
    B. may fail
    C. might have fail
    D. would fail

12. The sudden change in his behaviour came as a surprise to me, I began .... :
    A. to cut a sorry figure
    B. to smell a rat
    C. to turn a new leaf
    D. to blow hot

13. We all laughed .... the affair.
    A. over B. about
    C. for D. on

14. We warned her .... the danger.
    A. from B. about
    C. against D. of

15. The streets are lighted .... electricity.
    A. with B. by
    C. on D. in

Directions (Qs. No. 16-18) : *In the following questions, a sentence is marked in three parts indicated by number (A), (B), (C). Read the sentence to find whether there is an error in any part of it. When you find an error in any one of the parts (A), (B), or (C), select that part as your answer. If you do not find any error in a sentence, in that case (D) will signify a "No error" response. Error may be in grammar, word usage or idioms. There may be a word missing or there may be a word which should be removed.*

16. Put out (A)/ the fire (B)/ quickly (C)/ No error (D).

17. A fight (A)/ took place (B)/ on the board of the ship (C)/ No error (D).

18. Arun was leading (A)/ a happy and leisurely life (B)/ after his retirement from his service. (C)/ No error (D).

Directions (Qs. No. 19-20) : *In these questions four words are given in each question, out of which only one word is wrongly spelt. Find that word and choose your answer accordingly.*

19. A. Insolvency B. Legitimacy
    C. Hypocrisy D. Idiosyncracy

20. A. Quadruple B. Quagmaire
    C. Quadrangle D. Quadrant

Directions (Qs. No. 21) : *In the following question, a sentence has been given in active/passive voice. Out of the four alternatives suggested, select the one which best expresses the same sentence in passive / active voice.*

21. For a long time people believed the earth to be flat.
    A. The Earth was believed to be flat for a long time.
    B. The earth had been believed to be flat for a long time.
    C. The earth is believed to be flat for a long time.
    D. The Earth was being believed to be flat for along time.

Directions (Qs. No. 22-25) : *In these questions four words are given in each question, out of which only one word is wrongly spelt. Find that word and choose your answer accordingly.*

22. A. Anniversery B. Bureaucracy
    C. Heresy D. Secrecy

23. A. Inexplicable B. Inevitable
    C. Inextinguishable D. Inexpressable

24. A. Mountainer B. Mountaineer
    C. Mounteener D. Mountineer

25. A. Emphetic B. Emphattic
    C. Emphatick D. Emphatic

Directions (Qs. No. 26-30) : *One simple physical concept lies behind the formation of stars : Gravitational instability. The concept is not new. Newton first perceived it late in 17th century.*

Imagine a <u>uniform</u>, static cloud of gas in space. Imagine then that the gas is somehow disturbed so that one small spherical region becomes a little denser than the gas around it so that the small regions gravitation field becomes slightly stronger. It now attracts more matter to it and its gravity increases further, causing it begin contract. As <u>it</u> contracts, its density increases, which increases its gravity even more so it picks up even more matter and contracts even further. The process continues until the small region of gas finally forms gravitationally bound object.

26. The author provides information that answers which of the following questions?

(*a*) What causes the disturbances that changes the cloud from its original static condition?

(*b*) How does this small region's increasing density affect its gravitational field?

(*c*) What is the end result of the gradually increasing concentration of small region of gas?

A. (*a*) Only
B. (*b*) Only
C. (*b*) and (*c*) Only
D. (*a*), (*b*) and (*c*)

27. What does the underlined word <u>It</u> stands for in the passage?

A. Gravitational instability
B. Cloud of Gas
C. Small Spherical Denser region
D. Matter

28. With which of the following words can you replace the word <u>Uniform</u> as given in this passage:

A. Uniting B. Varying
C. Gaseous D. Unvarying

29. It can be inferred from this passage that the author views the information contained within it as:

A. Lacking in elaboration
B. Original but Obscure
C. Speculative and unprofitable
D. Uncomplicated and traditional

30. The primary purpose of the passage is to:

A. Describe the static condition
B. Support a theory considered outmoded.
C. Depict the successive stages of a phenomenon.
D. Demonstrate the evolution of the meaning of a term

Directions (Qs. No. 31-34) : *In the following questions, a sentence is marked in three parts indicated by number (A), (B), (C). Read the sentence to find whether there is an error in any part of it. When you find an error in any one of the parts (A), (B), or (C), select that part as your answer. If you do not find any error in a sentence, in that case (D) will signify a "No error" response. Error may be in grammar, word usage or idioms. There may be a word missing or there may be a word which should be removed.*

31. The wisest man (A)/ who ever lived (B)/ made mistakes (C)/ No error (D).

32. I am looking forward (A)/ to receive (B)/ your reply (C)/ No error (D).

33. Ten shillings (A)/ was paid (B)/ to him (C)/ No error (D).

34. The pirates, who had hidden the treasure on the island, (A)/ went back again (B)/because now they thought that they can now remove it with safety. (C)/ No Error (D).

Directions (Qs. No. 35-40) : *Out of the four alternatives, choose the one which can be substituted for the underlined words / part of the sentence.*

35. The beleaguered politician was anxious <u>to set the record straight:</u>

A. Give a speech
B. Win party support
C. Give a correct account
D. Make a confession

36. The study of religion and religious ideas and beliefs:
A. Theocracy B. Theosophy
C. Theology D. Theism

37. A short walk for pleasure or exercise:
A. Jog B. Stroll
C. Gallop D. Promenade

38. Ram does unpaid work for the hospital:
A. Honorific B. Honest
C. Honorary D. Honourable

39. A person who takes no intoxicating drinks:
A. Drunkard B. Non–alcoholic
C. Addict D. Teetotaller

40. Dr. Roshan Kumar was a demagogue:
A. One who commands one's followers with threats.
B. One who loves one's followers.
C. One who can sway one's followers by intelligence.
D. One who can sway one's followers by the power of oratory.

Directions (Qs. No. 41) : *In the following question, Choose the word opposite in meaning to the given word as your answer:*

41. Immortal:
A. Eternal B. Permanent
C. Deathly D. Temporary

Directions (Qs. No. 42-45) : *From the following alternatives (A), (B), (C) and (D), select the word closest in meaning to the underlined word.*

42. He spent most of his years debunking politicians.
A. Exposing B. Cheating
C. Threatening D. Pacifying

43. I was discomfited to find the boss in the Disco.
A. Irritated B. Uncomfortable
C. Bewildered D. Displeased

44. The Individual's freedom is circumscribed by his responsibility to others.
A. Limited B. Entangled
C. Destroyed D. Eroded

45. They are carrying a charade of negotiations with the Governments.
A. Series B. Charter
C. Absurd pretence D. Spate

Directions (Qs. No. 46-50) : *The first and last part of the sentence are numbered 1 and 6. The rest of the sentence is split into four parts and named P, Q, R and S. These four parts are not given in their proper order. Read the sentence and find out which of the four combinations is correct. Then find the correct answer:*

46. 1. Yesterday morning
P. And raised slogan against
Q. I was shocked to see the bank employees.
R. When I went to my bank to withdraw some money.
S. Squatting at the gate of the bank.
6. The anti worker stance of the bank management
A. QSPR B. RQSP
C. SPRQ D. PSRQ

47. 1. Here live the Kolis
P. The original inhabitants
Q. The british joined together
R. And turn it into
S. Of the seven Islands
6. A thriving port city
A. PSQR B. PQRS
C. PRSQ D. PQSR

48. 1. In spite of repeated warnings
P. Given by his friends and well wishers
Q. Ramesh continued to gamble
R. That he had inherited
S. And eventually lost everything.
6. From his long dead parents
A. PQSR B. QSRP
C. SRPQ D. RPQS

49. 1. Each one of us must realize
P. For India and her people
Q. Which has been the basis of our culture
R. That the only future
S. Is one of tolerance and cooperation
6. From age past.
A. PSQR B. RSQP
C. PRQS D. RPSQ

50. 1. From the hill, where we were standing
P. Lying to the west and to the north.
Q. And some rising considerably above the sand
R. Some half buried
S. We saw such a large number of tombs.
6. That we could not count them

A. RQSP B. SPRQ
C. RPSQ D. SQPR

Directions (Qs. No. 51-60) : *In the following sentences, there are some blanks which are numbered. Below the sentences you are given a choice of four words (A), (B), (C) and (D), one of which is the most appropriate. Choose the best word as your answer.*

It is one of the tragic ironies of our age that the rocket, which could have been the symbol of humanity's aspirations for the stars, has become one of the weapons threatening to destroy civilization. This state of affairs has —(51)— a difficult moral problem to —(52)— wishing to take an active —(53)— in the development of astronautics, —(54)— almost all research on rockets —(55)— now carried out by military —(56)— and is covered by various —(57)— classifications. The technical problems involved —(58)— designing long range guided missiles are —(59)— identical with those involved in the —(60)— of reconnaissance rockets.

51. A. presented B. propounded
C. caused D. produced

52. A. men B. that
C. those D. others

53. A. interest B. part
C. share D. position

54. A. when B. whatever
C. where D. for

55. A. is B. had been
C. was D. are

56. A. centers B. firms
C. establishments D. officers

57. A. favorable B. foolish
C. secret D. regular

58. A. for B. in
C. from D. with

59. A. practically B. however
C. hardly D. never

60. A. deployment B. engaging
C. launching D. construction

ANSWERS

1	2	3	4	5	6	7	8	9	10
C	A	C	D	C	B	C	A	D	C
11	**12**	**13**	**14**	**15**	**16**	**17**	**18**	**19**	**20**
D	B	B	C	A	D	C	A	D	B
21	**22**	**23**	**24**	**25**	**26**	**27**	**28**	**29**	**30**
A	A	D	B	D	C	B	D	D	C
31	**32**	**33**	**34**	**35**	**36**	**37**	**38**	**39**	**40**
B	B	B	C	C	C	D	C	D	D
41	**42**	**43**	**44**	**45**	**46**	**47**	**48**	**49**	**50**
D	A	C	A	C	B	A	A	D	B
51	**52**	**53**	**54**	**55**	**56**	**57**	**58**	**59**	**60**
C	C	B	A	A	C	C	B	D	C

MECHANICAL ENGINEERING

1

THERMODYNAMICS

Thermodynamics deals in the study of various concepts and laws describing the conversion of energy from one form to another. In Engineering Thermodynamics, the energy transformation is restricted to the study of heat and work and conversion from one form to another. The quantity of matter under consideration is called the system. In a closed system, there is no interchange of matter between system and surroundings. The mass does not cross the boundary whereas the energy transfer takes place along the boundary. In an open system, there is such interchange in which the mass as well as energy both transfer across its boundaries.

First Law of Thermodynamics

According to this in a cyclic process the total amount of heat supplied to the system is proportional to the amount of work done of the system. This law has been stated in a number of ways, some of the typical statements are :

A. Energy can neither be created nor be destroyed.
B. The sum total of all energy remains constant.
C. Whenever energy is transformed from one form to another, energy is always conserved.

The Second Law of Thermodynamics

It states that conversion of heat to work is limited by the temperature at which conversion occurs. Heat flows from hot objects to cold objects unaided but it cannot flow from a cold object to hotter object without the expenditure of mechanical energy.

According to Kelvin Plank statement, it is impossible to construct an engine working on cyclic process whose sole purpose is to convert all the heat supplied to it into equivalent amount of work.

Ideal Gas Laws

Boyle's Law : Keeping the temperature constant the volume of a given mass of a gas varies inversely as its absolute pressure

$$V \propto \frac{1}{P}$$

or $$P.V = \text{constant}$$

Charle's Law : Keeping pressure constant the volume of a given mass of a gas varies directly as its absolute temperature

$$V \propto T$$

or $$\frac{V}{T} = \text{constant}$$

Gas Equation : At low pressure and high temperatures, in the absence of chemical reaction, all gases approach a condition such their P–V–T properties may be expressed by the relation

$$pV = RT$$

If V is expressed as volume per unit weight, the value of the constant R will be different for different gases. If V is expressed as the volume of one molecular weight of gas, then Ru is same for all gases in any chosen system of unit. Hence R = Ru/M

$$pV = NMRT$$

Where V is now the total gas volume, N is the number of moles of gas in the volume V, M is the molecular weight and Ru = MR, the universal gas constant. The value of Ru for air is 29.27m kg f. per kg. per°k.

Entropy : For reversible cyclic process in which the temperature varies during heat absorption and rejection, *i.e.,* for any reversible cycle $\oint \frac{dQ}{T} = 0.$

Consequently for any reversible process. $\int \frac{dQ}{T}$ is not a function of the particular reversible path followed. This integral is called the entropy change, or

$$\int ds = \int_1^2 \frac{dQ}{T} = S_2 - S_1 = S_{1-2}$$

The entropy of a substance is dependent only on its state or condition. For any reversible process, the change is entropy of the system and surroundings is zero, whereas for any irreversible process, the net entropy change is possible.

The Third Law of Thermodynamics :

It states that the total entropy of pure substances approaches zero as the absolute thermodynamic temperature approach zero. The third law approaches further that the partial derivatives with respect to temperature of generalised force and generalized displacement also vanish at absolute zero.

Relation between Internal Energy (*u*), Enthalpy (*h*), and Entropy (S) of an ideal gas

If an ideal gas with constant specific heats changes from an initial state P_1, V_1, T_1 to a final state P_2, V_2, T_2, the following equations hold,

$$u_1 - u_2 = mC_v(T_2 - T_1)$$
$$= A(p_2v_2 - p_1v_1)/(k-1)$$
$$h_2 - h_1 = mC_p(T_2 - T_1)$$
$$= Ak(p_2v_2 - p_1v_1)/(k-1)$$

$$S_1 - S_2 = m\left[C_v \log_e\left(\frac{T_2}{T_1}\right) + AR\log_e\left(\frac{v_2}{v_1}\right)\right]$$

$$= m\left[C_p \log_e\left(\frac{T_2}{T_1}\right) + AR\log_e\left(\frac{p_2}{p_1}\right)\right]$$

$$= m\left[C_p \log_e\left(\frac{v_2}{v_1}\right) + C_v\log_e\left(\frac{p_2}{p_1}\right)\right]$$

Special Changes of State for Ideal gases :

A. Constant Volume :

$$\frac{P_2}{P_1} = \frac{T_2}{T_1}$$
$$Q_{12} = u_2 - u_1 = mC_v(t_2 - t_1)$$
$$W_{12} = 0$$
$$S_2 - S_1 = mC_v \log_e\left(\frac{T_2}{T_1}\right)$$

B. Constant Pressure :

$$\frac{V_2}{V_1} = \frac{T_2}{T_1}$$
$$W_{12} = p(V_2 - V_1) = mR(t_2 - t_1)$$
$$Q_{12} = mC_p(t_2 - t_1)$$
$$S_2 - S_1 = mC_p \log_e\left(\frac{T_2}{T_1}\right)$$

C. Isothermal (Constant Temperature) :

$$\frac{p_2}{p_1} = \frac{V_2}{V_1}$$
$$U_2 - U_1 = 0$$
$$W_{12} = mRT\log_e\left(\frac{V_2}{V_1}\right)$$
$$= p_1V_1\log_e\left(\frac{V_2}{V_1}\right)$$
$$Q_{12} = AW_{12}$$
$$S_2 - S_1 = Q_{12}/T$$
$$= MAR\log_e\left(\frac{V_2}{V_1}\right)$$

D. Reversible Adiabatic (Isentropic) :

$$p_1V_1^k = p_2V_2^k$$
$$\frac{T_2}{T_1} = \left(\frac{V_2}{V_1}\right)^{k-1} = \left(\frac{p_2}{p_1}\right)^{k-\frac{1}{k}}$$
$$AW_{12} = U_1 - U_2 = mC_v(t_1 - t_2)$$
$$Q_{12} = 0$$
$$S_2 - S_1 = 0$$
$$W_{12} = \frac{p_1V_1 - p_2V_2}{k-1}$$
$$= \frac{p_1V_1 - \left[1 - \left(\frac{p_2}{p_1}\right)\right]^{k-\frac{1}{k}}}{k-1}$$

Polytropic :

For a polytropic change of an ideal gas (for which C_v is constant), the specific heat is given by the relation

$$C_n = \frac{C_v(n-k)}{n-1}$$

Hence $1 < n < k$, C_n is negative

In polytropic process

$$p_1V_1^n = p_2V_2^n$$
$$\frac{T_2}{T_1} = \left(\frac{V_1}{V_2}\right)^{n-1} = \left(\frac{p_2}{p_1}\right)^{n-\frac{1}{n}}$$
$$W_{12} = \frac{p_1V_1 - p_2V2}{n-1}$$

$$= \frac{p_1 V_1 \left[1 + \left(\frac{p_2}{p_1}\right)^{\frac{n-1}{n}}\right]}{n-1}$$

$$Q_{12} = mC_n(t_2 - t_1)$$

Heat Engines

A heat engine is a device for converting heat energy into work. In the most general form it operates through the input as heat Q at temperature T, the output of work W, and the rejection of heat Q to a receiver or sink at temperature T_s. For a cycle,

$$\Delta E = 0 \text{ and } Q - Q_s = W$$

Hence for any such process

$$\text{Actual effciency} = \frac{W}{Q} = \frac{Q - Q_s}{Q} = 1 = \frac{Q_s}{Q}$$

For a reversible cycle operating between the constant temperature T and T_s, $Q = Td_s$ and $Q_s = T_s d_s$, hence for this ideal process.

$$\text{Ideal efficient} = \frac{T - T_s}{T}$$

Any irreversibility in the cycle makes Q_s greater than $T_s d_s$ reduces the efficiency.

Heat Transfer

Conduction : Heat conduction is due to the property of matter which allows the passage of heat energy, even if physical body is impermeable to any kind of rays and its parts are not in motion relative to one another.

The fundamental relation for steady flow of heat by conduction originates from the French physicists Biot and is expressed by

$$q = -kA \frac{dt}{dx}$$

Convection : When convective heat transfer is caused by density difference produced by temperature gradients, this is known as free or natural convection. On the other hand, the rate of heat transfer increases substantially if external agency, e.g. pump or blower is used, so that fluid moves faster. Such a convective heat transfer known as forced convection.

Radiation : Heat radiation is due to the property of matter to emit and to absorb different kinds of rays, and to the fact that an empty space is perfectly permeable to rays and that matter allows them to pass more or less.

Heat transfer by radiation is important in boiler furnaces billet reheating furnaces etc. Solar radiation plays an important part in the design of heating and ventilating system.

The rate of heat q_r radiated from an area, A is given by the equation.

$$q_r = \in \sigma AT^4$$

Where T is absolute temperature

$\in$ is a factor depending on kind of surface and on temperature

σ is a constant of nature.

Kirchoff's Law : It states that emissivity is equal for a body at temperature equilibrium with its surroundings and depend only on the temperature.

Black Body : When radiant energy falls on a body, part may be absorbed, part reflected and the remainder transmitted through the body.

MULTIPLE–CHOICE QUESTIONS

1. Calorific value of a fuel is based on
A. 1 kg of fuel B. 1 kg/m^3 of fuel
C. 1 m^3 of fuel D. its specific volume

2. The bomb calorimeter is an apparatus to measure the
A. calorific value of a gaseous fuel
B. calorific value of solid and gaseous fuels
C. calorimetric composition of any solid bomb material
D. calorific value of a solid or liquid fuel

3. The maximum heat content at 100°C in cal/m^3 is possessed by the followign gas.
A. CH_4 B. SO_2
C. O_2 D. CO_2

4. The major constituents of a fuel are
A. Carbon, Hydrogen and Oxygen
B. Carbon, hydrogen, Oxygen and Nitrogen
C. Carbon, Oxygen, Hydrogen, Nitrogen, Phosphorus and Sulphur
D. Carbon and hydrogen

5. For combustion of gaseous fuels the following is of great use
A. Mandeleef's periodic table
B. Dalton's Law
C. Brayton Cycle
D. Avogadro Hypothesis

6. Lower Calorific value of a fuel is the
A. value of heat produced by a fuel under constant pressure and volume.
B. value of heat produced which can be utilised for commercial purposes
C. lowest amount of heat produced by a fuel by burning 1 m^3 of fuel
D. lowest amount of heat produced by any fuel.

7. Which one of the properties given below is an intensive property of the system?
A. Volume B. Temperature
C. Kinetic energy D. Potential energy

8. Which one of the properties given below is an extensive property of the system?
A. Pressure B. Temperature
C. Potential energy D. Viscosity

9. The mechanical equivalent of heat 'J' is equal to
A. 4.1868 kg/k. cal B. 41.8 kJ/k.cal
C. 4.1868 k.cal/kg D. 4.1868 kJ

10. In metric system the unit of heat is given as
A. C.H.U B. B.T.U
C. k.cal D. Kelvin

11. The ratio of the specific heat at constant pressure to specific heat at constant volume for air is equal to
A. 1.4 B. 0.14
C. 14 D. 140

12. the general gas equation is given as
A. $PV = mT$ B. $\frac{P}{V} = mT$
C. $PT = mRT$ D. $\frac{P}{V} = mRT$

13. In S.I. units pressure is expressed in
A. kgf/cm^2 B. mm of mercury
C. N/m^2 or bar D. None of the above

14. For any gas
A. $C_p = C_v$ B. $C_p < C_v$
C. $C_p > C_v$ D. None of the above

15. Gases have
A. Two specific heats B. Three specific heats
C. One specific heat D. None of the above

16. The value of C_p for air is equal to
A. 2.38 k. cal/kg °K B. 0.024 k.cal/kg °K
C. 3.238 k. cal/kg °K D. 0.424 k.cal/kg °K

17. In a closed system
A. Energy transfers from surrounding to system
B. Energy transfers from system to surrounding
C. Energy transfers from system to surrounding and vice versa
D. Energy as well as mass cross the boundaries

18. Centrifugal pump is an example of
A. Isolated system B. Closed system
C. Steady flow system D. None of the above

19. Heat pump is a device which
A. Convert mechanical energy into heat energy
B. Convert heat energy into mechanical enrgy
C. Delivers the heat flow low temperature to a high temperature in a cyclic process
D. Delivers the heat from high temperature to a low temperature in a cyclic process

20. Molar volume is equal to
A. 22.41 m^3 at N.T.P. B. 2.241 m^3 at N.T.P.
C. 29.27 m^3 at N.T.P. D. 1.03 m^3 at N.T.P.

21. Equal volumes of different perfect gases at same temperature and pressure contain
A. Unequal number of molecules
B. Equal number of molecules
C. Any number of molecules depending upon other conditions also
D. None of the above

22. General energy equation for steam boiler is given by
A. $Q = H_2 - H_1$
B. $Q = H_1 + H_2$
C. $Q = H_2 - H_1$ + work done
D. $Q = H_2 - H_1 + K.E$
Where Q is the heat supplied and $H_2 - H_1$ is change in enthalpy

23. Change in entropy during constant pressure process is given by the relation
A. $mC_p \log_e \frac{T_1}{T_2}$ B. $mC_p \log_e \frac{T_2}{T_1}$
C. $mC_v \log_e \frac{T_2}{T_1}$ D. $m\frac{R}{J} \log_e \frac{T_2}{T_1}$

24. When a gas is heated at constant volume, the

chage in entropy is given by the relation

A. $mC_p \log_e \frac{T_2}{T_1}$ B. $m\frac{R}{J} \log_e \frac{T_2}{T_1}$

C. $mR \log_e \frac{T_2}{T_1}$ D. $mC_v \log_e \frac{T_2}{T_1}$

25. In isopiestic process, the

A. Temperature remains constant
B. Volume remains constant
C. $p \times v$ = constant
D. Pressure remains constant

26. A refrigeration system works on

A. Second Law of Thermodynamics
B. First Law of Thermodynamics
C. Zeroth Law of Thermodynmics
D. None of the above

27. Total heat supplied at constant volume is

A. $Q = m \times C_p \times (T_2 - T_1)$
B. $Q = m \times R \times (T_2 - T_1)$
C. $Q = m\, C_v \times (T_2 + T_1)$
D. $Q = m\, C_v \times (T_2 - T_1)$

28. Internal combustion engine works on

A. First Law of Thermodynamics
B. Second Law of Thermodynamics
C. Zeroth Law of Thermodynamics
D. None of the above

29. In orsat apparatus, the pyrogalic acid is used to absorb

A. CO_2 B. CO
C. O_2 D. N_2

30. In Orsat apparatus $CuCl_2$ is used to absorb

A. CO_2 B. CO
C. O_2 D. N_2

31. In Orsat apparatus KO_2 is used to absorb

A. CO_2 B. CO
C. O D. N_2

32. Boyle's Law states

A. $P_1V_1 = P_2V_2$ B. $\frac{P_1}{T_1} = \frac{V_1}{T_2}$

C. $\frac{P_1}{V_2} = \frac{P_2}{V_2}$ D. $\frac{V_1}{T_1} = \frac{V_2}{T_2}$

33. Charle's Law states

A. $P_1V_1 = P_2V_2$ B. $\frac{P_1}{T_1} = \frac{V_1}{T_2}$

C. $\frac{P_1}{V_2} = \frac{P_2}{V_2}$ D. $\frac{V_1}{T_1} = \frac{V_2}{T_2}$

34. Liquids have

A. No specific heat
B. Different values of specific heat at same temperature
C. Only one value of specific heat
D. Two distinct values of specific heat

35. The efficiency of the diesel cycle increases

A. With increase in cut-off ratio
B. With decrease in cut-off ratio
C. Remains unaffected
D. Unpredictable

36. The First and Second Laws of Thermodynamics help to derive the following properties respectively

A. Pressure and temperature
B. Temperature and entropy
C. Pressure and entropy
D. Temperature and enthalpy

37. For the same compression ratio, the efficiency of the Dual cycle

A. Is more than the Otto cycle
B. Is less than the Diesel cycle
C. Is less than the Diesel cycle and greater than the Otto cycle
D. In less than the Otto cycle and greater than the Diesel cycle

38. A refrigerator is working in an isolated room. The temperature inside the refrigerated space and that of room are 10°C and 25°C respectively. Suddenly the door of the room is opened, the temperature of the room then

A. Will increase
B. Will decrease
C. Will increase first and then decrease
D. Will remain constant

39. General energy equation for a steady flow system is

A. $H_1 + \frac{V_1^2}{2gJ} + \frac{Z_1}{J} + Q = \frac{V_2^2}{2gJ} + \frac{Z_2}{J}$ + losses

B. $H_1 + \frac{V_1^2}{2gJ} + \frac{Z_1}{J} + Q = \frac{V^2}{2gJ}$ + work done + losses

C. $H_1 + \frac{V_1^2}{2gJ} = \frac{Z_1}{J} + Q = H_2 + \frac{V_2^2}{2gJ} + \frac{V^2}{J} +$ work done + losses

D. $H_1 + \frac{V_1^2}{2gJ} + \frac{Z_1}{J} = H_2 + \frac{V_2^2}{2gJ} + \frac{Z_1}{J} +$ work done + losses

40. The Rankine cycle will approach to Carnot cycle is

A. The number of regenerators are increased
B. The number of regenerators are decreased
C. The number of reheaters are increased
D. The number of reheaters are decreased

41. Enthalpy (H) is equal to

A. $U + \frac{pv}{J}$ B. $U - \frac{pv}{J}$
C. $U + \frac{R}{Jpv}$ D. $U + Jpv$

42. Specific volume of a gas is the volume of

A. Gas at N.T.P.
B. Unit mass of that gas
C. Total amount of gas at some stated temperature and pressure
D. Gas at –273°C

43. The volume of the universal gas constant (R_u) is equal to

A. 848 m kgf/kg-mol per °K
B. 8.48 m kgf/kg-mol per °K
C. 84.8 m kgf/kg-mol per °K
D. .848 m kgf/kg-mol per °K

44. In a polytropic process

A. $\frac{T_1}{T_2} = \left(\frac{V_2}{T_1}\right)^{n-\frac{1}{n}} = \left(\frac{P_1}{P_2}\right)^{n-1}$

B. $\frac{T_1}{T_2} = \left(\frac{V_1}{V_2}\right)^{n-1} = \left(\frac{P_1}{P_2}\right)^{n-\frac{1}{n}}$

C. $\frac{T_1}{T_2} = \left(\frac{V_2}{V_1}\right)^{n-1} = \left(\frac{P_2}{P_1}\right)^{n\,\frac{1}{n}}$

D. $\frac{T_1}{T_2} = \left(\frac{V_2}{V_1}\right)^{n-1} = \left(\frac{P_1}{P_2}\right)^{n-\frac{1}{n}}$

45. Constant volume process is

A. Isopiestic process B. Hyperbolic process
C. Isometric process D. Polytropic process

46. Work done during polytropic process is given by the relation

A. $\frac{P}{J} = (V_2 - V_1)$ k. cal

B. $\frac{P_2V_2}{J} \log_e \frac{V_1}{V_2}$ k. cal

C. $\frac{P_1V_1 - P_2V_2}{J(n-1)}$ k. cal

D. $\frac{R}{J}\left(\frac{T_1 - T_2}{r-1}\right)$ k. cal

47. The polytropic process on P–V diagram is represented by the figure.

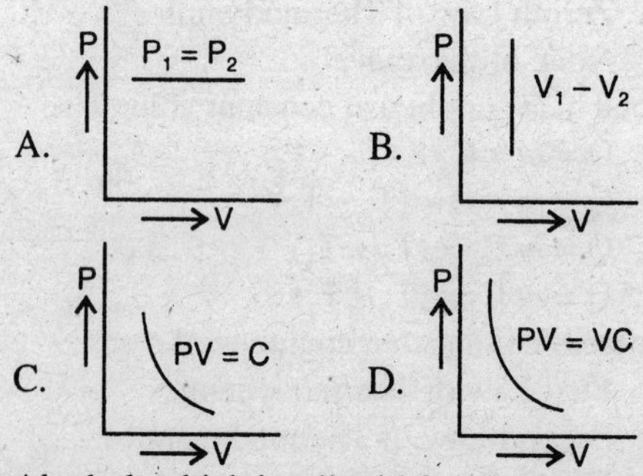

48. Alcohol, which is a liquid fuel is obtained from

A. The distillation of crude oil
B. Vegetable matters by the fermentation process
C. Destructive distillation of coal
D. None of the above

49. The percentage of carbon in crude oil varies between

A. 45% to 50% B. 50% to 60%
C. 60% to 80% D. 83% to 87%

50. The diesel oil is obtained during distillation process between the temperature limits

A. 100°C to 200°C B. 200°C to 300°C
C. 360°C to 475°C D. 500°C to 675°C

51. The solid fuel having the highest calorific value is

A. Wood B. Lignite
C. Coke D. Anthracite

52. The volumetic analysis of dry products of combustion is done by

A. Bomb calorimeter B. Viscosity meter
C. Orsat apparatus D. Calorimeter

ANSWERS

1	2	3	4	5	6	7	8	9	10
C	D	B	D	C	B	B	C	D	C
11	**12**	**13**	**14**	**15**	**16**	**17**	**18**	**19**	**20**
A	C	C	C	A	C	C	C	C	A
21	**22**	**23**	**24**	**25**	**26**	**27**	**28**	**29**	**30**
B	A	B	D	D	A	D	A	C	B
31	**32**	**33**	**34**	**35**	**36**	**37**	**38**	**39**	**40**
A	A	D	C	B	B	B	B	C	A
41	**42**	**43**	**44**	**45**	**46**	**47**	**48**	**49**	**50**
A	B	A	D	C	C	D	B	D	C
51	**52**								
D	C								

2

STEAM ENGINE

Steam is the working substance used in the operation of steam engines and steam turbines. A mixture of steam and water particles forms 'wet steam' when all water particles are evaporated, it is said to be 'dry and saturated' steam. Further heating results in super heated steam. steam does not obey the laws of perfect gases until it is perfectly dry.

The total heat or enthalpy of steam is given by the following relation.

I. For wet steam

$$H_W = h + L_X$$

II. For dry steam

$$H_S = h + L$$

III. For super heated steam

$$H_{sup} = h + L + C_p (t_{sup} - t_{sat})$$

The volume of wet steam = $q \times v$

Steam Engine : In all steam engines, steam is used as the working fluid. These engines operate on the principle of first law of thermodynamics *i.e.* heat and work are mutually convertible. In steam engine heat of steam is converted into work by means of a piston reciprocating in a cylinder. The mechanical work produced, is made available at the flywheel of the engine. Types of steam engines are

I. Horizontal or vertical.
II. Single cylinder or multicylinder.
III. Single acting or double acting.
IV. Slow speed, medium speed or high speed engines.
V. Condensing or non-condensing type.
VI. Throttle governed or automatic cut off governed.

Theoretical mean effective pressure, p_m is given by.

$$p_m = \frac{p_1}{r}\left[1 + 2 - 3 \log r\right] - p_b$$

Where p_1 = admission pressure of steam
p_b = back pressure of steam
r = expansion ratio

Indicated horse power of a steam engine

$$\text{I.H.P.} = \frac{p_m \text{ LAN}}{4500} \text{ h.p. for single acting engine}$$

$$\text{I.H.P.} = \frac{2p_m \text{ LAN}}{4500} \text{ h.p. for double acting engine}$$

$$\text{I.H.P.} = \frac{p_m \text{ LAN}(2A - Q)}{4500} \text{ h.p. taking into}$$

account piston rod

Where p_m =Actual mean effective pressure in kg/cm^2
L =Length of stroke in m
A =Area of the piston rod in cm^2
N =Engine rpm
a =Area a pistion rod in cm^2.

Fuels : A fuel is a substance which on burning with oxygen in the atmospheric air produces a large amount of heat. The amount of heat liberated is known as calorific value of fuel. The fuel exist in all the three forms :

A. Solid : Coal, wood.
B. Liquid fuels : Petrol, diesels, alcohols, molasses etc.
C. Gaseous fuels : Natural gas, coal gas, producer gas, water gas, blast furnace gas.

Calorific Value : The amount of heat obtained by the complete combination of 1 kg of a fuel when the products of its combustion have been cooled down to the temperature of surrounding air.

Calorific value of solid and liquid fuels may be determined with, the help of Bomb claorimeter, a Boy's gas calorimeter is used to determine calorific value of gaseous fuels.

Combustion of fuels : Atmospheric air contains 21% by volume of oxygen and 79% by volume nitrogen. By weight oxygen is 23% and nitrogen 77%. Knowing the composition of fuel, *e.g.*, carbon, hydrogen and other constituents present in air, the amount of air required for combustion can be estimated.

When pure carbon is burnt with minimum quantity of air, the maximum carbon dioxide content of fuel gases by volume is 20.9%. Thus CO_2 content of fuels can not exceed 21%. Presence of any other constituent of excess air supplied during combustion will reduce the percentage of carbon dioxide in the gases.

Steam boilers are closed vessels in which steam is produced by the application of the heat produced by the combustion of fuel. The boilers may be smoke tube type in which hot gases from the furnace pass through a tube or a bank of tubes. These tubes are surrounded by water. Due to transfer of heat from hot gases to water wet steam is produced. Simple vertical boiler, cochran boiler, scotch marine boiler, Lancashire boiler, and Locomotive boiler are exmaples of fire tube or smoke tube boilers.

In water tube boiler, water circulates inside the tubes which are heated from outside by hot gases from this furnace, Babcock and Wilcox boiler, La Mont boiler, Loeffer boiler are the examples of water tube boilers.

Performance : The performance of a boiler is measured in terms of its evaporative capacity *i.e.* quantity of steam produced per hour or per day. The equivalent evaporation and from at 100° is the amount of water evaporated from feed water at 100°C and formed into dry and saturated steam at 100°C at normal atmospheric pressure. Mathematically, equivalent evaporation from and at a 100°C is expressed as

$$E = \frac{We\left(H_1 - h_1\right)}{5390} \text{ kg.}$$

Where We = Weight of water actually evaporated or actual evaporation in kg/hr or kg/keg of fuel.

H = Total enthalpy of evaporated steam

$$\text{Boiler efficiency} = \frac{W_s\left(H - h_1\right)}{W_f \times C}$$

Efficiency of the engine : It is the raito of work done to the energy supplied, expressed in identical units is a measure of the efficiency of the engine. Thus

$$\text{Indicated thermal efficiency} = \frac{\text{I.H.P.} \times 4500}{W\left(H - h\right)J}$$

$$\text{Overall efficiency} = \frac{\text{B.H.P.} \times 4500 \times 60}{W_f \times C \times J}$$

$$\text{Brake thermal efficiency} = \frac{\text{Heat in B.H.P.}}{\text{Total heat}}$$

$$\text{Relative efficiency} = \frac{\text{Thermal efficiency}}{\text{Rankine efficiency}}$$

Steam Condenser is a closed vessel into which the steam is exhausted, and condenser after doing work in an engine cylinder or turbine. A steam condenser is used to maintain a low pressure so as to obtain the maximum possible energy from steam with the object of getting a high efficiency. Another pressure of steam condenser is to supply pure feed water of hot well, from where it is pumped back to the boiler.

Condensers are mainly of two types

I. Jet condenser or mixing type condenser

II. Surface condensers or non-mixing type condenser.

The vacuum efficiency of a condenser is given by

$$\text{Vacuum efficiency} = \frac{\text{Actual Vacuum}}{\text{Ideal Vacuum}}$$

$$= \frac{\text{Barometric pressure} - \text{Actual pressure}}{\text{Barometric pressure} - \text{Ideal pressure}}$$

Condenser Efficiency

$$= \frac{\text{Temperature rise of cooling water}}{\text{Vacuum temperature} - \text{Inlet cooling temperature}}$$

Steam Nozzles is a passage of varying cross-section, which converts heat energy of steam into kinetic energy. During the first part of the nozzle, the steam increases its velocity, but in its later part steam gains more in volume than in velocity. As the mass flow of steam remains constant, the variation of steam pressure depends upon

I. Dryness fraction of steam.

II. Specific volume of steam.

III. Velocity of steam.

The smallest section of the nozzle is known as throat. Velocity of steam through nozzle is given by

$$V = 44.7\sqrt{U}$$

Steam turbine : In a steam turbine rotatory motion is obtained by the gradual change of momentum of the steam. The steam turbine may by of two types.

I. Impulse turbine
II. Reaction type.

Performance of steam turbines

I. Diagram of blading efficiency

$$= \frac{\text{Work done on the blades}}{\text{Energy supplied}}$$

$$= \frac{2(Vw + Vw_1)\,V_b}{V^2} \text{ or } \frac{V^2 - V_1^2}{V^2}$$

II. Gross efficiency

$$= \frac{\text{Work done on blades / kg of steam}}{\text{Total energy supplied per stage per kg of steam}}$$

$$= \frac{(Vw_1 + Vw_2)\,V_b}{gJU}$$

III. Max. efficiency of an impulse turbine $= \cos^2 \alpha$

IV. Max. efficiency of a reaction turbine $= \dfrac{2\cos^2 \alpha}{1 + \cos^2 \alpha}$

MULTIPLE–CHOICE QUESTIONS

1. The maximum steam pressure of a locomotive boiler is
A. Above 10 kg/cm^2
B. Seldom below 30 kg/cm^2
C. 14.7 kg/cm^2 at N.T.P.
D. Limited to 18 kg/cm^2

2. The type of boilers which have greater reliability are the
A. Fire tube boilers
B. Water tube boilers
C. Both have equal reliability
D. Those which have single pass flow

3. The danger of an explosion is more serious in the case of
A. Water tube boilers
B. Fire tube boilers
C. Both are equally dangerous
D. It is more dangerous in water tube boilers because of its large water capacity

4. The boiler should conform to the safety regulations of the following
A. I.S. Specifications B. B.S. Code
C. DIN Specifications D. Boiler's Act

5. The use of an economiser with a boiler
A. Raises the plant efficiency
B. Helps bring down the feed water temperature
C. Is that it utilises the exhaust steam in raising the feed water temperature
D. Helps utilise the heat carried by the exhaust flue gases

6. In a boiler the fusible plug is fitted
A. Near the chimney before the exit steam opening
B. On the flange of the water level indicator
C. Inside the combustion chamber
D. At the fire box crown or over the combustion chamber

7. In a steam engine the fluid used for the expansion of work is
A. Coal B. Diesel
C. Steam D. Air fuel mixture

8. A steam engine can be a horizontal, vertical or inclined. This classification is according to the
A. Expansion of steam
B. Speeed of the engine
C. Position of cylinder
D. Field of application

9. Steam engine works on
A. Joule's cycle
B. Rankine cycle
C. Constant pressure cycle
D. Constant volume cycle

10. The thermal efficiency of steam engine is
A. more than steam turbine
B. less than steam turbine
C. equal to steam turbine
D. unpredictable

11. In uniflow steam engine the type of value used for controlling the steam is
A. Corliss value B. Drop value

C. D slide value D. None of the above

12. Eccentric is used to _

A. Reduce the speed of steam
B. Control the flow of steam
C. Convert the rotary motion into reciprocating
D. Convert the reciprocating motion into rotary motion

13. The function of crank is to

A. Control the speed
B. Control the flow of steam
C. Operate the value of engine
D. Convert reciprocating motion into rotary

14. A steam engine having a speed of 275 R.P.M. is termed as a

A. High speed engine
B. Low speed engine
C. Medium speed engine
D. Very slow speed engine

15. Diagram factor is always

A. More than one B. Less than one
C. Equal to one D. None of the above

16. The approximate value of diagram factor is

A. 0.2 B. 0.5
C. 0.7 D. 1.2

17. Which of the following is an example of a tire boiler?

A. Locomotive boiler
B. sterling boiler
C. Babcock and wilcox boiler
D. All the above

18. High pressure boilers are those which produce steam at a pressure of

A. 80 kg/cm^2 or more
B. 20 kg/cm^2
C. Above 40 kg/cm^2 but below 70 kg/cm^2
D. Two atmospheres and above

19. The cornish boiler differs from the Lancashire boiler in that

A. It contains one flue tube instead of two
B. Flow of gases is in the reverse direction
C. The cornish boiler is fire tube boiler whereas Lancashire is water tube boiler
D. All the above points are points of difference

20. Diagram factor is given by the relation

A. $\text{D.F.} = \dfrac{\text{Area of actual indicated diagram}}{\text{Area of hypothetical diagram}}$

B. $\text{D.F.} = \dfrac{\text{Area of actual indicated diagram}}{\text{Length of actual indicated diagram}}$

C. $\text{D.F.} = \dfrac{\text{Area of hypothetical diagram}}{\text{Length of hypothetical diagram}}$

D. $\text{D.F.} = \dfrac{\text{Area of hypothetical diagram}}{\text{Area of actual indicated diagram}}$

21. The relationship between stage efficiency, heat factor and overall efficiency of a multistage turbine is given by

A. $e_{\text{overall}} = \dfrac{e_{\text{stage}}}{\text{R.F.}}$

B. $e_{\text{overall}} = e_{\text{stage}} \times \text{R.F.}$

C. $e_{\text{overall}} = \dfrac{\text{R.F.}}{e_{\text{stage}}}$

D. $e_{\text{overall}} \times e_{\text{stage}} \times \text{R.F.} = 1$

22. Indicated horse power developed inside the steam engine cylinder is given by the relation

A. $\text{I.H.P.} = \dfrac{\text{P}_m \text{ LAN}}{75 \times 60}$ B. $\text{I.H.P.} = \dfrac{2\text{P}_m \text{ LAN}}{75 \times 60}$

C. $\text{I.H.P.} = \dfrac{4\text{P}_m \text{ LAN}}{75 \times 60}$ D. $\text{I.H.P.} = \dfrac{2\text{P}_m \text{ LAN}}{60}$

23. The boiler that is most suitable for meeting fluctuating demands of steam is the

A. Lancashire boiler B. Cornish boiler
C. Locomotive boiler . D. Cochran boiler

24. The draught in the Locomotive boiler is produced by

A. Means of the vacuum pump in it
B. The flow of steam from the fire box into the engine cylinder
C. The combined action of suction action of pump and pressure of steam
D. The motion of locomotive on rails

25. At the critical pressure of the steam the latent heat is equal to

A. 100 B. 250
C. zero D. 80

26. The function of the fusible plug in a boiler is to

A. Lift the lever and start the pump for water supply in case of failure
B. Extinguish the fire if the the water level in it falls below a certain level
C. Extinguish the fire if the water supply pump

trips off.

D. Acts as a safety valve

27. Boiler efficiency is the ratio of the

A. Energy absorbed by feed water to the energy supplied by the fuel

B. Energy released by feed water to the energy supplied by fuel

C. Energy utilised by feed water to energy absorbed by feed water

D. Boiler H.P to the pump H.P multiplied by the thermal efficiency of the system

28. Boiler H.P. is defined as

A. The evaporation of 15–65 kg of water per hour from and at 100°C into dry saturated steam

B. The work done for evaporation of 1 kg of steam per hour from and at 100°C into dry saturated steam

C. The amount of work done by the boiler in evaporating per unit kg of steam at 100°C into dry saturated steam at the same pressure

D. The network done plus the frictional loss incurred to evaporate 1 kg of steam at saturation pressure into dry superheated steam

29. A balanced draught is one which

A. Contains the correct amount of draught

B. Is a combination of the forced and induced draughts

C. produces the desired draught in the chimney

D. Gives a continuous state of balanced flow of air

30. Theoretical mean effective pressure (P_m) of steam engine is given by the relation.

A. $P_m = \frac{P_1(1 - \log_e r)}{r} - P_b$

B. $P_m = \frac{P_1(1 + \log_e r)}{r} - P_b$

C. $P_m = \frac{P_1(1 + \log_e r)}{r} + P_b$

D. $P_m = \frac{P_1(1 - \log_e r)}{r} + P_b$

Where P_1 is the inlet pressure, P_b is the back pressure and r is the expansion ratio

31. When the steam is carried from boiler to the engine, the pressure of steam

A. Will increase B. Will decrease

C. Will remain same D. None of the above

32. In Parson's steam turbine

A. The stationary and moving blades are identical

B. The stationary blades are smaller than the moving blades

C. They are perpendicular to each other

D. None of the above

33. In the impulse turbine, the steam is expanded

A. In nozzles only

B. Over the blades

C. Partly in the nozzles and partly over the blades

D. In the nozzles, pressure, increases subsequent when passing over the blades

34. In compounding for velocity the steam

A. Is expanded in the nozzles resulting in an increase in velocity

B. After expanding in the nozzle over the blades at a constant pressure

C. In expanded through nozzles from the boiler pressure to the condenser pressure, to a high velocity and then passed over the first ring of moving blades

D. Has to be perfectly dry

35. In compounding for pressure

A. The pressure drop increases for each stage

B. The pressure increases as sit flows over the moving blades

C. Pressure and velocity are compounded in different stages

D. Nearly all the velocity of steam is absorbed when it passes over the first moving blade ring

36. The P V diagram of an engine can be produced automatically by

A. Air indicator

B. Optograph

C. Press–vol crescograph

D. Digital system

37. In a steam engine, super heating of steam

A. Results in an increase in the efficiency of the Rankine cycle

B. Gives the benefit of reduced work done

C. Causes an increase in heat supply at a greater rate than the rate of work done

D. In beneficial only if it causes a state of reduced saturation pressure

38. In a steam engine the change in internal energy equals

A. The work done during whole of the Rankine cycle

B. The work done during adiabatic expansion only

C. The work done during compression

D. The change of enthalpy

39. The uniflow system engine is also known as

A. Single direction steam engine

B. Unidirection steam engine

C. The mid cylinder exhaust engine

D. The static flow engine

40. In two cylinder compound engine the cylinder dimensions can be calculated from the

A. Piston and connecting rod dimension

B. Horse power and the hypothetical indicator diagram

C. H.P. and the actual indicator diagram

D. P–V diagram

41. The pressure–velocity compounding of steam turbine

A. Gives rise to a larger number of stages with smooth flow over each stage

B. Results in a shorter turbine for a given total pressure drop

C. Results in the diameter of the turbine being reduced initially and then increasing in each stage

D. None of the above is true

42. Blade friction in the steam turbine

A. Results in a slight increase in the final heat drop

B. Gives rise to pitholes being formed in the blades

C. Results in a steady and uniform drop in each stage

D. Reults in loss of power

43. Velocity compounding involves

A. Pressure equalisation at different stages of the impulse turbine

B. The increased velocity obtained at the entrance to the moving blade due to expansion of steam

C. Recovery of residual kinetic energy in the steam leaving the first set of moving blades

D. Passage of steam from the fixed blade to the moving blade to increase its velocity

44. In the impulse turbine if friction is neglected the

A. Relative velocity at inlet and outlet is of the same magnitude

B. Passage of the steam over the moving blades provides the motive force

C. Pressure increases as it flows over the moving blades

D. Work done is zero

45. As compared to the relative velocity at inlet, friction in the impulse turbine causes the relative velocity at outlet to be

A. Less due to a fall of 2 to 3%

B. 10 to 15% less

C. Change is negligible

D. 40% less as compared to the inlet velocity

ANSWERS

1	2	3	4	5	6	7	8	9	10
D	A	B	D	A	D	C	C	B	B
11	**12**	**13**	**14**	**15**	**16**	**17**	**18**	**19**	**20**
D	C	D	A	B	C	A	A	A	A
21	**22**	**23**	**24**	**25**	**26**	**27**	**28**	**29**	**30**
B	B	C	D	C	B	A	A	B	B
31	**32**	**33**	**34**	**35**	**36**	**37**	**38**	**39**	**40**
B	A	A	C	D	A	A	B	C	B
41	**42**	**43**	**44**	**45**					
B	A	C	C	B					

3

INTERNAL COMBUSTION ENGINE

Internal Combustion Engine (I.C. Engine)

The compressed fuel air mixture is ignited inside the cylinder of engine. During combustion very high temperature and pressure gases are produced which expand, inside the cylinder. The hot gases so produced pushes the piston outward and the piston moves inside the engine cylinder. Due to the movement of piston, the power is obtained and it is transmitted to the shaft of the engine.

I.C. Engine is also called Spark Ignition Engine (S.I. Engine) which is used in automobile, locomotive, civil aviation, agricultural equipment, marine, heavy earth moving machines and so many other machines.

Various stroke of internal combustion engines are

I. Intake stroke II. Compression stroke
III. Ignition stroke IV. Exhaust stroke

Internal combustion engines are either four stroke engines or two stroke engines. In four stroke engines all the operation complete in four strokes mentioned above, whereas in two-stroke engine all the operations are completed in two strokes of the piston or in one revolution of the crankshaft.

The Otto Cycle : The Otto Cycle in idealised form assumes intake of air-fuel mixture without pressure loss

I. Adiabatic compression of mixture
II. Combustion of mixture at constant volume
III. Adiabatic expansion of combustion products with output of work
IV. Discharge at constant volume

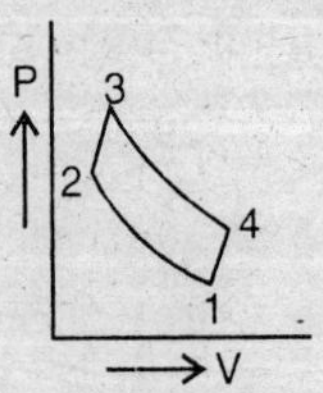

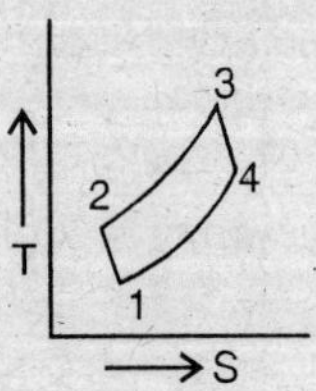

The ideal efficiency $= 1 - \dfrac{1}{(r)^{k-1}}$

Where r is the compression ratio

$$k = \frac{C_p}{C_v}$$

The Diesel Cycle : The diesel cycle in idealized form consists of intake air without pressure loss

I. Adiabatic compression of air
II. Liquid fuel injection at constant pressure maintained by vaporisation during expansion 2–3
III. Adiabatic combustion and expansion with output of work 3–4
IV. Discharge of the products of combustion at constant volume 4–1

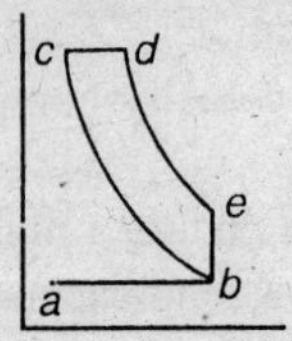

Ideal efficiency $= 1 - \dfrac{(r_c)^{1-k}}{k}\left(\dfrac{r_c^{\,k} - 1}{r_c - 1}\right)$

Where r_c = compression ratio $= \dfrac{v_1}{v_2}$

r_c = expansion ratio $= \dfrac{v_2}{v_3}$

The diesel cycle is inferior to the Otto cycle in ideal efficiency but superior in actual efficiency at part loads.

The Joule's Cycle : The Joule cycle used in gas turbines consists of :

I. Adiabatic compression of fuel air mixture
II. Combustion of mixture at constant pressure
III. Adiabatic expansion and

IV. Heat rejection at constant pressure

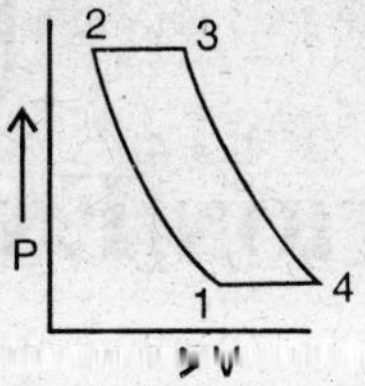

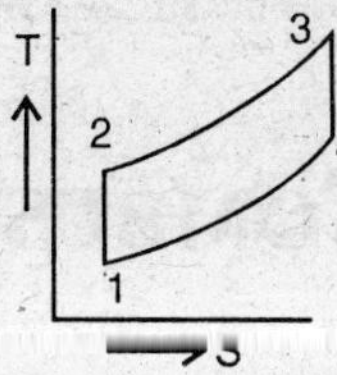

$$\text{Ideal efficiency} = 1-\left(\frac{p_1}{P_2}\right)^{k-1}$$

The Dual Combustion Cycle : The dual combustion cycle consists of

I. heat added during constant value process 2–3

II. heat added during constant pressure process 3–4

III. heat rejected during constant volume process 5–1

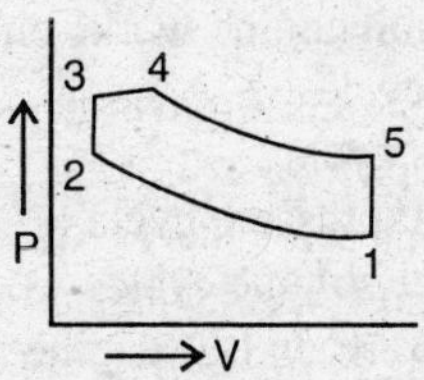

$$\text{Efficiency} = 1-\frac{2}{r^{k-1}}\left[\frac{\alpha\rho^k-1}{(\alpha-1)+\alpha\gamma(\rho-1)}\right]$$

Where r = Compression ratio

ρ = cut off ratio

α = pressure ratio

Performance of I.C. Engines

I.H.P. : The theoretical power developed in the engine cylinder is known as Indicated Horse Power or I.H.P.

$$\text{I.H.P.} = \frac{P_m\text{L.A.N.} \times k}{4500}$$

For two stroke engines

$$\text{I.H.P.} = \frac{P_m\text{L.A.N.} \times k}{4500}$$

(No. of working strokes = N rpm)

For four-stroke engine

$$\text{I.H.P.} = \frac{P_m\text{L.A.N.} \times k}{4500 \times 2}$$

$\left(\text{No. of working strokes} = \frac{N}{2}\right)$

Brake Horse Power : It is the total power available on the shaft of the engine.

$$\text{B.H.P.} = \frac{2\pi\text{ NT}}{4500}$$

Where T = Torque

N = r.p.m.

$$\text{Mechanical efficiency} = \frac{\text{B.H.P.}}{\text{I.H.P.}}$$

Brake Thermal Efficiency :

$$\text{B.T.E.} = \frac{\text{B.T.P.} \times 4500}{\text{W} \times \text{C.V} \times \text{J}}$$

$$\text{Relative Efficiency} = \frac{\text{Thermal efficiency}}{\text{Air standard efficiency}}$$

MULTIPLE-CHOICE QUESTIONS

1. A fuel which has a higher itself ignition temperatue

A. Detonates less

B. Helps detonation

C. Results in smooth burning of charge

D. Increase the rate of ignition

2. Pre-ignition

A. Is the spontaneous ignition of the last part of charge

B. Is resorted to at higher altitudes

C. Increases the efficiency and saves unburnt fuel

D. Causes reduced efficiency and loss of power

3. The efficiency of internal combustion engine ranges from

A. 15 to 35% B. 20 to 40%

C. 25 to 30% D. 30 to 35%

4. The firing order in a four-stroke I.C. engine is

A. 1–3–4–2 B. 1–4–3–2

C. 1–3–4–2 D. 1–2–4–3

5. The firing order in a six-stroke engine is

A. 1–5–3–4–2–6 B. 1–3–4–2–5–6

C. 1–5–3–4–6–2 D. 1–5–2–4–3–6

6. The quantity control method of governing is

used in

A. Diesel engines B. Rocket engines
C. Petrol engines D. Steam engines

7. The delay period in S.I. engine is about
A. 0.10 secs B. 0.0002 secs
C. 0.002 secs D. The ignition time lag

8. The unstable compounds which cause detonation are
A. Oxides and inert substances formed during the course of reaction
B. Ketones and sulphur compounds
C. Peroxides, aldehydes and ketones
D. Aldehydes, oxides and sulphides

9. In the liquid cooling system in I.C. engines the thermostat allows the water to go to the radiator when the temperature of the water reaches about
A. 60°C to 65°C
B. 80°C to 85°C
C. 95°C to 97°C
D. Slightly below 100°C

10. Using a perfect combustion chamber in a gas turbine it is possible to get a combustion efficiency of about
A. 80–90%
B. 78%
C. 99%
D. Two third, the theoretically calculated efficiency

11. Which among the following can be used for Turbojet engines?
A. Kerosene B. Methyl Alcohol
C. High speed diesel D. Demethylated spirit

12. Dopes is added to the engine fuel
A. To reduce its detonation tendency
B. To improve lubrication
C. To improve lubrication and reduce detonation
D. None of the above

13. The thermal efficiency of an I.C. engine is
A. More than external combustion engine
B. Less than external combustion engine
C. Equal to external combustion engine
D. Independent of method of fuel ignition

14. If a four-stroke engine is revolving of at 1200 R.P.M., then the number of explosions are equal to
A. 1200 B. 600
C. 2400 D. 300

15. If 'L' is the stroke length and r is the crank radius, then
A. $L = r$ B. $L = 4r$
C. $L = \frac{r}{2}$ D. $L = 2r$

16. In I.C. engine the type of governing used is
A. Quality governing
B. Quantity governing
C. Hit and miss governing
D. None of the above

17. Which one is not related of I.C. engine?
A. Gas turbine
B. Four-stroke I.C. engine
C. Two-stroke S.I. engine
D. Steam turbine

18. Which is related to I.C. engine only?
A. Distributor B. Spark plug
C. Atomiser D. Carburettor

19. Spark ignition engine works on
A. Carnot cycle
B. Rankine cycle
C. Constant pressure cycle
D. Constant volume cycle

20. The term 'Bore' in I.C. engine is used for
A. Diameter of the piston
B. Inside diameter of cyclinder
C. Diameter of piston ring
D. None of the above

21. Displacement volume or swept volume is the volume displaced by the piston in
A. Two strokes B. Four strokes
C. One stroke D. Half stroke

22. The piston if an I.C. engine completes two strokes in
A. 180° of crank rotation
B. 360° of crank rotation
C. 540° of crank rotation
D. 720° of crank rotation

23. Ignition quality of petrol is expressed by
A. Octane Number B. Cetane number
C. Calorific value D. None

24. The pistons are usually given a coating such as tin plating in order to
A. Conduct heat efficiency
B. Reduce possibility of scoring

C. Reduce friction
D. None of these

25. Ignition quality of diesel fuel oil is expressed by an index called
A. Cetane number B. Calorific value
C. Octane number D. None of these

26. High speed diesel engines need an approximate cetane number of
A. 1 B. 10
C. 50 D. 100

27. Carbon residue in diesel oil should not be more than
A. 0.01% B. 0.1%
C. 0.5% D. 1%

28. Piston rings are usually made of
A. Steel B. Cast iron
C. Aluminium D. Babbit

29. Which is false about V-type engines?
A. Less over head clearance
B. Casting less liable clearance
C. Compact design
D. All of the above

30. In loop scavenging, the top of piston is
A. Contoured B. Depressed
C. Slanted D. Flat

31. In the crank case method of scaversing the air pressure is produced by
A. Movement of piston
B. Centrifugal pump
C. National aspirator
D. None of these

32. In order to prevent formation of carbon the temperature of nozzle tip should be
A. 250°C – 300°C B. 400°C – 500°C
C. 500°C – 600°C D. 320°C – 500°C

33. Cetane
A. Helps detonation
B. Is a paraffin
C. Determines the efficiency
D. None of these

34. Ethyl fluid is used to
A. Increase the octane rating of fuel
B. As a defrosting agent
C. As a superior type of fluid compared to other
D. None of these

35. Normal heptane
A. Helps to resists auto-ignition
B. Accelerates auto-ignition
C. Has no relation with ignition
D. None of these

36. Connecting ròd is made of :
A. Aluminium alloy B. Cast iron
C. Copper alloy D. Medium carbon steel

37. In a four-stroke four-cylinder diesel engine, number of carburettors used is :
A. 0 B. 1
C. 2 D. 4

38. The material of the exhaust valve is
A. Aluminium alloy
B. Cast iron
C. Silicon chrome steel
D. Low carbon steel

39. The flywheel is located on the
A. Racker arm shaft B. Crank shaft
C. Cam shaft D. All of the above

40. The function of the governor is to
A. Supply energy during non-working strokes
B. Supply energy when the piston is at dead centre
C. Run the engine at some average constant speed
D. Control vibrations due to the reciprocating parts

41. The popular firing order of a four stroke S.I. engine is
A. 1–3–4–2 B. 1–2–3–4
C. 4–3–2–1 D. 2–4–3–1

42. In a petrol engine the pressure and temperature towards the end of compression are respectively
A. 20 to 30 kg/cm^2 and 400°C to 500°C
B. 40 to 50 kg/cm^2 and 700°C to 800°C
C. 12 to 18 kg/cm^2 and 300°C to 350°C
D. 6 to 12 kg/cm^2 and 250°C to 350°C

43. According to Recardo's theory
A. Detonation occurs due to improper combustion
B. Detonation occurs as a result of instantaneous auto ignition of last part of charge top burn
C. Due to improper mixing of the air and fuel delayed ignition of the last part of charge will occur, which causes detonation
D. Flame propagation occurs at a speed equal

to that of sound when detonation occurs

44. A fuel which will detonate less if it has
A. Higher self-ignition temperature
B. Lower self-ignition temperature
C. Unpredictable
D. None of these

45. Morse test is used to determine mechanical efficiency of
A. Multi-cylinder engines
B. Four-stroke engines
C. Two-stroke engines
D. None of these

46. In petrol engine, actual pressure developed compared to the predicted maximum pressure is
A. 50% B. 25%
C. 70% D. 90%

47. Detonation tendency of I.C. engines
A. Increases with increase in compression ratio
B. Increases with decrease in compression ratio
C. Remains unaffected
D. Cannot be predicted

48. Detonation tendency in S.I. engines
A. Increases with increase in compression ratio
B. Increases with decrease in compression ratio
C. Remains unaffected
D. Cannot be predicted

49. In a naturally aspirated diesel engine, air is supplied by
A. A super charger
B. a centrifugal blower
C. A vacuum chamber
D. An injection tube

50. Which of the following symptoms show that the combustion is necessarily complete?
A. Presence of free carbon in exhaust
B. Presence of carbon mono-oxide in exhaust
C. Presence of oxygen in exhaust
D. Presence of nitrogen in exhaust

ANSWERS

1	2	3	4	5	6	7	8	9	10
A	D	A	C	C	C	C	C	B	C
11	**12**	**13**	**14**	**15**	**16**	**17**	**18**	**19**	**20**
A	A	A	B	D	A	D	C	D	B
21	**22**	**23**	**24**	**25**	**26**	**27**	**28**	**29**	**30**
C	B	A	B	A	C	B	B	A	A
31	**32**	**33**	**34**	**35**	**36**	**37**	**38**	**39**	**40**
A	A	B	A	B	D	A	C	B	C
41	**42**	**43**	**44**	**45**	**46**	**47**	**48**	**49**	**50**
D	D	B	A	A	A	B	A	C	B

4

APPLIED MECHANICS

Simple Harmonic Motion is a special case of periodic motion, wherein particle moves to and fro about a fixed point, along a straight line path. Acceleration is directed towards a fixed point in the path and is proportional to the distance between that point and the moving point.

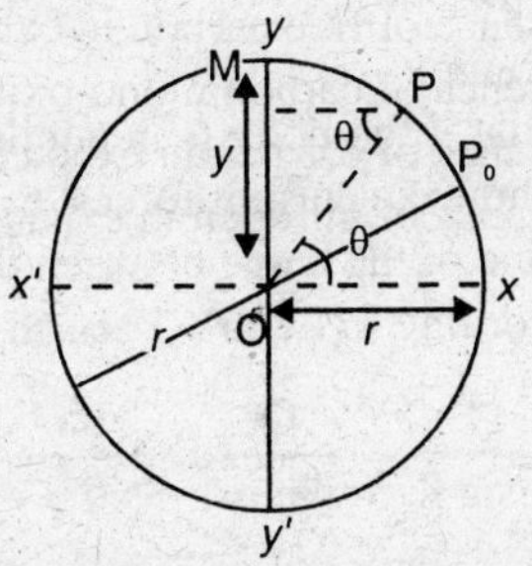

The motion of the projection of a diameter of a point moving with constant speed around a circle is an example of simple harmonic motion. The distance of the projection from the centres is the displacement and the radius of circle is amplitude. The angle of lead or lag ω, the phase angle.

Displacement : $x = r\cos(\omega t + \theta)$

$y = r\sin(\omega t + \theta)$

Velocity ; $\left.\begin{aligned} v_x &= -r\omega\sin(\omega t + \theta) = -\omega y \\ v_y &= -r\omega\cos(\omega t + \theta) = \omega x \end{aligned}\right\}$

Acceleration

$$\left.\begin{aligned} a_x &= -r\omega^2\cos(\omega t + \theta) = -\omega^2 x \\ a_y &= -r\omega^2\sin(\omega t + \theta) = \omega^2 y \end{aligned}\right\}$$

Projectile Motion : When a body is projected in space at an angle to the horizontal is called a projectile.

Maximum height attained

$$h = \frac{u^2 \sin\alpha}{2g}$$

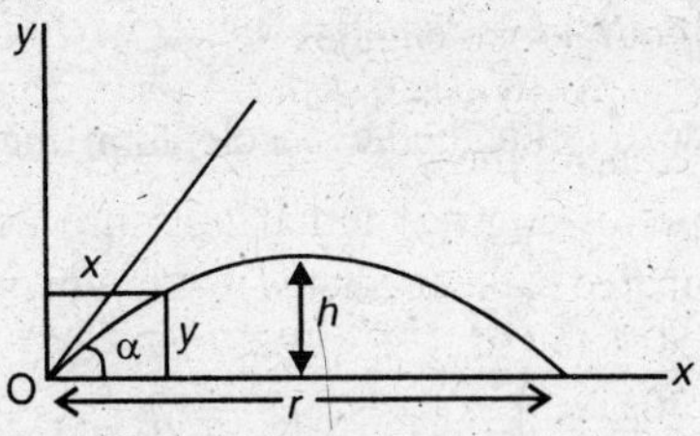

Time of flight

$$T = \frac{2u\sin\alpha}{g}$$

Horizontal range $R = \dfrac{u^2\sin\alpha}{g}$

maximum horizontal range $= \dfrac{u^2}{g}$

The horizontal range is maximum when the angle of projection $\alpha = \dfrac{\pi}{4}$

Pendulum : For a simple pendulum with the mass concentrated at a point L distance from the axis, the period of oscillation

$$t = 2\pi\sqrt{\frac{L}{g}}$$

For a conical pendulum, h is the height of the cone of revolution

$$t = 2\pi\sqrt{\frac{L}{g}}$$

and the angular velocity

$$\omega = \sqrt{\frac{g}{h}}$$

For a compound pendulum where k is the radius of gyration about the axis and S is the distance between the axis and the centre of gravity, the length of the equivalent simple pendulum

$$L = \frac{k^2}{S}$$

Equations of Motions

I. $v = u + at$

II. $v^2 = u^2 + 2as$

III. $S = ut + \frac{1}{2}at^2$

IV. $S_n = u + \frac{a}{2}(2n - 1)$

In case of falling bodies acceleration due to gravity is 'g'

I. $v = u + gt$

II. $v^2 = u^2 + 2gs$

III. $S = ut + \frac{1}{2}gt^2$

IV. $S_n = u + \frac{u}{2}(2n - 1)$

Equations for Angular Motions

I. $\omega = \omega_0 + \alpha t$

II. $\theta = \omega_0 + \frac{1}{2}\alpha t^2$

III. $\omega^2 = \omega^2_0 + 2\alpha\theta$

Newton's Laws of Motion

Ist Law : Every body continues in its state of rest, or of uniform motion in a straight line except in so far as its may be compelled by impressed forces to change that state.

IInd Law : Change of motion or change of momentum, is proportional to the impressed force and takes place in the direction of the straight line which the force acts.

IIIrd Law : To every action there is always an equal and opposite reaction, or the mutual actions of any two bodies are always equal and oppositely directed.

Concurrent Forces : If a number of forces are applied on a body, we have a system of forces which may be classified as coplanar or non-coplanar. The general problem of statics of the reduction of a given system of forces is the simplest equivalent or the resultant.

Triangle law of forces : If two forces are represented by their free vectors placed tip to tail, their resultant is the vector directed from the tail of the first vector to tip of the scond vector.

Parallelogram Law of forces : The resultant of the forces is diagonal of the parallelogram whose initial sides are the vectors of these forces. The diagonal is to used is that which emanates from the tail of the first vector to the tip of the secod vector.

Principle of Force Equilibrium

Two-force principle : A body will be in equilibrium if the two forces are collinear, equal and opposite.

The three-force principle : A body will be in equilibrium if the three forces acting on it are either concurrent or parallel.

Lami's Theorem

It states that if the body is in equilibrium under the action of three concurrent forces, each is proportional to the sine of the angle between the other two.

Thus, according to Lami's Theorm

$$\frac{P}{\sin\beta} = \frac{Q}{\sin\alpha} = \frac{R}{\sin\theta}$$

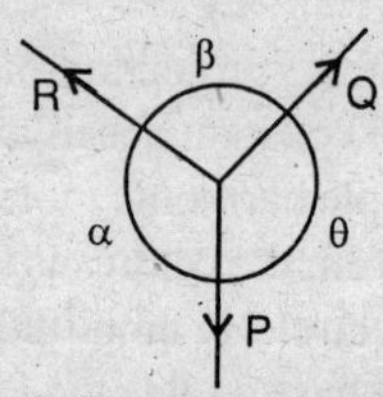

Moments and Couples : Moment or torque M of a force about a point for centre of moments is the product of the force magnitude and the arm or perpendicular distance S from the point to the action line of the force.

$$M = F \bullet S$$

Principles of Moments (Varignon's Theorem): The moment of the resultant of forces about a point in their plane or about a line is the algebraic sum of the moments of those forces about the point or line.

Couples : To equal opposite, and parallel forces acting on a body are called a couple of which the arm is the perpendicular distance between the lines of action and the moment is the product of one of the force magnitude and the arm. The sum of the moments of the two forces is same about any moment centre in their plane of action. The couple tends to produce rotation.

Centriod : The centriod of a system of parallel forces with fixed points of application is the point through which their resultant will always pass however the forces may be turned while being kept parallel.

Centre of gravity : The centre of gravity of a body, or system of bodies, is the centroid of the forces of gravitation or the point of application of the resultant of the gravity forces acting upon the various elements. The force of gravity on a body is, of course, equal to the weight w os the body.

Centre of gravity of various figures and bodies are.

I. Triangle–The point of intersection of medians situated at a distance of $\frac{h}{3}$ from the base.

II. Rectangle– At the point of intersection of diagonals

III. Cylinder– at the middle of height $\left(\frac{h}{3}\right)$

IV. Cone– $\frac{h}{4}$ from the base

V. Semicircle– $\frac{4r}{3\pi}$ from its base

VI. Hemisphere– $\frac{3r}{8}$ from the base

MULTIPLE-CHOICE QUESTIONS

1. A number of forces acting at a point will be in equilibrium if
A. Sum of the forces is zero
B. Algebraic sum of the forces is zero
C. Sum of the resolved part is zero
D. Sum of the resolved parts in any two perpendicular directions are both zero

2. The resultant of two forces A and B acting at an angle α is
A. $A + B$
B. $\sqrt{A^2 + B^2}$
C. $\sqrt{A^2 + B^2 + 2AB \sin \alpha}$
D. $\sqrt{A^2 + B^2 + 2AB \cos \alpha}$

3. If two forces of magnitude P act at an angle θ, their resultant will be
A. $2P \cos \frac{\theta}{2}$ B. $2P \sin \theta$
C. $2P \cos \theta$ D. $P \cos 2\theta$

4. The magnitude of two forces which when acting at right angles produce resultant force of 10 kg and when acting at 60° produce resultant of $\sqrt{183}$ kg. These forces are
A. 3 and 4 B. 4 and 6
C. 6 and 8 D. 5 and $\sqrt{75}$

5. The forces each equal to $\frac{P}{2}$ act at right angles. Their effect may be neutralized by a third force acting along their bisector in the opposite direction with a magnitude of
A. T B. $\sqrt{2}$ T
C. $\frac{T}{2}$ D. $\frac{T}{\sqrt{2}}$

6. The length of second pendulum is
A. 1000 mm B. 999 mm
C. 995 mm D. 994 mm

7. A clock with a second pendulum is gaining 5 minutes a day. To correct it
A. The length of pendulum should be increased
B. The length of pendulum should be decreased
C. The length of pendulum should not be changed
D. The eccentricity of bob with pendulum should be increased

8. The piston of a steam engine moves in S.H.M. The crank rotates at 180 r.p.m. and the stroke length is 2 metres. The linear velocity of the piston when it is at a distance of 1 metre from the centre is
A. 16.32 m/sec B. 8.16 m/sec
C. 5.88 m/sec D. 8.88 m/sec
E. Zero

9. A bob of simple pendulum oscillating in air is

made to oscillate in oil. The time period will
A. Increase
B. Decrease
C. Not change
D. Decrease but reduction depends on viscosity of oil

10. A particle is moving in Simple Harmonic Motion (S.H.M.) in a simple pendulum with some period of oscillation. Now in order to double the period of oscillation
A. The mass of the bob should be doubled
B. The mass of the bob should be halved
C. The length of pendulum should be doubled
D. The length of pendulum should be doubled

11. For the angle of projection when the range is equal to the distance through which the particle would have fallen in order to acquire a velocity equal to the velocity of projection will be
A. $22\frac{1°}{2}$ B. 30°
C. 45° D. 60°

12. For perfectly elastic bodies, the value of the coefficient of restitution is
A. Zero B. 0.372
C. 0.5 D. 1.0

13. A wound watch spring possesses energy in the form of
A. Potential energy
B. Kinetic energy
C. Spring energy
D. Mechanical potential energy

14. A ball weighing 250 gm is thrown vertically upwards with a velocity of 980 cm/sec. The time that the ball will take to return back to earth would be
A. 1 second B. 2 seconds
C. 3 seconds D. 4 seconds

15. In above case maximum height attained by the ball would be
A. 100 cm B. 49 cm
C. 490 cm D. 980 cm

16. The branch of physical science deealing with nature of motion only without any reference of the force causing it, is known as
A. Kinetic B. Kinematics
C. Static D. Hydrostatic

17. Which one is more rigid?
A. Cork B. Chalk
C. Wood D. Rubber

18. One newton is that much force which produce acceleration of
A. 1 m/sec^2 in a mass of 1 kg
B. 9.81 m/sec^2 ina mass of 1 kg
C. 9.81 m/sec^2 in a mass of 1 gm
D. 1 m/sec^2 in a mass of 1 gm

19. Bow's notation is used for representation of a
A. Mass B. Velocity
C. Force D. Couple

20. The triangle law of forces is applicable for the resultant of
A. Two forces
B. Three forces
C. Four forces
D. Any number of forces

21. Polygol law of forces is used for finding out resultant of
A. Parallel forces
B. Collinear forces
C. Coplanar concurrent forces
D. Non-coplanar concurrent forces

22. The result in parallelogram law of forces has maximum value when the angle between the two forces is equal to
A. 0° B. 30°
C. 90° D. 180°

23. The resultant in parallelogram law of forces has minimum value when the angle between the two forces is equal to
A. 0° B. 45°
C. 90° D. 180°

24. The resultant of coplanar parallel forces can be found by the using
A. Parallelogram law of forces
B. Ramii's theorem
C. Principle of moments
D. Resolution of forces

25. A body will be in equilibrium, when
A. Two equal collinear forces are acting on it in same direction
B. Two equal and opposite collinear forces are acting on it

C. Two unequal and opposite collinear forces are acting on it
D. None of the above

26. If four coplanar forces acting on a body keep it in equibrium the resultant of any two forces should be
A. Equal to the resultant of the remaining two forces
B. Collinear to the resultant of the other two forces
C. In opposite direction to the resultant of the other two forces
D. All of the above

27. For the direction of projection for the range of a projectile to be maximum on an inclined plane having angle of inclination 30° to the horizontal
A. 30° with horizontal
B. 30° with vertical
C. 45° with horizontal
D. 45° with vertical

28. The centre of percussion is
A. The same as centre of gravity
B. The point in a body about which it can rotate horizontally and oscillate under the influence of gravity
C. The point of application of the resultant of all the forces tending to cause a body to rotate about a central axis
D. The point of application of the resultant of gravity and buoyancy forces of the body
E. The metacentre of the body

29. It two collinear forces P and Q are acting on a body in the same direction, then their resultant is equal to
A. $P - Q$ B. $\sqrt{P^2 - Q^2}$
C. $P + Q$ D. $P \times Q$

30. Lami's theorem states that if three forces acting at a point be in equilibrium, each is proportional to the
A. Algebraic sum of the other two forces
B. Sine of the angle between the other two forces
C. Cosine of the angle between the other two forces
D. Algebraic difference of the other two forces

31. The system of forces, whose resultant is zero are called
A. Non-concurrent forces
B. Non-coplaner forces
C. Coplanar forces
D. Equilibrium forces

32. A man wished to move a block of size 3m × 3m weighing 80 kg. The co-efficient of friction between the block and the ground is 0.27. Which of the following methods should be used?
A. Slide along the ground by pushing
B. Pull it
C. Lift it bodily
D. Tip it over

33. A body whose true weight is 14 kg appears to weigh 14 kg when weighed with the help of a spring balance in a moving lift. The acceleration of the lift at the time was
A. 1.4 m/sec^2 B. 1 m/sec^2
C. 0.7 m/sec^2 D. 0.5 m/sec^2

34. If the value of '*g*' on the moon is one-sixth of that on earth the frequency of oscillation at moon as compared to that on earth will be
A. 6 times more B. $\frac{1}{6}$ of that on earth
C. $\sqrt{6}$ times more D. $\frac{1}{\sqrt{6}}$ of that on earth

35. A jet engine works on the principle of
A. Conservation of energy
B. Conservation of linear momentum
C. Conservation of mass
D. Conservation of mass and momentum
E. Conservation of energy and momentum

36. If 'ΣH' is the algebraic sum of resolved part of forces in a horizontal direction and 'ΣV' is the algebraic sum of resolved part of forces in a vertical direction, then resultant 'R' is equal to
A. $\Sigma H + \Sigma V$ B. $\Sigma H^2 + \Sigma V^2$
C. $\sqrt{\Sigma H^2 + \Sigma V^2}$ D. $\sqrt{\Sigma H^{1/2} + \Sigma V^{1/2}}$

37. The direction of resultant in the above case is given by the relation
A. $\theta = \tan^{1} \frac{\Sigma H}{\Sigma V}$ B. $\theta = \tan^{-1} \frac{\Sigma H}{\Sigma V}$

C. $\theta = \tan^{-1}\left(\frac{\Sigma H}{\Sigma V}\right)^2$ D. $\theta = \tan^{-1} \Sigma H \times \Sigma V$

38. The lever in which load and effort act on the same side of the fulcrum is known as
A. Lever of first type
B. Lever of second type
C. Lever of third type
D. None of the above

39. The periodic time of a body moving in S.H.M. is
A. Directly proportional to its angular velocity
B. Directly proportional to weight of body
C. Directly proportional to momentum of swinging body
D. Inversely proportional to angular velocity

40. A body in S.H.M. will attain maximum velocity when it passes through
A. Extreme point of the oscillation of L.H.S.
B. Extreme point of the oscillation at R.H.S.
C. Mean position
D. Point of half amplitude
E. Point of 0.75 amplitude

41. The maximum velocity of a body in S.H.M. with amplitude of 150 mm and a frequency 2 vibrations per sec is equal to
A. 0.01885 m/sec B. 0.1885 m/sec
C. 1.885 m/sec D. 18.55 m/sec
E. 18.5 m/sec

42. For the maximum range of a projectile the angle of prjection should be
A. $22\frac{1^\circ}{2}$ B. 30°
C. 45° D. 60°

43. The path followed by the projectile is
A. Circle B. Parabola
C. Hyperbola D. Ellipse

44. The time of flight of a projectilie is given by
A. $T = \frac{2u \sin \alpha}{g}$ B. $T = \frac{u \sin \alpha}{2g}$
C. $T = \frac{u \sin \alpha}{g}$ D. $T = \frac{u \sin \alpha}{4g}$

45. The greatest height attained by the projectile is equal to
A. $\frac{u^2 \sin^2 \alpha}{2g}$ B. $\frac{u^2 \sin \alpha}{2g}$
C. $\frac{u^2 \sin^2 \alpha}{g}$ D. $\frac{u \sin \alpha}{2g}$

46. The angle of projection (α) if a projectile is double the angle of inclination (θ) of the plane on which a particle is projected. The ratio of time of flights on the upward inclined plane and downward inclined plane will be equal to
A. $\frac{1}{\cos \alpha}$ B. $\frac{1}{2\cos \alpha}$
C. $\frac{1}{\sin \alpha}$ D. $\frac{1}{2\sin \alpha}$
E. $\frac{1}{2\tan \alpha}$

47. The maximum horizontal range of the projectile is
A. $\frac{u}{g}$ B. $\frac{2u}{g}$
C. $\frac{u}{2g}$ D. $\frac{u^2}{g}$

48. For the maximum horizontal range of the projectile, the angle of projection is
A. $\frac{\pi}{2}$ B. $\frac{\pi}{4}$
C. $\frac{\pi}{3}$ D. π

49. For a given value of initial velocity and angle of projection the maximum range for a projectile will be obtained if the angle of projection is
A. $\frac{\pi}{4}$ B. $\frac{\pi}{4} - \frac{\beta}{2}$
C. $\frac{\pi}{4} + \frac{\beta}{2}$ D. $\frac{\pi}{2} - \frac{\beta}{2}$
E. $\frac{\pi}{2} + \frac{\beta}{2}$

50. The gravitational field intensity is maximum at
A. Equator
B. Pole
C. Centre of earth
D. At a height above the surface

51. If the speed of rotation of earth decreased, the weight of the body will

A. Increase

B. Decrease

C. Remain unaltered

D. Depends on speed ratio

E. Cannot be ascertained on the basis of information given

52. The time of flight of the projectile when projected on an inclined plane, is

A. $\dfrac{u \sin \alpha}{g \sin \beta}$ B. $\dfrac{u \sin (\alpha - \beta)}{g \sin \beta}$

C. $\dfrac{2u \sin (\alpha - \beta)}{g \cos \beta}$ D. $\dfrac{u \sin (\alpha + \beta)}{g \cos \beta}$

53. The range of the projectile up the inclined plane with the horizontal

A. $\dfrac{2u^2 \cos \alpha \sin (\alpha - \beta)}{g \cos^2 \beta}$

B. $\dfrac{u^2 \cos \alpha \sin (\alpha - \beta)}{g \cos^2 \beta}$

C. $\dfrac{u^2 \cos \alpha \sin (\alpha + \beta)}{g \cos^2 \beta}$

D. $\dfrac{2u^2 \sin \alpha \sin (\alpha + \beta)}{g \cos^2 \beta}$

54. A uniform bar weighing 100 kg is hinged at A to a vertical wall and held in horizontal position by a cord BC. Tension in the cord BC will be

A. 50 kg B. 75 kg

C. 100 kg D. 150 kg

E. 200 kg

55. In actual machines

A. Mechanical advantage is equal to velociy ratio

B. Mechanical advantage is greater than velocity ratio

C. Mechanical advantage is less than velocity ratio

D. Mechanical advantage is unity

E. Mechancial advantage is less than unity

56. A stone thrown up from the foot of tower 50 m high with a velocity of 25 m/sec and the same time another stone is dropped from the top of tower, the two stones will cross each other after

A. 2 sec B. 3 sec

C. 4 sec D. 4.5 sec

E. 5 sec

57. The maximum range of the projectile down the inclined plane is

A. $\dfrac{u^2}{g(1 - \sin \beta)}$ B. $\dfrac{u}{g(1 - \sin \beta)}$

C. $\dfrac{2u}{g(1 - \sin \beta)}$ D. $\dfrac{u^2}{g(1 + \sin \beta)}$

58. The number of vibrations per second is known as

A. Beat B. Amplitude

C. Frequency D. Time period

59. For Simple Harmonic Motion of a pendulum, the angular amplitude should not exceed

A. 2° B. 4°

C. 8° D. 10°

60. A weight 'W' applied at the end of a helical spring is vibrating with S.H.M. Its line period is equal is

A. $T = \dfrac{2\pi}{W}$ B. $T = \pi\sqrt{\dfrac{W}{S}}$

C. $T = 2\pi\sqrt{\dfrac{W}{S}}$ D. $T = \dfrac{2\pi}{g}\sqrt{\dfrac{W}{S}}$

Where S = Stiffness of the spring

61. The phase difference between the velocity curve and the displacement curve is

A. $\dfrac{\pi}{4}$ B. $\dfrac{\pi}{2}$

C. π D. $\dfrac{\pi}{8}$

62. The phase difference between the acceleration curve and the velocity curve is

A. π B. 2π

C. $\dfrac{\pi}{2}$ D. $\dfrac{\pi}{4}$

63. The phase difference between the acceleration curve and the displacement is

A. $\dfrac{\pi}{6}$ B. $\dfrac{\pi}{2}$

C. 2π D. π

64. The piston of a steam engine has zero aceleration at the

A. Dead centre

B. $\frac{1}{4}$ th of the stroke
C. Mid point of stroke
D. None of the above

65. The velocity of the piston at dead centre is
A. Maximum
B. Zero
C. Average
D. Depending upon the speed of engine

66. The piston of I.C. engine has maximum velocity when it is at
A. Top dead centre position
B. Bottom dead centre position
C. Mid position between T.D.C. and B.D.C
D. $\frac{1}{4}$ th of the stroke

67. In case of S.H.M., the velocity at a distance 'x' on either side of the fixed point is expressed as
A. $v = \pm\mu\sqrt{r^2 - x^2}$ B. $v = \pm\mu\sqrt{r^2 + x^2}$
C. $v = \pm\mu^2\sqrt{r^2 + x^2}$ D. $v = \pm\sqrt{\mu}\sqrt{r^2 - x^2}$

68. A particle starts from rest and moves in a straight line whose equation of motion is given by $s = 2t^3 - t^2 - 1$. The acceleration of the particle after one sec will be
A. 4 m/sec^2 B. 6 m/sec^2
C. 8 m/sec^2 D. 10 m/sec^2
E. 12 m/sec^2

69. Identify the incorrect statement if any
A. The C.G. of a square at the intersection of diagonals
B. The C.G. of an equilateral triangle is the intersection of medians
C. The C.G. of an ellipse is at the intersection of major and minor axes
D. The C.G. of a right angled triangle is at the intersection of the medians
E. The C.G. of a semi-circle is at a distance $\frac{r}{2}$ from the centre

70. The centre of gravity of a right circular cone lies on the axis at a height (h = total height of cone) from base
A. $\frac{h}{4}$ B. $\frac{h}{3}$
C. $\frac{3}{4}h$ D. $\frac{3}{5}h$
E. $\frac{2}{3}h$

71. The centre of gravity of a hemisphere from its base maeasured along the vertical radius r is at a distance (from the base)
A. $\frac{3R}{8}$ B. $\frac{3R}{4}$
C. $\frac{3\pi}{4R}$ D. $\frac{4\pi}{3R}$
E. $\frac{8R}{3}$

72. The centre of percussion of the homogeneous rod of length L, suspended at the top will be
A. $\frac{3L}{8}$ B. $\frac{3L}{4}$
C. $\frac{3L}{5}$ D. $\frac{4L}{5}$
E. $\frac{5L}{9}$

73. A rope of length L is tied to a pillar in such a way so that a man pulling at its other end with a given force may have the greatest tendency to overturn the pillar. The height h at which the rope must be tied to pillar should be
A. L B. $\frac{L}{2}$
C. $\frac{3}{4}$L D. $\frac{L}{\sqrt{2}}$

74. Centre of gravity of a plane lamina will not be at its geometrical centre if it is a
A. Square B. Rectangle
C. Right angled trinagle D. Circle
E. Equilateral triangle

75. The centre of gravity of a solid cone lies on the axis at the height (h = total height of cone).
A. $\frac{h}{8}$ B. $\frac{h}{4}$
C. $\frac{2}{3}h$ D. $\frac{h}{2}$
E. $\frac{5}{8}h$

ANSWERS

1	**2**	**3**	**4**	**5**	**6**	**7**	**8**	**9**	**10**
D	D	A	C	D	D	A	E	A	D
11	**12**	**13**	**14**	**15**	**16**	**17**	**18**	**19**	**20**
D	D	D	B	C	B	C	A	C	A
21	**22**	**23**	**24**	**25**	**26**	**27**	**28**	**29**	**30**
C	A	D	C	B	D	B	C	C	B
31	**32**	**33**	**34**	**35**	**36**	**37**	**38**	**39**	**40**
D	D	C	D	B	C	B	C	D	C
41	**42**	**43**	**44**	**45**	**46**	**47**	**48**	**49**	**50**
C	C	B	A	A	B	D	B	C	C
51	**52**	**53**	**54**	**55**	**56**	**57**	**58**	**59**	**60**
A	C	A	C	C	A	A	C	B	C
61	**62**	**63**	**64**	**65**	**66**	**67**	**68**	**69**	**70**
B	C	D	C	B	C	A	C	E	A
71	**72**	**73**	**74**	**75**					
A	A	D	C	B					

5

STRENGTH OF MATERIALS

Stress is the force per unit area so that P as applied on cross-sectional area A

$$\text{Stress} = \frac{P}{A}$$

Unit of stress is kg/cm^2.

Strain is chage in length per unit length 1 so that for change in length δ1 when strain = $\frac{\delta 1}{1}$

It is dimensionless.

Hook's Law : It states that for the materials loaded within elastic limits the stress is proportional to strain.

Mathematically, $\frac{\text{Stress}}{\text{Strain}}$ = constant
(Young's Modulus of elasticity E)

$$\text{Shear Stress} = \frac{\text{Shearing force}}{\text{Cross-sectional area}}$$

Hoop Stress $p = \frac{D-d}{D} \times E$ and strain $e = \frac{D-d}{D}$

Where D = Outside diameter of wheel
d = Inside diameter of wheel

Poisson's ratio $\left(\frac{1}{m}\right)$ or $\mu = \frac{\text{Lateral strain}}{\text{Linear strain}}$

Volumetric Strain $C_v = \frac{P}{E}\left(1 - \frac{2}{m}\right)$

Relation between Young's Modulus of Elasticity E, Modulus of Rigidity c, and Bulk Modulus k is

$$E = 3k\left(1 - \frac{2}{m}\right) = 2c\left(1 + \frac{1}{m}\right) = \frac{9kc}{3k + c}$$

Shearing Force and Bending Moment

Condition for equilibrium of a beam are as follows

I. Algebraic sum of all forces in any direction is zero.

II. Algebraic sum of the moments of all forces about any point is zero.

Above conditions may also be considered as

I. The sum of downward force is equal to the sum of all upward forces.

II. The sum of all clockwise moments about any point is equal to the sum of the anticlockwise moments about the same.

Shear force at a section is the algebraic sum of all vertical forces to anyone side to the section.

Bending moment at a section is the algebraic sum of the moments of all forces of one side of the section.

At a hinge in a beam there is no bending moment but there is shear force.

The point of contraflexture or the point of inflexion is the point where the bending moment is zero.

Stresses in Beams

Bending equation is $\frac{p}{y} = \frac{M}{I} = \frac{E}{R}$

Where p = Stress due to ending at a distance y from neutral axis.
M = Bending moment
E = Modulus of elasticity of the beam material
I = Moment of inertia
R = Radius of curvature of the beam.

$$M = p \times \frac{I}{y} = pz$$

Where z is section modulus and is equal to $\frac{I}{y}$.

Impact Load and Resilience

Strain energy $U = \frac{p^2}{2E} \times \text{Volume}$

Where p is the instantaneous stress is the material and E is modulus of elasticity.

Modulus of resilience = $\frac{p^2}{2E} = \frac{Ee^2}{2}$

Columns and Struts

A member subjected to compressive stress is termed as post, stanchion, strut or pillar though there is no rigid distinction in the usage of these terms yet the convention is to call only wooden column as posts, built up rolled steel sections as stanchions and compression members as struts. Main supporting members of buildings are generally called columns or pillars irrespective of what they are made of.

The load carried by a short column is

$$P = p \times A$$

Where p is the intensity of stress and A is the area of cross-section of the column

$$\text{Slenderness ratio} = \frac{\text{Height of column}}{\text{Least radius of gyration}}$$

A column that fails primarily due to direct stress is called a short column and the one that fails primarily due to the bending stress is called the long column.

For short columns $\frac{1}{k} < 32$ or $I < 8\phi$

Where ϕ is diameter

For medium columns $\frac{1}{k} < 120 > 32I < 30\psi < 8\phi$

For long columns $\frac{1}{k} < 120$ or $I < 30\phi$

Rivetted Joints

Rivets are ductile metal pins after used for joining structural members as in case of trusses, stanchions, plate girders, cylindrical shell, etc. The rivets are provided with head at one end and the other end of the rivet is hammered to form a heat so that the members are permanently joined together. The distance between two heads is known as shank and rivet size is generally expressed in terms of shank diameter. There are two types of rivetted joints e.g. lap joints, in which the plates to be fastened are placed one over the other and rivetted by one or more rows of plates. In butt joints, the plates to be joined are butted together and rivetted with cover plates on one side or on both sides.

Resistance to tearing of plates per pitch length is

$$P_t = P_t\,(p - d) \times t$$

Resistance to bearing (crushing) of rivets is

$$P_b = n \times P_b \times d \times t$$

Resistance to shearing of rivets is

$$P_b = n \times p_s \times \frac{\pi d^2}{4} \text{ in single shear, and}$$

$$P_s = 2n \times p_c \times \frac{\pi d^2}{4} \text{ in double shear}$$

Where p_t = allowable tensile stress in plates

p_b = allowable bearing stress in rivets

p_s = allowable shear stress in rivets

d = gross diameter of rivets

t = plate thickness

n = number of rivets per pitch length

$$\text{Efficiency of joint } \eta = \frac{p-d}{p} \times 100$$

MULTIPLE–CHOICE QUESTIONS

1. Steel is more elastic than rubber because
- A. Its Young's modulus of elasticity is more
- B. Its Young's modulus of elasticity is less
- C. Its density is more
- D. Its density is less

2. Which is correct?
- A. Stainless steel is less elastic than mild steel
- B. Stainless steel is more elastic than mild steel
- C. Stainless steel has the same elasticity as mild steel
- D. None of the above mentioned

3. The stress before the material starts breaking is known as
- A. Yield stress
- B. Ultimate tensile stress
- C. Stress oat fracture
- D. Shear stress

4. The basis for comparing elasticity of various materials is
- A. To find their stress at elastic limit
- B. To find their stress at the yield point
- C. To find their stress at breaking point
- D. To find their shear stress

5. Working stress is always
- A. Less than ultimate stress
- B. More than ultimate stress

C. Equal to ultimate stress
D. None of the above

6. A material is said to be perfectly elastic
   A. If the deformation disappears completely with the removal of the load
   B. If the deformation disappears partly with the removal of the load
   C. If it does not deform due to application of external load
   D. None of the above
7. The stress to which a metal is subjected indefinitely to the stress reversal without rupture is called
   A. Endurance limit B. Safe stress
   C. Yield point D. Ultimate stress
8. The behaviour of metals under the action of cyclic stresses is termed as
   A. Fatigue B. Creep
   C. Endurance D. None of the above
9. The property which enables the materials to elongate sufficiently before breaking when subjected to gradually increasing load is called
   A. Malleability B. Brittleness
   C. Ductillity D. Plasticity
10. Moment of inertia for circular shafts is
   A. $I = \frac{\pi}{32}d^4$ B. $I = \frac{\pi}{32}d^2$
   C. $I = \frac{\pi}{64}d^4$ D. $I = \frac{\pi}{64}d^3$
11. Polar moment of inertia of a solid shaft of diameter '*d*' will be equl to
   A. $J = \frac{\pi}{16}d^4$ B. $J = \frac{\pi}{16}d^3$
   C. $J = \frac{\pi}{32}d^4$ D. $J = \frac{\pi}{32}d^3$
12. Torque in a solid shaft is given by the formula
   A. $T = \frac{\pi}{16}f_s d^3$ B. $T = \frac{\pi}{32}f_s d^3$
   C. $T = \frac{\pi}{64}f_s d^3$ D. None
13. Hook's Law states that within the elastic limit
   A. Stress + Strain = Constant
   B. Stress – Strain = Constant
   C. Stress × Strain = Constant
   D. $\frac{\text{Stress}}{\text{Strain}}$ = Constant
14. The value of modulus of elasticity for mild steel is
   A. 2×10^6 kgf/cm^2 B. 0.5×10^6 kgf/cm^2
   C. 1×10^6 kgf/cm^2 D. 0.05×10^6 kgf/cm^2
15. The Poisson's ratio $\frac{1}{m}$ is given by the relation
   A. $\frac{1}{m} = \frac{\text{Lateral strain}}{\text{Shear strain}}$
   B. $\frac{1}{m} = \frac{\text{Lateral strain}}{\text{Longitudinal strain}}$
   C. $\frac{1}{m} = \frac{\text{Lateral strain}}{\text{Volumetric strain}}$
   D. $\frac{1}{m} = \frac{\text{Longitudinal strain}}{\text{Lateral strain}}$
16. Volumetric strain is equal to
   A. Longitudinal strain $\left(1-\frac{2}{m}\right)$
   B. Longitudinal strain $\left(1+\frac{2}{m}\right)$
   C. Longitudinal Strain $\left(1-\frac{1}{m}\right)$
   D. Longitudinal strain $\left(1+\frac{1}{m}\right)$
17. The value of Poisson's ratio $\left(\frac{1}{m}\right)$ is never greater than
   A. 0.05 B. 0.5
   C. 1.5 D. 5.0
18. Strain is defined as the ratio of
   A. Change in length to the original length
   B. Change in shape to the original length
   C. Change in volume to the original length
   D. None
19. Young's Modulus is designed as the ratio of
   A. Lateral stress to longitudinal strain
   B. Lateral strain to longitudinal strain
   C. Longitudinal stress to longitudinal strain
   D. Shear stress to shear strain
20. The restoring force/unit area called into play inside the body is known as
   A. Pressure B. Stress

C. Thrust D. Torsion

21. The unit of stress in C.G.S. system is

A. Dynes/cm^2 B. Dynes cm^2

C. Dynes/cm D. Dynes

22. The working stress of a material is obtained by dividing the ultimate stress by

A. The lateral strain

B. The Poisson's ratio

C. The factor of safety

D. The maximum load to which material is subjected

23. The strain energy stored in a body due to external loading within the elastic limit, is known as the

A. Kinetic energy

B. Modulus of resilience

C. Proof resilience

D. Resilience

24. Actual stresses should not deviate from the allowable stresses by more than

A. ± 1% B. ± 3%

C. ± 5% D. ± 10%

25. For the same cross-sectional area of the beam, which of the following sections will be preferred against bending?

A. Circular B. Square

C. I–section D. Channel

26. At principle planes, the shear stresses is/are

A. Maximum B. Zero

C. Minimum D. None of the above

27. The normal stress at neutral axis in a beam is

A. Maximum B. Minimum

C. Zero D. Unpredictable

28. The dimensions of pressure are given by

A. $M^1L^1T^{-2}$ B. $M^1L^{-1}T^1$

C. $M^1L^1T^2$ D. $M^1L^{-1}T^{-2}$

29. Thin cylinders are used to store

A. Gas B. Steam

C. Liquids D. All of the above

30. The relation between Young's Modulus (E) and bulk modulus (K) is given by the relation.

A. $k = \frac{mE}{3(m+2)}$ B. $k = \frac{mE}{2(m+1)}$

C. $k = \frac{mE}{3(m+2)}$ D. $k = \frac{mE}{3(m-1)}$

31. The relation between modulus of rigidity (C) and Young's modulus is given as

A. $C = \frac{mE}{3(m-2)}$ B. $C = \frac{mE}{2(m-2)}$

C. $C = \frac{mE}{2(m+1)}$ D. $C = \frac{mE}{3(m+1)}$

32. In the analysis of strains we normally consider

A. The various stresses

B. Only the relative displacements

C. The angle of action

D. The angle of action and the principle plane

33. The plane of maximum shearing stresses make with the plane of principal stresses an angle of

A. 30° B. 90°

C. $22\frac{1}{2}^\circ$ D. 45°

34. Bulk modulus of the material within the elastic limit is the

A. Ratio of lateral strain to volumetric strain

B. Ratio of uniform strees intensity to lateral strain

C. Ratio of the uniform stress intensity to volumetric strain

D. Deformation produced in a material within the elastic limit for strain

35. For a given material its buckling load depends upon

A. Modulus of elasticity (E)

B. Area of x–section

C. Poisson's ratio

D. Slenderness ratio

E. The above A, B and D

36. A material is said to be plastic

A. If the plasticity of the material crosses the yield point

B. If the deformation disappears partially

C. If the deformation disappears completely on heating

D. Which undergoes complete change on application of force and regains its original shape on relieving

37. The total elongation produced in a bar of uniform cross-section hanging vertically, due to its own weight

A. Varies as the square of half the weight applied at the lower end

B. Is equal to that produced by a load, equal to its weight applied at lower end

C. Is equal to that produced by a load of half of its weight applied at the lower end

D. Is equal to that produced bya load of its weight, applied at the lower end or half its weight applied at the mid section

38. The thermal stess in a bar is directly proportional to

A. Its volume

B. Its cross-sectional area

C. The change in temperature

D. None of the above

39. A measure of strength economy of a material is the ratio between

A. Working strength and density

B. Ultimate strength density

C. Ultimate strength and factor of safety

D. Ultimate strength and Poisson's ratio

40. In the analysis of strains we consider

A. The relative displacement of the material as a whole

B. The relative displacement between the adjacent point

C. The rotation or translation of the material as a whole

D. The stresses created due to the rotation of the element as a whole

41. A hololw circular shaft having the same area of cross-section as a solid shaft

A. Is stronger than the solid shaft

B. Will be 33% less stronger than the solid shaft

C. Will have its strength depending upon the diameter of the shaft

D. Will be 33% less stronger than the solid shaft

42. A continuous beam is one which

A. Is supported on both the sides

B. Has more than two supports

C. Is simply supported at the centre

D. Is continuous over the span of the beams

43. A beam having one end fixed and other end free is called

A. Overhanging beam

B. Free beam

C. Cantilever

D. Fixed beam

44. If a simply supported beam carrying a concentrated load W at mid span of beam is 'L', then the maximum bending moment is equal to

A. $\frac{WL^2}{4}$ B. $\frac{WL}{4}$

C. $\frac{WL}{8}$ D. $\frac{WL^2}{2}$

45. The maximum bending moment will occur at the fixed end of a cantilever if it carries

A. A point load at a fixed end

B. A uniformly distributed load

C. A point load as well uniformly distributed load

D. All of the above

ANSWERS

1	2	3	4	5	6	7	8	9	10
A	B	D	B	A	A	A	A	C	C
11	**12**	**13**	**14**	**15**	**16**	**17**	**18**	**19**	**20**
C	A	D	A	B	A	B	A	C	B
21	**22**	**23**	**24**	**25**	**26**	**27**	**28**	**29**	**30**
A	B	D	C	C	B	C	D	D	A
31	**32**	**33**	**34**	**35**	**36**	**37**	**38**	**39**	**40**
C	B	D	B	E	B	C	C	B	B
41	**42**	**43**	**44**	**45**					
A	B	C	B	D					

6

HYDRAULICS AND HYDRAULIC MACHINES

Fluid

Any substance which is capable of flowing is called a fluid. It includes liquids as well as gases.

Since a number of phenomenon are involved in the study of fluid flow, we shall confine ourselves to the flow fo liquids only. To simplify the things further, we assume that

I. The liquid is incompressible. This means that density of the liquid is constant in all positions and at all times.

II. The liquid is non-viscous *i.e.* there are no tangential forces between layers of liquid in relative motion.

III. The flow of such a liquid is steady or streamlined *i.e.* orderly.

IV. The flow of liquid is irrotational *i.e.* in the liquid flow, there is no rotational motion of any element of the liquid about its centre of mass.

Laminar Flow

Particles of fluid move along smooth paths in laminas, or layers with one layer gliding smoothly over an adjacent layer.

Laminar flow is governed by newton's law of viscosity. In laminar flow, the action of viscosity damps out turbulent tendencies laminar flow is not stable in situations involving combinations of low viscosity, high velocity or large flow passages and breaks down into turbulent flow.

Turbulent Flow

Fluid particles in it move in very irregular paths, causing an exchange of momentum from one portion of the fluid to another.

Vortex Flow

Fluid particles rotate about a given axis, say the z-axis is defined as the average angular volocity of two infinitesimal line elements in the particle that are at right angles to each other and the given axis. If the fluid particles within a region have rotation about any axix, the flow is called rotational flow, or vortex flow. If the fluid within a region has no rotation, the flow is called irrotational flow.

Viscosity

The internal frictional force in a liquid which opposes the relative motion amongst its different layers is called Viscosity : Maxwell considered viscosity of a liquid in motion as equivalent to rigidity of a solid breaking down under a shearing stress. Hence viscosity of a liquid may also be defined as the temporary resistance offered by the 'liquid' to the shearing stress.

Coefficient of viscosity of a liquid is defined as the backward tangential force acting on unit area of a layer moving with unit relative velocity with respect to another layer at unit distance from it

$$\eta = -\frac{Fx}{Av}$$

The unit of η is called Poise. The dimensions of η can be defined from previous equation

$$\eta = \frac{Fx}{A.v}$$

$$= \frac{[MLT^{-2}][L]}{[L^2][LT^{-1}]}$$

$$= [ML^{-1}\,T^{-1}]$$

Buoyancy

If a body is floating in a fluid be in equilibrium, then the total upward force must be equal to the total downward force. The upward force on the floating body is known as buoyancy.

Archimedes Principle

According to the Archimedes Principle the

buoyancy is equal to the weight of the fluid displaced volume.

Stability of Submerged Bodies

A submerged body at rest is stable if a small displacement produces forces tending to restore the body to its original position. For a horizontal stability the centre of gravity of a rigid body must be below the centre of gravity, the body is unstable unless the centre of gravity of buoyancy shifts on rotation and set up a new position of stability.

Metacentre (M) is a piont where the buoyant force and the centre line intersect. Body is stable when M is above G (the position of centre of gravity), unstable when M is below G, and is neutral equilibrium when M is at G.

Bernoulli's Theorem

Bernoulli's Theorem is an outcome of the principle of conservation of energy, as applied to a liquid in motion. According to this theorem for the stream line flow of an ideal liquid, the pressure energy, potential energy and kinetic energy per unit volume always remains constant :

$$P + \rho g h + \frac{1}{2}\rho v^2 = \text{Constant}$$

Where $\rho = \frac{m}{V}$ = density of liquid

Flow through Constrictions

The energy losses from flow through changes in cross-section can be derived theoretically from the velocity distribution and integration of the momentum or mechanical energy equations. For incompressible flow with uniform velocity distributions the equations are given bel' w in which loss is expressed a energy per unit mass.

In general, the differential pressure is given by

$$\frac{p_1 - p_2}{P} = \Delta P = \frac{V_1^2 - V_2^2}{2g}$$

Sudden Expansion

$$\frac{p_1 - p_2}{P} = \frac{V_1^2}{g}\left[\left(\frac{S_1}{S_2}\right)^3 - \frac{S_1}{S_2}\right]$$

and $\Delta P = \frac{V_1^2}{2g}\left(1 - \frac{S_1}{S_2}\right)^2$

Sudden contraction

$$\Delta P = \frac{V^2}{2g}\left(\frac{1}{C_c} - 1\right)^2$$

Venturimeter

A venturimeter is a gauge used for measuring the rate of flow of liquids through pipes.

Open Channel formulae for uniform flow

I. Mannings formula

$$V = \frac{1}{n} m^{2/3} i^{1/2}$$

II. Chezy's formula

$$V = C\sqrt{mi}$$

III. Bazin's formula

$$C = \frac{157.6}{1.81 + k/\sqrt{m}}$$

Dimensionless Numbers

1. **Reynold's Number (Re)**

   The ratio of inertia force and viscous force is called Reynold's number

   $$Re = \frac{VL}{V}$$

   Where $V = \frac{\mu}{P}$ = kinematic viscosity of fluid

2. **Froude Number :**

   The ratio of inertia force and gravity force is

   $$= \frac{PL^2V^2}{PL^3 g} = \frac{V^2}{Lg}$$

   The square root of $\frac{V^2}{Lg}$ is known as Froude number.

   $$\text{Froude Number} = \frac{V}{\sqrt{Lg}}$$

3. **Euler Number :**

   The ratio of inertia force and pressure force is expressed as

   $$\frac{V^2}{P/p}$$

   The square root of this ratio is known as Euler number.

   $$\text{Euler Number} = \frac{V}{\sqrt{P/p}}$$

4. Newton Number :

Reciprocal of Euler number is known as

$$\text{Newton number} = \frac{\sqrt{P/p}}{V}$$

5. Cauchy Number :

$$\text{Dimensionless ratio} = \frac{V^2}{C^2}$$

$$C = \sqrt{\frac{k}{\rho}}$$

6. Mach Number :

The square root of $\frac{V^2}{C^2}$ is known as Mach number

$$\text{Mach number} = \frac{V}{C} = \frac{V}{\sqrt{k/\rho}}$$

7. Weber Number :

The dimensionless force ratio = $\frac{V^2}{\sigma/\rho L}$. The square root of this ratio is known as Weber number

$$\text{Weber number} = \frac{V}{\sigma/\rho L}$$

Hydraulic Jump

A rapidly flowing stream of liquid in a open channel suddenly changes to a slowly flowing stream with a larger cross-sectional area and sudden rise in elevation of liquid surface. This phenomenon of steady non-uniform flow is known as hydraulic jump.

$$\text{Losses due to jump } h = \frac{(y_2 - y_1)^3}{4y_1y_2}$$

Where y_1 and y_2 are downstream and upstream flow depths respectively.

Reaction Turbines

In a reaction turbine the water enters the wheel under pressure and flows over the vanes. In passing over the vanes the pressure head is converted to velocity head and is finally reduced to atmospheric pressure before leaving the wheel. In this case as the water under pressure, the wheel must run full and may, therefore, be entirely submerged below the tail race. Water must be admitted into the turbine over the whole circumference of the wheel. In this power is difficult to regulate.

Impulse Turbines

In this all the energy of water is converted into velocity before entering the wheel by expanding through a nozzle of guide vanes. The pressure of water is atmospheric hence the wheel must not run full, so it must be placed at the foot of the fall and above the tail race.

Types of Turbines

Reaction Turbines

I. Fournyon Turbine
II. Francis Turbine
III. Mixed Flow Turbine
IV. Kaplan and Propellor Turbine
V. Thomson's Turbine

Impulse Turbines

I. Pelton Wheel
II. Girdar Turbine
III. Turgo Turbine
IV. Banki Turbine
V. Jonval Turbine

MULTIPLE–CHOICE QUESTIONS

1. The ratio of inertia force to elastic force is known as

A. Weber's Number B. Reynold's Number
C. Mach Number D. Froude Number

2. Weber's Number is the ratio of

A. Inertia force to surface tension
B. Inertia force to viscous force
C. Inertia force to elasticity
D. None of the above

3. The channel section considered to have the highest efficiency is

A. Quadrant B. Square
C. Trapezoid D. Triangular

4. For an open channel at critical depth the flow becomes

A. Constant B. Zero

C. Half D. Maximum

5. While starting the certrifugal pump
   A. Delivery valve is kept wide open
   B. Delivery valve is kept closed
   C. Inlet valve is kept closed
   D. Delivery valve is opened slightly
6. For a fluid flow according to boundary layer concepts, separation occurs when the
   A. Pressure falls to zero
   B. Pressure rise is sudden and rapid
   C. Different boundary layers come across a sharp turn or bend
   D. Boundary layers of the fluid becomes stationary
7. The pressure of fluid can be measured by a
   A. Barometer
   B. Manometer
   C. Bourdan pressure gauge
   D. Piezometer tube
   E. All of the above
8. The total force acting on a plane horizontal surface in a liquid is equal to
   A. $w\bar{x}A$ B. $w\bar{x}$
   C. $\frac{w\bar{x}}{A}$ D. $\frac{Aw}{\bar{x}}$
   Where w = Specific weight of water
   $\bar{x}$ = Depth of liquid
   A = Area of surface
9. In case of laminar flow the
   A. Flow is irregular
   B. Losses are of prime importance
   C. Reynold's number lies between 2000 to 3000 for pipes
   D. Newton's law of viscocity is of importance
10. In order to have very high pressure and a high efficiency for a small discharge at a high head we prefer to use the following type of pump
    A. Centrifugal B. Reciprocating
    C. Mixed-flow pump D. Propeller
11. For handling non-viscous liquids, oils and chemicals we use
    A. Open type impeller centrifugal pump
    B. Axial flow pump
    C. Mixed flow pump
    D. Closed type impeller centrifugal pump
12. Any liquid flow, obeys the following
    A. Capillary action
    B. Bernoulli's equation
    C. Continuity equation
    D. Newton's law of viscocity
13. In case of pump the specific speed s given by
    A. $\frac{N\sqrt{Q}}{H^{1/2}}$ B. $\frac{N\sqrt{N}}{H^{3/4}}$
    C. $\frac{N\sqrt{P}}{H^{2/3}}$ D. $\frac{N\sqrt{Q}}{H^{3/4}}$
14. In the centrifugal pump, maximum efficiency is obtained when the blades are
    A. Bent backward
    B. Bent forward
    C. Straight
    D. Bent to have aerofoil section
15. High lift centrifugal pumps are those with head
    A. Greater than 15 m
    B. Greater than 40 m
    C. Equal to discharge area × velocity
    D. Above 10 m
16. A fluid is ideal if it is
    A. Inviscous and imcompressible
    B. Inviscous compressible
    C. Incompressible
    D. Inviscous
17. A fluid in equilibrium cannot sustain
    A. Tensile stress
    B. Compressive stress
    C. Decreases
    D. Shows erratic variation
18. Liquids transmit pressure equally in all direction and at right angle to the surface exposed. This statement known as
    A. Bernoulli's theorem
    B. Archimedes principle
    C. Pascal's law
    D. Principle of floatation
19. In case of partially immersed body in a liquid,
    A. the upward force > weight of fluid displaced
    B. the upward force < weight of fluid displaced
    C. the upward force = weight of fluid displaced
    D. None of the above
20. The bulk modulus of elasticity
    A. Has dimensions of $\frac{1}{\rho}$

B. Increases with pressure
C. Both A and B
D. None of these

21. The unit of viscosity is
A. m^2/sec B. kg. sec/m^2
C. Newton-sec/m^2 D. Newton-sec^2/metre

22. A uniform flow is one when
A. The flow parameters at any given instant remain same at every point
B. The flow parameters vary uniformly throughout
C. An imaginary situation
D. Non-existing

23. The point of application of buoyant force is known as
A. Centre of pressure B. Centre of buoyancy
C. Centre of gravity D. None of the above

24. The body is said to be floating when
A. $W > F_b$ B. $W = F_b$
C. $W < F_b$ D. None of the above
Where W = Weight of the body
F_b = Bouyant force.

25. According to principle of floatation, the weight of liquid displaced as compared to the weight of the body is
A. More
B. Less
C. Same
D. Depending upon the shpae of the body

26. The specific weight of water at 760 mm pressure at 4°C is
A. 1000 kg/m^3 B. 1kg/m^3
C. 10 kg/m^3 D. 100 kg/m^3

27. A perfect gas
A. Has viscocity constant
B. Has zero viscosity.
C. In incompressible
D. None of the above

28. The units of kinematic viscosity are
A. m^2/sec B. kg sec/m^2
C. Newton-sec/m^2 D. Newton-sec^2 metre

29. One dimension flow is one
A. Involving zero transverse components of flow
B. In uniform flow
C. In steady uniform flow
D. None of these

30. The atmospheric pressure with rise in altitude decreases
A. Linearly
B. First slowly and then steeply
C. First steeply and then gradually
D. Unpredictable

31. Falling drops of rain water because spherical due to
A. Viscosity B. Cohesion
C. Adhesion D. Surface tension

32. Reynold's number is the ratio of inertial force to
A. Surface tension B. Elasticity
C. Viscosity D. Gravitational force

33. The flow at critical depth in a open channel is
A. Maximum B. Minimum
C. Zero D. Half of normal flow

34. A body can be made to float by
A. Decreasing its volume
B. Increasing its weight
C. Decreasing both its vloume and weight
D. Increasing the volume of the body, weight remaining the same

35. A submerged body will be in stable equilibrium if the centre of gravity is
A. Below the centre of bouyancy
B. Above the centre of bouyancy
C. Coinciding with the centre of bouyancy
D. None of the above

36. The wetted perimeter for a pipe running full of water is equal to
A. $\frac{\pi d}{2}$ B. $2\pi d$
C. πd D. $\frac{\pi}{4}d^2$

37. The hydraulic mean depth for a pipe running full of water is equal to
A. $\frac{d}{2}$ B. $\frac{d}{4}$
C. $2d$ D. $2\pi d$
where d = diameter of pipe.

38. The hydraulic mean depth for a rectangular section is
A. $\frac{bd}{(2d+b)}$ B. $\frac{bd}{d+b}$

C. $\frac{2bd}{d+b}$ D. $\frac{bd}{2(d+b)}$

Where b = Width of rectangular section
d = Depth of water

39. Highest efficiency is obtained with following channel section

A. Trapezoidal B. Quadrant
C. Rectangualr D. Circular

40. For best hydraulic rectangular cross-section of an open channel, its depth should be equal to

A. Width B. 2 Width
C. $\frac{\text{Width}}{2}$ D. $\sqrt{\text{Width}}$

41. For a laminar flow

A. Flow occurs in a zig-zag way
B. Reynold's number lies between 200 to 3000
C. Newton's law of viscosity is of importance
D. None of these

42. In open channel corresponding to critical depth, the discharge is

A. Maximum B. Minimum
C. Zero-flow D. Turbulent flow

43. The maximum head loss in a pipe with bend angle

A. 60° B. 90°
C. U–bend D. 30°

44. The overflowing sheet of water over the weir is known as

A. Crest B. Nappe
C. Spillway D. All of the above

45. The discharge over the rectangualr weir is equal to

A. $2/3\ Cd\ \sqrt{2g}\ \text{L.H.}^{3/2}$
B. $3/2Cd\ \sqrt{2g}\ \text{L.H.}^{3/2}$
C. $3/2Cd\ \sqrt{2g}\ \text{L.H.}^{2/3}$
D. $2/3\ Cd\ \sqrt{2g}\ \text{L.H.}^{2/3}$

46. Any fluid flows

A. Bernoulli's equation
B. Newton's law
C. Darcy's equation
D. Continuity equation

47. In pipes larger than 25 mm, carrying water, the laminar flow

A. Very often exists B. Generally exists
C. Rarely exists D. Unpredictable

48. Metacentric height is the distance between

A. C.G. of body and centre of pressure
B. C.G. of body and the metacentre
C. C.G. of body and centre of buoyancy
D. None

49. An ideal fluid is

A. Frictionless and incompressible
B. One which has constant viscosity
C. Similar to perfect gas
D. Does not exist

50. Vertical Distribution of velocity in an open channel for laminar flow can be assumed as

A. Logarithmic B. Parabolic
C. Straight line D. Hyperbolic

ANSWERS

1	2	3	4	5	6	7	8	9	10
C	A	C	D	B	D	E	A	D	B
11	**12**	**13**	**14**	**15**	**16**	**17**	**18**	**19**	**20**
D	C	D	C	B	A	D	C	C	B
21	**22**	**23**	**24**	**25**	**26**	**27**	**28**	**29**	**30**
B	A	B	C	C	A	D	A	A	B
31	**32**	**33**	**34**	**35**	**36**	**37**	**38**	**39**	**40**
D	C	A	D	A	C	B	A	A	C
41	**42**	**43**	**44**	**45**	**46**	**47**	**48**	**49**	**50**
C	A	A	B	A	D	C	B	A	B

7

REFRIGERATION AND AIR CONDITIONING

Refrigeration

It is defined as the production of temperature lower than those of the surroundings and maintaining the lower temperature within the boudary of a given space.

Various methods for producing refrigerating effect are

(i) Ice refrigeration
(ii) Vapour absorption refrigeration
(iii) Liquid gas refrigeration
(iv) Vapour compression refrigeration
(v) Steam jet refrigeration
(vi) Air expansion refrigeration

Refrigerating Effect

The cooling effect produced by a machine is called as refrigerating effect.

Coefficient of Performance

The performance of a refrigerating machine is measured in terms of coefficient of performance, which is given by the relation.

$$\text{Coefficient of performance} = \frac{\text{Refrigerating effect}}{\text{Work input}}$$

If a machine has the capacity to produce cooling effect of 50 kcal/min is said to have one tonne capacity of refrigeration.

Refrigerants

In a refrigerating system the heat carrying medium is known as refrigerant. The refrigerant absorbs heat at one place which is at low temperature level and rejects it at some other place having higher temperature and pressure.

In a refrigeration cycle, the refrigerant changes from liquid to vapour during the heat absorption process and condenses again to liquid while liberating heat. An ideal refrigerant should liberate all the heat it is capable of absorbing.

Properties of a Good Refrigerant

(i) Low boiling and freezing point.
(ii) High Latent heat value and low specific value.
(iii) No corrosive effect on metals.
(iv) Should be safe and non-toxic.
(v) Ability to operate on a positive pressure.
(vi) Capacity to mix with oil.
(vii) No corrosive effect on metals.

Classification of Refrigerants

Refrigerants may be classified as

(i) **Primary Refrigerants**

Those which cool the substances by absorption of latent heat. These are generally used in vapour compression systems. Some of the primary refrigerants are Ammonia, Carbon-dioxide, Sulphurdioxide, Methyl chloride, methylene chloride and fluorinated hydrocarbonds.

(ii) **Secondary Refrigerants**

Those which cool substances by absorbing their sensible heat. Some of the secondary refrigerants are :

Air, water, calcium chloride brine, sodium chloride, brine, glycol etc.

Psychrometry

It is a branch of science which mainly deals with the study of the mixture of dry air and water vapour. The air is a mixture of gases like hydrogen, oxygen, argon, carbon dioxide, water vapour and traces of other gases. In air conditioning estimations air is taken as a mixture of dry air and water vapour.

Working of Refrigerating Machine

The coefficient of performance of a refrigeration machine working on reversed Carnot cycle is given by

$$\text{COP} = \frac{T_2}{T_1 - T_2}$$

Where T_1 is high temperature reservoir temperature, heat is rejected and T_2 is temperature of refrigerated space, i.e., low temperature reservoir. The C.O.P. of a carnot heat pump is more than the C.O.P. of carnot refrigerator by unity.

Vapour Compression Cycle

Vapour compression cycle is used for all purpose refrigeration. It is generally used from small domestic machines to an air conditioning plant of large capacity.

The four fundamental operations of a simple vapour compression system are

(i) Compression *(ii)* Condensation
(iii) Expansion *(iv)* Vaporisation

The vapour compression cycle depends upon

(i) the conversion of a substance from liquid to vapour form (evaporation) involving the absorption of a considerable quantity of latent heat by the substance.

(ii) for a given substance the temperature at which evaporation or condensation takes place depends only on the pressure prevailing and can be varied by varying the pressure.

Vapour Absorption Cycle

Vapour absorption cycle differs from compression cycle in a way that is uses heat energy instead of mechanical energy to make a change in the conditions necessary to complete the refrigeration cycle. The heat energy for the cycle may be obtained from the gas burner, kerosene oil lamp or electric heater. This system has minimum number of moving parts. The working of this system depends upon the use of two substances which have great affinity for each other and which can be easily separated by the application of heat :

Dry Air

International Joint Committee on Psychrometric Data has fixed the following composition of air in mole fraction.

Oxygen	...	0.2095
Nitrogen	...	9.7809
Argon	...	0.0093
Carbon dioxide	...	0.0003

Moist Air

It is mixture of dry air and water vapour. The quantity of water vapour in air depends upon the temperature of air.

Saturated Air

Moist air is said to be saturated when it contains maximum amount of water vapour that it can hold. If water added to air in more than that of saturated air, the drops of water will remain in suspension and will make the air foggy or moisty.

Degree of Saturation

It is the ratio of the prevailing humidy ratio of moist air to the humidity ratio of saturated air at the same temperature and pressure.

Psychrometric Chart

It is a graphical representation of the various thrmodynamic properties of moist air. In this abscessa represents dry bulb temperature and ordinate represents specific humidity. Other properties of air that air incorporated in a psychrometric chart are :

(i) Relative humidity
(ii) Pressure of water vapour
(iii) Enthalpy
(iv) Sensible heat factor
(v) Wet bulb temperature
(vi) Due point temperature
(vii) Specific volume

Air Conditioning

In involves the control of following factors :

(i) Temperature
(ii) Humidity control
(iii) Air movement and circulation
(iv) Filteration, cleaning and purification of air

Comfort air conditioning is sub-divided into three groups :

(i) Summer air conditioning
(ii) Winter air conditioning
(iii) Year round air conditioning

Cooling Loads

The total amount of heat which is required to be pumped out from the space to be kept at the desired level of temperature by the refrigerating equipment is known as cooling load. The total load determines the size of plant required. Various load on an air conditioned plant arise due to :

(i) Sensible heat gear
(ii) Latent heat gear

MULTIPLE-CHOICE QUESTIONS

1. The refrigeration is used for
   A. Food preservation
   B. Comfort
   C. Cold storage and ice factories
   D. All the above three

2 The coldest part in the domestic refrigerator is
   A. Condenser B. Evaporator
   C. Receiver D. Compressor

3. The refrigeration system works on
   A. First law of thermodynamics
   B. Second law of thermodynamics
   C. Zeroth law of thermodynamics
   D. None of the above

4. The capacity of a refrigerating machine is expressed in
   A. Tonnes of refrigeration
   B. Terms of lowest temperature attained
   C. Term of weight of a machine
   D. Term of volume of a space to be cooled

5. Tonnes of regfrigeration means
   A. The weight of machine is one tonne
   B. The weight of refrigerant used is one tonne
   C. The rate of abstraction of heat from the space to be cooled
   D. None of the above

6. The domestic refrigerator works on the principle of
   A. Vapour absorption refrigeration system
   B. Vapour compression refrigeration system
   C. Thermo-electric refrigeration system
   D. Liquid gas refrigeration system

7. The refrigerant used in the domestic refrigerator is
   A. Ammonia B. Freon
   C. Fluorine D. Methyl chloride

8. The liquid refrigerant which enters the evaporator is at
   A. Low pressure
   B. Low temperature
   C. Low pressure and temperature both
   D. High pressure and temperature both

9. Air refrigerator works on
   A. Rankine cycle B. Otto cycle
   C. Carnot cycle D. Bell coleman cycle

10. The working fluid in Bell coleman cycle is
   A. Freon-12 B. CO_2
   C. Ammonia D. Air

11. In refrigeration system using ammonia as refrigerant, the piping are made of
   A. Copper B. Aluminium
   C. Brass D. Steel

12. The unit of refrigerating effect is
   A. k cal B. k cal/J
   C. k cal/min D. Degree Kelvin

13. The refrigerant used for domestic refrigerator must be
   A. Non-corrosive
   B. Non-toxic and odourless
   C. Of high working pressure
   D. All the above three

14. The compressor of the refrigerator
   A. Sucks the refrigeration from the evaporator
   B. Deliver the compressed refrigerant to the condenser
   C. Both A and B
   D. Regulates the quantity of refrigerant

15. Cooling of water in an earthen pitcher is an example of
   A. Steam jet refrigeration
   B. Evaporation refrigeration
   C. Vapour absorption refrigeration
   D. Vapour compression refrigeration

16. Aqua ammonia is a solution of ammonia and
   A. Freon-12 B. Freon-22
   C. Water D. CO_2

17. Aqua ammonia solution is used in
   A. Vapour compression system
   B. Vapour absorption system
   C. Air refrigeration system
   D. Evaporative cooling system

18. The circulation of the refrigerant in an electrolux refrigerator takes place by
   A. A pump B. A compressor
   C. Gravity D. None of the above

19. The condenser of domestic refrigerator is fitted
   A. Below the evaporator
   B. On the back of the refrigerator
   C. Near the compressor

D. On the top of the refrigerator

20. The function of the expansion valve is
A. To control the pressure
B. To control the temperature
C. To regulate the flow of refrigerant
D. All the above three

21. The temperature of air measure by an ordinary thermometer is called the
A. Dry bulb temperature
B. Wet bulb temperature
C. Saturation temperature
D. None of the above

22. The temperature at which condensation of moisture begins when the air is cooled, is known as
A. Dry bulb temperature
B. Drew point temperature
C. Saturation temperature
D. Condensation temperature

23. The device used to regulate the flow of the refrigerant in a system is known as
A. Capillary tube
B. Solenoid valve
C. Thermostatic valve
D. None of the above
E. All of the above

24. The use of compressor is not required in
A. Vapour compression system
B. Bell Coleman refrigerator
C. Vapour absorption system
D. Air refrigeration system

25. In a vapour compression system, the compression of refrigerant vapour follows the law
A. pvr = C B. pv = C
C. pvn = C D. None of the above

26. In case of dry compression, the vapours
A. Enter the compressor in a wet state
B. Leave the compressor in dry saturated state
C. Enter the compressor in dry saturated state
D. None of the above

27. The Bell Coleman Cycle consists of
A. Two adiabatic processes and two constant pressure processes
B. Two adiabatic processes and two constant volume processes
C. Two isothermal processes and two adiabatic proceses
D. Two constant volume processes and two constant pressure processes

28. C.O.P. is always
A. More than one B. Less than one
C. Equal to one D. Unpredictable

29. Too much freezing around the freezer is due to
A. Defective door seal
B. Frequent opening of door
C. Storing of hot food stuff
D. Low voltage

30. The air which does not come in contact with the cooling coil while passing over it, is known as
A. Wet air B. Saturated air
C. Dry air D. By pass air

31. In evaporative cooling
A. Sensible heat is added to the air
B. Latent heat is removed from the air
C. Air is cooled and humidified
D. Air is cooled and dehumidified

32 The most suitable temperature for human comfort is in the range of
A. 30° C to 32°C B. 22.8°C to 25°C
C. 15°C to 18°C D. 18° C to 22.5°C

33. The sensible heating of air will change its
A. Moisture contents
B. Humidity ratio
C. Dry bulb temperature
D. None of the above

34. During sensible cooling of air the humidity ratio will
A. Increase B. Decrease
C. Remain same D. Unpredictable

35. Desert cooler work on the principle of
A. Evaporating cooling
B. Vapour compression system
C. Vapour absorption system
D. None of the above

36. The gain of heat due to conduction the cooled space through the surrounding walls, doors, ceiling etc. is known as
A. Product load B. Transmission load
C. Infiltration load D. None of the above

37. The indoor design temperature for air conditioning depends on the
A. Density of occupancy
B. Sex of the person
C. Age of the person

D. All of the above

38. The leakage of air into the refrigeration system will

A. Lower its cooling efficiency
B. Increase cooling efficiency
C. Not affect the cooling efficiency
D. Increase the C.O.P.

39. Normal cooling in freezer, but not in all the portion is due to

A. Defective door gasket
B. Frequent opening of door
C. Both A and B
D. Less refrigerant in the system

40. The compressor gives noisy operation due to

A. No refrigerant in the system
B. Loose mounting bolts
C. Chocking in the suction pipe
D. Defective door seal

41. Bulb of the refrigerator does not work due to

A. Defective thermostat
B. Defective door switch
C. Low voltage
D. Defective gasket

42 Motor runs slow because of

A. Bearing worn out B. Insulation failure
C. Motor over loaded D. Defective thermostat

43. Motor gets hot on running because of

A. Low voltage
B. Poor relay contacts
C. Open circuit in starting winding
D. Thermostat contact open

44. Motor goes on running even if the temperature is very low inside the refrigerator is due to

A. High voltage
B. Low voltage
C. Defective thermostat
D. Defective relay

45. Motor gives humming noise does not start due to

A. Defect in motor
B. Defective relay contacts
C. Low voltage
D. Any one of the three

46. Motor keeps on running but cooling is insufficient

A. Wrong setting of thermostat
B. Defective thermostat
C. Less refrigerant gas
D. No refrigerant gas in the system

47. In the modern domestic refrigerator the expansion valve is replaced by

A. Suction pipe B. Capillary tube
C. Discharge pipe D. Accumulator

48. The artificial atmosphere of particular requirements can be obtained from

A. Ceiling fan B. Desert cooler
C. Air conditioner D. Exhaust fan

49. The air conditioner gives

A. Cool air B. Hot air
C. Cold and hot air both D. Damped air

50. Which of the following properties, the airconditioner has

A. It can control the humidity of air
B. It can maintain proper temperature
C. It can keep down concentration of CO_2 and smoke with low limits
D. All the above three

ANSWERS

1	2	3	4	5	6	7	8	9	10
D	B	B	A	C	B	B	C	D	D
11	**12**	**13**	**14**	**15**	**16**	**17**	**18**	**19**	**20**
D	C	D	C	B	C	B	C	B	D
21	**22**	**23**	**24**	**25**	**26**	**27**	**28**	**29**	**30**
A	B	E	C	A	C	A	A	C	D
31	**32**	**33**	**34**	**35**	**36**	**37**	**38**	**39**	**40**
C	B	C	C	A	C	D	A	C	B
41	**42**	**43**	**44**	**45**	**46**	**47**	**48**	**49**	**50**
B	C	B	C	D	D	B	C	C	D

8

Gas Turbines, Compressor And Jet Engines

Gas Turbines

Gas Turbines operate on Brayton cycle. A compressor usually coupled with turbine, compresses air which is then transferred to combustor. A combustor is a heat exchanger, where fuel is burnt, and temperature of air from compressor is raised. This high pressure high temperature air expands in turbine doing mechanical work.

When the gas is ideal so that cp is constant, the thermal efficiency is given by

$$\eta = \frac{(T_c - T_b) - (T_d - T_a)}{(T_c - T_b)}$$

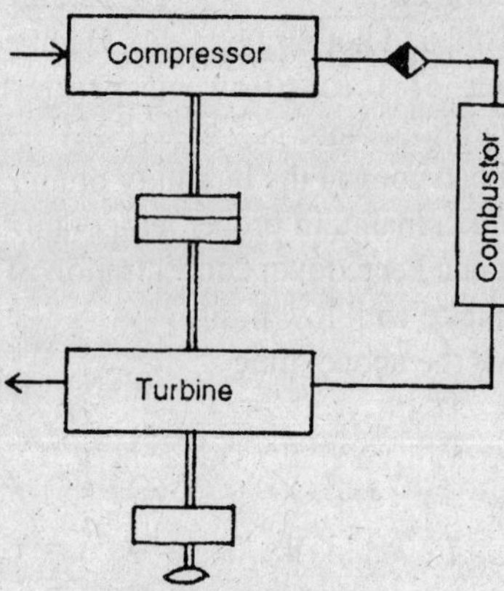

Brayton Cycle

The efficiency of cycle can be improved by

(i) Multistage compression with intercooling

(ii) Reheating of expanding ash

(iii) Use of regenerator.

Types of Gas Turbines

1. Open Cycle Gas turbine : During each cycle of operation fresh working fluid enters the system. The atmospheric air is drawn in the compressor and after compression it is used for the combustion of fuel in the combustor. The combustible gases after passing through the turbine are rejected to the atmosphere.

2. Closed Cycle Gas Turbine : In this system same working fluid is circulated again and again after completing the cycle. In this system, the heat is added from an external source and it is rejected top a cooling medium in a heat exchanger.

Steam Turbines

Steam Turbines convert energy in steam to shaft energy steam turbines may be classified as

(i) Impulse type

(ii) Reaction type

(iii) Combination of impulse and reaction

Steam Turbines may also be classified as

(i) Condensing type

(ii) Non-condensing type

Other classifications are

I. With respect to number of stages

(i) Single stage

(ii) Multi stage

II. With respect to the direction of steam flow

(i) Axial *(ii)* Radial

(iii) Mixed *(iv)* Helical

(v) Re-entry *(vi)* Tangential

III. With respect to the pressure of steam as

(i) High pressure

(ii) Medium pressure

(iii) Low presure

A steam turbine works on Rankine cycle and takes the advantage of expansion upto the lowest pressure. The thermal efficiency of a steam turbine is higher than that of steam engine. In an impulse turbine the expansion takes place in the nozzle only, where the pressure decreases and velocity increases. This pressure remains constant while steam passes over the blades of the turbine. In case of pure reaction turbine the steam expands as it flows over the blades which therefore act as nozzle.

The velocity of a simple impusle wheel is too high for practical purposes and as such the speed has to be reduced by some suitable means.

In case of single stage impulse the blade efficiency

$$\text{is} = \frac{2V_b(Vw_1 - Vw_0)}{V_1 2}$$

$$\text{and stage efficiency} = \frac{V_b(Vw_1 - Vw_0)}{gJhD}$$

In case of impulse turbine with several blade rings

$$\text{diagram efficiency} = \frac{2V_b\,\Sigma(Vw_1 - Vw_0)}{V_1 2}$$

Air Compressor

Air Compressor is used to increase the pressure of atmospheric air. For compressing the air, the work is being done on it by a prime mover, which may be a electric motor, diesel engine etc.

Types of Air Compressors

Rotary Compressor : Machines which develop

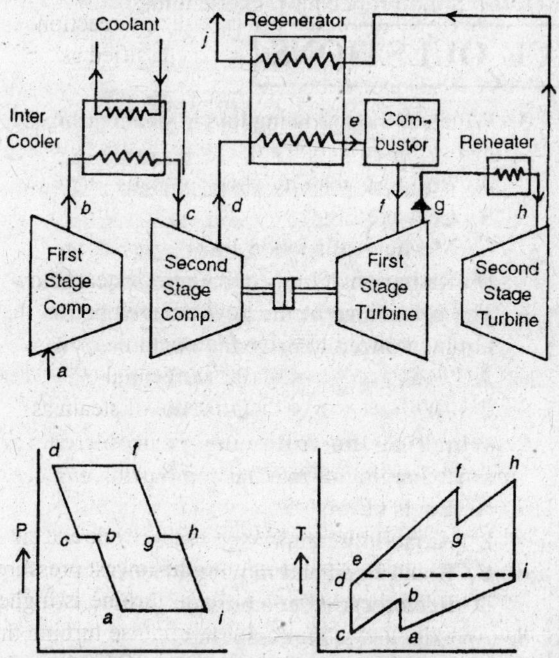

Brayton Cycle

pressure on rotary principle are called Rotary Compressors. They generally run at very high speeds and are often coupled with prime movers like steam turbines or gas turbines. The compression of gas in a rotary compressor follows the law pv^n = constant, where index n depends in the properties of gas being compressed and operating conditions.

Centrifugal Compressor

In centrifugal compressor impeller consists of a large number of vanes and is mounted on a shaft, inside a stationary casing. Pressure rise through impeller and diffuser as shown in the figure :

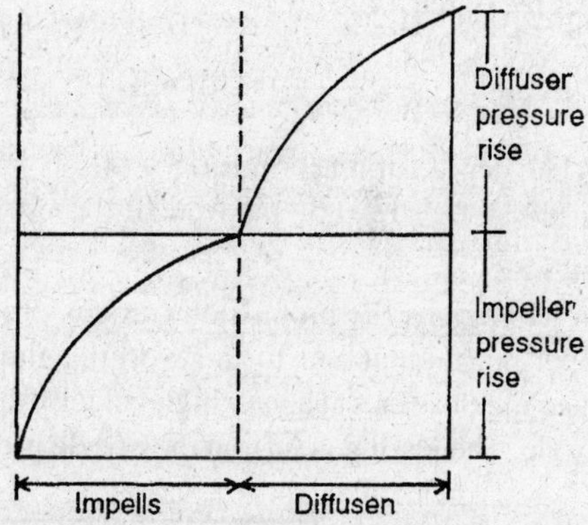

Work done is given by

$$W = \frac{Vw_2 . Vb_2}{g}$$

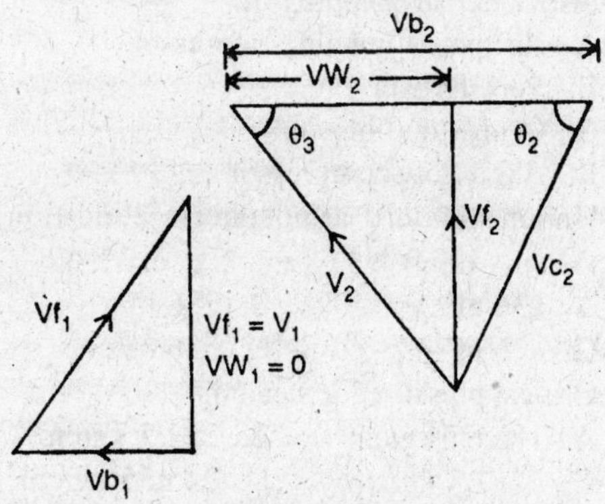

Insentropic efficiency of compressor

$$= \frac{\text{Isentropic temp. rise}}{\text{Actual temp. rise}}$$

Axial Flow Compressor

In axial flow compressor, air flows in an axial

direction. There are alternate layers of rotating blades and stator blades :

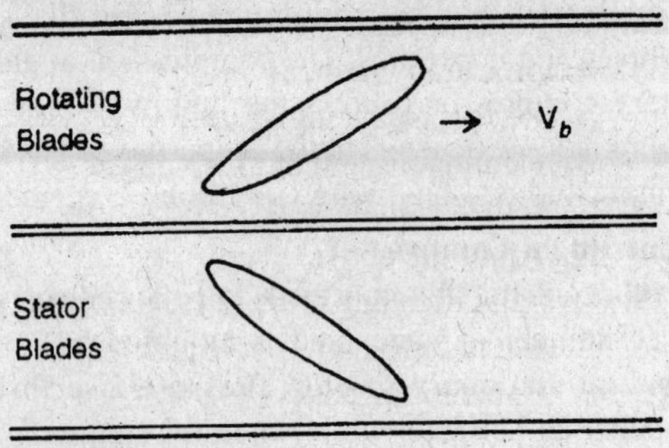

Degree of reaction,

$$R = \frac{1}{2}\frac{V_f}{V_b}\tan(\beta_1 + \beta_2)$$

When degree of reaction is 0.5

$$\alpha_1 = \beta_1 \text{ and } \alpha_2 = \beta_2$$

Jet Engines

In jet engines the propulsion force is produced by imparting momentum to the working fluid and then ejecting the gases at a very high velocity through the nozzle. The jet of gases from the nozzle produces a reaction in the opposite direction in the form of propulsive force.

Various types of jet engines are :

(*a*) Atmospheric engines

(*b*) Rocket engines

In atmospheric jet engines the oxygen required for the combustion of fuel is taken from the atmospheric air. The performance of such engines depends upon the atmospheric pressure and temperature. But rocket engines carries both the fuel and the oxidising agent for combustion of fuel. The performance of such engine is independent of the atmospheric air.

Types of Atmospheric Jet Engines

Atmospheric jet engines are classified as

(*a*) Turbojet engines

(*b*) Turbojet with after burner

(*c*) Turbo prop

(*d*) Ram jet

(*e*) Pulse jet

Types of Rocket Engines

Rocket Engines are classified as

(*a*) Liquid propellant rocket engine

(*b*) Solid propellant rocket engine

MULTIPLE-CHOICE QUESTIONS

1. Which one of the following compressors is a displacement compressor?

A. Reciprocating air compressor
B. Vane blower
C. Centrifugal blower
D. Axial flow compressor

2. Under standard atmospheric condition, the velocity of air is

A. 236 m/s B. 336 m/s
C. 436 m/s D. 536 m/s

3. Critical pressure for steam is

A. 185.85 kg/cm^2 B. 212.5 kg/cm^2
C. 225.65 kg/cm^2 D. 245.55 kg/cm^2

4. Which of the following fluid can be used in binary vapour cycle?

A. Mercury
B. Diphenyl oxide
C. Aluminium bromide
D. Any of the above

5. Which of the following loss in steam turbines is negligible?

A. Residual velocity loss
B. Leakage loss
C. Mechanical friction loss
D. Radiation

6. The percentage of the power developed in the turbine utilized to drive the compressor is

A. 20% B. 40%
C. 70% D. 90%

7. Which of the following is preferred for supercharging of internal combustion engines?

A. Roots blower
B. Axial flow compressor
C. Booth fixed and moving blades
D. Reciprocating compressor

8. An axial flow compressor has

A. Larger blades at gas entry and smaller blades at exit

B. Smaller blades at gas entry and larger blades at exit
C. Identical blades at exit as well as entry
D. Size of blades remains same only angles changes

9. Gas turbine used in aircraft is of
A. Open cycle type
B. Closed cycle type with reheating
C. Closed cycle with reheating and regeneration
D. Open cycle type with reheating, regeneration and inter-cooling.

10. In which of the following plant inferior quality fuel can be used?
A. Open cycle gas turbine with regeneration
B. Open cycle gas turbine with inter-cooling
C. Open cycle gas turbine with reheating and regeneration
D. Closed cycle gas turbine

11. The ratio of actual velocity to the local velocity of sound is called
A. Velocity ratio B. Velocity factor
C. Speed ratio D. Mach number

12. In a nozzle, once the critical conditions are achieved at the throat then which of the following remains constant?
A. Density of fluid B. Velocity of fluid
C. Flow rate D. All of the above

13. In a nozzle under choked flow conditions pressure waves travels, in the divergent portion at
A. Subsonic speed
B. Sonic speed
C. Supersonic speed
D. Subsonic to supersonic speed

14. Which of the following is a pressure compounded turbine?
A. Parson's turbine B. Curtis turbine
C. Rateau turbine D. All of the above

15. Which of the following steam turbine has identical fixed and moving blades
A. Curtis turbine B. Rateau turbine
C. Parson's turbine D. None of the above

16. Thermal efficiency of a gas turbine is in the range
A. 50 to 60% B. 40 to 50%
C. 30 to 40% D. 20 to 30%

17. A diffuser
A. Converts kinetic energy into thermal energy
B. Converts potential energy into kinetic energy
C. Converts pressure energy into kinetic energy
D. Converts thermal energy into kinetic energy

18. The advantage of a gas turbine over a reciprocating engine is
A. Perfect balancing of rotor
B. Continuous and uniform power
C. Usually small working pressures
D. All of the above

19. Overall efficiency of a gas turbine is
A. Equal to Rankine cycle efficiency
B. Equal to Carnot cycle efficiency
C. Less than Diesel cycle efficiency
D. More than Otto or Diesel cycle efficiency

20. The flow on two sides of a normal shock wave is
A. Sub-sonic
B. Sonic
C. Supersonic
D. Supersonic on one side and sub-sonic on the other side

21. The function of an intercooler is to
A. Cool the lubricating oil
B. Cool the cylinder body
C. Cool the compressed air between the stages
D. Cool the inlet air before suction.

22. The discharge capacity of a root blower is upto
A. 10 m^3/min B. 100 m^3/min
C. 500 m^3/min D. 1500 m^3/min

23. The maximum capacity of a reciprocating compressor is
A. 100 m^3/min B. 200 m^3/min
C. 300 m^3/min D. 1000 m^3/min

24. The comparison in a multistage compressor will be isothermal if
A. The compressor runs at slow speed
B. A perfect intercooling is provided
C. The cylinder is cooled properly
D. The pressure ratio for each stage is same

25. The adiabatic efficiency of a compressor is given by the relation.
A. $\dfrac{\text{air horse power supplied}}{\text{horse power of prime mover}}$
B. $\dfrac{\text{work done during adiabatic cycle}}{\text{actual indicated workdone on air}}$

C. $\dfrac{\text{work done during adiabatic cycle}}{\text{power supplied to compressor shaft}}$

D. $\dfrac{\text{actual indicated power of compressor}}{\text{work done during adabatic cycle}}$

26. The work done will be least if the compressor is

A. Isothermal B. Polytropic

C. Isentropic D. None of the above

27. The work done per kg of air delivered with increase in clearance volume will

A. Increase B. Decrease

C. Remain same D. Unpredictable

28. The volumetric efficiency of an air compressor with increase in clearance volume will

A. Decrease

B. Increase

C. Remain same

D. Increase or decrease depending on the inlet air temperature

29. A regenerator can be used on

A. Open cycle gas turbines only

B. Closed cycle gas turbines only

C. Both open as well as closed cycle gas turbines

D. None of the above

30. Thermal efficiency of a gas turbine can be improved by

A. Reheating between expansion stages

B. Intercooling between compression stages

C. Regeneration

D. Any of the above

31. The type of compressor used in an aeroplane is

A. Reciprocating B. Centrifugal

C. Axial flow D. Root blower

32. The volumetric efficiency of a compressor at high altitude will

A. Increase B. Decrease

C. Remain same D. Unpredictable

33. The maximum permissible inlet temperature of a gas turbine is about

A. 500°C B. 900°C

C. 1500°C D. 2000°C

34. The energy present in the exhaust gases of a turbine is utilized

A. To increase the compressor inlet air temperature

B. To increase the temperature of fuel before combustion

C. To increase the temperature of compressor air in a regenerator

D. For heating the combustion chamber

35. Water is injected into the compressor of a gas turbine plant

A. To control the temperature

B. To increase the power output

C. For intercooling the compressed air

D. To increase the air rate

36. The diverging portion of the nozzle acts as a diffuser for

A. The sub-sonic flow

B. The supersonic flow

C. Both the sub-sonic as well as supersonic flow

D. None of the above

37. All of the folowing positive displacement compressors except

A. Screw compressor

B. Axial flow compressor

C. Roots blower

D. Vane blower

38. The continuity equation in compressible fluids is derived on the basis of

A. Conservation of momentum

B. Conservation of energy

C. Conservation of mass

D. Conservation of velocity head

39. If the inlet temperature in compressor is increased, the air rate of gas turbine plant will

A. Increase B. Decrease

C. Remain same D. Unpredictable

40. The thermal efficiency of the open cycle gas turbine with regenerator, intercooler and reheater is about

A. 35% B. 29%

C. 12% D. 8%

41. The size of a gas turbine plant can be reduced by using

A. An intercooler

B. A reheater

C. Combination of both, i.e., intercooler and reheater

D. Any of the above

42. The jet propulsion engine is base on

A. Newton's Second and Third Laws of Motion

B. Newton's First Law of Motion
C. Second Law of Thermodynamics
D. Zeroth's Law of Thermodynamics

43. The specific fuel consumption, kg fuel per kg. thrust per hour, of the turbojet engine is in the range of
A. 0.4 to 0.5 B. 0.5 to 0.8
C. 1.0 to 1.4 D. 1.6 to 1.8

44. The specific fuel consumption of the turbojet engine, with increase in altitude, will
A. Decrease
B. Increase
C. Remain same
D. Depends upon other parameters

45. In a jet engine the ratio of the propulsive power to the heat supplied is known as
A. Thermal efficiency
B. Overall efficiency
C. Mechanical efficiency
D. Propulsive efficiency

46. The propulsive efficiency in the sub-sonic speed range is maximum in case of a
A. Reciprocating engine
B. Pulse jet engine
C. Rocket engine
D. Turbojet engine

47. With the increase in altitude the thrust of the rocket engine will
A. Decrease B. Increase
C. Remain same D. Unpredictable

48. The propulsive efficiency of a rocket engine as compared to turbojet engine is
A. More B. Less
C. Same D. Unpredictable

49. The type of engine recommended for aircrafts operating at sub-sonic speed is
A. Turbojet engine B. Turboprop engine
C. Rocket engine D. Ramjet engine

50. In a ramjet engine
A. The required quantity of air for the combustion of fuel is supplied by a compressor
B. The oxygen required for combustion is supplied by the oxidising agent
C. The gases after combustion passes through the turbine
D. The compressor as well as turbine is not used.

ANSWERS

1	2	3	4	5	6	7	8	9	10
B	B	C	D	D	C	A	A	A	D
11	**12**	**13**	**14**	**15**	**16**	**17**	**18**	**19**	**20**
D	D	B	C	C	C	A	D	C	D
21	**22**	**23**	**24**	**25**	**26**	**27**	**28**	**29**	**30**
C	D	C	B	B	A	C	A	C	D
31	**32**	**33**	**34**	**35**	**36**	**37**	**38**	**39**	**40**
C	B	B	C	B	A	B	C	A	B
41	**42**	**43**	**44**	**45**	**46**	**47**	**48**	**49**	**50**
D	A	B	A	A	A	B	B	B	D

9

NUCLEAR POWER PLANT

Isotopes

The atoms of an element having the same atomic number but different mass number are called isotopes.

Radioactivity

The phenomenon of emission of invisible radiations by certain heavy elements (like uranium, thorium, radium and polonium) is called radioactivity and the elements which emit such radiations are called radioactive elements.

Nuclear Reactions

In nuclear reactions, the nucleus of an atom undergoes a change forming new atoms and releasing a tremendous amount of energy is called nuclear energy.

Nuclear Fission

The process in which an unstable nucleus of a heavy atom (like Uranium^{235}) splits up into two medium weight nuclei with the liberation of an enormous amount of energy is called nuclear fission.

Nuclear Fusion

The process in which two nuclei of light atoms (like that of hydrogen) combine to form a heavy, more stable nucleus (like that of helium), with the liberation of a large amount of energy is called nuclear fusion.

Electricity is produced from nuclear energy or atomic energy. To understand this, we should first know the meaning of the terms like ; (1) Nuclear reactor, (2) Nuclear fuel, (3) Coolant, (4) Moderator, and (5) Controlling rods.

1. Nuclear Reactor : The nuclear reactor (or atomic reactor) is a kind of furnace for carrying out the controlled fission of a radioactive material like uranium^{235} for producing atomic power. It is in the reactor that the heat energy is produced from fission reactions, which in then taken out and converted into electricity.

2. Coolant : The substance which is circulated through the nuclear reactor to take out the heat energy produced in it, is called coolant. In general, some pipes are embedded in the reactor through which some coolant is circulated to take out the heat produced in the reactor. In most successful reactors, liquid sodium metal is used as the coolant, which removes the heat energy produced, in a short time. In some reactors, however, carbon dioxide gas and even water are used as coolants, to transfer the heat generated in reactor to the heat exchanger.

3. Nuclear Fuel : The fissionable material used in nuclear reactors for producing energy by the fission process is called a nuclear fuel. The fuel used in nuclear power plants is enriched uranium^{235}, which contains about 2 to 3% of easily fissionable uranium^{235} isotope (the remaining being uranium^{238} isotope which does not get fissioned easily). It shoud be noted that natural uranium, which contains a very low percentage of uranium^{235}, cannot be used as a nuclear fuel directly in reactors because due to the very low percentage of easily fissionable uranium^{235} in it, the natural uranium cannot sustain (cannot maintain) a nuclear chain reaction. Since naturally occurring uranium has very little uranium^{235}, so it has first to be processed to increase the percentage of fissionable uranium^{235} in it. This process is called enrichment. Even the enriched uranium used in reactors contains both type of atoms, uranium^{238} as well as uranum^{235}. But it is the uranium^{235} atoms which act as real fuel for producing energy. The nuclear fuel (or fissionable material) of enriched uranium is used in the reactors in the form of long rods or strips called fuel elements.

4. Moderator : The fission of uranium^{235} takes place easily only if the bombarding neutron is slow and not fast. Because only when the neutron is slow that it has more time to react with the nucleus and cause its fission. Now, the neutrons emitted by the uranium^{235} atoms have a fairly high speed; so they cannot cause the fission of other uranium^{235} atoms effectively. In such a case, the fission reaction will not become a self-propagating chain reaction and the nuclear fire will die down. So, in order to carry out the fission of uranium^{235} nuclei more effectively, the speed of neutrons must be slowed down. A substance which slows down the speed of neutrons in the nuclear reactor to a level appropriate to cause the fission of uranium^{235} effectively, is called a moderator. The commonly used moderators in the nuclear reactors are : Graphite and Heavy water. Graphite is a form of carbon element (C) whereas heavy water (D_2O) is a compound of oxygen (O) with heavy hydrogen called deuterium (D). Graphite or heavy water is used around the uranium rods in the reactor to moderate (slow down) the speed of neutrons, so that the chain reaction of fission is prevented from dying out. When the high speed neutrons collide with the graphite nucleus or heavy water; they lose some of their kinetic energy and get slowed down, so that they become slow neutrons. These slow neutrons then split (fission) the uranium^{235} nuclei to liberate more neutrons, and thus keep the nuclear fire burning. Thus, the function of moderator in a nuclear reactor is to slow down the speed of neutrons so that the chain reaction of fission is prevented from dying out. This is because the fission of uranium^{235} takes place effectively only if the bombarding neutrons are slow and not very fast.

5. Controlling Rods : An ordinary fission reaction produces a lot of neutrons at very step which cause further fission, and ultimately the chain reaction of fission goes out of control. In such a case of uncontrolled fission, the nuclear reactor will become a nuclear bomb (or atom bomb) and may cause an explosion. So, in order that the nuclear fission reaction of uranium^{235} may go on smoothly in a controlled manner, an arrangement or mechanism must be made to remove the excess neutrons as they are being produced in the reactor because it is these excess neutrons which make the fission reaction go out of control. The excess neutrons present in the reactor are removed by using cadmium or boron rods. This is because the elements cadmium and boron have the ability to absorb neutrons and hence make them ineffective to cause further fission. Thus, in a nuclear reactor, the chain reaction of nuclear fission is controlled (or made critical) by using controlling rods made of cadmium or boron. The cadmium or boron rods absorb excess neutrons being emitted by uranium^{235} atoms, so that the fission takes place at a steady rate and the energy which is produced in the form of heat can be utilized to generate electricity as in other thermal power stations. A very important point to note here is that if the cadmium or boron rods are inserted more deeply into the fuel, then they will absorb more neutrons that required and the fission will become very slow, on the other hand, if the cadmium or boron rods are inserted less deeply into the fuel, then they will absorb less neutrons than required, and the fission will become very fast. So the length of cadmium or boron rods inside the fuel is adjusted in such a way that the fission reaction is neither very slow nor very fast, but takes place at moderate rate. These controlling rods can be adjusted from outside the reactor. If we insert the cadmium or boron rods fully into the fuel, then they will absorb all the neutrons and hence the reactor will stop working. The nuclear fire will be extinguished. This is the shut down position of reactor. But if the cadmium and boron rods are completely withdrawn from the fuel, then all the neutrons will be available for fission, the reaction will go out of control, it will produce a tremendous amount of energy in a very short time and cause an explosion. We shall now describe how electricity is actually produced by using the nuclear reactor principle.

Production of Electricity from Nuclear Energy or Atomic Energy

The heat energy produced in the nuclear fission reactions can be used for producing electrical energy or electricity. In a nuclear power station, the heat required for producing steam to run steam turbines and hence electricity generators is provided by a nuclear reactor. The nuclear reactor is an arrangement in which a controlled chain reaction of nuclear fussion takes place.

Principle of Nuclear Power Production

In a nuclear power station, uranium^{235} is subjected to fission by bombarding with slow moving neutrons. This nuclear fission takes place in a nuclear reactor and produces a lot of heat energy. This heat energy is used to boil water to form steam. The hot, pressurised steam turns the steam turbine. When the turbine rotates, the electric generator or dynamo fixed on its shaft starts working and produces electricity. In a nuclear reactor, graphite (or heavy water) is used as a moderator to slow down the speed of neutrons, so as to keep the nuclear steam.

Peaceful uses of Atomic Energy or Nuclear Energy

The most important use of atomic energy (or nuclear energy) in the world is for generating electricity. In India too, atomic energy is being used to generate electrycity. Another important peaceful use of nuclear energy is in the treatment of diseases like cancer. Atomic energy is also being used for the improvement in agriculture and industry in India.

Atomic Energy in India

Mojor research centres : Bhabha Atomic Research Centre (BARC) at Bombay is the major centre for research and development work in atomic energy in India. Apart from BARC, Gulmarg in Sringar and Calcutta in West Bengal, have also good nuclear research laboratories.

Atomic power stations in India : The first atomic power station in India, called Tarapur Atomic Power Station' started functioning in 1969 in Maharashtra. There is a total of four nuclear power stations in India at present. These are :

1. Tarapur Atomic Power Station at Tarapur in Maharashtra.
2. Rajasthan Atomic Power Station at Rana Pratap Sagar, near Kota.
3. Madras Atomic Power station at Kalpakkam in Tamil Nadu.
4. Narora Atomic Power Station in Uttar Pradesh.
5. Kakrapara Atomic Power Station in Gujarat.

There are two more power stations—Kaiga (Karanataka) and Rawatbhata (Rajasthan)—are under construction. At present about 3% of the energy produced in India is obtained from nuclear power plants (or nuclear reactors).

MULTIPLE-CHOICE QUESTIONS

1. Select the moderator used in nuclear power plant.
A. Oxygen B. Hydrogen
C. Uranium D. Plutonium

2. Which of the following is a better heat transfer properly?
A. Light water B. Heavy water
C. Sodium D. Dowtherm

3. The readily fissionable material is
A. U^{-235} B. U^{-233}
C. U^{-238} D. U^{-239}

4. Which one is fertile material?
A. U^{-235} B. U^{-239}
C. U^{-233} D. U^{-238}

5. The energy produced by 1 kg uranium is about
A. 30 tonnes of coal
B. 300 tonnes of coal
C. 3000 tonnes of coal
D. 30,000 tonnes of coal

6. Natural uranium is a mixture of
A. Five isotopes B. Four isotopes
C. Three isotopes D. Two isotopes

7. Which of the element is natural radioactive?
A. Uranium B. Thorium
C. Radium D. All of the above

8. In boiling water reacter steam is generated :
A. In the reactor vessel
B. In the boiler
C. In the heat exchanger
D. None of the above

9. In a homogeneous reactor the fuel used is
A. Uranium
B. Lead
C. Throium
D. Uranyl sulphate in heavy

10. The pressurized water reactor uses light water as
A. Coolant
B. Moderator
C. Both moderator and coolant
D. None of the above

11. The moderator used in fast breeding reactor is
A. Graphite B. Liquid sodium

C. Heavy water D. None of the above

12. The main function of shielding in a nuclear reactor is to provide protection against
A. α-rays B. β-rays
C. γ-ray D. Electrons

13. In a hetrogeneous reactor metallic uranium rods are clad with
A. Alumimium B. Zirconium
C. Stainless steel D. All of the above

14. The scram control rods are used to
A. Control the chain reaction in the reactor
B. Prevent radiation from the reactor
C. Control the pressure of steam
D. None of the above

15. The concrete shield for acceptable level of radiation should be minimum
A. 5-metre-thick B. 2-metre-thick
C. 1 metre thick D. $\frac{1}{2}$ metre thick

16. The coolant used in nuclear power plant should have
A. Low coefficient of heat
B. High induced radioactivity
C. The tendency to absorb neutrons as low as possible
D. None of the above

17. The function of a reflector in nuclear power plant is to
A. Reflect heat
B. Reflect light
C. Reflect the escaping neutrons back into the core
D. None of the above

18. When the fission of U^{-235} takes place the average no. of neutrons ejected are
A. 0.25 B. 2.5
C. 5.2 D. 25

19. Pick the correct equation in which the alpha particles are emitted
A. ${}^{238}_{92}U \rightarrow {}^{4}_{2}He + {}^{234}_{90}Th$
B. ${}^{238}_{92}U \rightarrow {}^{4}_{2}He + {}^{238}_{92}Th$
C. ${}^{238}_{92}U \rightarrow {}^{4}_{2}He + {}^{234}_{92}Th$
D. ${}^{238}_{92}U \rightarrow {}^{4}_{2}He + {}^{242}_{94}Th$

20. Isotopes of the element has
A. Same atomic weight
B. Same number of neutrons
C. Different number of neutrons
D. None of the above

21. If Beryllium is represented as ${}^{9}_{5}Be$, then the number of neutrons are equal to
A. 9 B. 5
C. 14 D. 4

22. The nucleus of an atom consists of
A. Protons and electrons
B. Protons and neutrons
C. Neutrons and electrons
D. None of the above

23. The lithium elements is represented as ${}^{7}_{3}Li$. The sum of protons and electrons is equal to
A. 10 B. 7
C. 4 D. 3

24. The method of identifying the element is
A. ${}_{Z}X^{A}$ B. X^{AZ}
C. ${}_{A}X^{Z}$ D. $X^{A/Z}$

25. The compound nucleus has
A. Kinetic energy
B. Binding energy of bombarding particles
C. Both kinetic and binding energy of bombarding
D. None of the above

26. Which one of the following is most harmful for the human body?
A. Alpha particles B. Beta particles
C. Gamma particles D. None of the above

27. Combining of light nuclides to form a single heavy nucleus is called
A. Fusion B. Fission
C. Solidification D. Atomization

28. The assembly of fuel and other materials, in which the self-sustaining chain reaction, is maintained is called
A. Boiler B. Generator
C. Turbine D. Reactor

29. The material required for reactor vessel is
A. Cast iron B. Stainless steel
C. Mild steel D. Copper

30. In sodium graphite reactor the coolant used is
A. Water B. Graphite

C. Heavy water D. liquid Sodium

31. PWR stands for

A. Power Water Reactor

B. Pressurized Water Reactor

C. Power Welding Rod

D. Power Work Reaction

32. The gas which is used as a coolant in nuclear power plant is

A. Freon B. Ammonia

C. Helium D. Chlorine

33. Which is used as a moderator in Nuclear Power Plant?

A. Uranium B. Plutonium

C. Hydrogen D. Oxygen

34. The material used in shielding a core is

A. Concrete

B. Thick galvanized sheets

C. Copper sheets

D. Aluminium sheets

35. The scram control rods are used to

A. Control the chain reaction in the reactor

B. Prevent radiation from the reactor

C. Control the pressre of steam

D. None of the above

ANSWERS

1	2	3	4	5	6	7	8	9	10
B	C	A	D	C	C	D	A	D	C
11	**12**	**13**	**14**	**15**	**16**	**17**	**18**	**19**	**20**
D	C	D	A	A	C	C	B	A	C
21	**22**	**23**	**24**	**25**	**26**	**27**	**28**	**29**	**30**
D	B	B	C	C	C	A	D	B	D
31	**32**	**33**	**34**	**35**					
B	C	C	A	A					

10

THEORY OF MACHINES

A machine contains a number of inter-related parts, each having a different function, kinematics of machines deals with the relative motion between the parts, neglecting the consideration of force. Kinematic link is a resistant body or an assembly of resistant bodies which go to make a part or parts of a machine connecting other parts which have motion relating to it.

Kinematic Pair

A pair is a joint of two elements that permits relative motion. The relative motion between the elements or links that form a pair is required to be completely constrained or successfully constrained. Pairs may be clasified as follows :

1. Depending upon the nature of contact between elements
   (*a*) Lower pairs
   (*b*) Higher pairs
2. Depending upon the nature of the mechanical constraints
   (*a*) Closed pairs
   (*b*) Open pairs
3. Depending upon the nature of relative motion between elements
   (*a*) sliding pair
   (*b*) Turning pair
   (*c*) Rolling pair
   (*d*) Spherical pair
   (*e*) Helical pair

Kinematic Chain

When a number of links are connected in space such that the relative motion of any point on a link with respect to any other point on the other link follows a low, the chain is called a kinematic chain.

Mechanism

If one of the links of a constrained kinematic chain is fixed, the result is a mechanism.

Inversion of Mechanism

Inversions are the different mechanism obtained by fixing different links in a kinematic chain. Thus as many inversions are possible as the number of links. The motion of a point or a link in a kinematic chain relative to some other point or a link is the property of the chain and not of the mechanism.

Gears

A gear drive is smooth and positive in action. Also large power can be transmitted by gear drives. Gears are common in several mechanical engineering applications such as machine tools, automobiles, hoists, rolling mills etc. For parallel shafts, straight, stepped parallel helical gears are used, for intersecting shaft straight, bevel, spiral bevel gears are used and for non-parallel, non-intersecting shafts cross, helical, worm, Hypoid gears are used.

Terminology Used in Gears

(*a*) **Pitch circle diameter :** It is the diameter of a circle which by pure rolling action would produce the same motion as the toothed gear wheel.

(*b*) **Pitch point :** It is the oint of the tangency or the point of contact of the two pitch circles of the mating gears.

(*c*) **Circular pitch :** The distance along the circumference of the pitch circle from a point on one tooth to a corresponding point on the adjacent tooth is called circular pitch. Thus, the circular pitch denoted by P_c for the spur gear of pitch circle diameter d, having T as the number of teeth can be expressed by

$$P_c = \frac{\pi d}{T}$$

(*d*) **Diameteral pitch :** The number of teeth per unit length on the pitch circle diameter is known as diameteral pitch.

$$P_d = \frac{T}{d}$$

(e) **Module :** The length of the pitch circle diameter per tooth is called module.

$$m = \frac{d}{T}$$

(f) **Addendum :** The radial height of the tooth above pitch circle is defined as addendum. Its standard value is one module.

(g) **Addendum circle :** A circle bounding the tops of the teeth is known as addendum circle. Diameter for this circule for standard tooth gear = pitch circle diameter + 2m.

(h) **Dedendum :** The radial depth of a tooth below the pitch circle is defined as the dedendum. Its standard value is $\left(1+\frac{\pi}{20}\right)$ module = 1.157 m.

(i) **Dedendum circle :** A circle passing through the roots of all the teeth is defined as dedendum circle. Diameter of the dedendum circle for standard teeth is equal to (pitch diameter – 2 × 1.57 m).

(j) **Clearance :** The radial height difference between the addendum and the dedendum of a tooth is known as clearance. Thus standard teeth clearance value will be given by (1.157 m – 1 m) = 0.157 m.

Cams

A cam is a mechanical member of transmitting a desired motion to a follower by direct contact. The driver is called the cam and driven member is called the follwer.

The follower may be classified in three types :

(a) Construction of the surface in contact e.g., knife edge, roller, flat face mushroom or spherical shape mushroom.

(b) The type of motion-translatory or oscillatory.

The location of the line of motion, with respect to cam centre, radial and off set.

Friction

Ridges and depression are there in all surfaces. When one surface has contact with another surface, these ridges and depression interlock and thus the relative motion of one surface over the other is resisted. This resisted force is known as the force of friction. Force of friction will always oppose motion. Mainly there could be three possible states of surfaces:

I. Dry
II. Greasy or partially lubricated
III. Completely lubricated or film lubricated

Pivots and Collars

The rotating shafts are quite frequently subjected to axial thrust. This thrust is carried by bearing surfaces. The loss of horse power, in case of flat pivots, is given by the relation

I. Uniform pressure

$$\text{H.P. lost in friction} = \frac{4}{3}\frac{\mu W r_1 \pi N}{4500}$$

II. Uniform wear

$$\text{H.P. lost in friction} = \frac{\mu W r_1 \pi N}{4500}$$

Where W is total load in *kgf*, r_1 is the radius of the pivoit, μ is the coefficient of friction and N is the shaft r.p.m. In case of collars, the relations for horse power lost in friction are

I. Uniform pressure

$$\text{H.P. lost in friction} = \frac{2\pi N}{4500}\cdot\frac{2}{3}\mu W\left[\frac{r_1^3 - r_2^3}{r_1^2 - r_2^2}\right]$$

Belt, Rope and Chain Drive

They are known as flexible drives which are used to transmit power between shafts whose centre distance is too great, where gear trains are not possible.

Flat belts are mostly used to connect parallel shafts. The belts are made of leather, fabric, rubber impregnated fabric and synthetics. When d_1 is the diameter of driven pulley and w_1 is the speed of driven pulley in rad/sec, and w_2 and d_2 are the corresponding values of driven pulley, then

$$\frac{w_1}{w_2} = \frac{d_2}{d_1} \text{ and } \frac{w_1}{w_2} = \frac{d_2 + t}{d_1 + t}$$

Where *t* is the belt thickness.

Length of Flat Belts

I. **Open belt :**

$$L = 2D + 1.57(d_2 + d_1) + \left(\frac{d_2 - d_1}{4D}\right)^2$$

Where D is the centre distance.

II. **Cross belt :**

$$L = 2\left[D\cos\alpha + \left(\frac{d_2 + d_1}{2D}\right)\left(\frac{\pi}{2} + \alpha\right)\right]$$

III. **Angle of contact :**

$$Q = 2\left[\pi - \cos^{-1}\left(\frac{r_1 + r_2}{D}\right)\right]$$

Maximum power is transmitted by a belt where centrifugal tension

$$T_c = \frac{1}{2} \times \text{Maximum tension}$$

Maximum permissible velocity of belt is given by the relation

$$T = \frac{3wv^2}{I}$$

Where w is the weight of belt per meter length.

Governor

The function of a governor is to maintain the speed of an engine within prescribed speed limits for varying load conditions. Thus a governer comes into action when the load on the engine varies. Various types of governors are :

I. Simple governor-watt type
II. Proel governor
III. Portor governor
IV. Hartnell governor
V. Spring control governor

Sensitiveness

Sensitiveness of governor is the ratio of the difference between the maximum and minimum equilibrium speed to the mean equilibrium speed. Thus between speeds N_1 and N_2.

$$\text{Sensitiveness} = \frac{N_1 - N_2}{2(N_1 + N_2)}$$

Stability

A governor is said to be stable when for each speed within the working range the ball weights occupy a definite specified position. In other words, there is only one radius of the governor weights for each equilibrium speed.

Isochronism

A governor is said to be isochronous if the equilibrium speed is constant for all radii of rotation of the balls within the working range. Isochronism is desirable when approximately one constant speed is desired to be kept for all loads.

Hunting

A very sensitive governor may not be very stable. The speed controlled by it may fluctuate continuously. Thus in case of a very sensitive governor, the sleeve may shuttle between extreme position causing hunting.

Vibrations

Dynamically unbalanced masses in rotating machines cause oscillatory forces which result in mechanical vibrations are :

(i) Frequency *(ii)* Cycle
(iii) Period *(iv)* Free vibrations
(v) Natural frequencies *(vi)* Forced vibrations
(vii) Resonance *(viii)* Damping

MULTIPLE-CHOICE QUESTIONS

1. The power transmitted by belt drive will be maximum if the maximum tension in the belt is
A. Twice the tension in the slack side
B. Equal to the tension in the slack side
C. Three times the tension due to centrifugal force
D. Equal to the tension due to centrifugal force

2 The efficiency of transmitting power will be maximum in case of
A. Rope drive B. Open belt drive
C. V-belt drive D. Chain drive

3. The power transmitted by a belt drive is maximum when the centrifugal tension as compared to the maximum tension is
A. One third B. Equal
C. Double D. Three times

4. The radial distance between the top of the tooth and the bottom of the tooth space in the mating gear is known as
A. Addendum B. Dedendum
C. Pitch D. Clearance

5. A simple gear train is one in which each shaft

carries

A. One wheel B. Two wheels
C. Three wheels D. Any number of wheels

6. Which amongst the following constitute a link?
A. Piston and piston rod
B. Piston rod and cross head
C. Piston crankpin and crank shaft
D. Piston, piston-rod and cross head of a steam engine

7. A flexible link is one which
A. Is deformed to the extent of its flexibility
B. While transmitting motion is not deformed at all
C. Can under go any amount of deformation above yield point
D. While transmitting motion is partly deformed but in a manner which does not have any affect on the transmission of motion

8. When motion is transmitted by means of a fluid it is known as
A. Flexible link B. Rigid link
C. Fluid link D. None of the above

9. Links which do not suffer any deformation while transmitting motion are called
A. Flexible links B. Rigid links
C. Fluid links D. None of the above

10. A simple mechanism has
A. One link B. Two links
C. Three links D. Four links

11. The three types of links are
A. Cross, rigid, fluid
B. Rigid, elastic, fluid
C. Rigid, flexible, fluid
D. Strength, rigid, flexible

12. when two elements have surface contact and relative motion between them, it is called as
A. Higher pair B. Turning pair
C. Lower pair D. Sliding pair

13. The fluid under pressure in hydraulic crane act as a
A. Rigid link B. Fluid link
C. Flexible link D. All the above

14. Belts used for power transmission is an example of
A. Rigid link B. Fluid link
C. Flexible link D. None of the above

15. Any two links which have constrained relative motion betweent them, constitute a
A. Kinematic pair B. Couple
C. Joint D. Structure

16. The automobile steering gear is an example of
A. Higher pair B. Lower pair
C. Closed pair D. None of the above

17. In a higher pair, the relative motion is
A. Purely turning
B. Purely sliding
C. Due to surface contact
D. The combination of sliding and turning

18. When one element is constrained to roll over the other element the pair so formed is known as
A. Turning pair B. Sliding pair
C. Rolling pair D. Spherical pair

19. The fluid under pressure in hydraulic crane act as a
A. Rigid link B. Fluid link
C. Flexible link D. All the above

20. In a turning pair
A. One link is constrained to have only a turning motion relative to the other
B. One element is constrained to have sliding motion relative to another
C. One element is constrained to have rolling motion over the other
D. One link turns about the other by means of threads

21. Flat belts running over a pulley forms
A. A closed pair B. An open pair
C. A screw pair D. A spherical pair

22. For a kinematic chain, if L represents the number of links and J represents the number of joints, then
A. $J = \frac{2}{3}(L+2)$ B. $L = \frac{2}{3}(J+2)$
C. $J = \frac{3}{2}(L+1)$ D. $J = \frac{3}{2}(J+2)$

23. The relation between numbers of links (l) and number of pairs (p) is given as
A. $l = (2p - 1)$ B. $l = (2p - 4)$
C. $p = (2l - 2)$ D. $p = (2l - 1)$

24. In double slider crank chain the number of possible inversion are
A. Two B. Three
C. Four D. Six

25. In slider crank chain the number of possible inversions are
A. Three B. Four
C. Five D. Six

26. Crankshaft rotating in a journal bearing of an engine forms a
A. Rolling pair B. Sliding pair
C. Turning pair D. Screw pair

27. A kinematic chain should have a minimum of
A. One.link B. Two links
C. Three links D. Four links

28. The Oldham's coupling is used to connect
A. Two parallel shafts distance between whose axes is small and variable
B. Two parallel shafts distance between whose axes is fixed and small
C. Two parallel shafts distance between whose axes is small
D. Shafts which are non-intersecting

29. The Scott-Russell mechanism consists of
A. Sliding pairs
B. Turning pairs
C. Sliding as well as turning pairs
D. Sliding pair with a crank mechanism of the Scott-Russell type

30. The Ackermann steering mechanism is perferred to the Davis type because
A. the former has sliding pair
B. the former has turning pair
C. it is mathematically accurate
D. it is correct in all the positions

31. The instantaneous centre
A. Has zero velocity and the acceleration centre of the link has constant acceleration
B. Has zero velocity and acceleration centre of the link has zero acceleration
C. Alongwith the acceleration centre has constant acceleration
D. Has constant velocity and acceleration

32. The relative velocity method
A. In simpler than the instantaneous centre method
B. Can be applied to any configuration of a given mechanism
C. is difficult to apply when directions of motions of say any two ends x and y are parallel
D. is similar to the instantaneous centre method except the location of centre

33. In a compound kinematic chain the numbr of pairs are more than
A. Two B. Three
C. Four D. Six

34. The double slider crank chain consists of
A. Two turning and two sliding pairs
B. One turning and one sliding pair
C. Two turning and one sliding pair
D. Three turning pairs

35. The Ackerman stearing gear for automobile is an example of
A. Kinematic chain with two turning pairs
B. Kinematic chain with three turning pairs
C. Kinematic chain with four turning pairs
D. None of the above

36. In a rim type flywheel the main mass
A. Is kept as far away as possible
B. As near as possible
C. Is of little importance from the point of view of balancing
D. Is balanced by centrifugal and centripetal forces

37. The Klein's method of construction for reciprocating engine mechanism
A. Makes use of the acceleration diagram
B. Makes use of a quadrilateral similar to the diagram for a reciprocating engine mechanism
C. Utilises a triangle similar to the acceleration diagram
D. Is a simplified form of instantaneous centre method

38. The angular velocity is given by the relation
A. $\omega = d\theta/dt$ B. $\omega = d\theta/dt$
C. $\omega = ds/dt$ D. $\omega = d\theta \times dt$

39. The angular acceleration is equal to
A. $d\theta/dt$ B. ds/dt
C. dw/dt D. $dw/d\theta$

40. To connect two shafts, axes of which are neither in the same straight line nor parallel, but intersect in a point, we use
A. Universal coupling, or Hook's Joint
B. Oldham's Coupling
C. Flexible Coupling
D. Extended Joint

41. The double Hook's Joint gives a velocity ratio

equal to unity at every instant when

A. The axes of driven shafts lie in different planes
B. The intermediate shaft makes equal angles with driving and driven shafts
C. The axes of driving and driven shafts are in the same plane and intermediate shaft makes different angles with driving and driven shafts
D. The axes of driving and driven shafts are in the same plane and intermediate shaft makes equal angles with driving and driven shafts

42. The unit for angular acceleration is
A. Metre/sec B. Metre/sec^2
C. Radians/sec^2 D. Rad/sec

43. The slope or tangent of a displacement time curve represents
A. Acceleration B. Velocity
C. Retardation D. Displacement

44. The slope of velocity-time curve represents
A. Displacement B. Acceleration
C. Velocity D. None of the above

45. The Gyroscope
A. Is a body which while spinning about an axis is constrained to move in any other direction
B. Is represented by a counter balancing body which spins about an axis perpendicular to the body under the action of external forces
C. Is a body which while spinning about an axis is free to move in other direction under the action of external forces
D. Is a body which while spinning about an axis perpendicular to the direction of motion is acted upon by the action of external forces

46. The area under the angular acceleration and time curve represents
A. Change in velocity
B. Change in acceleration
C. Retardation
D. Displacement

47. Angular acceleration of a body is
A. The rate of change of displacement
B. The rate of change of velocity
C. The rate of change of angular velocity
D. The rate of change of momentum

48. In case of gyroscopic effect, the plane of
A. Spin and the plane of precession are mutually perpendicular
B. Spin and plane of gyroscopic couple are perpendicular
C. Spin and the plane of precession are parallel and mutually perpendicular to the plane of gyroscopic couple
D. Spin plane of precession and plane of gyroscopic couple are mutually perpendicular

49. The gyroscopic forces are
A. Independent of the body
B. Desirable
C. Undersirable
D. Undersirable in certain cases and converted to desirable forces in others

50. A and B are two points on the same link. The direction of the velocity of B relative to A is
A. Parallel to the link AB
B. Perpendicular to the link AB
C. 45° to the link AB
D. 30° to the link AB

ANSWERS

1	2	3	4	5	6	7	8	9	10
C	D	A	D	A	D	D	C	B	D
11	**12**	**13**	**14**	**15**	**16**	**17**	**18**	**19**	**20**
C	C	B	C	A	B	D	C	B	A
21	**22**	**23**	**24**	**25**	**26**	**27**	**28**	**29**	**30**
B	B	B	B	B	C	D	A	C	B
31	**32**	**33**	**34**	**35**	**36**	**37**	**38**	**39**	**40**
B	B	C	A	C	A	B	A	C	A
41	**42**	**43**	**44**	**45**	**46**	**47**	**48**	**49**	**50**
D	C	B	B	C	A	C	D	D	B

11

ENGINEERING MATERIALS

The natural material in which the metals or their compounds are found in earth are called minerals. Some minerals may contain a large percentage of metal whereas other may contain only a small precentage of the metal. Some minerals may not contain any objectionable impurities whereas other may contain objectionable impurities which hamper the extraction of metals. Thus all the minerals can not be used to extract metals. Those minerals from which the metals can be extracted conveniently and profitably are called ores. An ore contains a good percentage of metal and there are no objectionable impurities in it. This all the ores are minerals but all the minerals are not ores.

Types of Ores

The important types of ores which are used for the extraction of metals are : oxide ores, carbonate ores, sulphide ores and halide ores.

(i) **Oxide Ores :** Aluminium occurs as oxide in bauxite ore ($Al_2O_3 . 2H_2O$) and copper occurs as oxide in cuprite (Cu_2O)

(ii) **Carbonate Ores :** Calcium occurs as carbonate in limestone ($CaCO_3$) and Zinc occurs as cabrbonate in calamine ($ZnCO_3$).

(iii) **Sluphide Ores :** Zinc occurs as sulphide in zinc blende (Zns), and copper occurs as sulphide in copper glance (Cu_2S)

(iv) **Halide Ores :** Sodium occurs as chloride in rock salt (NaCl), and calcium occurs as fluroide in flurospar (CaF_2).

Metallurgy

The ores are converted into free metals by a number of steps which depend on the type of the ore used, nature of the impurities present and reactivity of the metal to be extracted. The various processes involved in the extraction of metals from their ores, and refining are known as metallurgy.

Various steps involved in the extraction of a metal from its ore are :

1. Concentration of Ore : Concentration of ore means purification of ore. This is done by using one or more of the following processes: hydraulic washing, froth floating process, magnetic separation or chemical separation methods.

2. Coversion of concentrated Ore into Metal Oxide : A carbonate ore is converted into metal oxide by calcination, and a sulphide ore is converted into metal oxide by roasting.

3. Reduction of Metal Oxide to Metal : The metal oxides are reduced to metal by carbon, aluminium or electrolytic reduction.

4. Refining of Impure Metal : Refinig means purification. The refining of metals can be done by electrolysis, liquation, distillation or oxidation method.

Before a material is considered for a particular application, it is necessary to have information about its physical properties. These physical properties are:

Ductility and Malleability : The ability of a metal to deform plastically without fracturing. In general, it means deformation under slow stressing instead of sudden impact. Metals can also be beaten into sheets is due to malleability.

Elastic Limit : The greatest stress a material can withstand without permanent elongation when the load is removed the sample will return to its original length.

Yield Point : The stress at which appreciable elongation occurs without increase in stress.

Ultimate Strength : Maximum stress required to break a specimen.

Modulus of Elasticity : The ratio of stress to strain within the elastic limit. It is a measure of stiffness.

Elongation : The ratio of the increase in gauge length to the original gauge length expressed in percentage.

Ultimate Strain : The unit of elongation at the specimen breaking-point. It is measure of ductility.

Stiffness : The ability of a metal to resist bending, stretching, shortening and twisting. Stiffness is defined by the modulus of elasticity. The modulus applies one within the elastic range-the range within which a metal will return to its original shape if the load is removed. It is the rate of stress to strain.

Indentation Hardness : In metal working hardness generally implies resistance of penetration. It may, however, include resistance to scratching, abrasion, or cutting. Indentation hardness is generally measured in terms of Brinell hardness number or Vicker's pramid number or Rockwell hardness number.

Fatigue : A description of the behaviour of metals under the action of alternating loads an distinguished from the behaviour under the steady loads. Cyclic stressing may occur in bending, tension, compression, torsion or in combination of these and may be found in such diverse applications as axles, connecting rods, springs etc.

Torsion : The twisting of a material by force which turns one end of a bar about its longitudinal axis while the other end is either clamped in a rigid fixture or twisted in the opposite direction. Torsion develops shear stresses in a material and occurs in such applications as propeller shafts, springs etc.

Creep : The deformation of materials ceases to be elastic and becomes plastic with a continuous increase under a constant load at high temperatures, such as are encountered in steam boilers, turbines and piping. The equilibrium between stress and load is not established, even after a very long time. The material under tensile stress continuous to stretch or creep. Creep is measured in terms of plastic deformation during a certain time.

Damping Capacity : Energy dissipated as heat by a unit volume of the material during a completely reversed cycle of stress. For example iron has high damping capacity.

Alloys

The various properties of a metal like malleability, ductility, strength hardness, resistance to corrosion, appearance, etc., can be improved by mixing other metals with it. This mixture of two or more metals is called an alloy. (For example, alluminium metal is light but not strong, but an alloy) of aluminium with copper, magnesium and manganese (called duralium) is light as well as hard. Alloys have properties which are different from the constituent metals.

Alloys of Aluminium : The important alloys of Aluminium are duralium and magnalium. A third alloy is alnico.

(i) Duralium or (Duralumin) : Duralium is an alloy containing aluminium, copper, and traces of manesium and manganese (Al, Cu, Mg, Mn). The percentage composition of duralium is

Aluminium 95% Copper 4%

Magnesium 0.5% Manganese 0.5%

Duralium alloy is much more strong than pure aluminium. In fact, duralium compares with mild steel in strength and at the same time it is very light. Since duralium is light and yet strong, it is used for making the aircraft bodies and parts, space satellites and kitchen-ware like pressure cookers, etc. Duralium is also resistant to sea water corrosion, so it is used for making bodies of ships.

(ii) Magnalium : magnalium is an alloy containing aluminium and magnesium (Al, Mg). The percentage composition of magnalium is

Aluminium 95%

Magnesium 5%

Magnalium is much more harder than pure aluminium and yet very light. It can be worked on lathes, Magnalium is used to make light instruments.

(iii) Alnico : Alnico is an alloy containing aluminium, nickel and cobalt (Al, Ni, Co). It is used for making.

Alloys of Iron : The important alloys of iron are steel and stainless steel.

(i) Steel . Steel is an alloy of iron with 0.5 to 1.5% of carbon. Thus, the constituents of steel are iron and carbon. Pure iron is not very hard and strong but steel is very hard and extremely strong. Steel is used for making nails, screws, girders, bridges and railway lines etc.

(ii) Stainless Steel : Stainless steel is an alloy of iron with chromium and nickel. It contains up to 18%

of chromium and nickel. Stainless steel is an alloy steel. This is one of the most important alloy of iron. Since stainless steel resists corrosion, it is used for making cooking utensils, knives, scissors, tools and ornamental pieces.

Alloys of Copper : The important alloys of copper are : brass, bronze and German silver.

(i) Brass : It is an alloy of copper and zinc. It contains 80% copper and 20% zinc. Brass is more malleable and more strong than pure copper. Brass is used for making cooking utensils, screws, nuts, bolts, wires, tubes, scientific instruments like microscopes and ornaments.

(ii) Bronze : It is an alloy of copper and tin. It contains 90% copper and 10% tin. Bronze is very tough and highly resistant to corrosion. It is used for making statues, coins, medals, cooking utensils and ships propellers.

(iii) German Silver : German silver is an alloy of copper, zinc and nickel. It contains 60% copper, 20% zinc and 20% nickel. German silver is used for making silver ware, utensils and for electroplating.

Solder : Solder is an alloy of lead and tin. It contains 50% lead and 50% tin. The alloy solder is used for soldering joints. Engineering solders are generally of three types :

(i) Soft Solder, *(ii)* Bronze Solder,
(iii) Silver Solder.

MULTIPLE-CHOICE QUESTIONS

1. Which of the following elements from carbides in steel?
A. Ni, Cu, Si, and Co
B. Mn, Cr, W, Mo, V, T_i and N_b
C. Ni, Cu and Mn
D. Mn, Cr and Cu

2. The mechanical properties of a steel are increased
A. By reduction of alloying elements which strengthen the ferrite
B. By addition of Molybdenum
C. By addition of alloying elements which strengthen the ferrite
D. When its temper brittleness decreases

3. Plastic materials derive their names
A. Due to their derivation from pertroleum products
B. Due to the state of plasticity existing at a certain stage in their manufacture
C. Because they can be moulded to any desired shape and form
D. From the state of flow ability on heating them at suitable temperatures

4. Muntz metal contains
A. Copper – nickel B. Copper – tin
C. Copper – zinc D. Copper – chromium

5. Constantan is an alloy of
A. Nickel – iron – chromium
B. Copper and nickel
C. Copper – aluminium
D. Copper – tin

6. If steel is slowly cooled in furnace, the structure obtained is
A. Pearlite B. Sorbite
C. Troosite D. Acicular

7. Trimming is a process associated with
A. Forging B. Electroplating
C. Press work D. Machining of metals

8. Tensile strength of common varieties of cast iron is in the range
A. 40 – 50 MP_a B. 50 – 80 MP_a
C. 500 – 650 MP_a D. 650 – 800 MP_a

9. The elastic limit of cast iron is
A. Low
B. High
C. Same as that of mild steel
D. Half of ultimate breaking strength
E. Close to ultimate breaking strength

10. Grey iron
A. Has low ductility
B. Breaks with appreciable distortion
C. Has brittleness
D. Low compression strength

11. Chilled iron casting
A. Are soft on surface
B. Are freely machined
C. Contain low carbon percentage
D. Highly resistance to wear

12. Toughness of a material means
A. Strength B. Fatigue resistance
C. Stress relieving D. Machinability

13. Hardness may be defined as resistance to
A. Local penetration B. Machining
C. Wear D. Scratching
E. Any of the above

14. The purpose of annealing is to
A. Induce Hardness B. Induce stresses
C. Harden the surface D. Remove stresses
E. Produce irregular micro-structure

15. Stress concentration may be caused by
A. Change in cross-section area
B. Change in shape
C. Change in dimensions
D. Polishing or painting a surface
E. A hole or a notch in the body

16. Fatigue failure ocurs when a part is subjected to
A. Tensile stress B. Compressive stress
C. Torsion D. Fluctuating stress

17. When the metals are severely deformed in a particular direction, as in rolling or forging the mechanieal properties may be
A. Identical B. Isotropic
C. Anisotropic D. Uniform

18. According to Hook's law
A. Stress is proportional to strain
B. Strain/Strain is constant
C. Average stress is proportional to average strain
D. Within elastic limits average stress is proportional to average strain

19. A body which does not contain voids or empty spaces is known as
A. Continuous body B. An isotropic body
C. Hetrogenous body D. Crystalline body

20. If a body has identical properties all over it is known as
A. Homogenous B. Isentropic
C. Ductile D. Elastic
E. Plastic

21. The behaviour of metals in which strength of a metal is increased and the ductility is decreased on heating at a relatively low temperature after cold working, is known as
A. Clustering
B. Solid solution hardening
C. Twinning
D. Screw dislocation
E. Strain aging

22. The allotropic form of alpha iron changes into gamma form at a temperature of
A. 890°C B. 910°C
C. 925°C D. 928°C

23. The effect or rolling on steel is
A. To elongate the inclusions in the direction of rolling giving the steel excellent properties
B. Reduction in tensile strength
C. Reduction is fatigue strength
D. Reduction in hardness

24. Hardness of material is about
A. RC 65 B. RC 48
C. RC 57 D. Rc 67
E. RC 89

25. High speed steel should have
A. Toughness B. Wear resistance
C. Hardenability D. A and C above

26. Shock resisting steel should have
A. Low wear resistance
B. Toughness
C. High wear resistance
D. Poor hardenability

27. The maximum content of sulphur permitted in carbon steel is
A. 0.8% B. 0.5%
C. 0.055% D. 0.25%

28. Ball bearings are generally made of
A. Cast iron B. Mellable cast iron
C. Carbon steel D. Stainless steel
E. Carbon chrome steel

29. Steel castings
A. Are weldable
B. Are not weldable
C. Have poor endurance properties
D. Can withstand impact
E. Cannot withstand impact

30. Heating elements of electrical appliances are made of
A. Nichrome B. Nicheloy
C. Coronite D. Invar

31. Which one is more ductile?
A. Lead B. Copper

C. Tin D. Gold

32. Pewter is an alloy of
A. Tin and lead B. Tin and aluminium
C. Lead and zinc D. Lead and nickle

33. The amount of cold work that a metal will stand is dependent upon
A. Room temperature B. Carbon percentage
C. Process D. Purity of metal
E. Ductility

34. In press work, the dies which combine two or more operations at one station are known as
A. Simple dies B. Press
C. Compound dies D. Progressive dies

35. The process of improving the physical properties of the non-ferrous alloys by solid state reaction is called
A. Case hardening B. Nitriding
C. Induction hardening D. Age hardening

36. Which one of the following is different from the others in press work:
A. Blanking B. Punching
C. Perforating D. Slitting
E. Seaming

37. The operation of cutting out flat areas to some desired shape and which is generally the first step in a series of operation is known as
A. Coining B. Curling
C. Blanking D. Slitting

38. Which one of the following is different from the remaining?
A. Cyniding B. Nitriding
C. Flame hardening D. Electroplating

39. The white metal alloys used for bearings are
A. Tin base alloys
B. Copper base alloys
C. Aluminium base alloys
D. Ferrous base alloys

40. Which one is different from the others in press work operations?
A. Coining B. Sizing
C. Flattening D. Rivetting
E. Punching

41. The process of shaping thin metals by pressing it against form while it is rotating is known as
A. Pressing B. Bending
C. Trimming D. Metal spinning

42. The maximum content of phosphorus permitted in carbon steel is
A. 0.04% B. 0.4%
C. 0.8% D. 1.2%

43. Pearlit consists of
A. 87% ferrite and 13% cementite by weight
B. 87% cementite and 13% ferrite by weight
C. 13% cementite and 87% ferrite by weight
D. 50% ferrite and 50% cementite by weight

44. Aluminium alloys for pressure die casting
A. Must possess considerable fluidity
B. Must not be free from hot shortness
C. Must have iron as one of the constituents
D. Must be light

45. The technique of converting metallic powder into articles of definite shape is known as
A. Carbiding B. Powder metallurgy
C. Plasticizing D. High pressure pressing

46. The main constituent of the tin base bearing alloy are
A. Tin, aluminium and copper
B. Tin, antimony and copper
C. Tin, antimony and aluminium
D. Tin, sulphur and lead

47. Process for making a thin phosphate coating on steel to act as base or primer for enamels and paints in known as
A. Anodizing B. Colourizing
C. Parkerizing D. Galvanizing

48. The process of zinc coating used extensively for protecting steel from atomspheric deterioration is known as
A. Anodizing B. Colourizing
C. Parkerizing D. Galvanizing

49. Duralumin consists of
A. 34% copper, 65% aluminium, 0.5% manganese and 0.5% magnesium
B. 65% copper, 34% aluminium, 0.5% manganese and 0.5% magnesium
C. 30% copper, 60% aluminium, 5.0% manganese and 5.0% magnesium
D. 65% aluminium, 34% tin, 0.5% manganese and 0.5% magnesium

50. In high speed steel the maximum percentage of any alloying element is
A. Carbon B. Tungsten
C. Chromium D. Vanadium

ANSWERS

1	**2**	**3**	**4**	**5**	**6**	**7**	**8**	**9**	**10**
B	C	B	C	B	A	A	C	E	A
11	**12**	**13**	**14**	**15**	**16**	**17**	**18**	**19**	**20**
D	A	E	D	E	D	C	D	A	A
21	**22**	**23**	**24**	**25**	**26**	**27**	**28**	**29**	**30**
E	B	A	A	E	B	C	E	A	A
31	**32**	**33**	**34**	**35**	**36**	**37**	**38**	**39**	**40**
D	A	E	C	D	E	C	D	A	E
41	**42**	**43**	**44**	**45**	**46**	**47**	**48**	**49**	**50**
D	B	A	A	B	B	C	D	A	B

12

PRODUCTION ENGINEERING

Manufacturing different products require machine that can work accurately and economically. Production and economy depends on proper selection of the machine or process for the job that will give a satisfactory finished product. The selection is influenced in turn, by the quantity of items to be produced. In selection of a machine, it should be of correct size, shape, low initial cost, require less maintenance and possess the flexibility. Special purpose machines differ from the general purpose machines in that they have built into them some of the skill of the operator. A simple screw may be produced on a special purpose automatic screw machine or a general purpose machine like lathe. The lathe operator has to be skilled in order to produce acceptable quantity of screw, whereas a semi-skilled operator on automatic screw machine can give good quality production.

On the automatic machines the sequence of operations and movement of tools are controlled by cams and stops, and each item produced in identical with the previous one.

Manufacturing Techniques

From one of the many ore-reducing or ore-refining processes most metal products are organised as an ingot casting. Molten metal by these processes is poured in the metal or graphite moulds to form ingots of convenient size and shape for further processing. Manufacturing techniques used in the working of metals may be classified as follows :

A. Process used primarily to change the shape of metals :

(i) Casting *(ii)* Forging
(iii) Swaging *(iv)* Rolling
(v) Squeezing *(vi)* Crushing
(vii) Drawing *(viii)* Extruding
(ix) Piercing *(x)* Bending
(xi) Shearing *(xii)* Spinning
(xiii) Electroforming *(xiv)* Power metal forming
(xv) Roll forming *(xvi)* Torch cutting

In this group of processes the material is changed into its primary form for some selected part. In certain cases parts are suitably finished for commerical use, as in metal spinning, cold rolling of shafting, die casting stretch forming of sheet metal and drawing wire.

B. Process used for machining parts to planned dimensions :

(i) Turning *(ii)* Planing
(iii) Shaping *(iv)* Drilling
(v) Boring *(vi)* Reaming
(vii) Milling *(viii)* Broaching
(ix) Grinding *(x)* Hobbing
(xi) Routing *(xii)* Sawing

These operations (secondary operations) are required for many products requiring close dimensional accuracy, metal is removed from the parts in small chips although chipless methods have also been developed. Above operations are performed on machine tools which include the various power driven machines used for cutting of metals.

C. Processes used primarily to obtain a surface finish :

(i) Polishing *(ii)* Super finishing
(iii) Electroplating *(iv)* Honing
(v) Lapping
(vi) Abrasive belt grinding
(vii) Barrel tumbling *(viii)* Metal spraying
(ix) Inorganic coating *(x)* Sheradizing
(xi) Anodizing *(xii)* Parkerizing

The above processes aim at improving the surface finish as such these processes cause little change in dimensions. In grinding operation little bit of material is removed.

D. Process used in joining parts of materials :

(i) welding *(ii)* Soldering
(iii) Brazing *(iv)* Sintering
(v) Pressing *(vi)* Riveting

(vii) Screw fastening *(viii)* Adhesive joining

Welding is the fusion or uniting of metals by heat. Soldering and brazing operations are similar except that the parts are joined by introducing a different metal between the two in a molten state. Sintering applies on the bonding of metallic particles by the application of heat.

E. Processes which change the properties of metals :

(i) Heat treatment *(ii)* Cold working
(iii) Hot working *(iv)* Shot peening

Heat treatment includes a number of processes which result in changing the properties and structure of metals. These are

(i) Annealing *(ii)* Hardening
(iii) Tempering *(iv)* Normalising
(v) Carburizing *(vi)* Nitriding
(vii) Cyaniding

Although both hot and cold working of metals are primarily processes for charging the shape of metals, these processes have coniderable influence on both the structure and the properties of metal being worked upon.

Tool's Shape and Angles

Nose angle : The angle with the side cutting edge and end cutting edge.

Lip angle : The tools have been ground wedge-shaped, the included angle is called the lip angle.

Slide clearance angle : The angle between the side of the tool and the work is called side clearance angle. It is provided to prevent the rubbing of tool against the work piece.

Rank angle : The angle between the face of tool and the plane parallel to the base of the tool. The side rake angle varies with lip angle.

End clearance angle : End clearance angle is provided to prevent rubbing of flank of the tool with a workpiece.

Cutting Tool Material

The various types of cutting tool materials are :

(i) Carbides *(ii)* Diamonds
(iii) Ceramics *(iv)* Stellites
(v) Carbon steel *(vi)* High speed steel

Tool Life

Tool life depends upon the following factors :

(i) Tool material
(ii) Shape and tool angle
(iii) Material of workpiece
(iv) Type of coolant
(v) Cutting speed
(vi) Ratio of feed to depth

Relation between cutting speed and tool life

$$VT^n = C$$

Where V = Cutting speed in m per min.
T = Tool life in minutes
C = Constant

Cutting Methods

A. Casting in metallic moulds

(i) Permanent mould casting
(ii) Slush casting
(iii) Die casting

B. Casting in non-metallic moulds

(i) True centrifugal
(ii) Semi-centrifugal
(iii) Centrifugal
(iv) Precision casting
(v) Moulds of wood, paper, rubber etc.
(vi) Shell moulding
(vii) Mercast process

C. Continuous casting

(i) Reciprocating moulds
(ii) Draw casting
(iii) Direct sheet casting
(iv) Stationary mould

Types of Dies

A. According to type of press operation :

1. Shearing
(a) Blanking *(b)* Punching
(c) Notching *(d)* Perforating
(e) Trimming *(f)* Shawing
(g) Slitting *(h)* Lancing

2. Bending
(a) Angle of bending *(b)* Curling
(c) Folding *(d)* Forming
(e) Seaming

3. Drawing
(a) Forming flanges *(b)* Tubes
(c) Embossing *(d)* Bulging
(e) Cupping *(f)* Reducing

4. Squeezing
(a) Coining *(b)* Sizing
(c) Flattering *(d)* Swaging
(e) Cold forging *(f)* Rivetting
(g) Upsetting *(h)* Extruding

(*i*) Hot pressing

B. According to construction or method of oeration

(*a*) Simple (*b*) Compound

(*c*) Progressive (*d*) Transfer

(*e*) Hydraulic (*f*) Rubber

Lathes

A lathe is a machine which removes material by rotating the work against a cutter. Parts to be machined can be held between centre, attached to a free path, supported in a jaw chuck to held in a draw-in chuck or collect

Classification of Lathes

1. Speed lathe
   (*a*) Wood working lathe
   (*b*) Centring
   (*c*) Metal spinning
   (*c*) Polishing etc.

2. Engine lathe
   (*a*) Step-cone pulley drive from live shaft
   (*b*) Step-cone pulley drive from individual motors
   (*c*) Gear head drive
   (*d*) Variable speed drive

3. Branch lathe

4. Tool-room lathe

5. Instrument maker's lathe

6. Special purpose lathe

Shapers and Planers

A shaper is a machine having a reciprocating cutting tool of the lathe type which takes a straight line cut. By moving the work across the path of this tool, a plane surface is generated regardless of the shape of tool. Shapers can also be used to cut external as well as internal key ways, spiral grooves gear racks, dovetails, T slops and other shapes

Classification of Shapers :

1. Horizontal, push type
2. Horizontal draw cut
3. Vertical
4. Special purpose, as for cutting gears

Drilling Machines

Drilling Machines is a widely used machine tool for making circular holes. It consists of a spindle which imparts rotary motion to the drilling tool, a mechanism for freeding the tool into work, a table on which the work rests and a frame.

Classification of drilling machines :

1. Portable drill
2. Sensitive drilling machine
3. Upright drilling machine
4. Radial drilling machine
5. Gang drilling machine
6. Multi spindle drilling machine
7. Automatic production drilling machine
8. Deep hole drilling machine

Milling Machines

A milling machine is a machine tool that removes metal as the work is fed against a rotating cutter. The centre is known as milling cutter and it has a series to cutting edges on its circumference, each of which acts as an individual centre in the cycle of rotation.

Classification of Million Machines :

1. Column or knee type
   (*a*) Hand miller
   (*b*) Plain milling machine
   (*c*) Universal milling machine
   (*d*) Ram type universal
   (*e*) Vertical milling machine

2. Planer milling machine

3. Fixed bed type milling machine
   (*a*) Simplex milling machine
   (*b*) Duplex machine
   (*c*) Triplex milling machine

4. Special types
   (*a*) Rotary table machine
   (*b*) Prum milling machine
   (*c*) Planetary milling machine
   (*d*) Stationary long table machine
   (*e*) Offset milling machine
   (*f*) Duplicator or profiling
   (*g*) Pantograph milling machine

Grinding Machines

To grind means 'to abrade' to wear by friction or to sharpen. As applied to machine shop practice it refers to the removal of metal by means of rotating abrasive wheel also known as grinding wheel. The action of grinding wheel is very similar to that of milling cutter. Grinding machines are designed principally to finish part having cylindrical, flat or internal surfaces. The kind of surface machined largely determines the type of grinding machines are given below :

1. Cylindrical grinder
   (*a*) Work between centres
   (*b*) Centreless
   (*c*) Tool post
   (*d*) Crank shaft and other special applications.
2. Internal grinder
   (*a*) Work rotated in chuck
   (*b*) Work rotated and held by rolls
   (*c*) Work stationary
3. Surface grinder
   (*a*) Planer type
      (*i*) Horizontal spindle
      (*ii*) Vertical spindle
   (*b*) Rotating table type
      (*i*) Horizontal spindle
      (*ii*) Vertical spindle
4. Tool grinder
   (*a*) Universal
   (*b*) Special
      (*i*) Drill (*ii*) Tool bit
      (*iii*) Cutter (*iv*) Pedestal
5. Special grinding machines
   (*a*) Swinging frame type
   (*b*) Cutting off
   (*c*) Portable
   (*d*) Haning and lapping
   (*e*) Super finishing
6. Surface finishing
   (*a*) Disk
   (*b*) Flexible band
   (*c*) Two wheel polishing machines

Gears

Gears are widely used in automobiles, agricultural machinery, industrial machinery machine tools, oil engine and in many industrial and consumer goods.

Materials for Gear Manufacture

	Material	*Application*
1.	Cast iron	Large size gears and complicated shapes
2.	Cast Steel	Gears where fabrication is difficult
3.	Carbon steel	Industrial gears
4.	Alloy steel with Mn, Ni, Cr and Mo content	Industrial and automobile gears
5.	Nitride steel	Aircraft gears Marine propulsion gear, industrial gears etc.
6.	Non-metallic gears	Instrument gears and appliances etc.

MULTIPLE-CHOICE QUESTIONS

1. Large size bolt heads are made by
   A. Hammering B. Casting
   C. Swaging D. Upset-forging
   E. Roll forging
2. A feeder gauge is used to check
   A. Screw pitch
   B. Diameter of rounder objetcs
   C. Surface roughness
   D. Unsymmetrical shape
3. The important factor to be considered while selecting a bearing is
   A. Applied load
   B. Operating speed range
   C. Required bearing capacity
   D. All of the above
4. The bonding of a rubber sheet with a metal is done by
   A. Welding
   B. High frequency dielectric heating
   C. Induction welding
   D. Melting rubber in metal
   E. Adhesive bending
5. Ball bearing races are
   A. Turned B. Ground
   C. Nickel plated D. Buffed
   E. Lapped
6. Mechanical seals are used
   A. To prevent vibrations
   B. To prevent leakage
   C. To reduce friction
   D. To balance the equipment
7. All mechanical seals have two flat sealing

surfaces
A. At right angles to the axis of rotation
B. Parallel to the axis of rotation
C. Parallel to the end plate
D. None of the above

8. Grey iron is usually welded by
A. Arc welding B. Gas welding
C. T.I.G. welding D. M.I.G. welding

9. Oxygen cylinders are
A. Cast iron cylinders
B. Steel cylinders, welded structure
C. Die cast
D. Seamless steel cylinders.
E. Alloy steel cylinders, thermit welded

10. Poor fusion in a welded joint may be due to
A. Lack of flux
B. Improper current
C. High welding speed
D. Dirty metal surfce

11. Which one of the following methods is generally not used in welding of chromium molybdenum steels?
A. Oxyacetylene B. Sub-merged arc
C. Thermit D. Resistance

12. Plain and butt welds may be used on materials upto approximately
A. 25 mm thick B. 40 mm thick
C. 50 mm thick D. 75 mm thick

13. A very soft whisper may have noise level of
A. About 10 db B. About 30 db
C. About 40 db D. About 100 db
E. About 140 db

14. Noise level in case of an aircraft is
A. Generally less than 100 db
B. Generally more than 100 db
C. Always more than 100 db
D. In the range of 60-80 db

15. The percentage of carbon that must be present in steel before it can be hardened noticeably is
A. 0.05% B. 0.10%
C. 0.20% D. 0.30%
E. 0.70%

16. Arc blow is a welding defect which is encountered
A. In arc welding using a.c. current
B. In arc welding using d.c. current
C. In gas welding
D. In thermit welding
E. In MIG welding

17. An accurate lathe in India is identified as
A. Mark I B. Accurate I
C. Grade I D. Precision I
E. Agmark I

10. Coolant used while turning cast iron is
A. Lard oil B. Soluble oil
C. Kerosene D. Sodawater
E. None of the above

19. Which bound is commonly used in grinding wheel
A. Vitrified bond B. Silicate bond
C. Shellac bound D. Resinoid bond
E. Rubber bound

20. An optical gauge works on the principle of
A. Reflection of light ray
B. Polarisation of light rays
C. Interference of light rays
D. Refraction of light rays
E. Dispersion of light rays

21. During the machining operation
A. The chips experience stresses
B. The chips experience strains
C. The values of stresses and strains are always calculated for the conditions at the normal plane
D. The chips experience stresses and strains

22. The tool life of a tool is said be over if
A. The tool has failed and a poor surface finish is obtained
B. Sudden increase in power and cutting forces takes place and chatter appears in machining
C. Overheating and fuming due to friction occurs in addition to dimensional instability
D. All the above

23. The commonly employed cutting fluid for turning and milling operations on alloy steels is:
A. Water
B. Kerosene
C. Soluble oil
D. Sulphurised mineral oil

24. The main function of cutting fluid is
A. To provide lubrication
B. To cool the tool and the workpiece
C. To provide lubrication and wash away the chips

D. All the above

25. For the production of quality parts the following casting method is normally employed

A. Centrifugal casting
B. Continuous casting
C. Green sand casting
D. Pressure die casting

26. The commonly use appliance for the casting of ferrous alloys is the

A. Hot chamber machine
B. Cold chamber machine
C. Direct blow machine
D. None of the above

27. Boring can be performed by

A. Boring machines only
B. Boring machines and lathe
C. A machine only by single point high speed carbide tools
D. Boring machine, lathe and milling machine

28. Generally the strongest form in which metals can be used as

A. Hot rolling B. Cold rolling
C. Etrusion D. Drawing
E. Forging

29. The grinding wheel is considered better if the grinding ratio is

A. Maximum B. Very low
C. Average D. Minimum

30. Graphite moulds are generally used for continuous casting method because

A. The metals wet the mould slightly
B. Only a small film of lubricating oil is required
C. They are self-lubricating
D. They are comparatively cheaper

31. In electro discharge machining, the erosion of metal is achieved.

A. By inducing high voltage current in the workpiece
B. By inducing low voltage current in the workpiece
C. By the rapidly recurring spark discharges impinging against the surface of workpiece
D. By passing electrolyte solution between the workpiece and tool

32. A transfer machine

A. Is an automatic machine which performs the job of transferring the workpiece from the feed station to the output station
B. Is an automatic machine which transfers the workpiece and the fixture from one station to another and at the same time several operations are performed on it
C. Is device for transfer of mechanical motions through numerically controlled techniques
D. Is the coordinating machine between the job table and the work controlling it automatically

33. The average frequency of sparks in electro dis charge machining is

A. 500 sparks/sec B. 1000 sparks/sec
C. 5000 sparks/sec D. 10,000 sparks/sec

34. The amount of material removed by the process of super finishing is about

A. 0.2 mm B. 0.02 mm
C. 0.002 mm D. 0.5 mm

35. The amount of stock which can be removed by honing is

A. 0.75 mm B. 0.05 mm
C. 0.02 mm D. 0.015 mm

36. Thermite is a mixture of

A. Five aluminium and iron oxide in the ratio of 3 : 1
B. Five iron and aluminium oxide in the ratio of 3 : 1
C. Five aluminium and iron in the ratio 3 : 1 with traces of sulphur, phosphorous and manganese
D. Molten iron and aluminum, with the ratio depending upon the type of the surface to be welded

37. Jig bushes are

A. The parts of a drill jig through which the cutting tools are operated and located
B. The locating devices used in jigs along with the fixture
C. The operating bushes in a jig
D. The locating and clamping parts of a jig and fixture arrangement

38. Ceramic tools are fixed to tool by the following process

A. Soldering B. Brazing
C. Welding D. Clamping

39. Bore diameters can be measured while working
A. By pneumatic gauge B. Micrometer
C. Vernier callipers D. Steel rule

40. The cutting speed is equal to
A. $\frac{\pi DN}{1000}$ B. $\frac{2\pi DN}{1000}$
C. $\frac{\pi DN}{75}$ D. $\frac{\pi DN}{4500}$
Where D = Diameter of job in mm
N = spindle or job speed in R.P.M.

41. The Vernier's Calliper's advantage over the micrometer is that
A. It can be used to make both inside and out side measurements over a range of sizes
B. Is more accurate
C. Is easier an quick to use
D. None of the above

42. Which one of the following is not a gear production process?
A. Gear-hobbing B. Gear shaping
C. Gear generating D. Gear shaving

43. Which of the following is not gear finishing process?
A. Gear hobbing B. Gear shaving
C. Gear lapping D. Gear grinding

44. The process of enlarging a hole is known as
A. Counter boarding B. Counter sinking
C. Boring D. Drilling

45. The following type of gauge has gauging sections combined on one end
A. Progressive gauge B. Fixed gauge
C. Limit gauge D. Combination gauge

46. Gear tooth vernier is used
A. To measure the addendum
B. To measure the addendum and dedendum
C. To measure the circular pitch
D. To measure the depth of tooth
E. To measure the pitch line thickness of both

47. An important precaution in filing is
A. Properly supporting the file
B. Clean file frequently
C. Not rub finger over file
D. Not rub finger over the work

48. When the file is pushed and pulled across the work, it is called
A. Draw filing B. Straight filing
C. Push pull filing D. All of the above

49. During soldering
A. Arc is produced between solder iron and metal to be soldered
B. Solder iron bit is red hot
C. Joint area must be clean and close fitting
D. Metal is heated from top as well as bottom

50. The angle at which the compound rest is set for turning a taper job, is
A. $\tan^{-1}\frac{D-d}{l}$ B. $\tan^{-1}\frac{D-d}{2l}$
C. $\tan^{-1}\frac{D+d}{l}$ D. $\tan^{-1}\frac{D+d}{2l}$
Where D = Large diameter
d = Smaller diameter
l = Length of job

ANSWERS

1	2	3	4	5	6	7	8	9	10
D	D	D	E	E	B	A	B	D	B
11	**12**	**13**	**14**	**15**	**16**	**17**	**18**	**19**	**20**
D	A	B	C	C	B	C	E	A	C
21	**22**	**23**	**24**	**25**	**26**	**27**	**28**	**29**	**30**
D	D	D	B	D	D	D	E	A	C
31	**32**	**33**	**34**	**35**	**36**	**37**	**38**	**39**	**40**
C	B	D	C	A	A	A	B	B	A
41	**42**	**43**	**44**	**45**	**46**	**47**	**48**	**49**	**50**
A	D	A	C	A	E	A	A	C	B

13

INDUSTRIAL ENGINEERING AND MANAGEMENT

Management

To achieve certain predetermined objectives organising and directing the human efforts is known as management. Management is responsible for the effective utlisation of material and human resources. It is an important factor in the economic development of the country. The management has social responsibility towards consumers, suppliers, workers and the Government.

Manpower Management

The function of the manpower management as to ensure the efficient provision, development and utilisation of manpower resources in employment looked from negative point of view, it is to prevent long term, waste of manpower resources in employment relationship. In general manpower management involves the following functions :

(i) Formation of manpower policy
(ii) Planning of manpower programmes
(iii) Continue review and appraisal of manpower policy and programmes
(iv) Job analysis
(v) Organisational planning
(vi) Recruitment
(vii) Selection
(viii) Placement and orientation
(ix) Training
(x) Collective bargaining
(xi) Wage and salary administration
(xii) Maintenance of motivation and morale
(xiii) Employment stabilisation
(xiv) Direction of employee benefits and services
(xv) Maintenance of records and reports
(xvi) Industrial relations research

Break Even Analysis

A break even chart is a diagram of the short run relation of total cost and of total revenue to rate output shows the typical break even chart, in which the vertical spread between the revenue line and the cost line defines the profit function.

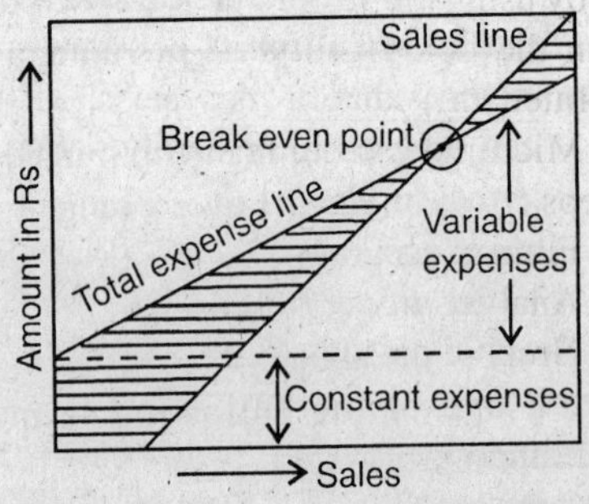

Most break even analysis aimed at the same goal, short runcost and profit behaviour. A single chart is generally good for only one product mix and ideally a whole set of charts is needed for the possible alternative combination of products.

Motions and Time Study

Motion and time study deals with :

1. The scientific determination of preferable work methods.
2. The appraisal, in terms of time, of the value of work involving human activity, and
3. Development of material required to make practical use of these data.

It is difficult to separate these three phases, since a specific method is one of the conditions of time measurement and time measurements often provide a basis for comparing alternative methods. In addition, method of determination and time appraisal complement the utility of each other in application. The combined term-motion and time study is used to denote all three phases of activity, method of determination, time appraisal and the development or material for the application of these data.

Motion Study

Motion study is a scientific, analytical procedure

for determining a preferable work method, considering:

(i) Raw material
(ii) Design of the products
(iii) Tools, work-piece and equipment for each individual step in the process
(iv) Hand and body motions used in each step.

Micromotion Study

Micromotion refers to the analysis of a man work method by using motion picture camera with a timing device in the field of view. A constant speed drive incorporated the camera may serve as the timing device. Micromotion study involves the following three steps :

(i) Filming
(ii) Analysis of the film
(iii) Graphic presentation

SIMO

Simultaneous motion cycle chart (SIMO) is a graphic presentation of the separate steps of each pertiment body members of the individual being charted and is normally accompanied by the use of a series 17 analysis categories called therbligs.

Time Study

Time study is the appraisal in terms of time, of the value of work involving human effort. In produces a time standard for the performance of a series of acts by a man or a group of men. Standard times may be used for the following purpose :

(i) To set schedules
(ii) To determine supervisory objectives
(iii) To furnish a basis of comparison for determining operating effectiveness
(iv) To set labour standards for satisfactory performance
(v) To determine the number of machines a person may run
(vi) To balance the work of crews or production lines
(vii) To compare alternative methods
(viii) To determine standard costs
(ix) To determine equipment and labour requirement
(x) To determine basic lines or standard data
(xi) To provide a basis for setting piece price or incentive wages.

The technique for time study involve the use of.

(i) Stop watch or camera
(ii) Synthesized standards
(iii) Statistical standards

Factory Planning

A factory is a complex unit that directly and indirectly affects the lives and well being of many persons. Its existence is justified by the fact that the goods or services produced satisfy needs or desires for which money, or some other medium or exchange, is sacrified. The more economically the goods or services can be produced. The greater the number of persons who can enjoy the benefits of the products.

The selection and arrangement of the physical facilities that constitute the factory, and the provisions for the comfort, safety and efficiency of the person who work in it are extremely important to its economical operation.

In most business, competition for the available market constantly forces the management of the concern to seek competitive advantages through such method as

(i) Product improvement or new products
(ii) Lower costs and lower selling prices for the same or better quality
(iii) Better services to customers

Some of the ways in which the factory plan can effect economics in operation are :

(i) Lower labour costs, both direct and indirect.
(ii) Reduction in work stoppages and down times.
(iii) Reduction in cycle time required for production.
(iv) Greater production capacity without additional equipment.
(v) Increased flexibility in the output.
(vi) Lower material handling costs.
(vii) Lower storage costs.
(viii) Fast service to customer.

MULTIPLE-CHOIE QUESTIONS

1. In time and motion study, the symbol 'X' represents

A. Crossing
B. Opposite directional Moments
C. Rejections
D. Completion of operation

E. None of the above

2. In time and motion study, the symbol □ represents
   A. Operation delay B. Avoidable delay
   C. Unavoidable delay D. Delay
   E. Inspection

3. SIMO charts are used in
   A. Method study B. Micromotion study
   C. Process analysis D. Layout analysis

4. Which of the following methods are used for system analysis?
   A. Linear programming B. Waiting line model
   C. Simulation mode D. All of the above

5. Which of the following is a resource?
   A. Time B. Men
   C. Money D. All of the above

6. Flatted roof buildings are preferred for
   A. Electronic industries
   B. Foundries
   C. Automobile assembly lines
   D. Rolling mills

7. The allowance provided to compensate idleness of the operator due to certain peculiar characteristics of the process, is termed as
   A. Personal Allowance B. Delay Allowance
   C. Process Allowance D. Fatigue Allowance

8. The proper sequence of the activities in method study should be
   A. Examine, select, record, develop and install
   B. Record, examine, select, develop and install
   C. Select, record, examine, develop and install
   D. Install, develop, examine, record and select

9. For which of the following situations, linear programming can be applied?
   A. Maximising material insulation
   B. Procurement problem
   C. Sheduling of production to meet sales forecast
   D. All of the above

10. A dummy activity completes the logical concept and it has
   A. No duration B. Very short duration
   C. Proportional duration D. Long duration

11. Which of the following statement about linear programming is incorrect?
   A. It is applicable to linear models only
   B. It gives dynamic solution
   C. No solution is available to time spans shorter than periods in model
   D. Uncertainties in the future cannot conveniently be incorporated in model

12. Which of the following least affects break even point?
   A. Change in selling price
   B. Change in volume of production
   C. Change in fixed cost
   D. Change in product mix

13. Cost reduction
   A. Means reduction in total fixed coast of a business
   B. Means reduction in material cost per unit
   C. Means reduction in per unit cost of goods prduced
   D. All of the above

14. Reduction in cost per unit may be result of
   A. Reduced expenditure, volume of production remaining same
   B. Higher production at same level of expenditure
   C. Higher production as a result of higher productivity
   D. All of the above

15. As the value of variance increases
   A. Uncertainty decreases
   B. Uncertainty increases
   C. Uncertainty remains unaffected
   D. Cannot say

16. Multi-storey buildings are used for
   A. Chemical plants
   B. Textile mills
   C. Engineering industries
   D. All of the above

17. The object of plant layout could be
   A. To reduce material handling cost
   B. For effective utlilisation of space
   C. To increase production
   D. Any of the above

18. An organisation may decide to buy a component from outside when
   A. Existing production facilities are limited
   B. There is need to maintain stability in employment
   C. Cost is less to buy as compared to production cost

D. All of the above

19. For measuring standard time :

A. an operator who is trained and experienced is selected

B. An unskilled operator is selected

C. A semi-skilled operator is slected

D. An unexperienced operator is selected

20. The technique followed to determine the standard work content of a specified task is

A. Work measurement B. Method study

C. Value analysis D. Job analysis

21. ABC analysis is used in

A. CPM B. PERT

C. Inventory control D. All of the above

22. In ABC analysis which class of items are generally large in number?

A. A B. B

C. C D.

23. In case of break even analysis, a change in product mix is likely to influence

A. Profits B. Break even point

C. Contribution D. All of the above

24. Shewart control charts are used in

A. Work study B. Motion study

C. Quality study D. All of the above

25. GERT is a

A. Computerised PERT chart

B. Technique which deals with the probability of a realisation of the activity

C. Technique which has become obsolute now

D. None of the above

26. Under Barth premium system wages are equal to

A. Daily rate × $\sqrt{\text{standard time} \times \text{actual time}}$

B. Piece rate × $\sqrt{\text{standard time} \times \text{actual time}}$

C. Daily rate × $\sqrt{\text{time saved} \times \text{actual time}}$

D. Piece rate × $\sqrt{\text{time saved} \times \text{actual time}}$

27. Group bonus system is used for

A. Direct workers for payment by results because their efficiency is not difficult to measure

B. Indirect workers because their efficiency is difficult to measure

C. Support individual bonus system

D. Fixing maximum percentage of bonus to be used under different individual bonus system

28. Which of the following is a parallel activity?

A. Wall construction and carpentary work of doors

B. Digging of foundation and construction of a well

C. Completion of flooring and plastering of walls

D. Completing first floor and starting second floor construction

29. Which of the following represents the reduction in duration

A. Crushing B. Negative slack

C. Variance D. All of the above

30. Which of the following chart is not used in work study?

A. Man machine chart

B. Flow process chart

C. Operation process chart

D. Gantt chart

31. In X and R charts, R represents

A. Repeatability B. Range

C. Rejections D. Randomners

32. PERT stands for

A. Period estimation and revision technique

B. Project estimation and revision technique

C. Project evaluation and revision technique

D. Programme evaluation and review technique

33. "DARSIRI" method is

A. A technique used in cost reduction

B. A method by which value of a product in relation to its cost could be increased

C. A procedure proceeding value engineering

D. All of the above mentioned

34. ABC analysis has its relevance to

A. Pareto's principle B. Taylor's principle

C. Scientific principle D. All of the above

35. In textile industry, the following type of material handling equipment is used

A. Fork lift trucks

B. Cranes and conveyors

C. Overhead cranes

D. Bell conveyers

36. Design of any product involves

A. Technical factors

B. Economical factors

C. Techno-economical factors

D. None of the above

37. Under Halsey premium plan a worker who takes the same time as allowed time receives remuneraaction

A. At piece rate
B. At piece rate with 10% efficiency bonus
C. At time rate
D. At time rate with 10% efficiency bonus

38. COBOL is

A. A programming language
B. a fortran based instruction language
C. Both A and B
D. None of the above

39. CPM is evolved through with the following

A. In built-activities oriented programmes
B. One line estimate
C. For repetitive works
D. Synthesising concepts
E. All of the above

40. Work element in a line assembly balancing is

A. The smallest element of the total assembly job
B. The smallest rational sub-division of total job
C. The largest element of the total assembly job
D. None of the above

41. The number of critical paths in a network can be

A. Only one
B. More than one
C. Two
D. Infinite number of critical paths

42 Re-order level is

A. Minimum reorder period × minimum usage
B. Minimum reorder period × maximum usage
C. Maximum reorder period × minimum usage
D. Maximum reorder period × maximum usage

43. Perpetual Inventory is a method of recording stores balance after

A. Every issue
B. Every receipt
C. Every receipt and issue
D. Every production run

44. Good material handling involves

A. Avoiding re-loading
B. Eliminating materials handling by hard labour or machine operator
C. Using equipment to match the pace of machine operator
D. All of the above

45. Input-output analysis is processed through

A. Time and motion only
B. Work study
C. Value analysis
D. Product analysis
E. Transaction matrix

ANSWERS

1	2	3	4	5	6	7	8	9	10
E	E	A	D	D	A	C	C	D	A
11	**12**	**13**	**14**	**15**	**16**	**17**	**18**	**19**	**20**
B	B	C	D	B	A	D	D	A	A
21	**22**	**23**	**24**	**25**	**26**	**27**	**28**	**29**	**30**
C	C	D	C	B	A	B	A	A	D
31	**32**	**33**	**34**	**35**	**36**	**37**	**38**	**39**	**40**
B	D	D	A	D	C	C	A	E	B
41	**42**	**43**	**44**	**45**					
B	D	C	D	E					

GENERAL INTELLIGENCE & REASONING

1. LETTER SERIES

In letter series, the letters follow a definite order. The given series of letters can be in natural order or in reverse order or combination of both. The letters may be skipped or repeated or consecutive. The given series may be single or may even comprise of two different series merged at alternate positions. While attempting questions on letter series one should note the pattern of alphabet series.

Alphabets in natural series are :

A B C D E F G H I J K L M N O P Q R S T U V W X Y Z

A ↓ 1st, E ↓ 5th, J ↓ 10th, O ↓ 15th, T ↓ 20th, Y ↓ 25th

Alphabets in reverse series are :

Z Y X W V U T S R Q P O N M L K J I H G F E D C B A

Z ↓ 1st, V ↓ 5th, Q ↓ 10th, L ↓ 15th, G ↓ 20th, B ↓ 25th

> **Note :** On reaching Z, the series restarts from A and on reaching A, it restarts from Z.

EXERCISE

Directions : *In each of the following series determine the order of the letters. Then from the given options select the one which will complete the given series.*

1. B Y C X D W E ?
(*a*) S (*b*) T
(*c*) U (*d*) V

2. B A F E J I P O ? U
(*a*) V (*b*) T
(*c*) S (*d*) Q

3. B A D C ? H G J I
(*a*) EF (*b*) FE
(*c*) FG (*d*) DF

4. ADG, XVT, BEH, WUS, ?
(*a*) VTR (*b*) CFI
(*c*) DFJ (*d*) STU

5. GMSY, IOUA, KQWC, ?
(*a*) MSYE (*b*) NSYE
(*c*) MTYE (*d*) MSYF

6. ADG, GJM, ?, SVY
(*a*) MPS (*b*) MQR
(*c*) MQS (*d*) SPM

7. XYZ, UVW, ?, OPQ
(*a*) RST (*b*) STU
(*c*) QRS (*d*) TUV

8. JOBS, KMEO, LKHK, ?, NGNC
(*a*) MJLH (*b*) LIKG
(*c*) MIKG (*d*) MNGM

9. AZ, GT, MN, ?, YB
(*a*) KF (*b*) TS
(*c*) RX (*d*) SH

10. BMY, DNW, FOU, ?
(*a*) HPT (*b*) HPS
(*c*) HQS (*d*) GPS

11. AZ, CX, EV, ?
(*a*) HU (*b*) GS
(*c*) GT (*d*) HT

12. DMP, FLN, HKL, JJJ, ?
(*a*) MIH (*b*) III
(*c*) LIH (*d*) MII

13. ECA, JHF, OMK, ?, YWU
(*a*) TRP (*b*) LNP
(*c*) QPN (*d*) RPT

14. ABP, CDQ, EFR, ?
(*a*) GHS (*b*) HGS
(*c*) GHR (*d*) GHT

15. BEH, KNQ, TWZ, ?
(*a*) IJL (*b*) BDF
(*c*) CFI (*d*) ADG

EXPLANATORY ANSWERS

1. (*d*) : There are two alternate series.

+1 +1 +1

B Y C X D W E V

−1 −1 −1

Series I : BCDE (natural order)
Series II : YXWV (reverse order)

2. (*a*) : Each vowel (AEIOU) is preceded by the letter that comes next to it in the natural alphabetical series.

B A F E J I P O V U

3. (*b*) : The letters in natural series are divided into sections of two letters each. The letters in each section are written backward.

BA DC FE HG JI

4. (*b*) : There are two alternate series.

ADG XVT BEH WUS CFI

Series I : ADG BEH CFI

+1 +1
+1 +1
+1 +1

Series II : XVT WUS

−1
−1
−1

5. (*a*) : The series is formed by moving each letter two steps forward from one group to the next.

GMSY IOUA KQWC MSYE

+2 +2 +2
+2 +2 +2
+2 +2 +2
+2 +2 +2

(The series restarts from A on reaching Z)

6. (*a*) : In each group of three letters the alphabet is in the succession of +3. The next group begins with the last alphabet of the previous group.

A D G G J M M P S S V Y

+3 +3 +3 +3 +3 +3 +3 +3

7. (*a*) : The alphabet from one group to the next are in recession of −3, *i.e.,*

XYZ UVW RST OPQ

−3 −3 −3
−3 −3 −3
−3 −3 −3

8. (*c*) : The alphabets in each group follow the pattern +1, −2, +3 and −4 respectively from one group to the next group.

JOBS KMEO LKHK MIKG NGNC

+1 +1 +1 +1
−2 −2 −2 −2
+3 +3 +3 +3
−4 −4 −4 −4

9. (*d*) : The letters in one group correspond to the letters in the next group in the manner +6, −6 respectively, *i.e.,*

AZ GT MN SH YB

+6 +6 +6 +6
−6 −6 −6 −6

10. (*b*) : The letters in one group correspond to the letters in the next group in the manner +2, +1, -2 respectively, *i.e.,*

BMY DNW FOU HPS

+2 +2 +2
+1 +1 +1
−2 −2 −2

11. (*c*) : The letters in each group correspond to the letters in the next group in the manner +2, –2 respectively, *i.e.,*

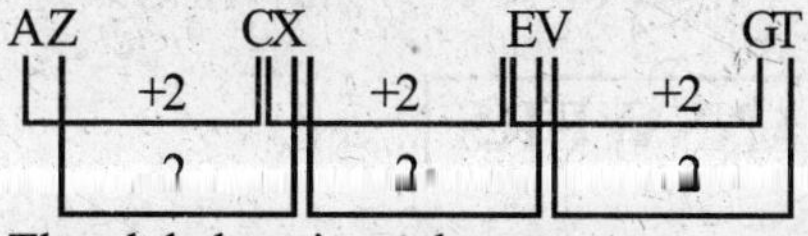

12. (*c*) : The alphabets in each group correspond to the alphabets in the next group in the manner +2, –1, –2 respectively, *i.e.,*

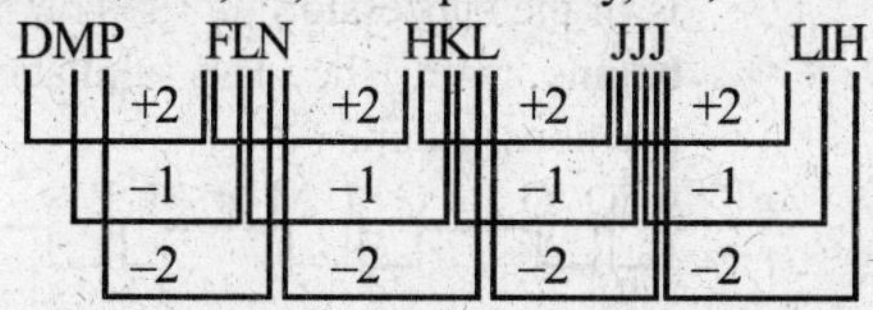

13. (*a*) : The alphabets in each group are moved five steps forward, *i.e.,*

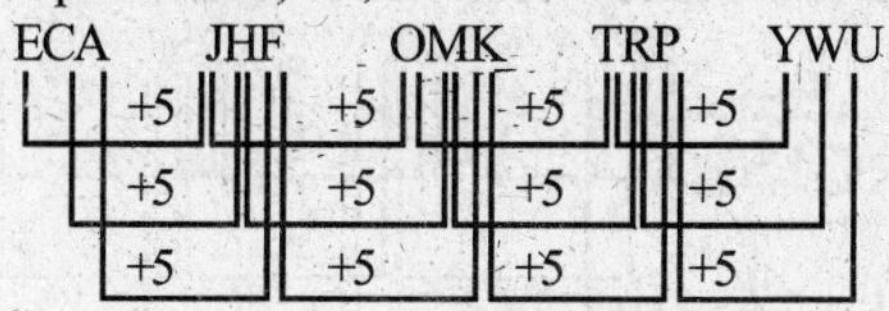

14. (*a*) : The letters in one group correspond to the letters in the next group in the manner +2, +2, +1 respectively, *i.e.,*

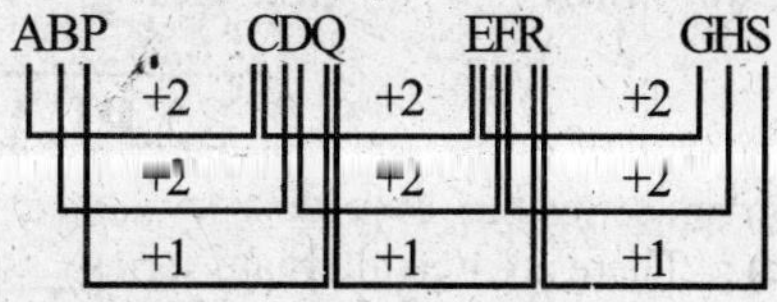

15. (*c*) : All the letters in each group are moved nine steps forward.

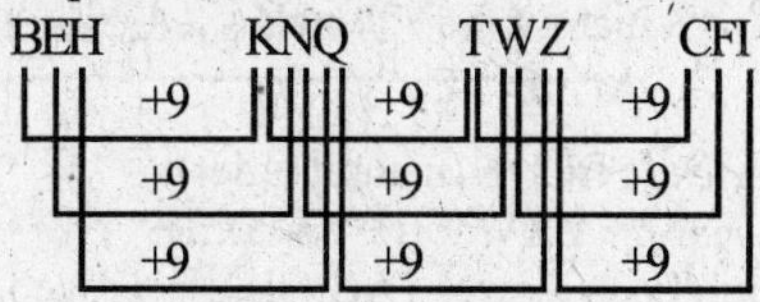

2. WRONG LETTER SERIES

In this type of series, the candidates are not required to find the letter or group of letters which will complete the given series but, they have to identify the letter or number which is wrong or misfit in the given series.

SOLVED EXAMPLE

1. Which of the following letters in the given series is wrong?

J M P T V Y

(*a*) J (*b*) P (*c*) T (*d*) Y

Ans. (*c*) : The letters in this series are moved three steps forward, *i.e.*,

J M P S V Y

+3 +3 +3 +3 +3

Letter 'T' should have been 'S'.

EXERCISE

Directions : *Which letter(s) in each of the following series is wrong or is misfit in the series?*

1. A E H O U

(*a*) U (*b*) O
(*c*) H (*d*) E

2. C H M S W B

(*a*) C (*b*) S
(*c*) B (*d*) W

3. X S N I C Y

(*a*) Y (*b*) C
(*c*) S (*d*) I

4. Z A W B X C

(*a*) D (*b*) C
(*c*) X (*d*) W

5. M L O N Q P R

(*a*) R (*b*) O
(*c*) Q (*d*) L

6. D K R Y F L

(*a*) L (*b*) D
(*c*) R (*d*) Y

7. L N Q T W Z C F

(*a*) C (*b*) Q
(*c*) L (*d*) F

8. XW, DC, CB, NM, PQ

(*a*) NM (*b*) CB
(*c*) PQ (*d*) XW

9. B E I N S A I

(*a*) A (*b*) E
(*c*) S (*d*) I

10. Z T P K H F

(*a*) Z (*b*) P
(*c*) T (*d*) F

EXPLANATORY ANSWERS

1. (*c*) : The series is made with vowels only. AEIOU. I should be in place of H.

2. (*b*) : The letters in the series are moved five steps forward.

C H M R W B

+5 +5 +5 +5 +5

R should be in place of S
(The series restarts from A on reaching Z)

3. (*b*) : The pattern in the series is –5, *i.e.*,

X S N I D Y

–5 –5 –5 –5 –5

D should be in place of C.

4. (*d*) : There are two alternate series

+1 +1

Z A Y B X C

–1 –1

Series I : ZYX (reverse series)

Series II : ABC (natural series)

Y should be in place of W.

5. (*a*) : Two consecutive letters are written backwards.

ML ON QP SR

S should be in place of R.

6. (*a*) : The pattern in this series in moving the letters seven steps forward.

D K R Y F M

+7 +7 +7 +7 +7

M should be in place of L.

7. (*c*) : The pattern in the series is +3

K N Q T W Z C F

+3 +3 +3 +3 +3 +3 +3

K should be in place of L.

8. (*c*) : The series is made with any two consecutive letters written backwards.

XW DC CB NM QP

← ← ← ← ←

Q should come before P in the series.

9. (*c*) : The difference between the letters is increased by one at each step.

B E I N T A I

+3 +4 +5 +6 +7 +8

T should be in place of S.

10. (*b*) : The difference between the letters is decreased by one at each step.

Z T O K H F

–6 –5 –4 –3 –2

O should be in place of P.

3. REPEAT SERIES

In this type of series, small letters of the alphabet are used to make a set of letters which are repeated. The candidate has to find the set of letters which will fit the blanks left in the given series in such a manner that one section of the series is further repeated in the same manner.

SOLVED EXAMPLE

1. Which of the following groups of letters will complete the given series?
ba-b-aab-a-b
(*a*) baab (*b*) abba (*c*) abaa (*d*) babb
Ans. (*b*) : The series is baab, baab, baab. Here the section 'baab' is repeated in the series.

***Solving steps* :** The candidate has to look for clues to solve such series pattern. 'aab' in the Series indicates that 'b' in this series is preceded by two 'a' so, the first blank and the last blank will be filled by 'a'. Now the first set is formed, *i.e.,* 'baab' in the beginning. This set is repeated, so the second and third blanks will have 'b' filling them. Now, solve the exercise given below to know the different ways in which these series are formed.

EXERCISE

Directions : *Which of the following groups of letters will complete the given series?*

1. ab---b-bbaa-
(*a*) babba (*b*) abaab
(*c*) abbab (*d*) baaab

2. aa-ab--aaa-a
(*a*) baaa (*b*) abab
(*c*) aaab (*d*) aabb

3. -baa-aab-a-a
(*a*) baab (*b*) abab
(*c*) aaba (*d*) aabb

4. -a cca-ccca-acccc-aaa
(*a*) ccaa (*b*) acca
(*c*) caac (*d*) caaa

5. c-bbb--abbbb-abbb-
(*a*) abccb (*b*) bacbb
(*c*) aabcb (*d*) abacb

6. ac-cab-baca-aba-acac
(*a*) bcbb (*b*) aacb
(*c*) babb (*d*) acbc

7. --aba--ba-ab
(*a*) abbab (*b*) bbaba
(*c*) baabb (*d*) abbba

8. --babbba-a--
(*a*) bbaba (*b*) babbb
(*c*) baaab (*d*) ababb

9. k-mk-lmkkl-kk-mk
(*a*) lklm (*b*) lkmk
(*c*) lkmm (*d*) lkml

10. abc-d-bc-d-b-dd
(*a*) decdb (*b*) dadac
(*c*) cdabe (*d*) bacde

11. b-abbc-bbca-bcabb-ab
(*a*) acba (*b*) acaa
(*c*) cacc (*d*) cabc

12. aca-ac--a-ac
(*a*) babc (*b*) aaac
(*c*) cacc (*d*) caca

13. ba-cb-b-bab-?
(*a*) acbb (*b*) bcaa
(*c*) cabb (*d*) bacc

14. ab-aa-caab-aab-a
(*a*) bcbc (*b*) bbca
(*c*) cbcc (*d*) caba

15. -bbcaa-bcaa-bc-a-bca
(*a*) bacab (*b*) abbab
(*c*) abcba (*d*) bcaab

16. a-bccb-ca-cca-baab-c
(*a*) accab (*b*) abcaa
(*c*) bacaa (*d*) ababc

17. b-dabbcd-b-c-ab
(*a*) cabd (*b*) bcad
(*c*) dcba (*d*) acbd

18. a-ba-caacb-bc-
(*a*) acbb (*b*) cbab
(*c*) cbaa (*d*) cbba

19. c-baa-aca-cacab-acac-bca
(*a*) acbaa (*b*) cbaac
(*c*) bccab (*d*) bbcaa

20. -bcc-ac-aabb-ab-cc
(*a*) bacab (*b*) abaca
(*c*) aabca (*d*) bcaca

21. ab-ccca-bccc-bbcc-
(*a*) abbc (*b*) bbac
(*c*) bbca (*d*) cabc

22. -cbc-a-bcaac-ca
(*a*) aaba (*b*) caab
(*c*) bcab (*d*) aacb

23. ab-ba--ba-
(*a*) abba (*b*) baab
(*c*) baba (*d*) abab

24. yx-yx-yxz-xzy-zyxz
(*a*) zzyx (*b*) xxzy
(*c*) yyzx (*d*) yzxz

25. xxxy-y-xxy-yxx-
(*a*) xyxy (*b*) yxyx
(*c*) yyxx (*d*) xxyy

EXPLANATORY ANSWERS

1. (*d*) : The series is abbaab, abbaab.
2. (*c*) : The series is aaaaba, aaaaba.
3. (*b*) : The series is aba, aba, aba, aba.
4. (*d*) : The series is c,a,cc,aa, ccc, aaa, cccc, aaaa.
5. (*a*) : The series is cabbbb, cabbbb, cabbbb.
6. (*b*) : The series is acac, abab, acac, abab, acac.
7. (*a*) : The series is ab, ab, ab, ab, ab, ab.
8. (*b*) : The series is bababb, bababb.
9. (*d*) : The series is klmk, klmk, klmk, klmk.
10. (*b*) : The series is abcdd, abcdd, abcdd.
11. (*d*) : The series is bcab, bcab, bcab, bcab, bcab.
12. (*c*) : The series is ac, ac, ac, ac, ac, ac.
13. (*d*) : The series is babc, babc, babc.
14. (*c*) : The series is abca, abca, abca, abca.
15. (*b*) : The series is abbca, abbca, abbca, abbca.
16. (*d*) : The series is aabcc, bbcaa, ccabb, aabcc.
17. (*a*) : The series is bcdab, bcdab, bcdab.
18. (*c*) : The series is acbabca, acbabca.
19. (*a*) : The series is cabaac, acabca, cabaac, acabca.
20. (*a*) : The series is bbccaa, ccaabb, aabbcc.
21. (*b*) : The series is abbccc abbccc.
22. (*d*) : The series is acbca acbca acbca.
23. (*d*) : The series is ab ab ab ab ab.
24. (*a*) : The series is yxz yxz yxz yxz yxz yxz.
25. (*b*) : The series is xxx yyy xxx yyy xxx.

4. NUMBER SERIES

In this type of series, the set of given numbers in a series are related to one another in a particular pattern or manner. The relationship between the numbers may be (i) consecutive odd/even numbers; (ii) consecutive prime numbers; (iii) squares/cubes of some numbers with/without variation of addition or subtraction of some number; (iv) sum/product/difference of preceding numbers; (v) addition/subtraction/multiplication/division by some number; and (vi) many more combinations of the relationships given above.

EXERCISE

Directions : *In the following questions, select the number(s) from the given options for completing the given series.*

1. 7776, 1296, 216, 36, 6, ?
(*a*) 6 (*b*) 0
(*c*) 3 (*d*) 1

2. 29282, 2662, 242, 22, ?
(*a*) 1 (*b*) 2
(*c*) 0 (*d*) 11

3. 1, 2, 2, 4, 16, ?, 65536
(*a*) 276 (*b*) 64
(*c*) 256 (*d*) 198

4. 3, 5, 9, 15, 23, ?, 45
(*a*) 37 (*b*) 35
(*c*) 31 (*d*) 33

5. 7, 21, 35, 49, 63, ?
(*a*) 70 (*b*) 77
(*c*) 81 (*d*) 108

6. 10, 14, 23, 39, 64, ?, 149
(*a*) 78 (*b*) 128
(*c*) 103 (*d*) 100

7. 6, 24, 29, 116, 121, ?, 489
(*a*) 468 (*b*) 484
(*c*) 243 (*d*) 363

8. 5, 50, 45, 450, 445, ?, 4445
(*a*) 4450 (*b*) 4600
(*c*) 4550 (*d*) 4500

9. 6.25, 9, 12.25, 16, 20.25, 25, 30.25?
(*a*) 36 (*b*) 32
(*c*) 28.25 (*d*) 40.25

10. 243, 5, 81, 15, 27, 45, 9, ?
(*a*) 5 (*b*) 15
(*c*) 135 (*d*) 27

11. 2, 7, 14, 23, ?, 47
(*a*) 31 (*b*) 38
(*c*) 28 (*d*) 34

12. 0, 1, 8, 27, 64, ?
(*a*) 125 (*b*) 128
(*c*) 256 (*d*) 121

13. 37, 47, 58, ?, 79, 95
(*a*) 71 (*b*) 69
(*c*) 68 (*d*) 67

14. 4, –8, 14, –22, 32, ?
(*a*) –44 (*b*) 42
(*c*) –42 (*d*) 44

15. 6, 7, 9, 11, 15, 15, 24, 19, ?
(*a*) 32 (*b*) 34
(*c*) 36 (*d*) 37

EXPLANATORY ANSWERS

1. (*d*) : The numbers in this sequence are divided by 6 each time.

2. (*b*) : The numbers in the series are divided by 11 at each step.

3. (*c*) : The number in the series is product of all the numbers preceding it.

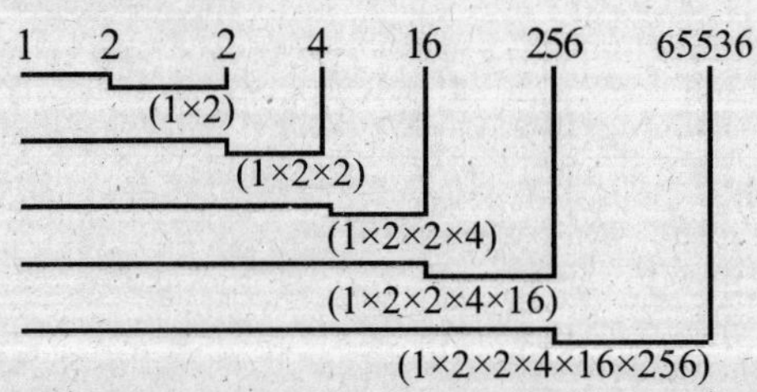

4. (d) : The difference between consecutive numbers increases by 2 at each step.

3 5 9 15 23 33 45

+2 +4 +6 +8 +10 +12

5. (b) : The series is multiplication of 7 by odd numbers starting from 3.

7 21 35 49 63 77

×3 ×5 ×7 ×9 ×11

6. (d) : The number plus the square of numbers in natural order starting from 2 gives the next number in the series.

10 14 23 39 64 100 149

$+2^2$ $+3^2$ $+4^2$ $+5^2$ $+6^2$ $+7^2$

7. (b) : The sequence in the series is ×4, +5, which is repeated.

8. (a) : The sequence in the series is ×10, –5, which is repeated.

9. (a) : There are two alternate series :

+6 +8 +10

6.25 9 12.25 16 20.25 25 30.25 36

+7 +9 +11

Series I : 6.25, 12.25, 20.25, 30.25 (sequence is +6, +8, +10)
Series II : 9, 16, 25, 36 (sequence is +7, +9, +11)

10. (c) : There are two alternate series :

÷3 ÷3 ÷3

243 5 81 15 27 45 9 135

×3 ×3 ×3

Series I : 243, 81, 27, 9 (division by 3)
Series II : 5, 15, 45, 135 (multiplication by 3)

11. (d) : The difference between two consecutive numbers is increasing by 2 starting from 5.

2 7 14 23 34 47

+5 +7 +9 +11 +13

12. (a) : The numbers are cubes of numbers in natural order.

13. (a) : The sum of the digits of the number is added to the number to obtain the next number in the series.

37 47 58 71 79 95

+(3+7) +(4+7) +(5+8) +(7+1) +(7+9)

14. (a) : Alternate numbers are marked positive and negative, but the difference between their magnitude increases by 2 at each step.

4 –8 14 –22 32 –44

4 6 8 10 12

15. (c) : There are two alternate series :

+3 +6 +9 +12

6 7 9 11 15 15 24 19 36

+4 +4 +4

Series I : 6, 9, 15, 24, 36 (sequence is +3, +6, +9, +12)
Series II : 7, 11, 15, 19 (addition of 4 at each step)

5. WRONG NUMBER SERIES

In this type of series, the given series may be complete but what needs to be identified is the number in the given completed series which is disturbing the sequential pattern of that series and does not fit in with the relationship shared between the other numbers.

EXERCISE

Directions : *In the given series find the number which is wrong.*

1. 5, 25, 120, 625, 3125, 15625
(*a*) 15625 (*b*) 625
(*c*) 120 (*d*) 5

2. 4, 8, 11, 22, 18, 36, 24, 50
(*a*) 8 (*b*) 22
(*c*) 36 (*d*) 24

3. 2, 4, 12, 24, 72, 142, 432
(*a*) 432 (*b*) 12
(*c*) 142 (*d*) 72

4. 2, 3, 4, 4, 6, 8, 9, 12, 16
(*a*) 3 (*b*) 9
(*c*) 6 (*d*) 12

5. 97, 91, 86, 83, 79, 77, 76, 76
(*a*) 86 (*b*) 76
(*c*) 91 (*d*) 83

6. 7, 11, 11, 9, 15, 7, 19, 5, 23, 1
(*a*) 5 (*b*) 7
(*c*) 1 (*d*) 9

7. 3, 7, 12, 28, 48, 118, 192, 448
(*a*) 12 (*b*) 118
(*c*) 28 (*d*) 7

8. 10, 100, 1100, 11000, 111000, 1210000
(*a*) 1210000 (*b*) 11000
(*c*) 100 (*d*) 111000

9. 24576, 6144, 1536, 386, 96, 24
(*a*) 386 (*b*) 6144
(*c*) 96 (*d*) 1536

10. 11, 13, 15, 17, 19, 23, 29, 31, 37
(*a*) 13 (*b*) 23
(*c*) 15 (*d*) 31

11. 36, 43, 49, 54, 60, 61, 63, 64
(*a*) 60 (*b*) 63
(*c*) 54 (*d*) 43

12. 3, 10, 41, 206, 1236, 8660
(*a*) 10 (*b*) 41
(*c*) 206 (*d*) 1236

13. 17, 25, 37, 50, 65, 82, 101
(*a*) 25 (*b*) 17
(*c*) 101 (*d*) 65

14. 12, 20, 38, 42, 56, 72
(*a*) 20 (*b*) 38
(*c*) 56 (*d*) 72

15. 5, 6, 11, 22, 42, 88, 176
(*a*) 5 (*b*) 42
(*c*) 176 (*d*) 11

EXPLANATORY ANSWERS

1. (*c*) : The numbers in the series are multiplied by 5 to get the next number.
∴ 125 should be in place of 120.

2. (*d*) : Two numbers form a pair. The first number increases by 7 for the next pair and the second number is the double of first number.

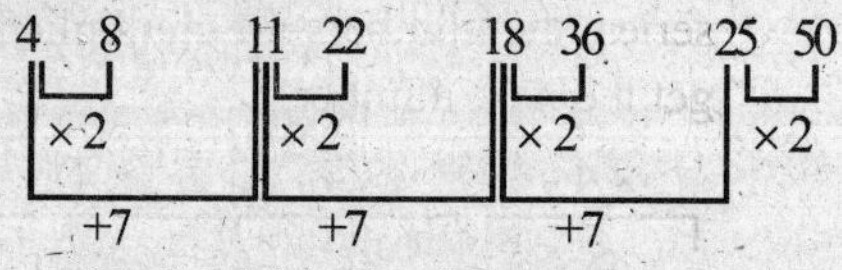

∴ 25 should be in place of 24.

3. (*c*) : There are two alternate series and in each series, the numbers are multiplied by 6 to get the next number.

×6 ×6 ×6

2 4 12 24 72 144 432

×6 ×6

∴ 144 should be in place of 142.

4. (*b*) : There are three alternate series and in each series, the numbers are multiplied by 2 to get the next number.

×2 ×2

2 3 4 4 6 8 8 12 16

×2 ×2

×2 ×2

Series I : 2, 4, 8 *Series II* : 3, 6, 12

Series III : 4, 8, 16

∴ 8 should be in place of 9.

5. (*d*) : The difference between the consecutive numbers in the series decreases by 1 at each step.

97 91 86 82 79 77 76 76

−6 −5 −4 −3 −2 −1 −0

∴ 82 should be in place of 83.

6. (*c*) : There are two alternate series :

+4 +4 +4 +4

7 11 11 9 15 7 19 5 21 3

−2 −2 −2 −2

Series I : 7, 11, 15, 19, 23 (addition of 4)

Series II : 11, 9, 7, 5, 3 (subtraction of 2)

∴ 3 should be in place of 1.

7. (*b*) : There are two alternate series and in each series, the numbers are multiplied by 4 to get the next number.

×4 ×4 ×4

3 7 12 28 48 112 192 448

×4 ×4 ×4

∴ 112 should be in place of 118.

8. (*d*) : The numbers in this series are multiplied by 10 and 11 alternately is, *i.e.*, × 10, × 11.

10 100 1100 11000 121000 1210000

×10 ×11 ×10 ×11 ×10

∴ 121000 should be in place of 111000.

9. (*a*) : The numbers in this series are divided by 4 to get the next number.

24576 6144 1536 384 96 24

÷4 ÷4 ÷4 ÷4 ÷4

∴ 384 should be in place of 386.

10. (*c*) : The series comprises of prime numbers in increasing order. Only 15 is an exception.

11. (*a*) : The difference between two consecutive numbers is decreasing by 1 at each step.

36 43 49 54 58 61 63 64

+7 +6 +5 +4 +3 +2 +1

∴ 58 should be in place of 60.

12. (*d*) : The sequence followed in this series is :

$3 \times 3 + 1 = 10$, $10 \times 4 + 1 = 41$

$41 \times 5 + 1 = 206$, $206 \times 6 + 1 = 1237$; and

$1237 \times 7 + 1 = 8660$

∴ 1237 should be in place of 1236.

13. (*a*) : The numbers in the series are 1 plus the squares of numbers in natural order starting from 4.

17 26 37 50 65 82 101

↓ ↓ ↓ ↓ ↓ ↓ ↓

$4^2 + 1$ $5^2 + 1$ $6^2 + 1$ $7^2 + 1$ $8^2 + 1$ $9^2 + 1$ $10^2 + 1$

∴ 26 should be in place of 25.

14. (*b*) : The sequence followed in this series is :

$3 \times 4 = 12$, $4 \times 5 = 20$, $5 \times 6 = 30$,

$6 \times 7 = 42$, $7 \times 8 = 56$, $8 \times 9 = 72$

∴ 30 should be in place of 38.

15. (*b*) : The numbers in the series are the sum of all the numbers preceding them.

5 6 11 22 44 88 176

(5 + 6)

(5 + 6 + 11)

(5 + 6 + 11 + 22)

(5 + 6 + 11 + 22 + 44)

(5 + 6 + 11 + 22 + 44 + 88)

∴ 44 should be in place of 42.

6. WORD ANALOGY

In Analogy Tests, the relationship between two given words is established and then applied to the other words. The type of relationship may vary, so while attempting such questions the first step is to identify the type of relationship, which can be any one of the following.

EXERCISE

Directions : *In the questions given below one term is missing. Based on the relationship of the two given words find the missing term from the given options.*

1. HUNGER : FOOD : : THIRST : ?
(*a*) Water (*b*) Drink
(*c*) Tea (*d*) Coffee

2. HUNTER : GUN : : WRITER : ?
(*a*) Book (*b*) Pen
(*c*) Poem (*d*) Page

3. WOOL : SHEEP : : SILK : ?
(*a*) Saree (*b*) String
(*c*) Silkworm (*d*) Moth

4. FOOD : STOMACH : : FUEL : ?
(*a*) Engine (*b*) Automobile
(*c*) Rail (*d*) Aeroplane

5. WATER : SAND : : OCEAN : ?
(*a*) Island (*b*) River
(*c*) Desert (*d*) Waves

6. ADULT : BABY : : FLOWER : ?
(*a*) Seed (*b*) Bud
(*c*) Fruit (*d*) Butterfly

7. WRITER : READER : : PRODUCER : ?
(*a*) Creator (*b*) Contractor
(*c*) Creature (*d*) Consumer

8. ENTRANCE : EXIT : : LOYALTY : ?
(*a*) Treachery (*b*) Patriotism
(*c*) Fidelity (*d*) Reward

9. MOTHER : MATERNAL : : FATHER : ?
(*a*) Eternal (*b*) Detrimental
(*c*) Paternal (*d*) Formidable

10. PEARL : NECKLACE : : FLOWER : ?
(*a*) Plant (*b*) Garden
(*c*) Petal (*d*) Bouquet

11. ALPHABET : WORD : : WORD : ?
(*a*) Sound (*b*) Music
(*c*) Sentence (*d*) Dictionary

12. LIFE : DEATH : : HOPE : ?
(*a*) Cry (*b*) Pain
(*c*) Despair (*d*) Sad

13. GOOD : BAD : : VIRTUE : ?
(*a*) Blame (*b*) Sin
(*c*) Despair (*d*) Vice

14. BIRD : FLY : : SNAKE : ?
(*a*) Timid (*b*) Clatter
(*c*) Crawl (*d*) Hole

15. CAT : MOUSE : : BIRD : ?
(*a*) Cage (*b*) Trap
(*c*) Eagle (*d*) Worm

16. STATE : EXILE
(*a*) Police : Arrest
(*b*) Judge : Convict
(*c*) Constitution : Amendment
(*d*) Church : Excommunicate

17. CAPRICIOUSNESS : RELIABILITY
(*a*) Extemporaneous : Predictability
(*b*) Unreliable : Inhuman
(*c*) Tenacious : Practicality
(*d*) Arbitrary : Whimsical

18. LOATH : COERCION
(*a*) Detest : Caressing
(*b*) Irritate : Caressing
(*c*) Irate : Antagonism
(*d*) Reluctant : Persuasion

19. SCALES : FISH
(*a*) Lady : Dress (*b*) Tree : Leaves
(*c*) Bird : Feather (*d*) Skin : Man

20. TREE : SAPLING
(*a*) Hut : Mansion
(*b*) Giant : Dwarf
(*c*) Horse : Foal
(*d*) Ant : Elephant

21. CHALK : BLACKBOARD
(*a*) Door : Handle
(*b*) Table : Chair
(*c*) Ink : Paper
(*d*) Type : Paint

22. PRIMEVAL : MEDIEVAL
(*a*) Dinosaur : Dragon
(*b*) Gorilla : Soldier
(*c*) Evolution : Revelation
(*d*) Thorn : Rose

23. TRILOGY : NOVEL
(*a*) Rice : Husk
(*b*) Milk : Cream
(*c*) Fabric : Weaving
(*d*) Serial : Episode

24. PEDANT : ERUDITION
(*a*) Prude : Modesty
(*b*) Blunt : Politician
(*c*) Diplomats : Tactless
(*d*) Enemy : Friendly

25. FURY : IRE
(*a*) Convulsion : Spasm
(*b*) Amusement : Happiness
(*c*) Joke : Laugh
(*d*) Dispassion : Emotion

EXPLANATORY ANSWERS

1. (*a*) : Hunger is satiated by food, thirst by water.

2. (*b*) : Weapon of a hunter is a gun, weapon of a writer is a pen.

3. (*c*) : Wool is obtained from sheep, silk is obtained from silkworm.

4. (*a*) : Food is consumed in stomach, fuel is consumed in engine.

5. (*c*) : The related words are near opposites.

6. (*b*) : The youngone of an adult is a baby and that of a flower is a bud.

7. (*d*) : A writer aims to please the readers by his writings, a producer aims to please the consumers by his products.

8. (*a*) : The related words are opposites.

9. (*c*) : Relations on the mother's side are maternal and on the father's side paternal.

10. (*d*) : Many pearls make a necklace, many flowers make a bouquet.

11. (*c*) : More than one alphabet make a word, more than one word make a sentence.

12. (*c*) : The related words are opposites.

13. (*d*) : The related words are opposites.

14. (*c*) : Birds fly, snakes crawl.

15. (*d*) : Cat chases the mouse, bird chases the worm.

16. (*d*) : Punishment of leaving the State is exile, punishment of leaving the Church is excommunication.

17. (*c*) : The related words are antonyms.

18. (*d*) : Loathing is the result of constant coersion, reluctance is the result of constant persuasion.

19. (*d*) : Covering of the fish is scales, covering of man is skin.

20. (*c*) : Young tree is a sapling, young horse is a foal.

21. (*c*) : Chalk is used to write on blackboard, ink is used to write on paper.

22. (*a*) : The related words represent almost the same time period and answer option represents almost the same sized creatures.

23. (*d*) : Trilogy is section of a novel, episode is a section of a serial.

24. (*a*) : The related words are synonyms.

25. (*b*) : Fury causes ire, amusement causes happiness.

7. NUMBER ANALOGY

In number analogy also, the relationship between the given numbers is detected and then applied to the second part to find the missing numbers. This relationship between the numbers can be based on any of the following patterns : *(i)* numbers can be odd/even/prime numbers; *(ii)* numbers can be multiples of one number; *(iii)* numbers can be squares/cubes of different numbers; *(iv)* some numbers can be added to/subtracted from/multiplied to/divided into the first number to get the second number; *(v)* the second number can be the sum/product/difference of the digits of first number; and *(vi)* combinations of any mathematical calculations given above can apply to the relationship between the two given numbers.

EXERCISE

Directions : *In the following questions, select the number from the given options which follows the same relationship as shared between the first two numbers.*

1. 1 : 11 : : 2 : ?
(*a*) 20 (*b*) 22
(*c*) 24 (*d*) 44

2. $\frac{1}{7} : \frac{1}{14} :: \frac{1}{9} : ?$
(*a*) $\frac{1}{88}$ (*b*) $\frac{1}{80}$
(*c*) $\frac{1}{81}$ (*d*) $\frac{1}{18}$

3. 0.16 : 0.0016 : : 1.02 : ?
(*a*) 10.20 (*b*) 0.102
(*c*) 0.0102 (*d*) 1.020

4. 663 : 884 : : 221 : ?
(*a*) 332 (*b*) 554
(*c*) 773 (*d*) 442

5. 16 : 0.16 : : ?
(*a*) 2 : 0.02 (*b*) 7 : 0.007
(*c*) 1.3 : 0.13 (*d*) 0.01 : 0.001

6. $3 : \frac{1}{3} :: ?$
(*a*) 6 : 12 (*b*) 5 : 2/15
(*c*) 8 : 1/8 (*d*) 9 : 27

7. 65 : 13 : : 180 : ?
(*a*) 93 (*b*) 36
(*c*) 133 (*d*) 102

8. 125 : 27 : : 343 : ?
(*a*) 729 (*b*) 64
(*c*) 216 (*d*) 512

9. 357 : 73 : : ?
(*a*) 429 : 94
(*b*) 201 : 21
(*c*) 138 : 38
(*d*) 93 : 39

10. 731 : 902 : : 655 : ?
(*a*) 646 (*b*) 800
(*c*) 793 (*d*) 556

11. 162 : 9 : : 310 : ?
(*a*) 33 (*b*) 27
(*c*) 16 (*d*) 4

12. 13 : 17 : : 15 : ?
(*a*) 19 (*b*) 11
(*c*) 21 (*d*) 16

13. 225 : 15 : : 256 : ?
(*a*) 26 (*b*) 16
(*c*) 20 (*d*) 28

14. 46 : 48 : : 54 : ?
(*a*) 59 (*b*) 40
(*c*) 67 (*d*) 62

15. 33 : 36 : : 21 : ?
(*a*) 9 (*b*) 18
(*c*) 25 (*d*) 32

EXPLANATORY ANSWERS

1. *(b)* : The first number is repeated to obtain the second number.

2. *(d)* : The first fraction is multiplied by half to obtain the second fraction.

$\frac{1}{7} : \frac{1}{14} :: \frac{1}{9} : \frac{1}{18}$ (each $\times \frac{1}{2}$)

3. *(c)* : The decimals are divided by 100.

0.16 : 0.0016 :: 1.02 : 0.0102 (each $\div 100$)

4. *(d)* : The digits at tens and hundreds place is same but the digit at the units place is half the other identical digits.

66<u>3</u> : 88<u>4</u> :: 22<u>1</u> : 44<u>2</u>

5. *(a)* : Of the two related numbers, the second number is the result of first number divided by 100.

16 : 0.16 :: 2 : 0.02 (each $\div 100$)

6. *(c)* : Of the two related numbers, the second number is the part fraction of the first number, *i.e.* 3 is related to one-third $\left(\frac{1}{3}\right)$. Similarly, 8 will be related to one-eighth $\left(\frac{1}{8}\right)$.

7. *(b)* : The first number is divided by 5 to get the second number.

65 : 13 :: 180 : 36 (each $\div 5$)

8. *(a)* : The numbers are cubes of different odd numbers.

125 : 27 :: 343 : 729

5^3 : 3^3 :: 7^3 : 9^3

9. *(a)* : The central digit of the first number is left out and the corner digits written in reverse order to get the second number.

357 : 73 :: 429 : 94

10. *(a)* : The sum of the digits of both the numbers is same.

$731 : 902 \rightarrow 7+3+1$
$= 9+0+2$ *i.e.* $11 = 11$

$655 : 646 \rightarrow 6+5+5$
$= 6+4+6$ *i.e.* $16 = 16$

11. *(d)* : The sum of the digits of the first number is the second number.

162 : 9 :: 310 : 4 ($1+6+2$; $3+1+0$)

12. *(a)* : First number plus 4 gives the second number.

13 : 17 :: 15 : 19 (each $+4$)

13. *(b)* : The root of first number is the second number.

225 : 15 :: 256 : 16 ($\sqrt{225}$; $\sqrt{256}$)

14. *(b)* : The product of the digits of first number is multiplied by 2 to get the second number.

46 : 48 :: 54 : 40 ($(4 \times 6)2$; $(5 \times 4)2$)

15. *(a)* : The square of the sum of the digits of the first number is the second number.

33 : 36 :: 21 : 9 ($(3+3)^2$; $(2+1)^2$)

8. ODD ONE OUT

In this type of classification, four words are given out of which three are almost same in matter or meaning and only one word is different from the common three. One has to find out the word which is different from the rest.

EXERCISE

Directions : *In each of the following questions, three words are alike in some manner. Spot the odd one out.*

1. (*a*) Green (*b*) Red (*c*) Colour (*d*) Orange

2. (*a*) Stable (*b*) Hole (*c*) Canoe (*d*) Sty

3. (*a*) Nose (*b*) Eyes (*c*) Skin (*d*) Teeth

4. (*a*) Venus (*b*) Moon (*c*) Pluto (*d*) Mars

5. (*a*) Happy (*b*) Gloomy (*c*) Lively (*d*) Cheerful

Directions : *Three of the following four in each question are alike in a certain way and so form a group. Select the group of letters that does not belong to that group.*

6. (*a*) ACE (*b*) LOR (*c*) GIK (*d*) VXZ

7. (*a*) TSR (*b*) LKJ (*c*) PQO (*d*) HGF

8. (*a*) EF LM (*b*) KJ SR (*c*) XW HG (*d*) ED YX

9. (*a*) JOPK (*b*) BOPC (*c*) QOPR (*d*) TOPS

10. (*a*) DfH (*b*) MoQ (*c*) UwY (*d*) InO

Directions : *In each of the following questions, there are four options. Three numbers, in these options, are alike in certain manner. Only one number does not fit in. Choose the one which is different from the rest.*

11. (*a*) 1948 (*b*) 2401 (*c*) 966 (*d*) 1449

12. (*a*) 182 (*b*) 169 (*c*) 130 (*d*) 158

13. (*a*) 129 (*b*) 130 (*c*) 131 (*d*) 132

14. (*a*) 3215 (*b*) 9309 (*c*) 4721 (*d*) 2850

15. (*a*) 1776 (*b*) 2364 (*c*) 1976 (*d*) 3776

Directions : *In the following questions select the pair which is different from the other three.*

16. (*a*) Chair - Furniture (*b*) Shirt - Garment (*c*) Necklace - Jewellery (*d*) Bogie - Engine

17. (*a*) Crayon - Paper (*b*) Pencil - Lead (*c*) Pen - Ink (*d*) Brush - Paint

18. (*a*) War - Peace (*b*) Real - Natural (*c*) Premiere - First (*d*) Wrath - Anger

19. (*a*) Finger - Thimble (*b*) Head - Cap (*c*) Waist - Tiara (*d*) Foot - Shoe

20. (*a*) Day - Night (*b*) Clever - Foolish (*c*) Clear - Blurred (*d*) Arrive - Come

Directions : *In the following questions, which of the following pair of letters is different from the other three?*

21. (*a*) FGH - HIJ (*b*) PQR - RST (*c*) MNO - OPQ (*d*) CDE - DEF

22. (*a*) JuM - jUm (*b*) iLo - Ilo (*c*) PSa - psA (*d*) ZeX - zEx

23. (*a*) NQT - JMP (*b*) CFI - RUX (*c*) ADG - FGH (*d*) SVY - ORU

24. (*a*) DXD - XDX (*b*) KUK - UKU (*c*) FHF - EHE (*d*) RSR - SRS

25. (*a*) AYT - BZU (*b*) FNG - EMF (*c*) RWU - QVN (*d*) HJD - GIC

EXPLANATORY ANSWERS

1. (*c*) : All others are types of colour.

2. (*c*) : Canoe is a boat. Others are resting places of birds/animals.

3. (*d*) : All others are sense organs.

4. (*b*) : All others are planets.

5. (*b*) : All others are expressions of joy.

6. (*b*) : The sequence in each group is +2. Only option (*b*) has sequence in +3, *i.e.,*

ABCDE: +2 +2; LMNOPQR: +3 +3; GHIJK: +2 +2; VWXYZ: +2 +2

7. (*c*) : The sequence of alphabet in each group is in reverse order. Only option (*c*) has sequence in disturbed order.

8. (*a*) : Two consecutive alphabet in each group are in reverse sequence (–1), *i.e.,*

KJ SR; XW HG; ED YX
–1 –1 –1 –1 –1 –1

Only in option (*a*) the sequence is in natural order (+1), *i.e.,*

E F: +1; L M: +1

9. (*d*) : In each group, letters 'OP' are common. The two corner alphabet are in natural order (+1); *i.e.,*

JOPK: +1; BOPC: +1; QOPR: +1

Only in option (*d*) they are in reverse order (–1); *i.e.,*

TOPS: –1

10. (*d*) : In other groups, only the alphabet in the centre is of lower case. In this option letter 'L' on the left is also in lower case.

11. (*a*) : Other numbers are divisible by 7.

12. (*d*) : Other numbers are multiples of 13.

13. (*c*) : 131 is a prime number.

14. (*b*) : In other numbers, no digit is repeated.

15. (*b*) : In other numbers, the last two digits are same.

16. (*d*) : Bogie is a part of train which is a type of conveyance. Chair, Shirt and Necklace are types of furniture, garment and jewellery respectively.

17. (*a*) : The medium used for writing with pencil is lead, with pen it is ink and with brush, it is paint. With crayon it should be wax.

18. (*a*) : The pair of words are opposite. Other pairs are synonyms.

19. (*c*) : Tiara is worn on the head.

20. (*d*) : Other words are opposite to each other.

21. (*d*) : In all other groups, the letters are in natural series and the last letter of first part is the first letter of the second part.

22. (*b*) : In all other groups, only the vowel is in lower case in the first part and in second part the case is reversed.

23. (*c*) : In all other groups, the letters jump two letters in between them.

24. (*c*) : In all other groups, the single letter in first part is repeated in the second and vice versa.

25. (*a*) : In all other groups, the letters in the first part are one step forward than the corresponding letters in the second part.

9. CODING AND DECODING

Coding is a secretive language which is used to change the representation of the actual term/word/value. This coded language can be framed by *(i)* moving the letters one or more steps forward or backward; *(ii)* substituting numbers for letters and vice–versa; *(iii)* writing the letters of the given word in reverse order in part or in whole; and *(iv)* replacing the letters in their natural series by the same positioned letters in their reverse series.

There is variety in ways of coding. Coding language is not only for words and numbers but also for hiding a group of words, statements or even sentences. This form of coding pattern may appear to be confusing but after solving only a few questions it is very easy to understand. Questions based on this coding pattern require no moving of steps or straining efforts of calculations, but only quick tallying or comparing ability. The codes can be letters or numbers.

EXERCISE

Directions : *In the following questions select the right option which indicates the correct code for the word or letter given in the question.*

1. If MUSK is coded as 146816, then ZERO will be coded as :
   (*a*) 113811 (*b*) 122912
   (*c*) 15915 (*d*) 2651815
2. If BAD is coded as 7, HIS as 9, LOW will be coded as :
   (*a*) 50 (*b*) 8
   (*c*) 23 (*d*) 5
3. In a certain code LIBERATE is written as 56403170, TRIBAL will be written in the same code as :
   (*a*) 734615 (*b*) 736415
   (*c*) 136475 (*d*) 034615
4. In certain military code, SYSTEM is written as SYSMET, and NEARER as AENRER, what will be the code for FRACTION?
   (*a*) CRAFNOIT (*b*) FRCAITNO
   (*c*) CARFNOIT (*d*) FRACNOIT
5. If CRUDE is written as BSTED, then MOIST will be coded as :
   (*a*) NNJRU (*b*) LNHRS
   (*c*) NPJTU (*d*) LPHTS
6. In a certain code ALPACA is written as ACAPLA. How will ANIMAL be written in that code?
   (*a*) LAMINA (*b*) ALAMIN
   (*c*) LAMNIA (*d*) AAMLIN
7. In a certain code FINGER is written as DGLECP. What will be the code for KIDNEY?
   (*a*) IGBLCW (*b*) IGCLBW
   (*c*) IBCGLE (*d*) IGBKCV
8. In a certain code QUESTION is written as NXBVQLLQ. How will REPLY be coded?
   (*a*) YHMOV (*b*) OBMVI
   (*c*) VHSOB (*d*) OHMOV
9. If in a certain code SKEW is coded as PNCY, then what will JXQV will stand for?
   (*a*) MUTS (*b*) MUST
   (*c*) MTSU (*d*) STUM
10. In a certain code LONDON is written as MPOEPO. What will IVOHSZ mean in the same code?
    (*a*) HUNGRY (*b*) HUNDRY
    (*c*) GRUNHY (*d*) HONDUS
11. In a certain code language 8514 is a code for HEAD, 3945 for RIDE and 057 for BEG. What will be the code for GRADE?
    (*a*) 71345 (*b*) 73415
    (*c*) 74135 (*d*) 73145

12. If MOTHERLAND is coded as 9501623748, how will DREAM be coded?
(*a*) 82697 (*b*) 86297
(*c*) 82769 (*d*) 82679

13. If OATH is coded in a certain language as TEYL, then how will WORD be coded?
(*a*) BWRH (*b*) HRWB
(*c*) BSWH (*d*) CSXI

14. If FINANCE is coded as GKQESIL, then how will BANK be coded in the same manner?
(*a*) CBOL (*b*) CDRP
(*c*) CCQO (*d*) CCPN

15. PLANNING is coded in a certain language as UFFHSCSA. How will AUTHORITY be coded in the same language?
(*a*) FOYBTLNND
(*b*) FYOTBNNLT
(*c*) FBOYTLNTN
(*d*) FBOYTNLTN

EXPLANATORY ANSWERS

1. (*b*) : The coded number signifies the position of the alphabet in its reverse order of the alphabetical series (ZYXW...)

M U S K → MUSK
↓ ↓ ↓ ↓
14th 6th 8th 16th → 146816

Similarly,

Z E R O → ZERO
↓ ↓ ↓ ↓
1st 22nd 9th 12th → 122912

2. (*d*) : The coded number is the sum of number digits signifying the position of the alphabet in the natural order.

B A D
↓ ↓ ↓
2nd 1st 4th *i.e.,* 2 + 1 + 4 = 7

Similarly,

H I S
↓ ↓ ↓
8th 9th 19th *i.e.,* 8 + 9 + 19 = 36
further, 3 + 6 = 9

Also,

L O W
↓ ↓ ↓
12th 15th 23rd *i.e.,* 12 + 15 + 23 = 50
further, 5 + 0 = 0

3. (*b*) : The letters of the word TRIBAL are picked from LIBERATE. So will be the coded numbers.

L I B E R A T E → given word
5 6 4 0 3 1 7 0 → codes

Similarly,

T R I B A L → word to be coded
7 3 6 4 1 5 → answer codes

4. (*c*) : The word is divided into two equal parts and the letters of each part are written in reverse order.

Similarly,

5. (*d*) : The code is formed by moving the letters one step backwards and one step forward alternately.

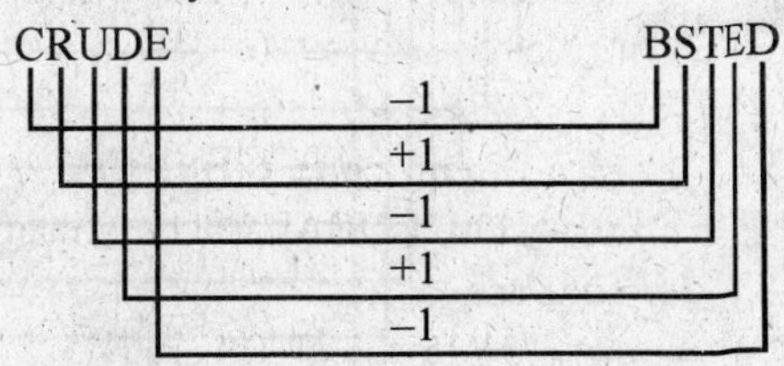

Similarly,

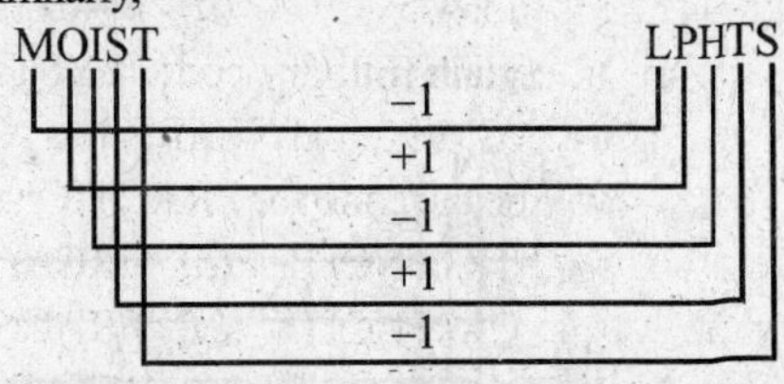

6. (*a*) : The letters of the word are written backwards.

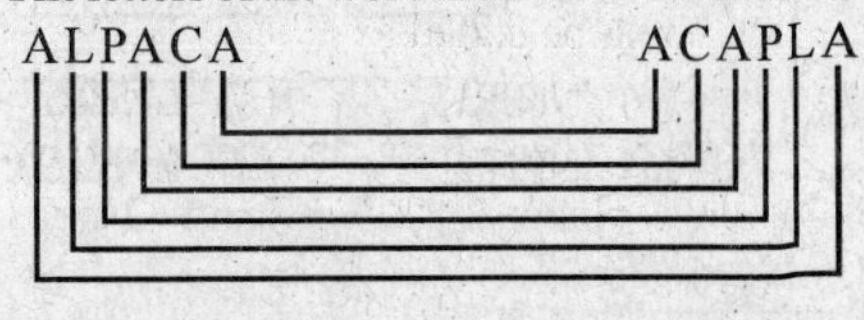

Similarly,

7. *(a)* : The word is coded by moving the letters two steps backwards.

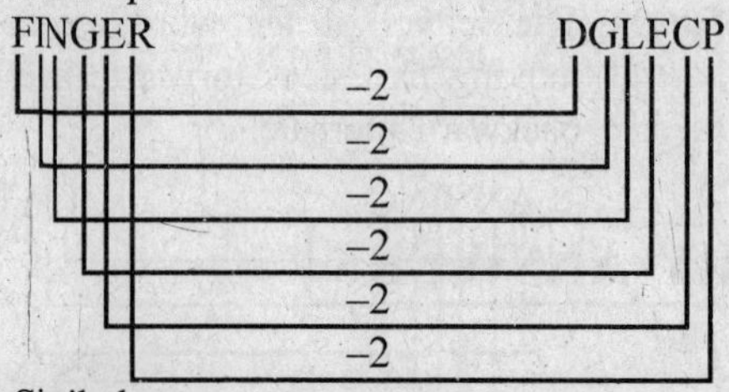

Similarly,

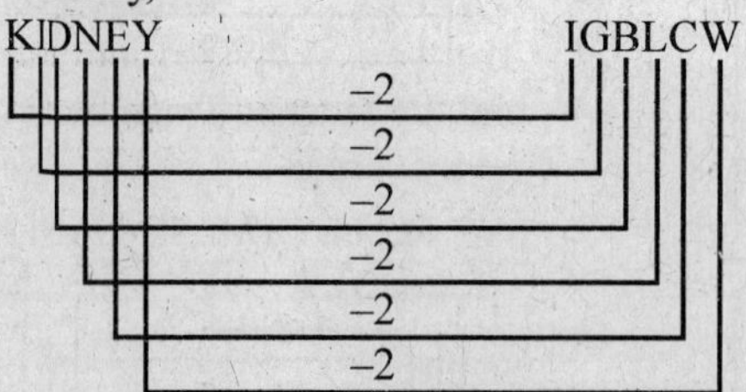

8. *(d)* : The letters of the word are coded by moving three steps backward and three steps forward alternately.

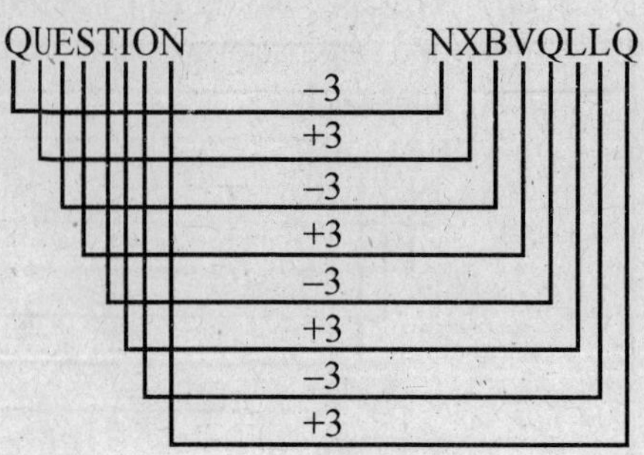

Similarly,

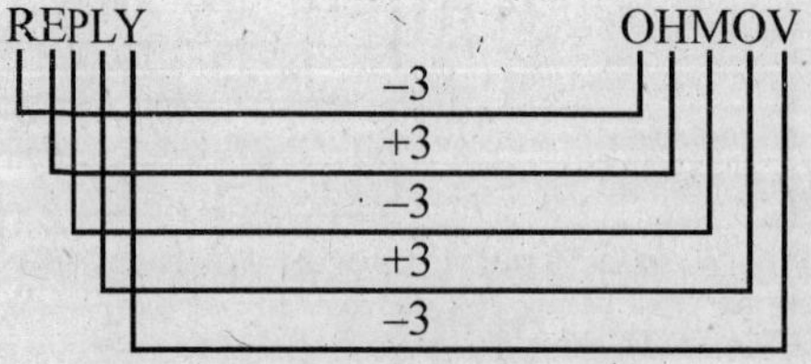

9. *(b)* : The letters are decoded by moving the letters +3, –3, +2 and –2 steps respectively.

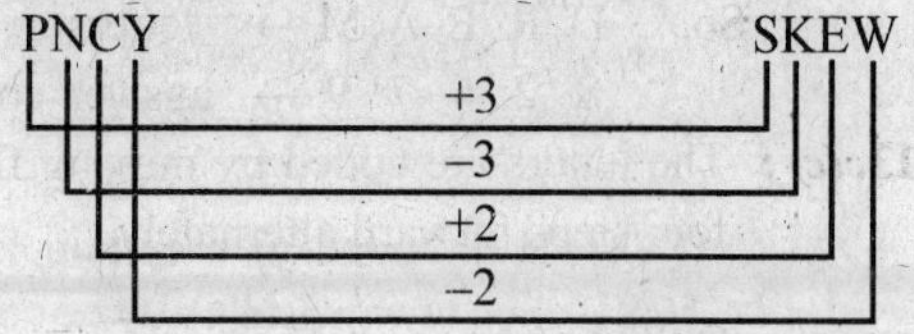

Similarly,

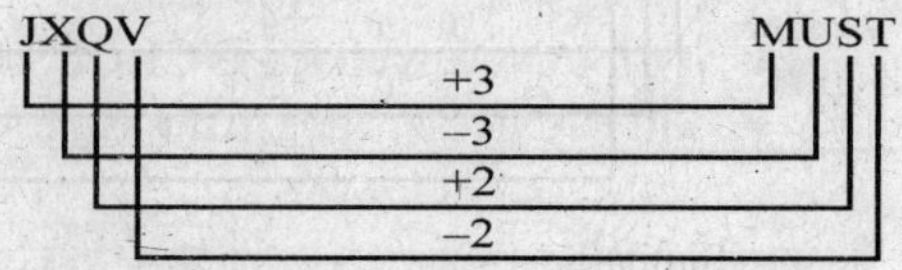

10. *(a)* : The letters of the coded word are moved one step backward.

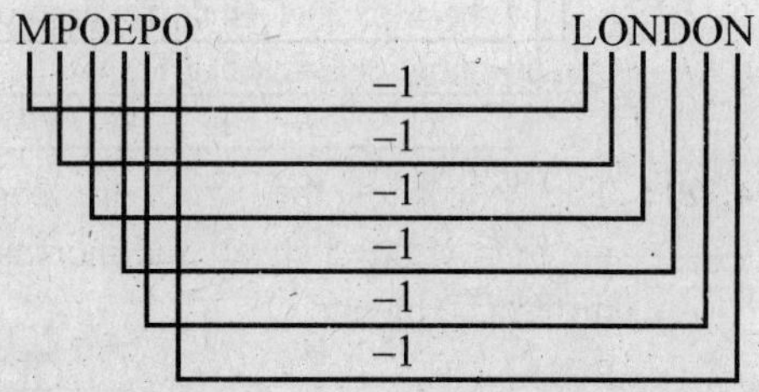

Similarly,

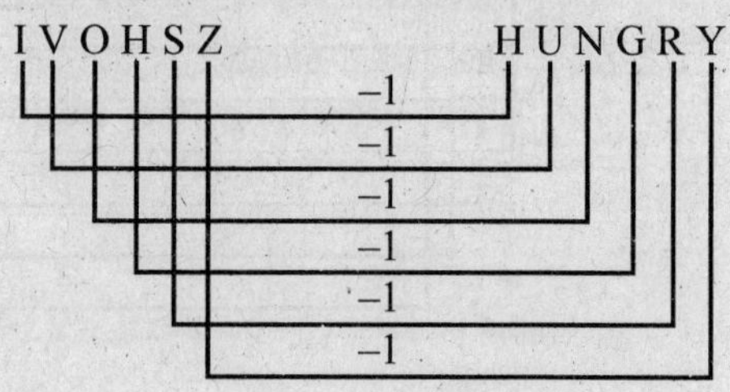

11. *(d)* : The word GRADE is framed by letters in the given words. So, in order to find the code for GRADE select the respective number codes.

H E A D R I D E B E G → letters
8 5 1 4 3 9 4 5 0 5 7 → codes

So,

G R A D E →letters
7 3 1 4 5 →answer codes

12. *(d)* : The letters of the word are coded by numbers. So to find the code for DREAM select the respective numbers.

M O T H E R L A N D → letters
9 5 0 1 6 2 3 7 4 8 → codes

So, D R E A M → letters
8 2 6 7 9 → answer codes

13. (c) : The letters are coded by moving five and four steps forward alternately.

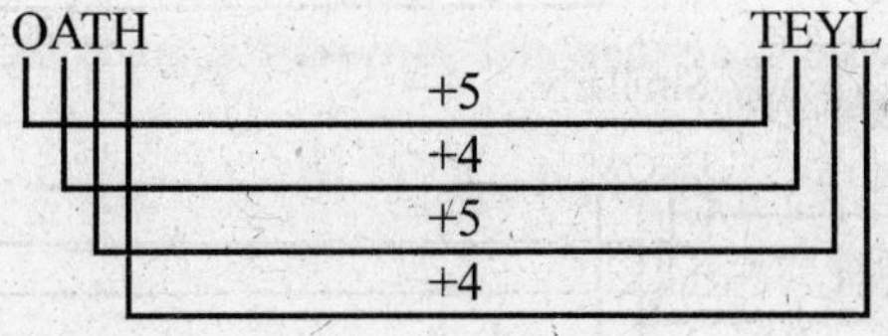

Similarly,

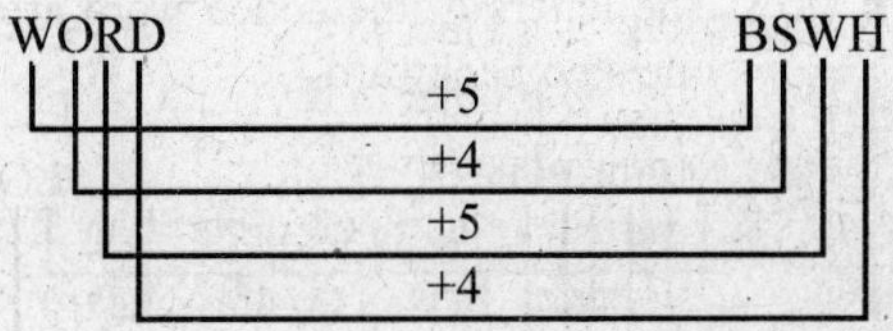

14. (c) : The letters of the word are coded by moving one step ahead and increasing the difference by one.

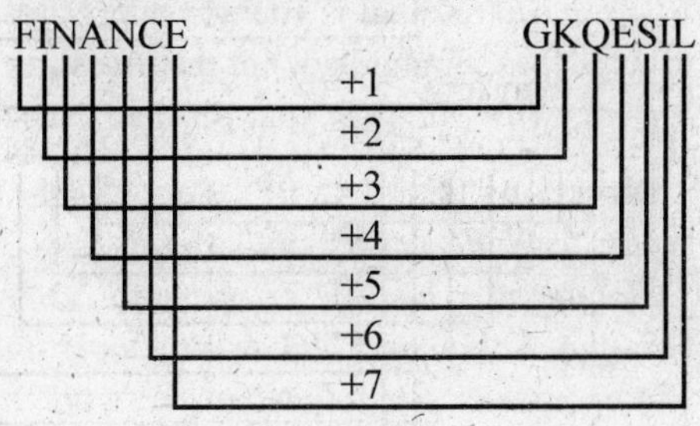

Similarly,

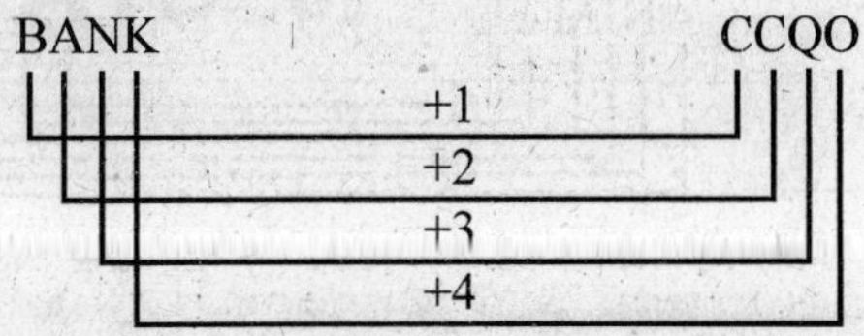

15. (a) : The letters of the word are coded by moving five steps forward and six steps backward alternately.

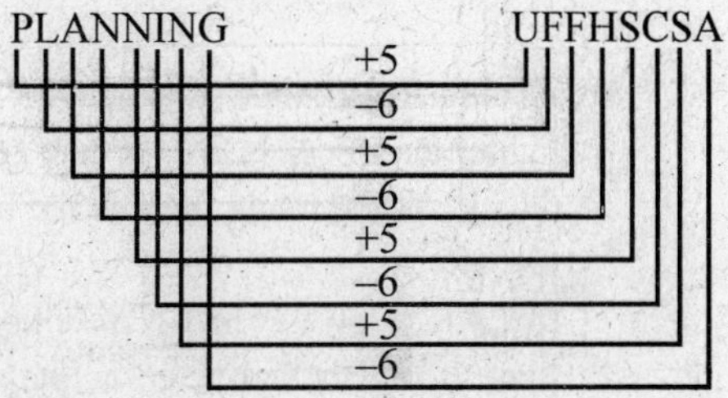

Similarly,

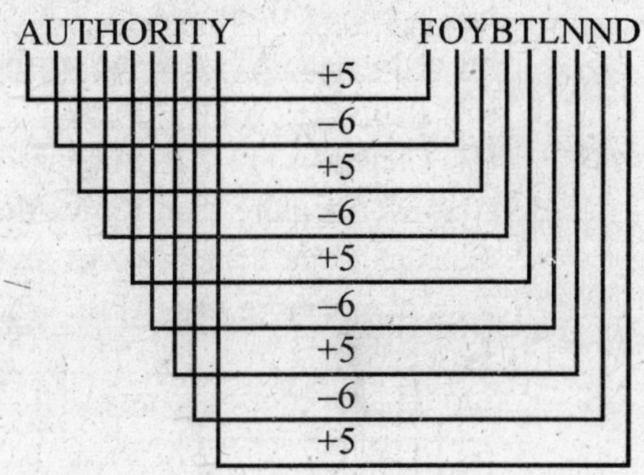

10. STATEMENT ANALYSIS

In these type of questions, a few statements are given. Certain facts are broken up and mentioned in these statements. What is required is to analyse the statements, arrange and sort out the given facts and then answer the questions related to the given statements.

EXERCISE

1. Among five friends, A is heavier than B; C is lighter than D; B is lighter than D but heavier than E. Who among them is the heaviest?

(*a*) B (*b*) C
(*c*) A (*d*) Can't say

2. Pune is bigger than Jhansi, Sitapur is bigger than Chittor. Raigarh is not as big as Jhansi, but is bigger than Sitapur. Chittor is not as big as Sitapur. Which is the smallest?

(*a*) Jhansi (*b*) Pune
(*c*) Chittor (*d*) Sitapur

3. Ajay works more than Ram. Alok works as much as Raju. Pankaj works less than Alok. Ram works more than Alok. Who works the most of all?

(*a*) Ajay (*b*) Ram
(*c*) Alok (*d*) Raju

4. Among five friends P, Q, R, S and T, who is the youngest? To arrive at the answer which of the following information given in the statements (A) and (B) is sufficient?

(A) R is younger than P and T.
(B) S is younger than Q.

(*a*) Only A alone is sufficient
(*b*) Either A or B is sufficient
(*c*) Both A and B together are needed
(*d*) Both A and B together are not sufficient

5. A is elder to B while C and D are elder to E who lies between A and B. If C be elder to B, which one of the following statements is necessarily true?

(*a*) E is elder to B
(*b*) A is elder to C
(*c*) C is elder to D
(*d*) D is elder to C

6. Suresh is as much older than Kamal as he is younger than Prabodh. Navin is as old as Kamal. Which of the following statements is wrong?

(*a*) Suresh is older than Navin
(*b*) Kamal is younger than Suresh
(*c*) Prabodh is not the oldest
(*d*) Navin is younger than Prabodh

Directions (Qs. 7 to 9) : *Ram, Sohan and Mohan play football, hockey and cricket. Ram, Ramesh and Mohan play hockey, cricket and basketball. Ram, Sohan, Rahim and Mohan play football and cricket. Now answer the following questions based on the above statements :*

7. Which game is played by all the boys?

(*a*) Football (*b*) Hockey
(*c*) Cricket (*d*) Basketball

8. Which two boys play all the games?

(*a*) Ram, Sohan (*b*) Ram, Ramesh
(*c*) Sohan, Mohan (*d*) Ram, Mohan

9. Who does not play football?

(*a*) Ramesh (*b*) Sohan
(*c*) Rahim (*d*) Mohan

Directions (Qs. 10 to 12) : *Read the following directions and answer the questions given below :*

There are five persons in a group. Out of these two are men. Only three persons know swimming, of which one is a man. There is a couple, of which the husband knows swimming. A is the younger sister of D and B is the husband of E. C is a swimming champion.

10. Who is the other man in the group?
(*a*) C (*b*) B
(*c*) A (*d*) D

11. The two women who know how to swim are:
(*a*) A and C (*b*) C and D
(*c*) D and E (*d*) A and E

12. The two persons who do not know how to swim are :
(*a*) B and D (*b*) D and E
(*c*) A and E (*d*) A and D

Directions (Qs. 13 to 15) : *Read the following statements and answer the questions given below :*

Rajat, Sushil and Nagesh play football, hockey and cricket. Rajat, Ramu and Nagesh play hockey, cricket and basketball. Rajat, Sushil, Mayank and Nagesh play football and cricket.

13. Which game is played by all the boys?
(*a*) Hockey (*b*) Basketball
(*c*) Football (*d*) Cricket

14. Who does not play football?
(*a*) Rajat (*b*) Nagesh
(*c*) Sushil (*d*) Ramu

15. Which of the following two boys play all the games?
(*a*) Nagesh, Rajat (*b*) Mayank, Ramu
(*c*) Ramu, Nagesh (*d*) Sushil, Mayank

EXPLANATORY ANSWERS

1. (*d*) : The five friends in descending order of weight are : A/D, B/C, E or A/D, B, C/E. Either A or D is the heaviest.

2. (*c*) : The order of cities in descending order of size is : Pune, Jhansi, Raigarh, Sitapur, Chittor.

3. (*a*) : On the basis of doing work, the descending order will be : Ajay, Ram, Alok/Raju, Pankaj.

4. (*d*) : Statements are not inter-related.

5. (*a*) : The order in descending seniority will be : A/C/D, E, B.

6. (*c*) : On the basis of age the descending order will be : Prabodh, Suresh, Kamal/Navin.

Chart for Answers 7 to 9

Boy	*Games Played*
Ram	Football, Hocky, Cricket, Basketball
Sohan	Football, Hockey, Cricket
Mohan	Football, Hockey, Cricket, Basketball
Ramesh	Hockey, Cricket, Basketball
Rahim	Football, Cricket.

7. (*c*) **8. (*d*)** **9. (*a*)**

For Answers 10 to 12 the information chart will be :

A. Woman ((younger sister of D); knows swimming.

B. Man (husband of E); knows swimming

C. Woman; Swimming champion

D. Man (brother of A)

E. Woman (wife of B)

From the couple B & E, B (husband) knows swimming. C is a swimming champion. Three persons know how to swim of which only B is a man. So, the two women who know how to swim are C and A (the younger sister of D). There are two men in the group of five. One is B and the other will be D.

10. (*d*) **11. (*a*)** **12. (*b*)**

Chart for Answers 13 to 15

Boy	*Games Played*
Rajat	— Football, Hockey, Cricket, Basketball
Sushil	— Football, Hockey, Cricket, Basketball
Nagesh	— Football, Hockey, Cricket, Basketball
Ramu	— Hockey, Cricket, Basketball
Mayank	— Football, Cricket

13. (*d*) **14. (*d*)** **15. (*a*)**

11. PLACE ARRANGEMENT

Place arrangement generally refers to the positioning of persons or objects in a manner indicated by set of information given. One has to understand the order of placement and then attempt questions following the given information.

EXERCISE

Directions : *In the following questions, understand the arrangement pattern and then select the right answer from the given options :*

1. Five boys are sitting in a row. Raghu is not adjacent to Shyam or Amit. Ajay is not adjacent to Shyam. Raghu is adjacent to Mayank. If Mayank is at the middle in the row, then Ajay is adjacent to whom out of the following?
   (*a*) Amit (*b*) Raghu
   (*c*) Mayank (*d*) Shyam
2. Mini is to the right of Rajni but to the left of Ananta. Saya is to the right of Mini but to the left of Jaya. Who is on the extreme left if all the girls are facing North?
   (*a*) Jaya (*b*) Mini
   (*c*) Rajni (*d*) Saya
3. O, P, Q, R, S and T are standing on a bench according to their height. P is taller than O but shorter than S. Only S is taller than T. R is shorter than P but taller than Q. Who is the shortest?
   (*a*) O (*b*) Q
   (*c*) P (*d*) Cannot be said
4. Five personalities are living in a multistoried building. Mr. Effortless lives in a flat above Mr. Active, Mr. Charge lives in a flat below Mr. Diligent, Mr. Active lives in a flat above Mr. Diligent and Mr. Behaved lives in a flat below Mr. Charge. Who lives in the topmost flat?
   (*a*) Mr. Charge (*b*) Mr. Diligent
   (*c*) Mr. Effortless (*d*) Mr. Behaved
5. Six friends are sitting in a circle and playing cards. Kenny is to the left of Danny. Michael is in-between Bob and John. Roger is in between Kenny and Bob. Who is sitting to the right of Michael?
   (*a*) Danny (*b*) John
   (*c*) Kenny (*d*) Bob
6. Four girls A, B, C and D are sitting in a circle. B and C are facing each other. Which of the following is definitely true?
   (*a*) A is to the left of C
   (*b*) D is to the left of C
   (*c*) A and D are facing each other
   (*d*) A is not between B and C
7. Brijesh, Jayesh, Amar and Praveer are playing a game of cards. Amar is to the right of Jayesh who is to the right of Brijesh. Who is to the right of Amar?
   (*a*) Brijesh
   (*b*) Praveer
   (*c*) Brijesh or Praveer
   (*d*) Jayesh
8. In a pile of 10 books there are 3 of History, 3 of Hindi, 2 of Maths, and 2 of English. Taking from above there is an English book between a History and Maths book, a History book between a Maths and an English book, a Hindi book between an English and a Maths book, a Maths book between two Hindi books, and two Hindi books between a Maths and a History book. Book of which subject is at the sixth position from the top?
   (*a*) English (*b*) Hindi
   (*c*) History (*d*) Maths

9. Five persons A, B, C, D and E are sitting in a row facing you such that D is on the left of C and B is on the right of E. A is on the right of C and B is on the left of D. If E occupies a corner position, then who is sitting in the centre?
(*a*) A (*b*) B
(*c*) C (*d*) D

10. Six friends A, B, C, D, E and F are standing in a circle. B is between F and C; A is between E and D; F is to the left of D. Who is between A and F?
(*a*) C (*b*) B
(*c*) D (*d*) E

EXPLANATORY ANSWERS

1. *(b)* : The order of sitting is :
Amit, Shyam, Mayank, Ajay, Raghu
or
Ajay, Raghu, Mayank, Amit, Shyam

2. *(c)* : The order in which the girls are positioned is :
Rajni, Mini, Ananta, Saya, Jaya
or
Saya, Jaya, Ananta
or
Saya, Ananta, Jaya

3. *(d)* : In descending order of height, the standing positions are :

S		S
T		T
P	*or*	P
R		R
O		Q
Q		O

Either O or Q is the shortest. The informa-tion given is not enough to clarify the answer.

4. *(c)* : The personalities living in flats in multi-storied building are in order given below :
Mr. Effortless
Mr. Active
Mr. Diligent
Mr. Charge
Mr. Behaved

5. *(d)* : The order in which the friends are sitting is :

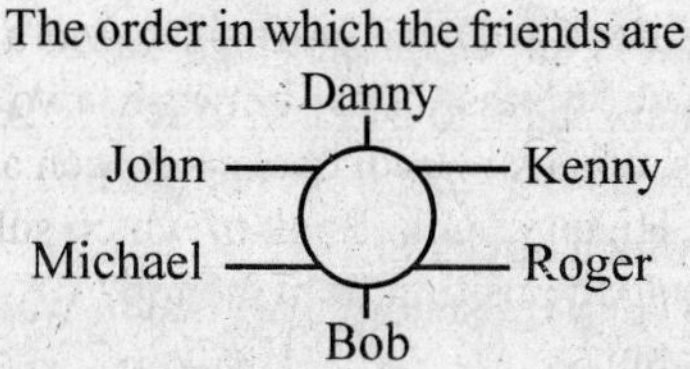

6. *(c)* : The sitting positions are :

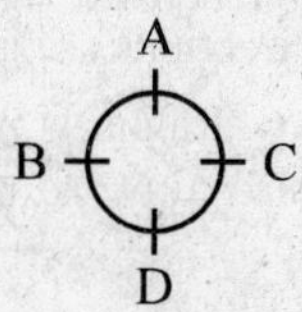

or

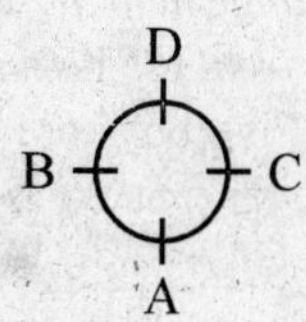

7. *(b)* : The order from left to right is :
Brijesh, Jayesh, Amar, Praveer

8. *(b)* : The pile of books is in the order :

1st — History
English
Maths
History
English
6th — Hindi
Maths
Hindi
Hindi
10th — History

9. *(d)* : Sitting order while facing us is :
A, C, D, B, E

10. *(c)* : The pattern of standing is :

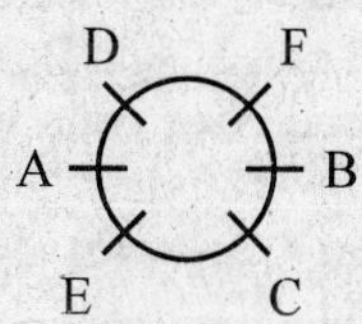

12. DIRECTION SENSE

In these type of tests, the directions in questions needs to be perceived. Such questions are based on the direction chart.

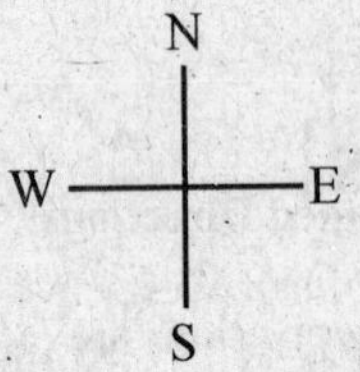

N = North S = South E = East W = West

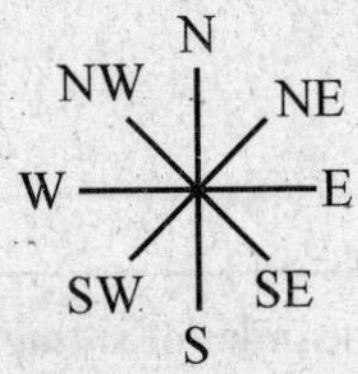

The sense of the different directions are guided by the left and right turns or angular turns.

EXERCISE

Directions : *In the following questions, select the right answer from the given options to depict the correct direction/distance.*

1. Kittu walks towards East and then towards South. After walking some distance he turns towards West and then turns to his left. In which direction is he walking now?

(*a*) North (*b*) South
(*c*) East (*d*) West

2. A person is driving towards West. What sequence of directions should he follow so that he is driving towards South?

(*a*) left, right, right
(*b*) right, right, left
(*c*) left, left, left
(*d*) right, right, right

3. Richa drives 8 km to the South, turns left and drives 5 km. Again, she turns left and drives 8 km. How far is she from her starting point?

(*a*) 3 km (*b*) 5 km
(*c*) 8 km (*d*) 13 km

4. Dingi runs 40 km towards North then turns right and runs 50 km. He turns right and runs 30 km, and once again turns right and runs 50 km. How far is he from his starting point?

(*a*) 90 km (*b*) 50 km
(*c*) 10 km (*d*) 5 km

5. If North is called North-West, North-West is called West, West is called South-West and so on. What will South-East be called?

(*a*) East (*b*) West
(*c*) North-East (*d*) South-East

6. A man travels 100 km towards South. From there he turns right and travels 100 km and again turns right to travel 50 km. Which direction is he in from his starting point?

(*a*) North (*b*) North-East
(*c*) East (*d*) South-West

7. A train runs 120 km in West direction, 30 km in South direction and then 80 km in east direction before reaching the station. In which direction is the station from the train's starting point?

(*a*) South-West (*b*) North-West
(*c*) South-East (*d*) South

8. Facing the West direction, Priya jogs for 20 m, turns left and goes further 40 m. She turns left again and jogs for 20 m. Then she turns right to go 20 m to reach the park. How far is the park from her starting point and in which direction?

(*a*) 20 m South (*b*) 40 m West
(*c*) 60 m South (*d*) 100 m East

9. If all the directions are rotated, *i.e.,* if North is changed to West and East to North and so on, then what will come in place of North-West?

(*a*) South-West (*b*) North-East

(*c*) East-North (*d*) East-West

10. A and B start together from one point. They walk 10 km towards North. A turns left and covers 5 km whereas B turns right and covers 3 km. A turns left again and covers 15 km whereas B turns right and covers his 15 km. How far is A from B?

(*a*) 18 km (*b*) 10 km

(*c*) 5 km (*d*) 8 km

EXPLANATORY ANSWERS

1. (*b*) :

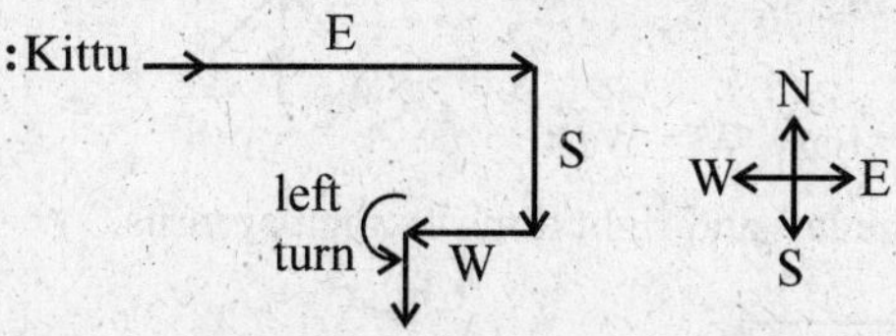

2. (*d*) :

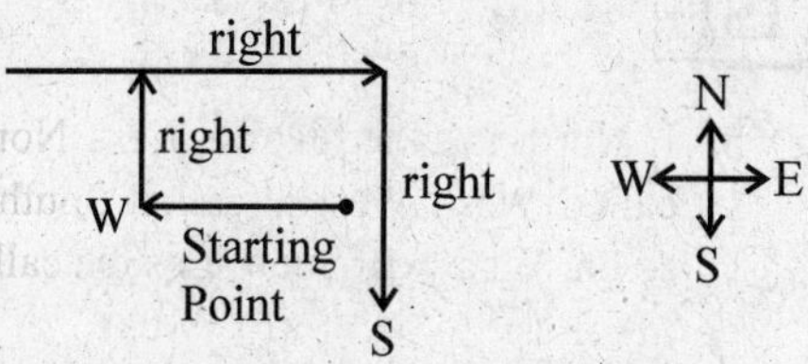

3. (*b*) :

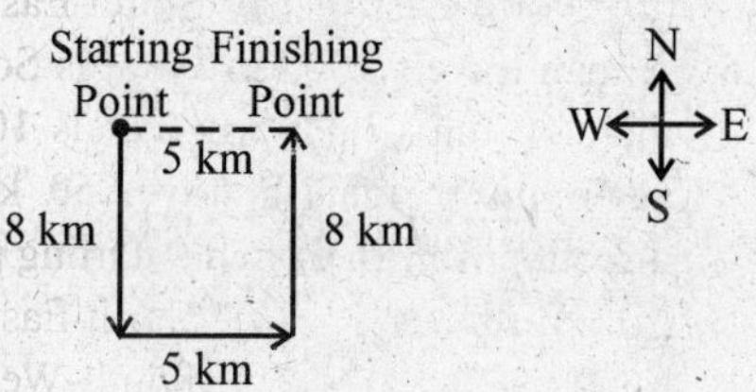

4. (*c*) :

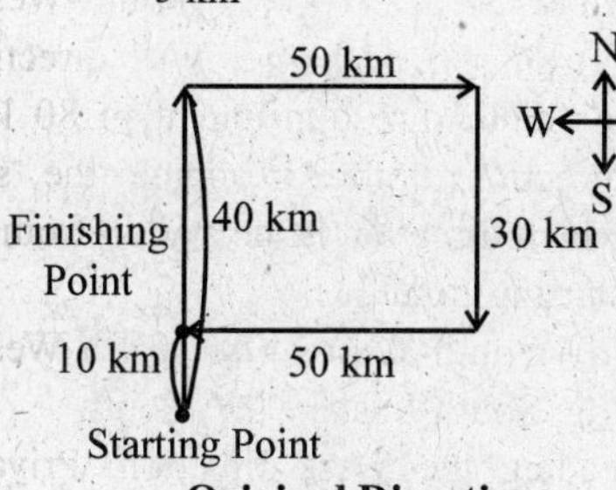

5. (*a*) : **Original Directions**

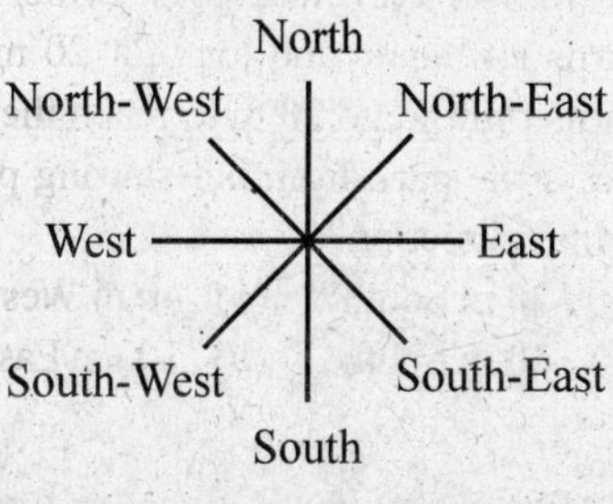

Changed Directions

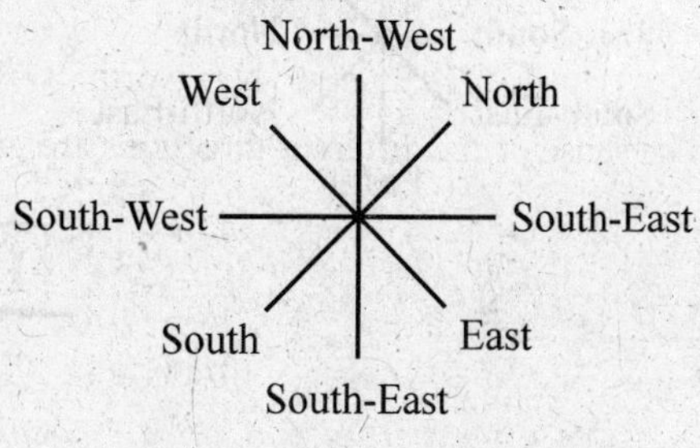

6. (*d*) :

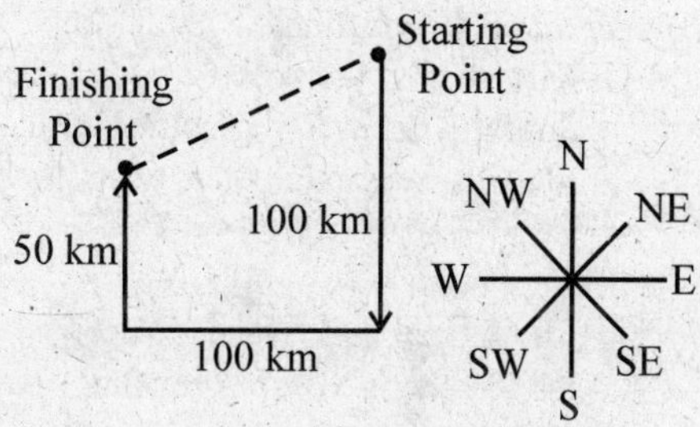

7. (*a*) :

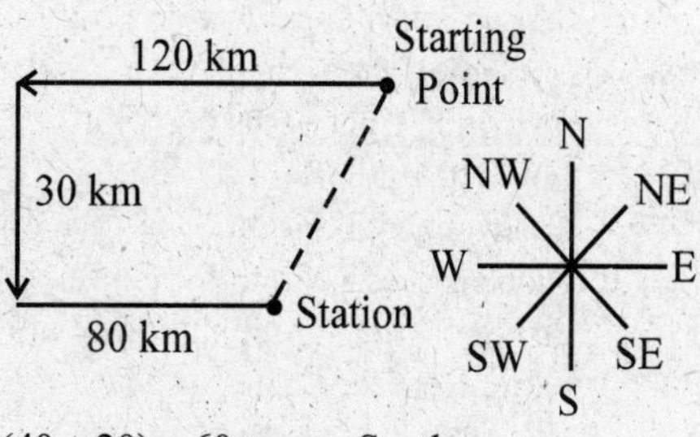

8. (*c*) : (40 + 20) = 60 metres South

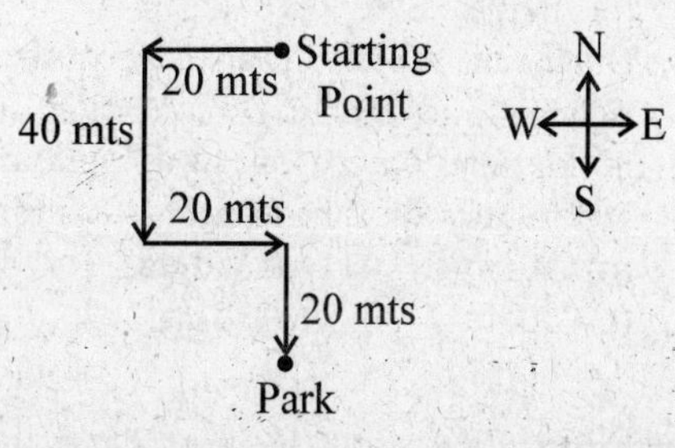

9. *(a)* : **Original Directions**

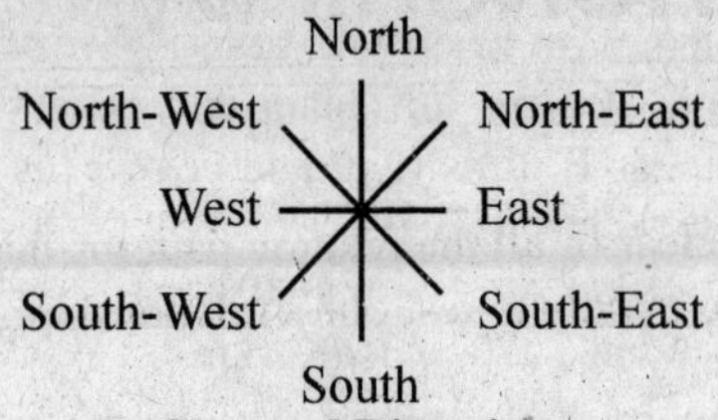

Changed Directions

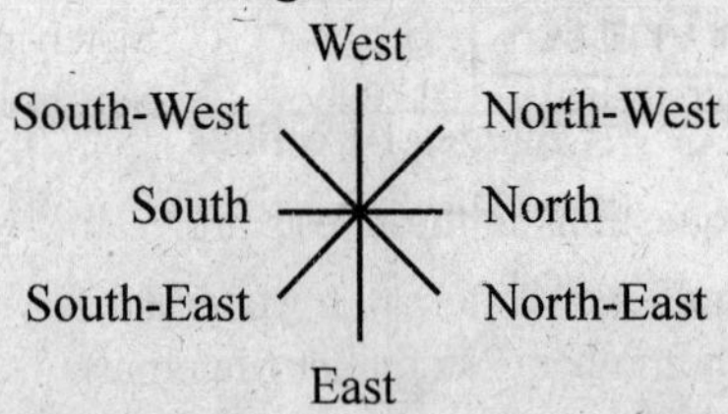

10. *(d)* :

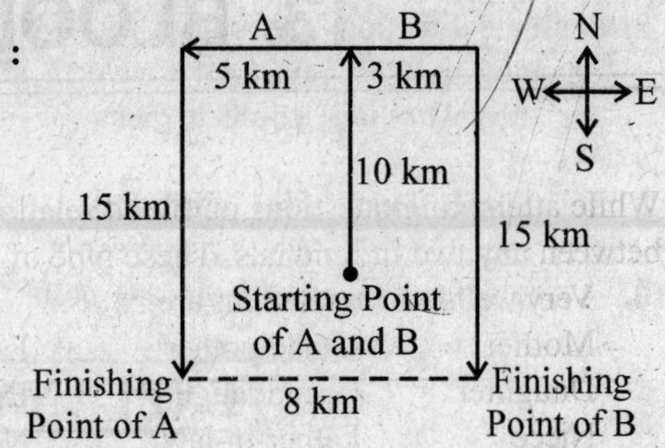

13. BLOOD RELATIONSHIPS

While attempting questions on blood relations, one should be clear of all the relation patterns that can exist between any two individuals. These type of questions are given mainly to test one's relationship ability.

Very well-known relations are :

Mother	Grandmother	Father	Grandfather	Son	Grandson
Daughter	Granddaughter	Brother	Brother-in-law	Sister	Sister-in-law
Niece	Father-in-law	Nephew	Mother-in-law	Uncle	Son-in-law
Aunt	Daughter-in-law	Husband	Cousin	Wife	

The patterns of some relationships which help in solving questions in these tests are :

Father's *or* Mother's Father	—	Grandfather (Paternal *or* Maternal)
Father's *or* Mother's Mother	—	Grandmother (Paternal *or* Maternal)
Father's *or* Mother's Son	—	Brother
Father's *or* Mother's Daughter	—	Sister
Father's Brother	—	Paternal Uncle
Father's Sister	—	Paternal Aunt
Mother's Brother	—	Maternal Uncle
Mother's Sister	—	Maternal Aunt
Uncle *or* Aunt's Son *or* Daughter	—	Cousin
Son's Wife	—	Daughter-in-law
Daughter's Husband	—	Son-in-law
Husband's *or* Wife's Brother	—	Brother-in-law
Husband's *or* Wife's Sister	—	Sister-in-law
Brother's Wife	—	Sister-in-law
Sister's Husband	—	Brother-in-law
Brother's Son	—	Nephew
Brother's Daughter	—	Niece

EXERCISE

Directions : *In each of the following questions keenly study the relationship mentioned between the persons, and then from the given options select the right relationship as the answer.*

1. A lady said, "The person standing there is my grandfather's only son's daughter". How is the lady related to the standing person?
   (*a*) Sister (*b*) Mother
   (*c*) Aunt (*d*) Cousin
2. Ajay is the brother of Vijay. Mili is the sister of Ajay. Sanjay is the brother of Rahul and Mehul is the daughter of Vijay. Who is Sanjay's Uncle?
   (*a*) Rahul (*b*) Ajay
   (*c*) Mehul (*d*) Data inadequate
3. A man introduced the boy coming with him as "He is son of the father of my wife's daughter". What relation did the boy bear to the man?
   (*a*) Son-in-law (*b*) Son
   (*c*) Brother (*d*) Father
4. If Amit's father is Billoo's father's only son and Billoo has neither a brother nor a

daughter, what is the relationship between Amit and Billoo?
(*a*) Uncle — Nephew
(*b*) Father — Daughter
(*c*) Father — Son
(*d*) Cousins

5. Pointing to a woman in the photograph a man said, "She is the daughter of my grand-mother's only son." How is the woman related to the man?
(*a*) Mother (*b*) Daughter
(*c*) Sister-in-law (*d*) Sister

6. Pointing to a photograph, a woman said, "She is the only daughter of my mother's father." How is the woman related to the person in the photograph?
(*a*) Mother
(*b*) Grandmother
(*c*) Daughter
(*d*) Cannot be determined

7. Ram is the brother of Shyam and Mahesh is the father of Ram. Jagat is the brother of Priya and Priya is daughter of Shyam. Who is the uncle of Jagat ?
(*a*) Shyam (*b*) Mahesh
(*c*) Ram (*d*) Data insufficient

8. Introducing a man, a woman said, "His wife is the only daughter of my father". How is the man related to the woman?
(*a*) Husband (*b*) Father
(*c*) Father-in-law (*d*) Brother

9. If Maya is the only daughter of Richa's grandmother's brother, how is Maya's daughter related to Richa?
(*a*) Niece (*b*) Cousin
(*c*) Aunt (*d*) Mother

10. Pointing to a woman, a man said, "Her husband's mother is the wife of my father's only son". How is the man related to the woman?
(*a*) Son (*b*) Brother-in-law
(*c*) Uncle (*d*) Father-in-law

EXPLANATORY ANSWERS

1. (*a*) :

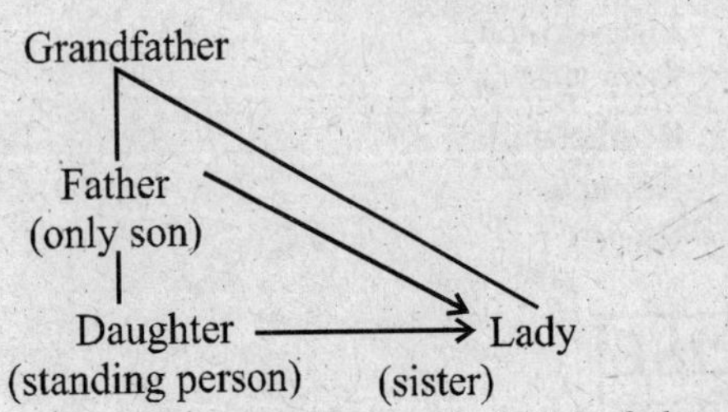

Lady's grandfather's son is lady's father and father's daughter will only be lady's sister.

2. (*d*) : 1. Mili ⟶ (sister) Ajay ⟶ (brother) Vijay ↓ Mehul (daughter)

2. Sanjay ⟶ (brother) Rahul

There are two sets of relationship. Information given is incomplete and no relation can be established between the two sets.

3. (*b*) : The relationship chart based on problem is :

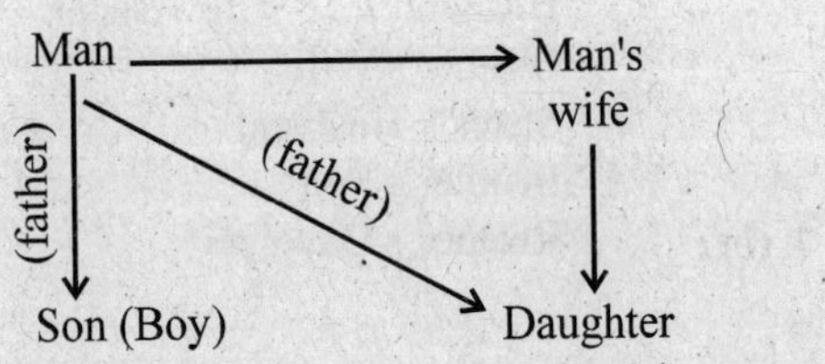

'Father of the man's wife's daughter' is the man himself and the boy in question is the man's son.

4. (*c*) : The relationship chart based on problem is :

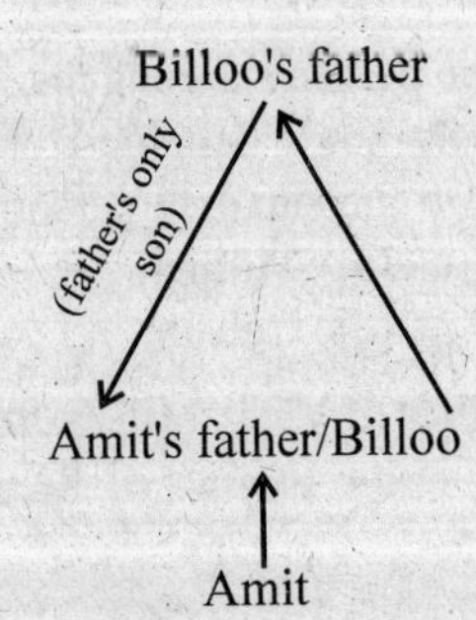

Amit's father is Billoo's father's only son means Billoo is the only son in question also, he is the father of Amit. It must be noted that Billoo has no brother which means he is single and also, when he has no daughter, Amit is his only son.

5. (*d*) :

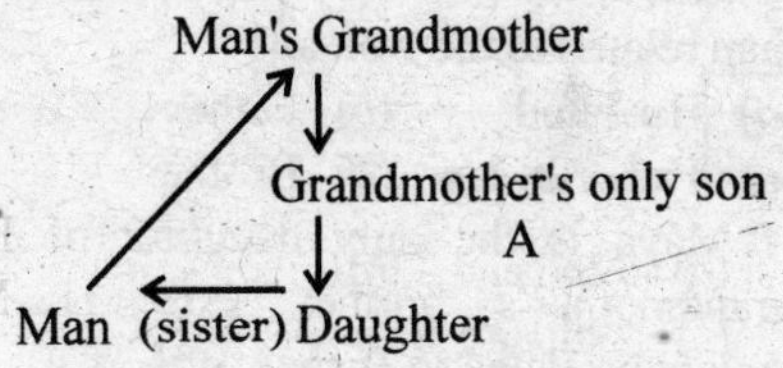

'My grandmother's only son' is the father of the man, and 'daughter of my grand-mother's only son' is the sister of the man.

6. (*c*) :

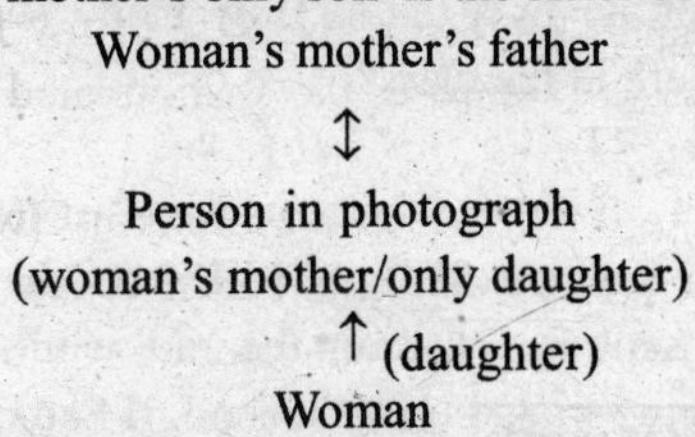

'Only daughter of my mother's father' is the person in the photograph and she is also the mother of the woman. So, the woman is the daughter of the person in the photo-graph.

7. (*c*) :

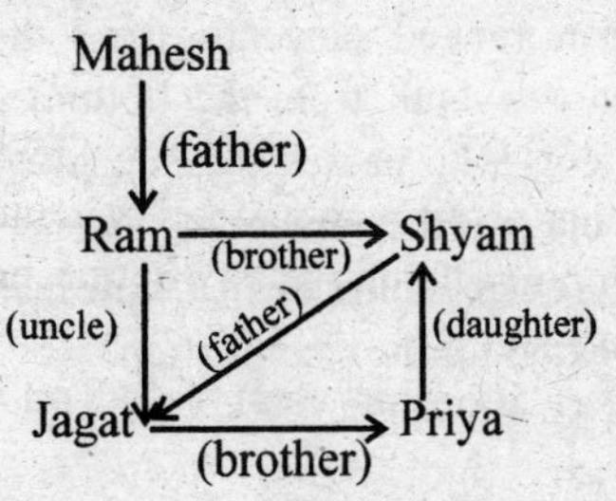

Jagat is brother of Priya and Priya is daughter of Shyam. So Shyam is also the father of Jagat. Ram is the brother of Shyam. So, Jagat's father's brother Ram is the uncle of Jagat.

8. (*a*) :

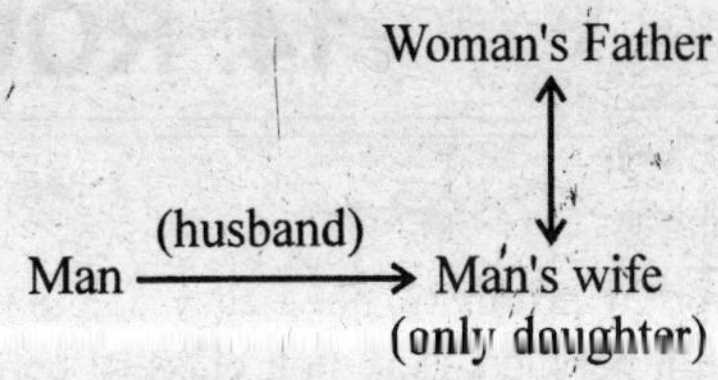

'Only daughter of my father' is the woman herself and the man is her husband.

9. (*b*) :

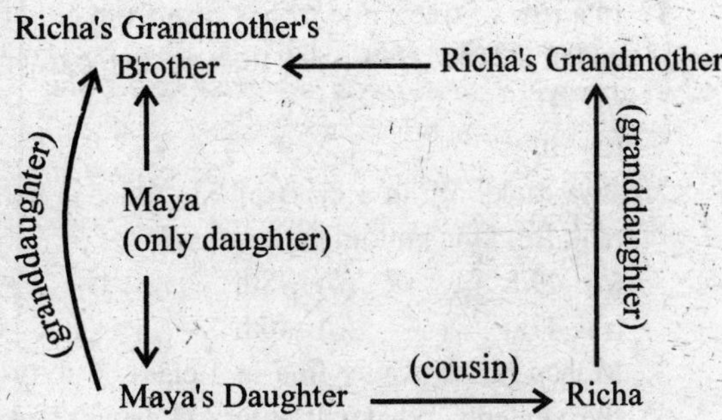

Both Maya's Daughter and Richa are granddaughters of a brother and a sister respectively. So Maya's daughter is the cousin of Richa.

10. (*d*) :

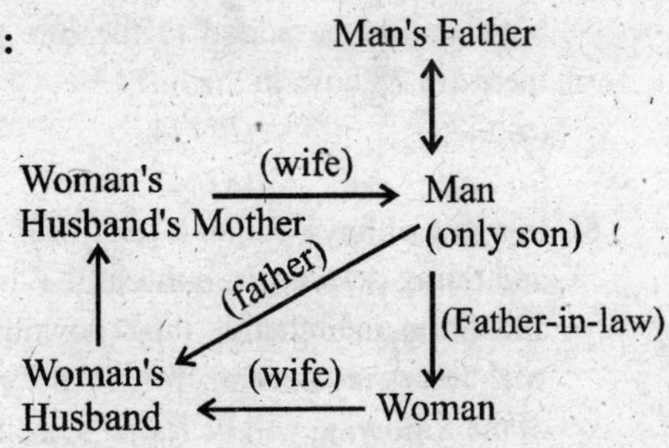

'My father's only son' is the man himself. 'Her husband's mother' is the wife of the man and so the man is the father of the woman's husband. As the woman is the wife of man's son, the man is the father-in-law of the woman.

14. ROWS AND RANKS

These type of problems need easy calculations to find out the number of objects in a row, lane or queue or to find a person's rank in a class of certain number of students; or to find the total number of students.

EXERCISE

1. In a row of trees, one tree is fifth from either end of the row. How many trees are in the row?
(*a*) 11 (*b*) 8
(*c*) 10 (*d*) 9

2. Jaya ranks 5th in a class of 53. What is her rank from the bottom in the class?
(*a*) 49th (*b*) 48th
(*c*) 47th (*d*) 50th

3. Mohan ranks twenty-first in a class of sixty-five students. What will be his (Mohan's) rank if the lowest candidate is assigned rank 1?
(*a*) 44th (*b*) 45th
(*c*) 46th (*d*) Data inadequate

4. If Rahul finds that he is 12th from the right in a line of boys and 4th from the left, how many boys should be added to the line such that there are 28 boys in the line?
(*a*) 12 (*b*) 14
(*c*) 20 (*d*) 13

5. In a row of boys, Rajan is tenth from the right and Suraj is tenth from the left. When Rajan and Suraj interchange their positions, Suraj will be twenty-seventh from the left. Which of the following will be Rajan's position from the right?
(*a*) Tenth
(*b*) Twenty-sixth
(*c*) Twenty-ninth
(*d*) None of these

6. Mahesh and Suresh are ranked 11th and 12th respectively from the top in a class of 41 students. What will be their respective ranks from the bottom?
(*a*) 32nd and 33rd
(*b*) 29th and 30th
(*c*) 30th and 31st
(*d*) 31st and 30th

7. Uma ranked 8th from the top and 37th from bottom in a class. How many students are there in the class?
(*a*) 47 (*b*) 46
(*c*) 45 (*d*) None of these

8. In a queue, Sadiq is 14th from the front and Joseph is 17th from the end, while Jane is in between Sadiq and Joseph. If Sadiq be ahead of Joseph and there be 48 persons in the queue, how many persons are there between Sadiq and Jane?
(*a*) 5 (*b*) 6
(*c*) 7 (*d*) 8

9. Rohan ranked eleventh from the top and twenty-seventh from the bottom among the students who passed the annual examination in a class. If the number of students who failed in the examination was 12, how many students appeared for the examination?
(*a*) 48
(*b*) 49
(*c*) 50
(*d*) Cannot be determined

10. Some boys are sitting in a row. P is sitting fourteenth from the left and Q is seventh from the right. If there are four boys between P and Q, how many boys are there in the row?
(*a*) 19 (*b*) 21
(*c*) 25 (*d*) 23

EXPLANATORY ANSWERS

1. (*d*):

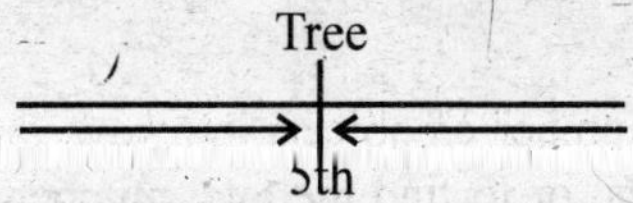

Total number of trees in the row are :
$(5+5)-1=9$.

2. (*a*) :

Jaya's rank from the bottom is :
$(53-5)+1=49$th.

3. (*b*) :

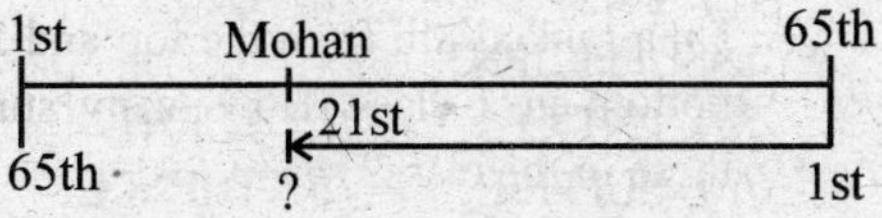

Note : Mohan's rank from the last or the question asked means the same.
Mohan's rank is $(65-21)+1=45$th.

4. (*d*) :

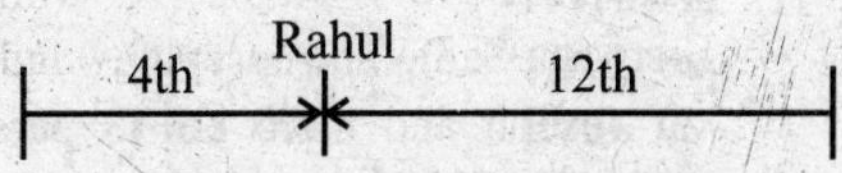

The number of boys in the line are :
$(4+12)-1=15$
To make a line of 28 boys, $(28-15)$ *i.e.* 13 more boys are needed.

5. (*d*) :

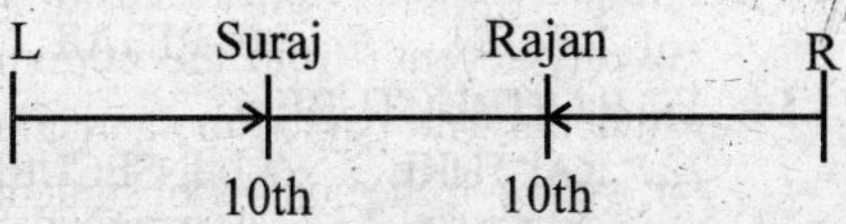

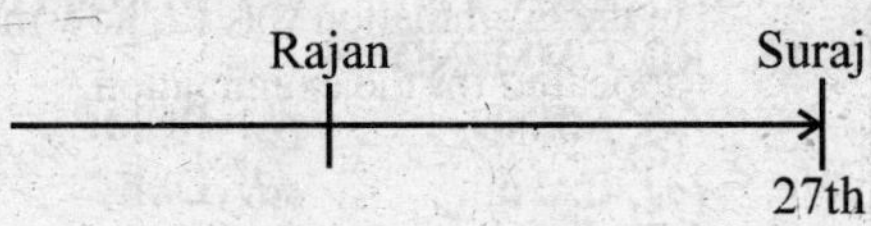

As the position of boys is equal from both ends, Rajan will also be 27th from the right after changing positions.

6. (*d*) :

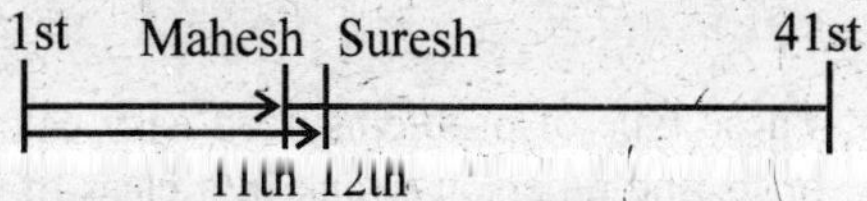

Mahesh's position from bottom is :
$(41-11)+1=31$st
Suresh's position from bottom is :
$(41-12)+1=30$th.

7. (*d*) :

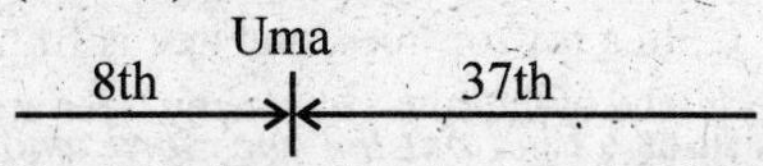

Total number of students in the class are :
$(8+37)-1=44$.

8. (*d*) :

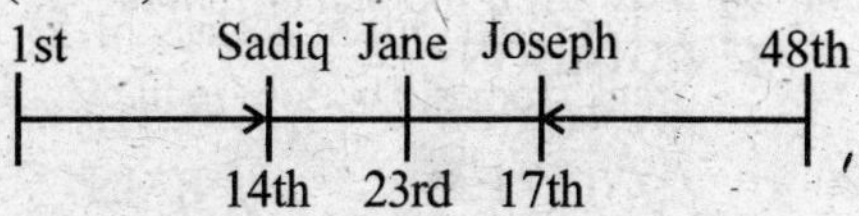

Sadiq's position from front : 14th
Joseph's position from last :
17th or $48-17+1=32$nd from front.
Middle postion between Sadiq & Joseph

$$=\frac{(32-14)}{2}+14=23\text{ rd.}$$

Hence, Jane position is 23rd from front
Person between Sadiq & Jane
$=23-14-1=8$.

9. (*b*) :

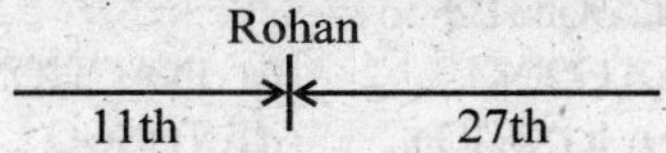

Number of students who passed the examination $(11+27)-1=37$
Those who failed $=12$
Total number of students who appeared in the examination $=37+12=49$.

10. (*c*) :

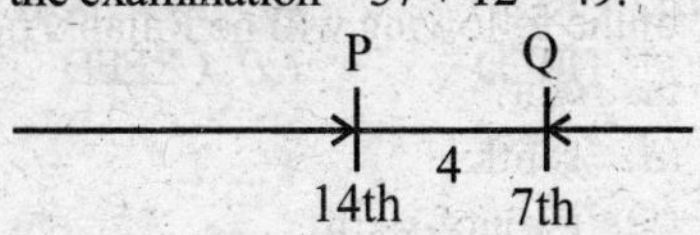

The number of boys in the row are :
$(14+4+7)=25$.

15. PERMUTATIONS AND COMBINATIONS

In these type of questions, the only factor essential is alertness. In every question, a word is given. By using the letters of this given word the options are formed. The candidates are required to find from the given options the word *(i)* which cannot be formed by using the letters of the given word or *(ii)* which can be formed by using the letters of the given word.

EXERCISE

Directions : *Find out the one word among the options which cannot be formed by using the letters of the word as given in each question.*

1. ROTATION
(a) TORN *(b)* NOTE
(c) TART *(d)* RAIN

2. PHILOSOPHY
(a) SOIL *(b)* SHIP
(c) SOLO *(d)* SPIN

3. SLAVATION
(a) SNORT *(b)* LATVIA
(c) SALIVA *(d)* AVAIL

4. ACADEMY
(a) DEMY *(b)* MACE
(c) DIRE *(d)* MADE

5. INCOGNITO
(a) GOING *(b)* INACTION
(c) IGNITION *(d)* TONGO

6. JUDICIARY
(a) INJURY *(b)* CADDY
(c) DICY *(d)* ACRID

7. DOCTRINE
(a) CRUST *(b)* DOCTOR
(c) TIRED *(d)* CREED

8. EDUCATED
(a) DATE *(b)* CUTE
(c) EAST *(d)* DUCT

9. INSUFFICIENT
(a) ENTICE *(b)* SCENT
(c) SUFFICE *(d)* THENCE

10. DECEMBER
(a) REDEEM *(b)* DECREE
(c) BRACED *(d)* MEMBER

11. FUGITIVE
(a) EXIT *(b)* FIVE
(c) GIVE *(d)* GIFT

12. CATASTROPHE
(a) TASTE *(b)* CHEAP
(c) POUCH *(d)* STARE

13. TORRENTIAL
(a) TRAIL *(b)* MENTAL
(c) LEARN *(d)* RETAIL

14. INFRASTRUCTURE
(a) RAPTURE *(b)* INSECURE
(c) CRAFTS *(d)* STRUCTURE

15. RECOMMEND
(a) MEND *(b)* ROME
(c) CANE *(d)* OMEN

ANSWERS

1	2	3	4	5	6	7	8	9	10
(b)	*(d)*	*(a)*	*(c)*	*(b)*	*(a)*	*(a)*	*(c)*	*(d)*	*(c)*
11	**12**	**13**	**14**	**15**					
(a)	*(c)*	*(b)*	*(a)*	*(c)*					

16. SYMBOL SUBSTITUTION

Questions in these category are easy to attempt. Candidates must be quick in substituting symbols and calculations. The common pattern of questions asked are given below.

EXERCISE

1. If "+" means "–"; "–" means "×"; "×" means "÷" and "÷" means "+", then
$15 \times 5 \div 10 + 5 - 3 = ?$
(a) 9.5 *(b)* 0
(c) –2 *(d)* 24

2. If "+" means "×"; "–" means "÷"; "÷" means "+" and "×" means "–", then what will be the value of $20 \div 40 - 4 \times 5 + 6 = ?$
(a) 60 *(b)* 1.67
(c) 150 *(d)* 0

3. If × stands for addition, < for subtraction, + stands for division, > for multiplication, – stands for equal to, ÷ for greater than, and = stands for less than, state which of the following is true?
(a) $5 \times 3 < 7 \div 8 + 4 \times 1$
(b) $3 \times 4 > 2 - 9 + 3 < 3$
(c) $5 > 2 + 2 = 10 < 4 \times 8$
(d) $3 \times 2 < 4 \div 16 > 2 + 4$

4. If → stands for subract, ← stands for add, ↓↑ ↑ stands for multiply, ↓ ↓ stands for divide, ↔ for greater than, ⟷ stands for equal to, then which of the following alternatives is true?
(a) 4 ← 6 ↑ ↑ 2 ⟷ 3 → 12 ← 12
(b) 10 ↓ ↓ 5 ↑ ↑ 5 ⟷ 9 → 3 ← 4
(c) 15 ↑ ↑ 2 → 5 ⟷ 12 ↓ ↓ 4 ← 3
(d) 13 ↓ ↓ 13 ← 1 ↔ 20 → 5 ↑ ↑ 2

5. If Δ denotes =; + denotes >, – denotes <, □ denotes ≠, × denotes > and ÷ denotes < then a + b – c denotes
(a) b Δ c □ a
(b) b □ a ÷ c
(c) a ÷ b × c
(d) b – a + c

6. If '✱' denotes '×', 'Δ' denotes '÷', '□' denotes '–', '●' denotes '+', 'α' denotes '=' and 'β' denotes ≠, then which of the following euations is correct?
(a) 2 □ 10 ✱ 4 Δ 5 α 5 ● 12 Δ 6
(b) 27 Δ 9 ● 6 β 3 ✱ 6 □ 9
(c) 4 Δ 2 ✱ 0 α 7 Δ 1 ✱ 0
(d) 5 ● 6 Δ 3 □ 2 α 8 Δ 4 ✱ 3

7. If ↓ stands for '÷', ↑ stands for '×', → stands for '+' and ← stands for '–', then
25 ↓ 5 → 3 ↑ 6 ← 8 = ?
(a) 9 *(b)* 12
(c) 16 *(d)* 15

8. If the + and × signs of the following equations are interchanged, which will be the correct equation?
(a) $7 \times 5 + 3 = 20$
(b) $4 + 9 \times 1 = 42$
(c) $6 \times 5 + 8 = 46$
(d) $2 + 11 \times 4 = 28$

9. If '+' stands for multiplication, '×' stands for addition, '÷' stands for subtraction and '–' stands for division, then what will be the result of the following equation?
$7 \times 4 \div 10 \times 2 + 5 = ?$
(a) 7 *(b)* 0
(c) 11 *(d)* 15

10. If 'A' means '÷', 'B' means '+', 'C' means '×' and 'D' means '–', then
12 C 4 A 24 D 10 B 1 = ?
(a) $11\frac{1}{3}$ *(b)* 23
(c) –7 *(d)* $16\frac{4}{5}$

EXPLANATORY ANSWERS

1. (c) : $15 \div 5 + 10 - 5 \times 3$

$3 + 10 - 15 = -2$

2. (d) : $20 + 40 \div 4 - 5 \times 6$

$20 + 10 - 30 = 0$

3. (c) : (a) $5 + 3 - 7 > 8 \div 4 + 1$

$1 > 3$

(b) $3 + 4 \times 2 = 9 \div 3 - 3$

$11 = 0$

(c) $5 \times 2 \div 2 < 10 - 4 + 8$

$5 < 14$

(d) $3 + 2 - 4 > 16 \times 2 \div 4$

$1 > 8$

4. (b) : (a) $4 + 6 \times 2 = 3 - 12 + 12$

$16 = 3$

(b) $10 \div 5 \times 5 = 9 - 3 + 4$

$10 = 10$

(c) $15 \times 2 - 5 = 12 \div 4 + 3$

$25 = 6$

(d) $13 \div 13 + 1 > 20 - 5 \times 2$

$2 > 10$

5. (d) : What is given is a > b < c

The equations are :

(a) b = c ≠ a which is wrong

(b) b ≠ a < c which is wrong

(c) a < b > c which is wrong

(d) b < a > c which is correct

Therefore, (*d*) is the answer.

6. (c) : The solved equations will be :

(a) $2 - 10 \times 4 \div 5 = 5 + 12 \div 6$

$2 - 8 = 5 + 2$

$-6 = 7$ which is wrong

(b) $27 \div 9 + 6 \neq 3 \times 6 - 9$

$3 + 6 \neq 18 - 9$

$9 \neq 9$ which is wrong

(c) $4 \div 2 \times 0 = 7 \div 1 \times 0$

$2 \times 0 = 7 \times 0$

$0 = 0$ which is correct

(d) $5 + 6 \div 3 - 2 = 8 \div 4 \times 3$

$5 = 6$ which is wrong

7. (d) : $25 \div 5 + 3 \times 6 - 8$

$5 + 18 - 8 = 15$

8. (c) : After interchanging the signs the equations are :

(a) $7 + 5 \times 3 = 22$ which is wrong

(b) $4 \times 9 + 1 = 37$ which is wrong

(c) $6 + 5 \times 8 = 46$ which is correct

(d) $2 \times 11 + 4 = 26$ which is wrong

9. (c) : $7 + 4 - 10 + 2 \times 5$

$7 + 4 - 10 + 10 = 11$

10. (c) : $12 \times 4 \div 24 - 10 + 1$

$2 - 10 + 1 = -7$

17. MISSING NUMBERS

Playing with numbers and mathematical skills are needed to attempt these type of tests. The candidates have to work out the right combination of arithmetical symbols to arrive at the answer options which will take the place of the interrogation sign in the given questions.

EXERCISE

Directions: *In each question given below which one number can be placed at the sign of interrogation?*

1.

(a) 693 *(b)* 939
(c) 981 *(d)* 993

2.

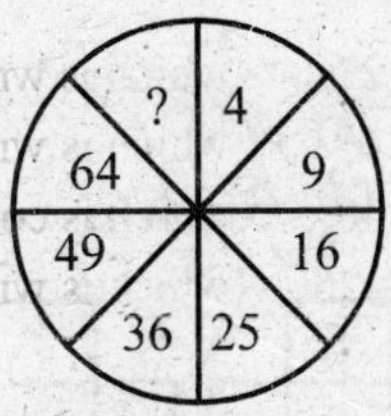

(a) 68 *(b)* 100
(c) 72 *(d)* 81

3.

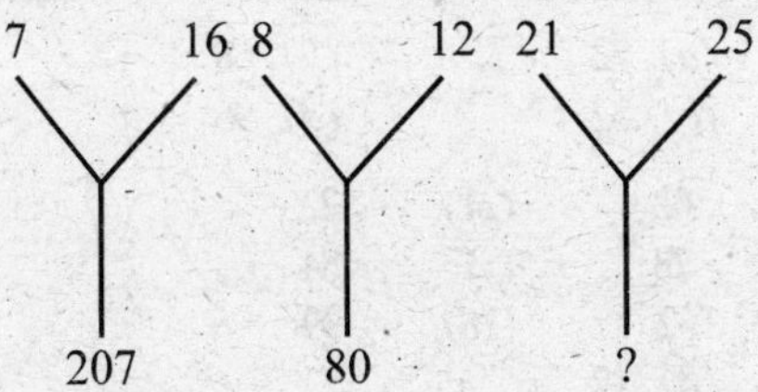

(a) 425 *(b)* 184
(c) 241 *(d)* 210

4.

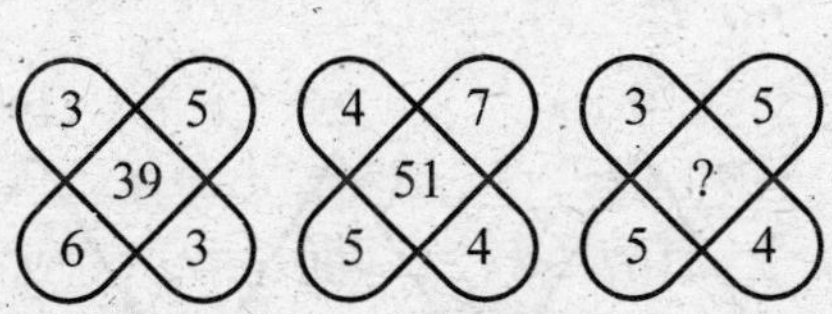

(a) 35 *(b)* 37
(c) 45 *(d)* 48

5.

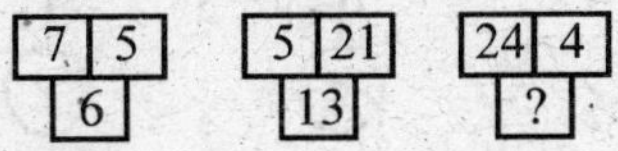

(a) 4 *(b)* 8
(c) 20 *(d)* 14

6.

14	9	4
12	7	2
10	5	0
16	11	?

(a) 9 *(b)* 6
(c) 3 *(d)* 7

7.

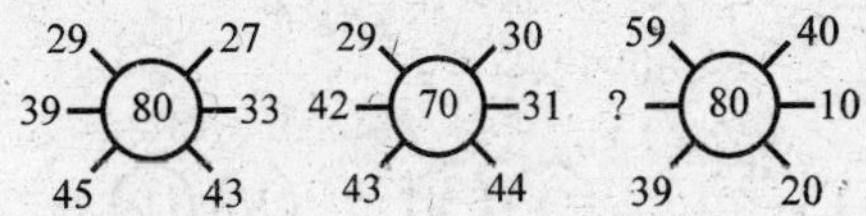

(a) 69 *(b)* 49
(c) 50 *(d)* 60

8.

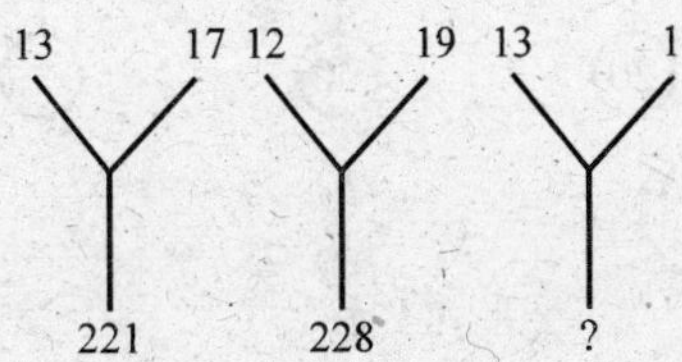

(a) 31 *(b)* 229
(c) 234 *(d)* 312

9.

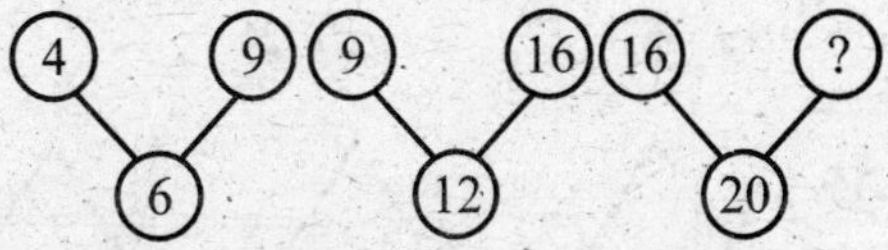

(a) 21 *(b)* 25
(c) 50 *(d)* 60

10.

51	(11)	61
64	(30)	32
35	(?)	43

(a) 25 *(b)* 27
(c) 32 *(d)* 37

11.

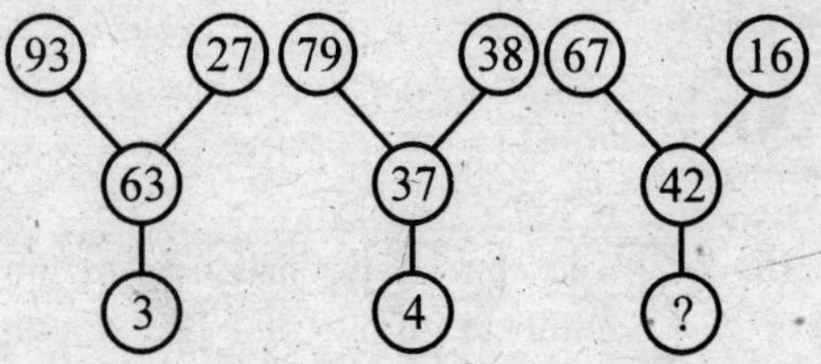

(a) 5 *(b)* 6
(c) 8 *(d)* 9

12.

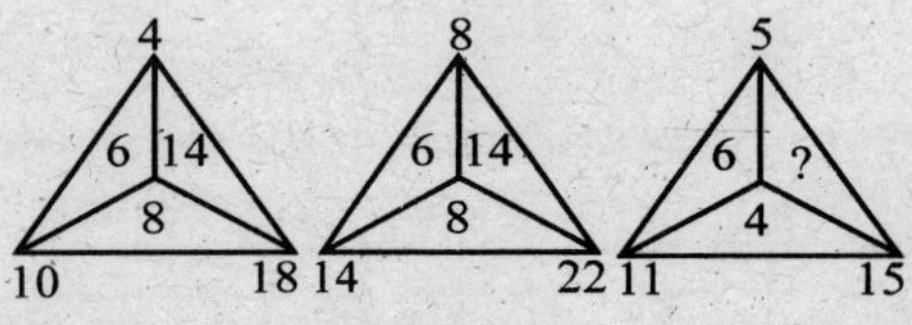

(a) 8 *(b)* 14
(c) 10 *(d)* 6

13.

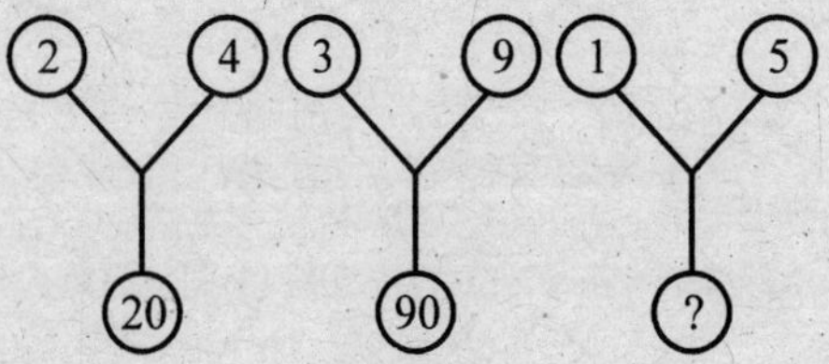

(a) 20 *(b)* 25
(c) 26 *(d)* 75

14.

27	22	50
13	12	26
9	2	?

(a) 12 *(b)* 39
(c) 18 *(d)* 24

15.

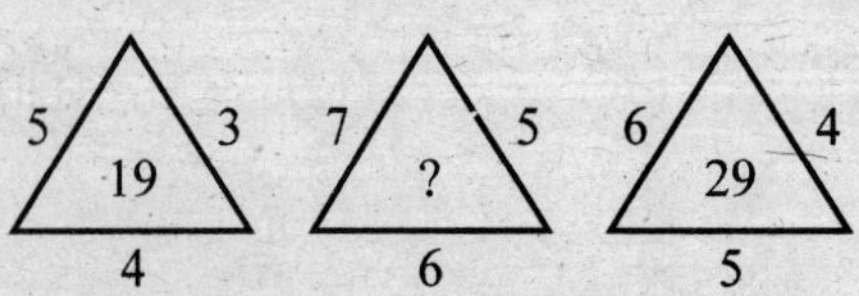

(a) 25 *(b)* 47
(c) 37 *(d)* 41

16.

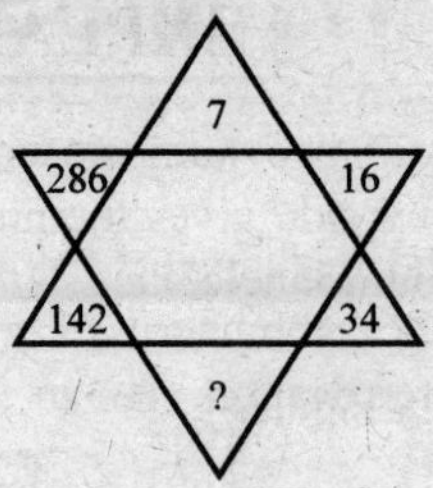

(a) 70
(b) 68
(c) 56
(d) 92

17.

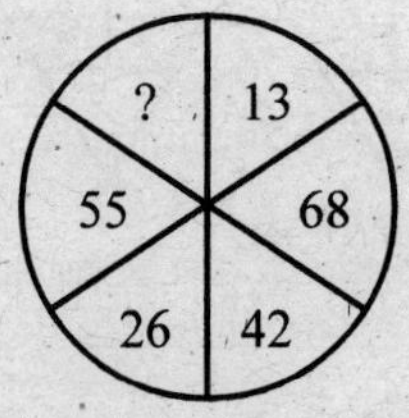

(a) 41 *(b)* 37
(c) 29 *(d)* 25

18.

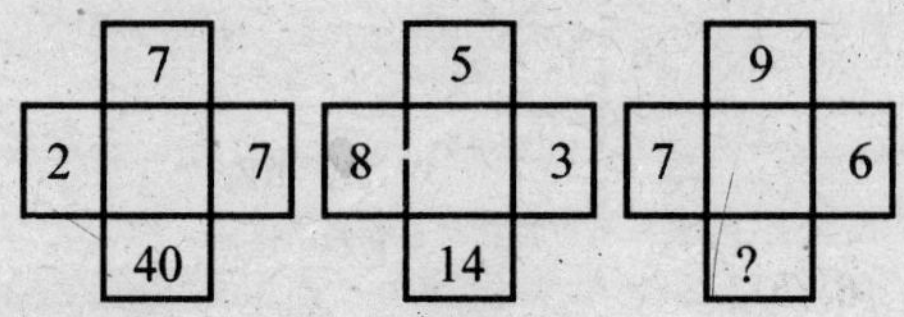

(a) 72 *(b)* 68
(c) 82 *(d)* 96

19.

42	(21)	22
78	(?)	84
162	(18)	99

(a) 12
(b) 13
(c) 60
(d) 72

20.

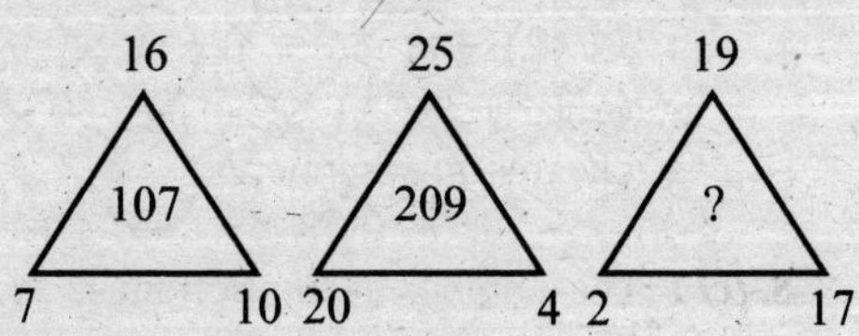

(a) 68 *(b)* 93
(c) 175 *(d)* 217

EXPLANATORY ANSWERS

1. *(c)* : The squares of two numbers on the top placed side by side gives the number inside the bottom triangle, *i.e.*,
6^2 and $3^2 = 369$
2^2 and $5^2 = 425$, similarly
3^2 and $9^2 = 981$.

2. *(d)* : Starting from number 4 the numbers are the squares of numbers in natural order *i.e.*, $2^2 = 4, 3^2 = 9, 4^2 = 16 \ldots\ldots 9^2 = 81$.

3. *(b)* : The number at the bottom is the difference of the squares of two numbers at the top, *i.e.*,
$16^2 - 7^2 = 256 - 49 = 207$
$12^2 - 8^2 = 144 - 64 = 80$, similarly
$25^2 - 21^2 = 625 - 441 = 184$.

4. *(b)* : The number in the centre is the sum of the products of diagonal numbers, *i.e.*,
$(3 \times 3) + (5 \times 6) = 39$
$(4 \times 4) + (7 \times 5) = 51$, similarly
$(3 \times 4) + (5 \times 5) = 37$.

5. *(d)* : Sum of two numbers on the top divided by 2 gives the third number, *i.e.*,
$(7 + 5) \div 2 = 6$
$(5 + 21) \div 2 = 13$, similarly
$(24 + 4) \div 2 = 14$.

6. *(b)* : The numbers in 2nd and 3rd columns are 5 less than the nunbers in 1st and 2nd columns respectively, *i.e.*,
$14 - 5 = 9$ and $9 - 5 = 4$
$12 - 5 = 7$ and $7 - 5 = 2, \ldots$ similarly
$16 - 5 = 11$ and $11 - 5 = 6$.

7. *(a)* : The sum of 3 numbers in each line in one figure is same, *i.e.*,
$29 + 80 + 43$ or $39 + 80 + 33$
or $45 + 80 + 27 = 152$
$29 + 70 + 44$ or $42 + 70 + 31$
or $43 + 70 + 30 = 143$,
similarly $59 + 80 + 20$ or $39 + 80 + 40 = 159$.
The missing number is :
$159 - (80 + 10) = 69$.

8. *(c)* : The number at the bottom is the product of two numbers at the top, *i.e.*,
$13 \times 17 = 221$
$12 \times 19 = 228$, similarly
$13 \times 18 = 234$.

9. *(b)* : Square of number at the bottom is equal to the product of two numbers at the top, *i.e.*,
$6^2 = 4 \times 9$, *i.e.*, 36
$12^2 = 9 \times 16$, *i.e.*, 144, similarly
$20^2 = 16 \times ?$, *i.e.*, 400. The missing number is $400 \div 16 = 25$.

10. *(b)* : The sum of the products of the digits of numbers in 1st and 3rd columns is the number in the 2nd column, *i.e.*,
$(5 \times 1) + (6 \times 1) = 11$
$(6 \times 4) + (3 \times 2) = 30$, similarly
$(3 \times 5) + (4 \times 3) = 27$.

11. *(d)* : The sum of numbers on right and centre subtracted from the number on the left gives the number at the bottom, *i.e.*,
$93 - (27 + 63) = 3$
$79 - (38 + 37) = 4$, similarly
$67 - (16 + 42) = 9$.

12. *(c)* : The number inside each triangle is the difference of the numbers at its base *i.e.*
$10 - 4 = 6, 18 - 4 = 14$ and $18 - 10 = 8$
$14 - 8 = 6, 22 - 8 = 14$ and $22 - 14 = 8$, similarly
$11 - 5 = 6, 15 - 5 = 10$ and $15 - 11 = 4$.

13. *(c)* : The sum of squares of two numbers at the top gives the third number below, *i.e.*,
$2^2 + 4^2 = 20$
$3^2 + 9^2 = 90$, similarly
$1^2 + 5^2 = 26$.

14. *(a)* : The sum of numbers in 1st and 2nd column plus 1 is the number in the 3rd column, *i.e.*,
$27 + 22 + 1 = 50$
$13 + 12 + 1 = 26$, similarly
$9 + 2 + 1 = 12$.

15. *(d)* : The product of numbers on either side of the triangle plus the number at the base is the number inside the triangle, *i.e.*,
$(5 \times 3) + 4 = 19$
$(6 \times 4) + 5 = 29$, similarly
$(7 \times 5) + 6 = 41$.

16. *(a)* : Clockwise starting from number 7; the next number is obtained by doubling the number and adding 2, *i.e.*,
$(7 \times 2) + 2 = 16$
$(16 \times 2) + 2 = 34 \ldots$, similarly
$(34 \times 2) + 2 = 70$
$(70 \times 2) + 2 = 142$
$(142 \times 2) + 2 = 286$.

17. *(c)* : The difference between the numbers in opposite sectors is 13, *i.e.*,
$26 - 13 = 13$
$68 - 55 = 13$, similarly
The missing number is $42 - 13 = 29$
($42 + 13 = 55$ is not given as option).

18. *(b)* : The number at the bottom is obtained by subtracting the sum of two numbers in the centre grid line from the square of the number at the top, *i.e.*,
$7^2 - (2 + 7) = 40$
$5^2 - (8 + 3) = 14$, similarly
$9^2 - (7 + 6) = 68$.

19. *(b)* : The number inside the brackets is obtained by multiplying the number on the left by 2 and then dividing the product by the sum of digits of number on the right, *i.e.*,
$(42 \times 2) \div (2 + 2) = 21$
$(162 \times 2) \div (9 + 9) = 18$, similarly
$(78 \times 2) \div (8 + 4) = 13$.

20. *(a)* : Subtracting the sum of squares of two numbers at the base from the square of number at the apex gives the number inside the triangle, *i.e.*,
$16^2 - (7^2 + 10^2) = 107$
$25^2 - (20^2 + 4^2) = 209$, similarly
$19^2 - (2^2 + 17^2) = 68$.

18. ALPHABET PROBLEMS

Alphabet problems are fun to attempt. They are based on alphabetical series in natural as well as reverse order.

Natural Order

A B C D E F G H I J K L M N O P Q R S T U V W X Y Z

Reverse Order

Z Y X W V U T S R Q P O N M L K J I H G F E D C B A

> **Note :** The series starts from A on reaching Z and from Z on reaching A. Of these A E I O U are vowels and the rest are consonants.

EXERCISE

1. Which letter should be ninth letter to the left of ninth letter from the right if the first half of the alphabet is reversed?

(a) I *(b)* D
(c) F *(d)* E

2. Starting from the fifth letter from the left, if twelve letters are written in reverse order, then which letter will be the seventh to the left of the fourteenth letter from the right?

(a) N *(b)* H
(c) L *(d)* O

3. What letter will come in the centre of sixth letter from the right and thirteenth letter from the left?

(a) Q *(b)* R
(c) P *(d)* S

4. If in the word "DISTURBANCE", the first letter is interchanged with the last letter, the second letter is interchanged with the tenth letter and so on, which letter would come after the letter "T" in the newly formed word?

(a) I *(b)* U
(c) N *(d)* S

5. If it is possible to make a meaningful word with the third, the fifth, the seventh and the tenth letters of the word PROJECTION. If no such word can be made, give 'O' as the answer. If more than one such word can be made, give 'M' as the answer.

(a) T *(b)* N
(c) O *(d)* M

6. A meaningful word is made if we take the first, fourth, fifth, seventh, tenth, eleventh and the twelfth letters of the word "FELICITATIONS". Which of the following will be the fifth letter of that word from the right end of that word?

(a) T *(b)* C
(c) N *(d)* I

7. On rearranging the jumbled spelling of the word SKARTINS, a language is obtained. What is the fifth letter from the right of the rearranged word?

(a) N *(b)* K
(c) R *(d)* S

8. If the 1st, 3rd, 5th, 7th, 10th and 13th letters of the word "ENTERTAINMENT" are used to make a meaningful word, then what two letters will come in the centre?

(a) AM *(b)* TT
(c) RE *(d)* NA

9. On rearranging the jumbled spelling of the word GRUBY a sport is obtained. What is the letter in the centre?

(a) R *(b)* B
(c) G *(d)* U

10. If the letters 'ERVSECI' can be rearranged to form a meaningful word what will be the fifth letter from the right?

(*a*) R (*b*) V

(*c*) E (*d*) None of these

11. From the word HASTEN how many independent meaningful English words can be made without changing the order of the letters and using each letter only once?

(*a*) 1 (*b*) 2

(*c*) 3 (*d*) 4

EXPLANATORY ANSWERS

1. (*d*) : MLKJIGHFEDCBANOPQRSTUVWXYZ

9th 9th

2. (*d*) : ABCDPONMLKJIHGFEQRSTUVWXYZ

7th 14th

3. (*a*) :

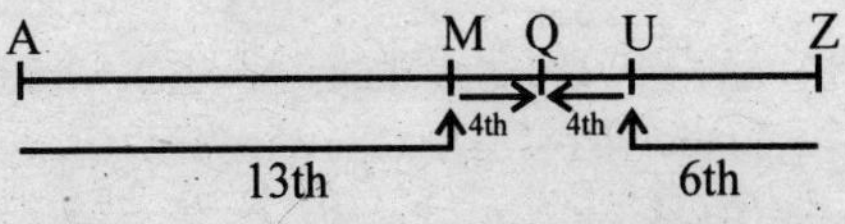

13th letter from left is 'M' and 6th letter from right is 'U'. The letter in the centre of 'M' and 'U' is 'Q'.

4. (*d*) : E C N A B R U T S I D

5. (*d*) : P R O J E C T I O N

The 3rd, 5th, 7th and 10th letters are OETN.

The words formed are TONE and NOTE.

6. (*b*) : F E L I C I T A T I O N S

The 1st, 4th, 5th, 7th, 10th, 11th and 12th lettes are FICTION.

The word is FICTION and 5th letter from right is 'C'.

7. (*d*) : The word is SANSKRIT and 5th letter from right is 'S'.

8. (*b*) : E N T E R T A I N M E N T

The 1st, 3rd, 5th 7th, 10th and 13th letters are ETRAMT.

The word formed is MATTER.

9. (*c*) : The sport is RUGBY. The letter in the centre is 'G'.

10. (*a*) : The word is SERVICE and fifth letter from right is 'R'.

11. (*b*) : The words formed are : HAS, TEN.

19. LOGICAL DIAGRAM

In these type of questions, a set of five different figures is given as options. Each figure represents a logical pattern of certain groups of related words wherein each word represents a class. One has to identify the most appropriate logical figure for the set of words given. Some of the relationships represented by these diagrams are given below. Understand the relationship patterns and then attempt the exercise following the explanation.

EXERCISE

Directions : *From the five logical Diagrams, select one which best illustrates the relationship among three given classes in the questions 1 to 10.*

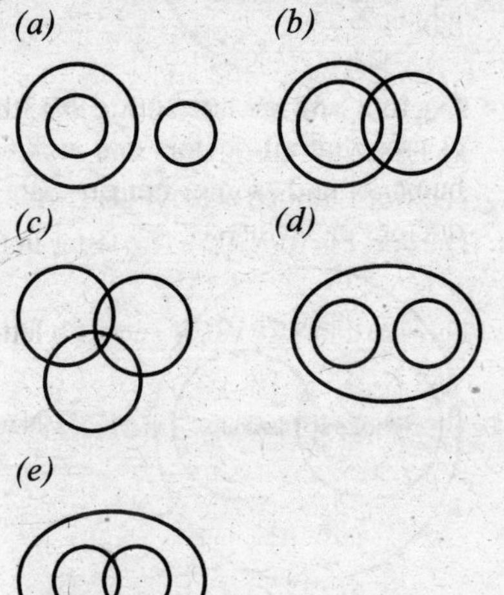

1. Birds, fruits, mangoes
2. Criminals, lawyers, bandits
3. Swimmers, bachelors, men
4. Smart, engineers, women
5. Vegetables, potatoes, brinjals
6. Grapes, sweet, fruit
7. Doctors, architects, humans
8. Scholars, people, Indians
9. Children, naughty, studious
10. Pens, pencils, stationery

Directions : *From the five logical diagrams select one which best illustrates the relationship among three given classes in questions 11 to 20.*

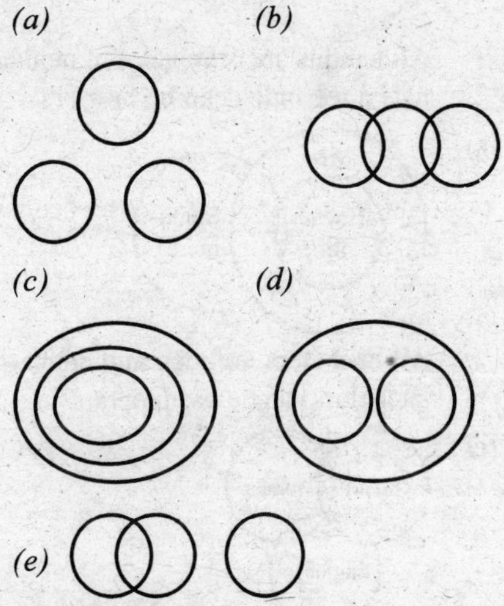

11. Ink, crayons, red
12. Canines, dogs, pups
13. Table, chair, stool
14. Ripe, mangoes, basket
15. Scholars, studious, illiterates
16. Cars, ships, means of conveyance
17. Age, number, thirteen
18. Country, state, continent
19. Father, parent, mother
20. Iron, metal, mercury

EXPLANATORY ANSWERS

1. ***(a)*** **:**

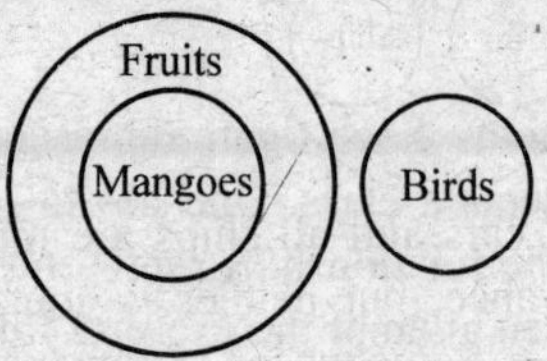

All mangoes are fruits, but neither fruits, nor mangoes can be birds.

2. ***(a)*** **:**

All bandits are criminal, but neither criminals nor bandits can be lawyers.

3. ***(b)*** **:**

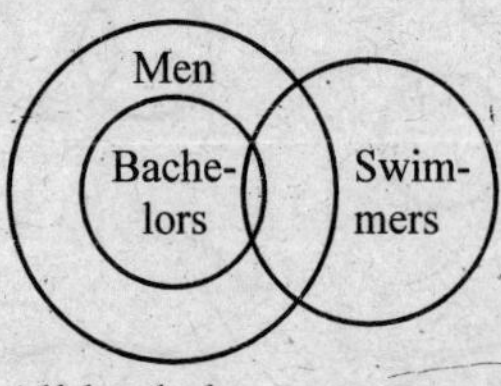

All bachelors are men and some men and bachelors can be swimmers.

4. ***(c)*** **:**

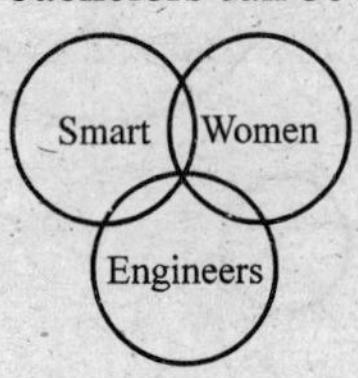

Some women can be smart and some women can be engineers and vice–versa. Some engineers can be women and some engineers can be smart and vice–versa.

5. ***(d)*** **:**

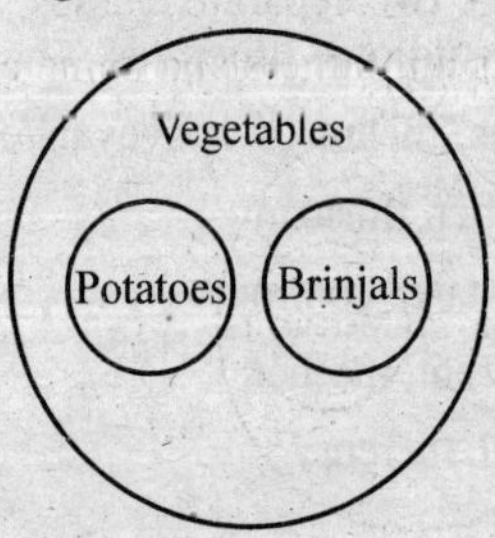

Potatoes and brinjals are vegetables but they have nothing in common. Some vegetables are potatoes and some are brinjals.

6. ***(b)*** **:**

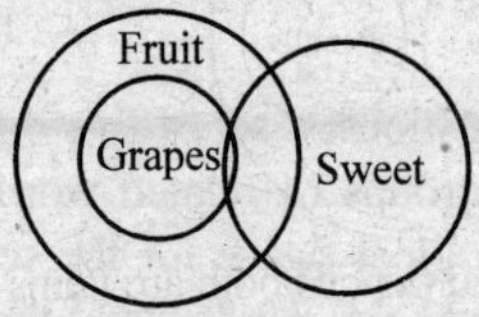

Some grapes are sweet and all grapes are fruit. But not all that is sweet is fruit.

7. ***(d)*** **:**

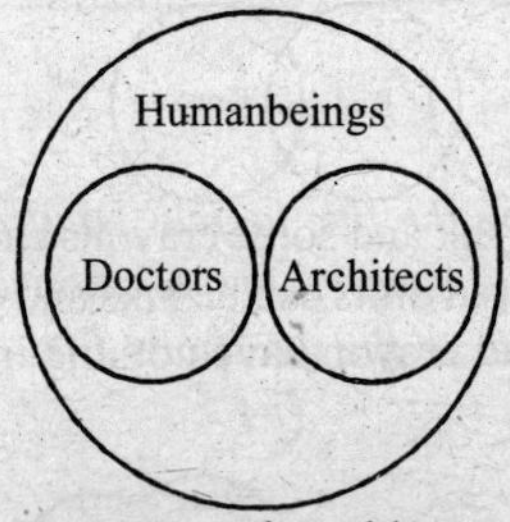

Doctors and architects are two separate classes, but all doctors and architects are humans and some humans are either doctors or architects.

8. ***(e)*** **:**

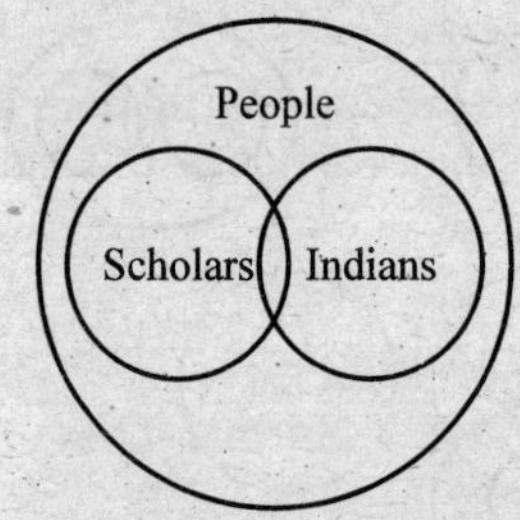

Some Indians can be scholars and some scholars can be Indians. All scholars and Indians are people.

9. ***(c)*** **:**

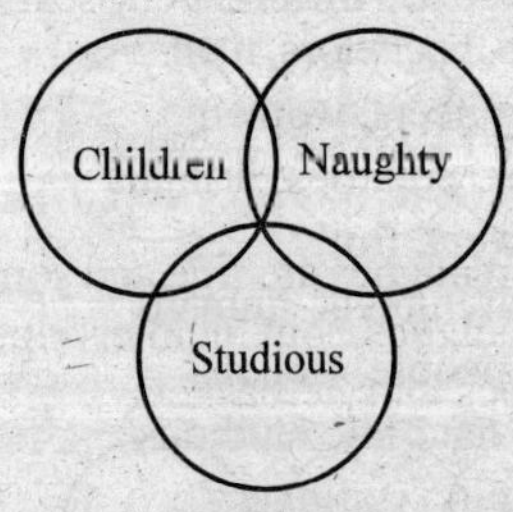

Some children can be naughty and some can be studious, some studious can be children and some naughty. Some naughty can be studious and some children.

10. *(d)* :

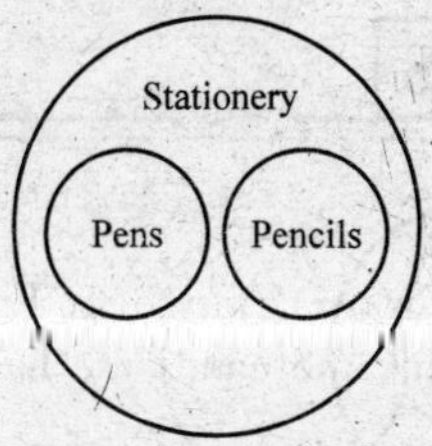

Pens and pencils both are items of stationery and some stationery is pens and pencils, but pens and pencils are two separate classes.

11. *(b)* :

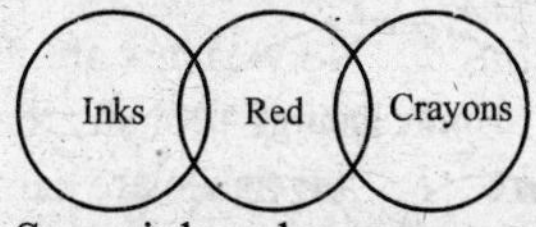

Some ink and some crayons can be red and some red units can be inks and crayons, but ink and crayon have nothing in common.

12. *(c)* :

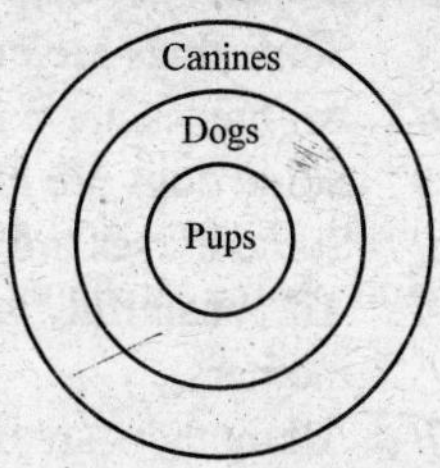

All pups are dogs and all dogs are canines. Some canines are dogs, of which some are pups.

13. *(a)* :

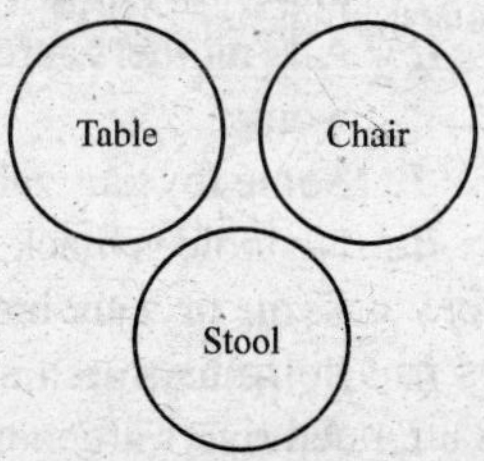

All three are different classes.

14. *(e)* :

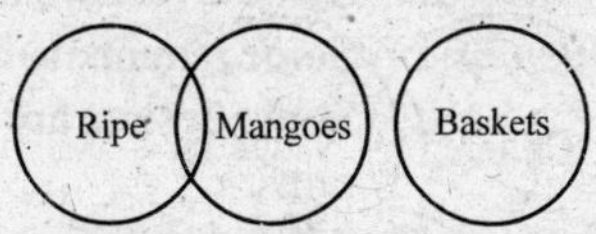

Some mangoes are ripe and some ripe units are mangoes, but neither ripe units nor mangoes can be baskets.

15. *(e)* :

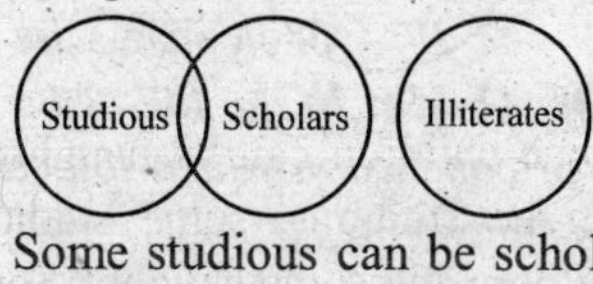

Some studious can be scholars and some scholars can be studious, but neither studious nor scholars can be illiterates.

16. *(d)* :

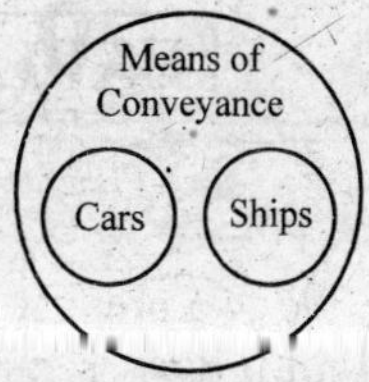

All cars and all ships are means of conveyance, but neither is contained in the other. Some means of conveyance are cars and some ships.

17. *(b)* :

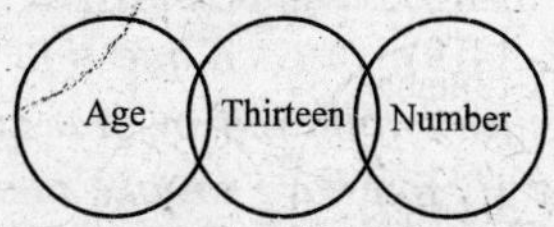

Some are aged thirteen and some numbers are thirteen. Some thirteen units are numbers and some ages. Age and number have nothing in common.

18. *(c)* :

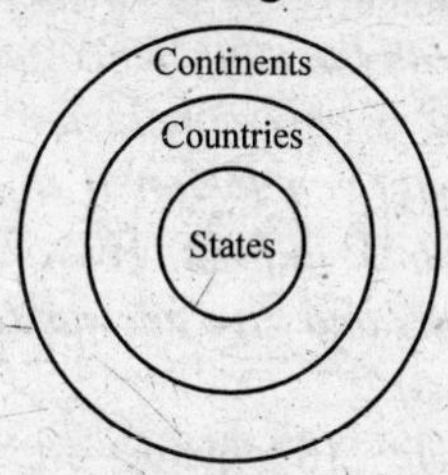

All continents contain countries within it and each country contains states within it.

19. *(d)* :

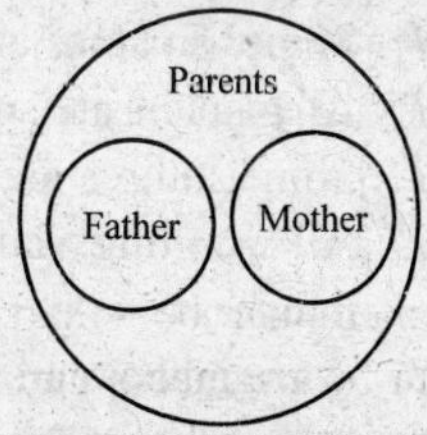

All fathers and mothers are parents, but they are two separate classes. Some of the parents are fathers and some are mothers.

20. *(d)* :

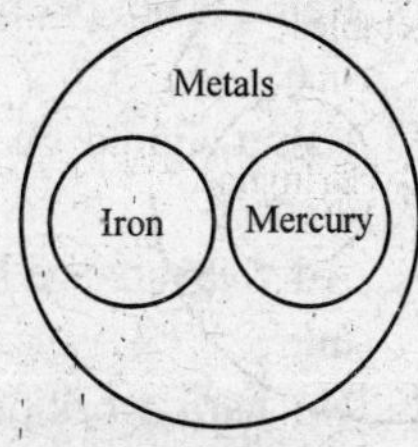

Iron and mercury are metals, but they have nothing in common. Some metals are iron and some mercury.

20. SYLLOGISM

In this reasoning pattern, the two premises are followed by two conclusions drawn from them. Five options *(a)*, *(b)*, *(c)*, *(d)* and *(e)* are given as answers. Based on the two statements the candidate has to select the right option as answer.

EXERCISE

Directions (Qs. 1-10): *In each question below are given two statements followed by two conclusions numbered I and II. You have to take the two given statements to be true even if they seem to be at variance from commonly known facts and then decide which of the given conclusions logically follows from the two given statements, disregarding commonly known facts. Read both the statements and—*

Give answer (a) if only conclusion I follows; give answer (b) if only conclusion II follows; give answer (c) if either I or II follows; give answer (d) if neither I nor II follows and give answer (e) if both I and II follows.

1. *Statements* *I*: All tomatoes are red.
II: All grapes are tomatoes.
Conclusions *I*: All grapes are red.
II: Some tomatoes are grapes.

2. *Statements* *I*: All painters are smilling.
II: Some authors are painters.
Conclusions *I*: All smiling authors are painters.
II: Some authors are smiling.

3. *Statements* *I*: All peons in this office are efficient.
II: Ramu is not efficient.
Conclusions *I*: Ramu is not peon in this office.
II: Ramu should be more efficient.

4. *Statements* *I*: All weavers are hard working.
II: No hard working men are foolish.
Conclusions *I*: No weavers are foolish.
II: Some foolish are weavers.

5. *Statements* *I*: All fishes are cars.
II: All cars are vegetables.
Conclusions *I*: Some vegetables are cars.
II: Some vegetables are fishes.

6. *Statements* *I*: Some dogs are pups.
II: All horses are pups.
Conclusions *I*: Some dogs are horses.
II: Some horses are dogs.

7. *Statements* *I*: All beautiful women are mothers.
II: All mothers are understanding.
Conclusions *I*: All beautiful women are understanding.
II: All mothers are beautiful women.

8. *Statements* *I*: Some toys are tables.
II: No table is black.
Conclusions *I*: Some toys are black.
II: Some toys are not black.

9. *Statements* *I*: All rivers are mountains.
II: Some rivers are deserts.
Conclusions *I*: Some mountains are deserts.
II: Some deserts are not mountains.

10. *Statements* *I*: All men are horses.
II: All horses are elephants.
Conclusions *I*: All men are elephants.
II: All elephants are men.

Directions (Qs. 11-15): *In the following questions, select the set of conclusion which logically follows from the given statements.*

11. *Statements* *I*: All foxes are plates.
II: All plates are trees.
Conclusions *I*: All foxes are trees.
II: All trees are foxes.
III: Some trees are foxes.
IV: Some trees are plates.
(a) All conclusions are correct.
(b) Only conclusions I, III, and IV follow.
(c) Only conclusions II, III, and IV follow.
(d) Only conclusions I and IV follow.
(e) None of the above.

12. *Statements* *I*: Some cubes are squares.
II: All squares are circles.
Conclusions *I*: All cubes are circles.
II: Some circles are cubes.
III: Some circles are squares.
IV: All squares are cubes.
(a) Only conclusion I follows.
(b) Only conclusion I, II and III follow.
(c) All conclusions are correct.
(d) Only conclusions II and III follow.
(e) None of the above.

13. *Statements* *I*: All cups are goats.
II: All goats are tins.
Conclusions *I*: All goats are cups.
II: All tins are goats.
III: No cups are tins.
IV: No tins are cups.
(a) Only conclusions III and IV follow.
(b) Only conclusios I and II follow.
(c) Only conclusions I, II and III follow.
(d) All conclusions are correct.
(e) None of the above.

14. *Statements* *I*: All bombs are bags.
II: Some bags are jets.
Conclusions *I*: All bombs are jets.
II: All jets are bombs.
III: Some jets are bombs.
IV: Some bombs are jets.
(a) Only conclusion III follows.
(b) Only conclusions I and II follow.
(c) All conclusions are correct.
(d) Only conclusions III and IV follow.
(e) None of these.

15. *Statements* *I*: Some thorns are jackets.
II: Some jackets are boats.
Conclusions *I*: No thorns are boats.
II: All jackets are boats.
III: Some boats are thorns.
IV: No jackets are thorns.
(a) Either conclusion I or IV follows.
(b) Either conclusion I or II follows.
(c) Either conclusion I or III follows.
(d) No conclusion is correct.
(e) All conclusions are correct.

EXPLANATORY ANSWERS

1. (e): When all tomatoes are red and all grapes are tomatoes, then all grapes are also red. When all grapes are tomatoes, then some tomatoes must be grapes. Therefore, both conclusions I and II are correct.

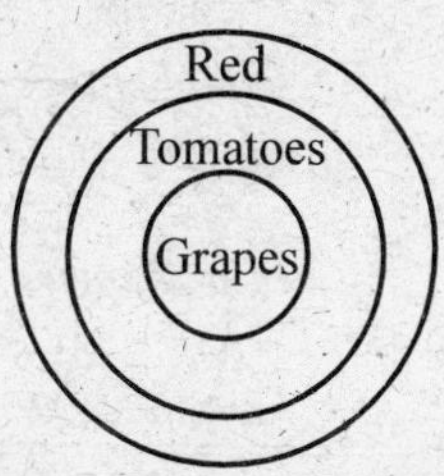

2. (b): When all painters are smiling and some authors are painters, then some authors are smiling. Therefore, only conclusion II is correct.

3. (a): When all the peons of the office are efficient, then Ramu cannot be a peon in this office. Therefore, only conclusion I is correct.

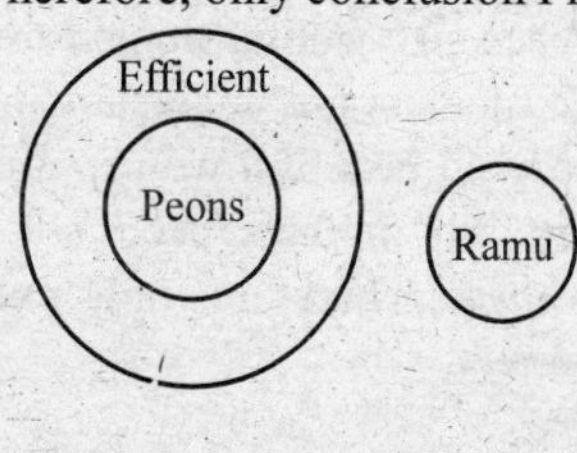

4. *(a)* : When all weavers are hardworking and no hardworking men are foolish, then no weavers are foolish. Therefore, only conclusion I is correct.

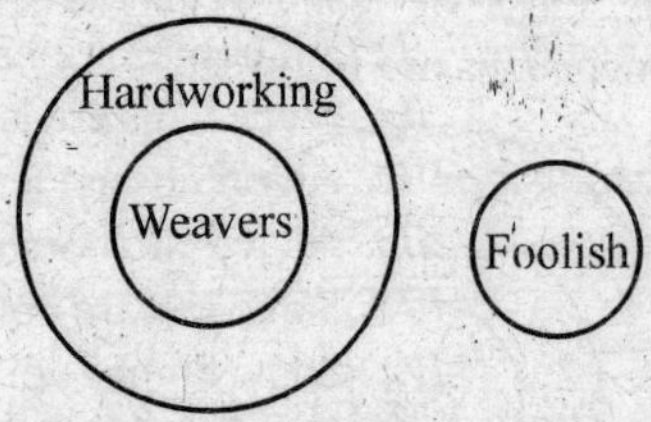

5. *(e)* : When all fishes are cars and all cars are vegetables, then all fishes will naturally be vegetables. This means that some vegetables are fishes. And when all cars are vegetables, then some vegetables will be cars naturally. Therefore, both the conclusions I and II are correct.

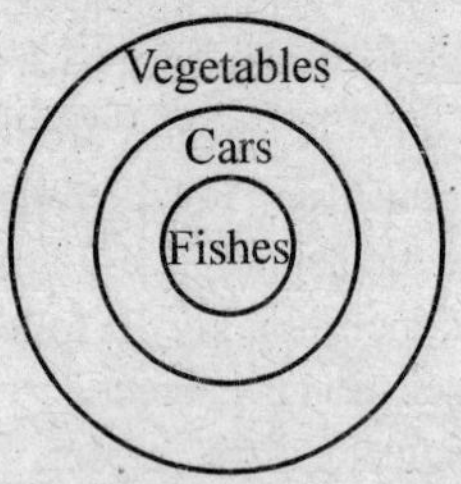

6. *(d)* : No relationship can be established between the two statements. Therefore, neither conclusion I nor conclusion II is correct.

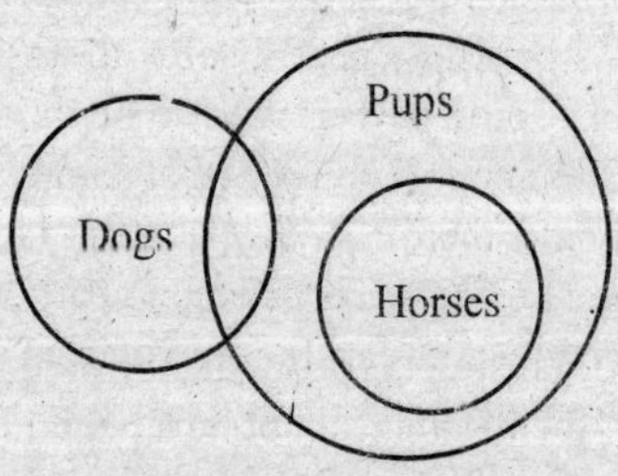

7. *(a)* : When all beautiful women are mothers and all mothers are understanding, then naturally all beautiful women are understanding. All mothers need not be beautiful women. Therefore, only conclusion I is correct.

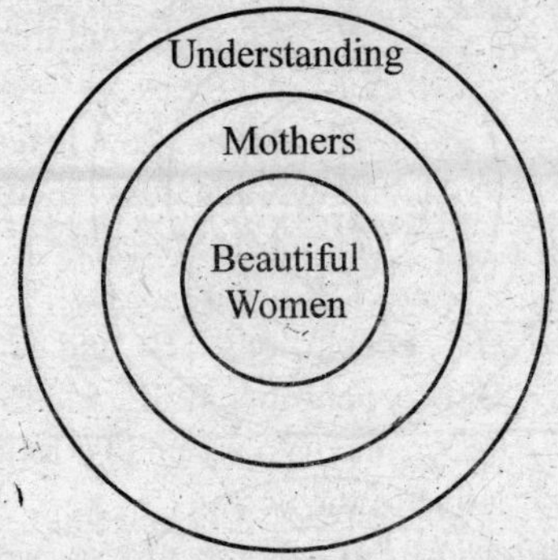

8. *(c)* : When some toys are tables and no table is black, then it is indicated that some toys can be black, as all toys are not tables. On the other hand, some toys may not be black. Therefore, there is a possibility that some toys may or may not be black. As such, either conclusion I or conclusion II can be correct.

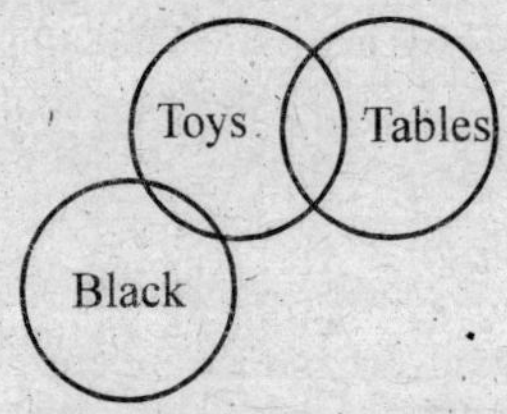

9. *(e)* : When all rivers are mountains and some rivers are deserts, then some deserts cannot be mountains and also, some mountains need not be deserts. Therefore, both conclusion I and conclusion II are correct.

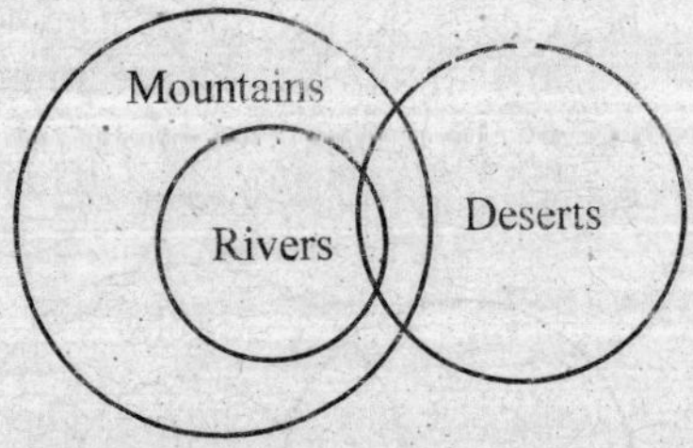

10. *(a)* : When all men are horses and all horses are elephants then, naturally all men are elephants, but all elephants need not be men. Therefore, only conclusion I is correct.

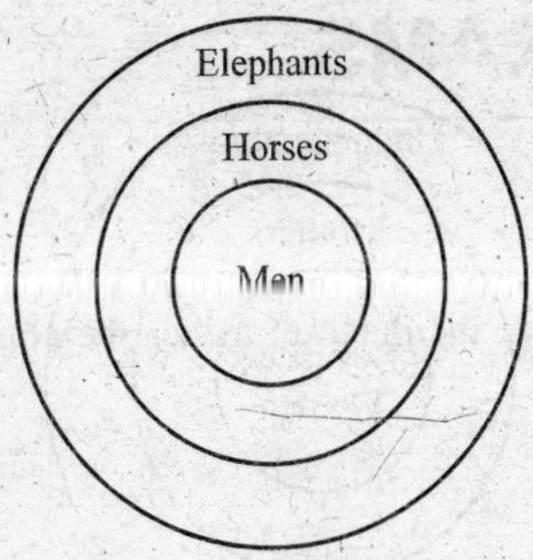

11. ***(b)*** **:**

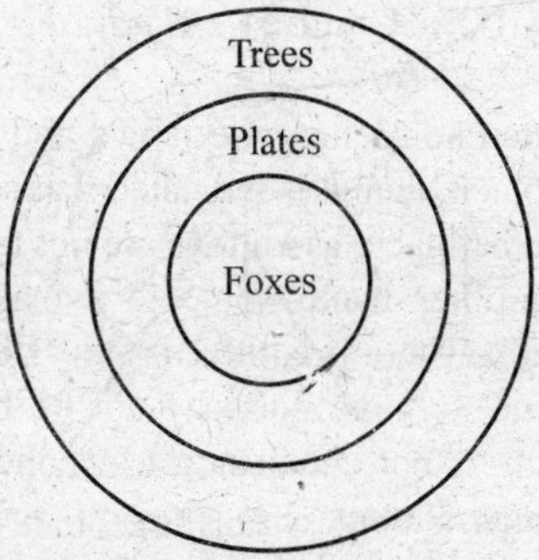

When all foxes are plates and all plates are trees, then naturally all foxes will be trees and some trees will then have to be foxes. And when all plates are trees then some trees will have to be plates. Therefore, only conclusions I, III and IV are correct.

12. ***(d)*** **:** When it is given that some cubes are squares and all squares are circles, then some cubes will naturally be circles, though all cubes cannot be circles. When some cubes are circles, then some circles will have to be cubes. And when all squares are circles, then some circles will have to be squares. As per given statement II, all squares are circles. Therefore all squares cannot be cubes. As such only conclusions II and III are correct.

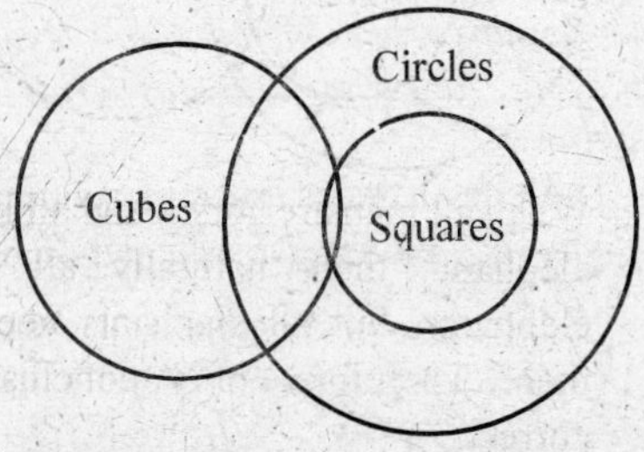

13. ***(e)*** **:** When all cups are goats, then only some goats can be cups. When all goats are tins, then only some tins can be goats. When all cups are goats and all goats are tins, then naturally all cups are tins and some tins must be cups. Therefore, all the conclusions are incorrect.

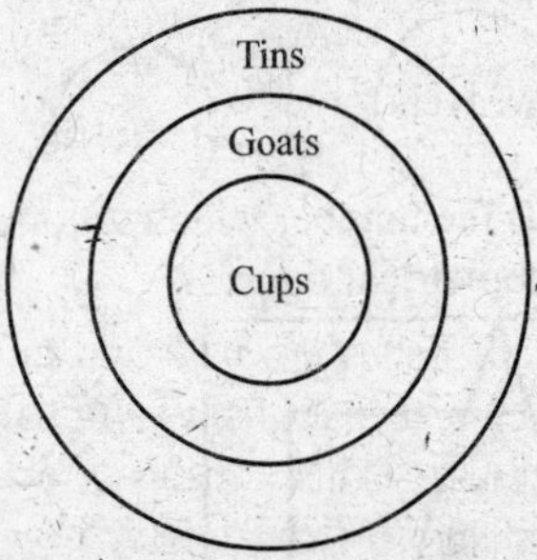

14. ***(e)*** **:** When all bombs are bags and some bags are jets then all bombs cannot be jets. 'Some bags' indicate that there is no chance of some bombs being jets, or some jets being bombs. Further all jets cannot be bombs. Therefore, all conclusions are incorrect.

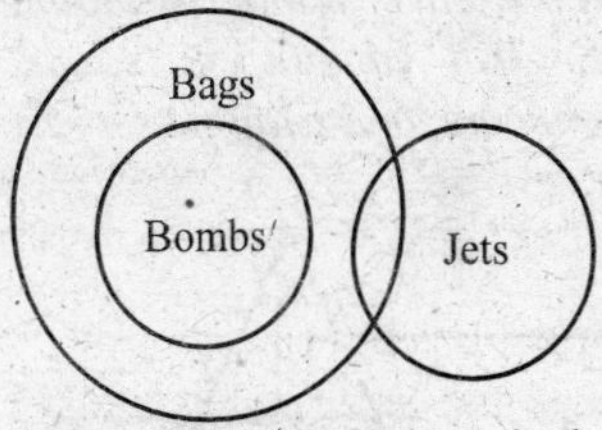

15. ***(d)*** **:** When some thorns are jackets and some jackets are boats, then some thorns may be boats but some boats cannot be thorns. As per Statement I, some thorns are jackets, some jackets need to be thorns. When Statement II conveys that some jackets are boats, then it is clear that all jackets cannot be boats. Therefore, no particular given conclusion can be drawn from the given statements.

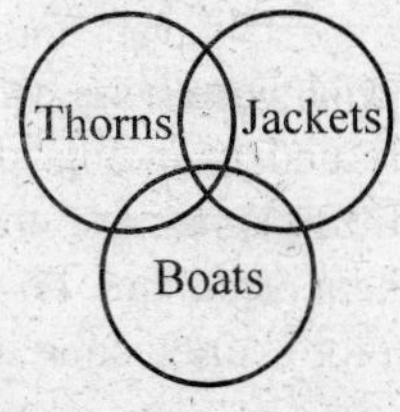

21. VENN DIAGRAMS

In these type of questions, diagrammatic representation presents a logical illustration of particular class or statements based on which the questions are asked. A clear view of the diagram makes the concepts clear for attempting such questions.

EXERCISE

1. What is the number which is common to only two geometrical figures?

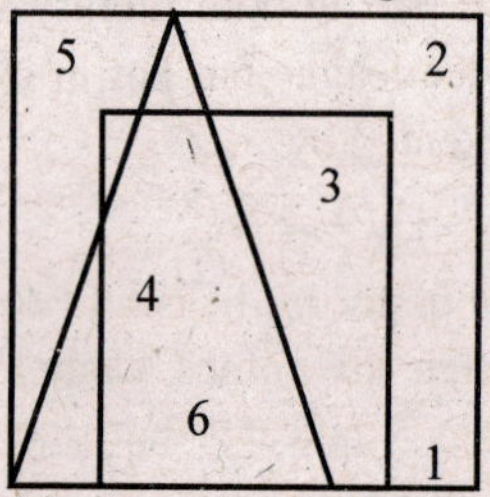

(a) 4 (b) 3
(c) 5 (d) 2

Directions (Qs. 2 and 3) : *In the following diagram, rectangle represents Hindi Announcers, circle represents English Announcers, square represents French Announcers, and triangle represents German Announcers.*

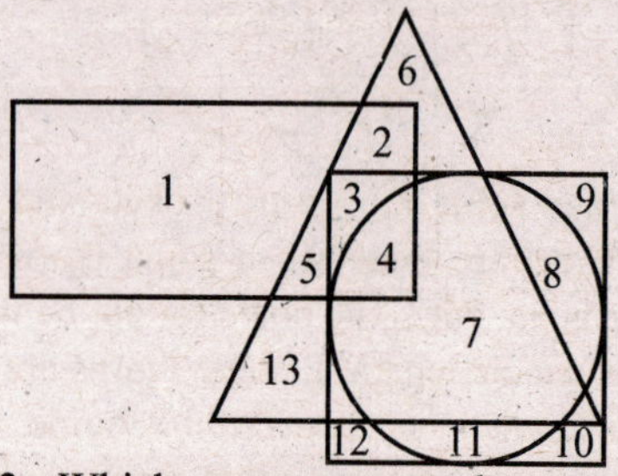

2. Which area represents those announcers who can present programmes in Hindi, French and German only?
   (a) 1 (b) 2
   (c) 3 (d) 4

3 Which area represents those announcers who can present programmes in French and English only?
   (a) 7 (b) 9
   (c) 11 (d) 13

Directions (Qs. 4 and 5) : *Study the diagram to answer these questions.*

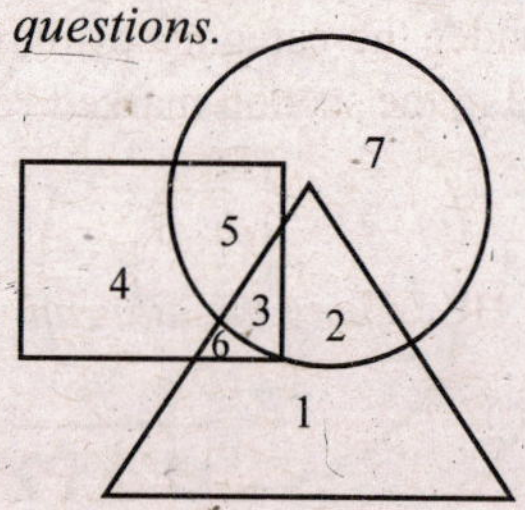

4. Which number is in all the geometrical figures?
   (a) 5 (b) 6
   (c) 2 (d) 3

5. Number 6 is in :
   (a) Rectangle and triangle
   (b) Circle and traingle
   (c) Rectangle and circle
   (d) Rectangle only

Directions (Qs. 6 to 9) : *In the following diagram*

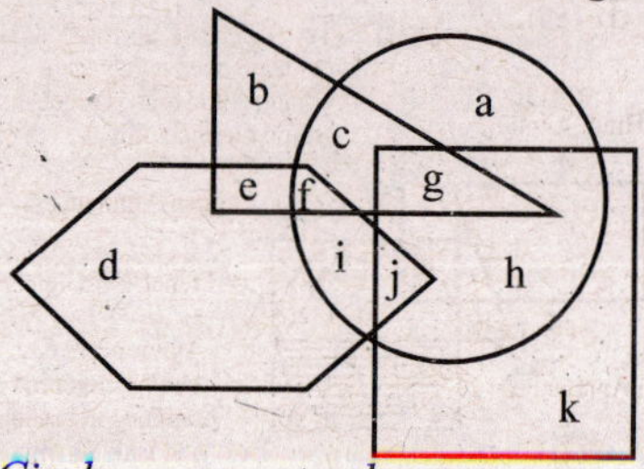

The Circle represents players
The Triangle represents outdoor games
The Hexagon represents indoor games and
The Square represents national level players
Study the diagram and answer the questions given below :

6. The letter in the section representing the players who play indoor games at national level is :
   (a) f (b) i
   (c) j (d) g

7. The letter representing the section of outdoor as well as indoor game players who do not play at the national level is :
(a) c (b) f
(c) e (d) i

8. The section representing national level players who do not play either outdoor or indoor games but still come under the category of players is :
(a) k (b) g
(c) c (d) h

9. Persons who play outdoor games but do not come under the category of players are represented in the section marked :
(a) b (b) c
(c) a (d) d

Direction (Qs. 10) : *Study the diagram given below.*

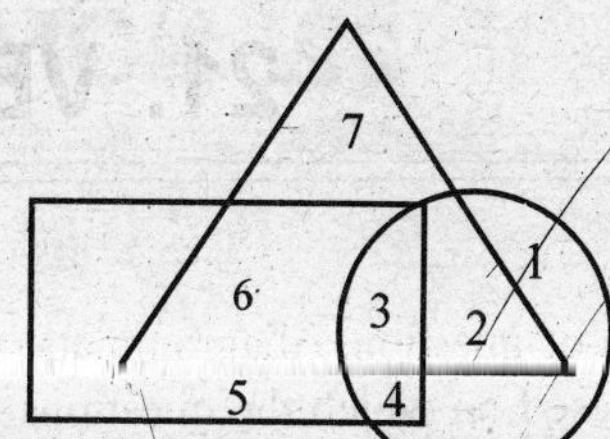

A college provides three different activities, students union represented by triangle, literary society represented by rectangle and social service league represented by circle.

10. Those who take part in both literary society and social service league but not in students union are represented by :
(a) 3 & 4 (b) 5 & 6
(c) 5 & 1 (d) 4

EXPLANATORY ANSWERS

1. (b) :

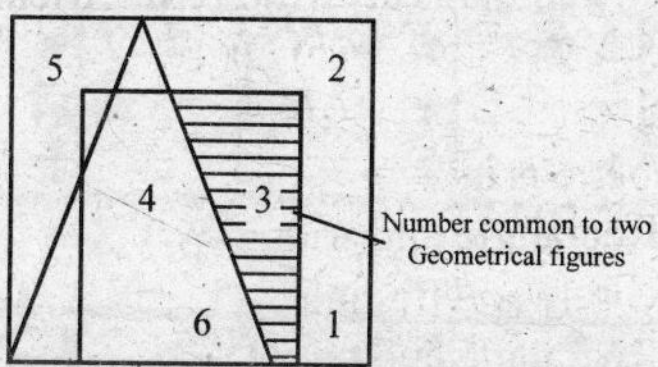

Note : Numbers 4 and 6 are common to all three geometrical figures.

2. (c), 3. (c) :

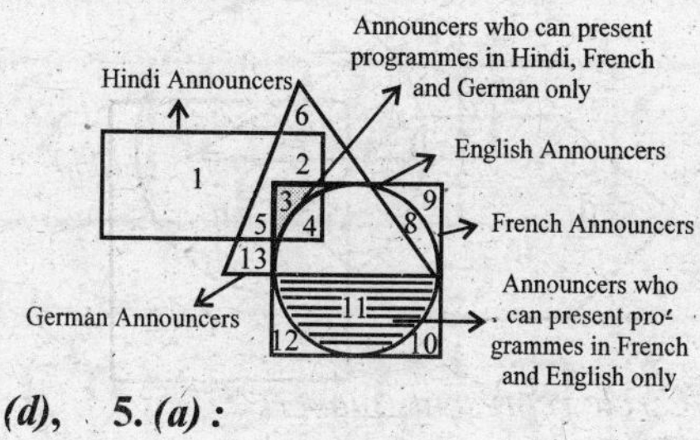

4. (d), 5. (a) :

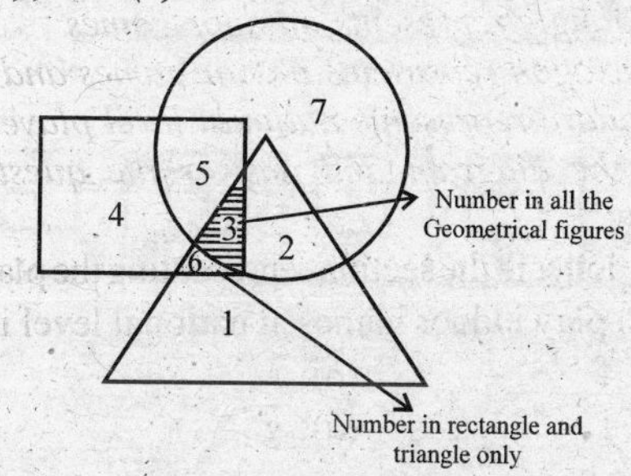

6. (c), 7. (b), 8. (d), 9. (a) :

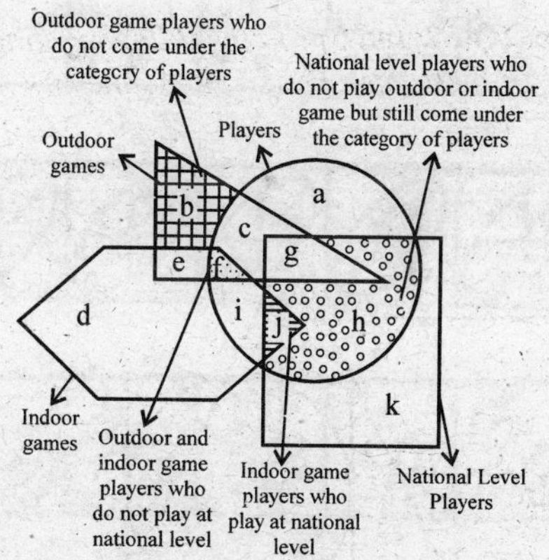

10. (d)

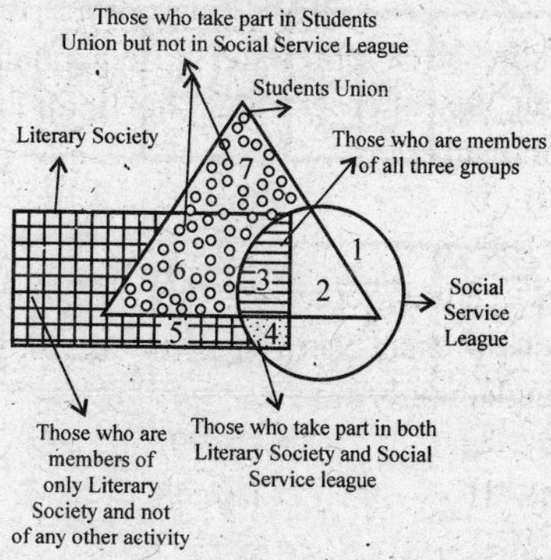

22. NON-VERBAL SERIES

EXERCISE

Directions (Q. 1–10) : *In each of the following questions which one of the five answer figures given below should come after the problem figures if the sequence are continued?*

Problem Figures — **Answer Figures**

1. 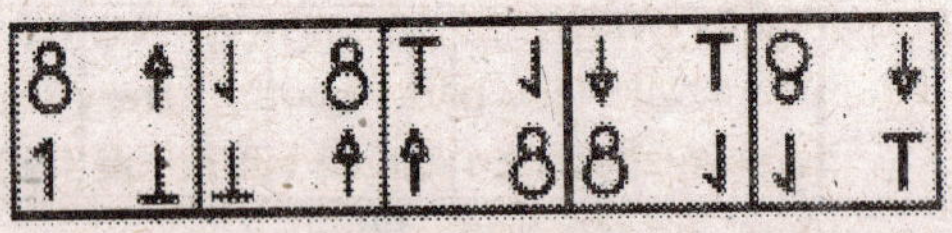 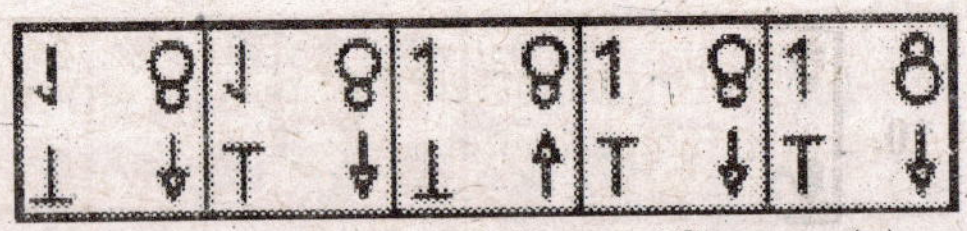

(a) *(b)* *(c)* *(d)* *(e)*

2. 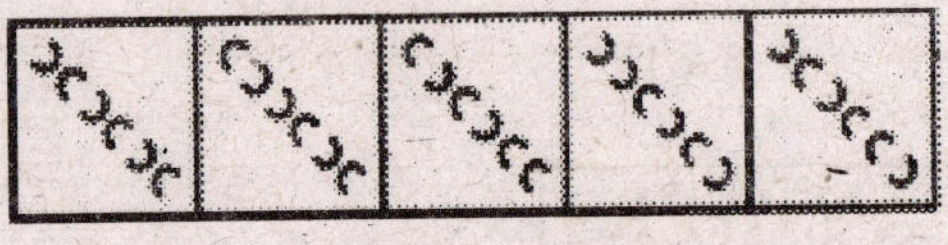 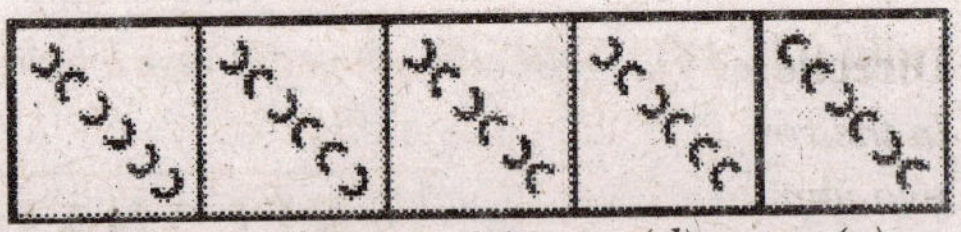

(a) *(b)* *(c)* *(d)* *(e)*

3. 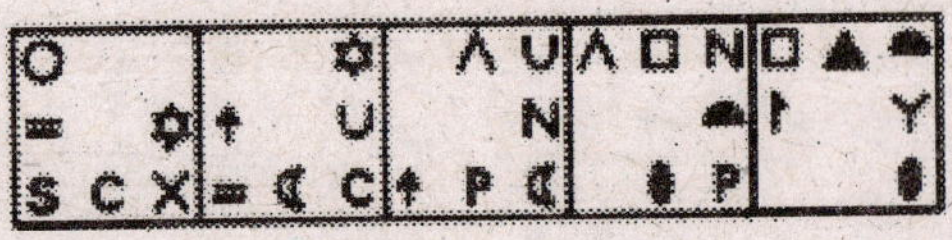 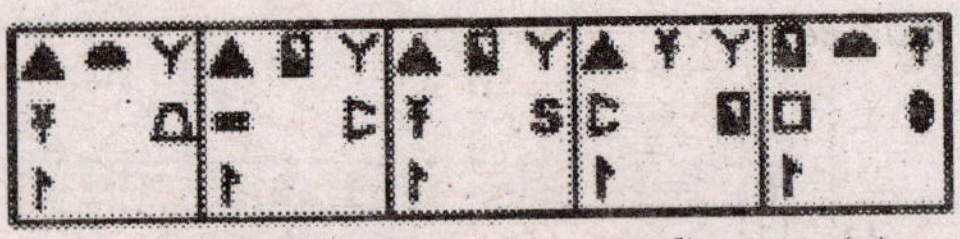

(a) *(b)* *(c)* *(d)* *(e)*

4.  

(a) *(b)* *(c)* *(d)* *(e)*

5.  

(a) *(b)* *(c)* *(d)* *(e)*

6. 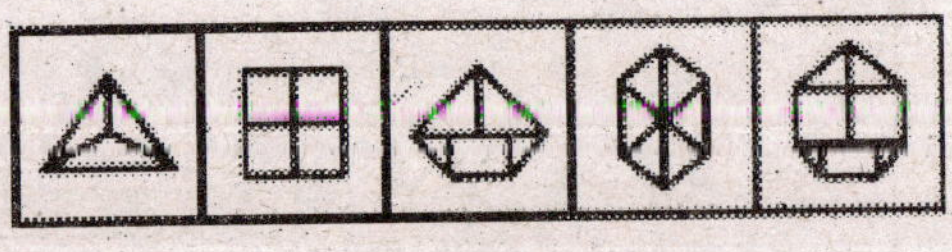 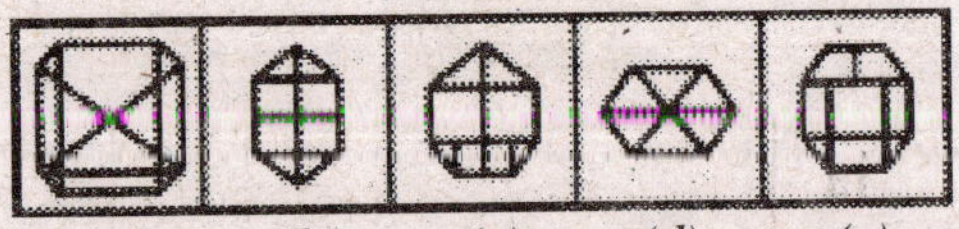

(a) *(b)* *(c)* *(d)* *(e)*

7. 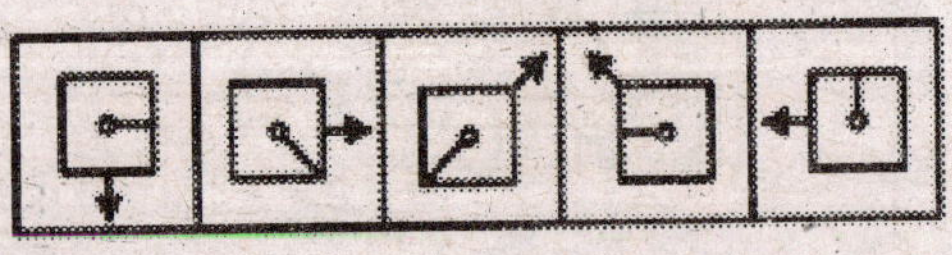 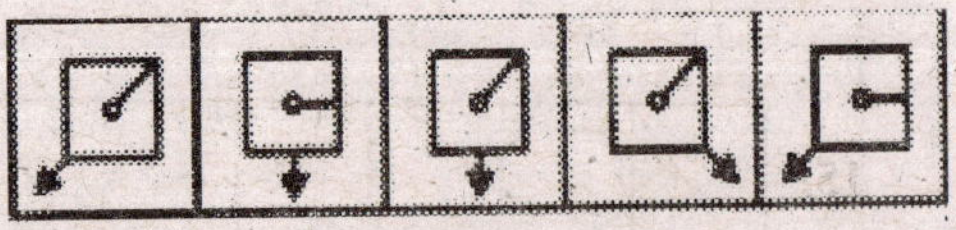

(a) *(b)* *(c)* *(d)* *(e)*

Problem Figures | **Answer Figures**

8.  

(a) (b) (c) (d) (e)

9. 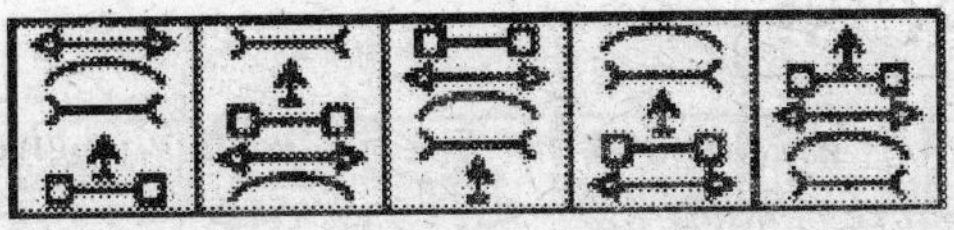 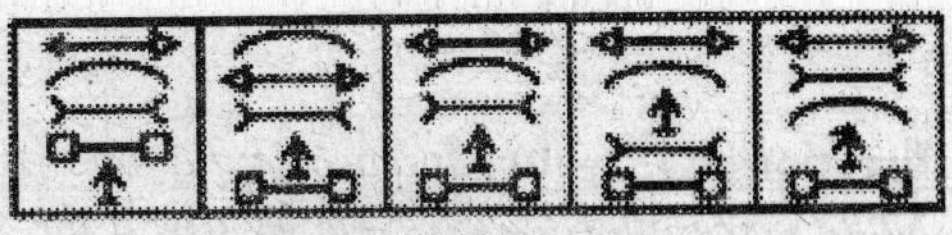

(a) (b) (c) (d) (e)

10. 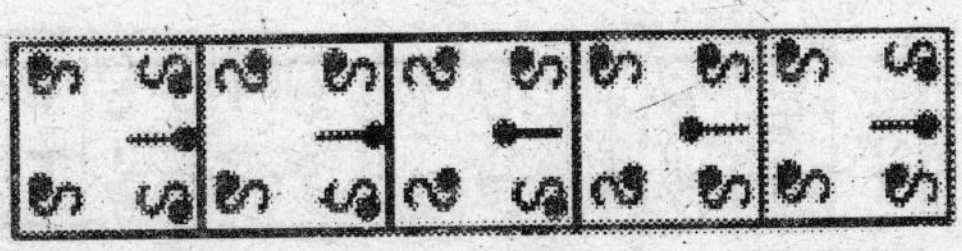 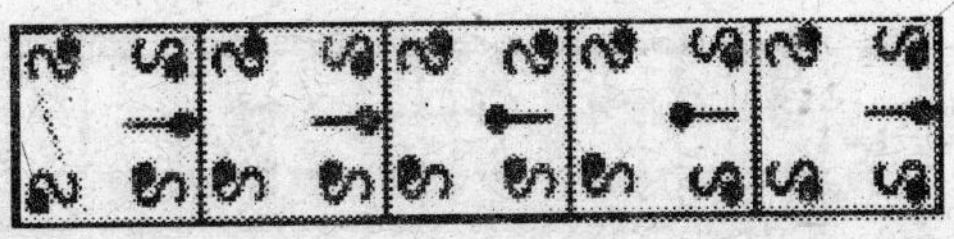

(a) (b) (c) (d) (e)

Directions (Q. 11-20) : *In each of these questions, a series begins with an unmarked figure on the extreme left in the row of figures. One and only one of the five lettered figures in the series does not fit into the series. The two unmarked figures, one on the extreme left and the other on the extreme right fit into the series. Take as many aspects into account as possible of the figures in the series and find out the one and only of the five marked figures which does not fit into the series. The letter of that figure is the answer.*

11. 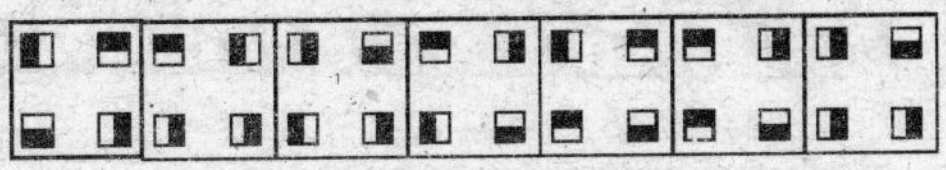

(a) (b) (c) (d) (e)

12. 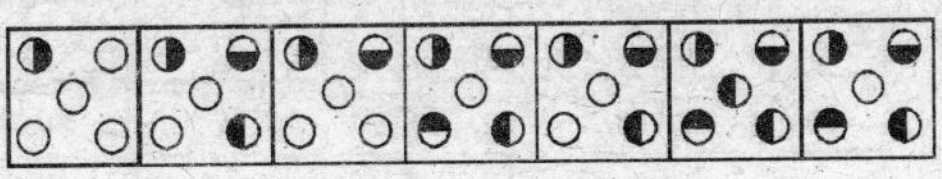

(a) (b) (c) (d) (e)

13. 

(a) (b) (c) (d) (e)

14. 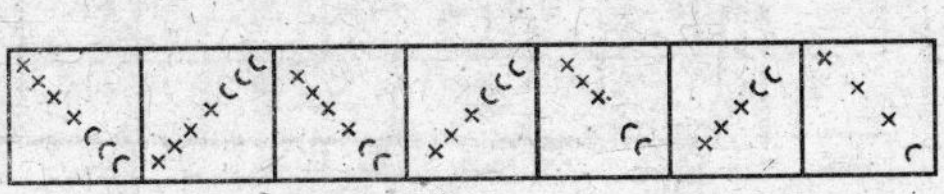

(a) (b) (c) (d) (e)

15. 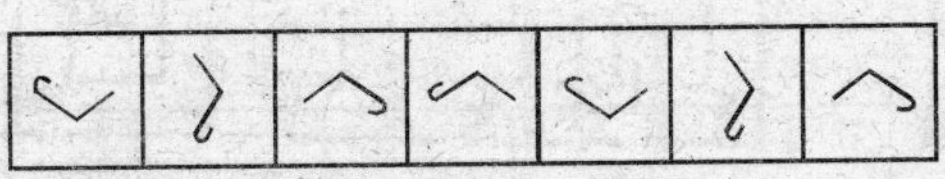

(a) (b) (c) (d) (e)

16. 

(a) (b) (c) (d) (e)

17. 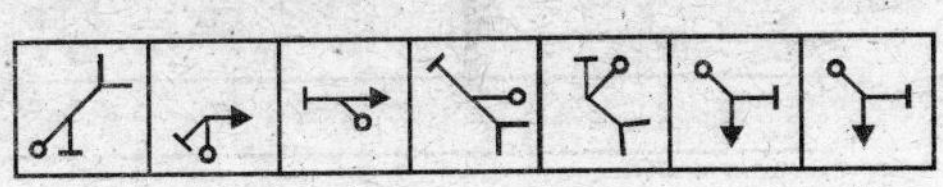

(a) (b) (c) (d) (e)

18. 

(a) (b) (c) (d) (e)

19. 

(a) (b) (c) (d) (e)

20. 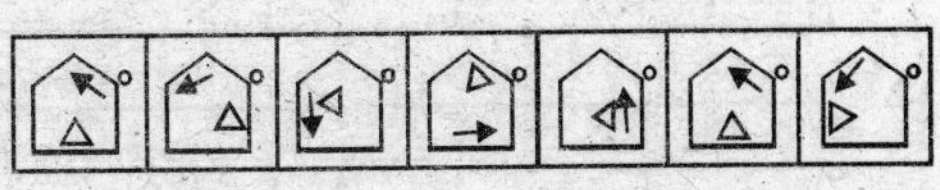

(a) (b) (c) (d) (e)

Directions (Q. 21–30) : *Each of the following questions consist of problem figures followed by answer figures. Select a figure from amongst the answer figures which will continue the same series or pattern as established by the problem figures.*

Problem Figures **Answer Figures**

21. 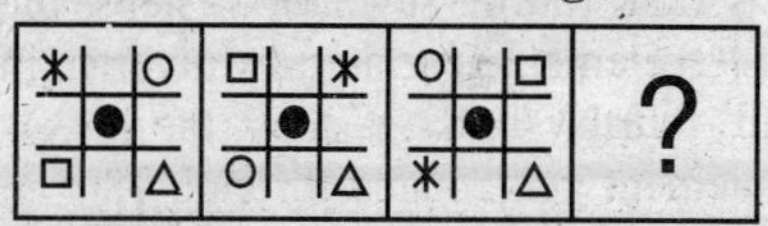 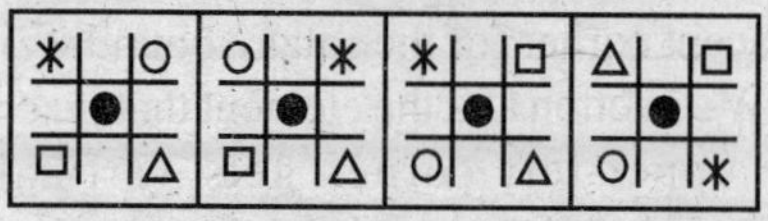

(a) (b) (c) (d)

22. 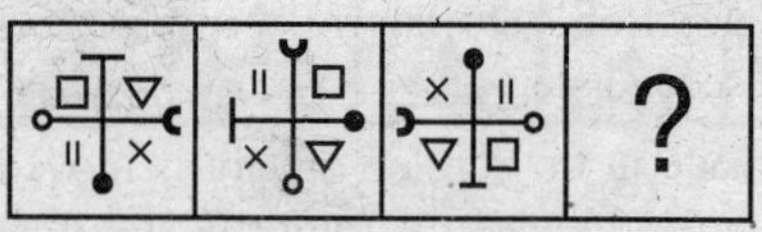 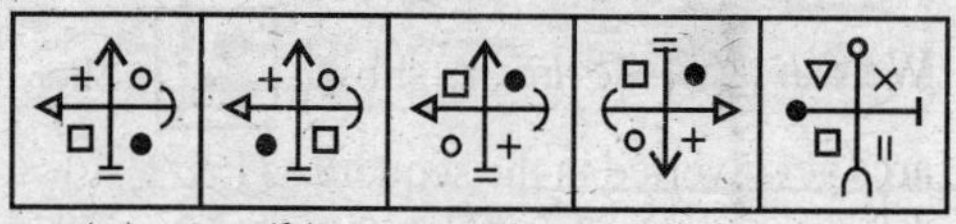

(a) (b) (c) (d) (e)

23. 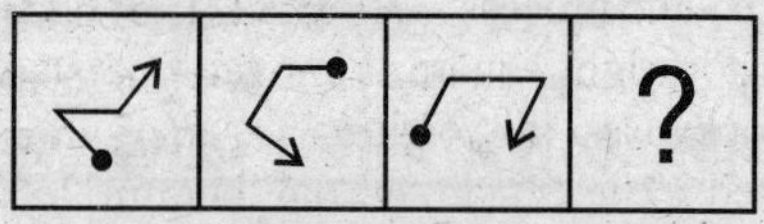 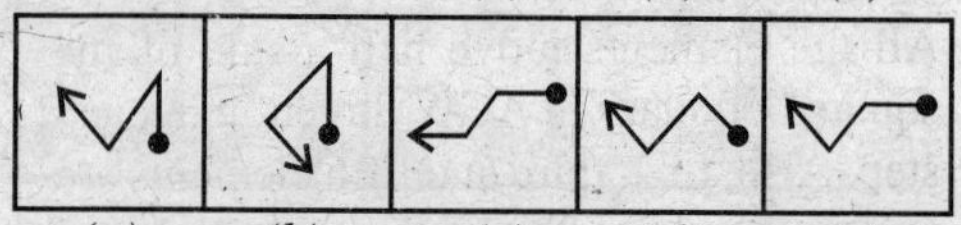

(a) (b) (c) (d) (e)

24. 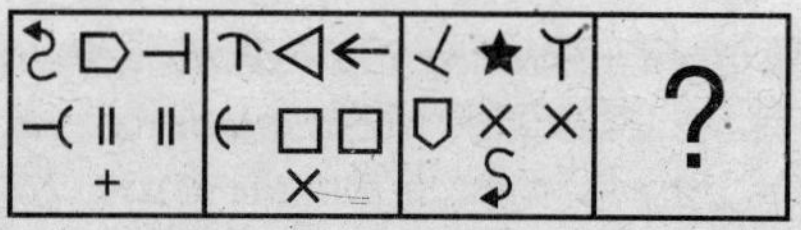 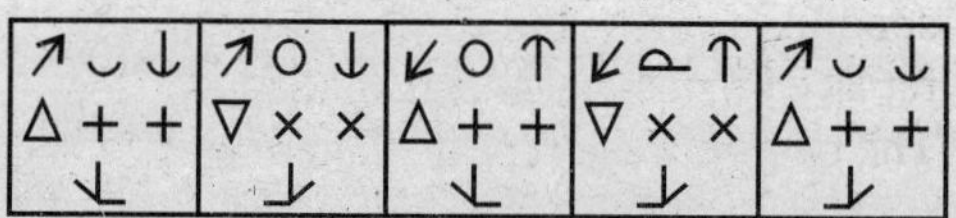

(a) (b) (c) (d) (e)

25. 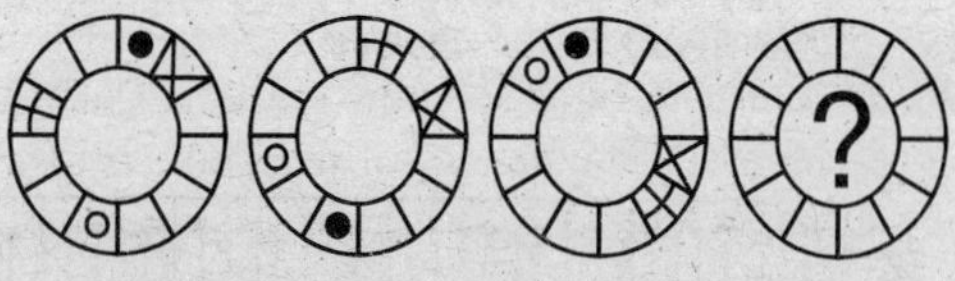 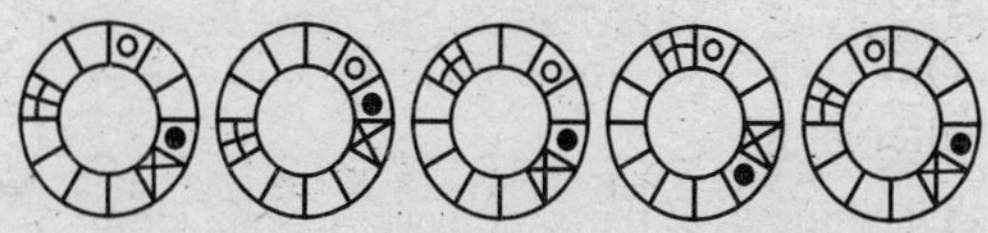

(a) (b) (c) (d) (e)

26. 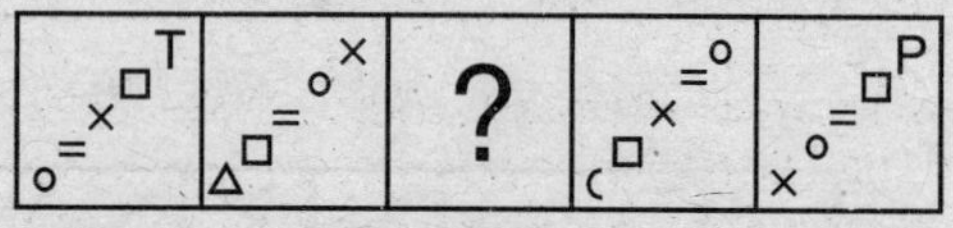 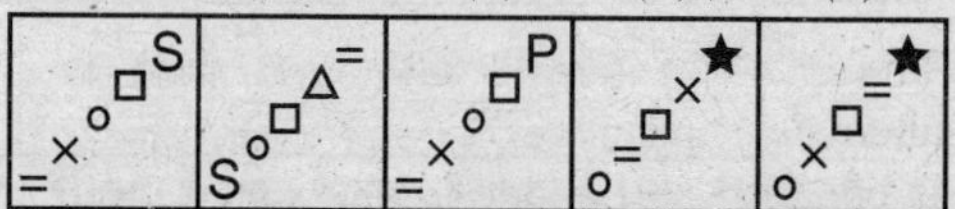

(a) (b) (c) (d) (e)

27. 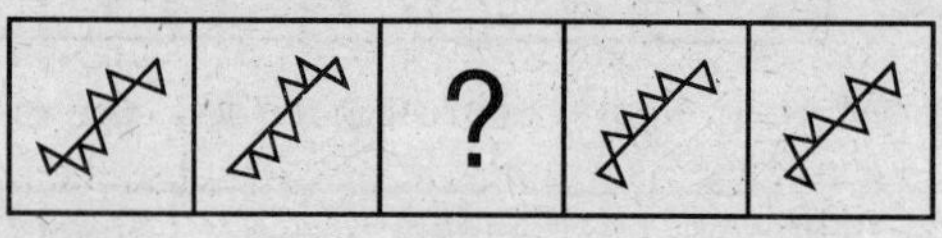 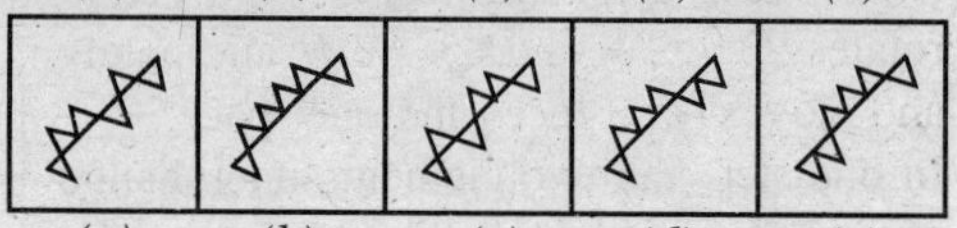

(a) (b) (c) (d) (e)

28. 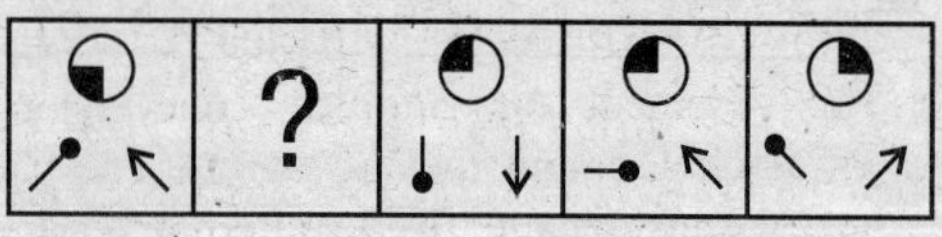 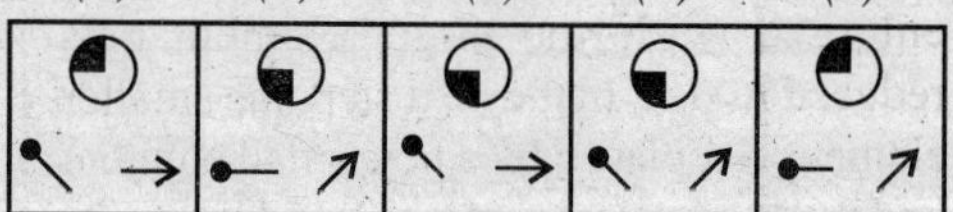

(a) (b) (c) (d) (e)

29. 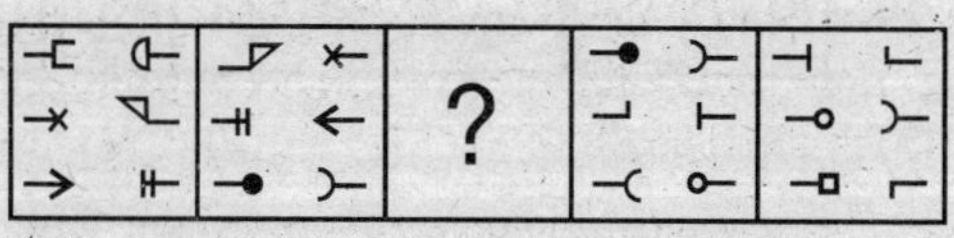 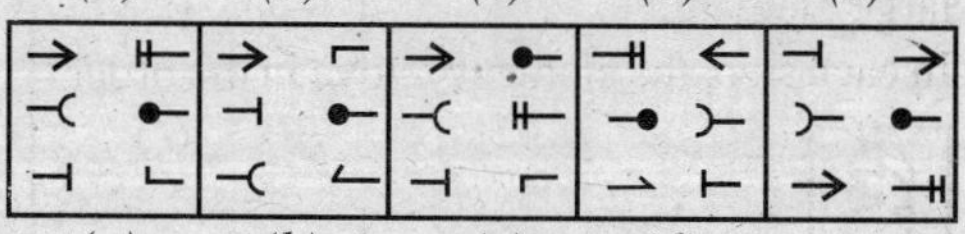

(a) (b) (c) (d) (e)

30. 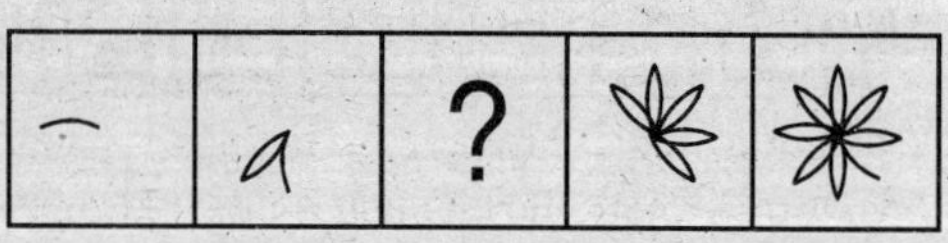 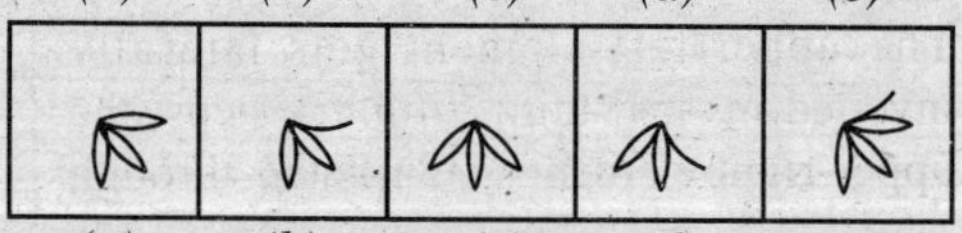

(a) (b) (c) (d) (e)

EXPLANATORY ANSWERS

1. ***(d)*** **:** In each step, all the elements move to the adjacent corner (of the square boundary) in a CW direction and the element that reaches the upper-left corner gets vertically inverted.

2. ***(c)*** **:** We can label the arcs as shown 

. The arcs get inverted in the sequence (1 & 2), (3, 4 & 5), (6 & 1), (2, 3 & 4), (5 & 6), ...

3. ***(d)*** **:** All the elements move half-a-side of the square boundary in ACW direction in each step. Also, first, third and fifth elements are replaced by new elements in one step and second, fourth and sixth elements are replaced by new elements in the next step. The two steps are repeated alternately.

4. ***(a)*** **:** In each step, the dot moves one space CW and the arrow moves two spaces CW.

5. ***(c)*** **:** One arc and four arcs get inverted alternately.

6. ***(e)*** **:** The number of parts increases by one along with the number of sides in the figure.

7. ***(c)*** **:** The pin rotates 45°CW and 90°CW alternately and moves one space (each space is equal to half-a-side of the square) and two spaces CW alternately. The arrow rotates 90°ACW and 45°ACW alternately and moves two spaces and one space.

8. ***(e)*** **:** In one step, the two elements interchange positions and the smaller element gets enlarged while the larger element gets reduced in size. In the next step, the smaller element is replaced by a new small element and the larger element is replaced by a new large element.

9. ***(c)*** **:** In each step, the elements move in the order .

10. ***(b)*** **:** The upper-left element gets laterally inverted in first, third, fifth. .... steps; the upper-right element gets rotated through 180° is first, fourth, seventh,.... steps; the lower-left element gets laterally inverted in second, fourth, sixth, ... steps; the lower-right element gets rotated through 180° in third, sixth,... steps and the pin at the middle-right position gets laterally inverted in every second step.

11. ***(a)*** **:** The shade in the top left square is moved one step clockwise till figure B and then reversed, the process is repeated. The shade in the top right square is moved one step anticlockwise till figure D and then reversed. The shade in the bottom left square is moved one step clockwise in alternate figures and the shade in bottom right square is moved one step clockwise after two figures. In figure 'A' the rule is isolated by the shade in the bottom left square.

12. ***(e)*** **:** In alternate figures a new circle is shaded clockwise. The pattern of the shade is also moved clockwise. In figure 'E' right half of the circle in the centre should have been shaded.

13. ***(a)*** **:** The three elements are placed either horizontally or vertically. In option 'A' neither of the placements can be applied.

14. ***(c)*** **:** The placement of elements is same in alternate figures. The number and type of elements is same in two subsequent figures. In this manner, figure 'C' should have four crosses and two C shapes.

15. ***(c)*** **:** The element is moved one step anticlockwise and the arc at one end is turned outside and inside alternately. In figure 'C' the element should be on the right side with the arc turned outside on the top side.

16. ***(e)*** **:** The left most element, line segment with the dot is moved one step towards right till figure C where it reaches the extreme right position. This process is repeated from figure D where the element on the extreme left, line segment with a circle, is moved. In figure 'E' the placement of the elements does not follow the rule of the series.

17. *(e)* : The 'T' line is rotated 45° clockwise and the line with the circle 45° anticlockwise. The 'Y' shape and the arrow are repeated twice after two figures. In option E, the 'T' shape and the line with the circle are rotated by 90°.

18. *(e)* : First the elements in the four corners are moved one step anticlockwise, next the four elements from the top are moved one step anticlockwise and then the four elements from the bottom are moved one step anticlockwise. Of the remaining two elements, the one on the left is made new each time and then their places are interchanged. This process is repeated from figure D. In option 'E' open square should have been in place of circle to continue the series.

19. *(a)* : At each step the outermost figure is removed and a new figure is placed right in the centre of other two figures. In option 'A' the triangle is turned upside down, which violates the rule of the series.

20. *(a)* : The arrow is moved one step anticlockwise and the triangle one step clockwise. In figure 'A' the triangle should have been on the left side of the figure.

21. *(a)* : The places of star, circle and square are moved one step clockwise at each step.

22. *(e)* : The elements in the four quadrants are moved one step clockwise and the elements at the ends of the cross are moved one step anticlockwise in this series.

23. *(a)* : In alternate figures, the line with the dot is turned 90° clockwise and the arrow 180° clockwise.

24. *(e)* : In alternate figures, the element in the top left position is horizontally inverted and moved one and half steps anticlockwise, the top middle element is turned 90° clockwise and moved one step anticlockwise, the top right element is turned 135° clockwise and moved one step anticlockwise, the element at the bottom is replaced by a new element and moved to the top middle position, and the two identical elements are replaced by two new identical elements.

25. *(a)* : The cross and the circle move one and two steps clockwise respectively (at each step), the plus moves 3, 4 and 5 steps clockwise, and the dot 6, 5 and 4 steps clockwise.

26. *(a)* : At first step, the fifth or the bottom most element is moved to the second place from top, the second element moved to the fourth place, the fourth element is moved to the third place, the third element is moved to the first or the topmost place and the element on the top, which is made new, is moved to the last or the fifth place. At second step i.e., from second problem figure to third problem figure the above process is reversed. The bottom most element is the first and the top most element is the last or fifth. Hereafter, the process is repeated from the beginning. Option 'A' is the right answer.

27. *(c)* : Starting from the bottom, one triangle is moved to the opposite side at each step in upward order. Option 'C' fits into the question marked space.

28. *(c)* : The shade inside the circle is rotated clockwise in alternate figures; the line segment with a dot is rotated 135° clockwise in alternate figures and the arrow is rotated 135° anticlockwise in alternate figures. By this process answer figure 'C' completes the series.

29. *(a)* : At each step the elements are moved diagonally upward and then laterally inverted, and the top two elements are made new and placed at the bottom line. By this process, option figure 'A' completes the series.

30. *(a)* : The number of arcs making the petals of the flower are increased by one, one and half, two, two and half respectively at each step. Also, the flower is turned 45° anticlockwise. By this process, option 'A' is the right answer.

23. NON-VERBAL ANALOGY

EXERCISE

TYPE-I

Directions (Q. 1-15): *The second figure in the first unit of the Problem Figures bears a certain relationship to the first figure. Similarly, one of the figures in the Answer Figures bears the same relationship to the first figures in the second unit of the Problem Figures. Locate the figure which would fit the questions marks.*

Problem Figures | **Answer Figures**

1.

1 2 3 4

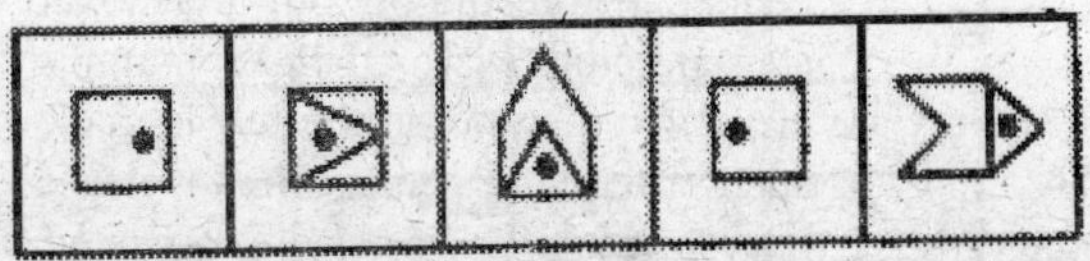

(a) (b) (c) (d) (e)

2.

1 2 3 4

(a) (b) (c) (d) (e)

3.

1 2 3 4

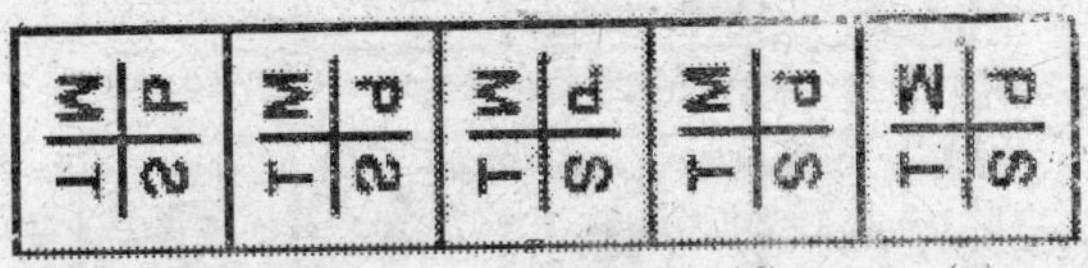

(a) (b) (c) (d) (e)

4.

1 2 3 4

(a) (b) (c) (d) (e)

5.

1 2 3 4

(a) (b) (c) (d) (e)

6.

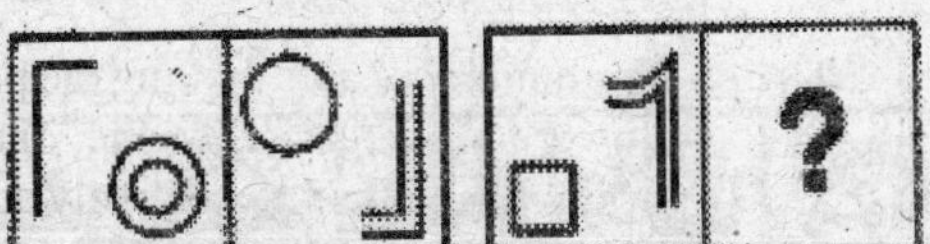

1 2 3 4

(a) (b) (c) (d) (e)

Problem Figures **Answer Figures**

7.

1 2 3 4

(a) (b) (c) (d) (e)

8.

1 2 3 4

(a) (b) (c) (d) (e)

9.
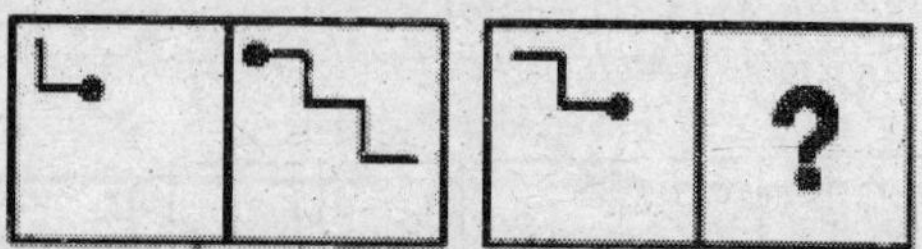
1 2 3 4
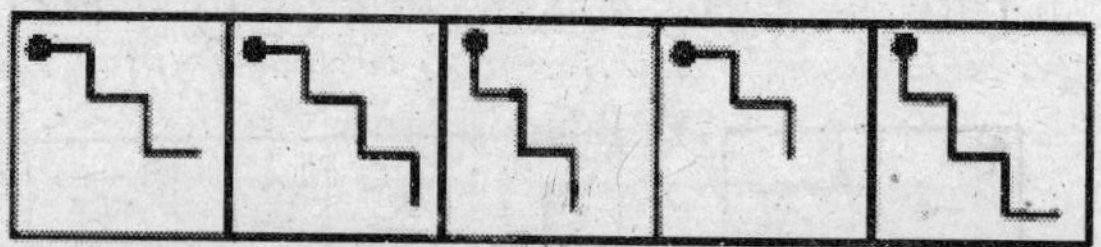
(a) (b) (c) (d) (e)

10.

1 2 3 4

(a) (b) (c) (d) (e)

11.

1 2 3 4

(a) (b) (c) (d) (e)

12.
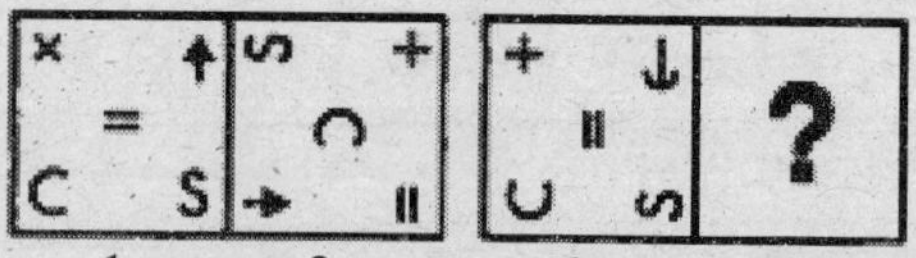
1 2 3 4
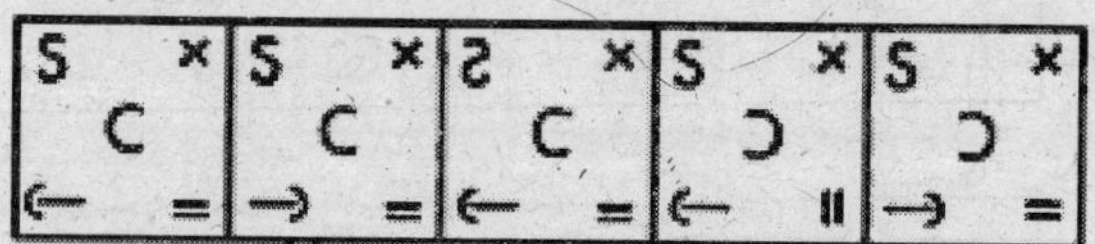
(a) (b) (c) (d) (e)

13.

1 2 3 4

(a) (b) (c) (d) (e)

14.

1 2 3 4

(a) (b) (c) (d) (e)

15.
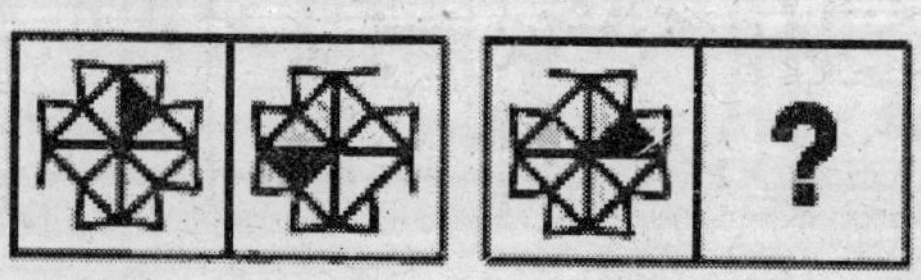
1 2 3 4

(a) (b) (c) (d) (e)

TYPE-II

Directions (Q. 16–30): *In each of the following questions, a related pair of figures is followed by five numbered pairs of figures. Select the pair that has a relationship* **similar** *to that in the unnumbered pair.*

Problem Figure **Answer Figures**

16. 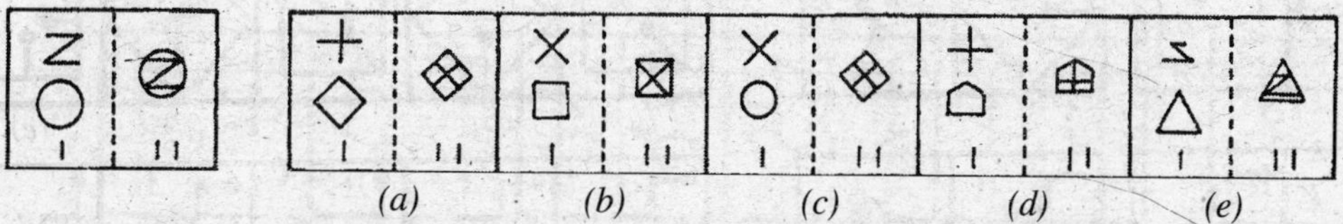

17. 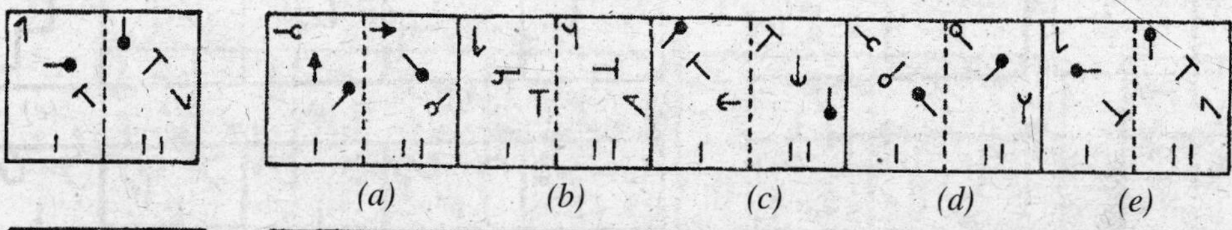

18. 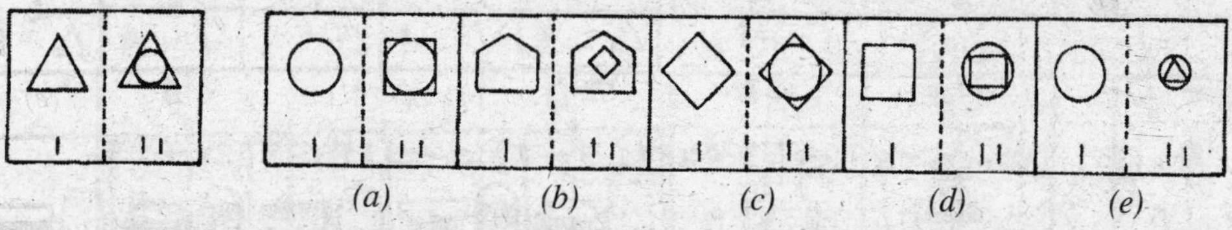

19. 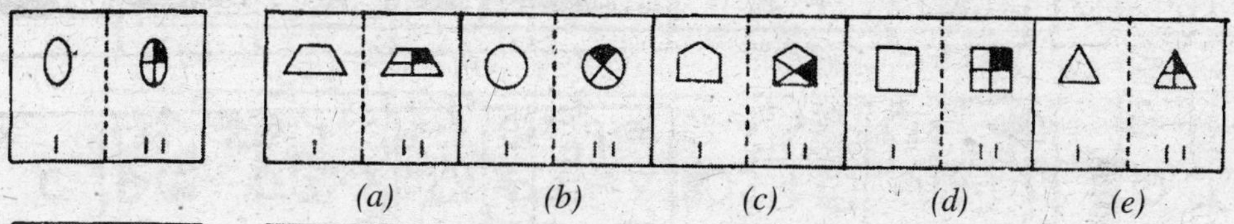

20. 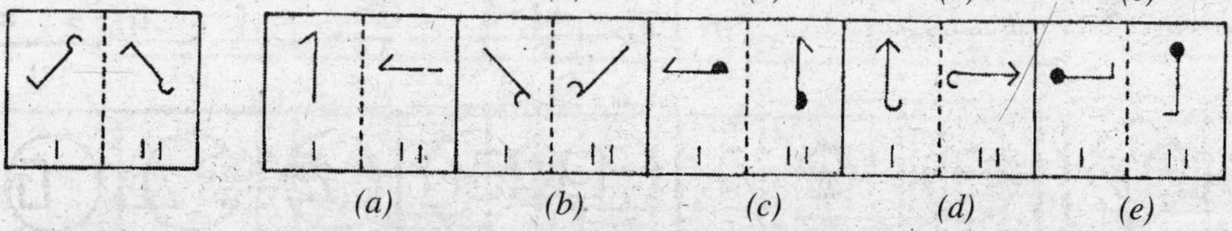

21. 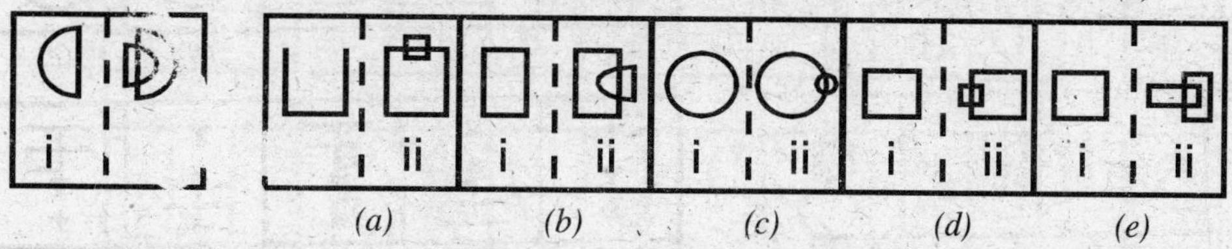

22. 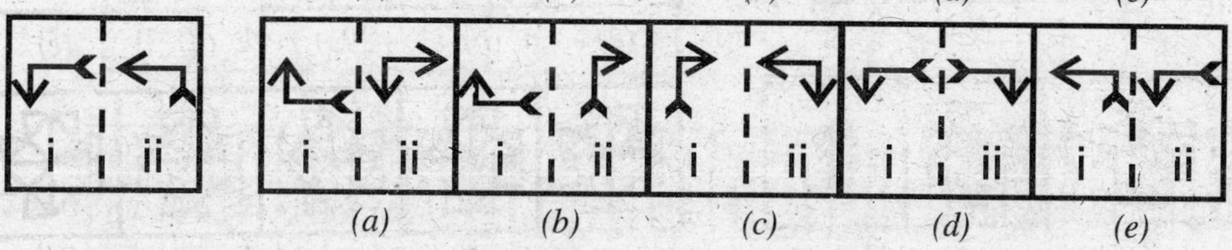

Problem Figure **Answer Figures**

23.

(a) (b) (c) (d) (e)

24.
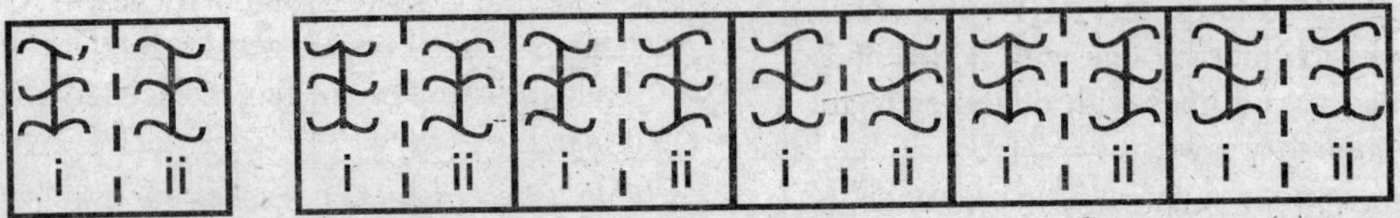
(a) (b) (c) (d) (e)

25.
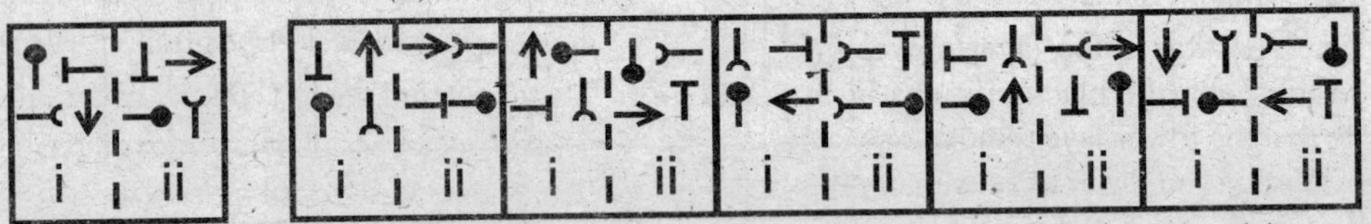
(a) (b) (c) (d) (e)

26.
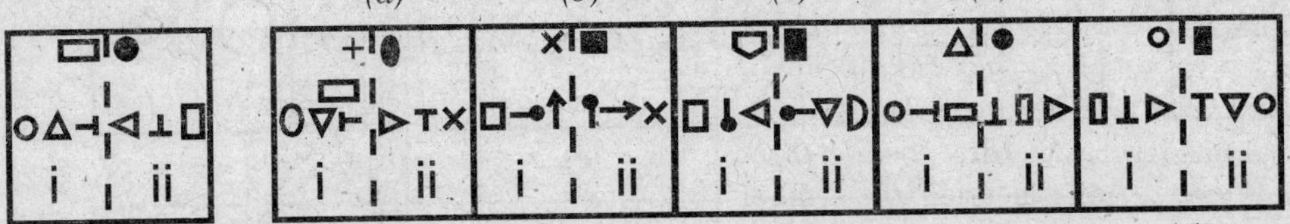
(a) (b) (c) (d) (e)

27.
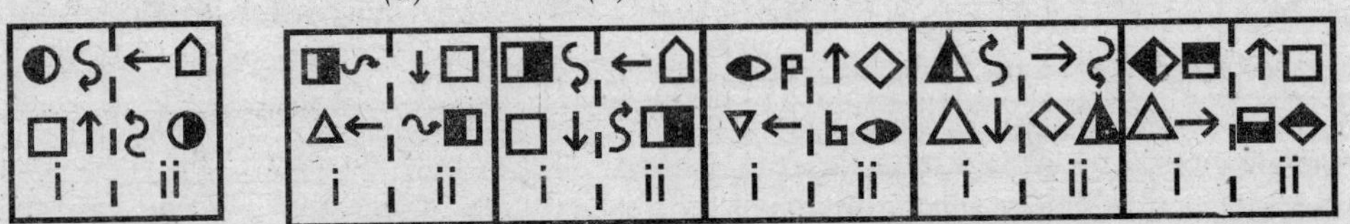
(a) (b) (c) (d) (e)

28.

(a) (b) (c) (d) (e)

29.
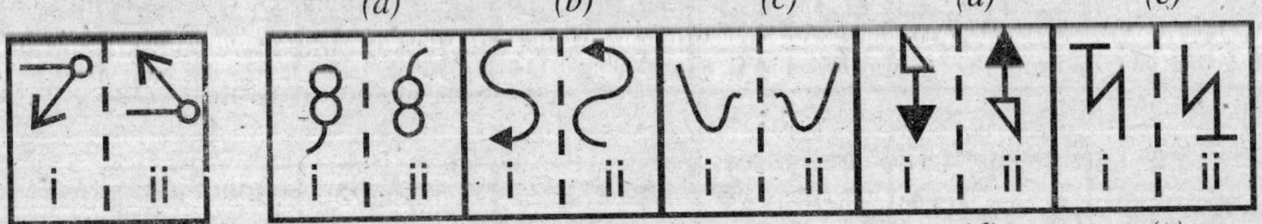
(a) (b) (c) (d) (e)

30.

(a) (b) (c) (d) (e)

EXPLANATORY ANSWERS

1. (b) : The R.H.S. figure is fitted into the L.H.S. figure and the resulting figure is rotated 90° CW.

2. (b) : The figure rotates 45° ACW, the arrow changes to a curved line with dotted ends and the curved lines with dotted ends get converted to arrows.

3. (d) : The top left symbol rotates 90° ACW while all other symbols rotate 90° CW.

4. (e) : The black portion in top layer moves one step to the right; the black portions in the middle and the lower layers move one step to the left and the dot moves one step upwards.

5. (d) : The first and second symbols from the left interchange positions and the other two symbols also interchange positions. The symbol that reaches the first position from the left gets laterally inverted; the symbol that reaches the second position gets inverted, the third symbol rotates 90° CW and the fourth symbol gets replaced by a new one.

6. (d) : The single figure is replaced by a figure similar to the double figures and the double figures are replaced by figures similar to the single figure.

7. (e) : The figure rotates 135° ACW; a 'T' appears diagonally opposite to the black leaf and a 'Y' appears diagonally opposite to the white leaf.

8. (c) : The square rotates through 45°. The arrow moves 90° ACW and the pin moves 45° ACW

9. (b) : The figure rotates through 180° and three lines forming a zig-zag, get attached to its lower end.

10. (d) : The symbols move in the order

The symbol that reaches the central position rotates 90° CW and its arc gets inverted; the 'P' shaped symbol rotates through 180°; the 'C' shaped symbol rotates 90° CW; the 'S' Shaped symbol gets laterally inverted and the fifth symbol gets replaced by a new one.

45°, the symbol that reaches the lower right corner rotates 90° ACW and a new symbol appears in middle-left position.

11. (e) : The upper and the lower parts of the figure get separated. Shading is removed from the upper part and the lower part is inverted. The two parts are then placed side by side.

12. (a) : The symbols move in the order

The symbol that reaches the top-left corner rotates 90° ACW; the symbol in the top-right corner rotates through 45°; the symbols in the lower-left corner and in the central positions rotates 90° CW and the symbol that reaches the lower-right corner rotates through 90°.

13. (e) : The figure gets laterally inverted. The dot on the larger arc, the pin and the small arc rotate 90° ACW. Also, the pin gets inverted.

14. (c) : The figure rotates 90° CW. One half of one of the lines on the arrow is lost. The figure in front of the arrowhead rotates through 45°.

15. (d) : The missing line segment in the first figure is replaced in second. Then moving ACW, the third line segment is removed along the two next consecutive sides of the square. Shaded portion in the first figure moves three steps ACW. Similarly, the third figure gives figure (D).

16. *(b)* : The uppermost design enters into innerside side of the lower design from Ist figure to the IInd figure.

17. *(a)* : In element I to II upper left design comes at lower right rotating 135° C.W. Middle design goes to upper left and rotates 90° CW. While lower right design goes to middle and it also rotates 90° C.W. The same changes occur in option A.

18. *(e)* : In element I to II and ellipse is put in the triangle. Similarly in option E a triangle is put in the ellipse.

19. *(d)* : From first figure to IInd figure, design is divided into four equal parts and right side of the upper portion becomes shaded.

20. *(e)* : From Ist figure to IInd figure, design is reversed after moving 90° anticlockwise direction.

21. *(d)* : The figure in the first part is laterally inverted and a similar but smaller design is placed on its left side in the second part.

22. *(e)* : The element in first part is moved by 90° and the places of short and long line segments are interchanged.

23. *(c)* : The number of sides making the top left figure is increased by one and a new figure is made, shaded and moved to the top right position. The element in the centre is turned 90° anticlockwise and the small line on the other side is turned by 180°. The element in the bottom right is turned upside down and moved to the bottom left position.

24. *(a)* : The direction of both arcs on the top, are on the middle right and arc on the bottom left in first part are turned to the other side in the second part.

25. *(b)* : From part one to part two, the element in the top left is turned 90° clockwise and the other three 90° anticlockwise, also the elements are moved one step anticlockwise.

26. *(b)* : From part one to part two, the top right element is turned by 90° and moved down, the lower right and middle elements are turned 90° clockwise and 90° anticlockwise respectively and moved to the left and the lower left element is shaded and moved up.

27. *(a)* : All the four elements exchange place diagonally and in doing so the top left element is laterally inverted, the top right element is horizontally inverted, the bottom right element is turned 90° anticlockwise and the number of lines making the element in bottom left is increased by one.

28. *(e)* : The innermost figure is removed and the new innermost figure also encloses the other two figures. The innermost and smallest figure is then shaded.

29. *(b)* : The design in the first part is horizontally inverted in the second.

30. *(b)* : All the elements in the first part are turned upside down and then 1st, 2nd, 3rd and 4th positioned elements become 3rd, 4th, 1st and 2nd elements in the second part.

24. ODD MAN OUT

In this type of reasoning a statement is followed by inferences drawn from it. From these inferences only one definitely follows which is the hidden proposition of the sentence and it is the right answer to the question.

EXERCISE

Directions (Q. 1–10) : *In each question below five figures are given. Four are similar in a certain way and so form a group. The question is— which one of the figures* **does not** *belong to that group?*

1. 

(a) (b) (c) (d) (e)

2. 

(a) (b) (c) (d) (e)

3. 

(a) (b) (c) (d) (e)

4. 

(a) (b) (c) (d) (e)

5. 

(a) (b) (c) (d) (e)

6. 

(a) (b) (c) (d) (e)

7. 

(a) (b) (c) (d) (e)

8. 

(a) (b) (c) (d) (e)

9. 

(a) (b) (c) (d) (e)

10. 

(a) (b) (c) (d) (e)

Directions (Q. 11–20) : *In each of the following questions, in four out of the five figures, element I is related to element II in the same particular way. Find out the figure in which the element I is* **not** *so related to element II.*

11. 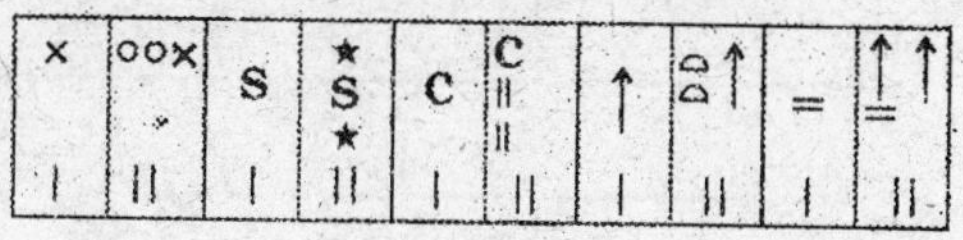

(a) (b) (c) (d) (e)

12. 

(a) (b) (c) (d) (e)

13. 
(a) (b) (c) (d) (e)

14. 
(a) (b) (c) (d) (e)

15. 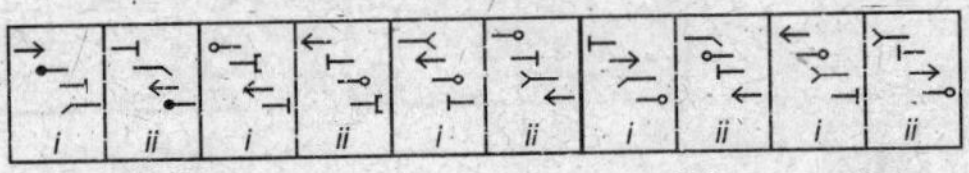
(a) (b) (c) (d) (e)

16. 
(a) (b) (c) (d) (e)

17. 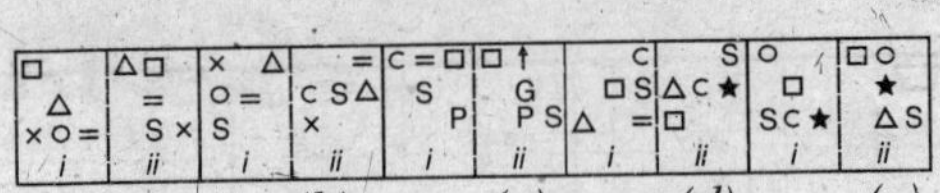
(a) (b) (c) (d) (e)

18. 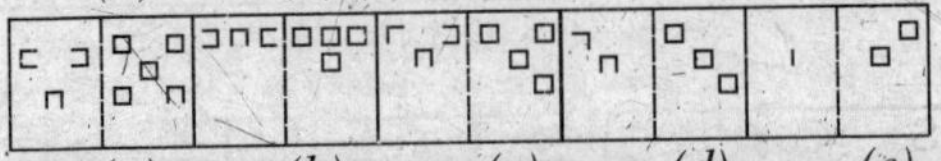
(a) (b) (c) (d) (e)

19. 
(a) (b) (c) (d) (e)

20. 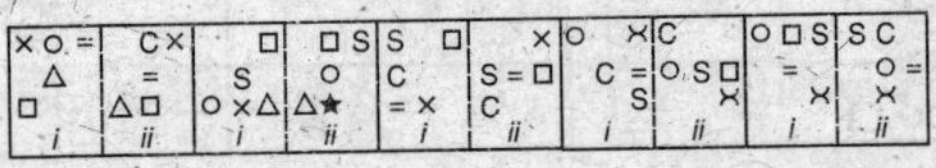
(a) (b) (c) (d) (e)

Directions (Q. 21–30) : *In each of the following questions, a related pair of figures (unnumbered) is followed by five numbered pairs of figures. Out of these five, four have relationship similar to that in the unnumbered pair. Only one pair of figures does not have similar relationship. Select that pair of figures which does not have a similar relationship to that in the unnumbered pair. Number of that pair is your answer.*

21. 
(a) (b) (c) (d) (e)

22. 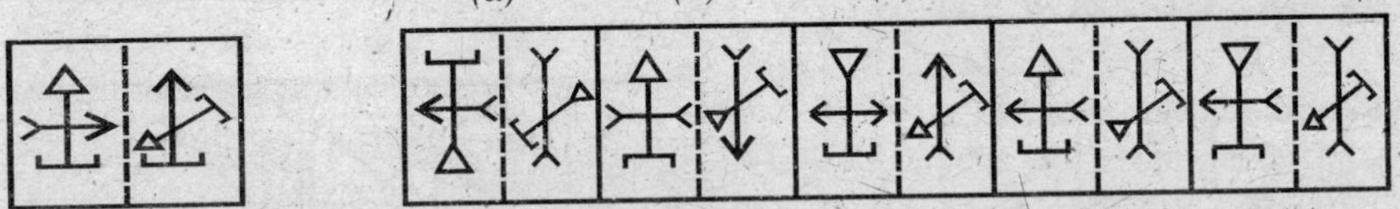
(a) (b) (c) (d) (e)

23. 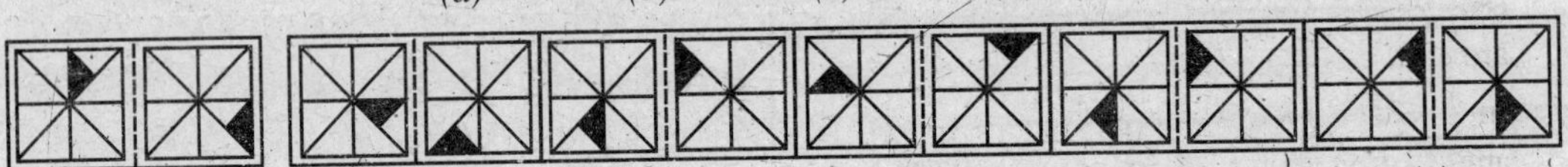
(a) (b) (c) (d) (e)

24. 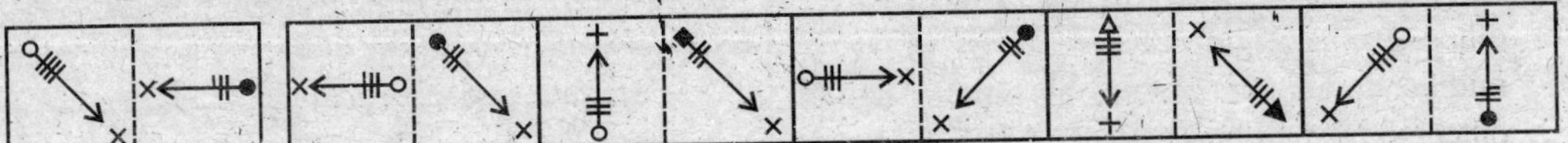
(a) (b) (c) (d) (e)

25. 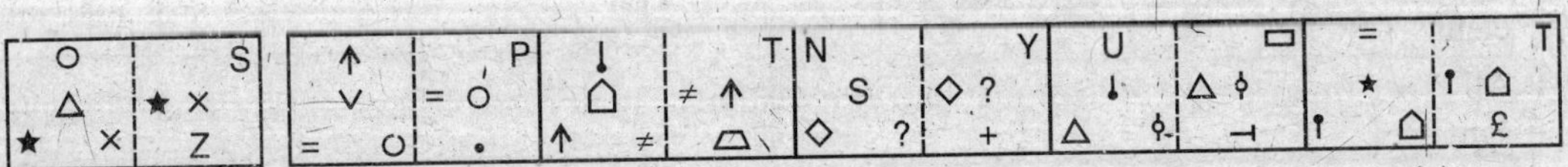
(a) (b) (c) (d) (e)

26. 
(a) (b) (c) (d) (e)

27. 

(a) (b) (c) (d) (e)

28. 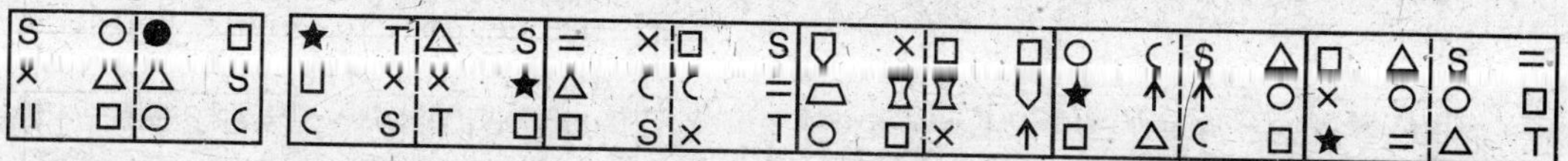

(a) (b) (c) (d) (e)

29. 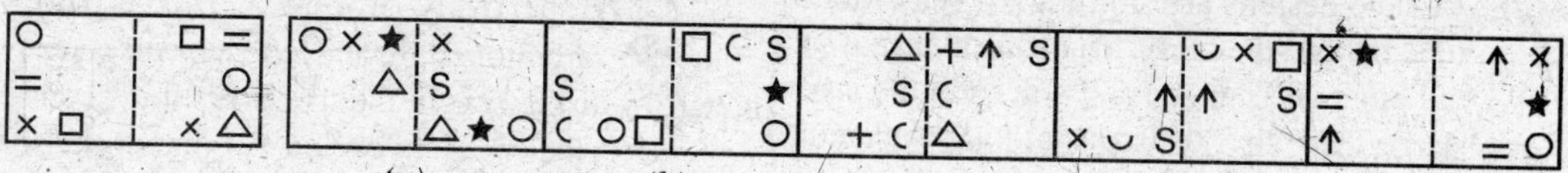

(a) (b) (c) (d) (e)

30. 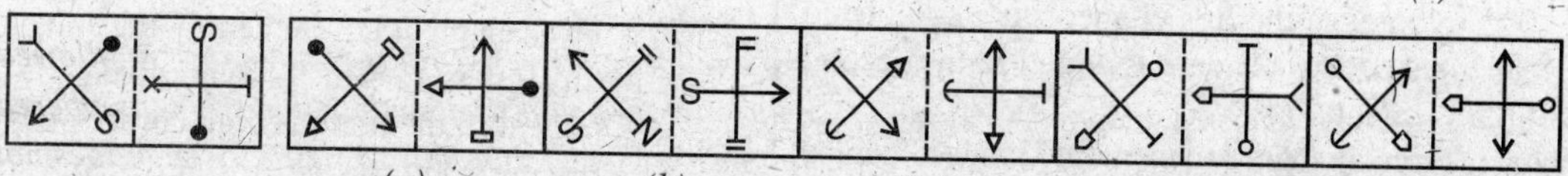

(a) (b) (c) (d) (e)

EXPLANATORY ANSWERS

1. *(d)* : In all other figures, the arrow and the + sign lie towards the black end of the main figure.

2.*(a)* : The pins, equal in number of sides in the main figure are attached to the midpoint of a side of the main figure in case of figures (B), (C), (D) and (E). In figure (A), these pins are attached to a vertex of the main figure.

3.*(c)* : In all other figures, the dot appears in the angle formed between the arrow and the pin.

4.*(a)* : All other figures can be rotated into each other. (In each figure except figure (A), the middle element is obtained by rotating the outer element through 90° CW and the inner element is obtained by rotating the middle element through 90° CW).

5.*(c)* : All other figures have at least one line of symmetry.

6.*(c)* : All other figures can be rotated into each other.

7.*(e)* : In each one of the other four figures, four arcs are curved towards the left and four other arcs are curved towards the right.

8.*(c)* : All other figures can be rotated into each other.

9.*(d)* : In all other figures, the number of dots outside the main figure is one more than the number of dots inside the main figure.

10.*(a)* : In all other figures, one of the dots lies outside the triangle as well as the circle.

11.*(e)* : Except in figure (B), in all other figures, from element I to II two new designs are added in one side of the main design.

12.*(c)* : In each figure from element I to II the main design rotates through 135° clockwise or anticlockwise. Except in figure (C), in all other figures, the smaller line segment moves to other side from element I to II.

13.*(a)* : In all other figures the element II can be obtained by the lateral inversion of the element I. In figure (A), the lower design has not been inverted.

14.*(b)* : In figure (B), the small segment is on the same side as that of the half shaded circle in both the elements.

15.(*d*) : The first design is inverted and moved to third place, the second design is moved to the fourth place, third design to the first place and fourth design is inverted and moved to the seeond place. Option (D) violates this.

16.(*b*) : In all other options the top-left element is moved to the centre with 90° clockwise rotation. Here, it is rotated anticlockwise.

17.(*d*) : All the designs are shifted in a set pattern one behind the other. The fourth design in all others is changed and placed in the last. Here, the fifth and last designs are changed.

18.(*a*) : In all other pair of figures, all incomplete squares in the first elements are completed and an extra square is added in the second element.

19.(*a*) : From element I to element II, the 'S' shape is turned 90° clockwise and moved down, the double arrow shape '⇒' is turned 90° clockwise and moved to the right, the two parallel lines one turned by 90°; one parallel line is added and all three lines are moved up, the line with a dot is turned 90° clockwise and moved to the centre and the 'C' shape in the centre is turned by 180° and moved to top left position. Here, the double arrow is turned anticlockwise.

20.(*c*) : Starting from one unit, all units are moved in a set pattern, the places of last two units moved are interchanged and the last unit is then made new. Here, no changes are made in the last two units.

21.(*d*) : From element I to element II clockwise the first unit is moved 2 steps forward, the second unit 1 step forward, the third unit 2½ steps forward and the fourth unit 3 steps forward. In option 'D' the third unit violates the rule.

22.(*e*) : From element I to element II, the horizontal bar is turned 135° anticlockwise and the unit at the lower end is turned by 180°. The vertical bar is turned 90° anticlockwise and the unit at the lower end is turned by 180°. In option 'E' one more unit at the top is turned by 180°.

23.(*e*) : In element II, the shade is moved two sections clockwise and shifted from the centre to the base. In option 'E' it is not so.

24.(*a*) : In element II, the arrow is turned 135° clockwise. In option 'A' it is turned anticlockwise.

25.(*b*) : From element I to element II, the bottom right unit and bottom left unit are moved to the centre and middle left position respectively. The other two units are removed and two new elements are placed in the top right and bottom centre position respectively. In option 'B' the placement of bottom right and left elements is not right.

26.(*c*) : In element II, the shades are shifted one petal clockwise. In option 'C' one of the shades is not moved.

27.(*b*) : From element I to element II, the unit on the top left is turned 90° anticlockwise and moved to the bottom right corner position, the unit in the centre is turned 135° anticlockwise and moved to the top right position, and the unit in the bottom right is turned by 180° and moved to the centre. In option 'B', the middle unit is turned 135° clockwise.

28.(*a*) : From element I to element II, a new unit is placed in the top left position, the top left unit is moved to the middle right position, the middle right unit is moved to the left position, the middle left unit is replaced by a new unit and placed in bottom right position, the bottom right unit is moved to the top right position, and the top right unit is moved diagonally to replace the bottom left unit. In option 'A', the middle left unit is not changed when moved to the bottom right position.

29.(*e*) : From element I to element II starting anticlockwise, the first and second units are moved 1½ steps clockwise respectively, the third unit ½ step anticlockwise, the fourth unit 2 steps clockwise, and a new unit is placed ahead of the first unit. Option 'E' violates the rules.

30.(*e*) : In element II, the cross is turned 135° clockwise and then the positions of left and top units on the cross are interchanged. In option 'E' it is not so.

ARITHMETIC

1. NUMBERS

The development of the number system started with natural numbers. These are generally known as counting numbers.

Natural Numbers

Numbers which start from 1 are known as natural numbers. It is denoted by N. The smallest natural number is 1. It is written as,

$$N = \{1, 2, 3, ..., \infty\}$$

Whole Numbers

A number which starts from zero (0) is known as whole number. It is denoted by W. It is written as,

$$W = \{0, 1, 2, 3, ..., \infty\}$$

Integers

Natural numbers along with 0 and their negatives are known as integers. It is denoted by I. It is written as,

$$I = \{..., -4, -3, -2, -1, 0, 1, 2, 3, 4, ...\}$$

Even Numbers

A number which is divisible by 2 is known as even numbers.

Such as, 2, 4, 6, 10, 12, 128, 432 etc.

Odd Numbers

A number which is not divisible by 2 is known as odd numbers:

Such as, 1, 3, 5, 7, 9, 11, 13, 21, 29, 123 etc.

Prime Numbers

A number which is divided by itself is known as prime numbers. The smallest prime number is 2.

Such as, 2, 3, 5, 7, 11, 13, 17, 19, 23, ... etc.

Composite Numbers

A number which is divided by itself and others also is known as composite numbers. The smallest composite number is 4.

Such as, 4, 6, 8, 9, 10, 12, 14, 15, 16, 18, ... etc.

There are 25 prime numbers between 1 to 100.

Such as, 2, 3, 5, 7, 11, 13, 17, 19, 23, 29, 31, 37, 41, 43, 47, 53, 59, 61, 67, 71, 73, 79, 83, 89, 97.

Test, whether a given number is prime or composite: If we want to test any number more than 100, whether it is prime or not, take an integer larger than the approximate square root of that number. Let it be x. Test the divisibility of the given number by every prime number less than x. If it is not divisible by any of them, then it is prime; otherwise it is composite number.

EXAMPLE: Which of the following numbers are prime numbers?

(*i*) 421 (*ii*) 671

SOLUTION:

(*i*) The square root of 421 is nearly 21.
Prime numbers less than 21 are 2, 3, 5, 7, 11, 13, 17, 19. Clearly, 421 is not divisible by any of them. So, 421 is a prime number.

(*ii*) The square root of 671 is nearly 26.
Prime numbers less than 26 are 2, 3, 5, 7, 11, 13, 17, 19, 23. Out of these, 671 is divisible by 11. So, 671 is not a prime number. Hence it is composite number.

The formulae given below are quite useful for quick multiplication:

(*i*) $(a+b)^2 = a^2 + 2ab + b^2$

(*ii*) $(a-b)^2 = a^2 - 2ab + b^2$

(iii) $a^2 - b^2 = (a+b)(a-b)$

(iv) $a^2 + b^2 = (a+b)^2 - 2ab$

(v) $(a+b)^3 = a^3 + b^3 + 3ab(a+b)$

(vi) $(a-b)^3 = a^3 - b^3 - 3ab(a-b)$

(vii) $a^3 + b^3 = (a+b)(a^2 - ab + b^2)$

(viii) $a^3 - b^3 = (a-b)(a^2 + ab + b^2)$

EXAMPLE: Simplify the following.

(i) $\dfrac{348 \times 348 \times 348 + 252 \times 252 \times 252}{348 \times 348 - 348 \times 252 + 252 \times 252}$

(ii) $\dfrac{261 \times 261 \times 261 - 77 \times 77 \times 77}{261 \times 261 + 261 \times 77 + 77 \times 77}$

SOLUTION:

(i) $\dfrac{348 \times 348 \times 348 + 252 \times 252 \times 252}{348 \times 348 - 348 \times 252 + 252 \times 252}$

Let $348 = a$

and $252 = b$

$\therefore$ Given expression is written as

$$\frac{a \times a \times a + b \times b \times b}{a \times a - a \times b + b \times b} = \frac{a^3 + b^3}{a^2 - ab + b^2}$$

$$= \frac{(a+b)(a^2 - ab + b^2)}{(a^2 - ab + b^2)} = a + b$$

$= 348 + 252 = 600.$

(ii) $\dfrac{261 \times 261 \times 261 - 77 \times 77 \times 77}{261 \times 261 + 261 \times 77 + 77 \times 77}$

Let $261 = a$

and $77 = b$

$$\therefore \frac{a^3 - b^3}{a^2 + ab + b^2} = \frac{(a-b)(a^2 + ab + b^2)}{(a^2 + ab + b^2)} = a - b$$

$\therefore$ $261 - 77 = 184.$

If we divide a given number by another number, then

Dividend = (Divisor × Quotient) + Remainder

EXAMPLE: On dividing 18254 by a certain number, the quotient is 289 and the remainder is 47. Find the divisor.

SOLUTION: Here, Dividend = 18254

quotient = 289

remainder = 47

$$\therefore \quad \text{Divisor} = \frac{\text{Dividend} - \text{Remainder}}{\text{Quotient}}$$

$$= \frac{18254 - 47}{289} = \frac{18207}{289} = 63$$

Hence, divisor = 63.

EXAMPLE: What least number must be subtracted from 862 to get a number exactly divisible by 31?

SOLUTION: On dividing 862 by 31, the remainder obtained is 25.

Hence, the required number = 25.

MULTIPLE CHOICE QUESTIONS

1. The face value of 8 in the numeral 458926 is:

A. 8000 B. 8

C. 1000 D. 458000

2. $106 \times 106 + 94 \times 94 = x$, the value of x is:

A. 21032 B. 20032

C. 23032 D. 20072

3. If $m \times 48 = 173 \times 240$ then the value of m is:

A. 545 B. 685

C. 865 D. 495

4. $\left(1 - \frac{1}{3}\right)\left(1 - \frac{1}{4}\right)\left(1 - \frac{1}{5}\right) \ldots \left(1 - \frac{1}{n}\right) = x$

then the value of x is:

A. $\dfrac{1}{n}$ B. $\dfrac{2}{n}$

C. $\dfrac{2(n-1)}{n}$ D. $\dfrac{2}{n(n+1)}$

5. When simplified the product

$\left(2 - \frac{1}{3}\right)\left(2 - \frac{3}{5}\right)\left(2 - \frac{5}{7}\right) \ldots \left(2 - \frac{997}{999}\right)$ is

equal to:

A. $\dfrac{5}{999}$ B. $\dfrac{1001}{999}$

C. $\dfrac{1001}{3}$ D. None of these

6. Which number should replace both the asterisks in $\left(\frac{*}{21}\right) \times \left(\frac{*}{189}\right) = 1$?

A. 21 B. 63
C. 3969 D. 147

7. In a division sum, the divisor is 12 times the quotient and 5 times the remainder. If the remainder be 48, then the dividend is:

A. 240 B. 576
C. 4800 D. 4848

8. What least number must be subtracted from 1294 so that the remainder when divided by 9, 11, 13 will leave in each case the same remainder 6?

A. 0 B. 1
C. 2 D. 3

9. If $\sqrt{\left(1+\frac{27}{169}\right)} = \left(1+\frac{x}{13}\right)$, then the value of x is:

A. 1 B. 3
C. 5 D. 7

10. If $\frac{x}{y} = \frac{3}{4}$, then the value of $\left(\frac{6}{7} + \frac{y-x}{y+x}\right)$ equals:

A. $\frac{5}{7}$ B. $1\frac{1}{7}$
C. 1 D. 2

11. The largest natural number by which the product of three consecutive even natural numbers is always divisible, is:

A. 16 B. 24
C. 48 D. 96

12. The least number of five digits which is exactly divisible by 12, 15 and 18 is:

A. 10080 B. 10800
C. 18000 D. 81000

13. The least number which when divided by 8, 9, 12, 16 and 20 leaves the same remainder 1 in each case is:

A. 712 B. 271
C. 721 D. 720

14. The value of 0.8693 + 0.092 + 0.87 + 0.4 equals:

A. 2.3213 B. 2.2331
C. 3.2313 D. 2.2313

15. The prime numbers between 1 to 50 are:

A. 8 B. 12
C. 15 D. 10

ANSWERS

1	2	3	4	5	6	7	8	9	10
B	D	C	B	C	B	D	B	A	C
11	12	13	14	15					
C	A	C	D	C					

EXPLANATORY ANSWERS

1. The face value of 8 in the numeral 458926 is 8.

2. $106 \times 106 + 94 \times 94 = x$

$\Rightarrow \quad (106)^2 + (94)^2 = x$

$\Rightarrow \quad (100+6)^2 + (100-6)^2 = x$

$\Rightarrow 10000 + 1200 + 36 + 10000 - 1200 + 36 = x$

$\Rightarrow \quad 20072 = x$

$\Rightarrow \quad x = 20072.$

3. $\because m = \frac{173 \times 240}{48} = 865.$

4. $\left(1-\frac{1}{3}\right)\left(1-\frac{1}{4}\right)\left(1-\frac{1}{5}\right)...\left(1-\frac{1}{n}\right) = x$

$\because \quad 1-\frac{1}{3} = \frac{3-1}{3} = \frac{2}{3}$

$$1-\frac{1}{4} = \frac{4-1}{4} = \frac{3}{4}$$

$$1-\frac{1}{5} = \frac{5-1}{5} = \frac{4}{5}$$

$$\vdots$$

$$1-\frac{1}{n} = \frac{n-1}{n}$$

$$\therefore \frac{2}{3}\times\frac{3}{4}\times\frac{4}{5}\times\ldots\times\frac{n-2}{n-1}\times\frac{n-1}{n} = \frac{2}{n}$$

5. $\left(2-\frac{1}{3}\right)\left(2-\frac{3}{5}\right)\left(2-\frac{5}{7}\right)\ldots\left(2-\frac{997}{999}\right)$

$$2-\frac{1}{3} = \frac{6-1}{3} = \frac{5}{3}$$

$$2-\frac{3}{5} = \frac{10-3}{5} = \frac{7}{5}$$

$$2-\frac{5}{7} = \frac{14-5}{7} = \frac{9}{7}$$

$$2-\frac{997}{999} = \frac{1998-997}{999} = \frac{1001}{999}$$

$$\therefore \frac{5}{3}\times\frac{7}{5}\times\frac{9}{7}\times\ldots\times\frac{999}{997}\times\frac{1001}{999} = \frac{1001}{3}$$

6. $\frac{*}{21}\times\frac{*}{189} = 1$

$$\frac{x^2}{21\times 189} = 1$$

$\Rightarrow \quad x^2 = 21 \times 189 = 21 \times 21 \times 9$

$\Rightarrow \quad x^2 = 21 \times 21 \times 3 \times 3$

$\Rightarrow \quad x = 21 \times 3 = 63$

7. Let quotient = Q and remainder = R

Then, divisor = 12Q = 5R

Now, R = 48

$\Rightarrow$ 12Q = 5 × 48 $\Rightarrow$ Q = 20

$\therefore$ Dividend = (20 × 240 + 48) = 4848

8. The number when divided by 9, 11, 13 leaving remainder 6 = (LCM of 9, 11, 13) + 6 = 1293

$\therefore$ Required number = (1294 – 1293) = 1

9. $\sqrt{\left(1+\frac{27}{169}\right)} = \left(1+\frac{x}{13}\right)$

$\Rightarrow \quad \sqrt{\frac{169+27}{169}} = \frac{13+x}{13}$

$\Rightarrow \quad \sqrt{\frac{196}{169}} = \frac{x+13}{13}$

$\Rightarrow \quad \frac{14}{13} = \frac{x+13}{13}$

$\Rightarrow \quad x + 13 = 14$

$\Rightarrow \quad x = 1$

10. $\because \frac{x}{y} = \frac{3}{4}$ then,

$$\frac{6}{7}+\frac{y-x}{y+x} = \frac{6}{7}+\frac{\frac{y}{y}-\frac{x}{y}}{\frac{y}{y}+\frac{x}{y}}$$

[Divide numerator and denominator by y.]

$$= \frac{6}{7}+\frac{1-\frac{3}{4}}{1+\frac{3}{4}} = \frac{6}{7}+\frac{\frac{1}{4}}{\frac{7}{4}} = \frac{6}{7}+\frac{1}{7} = \frac{7}{7} = 1$$

11. It is 2 × 4 × 6 = 48

12. Least number of 5 digits is 10000.

LCM of 12, 15, 18 is 180.

On dividing 10000 by 180, the remainder is 100.

$\therefore$ The least number = 10000 + (180 – 100)
= 10080.

13. Least number = (LCM of 8, 9, 12, 16, 20) + 1

2	8, 9, 12, 16, 20
2	4, 9, 6, 8, 10
2	2, 9, 3, 4, 5
3	1, 9, 3, 2, 5
	1, 3, 1, 2, 5

$\therefore$ LCM = $2^4 \times 3^2 \times 5 = 720$

Hence, least number = (720 + 1) = 721.

14.
```
  0.8693
  0.092
  0.87
+ 0.4
  2.2313
```

$\therefore$ The value of 0.8693 + 0.092 + 0.87 + 0.4
= 2.2313.

15. The prime numbers between 1 to 50 are 2, 3, 5, 7, 11, 13, 17, 19, 23, 29, 31, 37, 41, 43, 47.

Hence, there are 15 prime numbers between 1 to 50.

2. HCF AND LCM

FACTORS

The numbers are said to be factors of a given number when they exactly divide that number.

Example: Factors of 15 are 1, 3, 5 and 15 because each of these completely divides 15.

Highest Common Factor

The HCF of two or more than two numbers is the greatest number that divides each of them exactly. The highest common factor is also known as Greatest Common Divisor or Greatest Common Measure.

EXAMPLE: Let us consider two numbers 24 and 36. All possible factors of 24 are 1, 2, 3, 4, 6, 8, 12 and 24. All possible factors of 36 are 1, 2, 3, 4, 6, 9, 12, 18 and 36. The common factors of 24 and 36 are 1, 2, 3, 4, 6, 12. The greatest factor among these common factors is 12.

Hence, 12 is the HCF of 24 and 36.

EXAMPLE: Let us consider two numbers 18 and 30.

Now, $18 = 2 \times 3 \times 3$

and $30 = 2 \times 3 \times 5$

The factors common to the two numbers are 2 and 3.

Hence the required HCF = $2 \times 3 = 6$.

There are two methods of determining the HCF of two or more numbers.

(*i*) HCF by Factorization method

(*ii*) HCF by Division method.

HCF by Factorization Method

Express each one of the given number as the product of prime factors. Now choose common factors and take the product of these factors to obtain the required HCF.

EXAMPLE: Find the HCF of 126, 396 and 5400.

SOLUTION:

$$126 = 2 \times 3 \times 3 \times 7$$
$$396 = 2 \times 2 \times 3 \times 3 \times 11$$
$$5400 = 2 \times 2 \times 2 \times 3 \times 3 \times 3 \times 5 \times 5$$

Common factors are 2, 3 and 3.

Hence, the HCF = $2 \times 3 \times 3 = 18$.

EXAMPLE: Find the HCF of 1056, 1584 and 2178.

SOLUTION:

$$1056 = 2^5 \times 3 \times 11$$
$$1584 = 2^4 \times 3^2 \times 11$$

and $2178 = 2 \times 3^2 \times 11^2$

Hence, HCF = $(2 \times 3 \times 11) = 66$.

HCF by Division Method

Suppose we have to find the HCF of two given numbers. Divide the larger number by the smaller one. Now, divide the divisor by the remainder. Repeat the process of dividing the preceding divisor by the remainder last obtained till zero is obtained as remainder. The last divisor is the required HCF.

Suppose we have to find the HCF of three numbers. Then HCF of [(HCF of any two numbers) and (the third number)] gives the HCF of three given numbers. Similarly, the HCF of more than three numbers may be obtained.

EXAMPLE: Find the HCF of 48, 168 and 324.

SOLUTION: Firstly, we find the HCF of 48 and 168.

```
48) 1 6 8 (3
  - 1 4 4
    -----
     2 4) 4 8 (2
          4 8
          ---
           0
          ---
```

Thus, HCF of 48 and 168 = 24.

Now, we find the HCF of 24 and 324.

```
24) 3 2 4 (13
  - 2 4
    8 4
  - 7 2
    1 2) 2 4 (2
         2 4
           0
```

Thus, the HCF of 48, 168 and 324 is 12.

Lowest Common Multiple

The LCM of two or more numbers is the lowest or least number which is exactly divisible by each of them. In other words, it is the lowest number which contains each of them as a factor.

LCM by Factorization

Resolve each one of the given numbers into a product of prime factors. Then LCM is the product of highest powers of all the factors.

EXAMPLE: Find the LCM of 72, 189 and 1026.

SOLUTION: $72 = 2^3 \times 3^2$

$189 = 3^3 \times 7$

and $1026 = 2 \times 3^3 \times 19$

$\therefore$ $\text{LCM} = 2^3 \times 3^3 \times 7 \times 19$

$= 8 \times 27 \times 7 \times 19 = 28728$

EXAMPLE: Find the LCM of 12, 15, 20 and 54 by short cut method.

SOLUTION:

2	12,	15,	20,	54
2	6,	15,	10,	27
3	3,	15,	5,	27
5	1,	5,	5,	9
	1,	1,	1,	9

$\therefore$ $\text{LCM} = 2 \times 2 \times 3 \times 5 \times 9 = 540$

FORMULA

Product of two numbers = HCF × LCM.

$$\text{LCM} = \frac{\text{Product of numbers}}{\text{HCF}}$$

$$\text{HCF} = \frac{\text{Product of numbers}}{\text{LCM}}$$

$$\text{First number} = \frac{\text{LCM} \times \text{HCF}}{\text{2nd number}}$$

$$\text{2nd number} = \frac{\text{LCM} \times \text{HCF}}{\text{First number}}$$

HCF and LCM of Fractions

(*i*) $\text{HCF} = \frac{\text{HCF of numerators}}{\text{LCM of denominators}}$

(*ii*) $\text{LCM} = \frac{\text{LCM of numerators}}{\text{HCF of denominators}}$

EXAMPLE: Find the HCF and LCM of $\frac{3}{4}, \frac{6}{8}, \frac{15}{64}$ and $\frac{12}{32}$.

SOLUTION: $\text{HCF} = \frac{\text{HCF of 3, 6, 15, 12}}{\text{LCM of 4, 8, 64, 32}} = \frac{3}{64}$

$\text{LCM} = \frac{\text{LCM of 3, 6, 15, 12}}{\text{HCF of 4, 8, 64, 32}} = \frac{60}{4}$.

MULTIPLE CHOICE QUESTIONS

1. HCF of 1485 and 4356 is:
   A. 189 B. 89
   C. 99 D. 83
2. LCM of 18, 24, 42, 63 is:
   A. 302 B. 604
   C. 504 D. 404
3. Which of the following fractions is the greatest of all?
   $\frac{7}{8}, \frac{6}{7}, \frac{4}{5}, \frac{5}{6}$
   A. $\frac{6}{7}$ B. $\frac{4}{5}$
   C. $\frac{5}{6}$ D. $\frac{7}{8}$
4. Which of the following is in ascending order?
   A. $\frac{5}{7}, \frac{7}{8}, \frac{9}{11}$ B. $\frac{5}{7}, \frac{9}{11}, \frac{7}{8}$
   C. $\frac{7}{8}, \frac{5}{7}, \frac{9}{11}$ D. $\frac{9}{11}, \frac{7}{8}, \frac{5}{7}$

5. HCF of three numbers is 12. If they be in the ratio 1 : 2 : 3, the numbers are:
A. 12, 24, 36 B. 10, 20, 30
C. 5, 10, 15 D. 4, 8, 12

6. The largest natural number which exactly divides the product of any four consecutive natural numbers is:
A. 6 B. 12
C. 24 D. 120

7. The traffic lights at three different road crossings change after every 48 seconds, 72 seconds and 108 seconds respectively. If they all change simultaneously at 8 : 20 : 00 hrs; then they will again change simultaneously at:
A. 8 : 27 : 12 hrs B. 8 : 27 : 24 hrs
C. 8 : 27 : 36 hrs D. 8 : 27 : 48 hrs

8. The HCF of two numbers is 16 and their LCM is 160. If one of the number is 32, then the other number is:
A. 48 B. 80
C. 96 D. 112

9. The HCF of two numbers is 12 and their difference is also 12. The numbers are:
A. 66, 78 B. 70, 82
C. 94, 106 D. 84, 96

10. The largest number which exactly divides 210, 315, 147 and 161 is:
A. 3 B. 7
C. 21 D. 4410

11. The least perfect square number which is divisible by 3, 4, 5, 6 and 8 is:
A. 900 B. 1200
C. 2500 D. 3600

12. The smallest number which is divisible by 12, 15, 20 and is a perfect square, is:
A. 400 B. 900
C. 1600 D. 3600

13. The sum of two numbers is 216 and their HCF is 27. The numbers are:
A. 54, 162 B. 108, 108
C. 27, 189 D. None of these

14. The HCF and LCM of two numbers are 44 and 264 respectively. If the first number is divided by 2, the quotient is 44. The other number is:
A. 33 B. 66
C. 132 D. 264

15. The number of prime factors in $2^{222} \times 3^{333} \times 5^{555}$ is:
A. 3 B. 1107
C. 1110 D. 1272

16. The number of prime factors in the expression $(6)^{10} \times (7)^{17} \times (11)^{27}$ is:
A. 54 B. 64
C. 71 D. 81

17. Three measuring rods are 64 cm, 80 cm and 96 cm in length. The least length of cloth that can be measured exact number of times using any one of the above rod is:
A. 0.96 m B. 19.20 m
C. 9.60 m D. 96.00 m

18. The product of two numbers is 1600 and their HCF is 5. The LCM of the numbers is:
A. 320 B. 1605
C. 1595 D. 8000

19. About the number of pairs which have 16 as their HCF and 136 as their LCM, we can definitely say that:
A. Only one such pair exists
B. Only two such pairs exist
C. Many such pairs exist
D. No such pair exist

20. The total number of prime factors of the product $(8)^{20} \times (15)^{24} \times (7)^{15}$ is:
A. 59 B. 98
C. 123 D. 138

ANSWERS

1	2	3	4	5	6	7	8	9	10
C	C	D	B	A	C	A	B	D	B
11	**12**	**13**	**14**	**15**	**16**	**17**	**18**	**19**	**20**
D	D	C	C	C	B	C	A	D	C

EXPLANATORY ANSWERS

1.

```
1485) 4 3 5 6 (2
      2 9 7 0
      -------
      1 3 8 6) 1 4 8 5 (1
               1 3 8 6
               -------
                  9 9) 1 3 8 6 (14
                         9 9
                         ---
                         3 9 6
                         3 9 6
                         -----
                           0
```

$\therefore$ HCF of 1485 and 4356 is 99.

2.

2	18,	24,	42,	63
3	9,	12,	21,	63
3	3,	4,	7,	21
7	1,	4,	7,	7
	1,	4,	1,	1

LCM of 18, 24, 42, 63 = $2 \times 3^2 \times 7 \times 4 = 504$.

3. $\frac{7}{8} = 0.875$, $\frac{6}{7} = 0.857$, $\frac{4}{5} = 0.8$

$\frac{5}{6} = 0.833$

Clearly, 0.875 is the greatest of all.

Hence, $\frac{7}{8}$ is the greatest of all.

4. $\frac{5}{7} = 0.714$, $\frac{7}{8} = 0.875$, $\frac{9}{11} = 0.818$

Now, $0.714 < 0.818 < 0.875$

Hence, $\frac{5}{7} < \frac{9}{11} < \frac{7}{8}$.

5. Let the numbers be x, $2x$ and $3x$.
Then, their HCF = x
According to the question, $x = 12$
$\because$ The numbers are 12, 21, 36.

6. $1 \times 2 \times 3 \times 4 = 24$
$\therefore$ Required number = 24.

7. LCM of 48, 72, 108 = 432
432 seconds = 7 min 12 seconds.
So, the next simultaneous change will take place at 8 : 27 : 12 hrs.

8. Other number = $\frac{\text{LCM} \times \text{HCF}}{\text{One number}} = \frac{160 \times 16}{32} = 80$
Hence, other number = 80.

9. 12 is not the HCF of given options A, B and C. Hence, D is correct answer.
In 84, 96, 12 is HCF of 84 and 96
Difference of 96 – 84 = 12
So, required numbers are 84 and 96.

10. HCF of 210, 315, 147 and 161 = 7
Hence, the required number = 7.

11.

2	3,	4,	5,	6,	8
2	3,	2,	5,	3,	4
3	3,	1,	5,	3,	2
	1,	1,	5,	1,	2

LCM of 3, 4, 5, 6, 8 = $2 \times 2 \times 3 \times 5 \times 2$
Required number
$= (2 \times 2 \times 3 \times 3 \times 5 \times 5 \times 2 \times 2) = 3600$

12. LCM of 12, 15 and 20 = 60
Hence, required number = $60 \times 60 = 3600$.

13. HCF of 54, 162 = 54
HCF of 108, 108 = 108
HCF of 27, 189 = 27
Hence, required numbers are 27 and 189.

14. According to the question,
First number = $2 \times 44 = 88$
Other number
$= \frac{\text{LCM} \times \text{HCF}}{\text{First number}} = \frac{264 \times 44}{88} = 132$

15. The number of prime factors in the given product = $(222 + 333 + 555) = 1110$

16. 2, 3, 7, 11 are prime numbers in the given expression. The number of prime factors in the given expression $(10 + 10 + 17 + 27) = 64$

17. Required length = (LCM of 64, 80, 96) cm
= 960 cm = 9.60 m.

18. LCM = $\frac{\text{Product of numbers}}{\text{HCF}} = \frac{1600}{5} = 320$

19. HCF is always a factor of LCM. So no two numbers exist with HCF = 16 and LCM = 136.

20. Since 2, 3, 5, 7 are prime numbers and the given expression is $(2^3)^{20} \times (3 \times 5)^{24} \times (7)^{15}$ *i.e.* $2^{60} \times 3^{24} \times 5^{24} \times 7^{15}$, so the number of prime factors in the given expression
$= (60 + 24 + 24 + 15) = 123$

3. SIMPLIFICATION

Simplification means expressing in a simpler form. In order to simplify an expression we use the operations in the following order which is easily remembered as "BODMAS".

(*i*) Bracket (*ii*) Of (*iii*) Division (*iv*) Multiplication (*v*) Addition (*vi*) Subtraction.

'Of' means multiplication but it is operated even before division.

While removing brackets, first of all bar bracket '—' and after that small bracket '( )' is removed. Thereafter curley bracket '{ }' and at last square bracket '[ ]' is removed.

EXAMPLE: Simplify: $100 \div 25 \times 6 + 16 - 32$

SOLUTION: $100 \div 25 \times 6 + 16 - 32$

$= 4 \times 6 + 16 - 32$

$= 24 + 16 - 32$

$= 40 - 32 = 8$

EXAMPLE: Simplify: $54 + 24 \div 4 - 8 \times 5 + 4 \times 3$

SOLUTION: $54 + 24 \div 4 - 8 \times 5 + 4 \times 3$

$= 54 + 6 - 40 + 12$

$= 72 - 40 = 32$

EXAMPLE: Simplify: $10 - \left[6 - \left\{7 - \left(6 - \overline{8 - 5}\right)\right\}\right]$

SOLUTION: $10 - \left[6 - \left\{7 - \left(6 - 3\right)\right\}\right]$

$= 10 - [6 - \{7 - 3\}]$

$= 10 - [6 - 4] = 10 - 2 = 8.$

EXAMPLE: Simplify: $\dfrac{12 \times 12 \times 12 - 1 \times 1 \times 1}{12 \times 12 + 12 \times 1 + 1 \times 1}$

SOLUTION: Let $a = 12$ and $b = 1$

$$\therefore \quad \frac{a \times a \times a - b \times b \times b}{a \times a + a \times b + b \times b} = \frac{a^3 - b^3}{a^2 + ab + b^2}$$

$$= \frac{(a-b)(a^2 + ab + b^2)}{(a^2 + ab + b^2)}$$

$$= a - b = 12 - 1 = 11$$

EXAMPLE: Simplify:

$$\frac{2.33 \times 2.33 \times 2.33 + 7.67 \times 7.67 \times 7.67}{2.33 \times 2.33 - 2.33 \times 7.67 + 7.67 \times 7.67}$$

SOLUTION: Let $a = 2.33$ and $b = 7.67$

$$\frac{a^3 + b^3}{a^2 - ab + b^2} = \frac{(a+b)(a^2 - ab + b^2)}{(a^2 - ab + b^2)} = (a + b)$$

$$= 2.33 + 7.67 = 10$$

MULTIPLE CHOICE QUESTIONS

1. $\dfrac{48 - 12 \times 3 + 9}{12 - 9 \div 3}$ equals:

A. 3 B. 21

C. $\dfrac{7}{3}$ D. $\dfrac{1}{3}$

2. $\dfrac{69 - 14 \times 3 + 2}{9 \times 5 - (5)^2}$ equals:

A. 1.45 B. 2.75

C. 26.5 D. 265

3. If $\dfrac{17.28 \div x}{3.6 \times 0.2} = 2$ then, the value of x is:

A. 120 B. 1.20

C. 12 D. 0.12

4. $171 \div 19 \times 9$ equals:

A. 0 B. 1

C. 18 D. 81

5. $3120 \div 26 + 13 \times 30$ equals:

A. 2400 B. 3900

C. 536 D. None of these

6. $\dfrac{31}{10} \times \dfrac{3}{10} + \dfrac{7}{5} \div 20$ equals:

A. 0 B. 1

C. 100 D. $\dfrac{107}{200}$

7. The simplification of $1 + \dfrac{1}{2 + \dfrac{1}{1 - \dfrac{1}{3}}}$ yields the result:

A. $\dfrac{2}{7}$ B. $\dfrac{7}{9}$

C. $\dfrac{9}{7}$ D. $\dfrac{13}{7}$

8. The value of $1 + \dfrac{1}{4 \times 3} + \dfrac{1}{4 \times 3^2} + \dfrac{1}{4 \times 3^3}$ up to four places of decimals is:

A. 1.1202 B. 1.1203

C. 1.1204 D. None of these

9. $\dfrac{\dfrac{1}{2} \div 4 + 20}{\dfrac{1}{2} \times 4 + 20}$ equals:

A. $\dfrac{81}{88}$ B. $2\dfrac{3}{11}$

C. $\dfrac{161}{176}$ D. 1

10. $3 \div \left[(8-5) \div \left\{(4-2) \div \left(2 + \dfrac{8}{13}\right)\right\}\right]$ equals:

A. $\dfrac{13}{17}$ B. $\dfrac{68}{13}$

C. $\dfrac{17}{13}$ D. $\dfrac{13}{68}$

11. $10 - [9 - \{8 - (7 - 6)\}] - 5$ is equal to:

A. –5 B. 1

C. 3 D. 9

12. $\dfrac{\dfrac{1}{5} \div \dfrac{1}{5} \text{ of } \dfrac{1}{5}}{\dfrac{1}{5} \text{ of } \dfrac{1}{5} \div \dfrac{1}{5}}$ is equal to:

A. 1 B. 5

C. $\dfrac{1}{5}$ D. 25

13. The value of $1 + \dfrac{1}{1 + \dfrac{1}{1 + \dfrac{1}{9}}}$ is:

A. $\dfrac{29}{19}$ B. $\dfrac{10}{19}$

C. $\dfrac{29}{10}$ D. $\dfrac{10}{9}$

14. $\dfrac{3}{48}$ is what part of $\dfrac{1}{12}$?

A. $\dfrac{3}{7}$ B. $\dfrac{1}{12}$

C. $\dfrac{4}{3}$ D. None of these

15. How many $\dfrac{1}{8}$ s are there in $37\dfrac{1}{2}$?

A. 300 B. 400

C. 500 D. None of these

ANSWERS

1	2	3	4	5	6	7	8	9	10
C	A	C	D	D	B	C	B	C	A
11	**12**	**13**	**14**	**15**					
C	D	A	D	A					

EXPLANATORY ANSWERS

1. $\dfrac{48-12\times3+9}{12-9\div3}=\dfrac{48-36+9}{12-3}$

$=\dfrac{57-36}{9}=\dfrac{21}{9}=\dfrac{7}{3}.$

2. $\dfrac{69-14\times3+2}{9\times5-5^2}=\dfrac{69-42+2}{45-25}$

$=\dfrac{71-42}{20}=\dfrac{29}{20}=1.45.$

3. $17.28\div x=2\times3.6\times0.2$

$\Rightarrow\ \dfrac{17.28}{x}=1.44\Rightarrow 1.44\,x=17.28$

$\Rightarrow\ x=\dfrac{17.28}{1.44}=\dfrac{1728}{144}=12.$

4. $171\div19\times9=9\times9=81.$

5. $3120\div26+13\times30=120+390=510.$

6. $\dfrac{31}{10}\times\dfrac{3}{10}+\dfrac{7}{5}\div20=\dfrac{31}{10}\times\dfrac{3}{10}+\dfrac{7}{5}\times\dfrac{1}{20}$

$=\dfrac{93}{100}+\dfrac{7}{100}=\dfrac{93+7}{100}=\dfrac{100}{100}=1$

7. $1+\dfrac{1}{2+\dfrac{1}{1-\dfrac{1}{3}}}=1+\dfrac{1}{2+\dfrac{1}{\dfrac{3-1}{3}}}$

$=1+\dfrac{1}{2+\dfrac{1}{\dfrac{2}{3}}}=1+\dfrac{1}{2+\dfrac{3}{2}}=1+\dfrac{1}{\dfrac{7}{2}}=1+\dfrac{2}{7}=\dfrac{9}{7}$

8. $1+\dfrac{1}{4\times3}+\dfrac{1}{4\times3^2}+\dfrac{1}{4\times3^3}$

$=1+\dfrac{1}{12}+\dfrac{1}{36}+\dfrac{1}{108}=\dfrac{108+9+3+1}{108}$

$=\dfrac{121}{108}=1.1203$

9. $\dfrac{\dfrac{1}{2}\div4+20}{\dfrac{1}{2}\times4+20}=\dfrac{\dfrac{1}{8}+20}{2+20}=\dfrac{\dfrac{1+160}{8}}{22}$

$=\dfrac{161}{8\times22}=\dfrac{161}{176}$

10. $3\div\left[(8-5)\div\left\{(4-2)\div\left(2+\dfrac{8}{13}\right)\right\}\right]$

$=3\div\left[3\div\left\{2\div\dfrac{34}{13}\right\}\right]$

$=3\div\left[3\div\left\{2\times\dfrac{13}{34}\right\}\right]=3\div\left[3\div\dfrac{13}{17}\right]$

$=3\div\left[3\times\dfrac{17}{13}\right]=3\div\dfrac{51}{13}=3\times\dfrac{13}{51}=\dfrac{13}{17}$

11. $10-[9-\{8-(7-6)\}]-5$
$=10-[9-\{8-1\}]-5$
$=10-[9-7]-5=10-2-5=10-7=3$

12. $\dfrac{\dfrac{1}{5}\div\dfrac{1}{5}\text{ of }\dfrac{1}{5}}{\dfrac{1}{5}\text{ of }\dfrac{1}{5}\div\dfrac{1}{5}}=\dfrac{\dfrac{1}{5}\div\dfrac{1}{25}}{\dfrac{1}{25}\div\dfrac{1}{5}}=\dfrac{\dfrac{1}{5}\times\dfrac{25}{1}}{\dfrac{1}{25}\times\dfrac{5}{1}}=\dfrac{\dfrac{5}{1}}{\dfrac{1}{5}}$

$=\dfrac{5}{1}\times\dfrac{5}{1}=25$

13. $1+\dfrac{1}{1+\dfrac{1}{1+\dfrac{1}{9}}}=1+\dfrac{1}{1+\dfrac{1}{\dfrac{10}{9}}}=1+\dfrac{1}{1+\dfrac{9}{10}}$

$=1+\dfrac{1}{\dfrac{19}{10}}=1+\dfrac{10}{19}=\dfrac{29}{19}$

14. Let x of $\dfrac{1}{12}=\dfrac{3}{48}$

$\Rightarrow\ \dfrac{x}{12}=\dfrac{3}{48}\Rightarrow 48x=36$

$\Rightarrow\ x=\dfrac{36}{48}=\dfrac{3}{4}.$

15. Let n times $\dfrac{1}{8}=37\dfrac{1}{2}$

$\Rightarrow\ \dfrac{n}{8}=\dfrac{75}{2}\Rightarrow 2n=8\times75$

$\Rightarrow\ n=\dfrac{8\times75}{2}=4\times75=300.$

4. SURDS AND INDICES

SURDS

If 'a' is a rational number and n is a positive integer such that nth root of 'a', *i.e.*, $a^{1/n}$ or $\sqrt[n]{a}$ is an irrational number, then $a^{1/n}$ is called a surd or radical.

In other words, an irrational root of a rational number is called a surd. The symbol '$\sqrt{}$' is known as surd sign or radical.

For example, $\sqrt{2} = 2^{1/2}$ = Square root of 2

$\sqrt[3]{5} = 5^{1/3}$ = Cube root of 5

Pure and Mixed Surds

Pure Surd: A surd which has unity only as rational factor, the other factor being irrational, is called a pure surd.

For example, $\sqrt{2}$, $\sqrt[3]{3}$, $\sqrt[5]{3}$ are pure surds.

Mixed Surd: A surd which has a rational factor other than unity, the other factor being irrational, is called a mixed surds.

For example, $2\sqrt{5}$ $3\sqrt[4]{7}$, $5\sqrt[3]{11}$ are mixed surds.

Rationalising Factor: When the product of two surds is a rational number, then each of them is called the rationalising factor (R.F.) of the other.

For example, $3\sqrt{5} \times \sqrt{5} = 3 \times 5 = 15$

$\therefore$ $\sqrt{5}$ is a rationalising factor of $3\sqrt{5}$.

Important Formulae Based on Surds

$\sqrt[n]{a} = a^{1/n}$ and it is called a surd of order n.

(*i*) $\sqrt[n]{a^n} = a$

(*ii*) $\sqrt[n]{ab} = \sqrt[n]{a}\,\sqrt[n]{b}$

(*iii*) $\sqrt{a} \times \sqrt{a} = a$

(*iv*) $\sqrt{a} \times \sqrt{b} = \sqrt{ab}$

(*v*) $\sqrt{a^2 b} = a\sqrt{b}$

(*vi*) $\left(\sqrt{a} + \sqrt{b}\right)^2 = a + b + 2\sqrt{ab}$

(*vii*) $\left(\sqrt{a} - \sqrt{b}\right)^2 = a + b - 2\sqrt{ab}$

(*viii*) $\left(\sqrt{a} + \sqrt{b}\right)\left(\sqrt{a} - \sqrt{b}\right) = a - b$ where a and b are positive rational numbers.

INDICES

Let n be a positive integer and 'a' be a real number. The continued product of n factors each equal to a *e.g.*, $a \times a \times a \times \ldots \times n$ times is written as a^n and is called "n^{th} power of a" or "a raised to the power n".

The expression a^n is termed as power function or simply power, a is called the base and n is called index or exponent of the power a^n.

For example, 2^2 = square of 2, 2^3 = cube of 2, etc.

Laws of Indices

(*i*) $a^m \times a^n = a^{m+n}$

(*ii*) $a^m \times a^n \times a^p \times \ldots = a^{m+n+p+\ldots}$

(*iii*) $\dfrac{a^m}{a^n} = a^{m-n}$, if $m > n$

(*iv*) $\dfrac{a^m}{a^n} = \dfrac{1}{a^{n-m}}$, if $m < n$

(*v*) $(a^m)^n = a^{mn}$

(*vi*) $(ab)^n = a^n b^n$

(*vii*) $a^0 = 1$

(*viii*) If $a^m = a^n$ then $m = n$

(*ix*) If $a^m = b^m$ then $a = b$

(*x*) $\dfrac{a^m}{a^m} = a^{m-m} = a^0 = 1$

MULTIPLE CHOICE QUESTIONS

1. If the infinite series is $x = \sqrt{6+\sqrt{6+\sqrt{6+...}}}$ then the value of x is:

A. 2.5 B. 3
C. 6 D. 8

2. If $\frac{9^n \cdot 3^2 \cdot 3^n - (27)^n}{3^{3m} \cdot 2^3} = \frac{1}{27}$, then the value of $(m-n)$ is:

A. 1 B. 2
C. $\sqrt{3}$ D. $\sqrt{\frac{2}{3}}$

3. If $x = \frac{\sqrt{5}+\sqrt{3}}{\sqrt{5}-\sqrt{3}}$ and $y = \frac{\sqrt{5}-\sqrt{3}}{\sqrt{5}+\sqrt{3}}$, then $(x+y)$ is equal to:

A. 8 B. 6
C. $2\sqrt{15}$ D. $2\left(\sqrt{5}+\sqrt{3}\right)$

4. $2^{x+1} + 2^{x+3} = 2560$, then x is equal to:

A. 12 B. 11
C. 8 D. 6

5. If $\frac{5+2\sqrt{3}}{7+4\sqrt{3}} = a + b\sqrt{3}$, then b is equal to:

A. –6 B. 6
C. –11 D. 11

6. If $\frac{(21)^{5.36}}{(21)^{3.47}} = (21)^x$, then the value of x is:

A. 8.88 B. 1.54
C. 9.32 D. 1.89

7. $\sqrt{24}+\sqrt{12}$ equal to:

A. $\sqrt{36}$ B. $2\sqrt{6}+2\sqrt{3}$
C. $6\sqrt{2}$ D. $\sqrt{288}$

8. If $a^b = 64$, where a and b are positive integers then $(a-b)^{a+b-4}$ is:

A. 0 B. 1
C. 2 D. $\frac{1}{2}$

9. The value of $\frac{5^{10+n} \cdot 25^{3n-4}}{5^{7n}}$ is:

A. 5 B. 8
C. 25 D. 16

10. $3^x - 3^{x-1} = 18$, then the value of x^x is:

A. 3 B. 8
C. 27 D. 216

11. If $x = \sqrt{10+\sqrt{25+\sqrt{121}}}$, then x is equal to:

A. –2 only B. 2 only
C. ±4 D. 4 only

12. If $a^x = b^y = c^z$ and $b^2 = ac$, then y is equal to:

A. $\frac{xz}{x+z}$ B. $\frac{xz}{2(x-z)}$
C. $\frac{xz}{2(z-x)}$ D. $\frac{2xz}{x+z}$

13. $\frac{5^{n+3} - 6 \times 5^{n+1}}{9 \times 5^n - 5^n \times 2^2}$ is equal to:

A. 5 B. 19
C. 25 D. 95

14. The value of $\left(\frac{x^a}{x^b}\right)^{(a+b)} \times \left(\frac{x^b}{x^c}\right)^{(b+c)} \times \left(\frac{x^c}{x^a}\right)^{(c+a)}$ is equal to:

A. 0 B. 2
C. 1 D. 3

15. If $\sqrt{3^n} = 729$, then the value of n is:

A. 12 B. 8
C. 10 D. 6

ANSWERS

1	2	3	4	5	6	7	8	9	10
B	A	A	C	A	D	B	B	C	C
11	**12**	**13**	**14**	**15**					
D	D	B	C	A					

EXPLANATORY ANSWERS

1. $x = \sqrt{6+x}$

Squaring both sides

$$x^2 = 6 + x$$
$$\Rightarrow x^2 - x - 6 = 0$$
$$\Rightarrow x^2 - 3x + 2x - 6 = 0$$
$$\Rightarrow x(x-3) + 2(x-3) = 0$$
$$\Rightarrow (x-3)(x+2) = 0$$
$$\Rightarrow x = 3 \text{ or } x = -2$$

But x cannot be –2.

Hence, the required value of x is 3.

2. $$\frac{9^n \cdot 3^2 \cdot 3^n - (27)^n}{3^{3m} \cdot 2^3} = \frac{1}{27}$$

$$\Rightarrow \frac{3^{2n} \times 9 \times 3^n - 3^{3n}}{8 \times 3^{3m}} = \frac{1}{3^3}$$

$$\Rightarrow \frac{3^{3n}(9-1)}{8\,3^{3m}} = 3^{-3}$$

$$\Rightarrow 3^{3n-3m} = (3)^{-3}$$
$$\Rightarrow 3m - 3n = 3$$
$$\Rightarrow 3(m-n) = 3$$
$$\Rightarrow m - n = \frac{3}{3} = 1$$

3. $$x = \frac{\sqrt{5}+\sqrt{3}}{\sqrt{5}-\sqrt{3}} \times \frac{\sqrt{5}+\sqrt{3}}{\sqrt{5}+\sqrt{3}} = \frac{\left(\sqrt{5}+\sqrt{3}\right)^2}{5-3}$$

$$\Rightarrow x = \frac{5+3+2\sqrt{15}}{2} = \frac{8+2\sqrt{15}}{2} = \frac{2\left(4+\sqrt{15}\right)}{2}$$

$$\therefore \quad x = 4 + \sqrt{15}$$

Again, $$y = \frac{\sqrt{5}-\sqrt{3}}{\sqrt{5}+\sqrt{3}} \times \frac{\sqrt{5}-\sqrt{3}}{\sqrt{5}-\sqrt{3}}$$

$$= \frac{\left(\sqrt{5}-\sqrt{3}\right)^2}{5-3}$$

$$\Rightarrow y = \frac{5+3-2\sqrt{15}}{2}$$

$$= \frac{8-2\sqrt{15}}{2} = \frac{2\left(4-\sqrt{15}\right)}{2}$$

$$\Rightarrow y = 4 - \sqrt{15}$$

$$\therefore x + y = 4 + \sqrt{15} + 4 - \sqrt{15} = 8$$

4. $$2^{x+1} + 2^{x+3} = 2560$$
$$\Rightarrow 2^x \times 2 + 2^x \times 2^3 = 2560$$
$$\Rightarrow 2 \times 2^x + 8 \times 2^x = 2560$$
$$\Rightarrow 2^x(2+8) = 2560$$
$$\Rightarrow 2^x = 256 = 2^8$$
$$\Rightarrow x = 8$$

5. $$\because \frac{5+2\sqrt{3}}{7+4\sqrt{3}} = a + b\sqrt{3}$$

$$\frac{5+2\sqrt{3}}{7+4\sqrt{3}} \times \frac{7-4\sqrt{3}}{7-4\sqrt{3}} = \frac{35-20\sqrt{3}+14\sqrt{3}-24}{49-48}$$

$$= \frac{11-6\sqrt{3}}{1}$$

Comparing then we get,

$a = 11$, $b = -6$

Hence, $b = -6$.

6. $$\frac{(21)^{5.36}}{(21)^{3.47}} = (21)^x$$

$$\Rightarrow (21)^{5.36-3.47} = (21)^x$$
$$\Rightarrow x = 1.89$$

7. $\sqrt{24} + \sqrt{12} = 2\sqrt{6} + 2\sqrt{3}$

8. $a^b = 64 = (4)^3 \Rightarrow a = 4, b = 3$

$\therefore (a-b)^{a+b-4} = (4-3)^{4+3-4} = (1)^3 = 1$

9. $$\frac{5^{10+n} \cdot 25^{3n-4}}{5^{7n}} = \frac{5^{10} \times 5^n \times (5^2)^{3n-4}}{5^{7n}}$$

$$= \frac{5^{10} \times 5^n \times 5^{6n} \times 5^{-8}}{5^{7n}}$$

$$= \frac{5^{10-8} \times 5^{7n}}{5^{7n}} = 5^2 \times 5^{7n-7n}$$

$$= 25 \times 5^0 = 25 \times 1 = 25$$

10. $$3^x - 3^{x-1} = 18$$
$$\Rightarrow 3^x - 3^x \times 3^{-1} = 18$$
$$\Rightarrow 3^x\left(1 - \frac{1}{3}\right) = 18$$
$$\Rightarrow 3^x\left(\frac{2}{3}\right) = 18$$

$$\Rightarrow \quad 3^x = \frac{18 \times 3}{2} = 27$$

$$\Rightarrow \quad 3^x = (3)^3 \Rightarrow x = 3$$

$$\therefore \quad x^x = (3)^3 = 27$$

11. $x = \sqrt{10 + \sqrt{25 + \sqrt{121}}}$

$$\Rightarrow \quad x = \sqrt{10 + \sqrt{25 + 11}}$$

$$\Rightarrow \quad x = \sqrt{10 + \sqrt{36}}$$

$$\Rightarrow \quad x = \sqrt{10 + 6} = \sqrt{16}$$

$$\Rightarrow \quad x = 4$$

12. Let $a^x = b^y = c^z = k$

then $a = k^{\frac{1}{x}}$, $b = k^{\frac{1}{y}}$, $c = k^{\frac{1}{z}}$

Now, $b^2 = ac$

$$\Rightarrow \quad \left(k^{\frac{1}{y}}\right)^2 = k^{\frac{1}{x}} \cdot k^{\frac{1}{z}}$$

$$\Rightarrow \quad k^{\frac{2}{y}} = k^{\frac{1}{x}+\frac{1}{z}}$$

$$\Rightarrow \quad \frac{2}{y} = \frac{z + x}{xz}$$

$$\Rightarrow \quad 2xz = y(x + z)$$

$$\Rightarrow \quad y = \frac{2xz}{x + z}$$

13. $\dfrac{5^{n+3} - 6 \times 5^{n+1}}{9 \times 5^n - 5^n \times 2^2} = \dfrac{5^n \times 5^3 - 6 \times 5^n \times 5}{9 \times 5^n - 4 \times 5^n}$

$$= \frac{5^n(125 - 30)}{5^n(9 - 4)} = 5^0 \times \frac{95}{5}$$

$$= 1 \times 19 = 19.$$

14. $\left(\dfrac{x^a}{x^b}\right)^{(a+b)} \times \left(\dfrac{x^b}{x^c}\right)^{(b+c)} \times \left(\dfrac{x^c}{x^a}\right)^{(c+a)}$

$$= \left(x^{a-b}\right)^{(a+b)} \times \left(x^{b-c}\right)^{(b+c)} \times \left(x^{c-a}\right)^{c+a}$$

$$= x^{a^2-b^2} \times x^{b^2-c^2} \times x^{c^2-a^2}$$

$$= x^{a^2-b^2+b^2-c^2+c^2-a^2}$$

$$= x^0 = 1$$

15. $\sqrt{3^n} = 729 \Rightarrow 3^{n/2} = 3^6$

$$\Rightarrow \quad \frac{n}{2} = 6$$

$$\Rightarrow \quad n = 12.$$

5. RATIO AND PROPORTION

RATIO

When comparison is made by dividing one quantity by another of the same kind, the result is called ratio. If a and b are two numbers, ratio of a to b is denoted by $a : b$ or $\frac{a}{b}$. Here a is called first term and b is called the second term. The first term is also called antecedent and the second term is also called consequent.

EXAMPLE: The ratio 3 : 10 represents $\frac{3}{10}$ with antecedent 3 and consequent 10.

The multiplication or division of each term of a ratio by a same non-zero number does not effect the ratio.

PROPORTION

Equality of two ratios is called proportion. If $a : b = c : d$, then a, b, c, d are called in proportion. In a proportion $a : b :: c : d$, then a and d are called extremes and b and c are called means.

Product of extremes = Product of means

Comparison of Ratio: Suppose $\frac{a}{b} > \frac{c}{d}$ then we say that $a : b > c : d$.

Compounded Ratio: The compound ratio of the ratios $a : b$, $c : d$ and $e : f$ is $ace : bdf$.

Duplicate Ratio: The duplicate ratio of $a : b$ is $a^2 : b^2$.

Triplicate Ratio: The triplicate ratio of $a : b$ is $a^3 : b^3$.

Sub-duplicate and Sub-triplicate ratios

The sub-duplicate and Sub-triplicate ratios of ratio $a : b$ are $a^{1/2} : b^{1/2}$ and $a^{1/3} : b^{1/3}$ respectively.

Mean Proportional: Mean proportional between a and b is $\sqrt{ab}$.

Third Proportional: The third proportional to a, b is the fourth proportional to a, b, b.

Fourth Proportional: If $a : b :: c : d$ is a proportion, then d is called the fourth proportional to a, b, c.

EXAMPLE: If A : B = 3 : 4 and B : C = 8 : 9 then find A : C.

SOLUTION: $A : B = 3 : 4 \Rightarrow \frac{A}{B} = \frac{3}{4}$

$B : C = 8 : 9 \Rightarrow \frac{B}{C} = \frac{8}{9}$

$$\frac{A}{C} = \frac{A}{B} \times \frac{B}{C} = \frac{3}{4} \times \frac{8}{9} = \frac{2}{3}$$

$\Rightarrow \quad A : C = 2 : 3$

EXAMPLE: If 15% of A is the same as 20% of B, then find A : B.

SOLUTION: Given : 15% of A = 20% of B

$\Rightarrow \quad \frac{15}{100} \times A = \frac{20}{100} \times B$

$\Rightarrow \quad 3A = 4B$

$\Rightarrow \quad \frac{A}{B} = \frac{4}{3}$

$\Rightarrow \quad A : B = 4 : 3$

EXAMPLE: A stick 1.4 m long casts a shadow 1.3 m long at the same time when a pole casts a shadow 5.2 m long. Find the length of the pole.

SOLUTION: Clearly, more is the length of shadow, more is the length of the object.

Let the length of the pole be x metres.

Then, $1.3 : 5.2 :: 1.4 : x$

$$\Rightarrow \quad \frac{1.3}{5.2} = \frac{1.4}{x}$$

$$\Rightarrow \quad \frac{1}{4} = \frac{1.4}{x}$$

$$\Rightarrow \quad x = 1.4 \times 4 = 5.6$$

Hence, the length of the pole is 5.6 m.

MULTIPLE CHOICE QUESTIONS

1. If A : B = 2 : 3 and B : C = 4 : 5, then C : A is equal to:

A. 15 : 8 B. 12 : 10
C. 8 : 5 D. 8 : 15

2. If 10% of x is the same as 20% of y, then $x : y$ is equal to:

A. 1 : 2 B. 2 : 1
C. 5 : 1 D. 10 : 1

3. The mean proportional to $6+\sqrt{27}$ and $6-\sqrt{27}$ is:

A. 3 B. 9
C. 10 D. $\sqrt{10}$

4. If $x : y = 9 : 11$, the value of $\frac{5x+3y}{3x+5y}$ is:

A. 45 : 55 B. 18 : 22
C. 37 : 41 D. 39 : 41

5. If $a + b : b + c : c + a = 6 : 7 : 8$ and $a + b + c = 14$, then the value of c is:

A. 14 B. 7
C. 8 D. 6

6. Two numbers are in the ratio 2 : 3. If 5 is added to each number, the ratio becomes 5 : 7. The bigger number is:

A. 30 B. 40
C. 60 D. 20

7. What should be added to each of the numbers 12, 30, 40 and 86, so that they are in proportion?

A. 6 B. 4
C. –6 D. –4

8. The ratio of males and females of a village is 5 : 3. If there are 800 males in the village, females are:

A. 240 B. 480
C. 840 D. 488

9. In a mixture of 60 litres, the ratio of ethanol to ether is 4 : 1. How much ether must be added to the mixture to make this ratio 2 : 1?

A. 10 litres B. 12 litres
C. 18 litres D. 24 litres

10. The proportion of zinc and copper in a brass piece is 4 : 5. How much zinc will be there in 180 kg of such a piece?

A. 40 kg B. 80 kg
C. 100 kg D. 120 kg

11. The prices of a scooter and a television set are in the ratio 3 : 2. If a scooter costs ₹ 6000 more than the television set, the price of the television set is:

A. ₹ 18000 B. ₹ 12000
C. ₹ 10000 D. ₹ 6000

12. The weight of a 13 metres long iron rod be 23.4 kg. The weight of 6 metres long of such rod will be:

A. 7.2 kg B. 12.4 kg
C. 10.8 kg D. 18 kg

13. The ratio between the ages of Gayatri and Savitri is 6 : 5 and the sum of their ages is 44 years. The ratio of their ages after 8 years will be:

A. 5 : 6 B. 7 : 8
C. 8 : 7 D. 14 : 13

14. Two numbers are such that the ratio between them is 3 : 5 but if each is increased by 10, the ratio between them becomes 5 : 7. The numbers are:

A. 3, 5 B. 7, 9
C. 13, 22 D. 15, 25

15. In a factory the ratio of male workers to female workers was 5 : 3. If the number of female workers was less by 40, the total number of workers in the factory was:

A. 100
B. 500
C. 160
D. 200

ANSWERS

1	2	3	4	5	6	7	8	9	10
A	B	A	D	D	A	A	B	B	B
11	**12**	**13**	**14**	**15**					
B	C	C	D	C					

EXPLANATORY ANSWERS

1. $\frac{A}{B} = \frac{2}{3}$ and $\frac{B}{C} = \frac{4}{5}$

$\Rightarrow \quad \frac{A}{B} \times \frac{B}{C} = \frac{2}{3} \times \frac{4}{5} \Rightarrow \frac{A}{C} = \frac{8}{15}$

$\Rightarrow \quad \frac{C}{A} = \frac{15}{8}$

Hence, C : A = 15 : 8.

2. 10% of x = 20% of y

$\Rightarrow \quad \frac{10}{100}x = \frac{20}{100}y \Rightarrow \frac{x}{10} = \frac{y}{5}$

$\Rightarrow \quad \frac{x}{y} = \frac{10}{5} \Rightarrow x : y = 2 : 1$

3. Mean proportional = $\sqrt{(6+\sqrt{27})(6-\sqrt{27})}$

$= \sqrt{36-27} = \sqrt{9} = 3$

4. $\because \quad \frac{x}{y} = \frac{9}{11}$

$$\frac{5x+3y}{3x+5y} = \frac{\frac{5x}{y}+\frac{3y}{y}}{\frac{3x}{y}+\frac{5y}{y}} = \frac{5\left(\frac{x}{y}\right)+3}{3\left(\frac{x}{y}\right)+5}$$

$$= \frac{5\times\frac{9}{11}+3}{3\times\frac{9}{11}+5} = \frac{\frac{45+33}{11}}{\frac{27+55}{11}} = \frac{78}{82} = \frac{39}{41}$$

Hence, the value of $\frac{5x+3y}{3x+5y} = \frac{39}{41}$.

5. Given : $a + b = 6x, b + c = 7x$

and $c + a = 8x$ ...(*i*)

and $a + b + c = 14$ ...(*ii*)

Adding Eq. (*i*)

$a + b + b + c + c + a = 6x + 7x + 8x$

$\Rightarrow \quad 2(a + b + c) = 21x$

$\Rightarrow \quad 2 \times 14 = 21x$ [from Eq. (*ii*)]

$\Rightarrow \quad x = \frac{28}{21} = \frac{4}{3}$

$\therefore \quad a + b = 6x = 6 \times \frac{4}{3} = 8$

$\because \quad a + b + c = 14 \Rightarrow c = 14 - 8 = 6$

6. Let the two numbers are a and b

According to the question,

$\frac{a}{b} = \frac{2}{3} \Rightarrow 3a = 2b \Rightarrow b = \frac{3a}{2}$

Now, $\frac{a+5}{b+5} = \frac{5}{7} \Rightarrow 7a + 35 = 5b + 25$

$\Rightarrow \quad 7a - 5b = -10$

$\Rightarrow \quad 7a - 5\left(\frac{3a}{2}\right) = -10$

$\Rightarrow \quad 14a - 15a = -20 \Rightarrow -a = -20$

$\Rightarrow \quad a = 20, b = 3 \times \frac{20}{2} = 30$

Hence, the bigger number is 30.

7. Let x be added to each of the numbers.

Then, $(12 + x) : (30 + x) :: (40 + x) : (86 + x)$

$\Rightarrow \quad \frac{12+x}{30+x} = \frac{40+x}{86+x}$

$\Rightarrow (12 + x)(86 + x) = (30 + x)(40 + x)$

$\Rightarrow 12 \times 86 + 12x + 86x + x^2$

$= 30 \times 40 + 30x + 40x + x^2$

$\Rightarrow \quad 1032 + 98x = 1200 + 70x$

$\Rightarrow \quad 28x = 168 \Rightarrow x = 6$

8. Ratio of Males : Females = 5 : 3

$\Rightarrow \quad \frac{800}{x} = \frac{5}{3} \Rightarrow 5x = 3 \times 800$

$\Rightarrow \quad x = \frac{3 \times 800}{5} = 3 \times 160 = 480$

Hence, number of females = 480.

9. Let ethanol = $4x$ and ether = $1x$

$4x + 1x = 60 \Rightarrow 5x = 60 \Rightarrow x = 12$

Quantity of ethanol = $12 \times 4 = 48$ litres

Quantity of ether = $1 \times 12 = 12$ litres

Let m litres of ether be added to mixture to get the desired ratio. Then,

$$\frac{48}{12+m} = \frac{2}{1} \Rightarrow 24 + 2m = 48$$

$$\Rightarrow 2m = 24 \Rightarrow m = 12$$

Hence, 12 litres of ether is to be added.

10. In 9 kg of brass, zinc = 4 kg

$\therefore$ In 180 kg of brass, zinc = $\frac{4}{9} \times 180 = 80$ kg.

11. Let the prices of a scooter and a television be ₹ $3x$ and $2x$ respectively.

According to the question,

$3x - 2x = 6000 \Rightarrow x = 6000$

$\therefore$ Price of a television = $2 \times 6000 =$ ₹ 12000.

12. Weight of 13 m long iron rod = 23.4 kg

Weight of 6 m long iron rod

$= \frac{23.4}{13} \times 6$ kg $= 1.8 \times 6 = 10.8$ kg.

13. Let present age of Gayatri = $6x$ years and present age of Savitri = $5x$ years.

According to the question,

$$6x + 5x = 44 \Rightarrow 11x = 44 \Rightarrow x = 4$$

Gayatri's age = $6 \times 4 = 24$ years

Savitri's age = $5 \times 4 = 20$ years

After 8 years their ages will be 32 years and 28 years.

Ratio of their ages after 8 years = $\frac{32}{28} = 8 : 7$.

14. Let numbers are x and y

$$\frac{x}{y} = \frac{3}{5}$$

$$\Rightarrow 5x = 3y \Rightarrow x = \frac{3y}{5}$$

According to the question,

$$\frac{x+10}{y+10} = \frac{5}{7} \Rightarrow 7x + 70 = 5y + 50$$

$$\Rightarrow 7x - 5y = -20$$

$$\Rightarrow 7\left(\frac{3y}{5}\right) - 5y = -20$$

$$\Rightarrow 21y - 25y = -100$$

$$\Rightarrow 4y = 100 \Rightarrow y = 25$$

$$\therefore x = \frac{3 \times 25}{5} = 15$$

Hence, numbers are 15 and 25.

15. Let the number of male and female workers be $5x$ and $3x$ respectively.

According to the question,

$5x - 3x = 40 \Rightarrow 2x = 40 \Rightarrow x = 20$

$\therefore$ Number of male = $5 \times 20 = 100$

and number of female = $3 \times 20 = 60$

Hence, total number of workers = $100 + 60 = 160$.

6. PARTNERSHIP

Partnership is a form of association of two or more persons who contribute resources like money together in order to carry on a business. It may be of simple or compound type.

Simple partnership is one in which the capitals of the partners are invested for the same time. The profits or losses are divided among the partners in the ratio of their investments.

Compound partnership is one in which the capitals of the partners are invested for different periods. In such cases, equivalent capitals are calculated for each partner by multiplying their capital contributions with time. The profits or losses are then divided in the ratio of these equivalent capitals. Thus, the ratio of profits is directly proportional to both capital invested as well as time.

The partner who invests the money in the business as well as takes part in its management, is known as **Working partner**.

The partner who only invests the money in the business and does not work, is known as **Sleeping partner**.

A working partner gets either monthly payment or a share in the profit for his contribution in the management of the business. This payment is deducted from the total profit before its distribution.

EXAMPLE: A, B and C invest ₹ 15000, ₹ 20000 and ₹ 25000 respectively in a business. The profit earned is ₹ 1200. Find the share of each in the profit.

SOLUTION: This is a case of simple partnership

Ratio of investments, A : B : C

= 15000 : 20000 : 25000

= 3 : 4 : 5

Sum of the ratios = 3 + 4 + 5 = 12

Share in the profit

$$\text{For A} = \frac{3}{12} \times 1200 = ₹\ 300$$

$$\text{For B} = \frac{4}{12} \times 1200 = ₹\ 400$$

$$\text{For C} = \frac{5}{12} \times 1200 = ₹\ 500$$

EXAMPLE: A and B are partners in a firm. A invests ₹ 15000 and B ₹ 25000. A is the working partner and gets 20% of the profit for his contribution in the management of the firm. B is the sleeping partner. If the profit is ₹ 475, find the share of each.

SOLUTION: First we have to deduct the payment to be made to A from the total profit for his contribution in the management of the firm.

20% of ₹ 475 = ₹ 95

Balance profit = 475 − 95 = ₹ 380

This has to be divided between A and B in the ratio of their investments *i.e.,* ₹ 15000 : ₹ 25000 = 3 : 5

$$\text{A's share} = ₹\ 380 \times \frac{3}{8} = ₹\ 142.5$$

$$\text{B's share} = ₹\ 380 \times \frac{5}{8} = ₹\ 237.5$$

Finally, A gets a total of (95 + 142.5) − ₹ 237.5 and B gets = ₹ 237.5

EXAMPLE: In a business A and B gained some amount in a certain ratio. B and C received the profit in the ratio as that of A and B. If B received ₹ 6400 and C received ₹ 10,000 then find the amount invested by B.

SOLUTION: Let the ratio of A's and B's profit be $\frac{a}{b}$.

Hence, the ratio of B's and C's profit = $\frac{a}{b}$

Thus, $A : B : C = a : b : \frac{b^2}{a}$

when A's profit, $a = ₹\ 6400$

and C's profit, $\frac{b^2}{a} = ₹\ 10,000$

$\Rightarrow \quad b^2 = 10,000 \times 6400 = 100 \times 100 \times 80 \times 80$

$\Rightarrow \quad b = 100 \times 80 = 8000$

Hence, the amount invested by B = ₹ 8000.

MULTIPLE CHOICE QUESTIONS

1. A, B and C share the profit in the ratio of 3 : 5 : 7. If the gain is ₹ 2040, then C's share is:
A. ₹ 360 B. ₹ 600
C. ₹ 952 D. ₹ 120

2. A, B and C started a business with ₹ 47000. A puts in ₹ 5000 more than B and B ₹ 3000 more than C. The share of A out of the profit of ₹ 14100 will be:
A. ₹ 3600 B. ₹ 4500
C. ₹ 6000 D. ₹ 6300

3. A starts a business with ₹ 5000. After 4 months B joins him with a sum of ₹ 4000. In the end of the year there is a profit of ₹ 8970. The share of A in the profit will be:
A. ₹ 3120 B. ₹ 4020
C. ₹ 5850 D. ₹ 6360

4. A, B, C are three partners in a business. The profit share of A is $\frac{3}{16}$ of the profit and B's share is $\frac{1}{4}$ of the profit. If C receives ₹ 243, then the amount received by B will be:
A. ₹ 90 B. ₹ 96
C. ₹ 108 D. ₹ 120

5. A, B and C share the profit in the ratio 2 : 3 : 7. If the average gain is ₹ 8000, then B's share is:
A. ₹ 2000 B. ₹ 1000
C. ₹ 1500 D. ₹ 3000

6. Ashok started a business investing ₹ 90,000. After 3 months Shabir joined him with a capital of ₹ 1,20,000. If at the end of one year the total profit made by them was ₹ 96,000, what will be the difference between their shares?
A. ₹ 24000 B. ₹ 8000
C. ₹ 20000 D. None of these

7. Mahesh received ₹ 6000 as his share out of the total profit of ₹ 9000 which he and Ram entered at the end of one year. If Mahesh invested ₹ 20,000 for 6 months, whereas Ram invested his amount for the whole year, what was the amount invested by Ram?
A. ₹ 4000 B. ₹ 5000
C. ₹ 3000 D. ₹ 6000

8. A and B started a business jointly. A's investment was thrice the investment of B and the period of his investment was two times the period of investment of B. If B received ₹ 40,000 as profit, then their total profit is:
A. ₹ 2,40,000 B. ₹ 28000
C. ₹ 24000 D. ₹ 2,80,000

9. Anil started a business investing ₹ 70,000. After 8 months Vimal joined him with a capital of ₹ 1,80,000. In what ratio should Anil and Vimal share the profit after two years?
A. 8 : 7 B. 7 : 5
C. 7 : 6 D. None of these

10. A, B and C starts a business. A invests ₹ 3,20,000 for four months. B invests ₹ 5,10,000 for three months and C invests ₹ 2,70,000 for five months. If at the end of year there is a profit of ₹ 1,24,800, then share of B is:
A. ₹ 79000 B. ₹ 49200
C. ₹ 50000 D. ₹ 45900

11. A, B and C contract a work for ₹ 550. Together A and B are to do $\frac{7}{11}$ of the work. The share of C should be:
A. ₹ 400 B. ₹ 300
C. ₹ 200 D. ₹ $183\frac{1}{3}$

12. Jagmohan, Rooplal and Pankaj rented a video cassette for one week at a rent of ₹ 350. If they use it for 6 hrs, 10 hrs and 12 hrs respectively, the rent to be paid by Pankaj is:
A. ₹ 75 B. ₹ 125
C. ₹ 35 D. ₹ 150

13. Manoj got ₹ 6000 as his share out of the total profit of ₹ 9000 which he and Ramesh earned at the end of one year. If Manoj invested ₹ 20,000 for 6 months, whereas Ramesh invested his amount for the whole year, the amount invested by Ramesh was:
A. ₹ 60,000 B. ₹ 10,000
C. ₹ 4000 D. ₹ 5000

14. A, B and C invest ₹ 2000, ₹ 3000 and ₹ 4000 in a business. After one year A removed his money, B and C continued the business for one more year. If the net profit after 2 years be ₹ 3200, then A's share in the profit is:
A. ₹ 1000 B. ₹ 600
C. ₹ 800 D. ₹ 400

15. A and B enter into partnership investing ₹ 12000 and ₹ 16000 respectively. After 8 months, C also joins the business with a capital of ₹ 15000. The share of C in a profit of ₹ 46500 after 2 years will be:
A. ₹ 12000 B. ₹ 14400
C. ₹ 19200 D. ₹ 21200

ANSWERS

1	2	3	4	5	6	7	8	9	10
C	C	C	C	A	D	B	D	D	D
11	**12**	**13**	**14**	**15**					
C	D	D	D	A					

EXPLANATORY ANSWERS

1. C's share $= \frac{7}{15} \times 2040 = ₹ 952.$

2. Let C's capital be ₹ x
Then B's capital = ₹ $(x + 3000)$
and A's capital = ₹ $(x + 3000 + 5000) = x + 8000$
$\Rightarrow \quad x + (x + 3000) + (x + 8000) = 47000$
$\Rightarrow \quad 3x + 11000 = 47000$
$\Rightarrow \quad 3x = 47000 - 11000 = 36000$
$\Rightarrow \quad x = 12000$
Thus, capital of A, B and C are ₹ 20000, ₹ 15000 and ₹ 12000 respectively.
∴ Profit sharing ratio = 20 : 15 : 12
∴ Profit of A $= \frac{20}{47} \times 14100 = ₹ 6000$

3. ₹ 5000 × 12 = ₹ 60,000 for A
₹ 4000 × (12 – 4) = 4000 × 8 = ₹ 32000 for B
Ratio of profit sharing = 60000 : 32000
= 60 : 32 = 15 : 8
∴ Share of A in the profit $= \frac{15}{23} \times 8970$
= 15 × 390 = ₹ 5850

4. Let the profit be ₹ 1. Then,

$$A : B : C = \frac{3}{16} : \frac{1}{4} : \left[1 - \left(\frac{3}{16} + \frac{1}{4}\right)\right]$$
$$= \frac{3}{16} : \frac{1}{4} : \frac{9}{16}$$
$$= \frac{3}{16} : \frac{4}{16} : \frac{9}{16} \quad \text{i.e., } 3 : 4 : 9$$

when C's share is ₹ 9, then B's share = ₹ 4
when C's share is ₹ 243, then B's share
$$= \frac{4 \times 243}{9} = ₹ 108$$

5. B's share $= \frac{3}{2 + 3 + 7} \times 8000$
$= \frac{3 \times 8000}{12} = ₹ 2000$

6. The ratio of their investment
$= 12 \times 90000 : (12 - 3) \times 120000$
$= 12 \times 9 : 9 \times 12 = 1 : 1$

Ashok's share $= \frac{1}{1+1} \times 96000 = ₹ 48000$

Shabir's share $= \frac{1}{1+1} \times 96000 = ₹ 48000$

Difference between their shares

$= ₹\ 48000 - ₹\ 48000 = 0.$

7. The ratio of their profit

$= ₹\ 6000 : ₹\ (9000 - 6000)$

$= ₹\ 6000 : ₹\ 3000 = 2 : 1$

Let ₹ x be the amount invested by Ram.

The ratio of their profit = The ratio of their investment

$\Rightarrow \quad 2 : 1 = 6 \times 20000 : 12 \times x$

$\Rightarrow \quad \frac{2}{1} = \frac{6 \times 20000}{12 \times x} \Rightarrow 2x = 10000$

$\Rightarrow \quad x = 5000$

∴ The investment of Ram is ₹ 5000.

8. Let ₹ x be the investment of B and n years be the period of investment of B.

Given : A's investment = $3 \times ₹\ x = ₹\ 3x$

and period of investment of A = $2n$ years

∴ The ratio of investment of A and B

$= 2n \times 3x : n \times x$

$= 6nx : nx = 6 : 1$

Let the total profit be ₹ y

Given B's share in profit = ₹ 40,000

$\Rightarrow \frac{1}{6+1} \times y = ₹\ 40{,}000 \Rightarrow y = ₹\ 2{,}80{,}000$

∴ Total profit is ₹ 2,80,000.

9. The ratio of Anil's and Vimal's share in the profit

= Ratio of their investments

$= 24 \times 70000 : 16 \times 180000$

$= 24 \times 7 : 16 \times 18 = 7 : 12$

10. The ratio of investments of A, B and C

$= 4 \times 320000 : 3 \times 510000 : 5 \times 270000$

$= 4 \times 32 : 3 \times 51 : 5 \times 27$

$= 128 : 153 : 135$

Total profit after 1 year = ₹ 124800

$$\text{Share of B} = ₹\ \frac{153}{128+153+135} \times 124800$$

$$= ₹\ \frac{153}{416} \times 124800 = ₹\ 45900$$

11. C's share $= ₹\left(550 \times \frac{4}{11}\right) = ₹\ 200$

12. Ratio of rents = 6 : 10 : 12 = 3 : 5 : 6

$$\therefore \text{Pankaj's share of rent} = ₹\left(350 \times \frac{6}{14}\right) = ₹\ 150$$

13. Let amount invested by Ramesh be ₹ x

$\therefore 20000 \times 6 : 12x = 6000 : 3000$

i.e., $\frac{12x}{120000} = \frac{3000}{6000}$ or $x = ₹\ 5000$

14. Ratio of investments

$= (2000 \times 1) : (3000 \times 2) : (4000 \times 2)$

$= 1 : 3 : 4$

$$\therefore \text{A's share} = ₹\left(3200 \times \frac{1}{8}\right) = ₹\ 400.$$

15. Ratio of investments

$= (12000 \times 24) : (16000 \times 24) : (15000 \times 16)$

$= 6 : 8 : 5$

$$\text{C's share of profit} = ₹\left(45600 \times \frac{5}{19}\right) = ₹\ 12000$$

7. AVERAGE

The sum of all the quantities of same kind divided by their number is called average (or mean) of those quantities.

FORMULAE

1. Average = $\left(\dfrac{\text{Sum of observations}}{\text{Number of observations}}\right)$
2. Sum of the first n natural numbers
   $= 1 + 2 + 3 + ... + n = \dfrac{n(n+1)}{2}$
3. Sum of the squares of the first n natural numbers
   $= 1^2 + 2^2 + ... + n^2 = \dfrac{n(n+1)(2n+1)}{6}$
4. Sum of the cubes of the first n natural numbers
   $= 1^3 + 2^3 + ... + n^3 = \left\{\dfrac{n(n+1)}{2}\right\}^2$
5. Sum of the first n odd numbers
   $= 1 + 3 + 5 + ... + (2n-1) = n^2$
6. Distance between two stations P and Q is x km. A person covers the journey from P to Q at 'a' km/hr and returns back to P with a uniform speed of 'b' km/hr. Then the average speed of the person during the whole journey
   $= \dfrac{2ab}{a+b}$ km/hr.

Different kinds of mean or average:

(*a*) Arithmetic mean
(*b*) Geometric mean
(*c*) Harmonic mean

(*a*) **Arithmetic Mean:** It is most popularly used of all the averages. For example, average income, average profit, average mileage etc. As defined earlier, it is the sum total of all values of items divided by the total number of items. For detailed discussion we will confine ourselves to Arithmetic Mean only because this is the most relevant of all the average for us.
Let $x_1, x_2, x_3, ..., x_n$ be the n values of x.
Their average is denoted by $\bar{x}$ and given by

$$\bar{x} = \frac{\text{Sum of observations}}{\text{Total number of observations}}$$

or $$\bar{x} = \frac{x_1 + x_2 + x_3 + ... + x_n}{n}$$

(*b*) **Geometric Mean :** For observations $x_1, x_2, x_3, ..., x_n$ the geometric mean denoted by G.M. is defined as:

$$\text{G.M.} = (x_1 \cdot x_2 \cdot x_3 \cdots x_n)^{1/n}$$

It is useful in calculating averages of ratios such as average population, growth rate, average percentage increase etc.

(*c*) **Harmonic Mean:** It is defined as

$$\text{H.M.} = \frac{n}{\frac{1}{x_1} + \frac{1}{x_2} + ... + \frac{1}{x_n}}.$$

EXAMPLE: Find the average of first ten prime numbers.

SOLUTION: First ten prime numbers are 2, 3, 5, 7, 11, 13, 17, 19, 23 and 29.

$$\therefore \text{Average} = \frac{2+3+5+7+11+13+17+19+23+29}{10}$$

$$= \frac{129}{10} = 12.9$$

EXAMPLE: If x_1, x_2, x_3, x_4, x_5 are five consecutive odd numbers then find the average of these numbers.

SOLUTION: Since x_1 is the first odd number.

$\therefore$
$$x_2 = x_1 + 2$$
$$x_3 = x_2 + 2 = x_1 + 4$$
$$x_4 = x_3 + 2 = x_1 + 6$$
$$x_5 = x_4 + 2 = x_1 + 8$$

$$\therefore \text{ Average} = \frac{x_1 + x_1 + 2 + x_1 + 4 + x_1 + 6 + x_1 + 8}{5}$$

$$= \frac{5x_1 + 20}{5} = \frac{5(x_1 + 4)}{5} = x_1 + 4$$

EXAMPLE: If the average of four consecutive even numbers is 27, then find the largest of these numbers.

SOLUTION: Let x be the first even number in the series of four consecutive even numbers.

$\therefore$ 2nd even number $= x + 2$

3rd even number $= x + 4$

4th even number $= x + 6$

$$\text{Average} = \frac{x + x + 2 + x + 4 + x + 6}{4}$$

$$\Rightarrow \quad 27 = \frac{4x + 12}{4}$$

$$\Rightarrow \quad 4x + 12 = 27 \times 4 = 108$$

$$\Rightarrow \quad 4x = 96$$

$$\Rightarrow \quad x = 24$$

Largest number in this series is $x + 6$

i.e., $24 + 6 = 30$

EXAMPLE: The average of eight numbers is 14. The average of six of these numbers is 16. What is the average of the remaining two numbers?

SOLUTION: Sum of the eight numbers $= 14 \times 8 = 112$

Sum of six of these eight numbers $= 16 \times 6 = 96$

$\therefore$ Sum of the remaining two numbers $= 112 - 96 = 16$

$\therefore$ Average of the remaining two numbers $= \frac{16}{2} = 8$

EXAMPLE: What is the average of first 30 multiples of 7?

SOLUTION: Required Average

$$= \frac{7 + 14 + 21 + ... + 210}{30}$$

$$= \frac{7(1 + 2 + 3 + ... + 30)}{30}$$

$$= \frac{7 \times 30(30 + 1)}{2 \times 30}$$

$$= \frac{7 \times 31}{2} = \frac{217}{2} = 108.5$$

EXAMPLE: The average of 11 results is 50. If the average of first six results is 49 and that of last six is 52, find the sixth result.

SOLUTION: Sum of 11 results $= 11 \times 50 = 550$

Sum of first 6 results $6 \times 49 = 294$

Sum of last 6 results $= 6 \times 52 = 312$

$\therefore$ 6th result $= 294 + 312 - 550$

$= 56$

EXAMPLE: The average age of three boys is 15 years. If their ages are in the ratio 3 : 5 : 7. What is the age of the youngest boy?

SOLUTION: Let the ages of the three boys be $3x$, $5x$ and $7x$.

$$\text{Average age} = \frac{3x + 5x + 7x}{3} = 5x$$

and $\quad 5x = 15 \Rightarrow x = 3$

The age of the youngest boy $= 3x = 3 \times 3 = 9$ years.

EXAMPLE: The average of 100 observations is 45. It was later found that two observations 19 and 31 were incorrectly recorded as 91 and 13. Find the correct average.

SOLUTION: Sum of 100 observations

$= 100 \times 45 = 4500$

New sum of 100 observations

$= 4500 + (19 + 31) - (91 + 13)$

$= 4500 + 50 - 104 = 4446$

$$\text{Correct average} = \frac{4446}{100} = 44.46$$

MULTIPLE CHOICE QUESTIONS

1. The average of first five multiples of 3 is:
   A. 3 B. 9
   C. 12 D. 15
2. The average of 25 results is 18, that of first 12 is 14 and of the last 12 is 17. Thirteenth result is:
   A. 78 B. 85
   C. 28 D. 72
3. Out of three numbers, the first is twice the second and is half of the third. If the average of the three numbers is 56, the three numbers in order are:
   A. 48, 96, 24 B. 48, 24, 96
   C. 96, 24, 48 D. 96, 48, 24
4. The sum of three numbers is 98. If the ratio between first and second be 2 : 3 and that between second and third be 5 : 8, then the second number is:
   A. 30 B. 20
   C. 58 D. 48
5. The average age of a committee of seven trustees is the same as it was 5 years ago; a young man having been substituted for one of them. The new man compared to the replaced old man, is younger in age by:
   A. 5 years B. 7 years
   C. 12 years D. 35 years
6. The average expenditure of a man for the first five months is ₹ 120 and for the next seven months is ₹ 130. His monthly average income if he saves ₹ 290 in that year, is:
   A. ₹ 160 B. ₹ 170
   C. ₹ 150 D. ₹ 140
7. The average salary of 20 workers in an office is ₹ 1900 per month. If the manager's salary is added, the average becomes ₹ 2000 per month. The manager's salary is:
   A. ₹ 24000 B. ₹ 25200
   C. ₹ 45600 D. None of these
8. The average temperature of first 3 days is 27°C and of the next 3 days is 29°C. If the average of the whole week is 28.5°C, the temperature of the last day is:
   A. 31.5°C B. 10.5°C
   C. 21°C D. 42°C
9. A cricketer scored 180 runs in the first test and 258 runs in the second. How many runs should he score in the third test so that his average score in the three tests would be 230 runs?
   A. 219 B. 242
   C. 334 D. None of these
10. The average of first five prime numbers is:
    A. 5.0 B. 5.2
    C. 5.6 D. 6.0
11. The average weight of 3 men A, B and C is 84 kg. Another man D joins the group and the average now becomes 80 kg. If another man E, whose weight is 3 kg more than that of D, replaces A, then average weight of B, C, D and E becomes 79 kg. The weight of A is:
    A. 70 kg B. 72 kg
    C. 75 kg D. 80 kg
12. The average age of A, B, C, D 5 years ago was 45 years. By including x, the present average of all the five is 49 years. The present age of x is:
    A. 64 years B. 48 years
    C. 45 years D. 40 years
13. The average height of 30 boys, out of a class of 50, is 160 cm. If the average height of the remaining boys is 165 cm, the average height of the whole class (in cm) is:
    A. 161 B. 162
    C. 163 D. 164
14. The average age of an adult class is 40 years. 12 new students with an average age of 32 years join the class, thereby decreasing the average of the class by 4 years. The original strength of the class was:
    A. 10 B. 11
    C. 12 D. 15
15. If a, b, c, d, e are five consecutive odd numbers, their average is:
    A. $5(a+4)$ B. $\frac{abcde}{5}$
    C. $5(a+b+c+d+e)$ D. None of these
16. Of the three numbers, second is twice the first and is also thrice the third. If the average of the three numbers is 44, the largest number is:
    A. 24 B. 36
    C. 72 D. 108

17. The average of 50 numbers is 38. If two numbers namely, 45 and 55 are discarded, the average of remaining number is:

A. 36.50 B. 37.00
C. 37.50 D. 37.52

18. The average height of 30 girls out of a class of 40 is 160 cm and that of the remaining girls is 156 cm. The average height of the whole class is:

A. 158 cm B. 158.5 cm
C. 159 cm D. 159.5 cm

19. The average of n numbers is x. If 36 is subtracted from any two numbers each, then new average is $(x - 8)$. The value of n is:

A. 6 B. 8
C. 9 D. 72

20. The average salary of male employees in a firm is ₹ 520 and that of female employees is ₹ 420. The mean salary of all the employees is ₹ 500. The percentage of female employees is:

A. 40% B. 30%
C. 25% D. 20%

ANSWERS

1	2	3	4	5	6	7	8	9	10
B	A	B	A	D	C	D	A	D	C
11	**12**	**13**	**14**	**15**	**16**	**17**	**18**	**19**	**20**
C	C	B	C	D	C	C	C	C	D

EXPLANATORY ANSWERS

1. Average $= \frac{3(1+2+3+4+5)}{5} = \frac{(3\times15)}{5} = 9$

2. Thirteenth result
$= [(25 \times 18) - (12 \times 14 + 12 \times 17)]$
$= [450 - (168 + 204)]$
$= 450 - 372 = 78.$

3. Let the numbers be $2x$, x and $4x$.

$$\text{Average} = \frac{2x+x+4x}{3} = \frac{7x}{3}$$

According to the question,

$$\frac{7x}{3} = 56$$

$\Rightarrow \quad 7x = 3 \times 56$

$\Rightarrow \quad x = \frac{3\times56}{7} = 24$

Hence, the numbers in order are 48, 24 and 96.

4. Let the numbers be x, y, z, then

$x + y + z = 98$

$\frac{x}{y} = \frac{2}{3}$ and $\frac{y}{z} = \frac{5}{8}$

$\therefore \quad x = \frac{2y}{3}$ and $z = \frac{8y}{5}$

So, $\frac{2y}{3} + y + \frac{8y}{5} = 98$

$\Rightarrow \quad \frac{10y+15y+24y}{15} = 98$

$\Rightarrow \quad 49y = 15 \times 98$

$\Rightarrow \quad y = \frac{15\times98}{49} = 30$

5. During these five years, the total age would have increased by $(7 \times 5) = 35$ years.
But, it remains the same as it was 5 years ago.
$\therefore$ The new man is younger than the replaced old man by 35 years.

6. Total income for 12 months
$= ₹\ (120 \times 5 + 130 \times 7 + 290)$
$= ₹\ 1800$

Average monthly income $= ₹\frac{1800}{12} = ₹150$

7. Total salary of 20 workers
$= 20 \times 1900 = ₹\ 38000$
Total salary of 20 workers and manager
$= 21 \times 2000 = ₹\ 42000$
Monthly salary of the manager
$= 42000 - 38000 = ₹\ 4000.$

8. Total temperature of first 3 days
$= 27 \times 3 = 81°C$
Total temperature of next 3 days
$= 29 \times 3 = 87°C$

Total temperature of 7 days

$= 28.5 \times 7 = 199.5°C$

Temperature of the last day

$= 199.5 - (81 + 87)$

$= 199.5 - 168 = 31.5°C$

9. Let runs he should score in third test be x :

Then, $\frac{180+258+x}{3} = 230$

$\Rightarrow \quad x = 690 - 438 = 252.$

10. Average $= \frac{2+3+5+7+11}{5} = \frac{28}{5} = 5.6.$

11. Weight of D = (80 × 4 – 84 × 3) kg = 68 kg

Weight of E = (68 + 3) kg = 71 kg

(B + C + D + E)'s weight = (79 × 4) kg = 316 kg

∴ (B + C)'s weight

= [316 – (68 + 71)] kg = 177 kg

Hence, A's weight

= [(84 × 3) – 177]kg = 75 kg

12. Total age of A, B, C and D 5 years ago

= (45 × 4) years = 180 years.

Total present age of A, B, C, D and x

= (49 × 5) years = 245 years.

Present age of A, B, C and D

= (180 + 5 × 4) years = 200 years.

∴ Present age of x = 45 years.

13. Total height of 30 boys = 30 × 160 = 4800

Total height of 20 boys = 20 × 165 = 3300

Total height of 50 boys = 8100

Average height of 50 boys $= \frac{8100}{50} = 162.$

14.
$$40x + 12 \times 32 = (12 + x) \times 36$$
$$\Rightarrow \quad 40x + 384 = 432 + 36x$$
$$\Rightarrow \quad 4x = 432 - 384 = 48$$
$$\Rightarrow \quad x = \frac{48}{4} = 12$$

Hence, the original strength of the class was 12.

15. Average $= \frac{a+a+2+a+4+a+6+a+8}{5}$

$= \frac{5a+20}{5} = \frac{5(a+4)}{5} = a+4$

16. Let the numbers be x, $2x$ and $\frac{2x}{3}$.

$$\text{Average} = \frac{x+2x+\frac{2x}{3}}{3}$$
$$\Rightarrow \quad \frac{11x}{9} = 44$$
$$\Rightarrow \quad x = \frac{44 \times 9}{11} = 36$$

So, the numbers are 36, 72 and 24.

Hence, the largest one is 72.

17. Total of 50 numbers = 50 × 38 = 1900

Average of 48 numbers $= \frac{1900-(45+55)}{48}$

$= \frac{1800}{48} = 37.50$

18. The average of the whole class

$= \frac{(30 \times 160 + 10 \times 156)}{40} = \frac{4800+1560}{40}$

$= \frac{6360}{40} = 159$ cm

19.
$$\frac{nx-36-36}{n} = x - 8$$
$$\Rightarrow \quad nx - 72 = nx - 8n$$
$$\Rightarrow \quad 8n = 72$$
$$\Rightarrow \quad n = 9$$

20. Let the total employees be 100.

n_1 = number of females = x

n_2 = number of males = $100 - x$

$$\bar{x} = \frac{n_1\bar{x}_1 + n_2\bar{x}_2}{n_1+n_2}$$
$$\Rightarrow \quad 500 = \frac{x \times 420 + (100-x) \times 520}{100}$$
$$\Rightarrow \quad 500 = \frac{42x + 5200 - 52x}{10}$$
$$\Rightarrow 5000 = 5200 - 10x$$
$$\Rightarrow \quad 10x = 200$$
$$\Rightarrow \quad x = 20 \text{ i.e., } 20\%.$$

8. PROFIT AND LOSS

Cost Price (CP)

The price at which an article is purchased is called the cost price of the article.

Selling Price (SP)

The price at which an article is sold is called the selling price of the article.

Profit or Gain

If SP is greater than the CP, the seller is said to have a profit or gain.

Clearly, Gain = SP – CP

Loss

If SP is less than CP, the seller is said to have a loss.

Clearly, Loss = CP – SP

Profit or loss per cent is calculated on cost price.

$$\text{Profit \%} = \frac{\text{Profit}}{\text{CP}} \times 100$$

$$\text{Loss \%} = \frac{\text{Loss}}{\text{CP}} \times 100$$

$$\text{SP} = \frac{\text{CP} \times (100 + \text{Profit\%})}{100}, \text{ if there is gain}$$

$$\text{SP} = \frac{\text{CP} \times (100 - \text{Loss\%})}{100}, \text{ if there is loss}$$

$$\text{CP} = \text{SP} \times \left(\frac{100}{100 + \text{Profit\%}}\right), \text{ if there is gain}$$

$$\text{CP} = \text{SP} \times \left(\frac{100}{100 - \text{Loss\%}}\right), \text{ if there is loss}$$

If an article is sold at a gain of 20%,

then, SP = (120% of CP)

If an article is sold at a loss of 20%,

then, SP = (80% of CP)

Overheads

The expenses incurred on transportation, rent, personnel salary, maintenance, packaging, advertisements and the like are included under the general heading of overheads. These overhead and the profit when added to the cost price determine the selling price. If the overheads are not separately mentioned in the problem, we assume it to be zero or else these have been included in the cost price itself.

Discount

It is an offer made by the seller to the buyer for reduction in price to be paid. There are several cases where discounts are allowed. For instance, to dispose off old goods, to increase its market share when the customer is ready to pay the whole amount in cash instead of instalment and so on. It is subtracted from the original price and is usually expressed as per cent or a fraction of the marked price. The price obtained after deducting the discount from the original price is the selling price which the customer has to pay.

EXAMPLE: If an article is purchased for ₹ 570 and sold for ₹ 518.70, find the lost per cent.

SOLUTION: CP = ₹ 570

SP = ₹ 518.70

∴ Loss = CP – SP

= 570 – 518.70 = ₹ 51.30

$$\text{Loss \%} = \frac{\text{Loss}}{\text{CP}} \times 100 = \frac{51.30}{570} \times 100$$

$$= \frac{5130}{570} = \frac{513}{57} = 9\%$$

EXAMPLE: A man buys a TV for ₹ 16,000. After two years he sells it for ₹ 12800. Find his loss per cent.

SOLUTION: $$\text{Loss \%} = \frac{\text{Loss}}{\text{CP}} \times 100$$

$$= \frac{16000 - 12800}{16000} \times 100$$

$$= \frac{3200}{16000} \times 100 = 20\%$$

EXAMPLE: Mohan sells his watch at a loss of ₹ 500 for ₹ 1000. Find the cost price and loss per cent.

SOLUTION: $$\text{CP} = \text{SP} + \text{Loss}$$

$$= 1000 + 500 = ₹\ 1500$$

$$\text{Loss \%} = \frac{\text{Loss}}{\text{CP}} \times 100 = \frac{500}{1500} \times 100$$

$$= \frac{100}{3} = 33\frac{1}{3}\%$$

EXAMPLE: Ravi buys an article for ₹ 5000 and sells it at 20% gain. Find it selling price.

SOLUTION: $$\text{Profit} = 20\% \text{ of CP} = \frac{20}{100} \times 5000$$

$\Rightarrow$ $$\text{Profit} = ₹\ 1000$$

$$\text{SP} = \text{CP} + \text{Profit}$$

$$= 5000 + 1000$$

$$= ₹\ 6000$$

EXAMPLE: A man sells an article at 20% gain for ₹ 3600. Find its cost price.

SOLUTION: Let CP = ₹ 100

then SP = 100 + 20 = ₹ 120

When SP ₹ 120 then CP = ₹ 100

When SP ₹ 3600 then CP = $\frac{100}{120} \times 3600$

Hence CP = ₹ 3000

EXAMPLE: The cost price of 6 pens is equal to the selling price of 4 pens. Find the profit per cent.

SOLUTION: SP of 4 pens = CP of 6 pens

SP of 2 pens = CP of $\frac{6}{4} \times 2 = 3$ pens

Profit = CP of 3 pens

investment = CP of 6 pens

$$\text{Profit \%} = \frac{3}{6} \times 100 = 50\%$$

Alternatively:

Let the CP of 1 pen be ₹ x.

$\therefore$ CP of 6 pens = ₹ $6x$

Also, SP of 4 pens = ₹ $6x$

$\therefore$ SP of 6 pens = $\frac{6x}{4} \times 6 = ₹\ 9x$

Profit = SP – CP = $9x - 6x = 3x$

$$\text{Profit \%} = \frac{3x}{6x} \times 100 = 50\%$$

EXAMPLE: If CP of 20 tables is equal to the SP of 25 tables. Find the loss percent.

SOLUTION: Let the CP of 1 table be ₹ x.

$\therefore$ CP of 20 tables = ₹ $20x$

Also, SP of 25 tables = ₹ $20x$

$\therefore$ SP of 20 tables = ₹ $\frac{20x}{25} \times 20 = ₹\ 16x$

Loss = $20x - 16x = 4x$

$$\text{Loss \%} = \frac{\text{Loss}}{\text{CP}} \times 100$$

$$= \frac{4x}{20x} \times 100 = 20\%$$

EXAMPLE: Ram sold a book at a profit of 6%. Had he sold it for ₹ 2 more he would have gained 10%. Find the cost price of the book.

SOLUTION: (10% – 6%) of CP = 4% of CP = ₹ 2

$\Rightarrow$ $$\frac{4}{100} \times \text{CP} = 2$$

$\Rightarrow$ $$\text{CP} = \frac{200}{4} = ₹\ 50$$

EXAMPLE: An article is sold for ₹ 4600 at a gain of 15%. What would be the profit or loss per cent if it is sold for ₹ 3600?

SOLUTION: $$\text{CP} = 4600 \times \frac{100}{115} = ₹\ 4000$$

$$\text{Loss \%} = \frac{4000 - 3600}{4000} \times 100 = 10\%$$

MULTIPLE CHOICE QUESTIONS

1. A loss of 5% was suffered by selling a plot for ₹ 4085. The cost price of the plot was:
A. ₹ 4350 B. ₹ 4259.25
C. ₹ 4200 D. ₹ 4300
2. On selling an article for ₹ 240, a trader loses 4%. In order to gain 10%, he must sell that article for:
A. ₹ 264.00 B. ₹ 273.20
C. ₹ 275.00 D. ₹ 280.00
3. A man purchased a watch for ₹ 400 and sold it at a gain of 20% of the selling price. The selling price of the watch is:
A. ₹ 300 B. ₹ 320
C. ₹ 440 D. ₹ 500
4. If 5% more is gained by selling an article for ₹ 350 than by selling it for ₹ 340, the cost of the article is:
A. ₹ 50 B. ₹ 160
C. ₹ 200 D. ₹ 225
5. Profit after selling a commodity for ₹ 425 is same as loss after selling it for ₹ 355. The cost of the commodity is:
A. ₹ 385 B. ₹ 390
C. ₹ 395 D. ₹ 400
6. The cost price of an article, which on being sold at a gain of 12% yields ₹ 6 more than when it is sold at a loss of 12%, is:
A. ₹ 30 B. ₹ 25
C. ₹ 20 D. ₹ 24
7. The CP of an article which is sold at a loss of 25% for ₹150, is:
A. ₹ 125 B. ₹ 175
C. ₹ 200 D. ₹ 225
8. When the price of pressure cooker was increased by 15%, its sale fell down by 15%. The effect on the money receipt was:
A. no effect B. 15% decrease
C. 7.5% increase D. 2.25% decrease
9. A man sells 320 mangoes at the cost price of 400 mangoes. His gain per cent is:
A. 10% B. 25%
C. 15% D. 20%
10. By selling 12 oranges for one rupee a man loses 20%. How many for a rupee should he sell to get a gain of 20%?
A. 5 B. 8
C. 10 D. 15
11. A man sells a car to his friend at 10% loss. If the friend sells it for ₹ 54000 and gains 20%, the original CP of the car was:
A. ₹ 25000 B. ₹ 37500
C. ₹ 50000 D. ₹ 60000
12. The loss incurred on selling an article for ₹ 270 is as much as the profit made after selling it at 10% profit. The CP of the article is:
A. ₹ 90 B. ₹ 110
C. ₹ 363 D. ₹ 300
13. An item costing ₹ 200 is being sold at 10% loss. If the price is further reduced by 5%, the selling price will be:
A. ₹ 179 B. ₹ 175
C. ₹ 171 D. ₹ 170
14. A trader lists his articles 20% above CP and allows a discount of 10% on cash payment. His gain per cent is:
A. 10% B. 6%
C. 8% D. 5%
15. A discount series of 10%, 20% and 40% is equal to a single discount of:
A. 50% B. 56.80%
C. 70% D. 70.28%

ANSWERS

1	2	3	4	5	6	7	8	9	10
D	C	D	C	B	B	C	D	B	B
11	**12**	**13**	**14**	**15**					
C	D	C	C	B					

EXPLANATORY ANSWERS

1. Loss = 5%, SP = ₹ 4085

Let CP = ₹ 100

∴ SP = ₹ 100 – 5 = ₹ 95

When SP ₹ 95 then CP = ₹ 100

When SP ₹ 4085 then CP = $\frac{100}{95} \times 4085$

= 4300

Hence, the cost price of the plot was ₹ 4300.

2. Loss = 4%, SP = ₹ 240

Let CP = ₹ 100

∴ SP = 100 – 4 = 96

When SP ₹ 96 then CP = ₹ 100

When SP ₹ 240 then CP = $\frac{100}{96} \times 240 =$ ₹ 250

Again 100 + 10 = 110

When CP 100 then SP = ₹ 110

When CP 250 then SP = $\frac{110}{100} \times 250 =$ ₹ 275

3. Let SP = ₹ x

then, profit = $\frac{20}{100} \times x =$ ₹ $\frac{x}{5}$

CP = SP – profit = $x - \frac{x}{5} =$ ₹ $\frac{4x}{5}$

According to the question,

$\frac{4x}{5} = 400 \Rightarrow 4x = 2000$

$\Rightarrow x = 500$

Hence, selling price of the watch = ₹ 500.

4. Let CP = ₹ x

Then, if SP = ₹350

Profit = SP – CP = ₹ $(350 - x)$

if SP = ₹ 340 then, profit = ₹ $(340 - x)$

$\therefore (350 - x) - (340 - x) = \frac{5}{100}x$

$\Rightarrow 10 = \frac{5}{100}x \quad \Rightarrow x = 200$

Hence, the cost of the article = ₹ 200.

5. Let CP = ₹ x,

then, $425 - x = x - 355 \Rightarrow 2x = 780$

$\Rightarrow x = 390$

Hence, the cost of commodity is ₹ 390.

6. Let CP of the article = ₹ x

Then, SP when profit is 12%

$= \left(\frac{12x}{100} + x\right) = \frac{112x}{100}$

$\therefore \frac{112x}{100} - \frac{88x}{100} = 6$

$\Rightarrow 24x = 600$

$\Rightarrow x = \frac{600}{24} = 25$

∴ CP of the article is ₹ 25.

7. 100 – 25 = 75

When SP 75 then CP = ₹ 100

When SP 150 then CP = ₹ $\frac{100}{75} \times 150 =$ ₹ 200

8. Let the original cost of each cooker be ₹ 1 and let the number sold originally be 100.

Total sale proceed = ₹ (100 × 1) = ₹ 100

New rate = (115% of ₹ 1) = ₹ 1.15

Number sold now = 85

∴ Sale proceed now = ₹(1.15 × 85) = ₹ 97.75

So, there is a decrease of 2.25% in the money receipt.

9. Let CP of each mango be ₹ 1.

Then, CP of 400 mangoes = ₹ 400

∴ CP of 320 mangoes = ₹ 320

SP of 320 mangoes = ₹ 400

Profit = 400 – 320 = ₹ 80

Profit% = $\frac{80}{320} \times 100 = 25\%$

10. SP = ₹ 1, Loss = 20%

$\Rightarrow$ CP = $\left(\frac{100}{80} \times 1\right) \Rightarrow$ CP = ₹ $\frac{5}{4}$

Now, CP = ₹ $\frac{5}{4}$, gain, 20%

$\Rightarrow$ SP = $\frac{120}{100} \times \frac{5}{4} =$ ₹ $\frac{3}{2}$

For ₹$\frac{3}{2}$, he must sell 12 oranges

For ₹ 1, he must sell $\left(12 \times \frac{2}{3}\right)$ = 8 oranges.

11. SP = ₹ 54000 and gain earned = 20%

$$CP = ₹\left(\frac{100}{120} \times 54000\right) = ₹\ 45000$$

Now, SP = ₹ 45000 and Loss = 10%

$$\therefore\ CP = ₹\left(\frac{100}{90} \times 45000\right) = ₹\ 50000$$

12. Let CP be ₹ x. Then,

$$x - 270 = 10\% \text{ of } x = \frac{x}{10}$$

$$\Rightarrow \quad x - \frac{x}{10} = 270$$

$$\Rightarrow \quad 9x = 10 \times 270$$

$$\Rightarrow \quad x = \frac{10 \times 270}{9}$$

$$\Rightarrow \quad x = 300$$

$\therefore$ CP of the article is ₹ 300.

13. SP = 90% of ₹ 200 = ₹ 180

Further, SP = (95% of ₹180) = ₹ 171

14. Let CP = ₹ 100. Then, MP = ₹ 120.

$$SP = 90\% \text{ of } ₹\ 120 = \frac{90}{100} \times 120 = ₹\ 108$$

Profit = SP – CP = 108 – 100 = ₹ 8

$$\text{Profit } \% = \frac{\text{Profit}}{\text{CP}} \times 100 = \frac{8}{100} \times 100 = 8\%$$

15. Let original price = ₹ 100

Price after 1st discount = ₹ 90

Price after 2nd discount

$$= ₹\left(\frac{80}{100} \times 90\right) = ₹\ 72$$

Price after 3rd discount

$$= ₹\left(\frac{60}{100} \times 72\right) = ₹\ 43.20$$

$\therefore$ Single discount = 100 – 43.20 = 56.8%.

9. SIMPLE AND COMPOUND INTEREST

In any money transaction there is a **lender** who gives money, and a **borrower** who receives money. The amount of loan borrowed, is called the principal (P). The borrower pays a certain amount for the use of this money. This is called **Interest (I)**. Interest is always calculated on the principal borrowed. The borrowing is for a specified **Time (t)** and on specified terms. The specified term is expressed as per cent of the principal and is called rate of interest.

The sum of the principal and the interest is called the **Amount (A)**. In general, the rate of interest may be yearly, half yearly, quarterly or monthly as mutually agreed upon by both parties at the time of transaction. Depending upon the period of rate of interest, time is expressed in multiples of this period.

Interest is of two kinds—**Simple Interest and compound Interest**. If the interest is calculated only, on a certain sum borrowed it is called Simple Interest.

The simple interest (SI) on a principal P at R% per annum for T years is given by:

$$SI = \frac{P \times R \times T}{100}$$

$$\therefore \quad P = \frac{SI \times 100}{R \times T}$$

$$\therefore \quad R = \frac{SI \times 100}{P \times T}$$

$$\therefore \quad T = \frac{SI \times 100}{P \times R}$$

Compound Interest differs from Simple Interest that in CI the interest for the future period is calculated not only on the principal but also on the interest earned until the previous period. Thus, the total interest earned in case of CI is not uniformly distributed over time units whereas in Simple Interest it is uniformly distributed. The interest due at the end of the first unit of time is added to the principal and the amount so obtained becomes the principal for the second unit. Similarly, the amount after the 2nd unit of time becomes the principal for the third unit of time and continues till the last unit of time.

The difference between the final amount (A) obtained at the last unit of time and the original principal is called the **Compound Interest**.

Important Relations

Principal = ₹ P (in rupees)

Rate = R % (in per cent per annum)

Time period = T years (in years)

Amount = ₹ A (in rupees)

I. When interest is compounded annually,

$$A = P\left[1 + \frac{R}{100}\right]^T$$

II. When interest is compounded half-yearly,

$$A = P\left[1 + \frac{R/2}{100}\right]^{2T} = P\left[1 + \frac{R}{200}\right]^{2T}$$

[R is divided by 2 and T is multiplied by 2.]

III. When interest is compounded quarterly,

$$A = P\left[1+\frac{R/4}{100}\right]^{4T} = P\left[1+\frac{R}{400}\right]^{4T}$$

[R is divided by 4 and T is multiplied by 4.]

IV. When interest is R_1% for first year, R_2% for 2nd year and R_3% for third year;

$$A = P\left[1+\frac{R_1}{100}\right]\left[1+\frac{R_2}{100}\right]\left[1+\frac{R_3}{100}\right]$$

V. $CI = A - P$

EXAMPLE: Find the simple interest on ₹ 1000 for 3 years at 10% p.a.

SOLUTION: $SI = \frac{P \times R \times T}{100} = \frac{1000 \times 10 \times 3}{100} = ₹\,300$

EXAMPLE: Find the amount of ₹ 600 in 4 years at 3% p.a.

SOLUTION: $SI = \frac{P \times R \times T}{100} = \frac{600 \times 3 \times 4}{100} = ₹\,72$

$\therefore$ Amount $= P + SI = 600 + 72 = ₹\,672$

EXAMPLE: In what time will ₹ 7000 give ₹ 3675 as interest at the rate of 7% p.a. simple interest?

SOLUTION: $T = \frac{SI \times 100}{P \times R} = \frac{3675 \times 100}{7000 \times 7}$

$= \frac{15}{2} = 7\frac{1}{2}$ years.

EXAMPLE: At what rate per annum will a sum of ₹ 5000 amount to ₹ 6000 in 4 years?

SOLUTION: $SI = A - P = 6000 - 5000 = ₹\,1000$

$R = \frac{SI \times 100}{P \times T} = \frac{1000 \times 100}{5000 \times 4} = 5\%$

EXAMPLE: In how many years will a sum of money double itself at 5% rate of interest?

SOLUTION: A sum doubles itself when amount of interest becomes equal to the principal

$SI = P, R = 5\%$

$\therefore \quad T = \frac{100 \times P}{P \times 5} = 20$ years

EXAMPLE: A certain sum amounts to ₹ 115200 in 2 years and to ₹ 165888 in 4 years. Find the sum and rate per cent.

SOLUTION: Here, amount on ₹ 115200 for 2 years at CI is ₹ 165888

$\therefore \quad 115200\left(1+\frac{R}{100}\right)^2 = 165888$

$\left(1+\frac{R}{100}\right)^2 = \frac{165888}{115200} = 1.44$

$\therefore \quad 1+\frac{R}{100} = 1.2$

$\frac{R}{100} = 1.2 - 1 = 0.2$

$\Rightarrow \quad R = 0.2 \times 100 = 20\%$

Amount after 2 years is ₹ 115200

$\therefore \quad P\left(1+\frac{20}{100}\right)^2 = 115200$

$\Rightarrow \quad P = \frac{115200}{\left(1+\frac{20}{100}\right)^2} = \frac{115200}{1.44} = 80000$

$\therefore$ Principal = ₹ 80000

EXAMPLE: A sum of money doubles itself at CI in 15 years. In how many years will it become eight times?

SOLUTION: $P\left(1+\frac{R}{100}\right)^{15} = 2P$

$\Rightarrow \quad \left(1+\frac{R}{100}\right)^{15} = 2$

Let T be the required number of years that makes the principal 8 times of it.

$\therefore \quad P\left(1+\frac{R}{100}\right)^{T} = 8P$

$\Rightarrow \quad \left(1+\frac{R}{100}\right)^{T} = 8 = (2)^3$

$\Rightarrow \quad \left(1+\frac{R}{100}\right)^{T} = \left[\left(1+\frac{R}{100}\right)^{15}\right]^3$

$\Rightarrow \quad \left(1+\frac{R}{100}\right)^{T} = \left(1+\frac{R}{100}\right)^{45}$

$\Rightarrow \quad T = 45$ years

Hence, required number of years is 45 years.

EXAMPLE: The difference between simple and compound interest on a sum of money at 5% p.a. for 2 years is ₹ 25. Find the sum.

SOLUTION: Let P = ₹ 100

$$SI = \frac{P \times R \times T}{100} = \frac{100 \times 5 \times 2}{100} = ₹\,10$$

$$A = P\left(1+\frac{R}{100}\right)^T = 100\left(1+\frac{5}{100}\right)^2$$

$$= \frac{100 \times 21 \times 21}{400} = ₹\,\frac{441}{4}$$

$$CI = A - P = \frac{441}{4} - 100 = ₹\,\frac{41}{4}$$

$$CI - SI = \frac{41}{4} - 10 = \frac{41-40}{4} = ₹\,\frac{1}{4}$$

When difference ₹ $\frac{1}{4}$ then P = ₹ 100

When difference ₹ 25 then P = 100 × 4 × 25
= ₹ 10000

Hence, sum = ₹ 10000.

MULTIPLE CHOICE QUESTIONS

1. The simple interest on ₹ 500 for 6 years at 5% p.a. is:
A. ₹ 250 B. ₹ 150
C. ₹ 140 D. ₹ 120

2. A certain sum of money at SI amounts to ₹ 1012 in $2\frac{1}{2}$ years and to ₹ 1067.20 in 4 years. The rate of interest per annum is:
A. 2.5% B. 3%
C. 4% D. 5%

3. ₹ 1200 amounts to ₹ 1632 in 4 years at a certain rate of simple interest. If the rate of interest is increased by 1%, it would amount to how much?
A. ₹ 1635 B. ₹ 1644
C. ₹ 1670 D. ₹ 1680

4. A man will get ₹ 87 as simple interest on ₹ 725 at 4% per annum in:
A. 3 years B. 3½ years
C. 4 years D. 5 years

5. At simple interest, a sum doubles after 20 years. The rate of interest per annum is:
A. 5% B. 10%
C. 20% D. Data inadequate

6. A lent ₹ 600 to B for 2 years and ₹ 150 to C for 4 years and received altogether from both ₹ 90 as simple interest. The rate of interest is:
A. 12% B. 10%
C. 5% D. 4%

7. Interest on a certain sum of money for $2\frac{1}{3}$ years at $3\frac{3}{4}$% per annum is ₹ 210. The sum is:
A. ₹ 2800 B. ₹ 1580
C. ₹ 2400 D. None of these

8. A certain sum of money at simple interest amounts to ₹ 1260 in 2 years and to ₹ 1350 in 5 years. The rate per cent per annum is:
A. 2.5% B. 3.75%
C. 5% D. 7.5%

9. A sum of money doubles itself in 5 years. It will become 4 times itself in:
A. 10 years B. 12 years
C. 15 years D. 20 years

10. The simple interest on a sum of money will be ₹ 600 after 10 years. If the principal is trebled after 5 years, the total interest at the end of 10 years will be:
A. ₹ 600 B. ₹ 900
C. ₹ 1200 D. Data inadequate

11. ₹ 800 amounts to ₹ 920 in 3 years at simple interest. If the interest rate is increased by 3%, it would amount to how much?
A. ₹ 1056 B. ₹ 1112
C. ₹ 1182 D. ₹ 992

12. A sum of money at simple interest amounts to ₹ 2240 in 2 years and ₹ 2600 in 5 years. The sum is:
A. ₹ 1880 B. ₹ 2000
C. ₹ 2120 D. Data inadequate

13. If ₹ 7500 are borrowed at CI at the rate of 4% per annum, then after 2 years the amount to be paid is:

A. ₹ 8082 B. ₹ 7800
C. ₹ 8100 D. ₹ 8112

14. Simple interest on a sum at 4% per annum is ₹ 80 in 2 years. The compound interest on the same sum for the same period is:

A. ₹ 81.60 B. ₹ 160
C. ₹ 1081.60 D. None of these

15. ₹ 800 at 5% per annum compound interest will amount to ₹ 882 in:

A. 1 year B. 2 years
C. 3 years D. 4 years

ANSWERS

1	2	3	4	5	6	7	8	9	10
B	C	D	A	A	C	C	A	C	C
11	**12**	**13**	**14**	**15**					
D	B	D	A	B					

EXPLANATORY ANSWERS

1. $SI = \frac{P \times R \times T}{100} = \frac{500 \times 5 \times 6}{100} = ₹\ 150$

2. SI for $1\frac{1}{2}$ years = 1067.20 – 1012 = ₹ 55.20

SI for $2\frac{1}{2}$ years $= 55.20 \times \frac{2}{3} \times \frac{5}{2} = ₹\ 92$

∴ Principal = ₹ (1012 – 92) = ₹ 920

$R = \frac{SI \times 100}{P \times T} = \frac{92 \times 100 \times 2}{920 \times 5} = 4\%$

3. $R = \frac{SI \times 100}{P \times T} = \frac{432 \times 100}{1200 \times 4} = 9\%$

New rate = (9 + 1)% = 10%

$SI = \frac{P \times R \times T}{100} = \frac{1200 \times 10 \times 4}{100} = ₹\ 480$

Amount = P + SI = 1200 + 480 = ₹ 1680

4. $T = \frac{SI \times 100}{P \times R} = \frac{87 \times 100}{725 \times 4} = 3$ years

5. Let P be ₹ x then A = ₹ $2x$

SI = A – P = $2x - x$ = ₹ x

$R = \frac{SI \times 100}{P \times T} = \frac{x \times 100}{x \times 20} = 5\%$

6. $SI = \frac{P \times R \times T}{100} = \frac{600 \times R \times 2}{100} = 12R$

Again $SI = \frac{P \times R \times T}{100} = \frac{150 \times R \times 4}{100} = 6R$

Total SI = 12R + 6R = 18R

According to the question,

$18R = 90 \Rightarrow R = \frac{90}{18} = 5\%$

7. $T = 2\frac{1}{3} = \frac{7}{3}$ years,

$R = 3\frac{3}{4}\% = \frac{15}{4}\%$

$P = \frac{SI \times 100}{P \times T} = \frac{210 \times 100}{\frac{15}{4} \times \frac{7}{3}}$

$= \frac{210 \times 100 \times 4 \times 3}{15 \times 7} = ₹\ 2400$

8. SI for 3 years = ₹ 1350 – ₹ 1260 = ₹ 90

SI for 1 year $= \frac{90}{3} = ₹\ 30$

SI for 2 years = ₹ 30 × 2 = ₹ 60

P = A – SI = 1260 – 60 = ₹ 1200

$R = \frac{SI \times 100}{P \times T} = \frac{60 \times 100}{1200 \times 2} = \frac{5}{2} = 2.5\%$

9. Let P be ₹ x, A = ₹ $2x$,
SI = $2x - x$ = ₹ x

$$R = \frac{SI \times 100}{P \times T} = \frac{x \times 100}{x \times 5} = 20\%$$

Again, P = ₹ x, A = $4x$,
SI = $4x - x = 3x$

$$T = \frac{SI \times 100}{P \times R} = \frac{3x \times 100}{x \times 20} = 15 \text{ years}$$

10. Let P be ₹ x
SI = ₹ 600, T = 10 years.

$$R = \frac{SI \times 100}{P \times T} = \frac{600 \times 100}{x \times 10} = \frac{6000}{x}\%$$

$$\text{SI for first 5 years} = \frac{x \times 5 \times 6000}{100 \times x} = ₹\ 300$$

$$\text{SI for last 5 years} = \frac{3x \times 5 \times 6000}{100 \times x} = ₹\ 900$$

Total interest at the end of 10 years
= 900 + 300 = ₹ 1200.

11. P = ₹ 800, SI = 920 – 800 = ₹ 120
T = 3 years

$$R = \frac{SI \times 100}{P \times T} = \frac{120 \times 100}{800 \times 3} = 5\%$$

New rate = 8% (increase 3%)

$$SI = \frac{P \times R \times T}{100} = \frac{800 \times 8 \times 3}{100} = ₹\ 192$$

$\therefore$ A = P + SI = 800 + 192 = ₹ 992.

12. SI for 3 years = 2600 – 2240 = ₹ 360

$$\text{SI for 2 years} = \frac{360}{3} \times 2 = ₹\ 240$$

$\therefore$ Sum = 2240 – 240 = ₹ 2000

13.
$$A = P\left(1 + \frac{R}{100}\right)^T = 7500\left(1 + \frac{4}{100}\right)^2$$

$$= 7500 \times \frac{26}{25} \times \frac{26}{25} = ₹\ 8112$$

14.
$$P = \frac{SI \times 100}{T \times R} = \frac{80 \times 100}{4 \times 2} = ₹\ 1000$$

$$A = P\left(1 + \frac{R}{100}\right)^T = 1000\left(1 + \frac{4}{100}\right)^2$$

$$= 1000 \times \frac{26}{25} \times \frac{26}{25} = 1081.60$$

CI = A – P = 1081.60 – 1000 = ₹ 81.60

15. Let time = x years

$$A = P\left(1 + \frac{R}{100}\right)^T$$

$$882 = 800\left(1 + \frac{5}{100}\right)^x$$

$$\Rightarrow \frac{882}{800} = \left(\frac{21}{20}\right)^x$$

$$\Rightarrow \left(\frac{21}{20}\right)^2 = \left(\frac{21}{20}\right)^x \Rightarrow x = 2$$

$\therefore$ Time = 2 years

10. TIME AND WORK

Performing or doing work of any amount involves efforts of person (S) over a period of time. Therefore, the number of persons (P), the quantity of work (W) and the period of time (T) are important variables in problems related to "Time and Work". Moreover time (T) taken to do a work depends not only on how many persons are employed to do it but also on how efficient they are. Efficiency here means rate of doing same work. This aspect comes into picture when the problem involves comparison of work done by different categories of persons. For instance, efficiencies of man, woman, boy, girl in general are different. Even efficiency of one man may not be same as that of other; but unless otherwise specifically stated in the problem, all men or women working in a group are assumed to do work with equal efficiency.

The problems on Time and Work can be solved by following two methods:

(*i*) Ratio and proportion method

(*ii*) Unitary method

(*i*) **Ratio and Proportion Method:** Since problems concerning to Time and Work have proportional relation, these can be solved by this method. We have tried to solve questions based on Time and Work in the chapter mentioned.

(*ii*) **Unitary Method:** This is a very simple and useful method. The term 'Unitary' is self-evident. In this method, we first proceed to reduce the problem to either work done by one person or work done in 1 day and so on as per the requirement of the problem. Let us try to understand it.

(*a*) If a man can do a piece of work in 10 days he will do $\frac{1}{10}$ of the work in 1 day. Conversely, if a man can do $\frac{1}{10}$ of the work in 1 day, he will do the work in 10 days.

(*b*) If the number of men engaged to do a piece of work be changed in the ratio 5 : 4, the time required for the work will be changed in the ratio 4 : 5.

(*c*) If A is x times as good a workman as B, then A will take $\frac{1}{x}$ of the time that B takes to do a certain work.

All the above points can be summarised into one and can be written in the following form:

If M_1 persons can do W_1 works in D_1 days and M_2 persons can do W_2 works in D_2 days then we have a very general formula in the relationship of

$$M_1 D_1 W_2 = M_2 D_2 W_1$$

The above relationship can be taken as a very basic and all-in-one formula we also derive:

(*i*) More men less days and conversely more days less men.

(*ii*) More men more work and conversely more work more men.

(*iii*) More days more work and conversely more work more days.

$$M_1 D_1 T_1 W_2 = M_2 D_2 T_2 W_1$$

EXAMPLE: 5 men can prepare 10 toys in 6 days working 6 hrs a day. How many days can 12 men prepare 16 toys working 8 hrs a day?

SOLUTION: $M_1 D_1 T_1 W_2 = M_2 D_2 T_2 W_1$

$$5 \times 6 \times 6 \times 16 = 12 \times D_2 \times 8 \times 10$$

$$D_2 = \frac{5 \times 6 \times 6 \times 16}{12 \times 8 \times 10} = 3 \text{ days.}$$

EXAMPLE: A can reap a field in 8 days, which B alone can reap in 12 days. In how many days, both together, can reap this field?

SOLUTION: A's 1 day's work $= \frac{1}{8}$

B's 1 day's work $= \frac{1}{12}$

(A + B)'s 1 day's work $= \left(\frac{1}{8}+\frac{1}{12}\right)$

$= \frac{3+2}{24} = \frac{5}{24}$

$\therefore$ Both together can reap the field in $\frac{24}{5}$ days

$= 4\frac{4}{5}$ days.

EXAMPLE: A and B together can do a piece of work in 12 days, B alone can finish it in 30 days. In how many days can A alone finish the work?

SOLUTION: (A + B)'s 1 day's work $= \frac{1}{12}$

B's 1 day's work $= \frac{1}{30}$

$\therefore$ A's 1 day's work $= \frac{1}{12} - \frac{1}{30}$

$= \frac{5-2}{60} = \frac{3}{60} = \frac{1}{20}$

Hence, A alone can finish the work in 20 days.

EXAMPLE: A and B can do a piece of work in 12 days, C and A in 20 days and B and C in 15 days. In how many days will they finish it together and separately?

SOLUTION: (A + B)'s 1 day's work $= \frac{1}{12}$

(B + C)'s 1 day's work $= \frac{1}{15}$

(C + A)'s 1 day's work $= \frac{1}{20}$

Adding, 2(A + B + C)'s 1 day's work

$= \left(\frac{1}{12}+\frac{1}{15}+\frac{1}{20}\right) = \frac{5+4+3}{60}$

$= \frac{12}{60} = \frac{1}{5}$

or (A + B + C)'s 1 day's work $= \frac{1}{10}$

$\therefore$ A, B, C together can finish the work in 10 days.

Now, C's 1 day's work $= \frac{1}{10} - \frac{1}{12} = \frac{1}{60}$

$\therefore$ C alone can finish the work in 60 days.

Similarly B's 1 day's work $= \frac{1}{10} - \frac{1}{20} = \frac{1}{20}$

$\therefore$ B alone can finish the work in 20 days.

A's 1 day's work $= \frac{1}{10} - \frac{1}{15} = \frac{1}{30}$

$\therefore$ A alone can finish the work in 30 days.

EXAMPLE: A can do a piece of work in 25 days and B can finish it in 20 days. They work together for 5 days and then A goes away. In how many days will B finish the work?

SOLUTION: (A + B)'s 5 days work $= 5\left(\frac{1}{25}+\frac{1}{20}\right) = \frac{9}{20}$

Remaining work $= 1 - \frac{9}{20} = \frac{11}{20}$

Now, $\frac{1}{20}$ work is finished by B in 1 day

$\therefore$ $\frac{11}{20}$ work will be finished by B in $\left(\frac{20\times 11}{20}\right)$

= 11 days.

EXAMPLE: A is thrice as good a workman as B and is therefore able to finish a piece of work in 60 days less than B. Find the time in which they can do it, working together.

SOLUTION: Ratio of work done by A and B in the same time = 3 : 1

Ratio of time taken by A and B = 1 : 3

Suppose B takes x days to finish a work

then, A takes $(x - 60)$ days

$\therefore$ $\frac{x-60}{x} = \frac{1}{3}$ or $3(x-60) = x \Rightarrow x = 90$

$\therefore$ B can finish the work in 90 days.

A can finish the work in (90 – 60) = 30 days

Both finish the work $= \left[\frac{1}{30}+\frac{1}{90} = \frac{2}{45}\right]$

$= \frac{45}{2} = 22\frac{1}{2}$ days.

EXAMPLE: A certain number of men complete a piece of work in 60 days. If there were 8 men more, the work could be finished in 10 days less. How many men were originally there?

SOLUTION: Let the original number of men be x.

Now, x men can finish the work in 60 days

and $(x + 8)$ men can finish it in $(60 - 10)$ *i.e.*, 50 days.

$\therefore \quad x + 8 : x :: 60 : 50$

$\Rightarrow \quad \dfrac{x+8}{x} = \dfrac{60}{50} = \dfrac{6}{5}$

$\Rightarrow \quad 6x = 5x + 40 \Rightarrow x = 40$

Hence, the original number of men = 40.

EXAMPLE: If 4 men or 6 boys can finish a piece of work in 20 days, in how many days can 6 men and 11 boys finish it?

SOLUTION: 4 men = 6 boys

$\therefore \quad 6 \text{ men} = \dfrac{6}{4} \times 6 = \dfrac{36}{4} = 9 \text{ boys}$

6 men + 11 boys = 9 + 11 = 20 boys

Now, 6 boys can finish a work in 20 days.

1 boy can finish the same work in 6 × 20 days.

20 boys can finish the same work in $\dfrac{6 \times 20}{20}$

= 6 days.

EXAMPLE: If 12 men can build a wall 360 m long in 54 days, how many days will it take to build a similar wall 160 m long, if 16 men working on it?

SOLUTION: 12 men can build 360 m long wall in 54 days.

1 man can build 360 m long wall in 54 × 12 days.

1 man can build 1 m long wall in $\dfrac{54 \times 12}{360}$ days

16 men can build 1 m long wall in $\dfrac{54 \times 12}{360 \times 16}$ days

16 men can build 160 m long wall in $\dfrac{54 \times 12 \times 160}{360 \times 16}$ days

= 18 days.

EXAMPLE: If 3 persons weave 168 carpets in 7 days, how many carpets will 8 persons weave in 5 days?

SOLUTION: 3 persons can weave in 7 days 168 carpets

1 person can weave in 7 days = $\dfrac{168}{3}$ carpets

1 person can weave in 1 day = $\dfrac{168}{3 \times 7}$ carpets

8 persons can weave in 1 day = $\dfrac{168 \times 8}{3 \times 7}$ carpets

8 persons can weave in 5 days = $\dfrac{168 \times 8 \times 5}{3 \times 7}$ carpets

= 320 carpets

EXAMPLE: Mukesh can do a job in 12 days while Manoj can do the same job in 15 days. They undertake to complete the job for ₹ 5400. What will be the share of each in the income?

SOLUTION: Mukesh's 1 day's work = $\dfrac{1}{12}$

Manoj's 1 day's work = $\dfrac{1}{15}$

Ratio of their 1 day's work = $\dfrac{1}{12} : \dfrac{1}{15} = 5 : 4$

$\therefore$ Mukesh's share = ₹ $\dfrac{5}{9} \times 5400$ = ₹ 3000

Manoj's share = ₹ $\dfrac{4}{9} \times 5400$ = ₹ 2400

MULTIPLE CHOICE QUESTIONS

1. A and B can together do a piece of work in 15 days. B alone can do it in 20 days. In how many days can A alone do it?

A. 30 days B. 40 days

C. 45 days D. 60 days

2. A can do a piece of work in 30 days while B can do it in 40 days. A and B working together can do it in:

A. 70 days B. $42\frac{3}{4}$ days

C. $27\frac{1}{7}$ days D. $17\frac{1}{7}$ days

3. A can do $\frac{1}{3}$ of the work in 5 days and B can do $\frac{2}{5}$ of the work in 10 days. In how many days both A and B together can do the work?

A. $7\frac{3}{4}$ days B. $8\frac{4}{5}$ days

C. $9\frac{3}{8}$ days D. 10 days

4. A, B and C can do a piece of work in 6, 12 and 24 days respectively. They altogether will complete the work in:

A. $3\frac{3}{7}$ days B. $\frac{7}{24}$ days

C. $4\frac{4}{5}$ days D. $\frac{5}{24}$ days

5. A, B and C contract a work for ₹ 550. Together A and B are to do $\frac{7}{11}$ of the work. The share of C should be:

A. ₹ $183\frac{1}{3}$ B. ₹ 200

C. ₹ 300 D. ₹ 400

6. A and B finish a job in 12 days while A, B and C can finish it in 8 days. C alone will finish the job in:

A. 20 days B. 14 days

C. 24 days D. 16 days

7. 12 men can complete a work in 8 days. Three days after they started the work, 3 more men joined them. In how many days will all of them together complete the remaining work?

A. 2 B. 4

C. 5 D. 6

8. Mahesh and Umesh can complete a work in 10 and 15 days respectively. Umesh starts the work and after 5 days Mahesh joins him. In all, the work would be completed in:

A. 9 days B. 7 days

C. 11 days D. None of these

9. Sunil completes a work in 4 days whereas Dinesh completes the work in 6 days. Ramesh works $1\frac{1}{2}$ times as fast as Sunil. How many days it will take for the three together to complete the work?

A. $\frac{7}{12}$ B. $1\frac{5}{12}$

C. $1\frac{5}{7}$ D. None of these

10. A can complete a work in 6 days and B in 5 days. They work together, finish the job and receive ₹ 220 as wages. B's share should be:

A. ₹ 120 B. ₹ 110

C. ₹ 100 D. ₹ 90

11. 12 men and 8 children can finish a piece of work in 9 days. If each child takes twice the time taken by a man to finish the work, in how many days will 12 men finish the same work?

A. 8 days B. 15 days

C. 9 days D. 12 days

12. A, B and C together earn ₹ 150 per day while A and C together earn ₹ 94 and B and C together earn ₹ 76. The daily earning of C is:

A. ₹ 75 B. ₹ 56

C. ₹ 34 D. ₹ 20

13. If 5 men or 9 women can finish a piece of work in 19 days, 3 men and 6 women will do the same work in:

A. 10 days B. 12 days

C. 13 days D. 15 days

14. A can do a piece of work in 12 days. B is 60% more efficient than A. The number of days, it takes B to do the same piece of work, is:

A. $7\frac{1}{2}$ days B. $6\frac{1}{4}$ days

C. 8 days D. 6 days

15. A and B can do a piece of work in 45 and 40 days respectively. They began the work together, but A leaves after some days and B finished the remaining work in 23 days. After how many days did A leave?

A. 6 days B. 8 days

C. 9 days D. 12 days

ANSWERS

1	2	3	4	5	6	7	8	9	10
D	D	C	A	B	C	B	A	D	A
11	**12**	**13**	**14**	**15**					
D	D	D	A	C					

EXPLANATORY ANSWERS

1. $(A+B)$'s 1 day's work $= \frac{1}{15}$

B's 1 day's work $= \frac{1}{20}$

A's 1 day's work $= \frac{1}{15} - \frac{1}{20} = \frac{4-3}{60} = \frac{1}{60}$

$\therefore$ A can do this work alone in 60 days.

2. A's 1 day's work $= \frac{1}{30}$

B's 1 day's work $= \frac{1}{40}$

$(A+B)$'s 1 day's work

$= \frac{1}{30} + \frac{1}{40} = \frac{4+3}{120} = \frac{7}{120}$

$\therefore$ Both together will finish the work in $\frac{120}{7}$

$= 17\frac{1}{7}$ days.

3. $\frac{1}{3}$ of the work is done by A in 5 days.

$\therefore$ Whole work will be done by A in 3×5

$= 15$ days

$\frac{2}{5}$ of the work is done by B in 10 days.

Whole work will be done by B in $\left(10 \times \frac{5}{2}\right)$

$= 25$ days

$(A+B)$'s 1 day's work $= \frac{1}{15} + \frac{1}{25} = \frac{5+3}{75} = \frac{8}{75}$

$\therefore$ Both together can finish it in $\frac{75}{8} = 9\frac{3}{8}$ days.

4. A's 1 day's work $= \frac{1}{6}$

B's 1 day's work $= \frac{1}{12}$

C's 1 day's work $= \frac{1}{24}$

$(A+B+C)$'s 1 day's work $= \frac{1}{6} + \frac{1}{12} + \frac{1}{24}$

$= \frac{4+2+1}{24} = \frac{7}{24}$

$\therefore$ They all together will complete the work in $\frac{24}{7}$ days $= 3\frac{3}{7}$ days

5. Work to be done by C $= \left(1 - \frac{7}{11}\right) = \frac{4}{11}$

$\therefore (A+B) : C = \frac{7}{11} : \frac{4}{11} = 7 : 4$

$\therefore$ C's share $= ₹\frac{4}{11} \times 550 = ₹\,200$

6. $(A+B)$'s 1 day's work $= \frac{1}{12}$

$(A+B+C)$'s 1 day's work $= \frac{1}{8}$

C's 1 day's work $= \frac{1}{8} - \frac{1}{12} = \frac{3-2}{24} = \frac{1}{24}$

Hence, C will complete the work in 24 days.

7. 1 man's 1 day's work $= \frac{1}{96}$

12 men's 3 day's work $= \frac{12}{96} \times 3 = \frac{3}{8}$

Remaining work = $\left(1-\frac{3}{8}\right) = \frac{5}{8}$

15 men's 1 day's work = $\frac{15}{96}$

Now, $\frac{15}{96}$ work is done by them in 1 day

$\therefore$ $\frac{5}{8}$ work will be done by them in $\frac{96}{15} \times \frac{5}{8}$
= 4 days

8. Umesh's 5 day's work = $\frac{5}{15} = \frac{1}{3}$

Remaining work = $\left(1-\frac{1}{3}\right) = \frac{2}{3}$

Now, $\left(\frac{1}{10}+\frac{1}{15}\right)$ work is done by A and B in 1 day.

$\therefore$ $\frac{2}{3}$ work will be done by A and B in $6 \times \frac{2}{3}$
= 4 days.

So, the work would be completed in (5 + 4)
= 9 days.

9. Time taken by Ramesh alone = $\frac{2}{3} \times 4 = \frac{8}{3}$ days

$\therefore$ Their 1 day's work = $\left(\frac{1}{4}+\frac{1}{6}+\frac{3}{8}\right)$

$= \frac{6+4+9}{24} = \frac{19}{24}$

So, together they can finish the work in $\frac{24}{19}$ days

$= 1\frac{5}{19}$ days.

10. Ratio of time taken by A and B = 6 : 5
Ratio of work done in same time = 5 : 6
So, the money is to be divided among A and B in the ratio 5 : 6.

$\therefore$ B's share = ₹ $\frac{6}{11} \times 220$ = ₹ 120

11. 2 children = 1 man
$\therefore$ 8 children + 12 men = 4 + 12 = 16 men
Now, less men, more days

$12 : 16 : : 9 : x \Rightarrow \frac{12}{16} = \frac{9}{x} \Rightarrow x = 12$ days

12. B's daily earning = ₹ (150 – 94) = ₹ 56
A's daily earning = ₹ (150 – 76) = ₹ 74
C's daily earning = ₹ [150 – (56 + 74)] = ₹ 20

13. 5 men = 9 women $\Rightarrow$ 1 man = $\frac{9}{5}$ women

$\therefore$ 3 men + 6 women = $\left(3 \times \frac{9}{5} + 6\right) = \frac{57}{5}$ women

Now, 9 women can do the work in 19 days

$\therefore$ $\frac{57}{5}$ women can do it in $\frac{9 \times 19 \times 5}{57}$ = 15 days

14. A's 1 day's work = $\frac{1}{12}$

B's 1 day's work = $\frac{1}{12}$ + 60% of $\frac{1}{12} = \frac{2}{15}$

Hence, B can do the whole work in $\frac{15}{2}$

$= 7\frac{1}{2}$ days.

15. B's 23 day's work = $\frac{23}{40}$

Remaining work = $\left(1-\frac{23}{40}\right) = \frac{17}{40}$

Now, (A + B)'s 1 day's work = $\left(\frac{1}{45}+\frac{1}{40}\right) = \frac{17}{360}$

$\frac{17}{360}$ work is done by A and B in 1 day

$\frac{17}{40}$ work is done by A and B in $\frac{360}{17} \times \frac{17}{40}$
= 9 days.

Hence, A left after 9 days.

11. AREA AND PERIMETER

The area of any figure is the amount of surface enclosed within its boundary lines. It is measured by the number of square metres or square centimetres or square inches (or some other units of square measure) it contains.

Perimeter

Perimeter of a geometrical figure is the total length of the sides enclosing the figure.

Triangle

A triangle is a plane figure bounded by three sides. It includes three angles. It is denoted by the symbol Δ. The sum of angles of a triangle is 180°.

(i) **Equilateral Triangle:** A triangle in which all sides are equal is called an equilateral triangle.

(ii) **Isosceles Triangle:** A triangle in which two sides are equal is called an isosceles triangle.

(iii) **Scalene Triangle:** A triangle in which all sides are different or unequal is called scalene triangle.

(iv) **Right Angled Triangle:** A triangle having one of the angles equal to 90° is called a right angled triangle. The side opposite to the right angle of a triangle is called its hypotenuse.

Quadrilateral

A plane figure bounded by four straight lines is called a quadrilateral.

Various Types of Quadrilaterals:

(i) **Rectangle:** A quadrilateral whose opposite sides are equal and all angles are at right angles. The diagonals of a rectangle are equal.

(ii) **Square:** A rectangle having all sides are equal is called a square.

(iii) **Parallelogram:** A quadrilateral whose opposite sides are equal and parallel is called parallelogram.

(iv) **Rhombus:** A parallelogram having all the sides equal is called a rhombus. Diagonals of a rhombus are not equal and they bisect each other at right angles.

(v) **Trapezium:** A quadrilateral having one pair of opposite sides parallel, is called a trapezium.

Circle

The path traced by a point which moves in such a way that its distance from a fixed point is always same, is called a circle. The fixed point is called its centre and fixed distance is called its radius. The length of the whole path of a circle is called its circumference.

(i) **Arc:** Any part of the circumference of a circle is called an arc.

(ii) **Chord:** The straight line joining the ends of an arc of a circle is called a chord.

(iii) **Diameter:** The chord passing through the centre of a circle is called its diameter.
The diameter of a circle divides the circle into two equal parts, each one of which is called a semi-circle.

(iv) **Segment:** The area enclosed by an arc and a chord is called a segment.

(v) **Sector:** The area bounded by an arc and two radii is called a sector.

Formulae for Area of Various Figures:

(i) **Rectangle:**

Area of rectangle = $l \times b$

Perimeter of rectangle = $2(l + b)$.

(ii) Square:

Area of square = $(\text{side})^2$

Perimeter of square = $4 \times$ side

Area of room = $l \times b$

Area of 4 walls of a room = $2(l + b) \times h$

(iii) Parallelogram:

Area of $11^{gm} = b \times h$

Area of rhombus = $\frac{1}{2} \times d_1 \times d_2$.

(iv) Trapezium:

Area of trapezium = $\frac{1}{2}$ (sum of parallel sides) × (distance between them)

(v) Triangle:

(a) Area of right triangle = $\frac{1}{2} \times b \times h$

(b) Area of equilateral triangle = $\frac{\sqrt{3}}{4} \times (\text{side})^2$

(c) Area of scalene triangle

$$= \sqrt{s(s-a)(s-b)(s-c)}$$

where, $s = \frac{a+b+c}{2}$

(vi) Circle:

(a) Area of circle = πr^2

(b) Circumference of a circle = $2\pi r$

(c) Length of arc = $\frac{\theta}{360} \times 2\pi r$

(d) Area of sector = $\frac{\theta}{360} \times \pi r^2$

Polygon

A polygon is plane figure bounded by multiple number of sides. Normally, it is used for figures enclosed by more than four sides: *e.g.*, pentagon, hexagon, octagon etc.

Regular Polygon

It is a polygon whose all sides are equal.

For a regular polygon of n equal sides, its vertex angle θ is given by

$$\theta = \left(\frac{n-2}{n}\right) \times 180°$$

Example: Find the area and perimeter of a rectangle whose length is 25 m and breadth is 15 m.

Solution: Area of rectangle = $l \times b$

$= 25 \times 15 = 375 \text{ m}^2$

Perimeter of rectangle = $2(l + b)$

$= 2(25 + 15) = 80$ m

Example: Find the area of a rectangle whose one side is 6 m and the diagonal is 10 m.

Solution: Another side of rectangle = $\sqrt{(10)^2 - (6)^2}$

$= \sqrt{100-36} = \sqrt{64} = 8$ m

Area of rectangle = $l \times b = 8 \times 6 = 48 \text{ m}^2$.

Example: Find area and perimeter of a square whose each side is 12 cm.

Solution: Area of square = $(\text{side})^2 = (12)^2 = 144 \text{ cm}^2$

Perimeter of square = $4 \times$ side = $4 \times 12 = 48$ cm

Example: Find the area of a parallelogram whose base is 35 m and altitude 18 m.

Solution: Area of parallelogram = $b \times h$

$= 35 \times 18 = 630 \text{ m}^2$

Example: Find the area of a rhombus one side of which measures 20 cm and one diagonal 24 cm.

Solution: Since the diagonals of a rhombus bisect at right angles, so one side and half of each of the diagonals form a right angled triangle. In this right angled triangle,

One side = 20 cm, another side = $\frac{24}{2} = 12$ cm

Third side = $\sqrt{(20)^2 - (12)^2} = \sqrt{400-144}$

$= \sqrt{256} = 16$ cm

Hence other diagonal = $16 \times 2 = 32$ cm

Area of rhombus = $\frac{1}{2} \times d_1 \times d_2$

$= \frac{1}{2} \times 24 \times 32 = 12 \times 32$

$= 384 \text{ cm}^2$

Example: Find the area of an equilateral triangle each of whose sides measures 12 cm.

Solution: Area of equilateral triangle

$= \frac{\sqrt{3}}{4} (\text{side})^2 = \frac{\sqrt{3}}{4} \times (12)^2$

$$= \frac{\sqrt{3}}{4} \times 144 = 36\sqrt{3} \text{ cm}^2$$

$$= 36 \times 1.73 = 62.28 \text{ cm}^2$$

EXAMPLE: Find the area of a triangle whose sides are 40 cm, 41 cm and 9 cm respectively.

SOLUTION: $s = \frac{a+b+c}{2} = \frac{9+40+41}{2}$

$$= \frac{90}{2} = 45 \text{ cm}$$

$$\text{Area of triangle} = \sqrt{s(s-a)(s-b)(s-c)}$$

$$= \sqrt{45(45-9)(45-40)(45-41)}$$

$$= \sqrt{45 \times 36 \times 5 \times 4}$$

$$= \sqrt{225 \times 144}$$

$$= 15 \times 12 = 180 \text{ cm}^2$$

EXAMPLE: Find the circumference and the area of a circle of radius 3.5 cm.

SOLUTION: Circumference $= 2\pi r$

$$= 2 \times \frac{22}{7} \times 3.5 = 22 \text{ cm}$$

$$\text{Area of circle} = \pi r^2 = \frac{22}{7} \times 3.5 \times 3.5$$

$$= 38.5 \text{ cm}^2$$

EXAMPLE: In a circle of radius 35 cm, an arc subtends an angle of 72° at the centre. Find the length of the arc and the area of the sector.

SOLUTION: Length of arc $= \frac{\theta}{360} \times 2\pi r$

$$= \frac{72}{360} \times 2 \times \frac{22}{7} \times 35$$

$$= 44 \text{ cm}$$

$$\text{Area of the sector} = \frac{\theta}{360} \times \pi r^2$$

$$= \frac{72}{360} \times \frac{22}{7} \times 35 \times 35$$

$$= 770 \text{ cm}^2$$

EXAMPLE: Find the area of a trapezium whose parallel sides are 77 cm, 60 cm and the other sides are 25 cm and 26 cm.

SOLUTION:

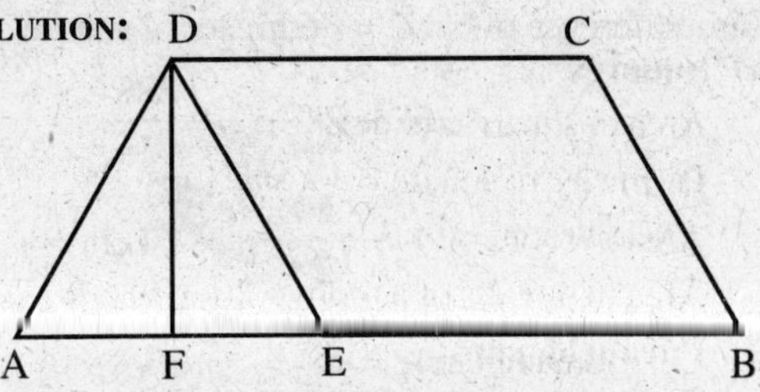

Let ABCD be the given trapezium in which AB = 77 cm, CD = 60 cm, BC = 25 cm, AD = 26 cm.

Draw DE || BC and DF ⊥ AB

Now, DE = BC = 25 cm

AE = AB – EB = AB – CD

= 77 – 60 = 17 cm

In ΔDAE, $s = \frac{17+25+26}{2} = \frac{68}{2} = 34 \text{ cm}$

$$\text{Area of } \Delta DAE = \sqrt{34(34-17)(34-25)(34-26)}$$

$$= \sqrt{34 \times 17 \times 9 \times 8} = 204 \text{ cm}^2$$

$$\text{Again area of } \Delta DAE = \frac{1}{2} \times AE \times DF$$

$$204 = \frac{1}{2} \times 17 \times DF$$

$$\Rightarrow \quad DF = \frac{2 \times 204}{17} = 24 \text{ cm}$$

$$\therefore \text{ Area of trapezium ABCD} = \frac{1}{2}(AB + CD) \times DF$$

$$= \frac{1}{2}(77+60) \times 24$$

$$= \frac{1}{2} \times 137 \times 24$$

$$= 1644 \text{ cm}^2$$

EXAMPLE: A copper wire when bent in the form of a square, encloses an area of 484 cm². If the same wire is bent in the form of circle, find the area enclosed by it.

SOLUTION: Area of the square = 484 cm²

$$\text{Side} = \sqrt{484} = 22 \text{ cm}$$

Length of wire = Perimeter of square

= 4 × side = 4 × 22

= 88 cm

Let r be the radius of the circle.

$\therefore$ Circumference of circle = Perimeter of square

$$\therefore \quad 2\pi r = 88 \Rightarrow r = \frac{88}{2\pi}$$

$$= \frac{88 \times 7}{2 \times 22} = 14 \text{ cm}$$

$$\text{Area of circle} = \pi r^2 = \frac{22}{7} \times 14 \times 14$$

$$= 616 \text{ cm}^2$$

EXAMPLE: A bicycle wheel makes 5000 revolutions in moving 11 km. Find the diameter of the wheel.

SOLUTION: Distance covered by the wheel in 1 revolution

$$= \frac{\text{Distance covered}}{\text{Number of revolutions}} = \frac{11}{5000} \text{ km}$$

$$= \frac{11 \times 1000 \times 100}{5000} \text{ cm} = 220 \text{ cm}$$

$\therefore$ Circumference of the wheel = 220 cm

$$2\pi r = 220 \Rightarrow 2 \times \frac{22}{7} \times r = 220$$

$$\Rightarrow \quad r = \frac{220 \times 7}{44} = 35 \text{ cm}$$

Hence, diameter of the wheel = 35 × 2 = 70 cm

EXAMPLE: The perimeter of a square is 44 cm and circumference of a circle is 44 cm. Which area is greater and by how much?

SOLUTION: Side of square $= \frac{44}{4} = 11$ cm

$$\text{Area of square} = (11)^2 = 121 \text{ cm}^2$$

$$\text{Circumference of a circle} = 2\pi r$$

$$\Rightarrow \quad 44 = 2 \times \frac{22}{7} \times r$$

$$\Rightarrow \quad r = \frac{44 \times 7}{44} = 7 \text{ cm}$$

$$\text{Area of circle} = \pi r^2$$

$$= \frac{22}{7} \times 7 \times 7 = 154 \text{ cm}^2$$

Clearly, area of circle > area of square

Difference = 154 – 121 = 33 cm^2.

EXAMPLE: A sheet of paper is in the form of a rectangle ABCD in which AB = 40 cm and AD = 28 cm. A semi-circular portion with BC as diameter is cut off. Find the area of the remaining paper.

SOLUTION:

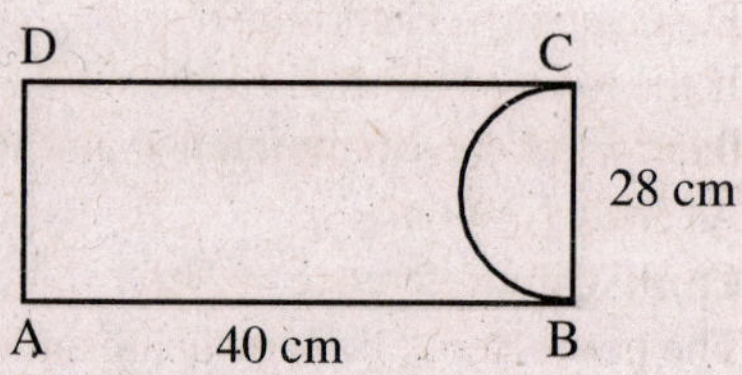

$$\text{Area of ABCD} = 40 \times 28 = 1120 \text{ cm}^2$$

$$\text{Area of semicircle} = \frac{1}{2}\pi r^2$$

$$= \frac{1}{2} \times \frac{22}{7} \times 14 \times 14$$

$$= 22 \times 14 = 308 \text{ cm}^2$$

Area of the remaining paper = 1120 – 308 = 812 cm^2

MULTIPLE CHOICE QUESTIONS

1. The length of a plot is four times its breadth. A playground measuring 1200 square metres occupies a third of the total area of the plot. What is the length of the plot, in metres?

A. 20 B. 30
C. 60 D. None of these

2. The width of a rectangular hall is $\frac{3}{4}$ of its length. If the area of the hall is 300 m^2, then the difference between its length and width is:

A. 3 m B. 4 m
C. 5 m D. 15 m

3. The length and breadth of a rectangular piece of land are in ratio of 5 : 3. The owner spent ₹ 3000 for surrounding it from all the sides at ₹ 7.50 per metre. The difference between its length and breadth is:

A. 50 m
B. 100 m
C. 150 m
D. 200 m

4. A room 8 m × 6 m is to be carpeted by a carpet 2 m wide. The length of carpet required is:
A. 12 m B. 36 m
C. 24 m D. 48 m

5. The length of a rectangle is increased by 60%. By what per cent would the width have to be decreased to maintain the same area?
A. $37\frac{1}{2}\%$ B. 60%
C. 75% D. 120%

6. A man walked 20 m to cross a rectangular field diagonally. If the length of the field is 16 m, the breadth of the rectangle is:
A. 4 m
B. 16 m
C. 12 m
D. Cannot be determined

7. If the ratio of the areas of two squares is 9 : 1, the ratio of their perimeters is:
A. 9 : 1 B. 3 : 1
C. 3 : 4 D. 1 : 3

8. The perimeter of both, a square and a rectangle are each equal to 48 m and the difference between their areas is 4 m^2. The breadth of the rectangle is:
A. 10 m B. 12 m
C. 14 m D. None of these

9. Area of a square with side x is equal to the area of a triangle with base x. The altitude of the triangle is:
A. $\frac{x}{2}$ B. x
C. $2x$ D. $4x$

10. If only the length of the rectangular plot is reduced to $\frac{2}{3}$rd of its original length, the ratio of original area to reduced area is:
A. 2 : 3 B. 3 : 2
C. 1 : 2 D. None of these

11. If the radius of a circle be reduced by 50%, its area is reduced by:
A. 25% B. 50%
C. 75% D. 100%

12. The perimeter of a rhombus is 52 m while its longer diagonal is 24 m. Its other diagonal is:
A. 5 m B. 10 m
C. 20 m D. 28 m

13. The circumference of a circle is 352 m, then its area in m^2 is:
A. 9856 B. 8956
C. 6589 D. 5986

ANSWERS

1	2	3	4	5	6	7	8	9	10
D	C	A	C	A	C	B	A	C	B
11	**12**	**13**							
C	B	A							

EXPLANATORY ANSWERS

1. Area of the plot = 3 × 1200 = 3600 m^2
Let breadth be x m. Then length = $4x$ m
According to the question,
$4x \times x = 3600 \Rightarrow x^2 = 900 \Rightarrow x = 30$
Hence, length of the plot = 4 × 30 = 120 m.

2. Let length be x m, then breadth = $\frac{3x}{4}$ m

Area of the hall = $x \times \frac{3x}{4} = \frac{3x^2}{4}$

According to the question,

$$\frac{3x^2}{4} = 300 \Rightarrow x^2 = 400 \Rightarrow x = 20$$

Length = 20 m and breadth = $\frac{3}{4} \times 20 = 15$ m

Difference = 20 – 15 = 5 m

3. Let length = $5x$ m and breadth = $3x$ m
Perimeter of rectangle = $2(5x + 3x) = 16x$ m

But perimeter = $\frac{\text{Total cost}}{\text{Rate}} = \frac{3000}{7.50} = 400$ m

Now, $16x = 400 \Rightarrow x = 25$

$$\text{length} = 5x = 5 \times 25 = 125 \text{ m}$$
$$\text{breadth} = 3x = 25 \times 3 = 75 \text{ m}$$
$$\text{Difference} = 125 - 75 = 50 \text{ m}$$

4. Length of the carpet $= \dfrac{8 \times 6}{2} = 24$ m.

5. Initially, let length = x and breadth = y
Let new breadth = z.

Then new length $= \dfrac{160x}{100} = \dfrac{8x}{5}$

$\therefore \quad \dfrac{8x}{5} \times z = xy \Rightarrow z = \dfrac{5y}{8}$

Decrease in breadth $= \left(y - \dfrac{5y}{8}\right) = \dfrac{3y}{8}$

$\therefore$ Decrease per cent $= \dfrac{3y}{8} \times \dfrac{1}{y} \times 100$

$= \dfrac{75}{2} = 37.5\% =$

6. Breadth $= \sqrt{(20)^2 - (16)^2}$

$= \sqrt{400 - 256} = \sqrt{144} = 12$ m.

7. Let the areas of the squares be $(9x^2)$ m^2 and (x^2) m^2
Then, their sides are $3x$ m and x m respectively

Ratio of their perimeters $= \dfrac{12x}{4x} = 3:1$

8. Let length of rectangle = x m
and breadth of rectangle = y m
Also, let the side of the square be z m
According to the question,

$2(x + y) = 4z = 48$

$x + y = 24$ and $z = 12$

Also, $z^2 - xy = 4$

$\Rightarrow \quad (12)^2 - 4 = xy$

$\Rightarrow \quad xy = 140$

$\because \quad x + y = 24$ and $xy = 140$

$(x - y)^2 = (x + y)^2 - 4xy$

$\Rightarrow \quad (x - y)^2 = (24)^2 - 4(140)$

$\Rightarrow \quad (x - y)^2 = 576 - 560 = 16$

$\Rightarrow \quad x - y = 4$

Now, $x + y = 24$
$x - y = 4$
Solving and get $x = 14$, $y = 10$
Hence, breadth of rectangle = 10 m.

9. According to the question,

$$x^2 = \frac{1}{2} \times x \times h$$

$\Rightarrow \quad h = \dfrac{2x^2}{x} = 2x$

10. Let length = x and breadth = y

New length $= \dfrac{2}{3}x$

$\therefore \quad \dfrac{\text{Original area}}{\text{Reduced area}} = \dfrac{xy}{\frac{2}{3}xy} = \dfrac{3}{2} = 3:2$

11. Original area $= \pi r^2$, New area $= \pi\left(\dfrac{r}{2}\right)^2 = \dfrac{\pi r^2}{4}$

Reduction in area $= \pi r^2 - \dfrac{\pi r^2}{4} = \dfrac{3\pi r^2}{4}$

Reduction per cent $= \dfrac{3\pi r^2}{4} \times \dfrac{1}{\pi r^2} \times 100 = 75\%$

12. Side of rhombus $= \dfrac{52}{4} = 13$ m

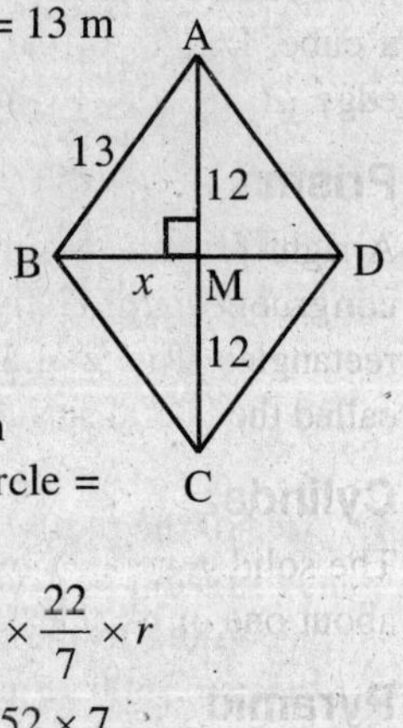

In ΔABM,

$x^2 = (13)^2 - (12)^2$

$x^2 = 169 - 144$

$x^2 = 25$

$\Rightarrow \quad x = 5$ m

$\therefore$ Another diagonal $= 2 \times 5 = 10$ m

13. Circumference of a circle $= 2\pi r$

$\Rightarrow \quad 352 = 2 \times \dfrac{22}{7} \times r$

$\Rightarrow \quad r = \dfrac{352 \times 7}{44} = 56$ m

Area of circle $= \pi r^2 = \dfrac{22}{7} \times 56 \times 56$

$= 9856$ m^2

12. VOLUME AND SURFACE AREA

We know that every real object occupies some space. It is usually specified by its three dimensions—length, breadth and depth (or height or thickness). It may be a solid or a hollow object. In case of circular, cylindrical and spherical object the specifying dimensions may change to radius, angle etc. The amount of space occupied by the object is called its volume. Its unit of measurement is m^3, cm^3, $(inches)^3$ etc. The area of the surfaces (plane/curved) of the object is called its surface area.

A Cuboid and A Cube

The solid like wooden boxes, tea containers, match box etc. which have six faces, each of which is a rectangle, are called cuboids. It has 12 edges.

A cuboid in which every face is a square is called a cube. Length of each face of a cube is called its edge.

Prism

A right prism is a solid in which the two ends are congruent parallel figures and the side faces are rectangles. The total area of side faces of a prism is called the lateral surface of the prism.

Cylinder

The solid generated by the revolution of a rectangle about one of its sides as axis is called a cylinder.

Pyramid

A solid whose base is a plane rectilinear figure having the side faces as triangles meeting at a common vertex is called a pyramid. When the base of a pyramid is a triangle, the pyramid is called a tetrahedron.

Cone

The solid generated by the revolution of a right angled triangle about one of the sides containing the right angle as the axis is called a right circular cone.

The perpendicular distance from the vertex to the base is called the height of the cone and the length of slant face from vertex to the base is called the slant height of the cone.

Frustum

If a cone is cut by a plane parallel to the base so as to divide the cone into two parts, then the lower part is called the frustum of the cone.

Sphere

When a semicircle moves about its diameter, the solid generated is called a sphere.

Formulae

Cuboid:

Volume of cuboid $= l \times b \times h$ cubic units

Whole surface area $= 2(lb + bh + hl)$ square units

Diagonal of cuboid $= \sqrt{l^2 + b^2 + h^2}$ units

Area of 4 walls of a room $= 2(l + b) \times h$ square units

Cube:

Volume of cube $= a^3$ cubic units

Side of cube $= \sqrt[3]{\text{Volume}}$

Lateral surface area $= 4a^2$ square units

Total surface area $= 6a^2$ square units

Diagonal of the cube $= \left(\sqrt{3}\,a\right)$ units

Cylinder:

Volume of cylinder $= \pi r^2 h$ cubic units

Lateral surface area $= 2\pi rh$ square units

Total surface area $= 2\pi r(h + r)$ square units

Cone:

Volume of cone $= \frac{1}{3}\pi r^2 h$ cubic units

Lateral surface area $= \pi rl$ square units

Total surface area $= \pi r(l + r)$ square units

Slant height $(l) = \sqrt{r^2 + h^2}$

Sphere:

Volume of sphere $= \frac{4}{3}\pi r^3$ cubic units

Surface area $= 4\pi r^2$ square units

Hemisphere:

Volume $= \frac{2}{3}\pi r^3$ cubic units

Lateral surface area $= 2\pi r^2$ square units

Total surface area $= 3\pi r^2$ square units

Frustum:

Volume $= \frac{1}{3}\pi h(r_1^2 + r_1 r_2 + r_2^2)$ cubic units

Curved surface area $= \pi(r_1 + r_2) \times l$ square units

Total surface area $= \pi\left[r_1^2 + r_2^2 + (r_1 + r_2)l\right]$ square units

Pyramid:

Volume $= \frac{1}{2} \times$ (area of base) $\times$ height cubic units

Example: The dimensions of a metallic cuboid are 100 cm × 80 cm × 64 cm. It is melted and recast into cube. Find the total surface area of the cube.

Solution: Volume of cuboid $= l \times b \times h$

$= 100 \times 80 \times 64$

$= 512000 \text{ cm}^3$

Volume of cube $= a^3$

According to the question,

$a^3 = 512000$

$\Rightarrow a^3 = 8 \times 8 \times 8 \times 10 \times 10 \times 10$

$\Rightarrow a = 8 \times 10 = 80$ cm

Total surface area of cube $= 6a^2 = 6 \times 80 \times 80 = 38400$

Hence, total surface area of cube is 38400 cm^2.

Example: Three cubes whose edges measure 3 cm, 4 cm and 5 cm respectively form a single cube. Find the total surface area of the new cube.

Solution: Let the edge of new cube $= x$ cm

$x^3 = 3^3 + 4^3 + 5^3$

$= 27 + 64 + 125 = 216 \text{ cm}^3$

$\Rightarrow x^3 = 6 \times 6 \times 6 \Rightarrow x = 6$ cm

Total surface area of cube $= 6(x)^2 = 6 \times 6 \times 6 = 216 \text{ cm}^2$

Hence, total surface area of new cube $= 216$ cm^2.

Example: The capacity of a cylindrical tank is 6160 m^3. If the radius of its base is 14 m, find the depth of the tank.

Solution: Volume of cylinder $= \pi r^2 h$

$\pi r^2 h = 6160$

$\Rightarrow \frac{22}{7} \times 14 \times 14 \times h = 6160$

$\Rightarrow h = \frac{6160}{44 \times 14} = 10$ m

Hence, depth of the tank is 10 m.

Example: How many bullets can be made out of a lead cylinder 28 cm high and 6 cm radius, each bullet being 1.5 cm in diameter?

Solution: Number of bullets

$$= \frac{\text{Volume of cylinder}}{\text{Volume of 1 bullet}}$$

$$= \frac{\pi \times 6 \times 6 \times 28}{\frac{4}{3} \times \pi \times 0.75 \times 0.75 \times 0.75}$$

$$= \frac{6 \times 6 \times 28 \times 3}{4 \times \frac{3}{4} \times \frac{3}{4} \times \frac{3}{4}} = \frac{6 \times 6 \times 28 \times 4 \times 4 \times 3}{3 \times 3 \times 3}$$

$= 1792$

Example: A metal sphere of diameter 42 cm is dropped into a cylindrical vessel, which is partly filled with water. The diameter of the vessel is 1.68 metres. If the sphere is completely submerged, find by how much the surface of water will rise.

Solution: Radius of the sphere $= 21$ cm

$$\text{Volume of sphere} = \frac{4}{3}\pi r^3$$

$$= \frac{4}{3} \times \frac{22}{7} \times 21 \times 21 \times 21$$

$= 38808 \text{ cm}^3$

Volume of water displaced by sphere = 38808 cm^3
Let water rise by h cm.

$$\text{Volume of cylinder} = \pi r^2 h$$

$$\frac{22}{7} \times 84 \times 84 \times h = 38808$$

$$\Rightarrow \quad h = \frac{38808 \times 7}{22 \times 84 \times 84} = \frac{7}{4} = 1.75 \text{ cm}$$

EXAMPLE: A tent is in the form of a right circular cylinder surmounted by a cone. The diameter of cylinder is 24 m. The height of the cylindrical portion is 11 m while the vertex of the cone is 16 m above the ground. Find the area of the canvas required for the tent.

SOLUTION: Lateral surface area of cylinder = $2\pi rh$

$$= 2 \times \frac{22}{7} \times 12 \times 11 = \frac{5808}{7} \text{ m}^2$$

Height of cone = 16 – 11 = 5 m
Radius of cone = 12 m

$$\text{Slant height } l = \sqrt{r^2 + h^2} = \sqrt{12^2 + 5^2}$$

$$= \sqrt{169} = 13 \text{ m}$$

Lateral surface area of cone = πrl

$$= \frac{22}{7} \times 12 \times 13 = \frac{3432}{7} \text{ m}^2$$

$$\text{Area of canvas} = \frac{5808}{7} + \frac{3432}{7}$$

$$= \frac{9240}{7} = 1320 \text{ m}^2$$

EXAMPLE: The slant height of the frustum of a cone is 20 cm and the height of the frustum is 16 cm. The radius of the smaller circle is 8 cm. Find the volume and total surface area of the frustum.

SOLUTION: $l = \sqrt{h^2 + (R - r)^2} = \sqrt{16^2 + (R - 8)^2}$

$$\Rightarrow \quad 20 = \sqrt{256 + R^2 - 16R + 64}$$

$$= \sqrt{R^2 - 16R + 320}$$

$$\Rightarrow R^2 - 16R + 320 = 400$$

$$\Rightarrow \quad R^2 - 16R - 80 = 0 \Rightarrow R = 20 \text{ cm}$$

$$\text{Volume of frustum} = \frac{1}{3}\pi h(R^2 + r^2 + Rr)$$

$$= \frac{1}{3} \times \frac{22}{7} \times 16(400 + 64 + 160)$$

$$= \frac{73216}{7} \text{ cm}^3$$

$$\text{Total surface area} = \pi(R^2 + r^2 + Rl + rl)$$

$$= \frac{22}{7}(400 + 64 + 400 + 160)$$

$$= \frac{22}{7} \times 1024 = \frac{22528}{7}$$

$$= 3218.28 \text{ cm}^2$$

EXAMPLE: The length of a garden roller is 2 m and diameter is 1.4 m. How much area will it cover in 10 revolutions?

SOLUTION: Area covered

= Curved surface × no. of revolutions

$= 2\pi rh \times 10$

$$= 2 \times \frac{22}{7} \times 0.7 \times 2 \times 10 = 88 \text{ m}^2$$

EXAMPLE: A cylinder is made by lead whose radius is 4 cm and height is 10 cm. By melting it how many spheres of radius 2 cm can be made?

SOLUTION: Given, radius of the cylinder = 4 cm
and height of the cylinder = 10 cm

$$\therefore \quad \text{Volume of the cylinder} = \pi r^2 h = \pi(4)^2 \times 10$$

$$= 160\pi \text{ cm}^3$$

$$\text{Volume of sphere} = \frac{4}{3}\pi r^3 = \frac{4}{3}\pi(2)^3$$

$$= \frac{32}{3}\pi \text{ cm}^3$$

$$\therefore \quad \text{Number of spheres} = \frac{\text{Volume of cylinder}}{\text{Volume of one sphere}}$$

$$= \frac{160\pi}{\frac{32}{3}\pi} = \frac{160 \times 3}{32} = 15$$

Hence, number of spheres that can be made are 15.

MULTIPLE CHOICE QUESTIONS

1. The surface area of a cube is 726 m^2. The volume of cube is:
   A. 1300 m^3 B. 1331 m^3
   C. 1452 m^3 D. 1542 m^3
2. Sum of the length, width and depth of a cuboid is s and its diagonal is d. Its surface area is:
   A. s^2 B. d^2
   C. $s^2 - d^2$ D. $s^2 + d^2$
3. A wooden box of dimensions 8 m × 7 m × 6 m is to carry rectangular boxes of dimensions 8 cm × 7 cm × 6 cm. The maximum number of boxes that can be carried in 1 wooden box is:
   A. 1200000 B. 1000000
   C. 9800000 D. 7500000
4. The length of the longest rod that can be placed in a room 30 m long, 24 m broad and 18 m high is:
   A. 30 m B. $15\sqrt{2}$ m
   C. 60 m D. $30\sqrt{2}$ m
5. If the volume of two cubes are in the ratio 8 : 1, the ratio of their edges is:
   A. 8 : 1 B. $2\sqrt{2} : 1$
   C. 2 : 1 D. None of these
6. A metal sheet 27 cm long 8 cm broad and 1 cm thick is melted into a cube. The difference between the surface areas of two solids will be:
   A. 284 cm^2 B. 296 cm^2
   C. 286 cm^2 D. 300 cm^2
7. If each edge of a cube is increased by 50%, the percentage increase in surface area is:
   A. 50% B. 75%
   C. 100% D. 125%
8. If a right circular cone of vertical height 24 cm has a volume of 1232 cm^3, then the area of its curved surface in cm^2 is:
   A. 1254 B. 704
   C. 550 D. 154
9. Two cubes have volumes in the ratio 1 : 27. The ratio of their surface areas is:
   A. 1 : 3 B. 1 : 8
   C. 1 : 9 D. 1 : 18
10. If the volumes of two cones are in the ratio 1 : 4 and their diameters are in the ratio 4 : 5, then the ratio of their heights is:
    A. 1 : 5 B. 5 : 4
    C. 5 : 16 D. 25 : 64
11. The radius of a wire is decreased to one-third. If volumes remains the same, length will increase:
    A. 1 time B. 3 times
    C. 6 times D. 9 times
12. A cylindrical piece of metal of radius 2 cm and height 6 cm is shaped into a cone of same radius. The height of cone is:
    A. 18 cm B. 14 cm
    C. 12 cm D. 8 cm
13. If 1 cubic cm of cast iron weight 21 g then the weight of a cast iron pipe of length 1 m with a bore of 3 cm and in which the thickness of the metal is 1 cm, is:
    A. 21 kg B. 24.2 kg
    C. 26.4 kg D. 18.6 kg
14. The number of solid spheres, each of diameter 6 cm, that could be moulded to form a solid metal cylinder of height 45 cm and diameter 4 cms, is:
    A. 3 B. 4
    C. 5 D. 6
15. A right cylinder and a right circular cone have the same radius and the same volume. The ratio of the height of the cylinder to that of the cone is:
    A. 3 : 5 B. 2 : 5
    C. 3 : 1 D. 1 : 3

ANSWERS

1	2	3	4	5	6	7	8	9	10
B	C	B	D	C	C	D	C	C	D
11	**12**	**13**	**14**	**15**					
D	A	C	C	D					

EXPLANATORY ANSWERS

1. Surface area of cube = $6a^2$

$6a^2 = 726 \Rightarrow a^2 = \frac{726}{6} = 121 \Rightarrow a = 11$ m

Volume of cube = $a^3 = 11 \times 11 \times 11 = 1331$ m^3

2. $l + b + h = s$

and $\sqrt{l^2 + b^2 + h^2} = d \Rightarrow l^2 + b^2 + h^2 = d^2$

$(l + b + h)^2 = s^2$

$\Rightarrow l^2 + b^2 + h^2 + 2(lb + bh + hl) = s^2$

$\Rightarrow d^2 + 2(lb + bh + hl) = s^2$

$\Rightarrow 2(lb + bh + hl) = s^2 - d^2$

$\therefore$ Surface area = $(s^2 - d^2)$.

3. Number of boxes $= \frac{800 \times 700 \times 600}{8 \times 7 \times 6} = 1000000$

4. Diagonal of cuboid $= \sqrt{l^2 + b^2 + h^2}$

$\therefore$ Length of longest rod $= \sqrt{30^2 + 24^2 + 18^2}$

$= \sqrt{900 + 576 + 324} = \sqrt{1800}$

$= \sqrt{30 \times 30 \times 2} = 30\sqrt{2}$ m

5. Let their volumes be $8x^3$ and x^3.
Then, their sides are $2x$ and x

$\therefore$ Ratio of their edges = 2 : 1

6. Volume of sheet = $27 \times 8 \times 1 = 216$ cm^3
Volume of cube formed = 216 cm^3

Side of cube = $\sqrt[3]{216} = 6$ cm

Surface area of cuboid = $2(lb + bh + hl)$

$= 2(27 \times 8 + 8 \times 1 + 1 \times 27) = 502$ cm^2

Surface area of cube = $6(\text{side})^2 = 6 \times 36 = 216$ cm^2

Difference in areas = $502 - 216 = 286$ cm^2

7. Let original length of cube = x
then, its surface area = $6x^2$

New edge $= \left(\frac{150}{100}x\right) = \frac{3}{2}x$

New surface area $= 6 \times \left(\frac{3}{2}x\right)^2$

$= 6 \times \frac{9}{4}x^2 = \frac{27}{2}x^2$

Increase in surface area $= \left(\frac{27}{2} - 6\right)x^2 = \frac{15}{2}x^2$

$\therefore$ Increase % $= \frac{15x^2/2}{6x^2} \times 100$

$= \frac{15x^2}{12x^2} \times 100 = 125\%$

8. Volume of cone = 1232

$\Rightarrow \frac{1}{3}\pi r^2 h = 1232$

$\Rightarrow \frac{1}{3} \times \frac{22}{7} \times r^2 \times 24 = 1232$

$\Rightarrow r^2 = \frac{3 \times 7 \times 1232}{22 \times 24} = 49 \Rightarrow r = 7$ cm

$\Rightarrow l = \sqrt{r^2 + h^2} = \sqrt{7^2 + 24^2} = \sqrt{625} = 25$ cm

Lateral surface area of cone = πrl

$= \frac{22}{7} \times 7 \times 25 = 22 \times 25 = 550$ cm^2

9. Let their volumes are x^3 and $27x^3$.
Then, their sides are x and $3x$.

Ratio of their surface areas $= \frac{6x^2}{6(3x)^2} = \frac{x^2}{9x^2}$

$= 1 : 9$

10. Let the diameters of the bases of the cones be $4r$ and $5r$. Let their heights be h and H.

then, $\frac{\frac{1}{3}\pi \times \left(\frac{4r}{2}\right)^2 \times h}{\frac{1}{3}\pi\left(\frac{5r}{2}\right)^2 \times H} = \frac{1}{4}$

$\Rightarrow \frac{16}{25} \times \frac{h}{H} = \frac{1}{4}$

$\Rightarrow \frac{h}{H} = \frac{25}{64}$

11. Let original radius = r

and original length = h

$$\text{New radius} = \frac{1}{3}r$$

Let new length = H

then, $\pi r^2 h = \pi\left(\frac{1}{3}r\right)^2 \times H = \frac{\pi r^2 H}{9}$

$\therefore$ $H = 9h$

Thus length becomes 9 times.

12. Volume of cone = Volume of cylinder

$$\frac{1}{3}\pi r^2 h = \pi r^2 h$$

$$\Rightarrow \quad \frac{1}{3} \times \frac{22}{7} \times 2 \times 2 \times h = \frac{22}{7} \times 2 \times 2 \times 6$$

$$\Rightarrow \quad \frac{h}{3} = 6 \Rightarrow h = 18 \text{ cm}$$

$\therefore$ Height of cone = 18 cm

13. Diameter = 3 cm, $h = 1$ m = 100 cm

$$\therefore \text{Radius} = \frac{3}{2} \text{ cm} = 1.5 \text{ cm}$$

thickness = 1 cm

$\therefore$ $R = 1.5 + 1 = 2.5$ cm

$r = 1.5$ cm

$$\text{Volume of metal} = \pi(R^2 - r^2) \times h$$
$$= \pi[(2.5)^2 - (1.5)^2] \times 100$$
$$= \pi[4] \times 100 = \pi \times 400 \text{ cm}^3$$

$\because$ $1 \text{ cm}^3 = 21$ g

$\therefore$ $\pi \times 400 \text{ cm}^3 = 21 \times \pi \times 400$ g

$$= 21 \times \frac{22}{7} \times \frac{400}{1000} \text{ kg}$$
$$= 26.4 \text{ kg}$$

14. Number of spheres $= \dfrac{\text{Volume of cylinder}}{\text{Volume of sphere}}$

$$= \frac{\pi \times 2 \times 2 \times 45}{\frac{4}{3}\pi \times (3)^3} = \frac{4 \times 45 \times 3}{4 \times 27} = 5$$

15. Volume of cylinder = Volume of cone

$$\pi r^2 h = \frac{1}{3}\pi r^2 H$$

$$\Rightarrow \quad 3h = H \Rightarrow \frac{h}{H} = \frac{1}{3}$$

13. DATA INTERPRETATION

The collection of figures and facts in every field is called the statistical data. There are three types of statistical data.

(*a*) **Primary data:** The data collected by the investigator or the statistician to be used or integrated himself are called primary data. It is more reliable and relevant because it is collected by the investigator himself for the first time for his study.

(*b*) **Secondary data:** The data which are collected originally by someone else and used and interpreted by others for statistical analysis are called secondary data.

(*c*) **Grouped data:** When primary data is arranged in classes or groups to bring out certain sailent feature of the data is called grouped data.

Graphical Representation of Data

A graph is a visual form for presentation of data, highlighting their basic facts and relationship.

The word graph, chart and diagram are used interchangeably for the pictorial representation of data. However, the visual form made by using rectangular coordinate system is called a graph. In general, the other pictorial representation in which the coordinate system is not used are called diagrams or charts.

Variate: The quantity that we measure from observation-to-observation is called a variate.

Class-Interval: Every data is generally divided into small group using some interval is said to be in class-interval, *e.g.,* 0–5, 5–10, 10–15 etc.

Class-Size: The difference between the true upper limit and true lower limit of a class gives the size of a class-interval, *e.g.,* class-size of the class-interval 0–5 is 5.

Mid Value: The variable value which is mid-way between the lower and upper limit of a class is called its mid-value, *e.g.,* mid-value of class-interval 0–5 is $\frac{0+5}{2} = 2.5$.

Frequency: The number of observations corresponding to particular class is said to be the frequency of that class, *e.g.,* frequency of the interval 5–10 is 6. It means 6 persons have got 5 or more articles but less than 10.

Cumulative Frequency: The sum of the preceding frequencies is called cumulative frequency. Last frequency of cumulative frequency column is equal to the sum of the frequencies.

Class Limit: Every interval has two limits. Lower number of the interval is called lower limit while upper number of the interval is called upper limit, *e.g.,* in class-interval 0–5, 0 is lower limit while 5 is the upper limit.

Histogram

A statistical graph that represents by the height of a rectangular column the number of times that each class of result occurs in a sample or experiment, *e.g.,* the following table represents the number of matured persons in age group (15–20) in a city.

Age Group	Number of persons
15–20	200
20–25	350
25–30	475
30–35	600
35–40	750
40–45	900
45–50	100

Then the histogram of the data is given below:

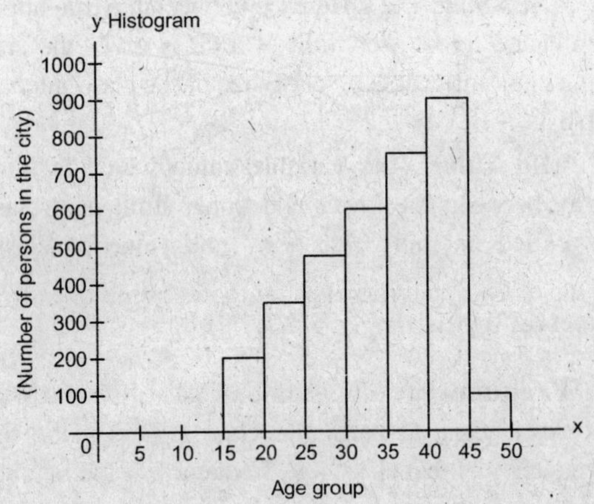

Bar Chart

A graph consisting of bars whose lengths are proportional to quantities in a set of data. It can be used when one axis cannot have a numerical scale, *e.g.*, to show how many different columns of flowers grow from a packet of mixed seeds, *e.g.*,

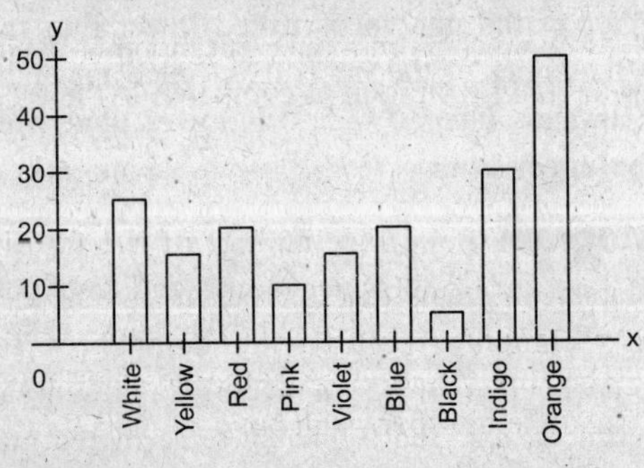

Pie Chart

A diagram in which proportions are illustrated as sectors of a circle. The relative area of the sectors representing the different proportions, *e.g.*, if out of 100 military personnels 25 personnels use tank, 30 personnels use warship, 40 personnels use aircraft and rest of them use rifles. Then pie-chart of the above data is.

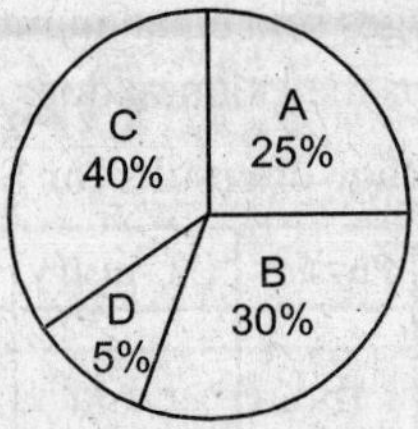

$$\text{A uses tank} = \frac{25}{100} \times 360 = 90^\circ$$

$$\text{B uses warship} = \frac{30}{100} \times 360 = 108^\circ$$

$$\text{C uses aircraft} = \frac{40}{100} \times 360 = 144^\circ$$

$$\text{D uses rifles} = \frac{5}{100} \times 360 = 18^\circ$$

EXAMPLE: Find out the marks obtained in different subjects from the following pie-diagram, if the total marks be 540.

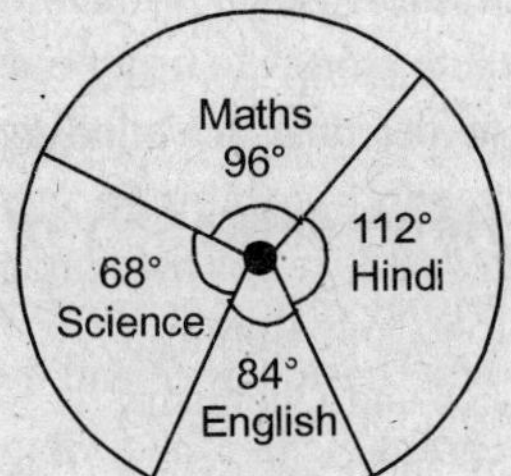

SOLUTION: Sum of the angles at the centre of circle = 360°

Total marks = 540

$$\therefore \text{ Marks obtained in Hindi} = \frac{112}{360} \times 540 = 168$$

$$\text{Marks obtained in English} = \frac{84}{360} \times 540 = 126$$

$$\text{Marks obtained in Science} = \frac{68}{360} \times 540 = 102$$

$$\text{Marks obtained in Maths} = \frac{96}{360} \times 540 = 144$$

MULTIPLE CHOICE QUESTIONS

Directions (Qs. 1 to 5): *Answers the questions on the basis of the following table:*

Assume all colleges sent equal number of candidates in all subjects for the examination.

Percentage of results for Subjects

College	Maths	Physics	Ch mistry	Zoology	Botany
A	52	65	62	47	40
B	47	62	52	35	38
C	53	70	46	54	39
D	35	72	58	62	57

1. Taking all the colleges into account which subject has shown highest percentage result?

A. Chemistry
B. Maths
C. Zoology
D. Physics

2. Taking the performance in all the subjects into account which college has shown highest level of percentage results?

A. D B. A
C. B D. C

3. Seeing the performance of all the four colleges together which combination of groups has shown lowest level of percentage results?

A. Zoology and Botany
B. Physics and Chemistry
C. Maths and Physics
D. Chemistry and Botany

4. Taking all the colleges into account which subject has shown lowest percentage result?

A. Maths
B. Physics
C. Chemistry
D. Botany

5. Taking the performance in all subjects into account which college has shown lowest level?

A. A B. B
C. C D. D

Directions (Qs. 6 to 10): *These questions refer to the following circle graph showing the expenditure distribution of a certain family. The family spends ₹6500 per month.*

Expenditure Distribution of a Certain Family

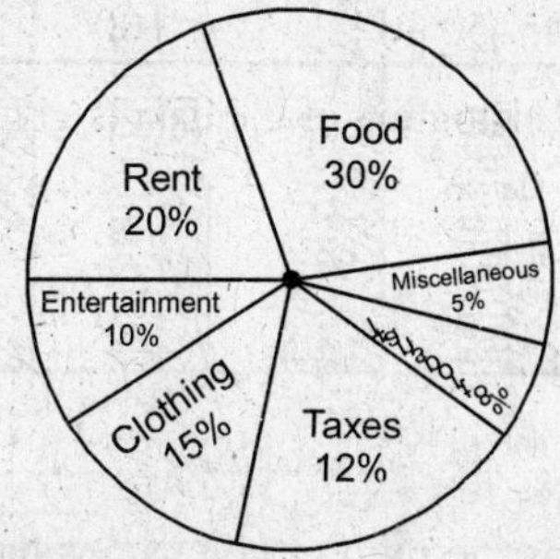

6. How much it spends on food per month?

A. ₹ 1950
B. ₹ 2950
C. ₹ 4850
D. ₹ 850

7. How much are its annual taxes?

A. ₹ 6500 B. ₹ 9360
C. ₹ 8900 D. ₹ 9500

8. How many degrees should there be in the central angle showing clothing, taxes and transportation combined?

A. 100 B. 115
C. 118 D. 126

9. How much more money per month is spent by the family on food as compared to the rent?

A. ₹ 650 B. ₹ 750
C. ₹ 550 D. ₹ 850

10. If the expenditure budget of the family is raised to ₹ 8000 per month and distribution on various items remain the same, then the monthly expenses on both, the entertainment and the transport, will be:

A. ₹ 1700
B. ₹ 1650
C. ₹ 1440
D. ₹ 1320

Directions (Qs. 11 to 15): *Study the following graph carefully and answer the following questions.*

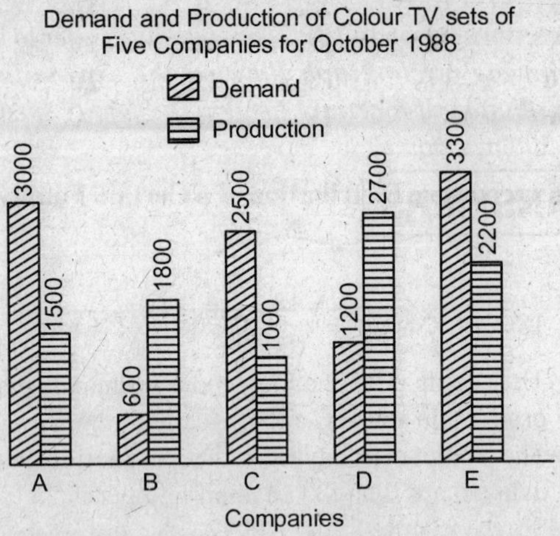

11. What is the ratio of companies having more demand than production of those having more production than demand?

A. 2 : 3 B. 4 : 1
C. 2 : 2 D. 3 : 2

12. What is the difference between average demand and average production of the five companies taken together?

A. 1400 B. 400
C. 280 D. 138

13. The production of Company 'D' is approximately how many times that of the production of the Company A?

A. 1.8 B. 4.5
C. 2.5 D. 4.9

14. The demand for Company 'B' is approximately what per cent of the demand for Company 'C'?

A. 4% B. 24%
C. 20% D. 60%

15. If Company A desires to meet the demand by purchasing surplus TV sets from a single company, which one of the following companies can meet the need adequately?

A. B B. C
C. D D. None of these

Directions (Qs. 16 to 20): *Study the following graph to answer the given questions.*

Per cent profit earned by two companies over the given years

$$\% \text{ Profit} = \frac{\text{Income} - \text{Expenditure}}{\text{Expenditure}} \times 100$$

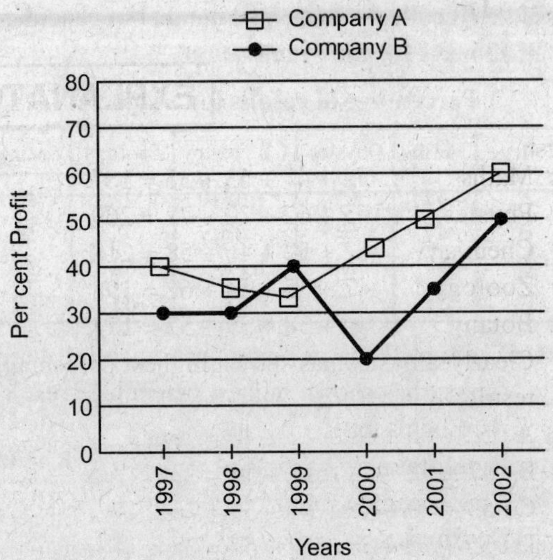

16. If the expenditure of Company B in 2000 was ₹ 200 crores, what was its income?

A. ₹ 240 crores B. ₹ 220 crores
C. ₹ 160 crores D. ₹ 180 crores

17. If the income of Company A in 2002 was ₹ 600 crores, what was its expenditure?

A. ₹ 360 crores B. ₹ 480 crores
C. ₹ 375 crores D. ₹ 320 crores

18. If the income of Company B in 1998 was ₹ 200 crores, what was its profit in 1999?

A. ₹ 21.5 crores
B. ₹ 153 crores
C. ₹ 46.15 crores
D. Cannot be determined

19. If the incomes of the two companies in 1998 were equal, what was the ratio of their expenditure?

A. 1 : 2 B. 26 : 27
C. 4 : 5 D. 100 : 67

20. What is the per cent increase in per cent profit for Company B from year 2000 to 2001?

A. 75 B. 175
C. 160 D. 150

ANSWERS

1	2	3	4	5	6	7	8	9	10
D	A	A	D	B	A	B	D	A	C
11	**12**	**13**	**14**	**15**	**16**	**17**	**18**	**19**	**20**
D	C	A	B	C	A	C	D	B	A

EXPLANATORY ANSWERS

1. Maths : $52 + 47 + 53 + 35 = 187$
Physics : $65 + 62 + 70 + 72 = 269$
Chemistry : $62 + 52 + 46 + 58 = 218$
Zoology : $47 + 35 + 54 + 62 = 198$
Botany : $40 + 38 + 39 + 57 = 174$
Clearly, Physics has shown highest percentage result.

2. A : $52 + 65 + 62 + 47 + 40 = 266$
B : $47 + 62 + 52 + 35 + 38 = 234$
C : $53 + 70 + 46 + 54 + 39 = 262$
D : $35 + 72 + 58 + 62 + 57 = 284$
Clearly, college D has shown highest level of percentage result.

3. Zoology and Botany of groups has shown lowest level of percentage result.

4. Total marks of Botany = 174 which shows lowest percentage result.

5. College B has shown lowest level because its total percentage result in all five subjects is 234 which is lowest.

6. Food 30% of ₹ 6500 = $\frac{30}{100} \times 6500$ = ₹ 1950

7. Taxes = 12% of ₹ 6500

$= \frac{12}{100} \times 6500$ = ₹ 780/month

= ₹ 780 × 12 = ₹ 9360/year

∴ Annual taxes = ₹ 9360

8. Clothing, taxes and transportation combined are 35%.

Now, $100\% = 360°$

$35\% = \frac{360°}{100} \times 35 = 126°$

9. 10% of ₹ 6500 = $\frac{10}{100} \times 6500$ = ₹ 650/month

10. 18% of ₹ 8000 = $\frac{18}{100} \times 8000$ = ₹ 1440

11. The companies having more demand than production are A, C and E *i.e.* their number is 3. The companies having more production than demand are B and D *i.e.* their number is 2.
So, the required ratio is 3 : 2.

12. Average demand

$= \frac{1}{5}(3000 + 600 + 2500 + 1200 + 3300)$

$= \frac{10600}{5} = 2120$

Average production

$= \frac{1500 + 1800 + 1000 + 2700 + 2200}{5}$

$= \frac{9200}{5} = 1840$

∴ Difference between average demand and average production = 2120 – 1840 = 280

13. Let $K(1500) = 2700$

$\Rightarrow \quad K = \frac{2700}{1500} = \frac{9}{5} = 1.8.$

14. Let x% of (demand for C) = (demand for B)

$\Rightarrow \quad \frac{x}{100} \times 2500 = 600$

$\Rightarrow \quad x = \frac{600 \times 100}{2500} = 24\%$

15. Since Company D produces highest number of TV sets and Company A desires to meet the demand by purchasing surplus TV sets from a single Company.
Clearly, D can meet the demand of A.
∴ Correct answer is C.

16. Let the income be ₹ x crores

$$\therefore \quad 20 = \frac{x-200}{200} \times 100$$

$$\Rightarrow \quad 40 = x - 200$$

$$\Rightarrow \quad x = 240.$$

$\therefore$ Income = ₹ 240 crores

17. The income of Company A in 2002 = ₹ 600 crores

% Profit = 60

Let the expenditure be ₹ x crores.

$$\therefore \quad 60 = \frac{600-x}{x} \times 100$$

$$\Rightarrow \quad x = \frac{600-x}{60} \times 100$$

$$\Rightarrow \quad x = \frac{(600-x)5}{3}$$

$$\Rightarrow \quad 3x = 3000 - 5x$$

$$\Rightarrow \quad 8x = 3000$$

$$\Rightarrow \quad x = \frac{3000}{8} = 375$$

Hence, expenditure = ₹ 375 crores.

18. It cannot be determined as Income and Expenditure of respective year is not known.

19. Let their equal incomes be ₹ 1 crore. Also, let expenditure of Company A be ₹ E_1 crores and that of Company B be ₹ E_2 crores.

Now, $$35 = \frac{1-E_1}{E_1} \times 100$$

$$35\,E_1 = 100 - 100\,E_1$$

$$135\,E_1 = 100 \quad \text{...}(i)$$

Similarly $$30 = \frac{1-E_2}{E_2} \times 100$$

$$130\,E_2 = 100 \quad \text{...}(ii)$$

From (i) and (ii)

$$135\,E_1 = 130\,E_2$$

$$\Rightarrow \quad \frac{E_1}{E_2} = \frac{130}{135} = \frac{26}{27}$$

$$\therefore \quad E_1 : E_2 = 26 : 27$$

20. Required percentage $= \frac{35-20}{20} \times 100$

$$= \frac{15}{20} \times 100 = 75.$$

GENERAL AWARENESS

NATIONAL SYMBOLS

STATE EMBLEM

State Emblem of India is an adaptation from the Sarnath Lion Capital of Ashoka. It was adopted by the Government of India on January 26, 1950. In the adapted form, only three lions are visible, the fourth being hidden from the view. The wheel (Dharma Chakra) appears in relief in the centre of the abacus with a bull on the right and a horse on the left.

The bell-shaped lotus has been omitted. The words ''Satyameva Jayate'' meaning ''Truth alone triumphs'' are inscribed below the Emblem in Devanagari script.

NATIONAL FLAG

The National Flag of India is a horizontal tricolour of deep saffron (Kesari), white and dark green in equal proportion. In the centre of the white band there is a wheel in navy blue colour. It has 24 spokes. The ratio of the length and the breadth of the flag is 3 : 2. Its design was adopted by the Constituent Assembly of India on July 22, 1947.

NATIONAL ANTHEM

Rabindranath Tagore's song 'Jana-gana-mana' was adopted by the Constituent Assembly as the National Anthem of India on January 24, 1950.

Jana-gan-mana-adhinayaka jaya he, Bharata-bhagya-vidhata
Punjab-Sindh-Gujarat-Maratha-Dravida-Utkala-Banga
Vindhya-Himachala-Yamuna-Ganga Uchhala-jaladhi-taranga.
Tava subha name jage, Tava subha asisa mange, Gahe tava jaya gatha,
Jana-gana-mangala-dayak, jaya he Bharata bhagya vidhata,
Jaya he, jaya he, jaya he, Jaya jaya jaya, jaya he.

NATIONAL SONG

Bankim Chandra Chatterji's 'Vande Mataram' which was a source of inspiration to the people in their struggle for freedom, has been adopted as National Song. It has an equal status with the National Anthem.

Vande Mataram
Sujalam, suphalam, malayaja-shitalam,
Shasya shyamalam, Mataram
Shubhrajyotsna,pulkita yaminim,
Phulla kusumita drumadalashobhinim,
Subhasinim sumadhura—bhashinim,
Sukhadam, Varadam, Mataram.

NATIONAL CALENDAR

It is based on the Saka era with Chaitra as its first month and a normal year of 365 days. It was adopted from March 22, 1957. Dates of the national calendar have a permanent correspondence with dates of Gregorian calendar as Chaitra I falls on March 22 in a normal year and March 21 in a leap year. In official communications, both Saka and Gregorian calendar dates are written. Months of the national calendar are Chaitra, Vaishakha, Jaishtha, Ashada, Shravan, Bhadra, Ashvina, Kartika, Margashirsha, Pausha, Magha and Phalguna.

NATIONAL ANIMAL

The magnificent tiger — Panthera tigris (Linnaeus) is the national animal of India. Tiger is found in several parts of the country and is known for its grace, strength, agility and enormous power. 'Project Tiger' was launched in 1973 to check their dwindling population in India.

NATIONAL BIRD

The Indian Peacock — Pavo Christatus (Linnaeus) is the national bird of India. It is a colourful, swan-sized bird with a fan-shaped crest of feathers on its head and a long-slander neck. The male species is more colourful with blue breast and a spectacular bronze-green train of around 200 elongated feathers.

National Flower—Lotus

National Tree—Banyan

National Fruit—Mango

National Currency—Rupee '`'

(One Rupee = 100 Paise)

National Aquatic Animal—Dolphin

BOOKS AND AUTHORS

Name of Book	Author
Ain-e-Akbari	Abul Fazal
Anand Math	Bankim Chandra Chatterjee
An Unknown Indian	Nirad C. Chaudhuri
Arthshastra	Kautilya
Coolie	Mulk Raj Anand
Das Kapital	Karl Marx
Discovery of India	Jawaharlal Nehru
Eternal India	Mrs. Indira Gandhi
Godan	Prem Chand
Gitanjali	Rabindranath Tagore
Gora	Rabindranath Tagore
Geet Govinda	Jayadeva
Harsha Charit	Bana Bhatta
Hindu View of Life	Dr. S. Radhakrishnan
India Wins Freedom	Maulana Abul Kalam Azad
Jobs of Millions	V.V. Giri
Jungle Book	Rudyard Kipling
Kamayani	Jai Shankar Prasad
Kadambari	Bana Bhatta
Life Divine	Sri Aurobindo
Last days of Netaji	G.D. Khosla
Les Miserables	Victor Hugo
Mahabharat	Veda Vyas
Macbeth	William Shakespeare
Mein Kempf	Hitler
Meghduta	Kalidas
Mother (Maa)	Maxim Gorky
Mother India	Katherine Mayo
My Experiments with Truth	Mahatma Gandhi
My Presidential Years	R. Venkataraman
Neeti Shatak	Bhartrihari
Nehru and His Vision	Dr. K.R. Narayanan
Old Man and the Sea	Ernest Hemingway
One World	Wendell Wilkie
Panchtantra	Vishnu Sharma
Paradise Lost	John Milton
Ramayana	Valmiki (in Sanskrit)
Raghuvansham	Kalidas
Rajtarangini	Kalhan
Ram Charit Manas	Tulsi Das
Abhijnan Shakuntalam	Kalidas
Satanic Verses	Salman Rushdie
Saket	Maithili Sharan Gupta
Speed Post	Shobha De
The God of Small Things	Arundhati Roy
Treasure Island	R.L. Stevenson
Twelfth Night	William Shakespeare
Train to Pakistan	Khuswant Singh
Uttara Ram Charitra	Bhava Bhuti
Vanity Fair	W.M. Thackeray
War and Peace	Leo Tolstoy
Wealth of Nations	Adam Smith
Wake up India	Annie Besant

INVENTIONS AND DISCOVERIES

Geographical Discoveries

Discovery	Discoverer
America	Columbus
Brazil	Cabral
North Pole	Robert Peary
Everest (Conquered)	Tabie Junko
Planetary Motion	Kepler
Hawaiian Islands	Captain Cook
South Pole	Amundsen
Solar System	Copernicus

Chemistry and Physics

Discovery	Discoverer
Atom Bomb	Otto Hahn
Atomic Theory	Dalton
Atomic Numbers	Moseley
Cosmic Rays	R.S. Millikan
Dynamite	Alfred Nobel
Electrons Theory	Bohr
Electricity (current)	Volta
Electric Telegraphy (Code)	S. Morse

Discovery	Discoverer
Gravitation	Newton
Gas Light	Murdock
Oxygen	J. Priestly
Photography	L. Daguerre
Printing for the blind	Louis Braille
Radium	Madame Curie
Telegraph	Samuel Morse
Television	J.L. Baird
Telephone	Graham Bell
Wireless	G. Marconi
X-rays	W.K. Roentgen
Mechanical	
Aeroplane	Wright Brothers
Bicycle	Macmillan
Computer	Charles Babbage
Dynamo	Michal Faraday
Diesel Engine	Rudolf Diesel
Engine (Railway)	Stephenson
Fountain Pen	Waterman
Gramophone	Edison
Locomotive Power of Steam	James Watt
Helicopter	Brequet
Life Boat	Henry Greathead

Discovery	Discoverer
Microscope	Z. Jansen
Printing Press	Gutenberg
Revolver	Colt
Sewing Machine	Elias Howe
Thermometer	Fahrenheit
Transistor	W. Shockley
Typewriter	Sholes
Telescope	Hans Lippershey
Tank (Military)	Swinton
Medical	
Antiseptic Surgery	Lord Joseph Lister
Bacteria	Leeuwenhock
Circulation of Blood	William Harvey
Homoeopathy (Discovered)	Hahnemann
Insulin	F. Banting
Penicillin	Alexander Flemming
Malaria Parasite	Dr. Ronald Ross
Stethoscope	Laennec
Vitamins	Funk
Anti-Rabies Treatment	Pasteur
General	
Nylon	Carouthers
Science of Geometry	Euclids

WORLD'S GEOGRAPHICAL SURNAMES

• City of Sky-scrapers—New York • City of Seven Hills—Rome • City of Dreaming Spires—Oxford • City of Golden Gate—San Francisco • City of Magnificent Buildings—Washington D.C. • City of Eternal Springs—Quito (S. America) • China's Sorrow—Hwang Ho • Cockpit of Europe—Belgium • Dark Continent—Africa • Emerald Isle—Ireland • Eternal City—Rome • Empire City—New York • Forbidden City—Lhasa (Tibet) • Garden City—Chicago • Gate of Tears—Strait of Bab-el-Mandeb • Gift of the Nile—Egypt • Granite City—Aberdeen (Scotland) • Hermit Kingdom—Korea • Herring Pond—Atlantic Ocean • Holy Land—Jerusalem • Island Continent—Australia • Islands of Cloves—Zanzibar • Isle of Pearls—Bahrein (Persian Gulf) • Key to the Mediterranean—Gibralter • Land of Cakes—Scotland • Land of Golden Fleece—Australia • Land of Maple Leaf—Canada • Land of Morning Calm—Korea • Land of Midnight Sun—Norway • Land of the Thousand Lakes—Finland • Land of the Thunderbolt—Bhutan • Land of White Elephant—Thailand • Land of Thousand Elephants—Laos • Land of Rising Sun—Japan • Loneliest Island—Tristan De Gunha (Mid-Atlantic) • Manchester of Japan—Osaka • Pillars of Hercules—Strait of Gibraltar • Pearl of the Antilles—Cuba • Playground of Europe—Switzerland • Quaker City—Philadelphia • Queen of the Adriatic—Venice • Roof of the World—The Pamirs, Central Asia • Sugar bowl of the world—Cuba • Venice of the North—Stockholm • Windy City—Chicago • Whiteman's grave—Guinea Coast of Africa • Yellow River—Huang Ho (China) • Sickman of Europe—Turkiye

CAPITALS AND CURRENCIES OF COUNTRIES

Country	Capital	Currency	Country	Capital	Currency
Afghanistan	Kabul	Afghani	Indonesia	Jakarta	Rupiah
Algeria	Algiers	Dinar	Iran	Teheran	Rial
Angola	Luanda	New Kwanza	Iraq	Baghdad	Dinar
Argentina	Buenos Aires	Peso	Ireland	Dublin	Euro
Armenia	Yeravan	Dram	Israel	Jerusalem	Shekel
Australia	Canberra	Dollar	Italy	Rome	Euro
Austria	Vienna	Euro	Jamaica	Kingston	Dollar
Azerbaijan	Baku	Monat	Japan	Tokyo	Yen
Bahrain	Manama	Dinar	Jordan	Amman	Dinar
Bangladesh	Dhaka	Taka	Kazakhstan	Akmola	Tenge
Barbados	Bridgetown	Dollar	Kenya	Nairobi	Shilling
Belgium	Brussels	Euro	Korea (S)	Seoul	Won
Bhutan	Thimphu	Ngultrum	Korea (N)	Pyongyang	Won
Bolivia	La paz	Boliviano	Kyrgyzstan	Bishkek	Som
Brazil	Brasilia	Cruzeiro	Kuwait	Kuwait City	Dinar
Bulgaria	Sofia	Lev	Laos	Vientiane	Kip
Byelorussia	Minsk	Zaichik	Latvia	Riga	Lat
Cambodia	Phnom-Penh	Riel	Lebanon	Beirut	Pound
Canada	Ottawa	Dollar	Libya	Tripoli	Dinar
Chile	Santiago	Peso	Lithuania	Vilnius	Litas
China	Beijing	Yuan	Malaysia	Kuala Lumpur	Ringgit
Colombia	Bogota	Peso	Maldives	Male	Rufiyya
Congo	Brazzaville	Franc	Mauritius	Port Louis	Rupee
Croatia	Zagreb	Kuna	Moldavia	Chisinau	Leu
Cuba	Havana	Peso	Mexico	Mexico City	Peso
Cyprus	Nicosia	Euro	Morocco	Rabat	Dirham
Czech Republic	Prague	Crown	Mozambique	Maputo	Metical
Denmark	Copenhagen	Krone	Myanmar (Burma)	Nay Pyi Taw	Kyat
Egypt	Cairo	Pound			
Estonia	Tallinn	Kroon	Nepal	Kathmandu	Rupee
Ethiopia	Addis Ababa	Birr	Netherlands	Amsterdam	Euro
Fiji	Suva	Dollar	New Zealand	Wellington	Dollar
Finland	Helsinki	Euro	Nigeria	Abuja	Naira
France	Paris	Euro	Norway	Oslo	Krone
Georgia	Tbilisi	Lari	Oman	Muscat	Rial
Germany	Berlin	Euro	Pakistan	Islamabad	Rupee
Ghana	Accra	Cedi	Philippines	Manila	Peso
Greece	Athens	Euro	Poland	Warsaw	Zloty
Guatemala	Guatemala City	Quetzal	Portugal	Lisbon	Euro
Hong Kong	Victoria	Dollar	Qatar	Doha	Riyal
Hungary	Budapest	Forints	Romania	Bucharest	Leu
Iceland	Reykjavik	Krona	Russia	Moscow	Ruble
India	New Delhi	Rupee	Saudi Arabia	Riyadh	Rial

Country	Capital	Currency
Slovakia	Bratislava	Euro
Spain	Madrid	Euro
Sri Lanka	Colombo	Rupee
Sudan	Khartoum	Dinar
Sweden	Stockholm	Krona
Switzerland	Berne	Swiss Francs
Syria	Damascus	Pound
South Africa	Capetown (Legislative) Pretoria (Administrative)	Rand
Tajikistan	Dushanbe	Somoni
Taiwan	Taipei	Dollar
Tanzania	Dodoma	Shilling
Thailand	Bangkok	Baht
Turkiye	Ankara	Turkish Lira
Turkmania	Ashikabad	Manat
Uganda	Kampala	Shilling
Ukraine	Kiev	Hyrvna
United Arab Emirates	Abu Dhabi	Dirham
U.K.	London	Pound Sterling
U.S.A.	Washington	Dollar
Uzbekistan	Tashkent	Som
Vietnam	Hanoi	Dong
Yemen	Sana'a	Rial/Dinar
Zimbabwe	Harare	Dollar
Congo (Democratic Republic)	Kinshasa	Franc
Zambia	Lusaka	Kwacha

INDIAN CITIES AND THEIR RIVERS

City	State	River
Agra	U.P.	Yamuna
Ahmedabad	Gujarat	Sabarmati
Alwaye	Kerala	Periyar
Kolkata	West Bengal	Hooghly
Cuttack	Odisha	Mahanadi
Delhi	Delhi	Yamuna
Haridwar	Uttarakhand	Ganga
Kanpur	Uttar Pradesh	Ganga
Ludhiana	Punjab	Sutlej
Lucknow	Uttar Pradesh	Gomati
Nasik	Maharashtra	Godavari
Patna	Bihar	Ganga
Prayagraj	U.P.	Confluence of the Ganga, Yamuna, and invisible Saraswati
Srinagar	J & K	Jhelum
Surat	Gujarat	Tapti
Tiruchirapally	Tamil Nadu	Kaveri
Ujjain	Madhya Pradesh	Shipra
Vijayawada	Andhra Pradesh	Krishna
Varanasi	Uttar Pradesh	Ganga

WONDERS OF THE WORLD

Seven Wonders of the Ancient World: (1) the Pyramids of Egypt, built in approximately 2700 BC; (2) the Hanging Gardens at Babylon; (3) the temple of Artemis at Emphesus; (4) the statue of Zeus at Olympia; (5) the tomb of Mausolus at Halicarnassus, built in nearly 350 BC; (6) the Colossus of Rhodes, built in nearly 280 BC; (7) the Pharos Lighthouse at Alexandria.

Seven Wonders of the Medieval World: (1) the Colosseum of Rome; (2) the Great Wall of China; (3) the Porcelain Tower of Nanking; (4) the Mosque at St. Sophia (Constantinople); (5) Stonehenge; (6) the Catacombs of Rome; (7) the Leaning Tower of Pisa.

Seven New Wonders of the World: (1) Taj Mahal of Agra (India); (2) Pyramid at Chichen Itza (Mexico); (3) Machu Picchu (Peru); (4) Statue of Christ The Redeemer (Brazil); (5) Great Wall of China; (6) Roman Colosseum, Italy; (7) Ruins of Petra, Jordan.

STATES & UNION TERRITORIES OF INDIA (CAPITALS, PRINCIPAL LANGUAGES)

States & Union Territories	*Capitals*	*Principal Languages*
■ Andhra Pradesh	Amravati	*Telgu and Urdu*
■ Arunachal Pradesh	Itanagar	*Monpa, Adi, Nissi etc.*
■ Assam	Dispur	*Assamese and Bengali*
■ Bihar	Patna	*Hindi and Maithili*
■ Chhattishgarh	Raipur	*Hindi*
■ Goa	Panaji	*Konkani*
■ Gujarat	GandhiNagar	*Gujarati*
■ Haryana	Chandigarh	*Hindi*
■ Himachal Pradesh	Shimla	*Hindi and Pahari*
■ Jharkhand	Ranchi	*Hindi*
■ Kerala	Thiruvananthpuram	*Malyalam*
■ Karnataka	Bengluru	*Kannada*
■ Madhya Pradesh	Bhopal	*Hindi*
■ Maharashtra	Mumbai	*Marathi*
■ Meghalaya	Shillong	*Khashi, Jayantia and Garo*
■ Manipur	Imphal	*Manipuri*
■ Mizoram	Aizawl	*Mizo and English*
■ Nagaland	Kohima	*Naga, Assamese and English*
■ Odisha	Bhubaneshwar	*Odiya*
■ Punjab	Chandigarh	*Punjabi*
■ Rajasthan	Jaipur	*Hindi, Rajasthani*
■ Sikkim	Gangtok	*Sikkimese and Gorkhali*
■ Tamil Nadu	Chennai	*Tamil*
■ Tripura	Agartala	*Bengali, Tripuri*
■ Uttar Pradesh	Lucknow	*Hindi*
■ Uttarakhand	Dehradun	*Hindi*
■ West Bengal	Kolkata	*Bengali*
■ Telangana	Hyderabad	*Telgu and Urdu*
■ Jammu & Kashmir	Srinagar/Jammu	*Kashmiri, Dongri, Urdu, Dardi and Pahari*
■ Andaman and Nicobar Islands	Port Blair	*Hindi, Nicobarese, Bengali, Malayalam, Tamil, Telugu*
■ Chandigarh	Chandigarh	*Hindi, Punjabi, English*
■ Dadar and Nagar Haveli and Daman and Diu	Daman	*Gujarati, Hindi*
■ Delhi	Delhi	*Hindi, Punjabi*
■ Lakshadweep	Kavaratti	*Malayalam*
■ Puducherry	Puducherry	*Tamil, Telugu, Malayalam, English and French*
■ Ladakh	Leh	*Ladakhi*

HIGH COURTS IN INDIA

Name	*Territorial Jurisdiction*	*Seat*
Allahabad	Uttar Pradesh	Prayagraj (Bench at Lucknow)
Andhra Pradesh	Andhra Pradesh	Amaravati
Bombay	Maharashtra, Goa Dadar and Nagar Haveli and Daman and Diu	Mumbai (Benches at Nagpur, Panaji, and Aurangabad)
Calcutta	West Bengal and Andaman & Nicobar Islands	Kolkata (Circuit Benches at Port Blair and Jalpaiguri)
Chhattisgarh	Chhattisgarh	Bilaspur
Delhi	New Delhi	NCT of Delhi
Gauhati	Assam, Nagaland, Mizoram and Arunachal Pradesh	Guwahati (Benches at Kohima, Aizawl and Itanagar)
Gujarat	Gujarat	Ahmedabad
Himachal Pradesh	Himachal Pradesh	Shimla
Jammu & Kashmir and Ladakh	Jammu & Kashmir/Ladakh	Srinagar and Jammu
Jharkhand	Jharkhand	Ranchi
Karnataka	Karnataka	Bengaluru (Circuit Benches at Dharwar and Gulbarga)
Kerala	Kerala & Lakshadweep	Ernakulam
Madhya Pradesh	Madhya Pradesh	Jabalpur (Benches at Gwalior and Indore)
Madras	Tamil Nadu & Puducherry	Chennai (Bench at Madurai)
Orissa	Odisha	Cuttack
Patna	Bihar	Patna
Punjab and Haryana	Punjab, Haryana and Chandigarh	Chandigarh
Rajasthan	Rajasthan	Jodhpur (Bench at Jaipur)
Sikkim	Sikkim	Gangtok
Uttarakhand	Uttarakhand	Nainital
Tripura	Tripura	Agartala
Meghalaya	Meghalaya	Shillong
Manipur	Manipur	Imphal
Telangana	Telangana	Hyderabad

FAMOUS HILL STATIONS

Hill Station	State/UT
1. Almora, Mussoorie Nainital	: Uttarakhand
2. Cherrapunji (Shillong), Khasi Hills (Shillong)	: Meghalaya
3. Ooty, Kodaikanal Yereaud	: Tamil Nadu
4. Dalhousie, Kassauli	: Himachal Pradesh
5. Darjeeling	: West Bengal
6. Gulmarg, Srinagar	: Jammu and Kashmir
7. Mahabaleshwar	: Maharashtra
8. Mt. Abu	: Rajasthan
9. Panchmarhi	: Madhya Pradesh

FAMOUS NATIONAL PARKS

1. Corbett National Park	: Nainital, Uttarakhand
2. Dudhwa National Park	: Lakhimpur Kheri, Uttar Pradesh
3. Kaziranga National Park	: Jorhat, Assam
4. Kanha National Park	: Jabalpur, Bhedaghat
5. Gir National Park	: Rajkot, Junagarh, Gujarat
6. Guindy National Park	: Guindy, Chennai, Tamil Nadu
7. Nagairhole National Park	: Coorg, Karnataka
8. Bandipur National Park	: Mysore, Karnataka

FAMOUS NATIONAL WILDLIFE SANCTUARIES

1. Dachigam Wildlife Sanctuary	: Srinagar, Jammu and Kashmir
2. Sariska	: Alwar, Rajasthan
3. Hazaribagh Wildlife Sanctuary	: Hazaribagh, Jharkhand
4. Tiger Project	: Sawai Madhopur, Rajasthan
5. Mudhumali Wildlife Sanctuary	: Mudhumalia, Nilgiri, Tamil Nadu
6. Periyar Wildlife Sanctuary	: Idukki, Kottayam, Kerala

HOLY PLACES IN INDIA

1.	Amarnath	Jammu and Kashmir
2.	Ayodhya	Uttar Pradesh
3.	Badrinath	Uttarakhand
4.	Dwarka	Gujarat
5.	Haridwar	Uttarakhand
6.	Kancheepuram	Tamil Nadu
7.	Kedarnath	Uttarakhand
8.	Mathura	Uttar Pradesh
9.	Puri	Odisha
10.	Rameswaram	Tamil Nadu
11.	Tirupati	Andhra Pradesh
12.	Ujjain	Madhya Pradesh
13.	Varanasi	Uttar Pradesh
14.	Bodh Gaya	Bihar

SPORTS

Terms Associated With Sports :

Cricket : Ashes, Bye, Bodyline, Bowling, Break, Cover-point, Creases, Chinaman, Chucker, Drive, Duck, Follow on, Googly, Hit-Wicket, Hat-trick, Leg-before-wicket, Leg break, Leg-bye, Maiden over, No ball, Night-watchman, Runner, Run-out, Stumped, Silly-point, Slip.

Football : Handball, Corner kick, Dribble, Free Kick, Hat-trick, Off-side, Penalty Kick, Try, Throw in, Wembley.

Hockey : Bully, Carry, Corner kick, Corner, Penalty stroke, Off-side, Penalty, Roll in scoop, Sticks, Sudden death, Striking circle, Short Corner, Scoop, Tie-breaker, Under-cutting, Hat-trick.

Tennis : Backhand drive, Deuce, Fault, Half-volley, Net, Let, Volley, Smash, Service.

Billiards : Break, Cannons, Cue, Pot, Jigger, Scratch, In Bauk, In, Off.

Bridge : Dummy, Finesse, Grand-slam, Little Slam, Revoke, Ruff slam, Trump, Tricks, Vulnerable.

Volley Ball : Booster, Love, Service, Volley, Smasher.

Badminton : Smash, Drop, Let.

Chess : Check, Checkmate, Gambit, State-mate.

Golf : Bogy, Caddie, Hole, Links, Stynie, Tee, Put.

Polo : Chukker, Mallet, Bunder.

Baseball : Bunting, Diamond, Pitcher, Put-out, Strike, Home.

Boxing : Knockout, Punch, Upper-cut, Jab, Hook.

FAMOUS TROPHIES

Agha Khan Cup	Hockey
Beighton Cup	Hockey
Corbillion Cup	World Table Tennis (Women)
Davis Cup	Lawn Tennis
Duleep Trophy	Cricket
Durand Cup	Football
Ezra Cup	Polo
I.F.A. Shield	Football
Irani Cup	Cricket (India)
Jayalaxmi Cup	Table Tennis (Women)
Lady Rattan Tata Trophy	Hockey (Women)
Nehru Cup	Hockey (India)
Obaidullah Cup	Hockey
Ranji Trophy	Cricket (India)
Rangaswamy Cup	Hockey (India)
Rovers Cup	Football (India)
Santosh Trophy	Football (India)
Subroto Cup	Football
Thomas Cup	Badminton
Uber Cup	Badminton (Women)
Wellington Trophy	Rowing (India)

BIGGEST, LARGEST, TALLEST OF THE WORLD

Airport, *Largest*—King Fahd International Airport, Dammon (Saudi Arabia)

Animal, *Tallest*—Giraffe (Average height 6.09 m); *Largest and Heaviest*—Blue Whale (190 tonnes)

Longest recorded Animal—Boot lace Worm (55 m); *Fastest*—Cheetah (Approximately 100 km/hr)

Bay, *Largest*—Bay of Bengal

Continent, *biggest*—Asia (31,845,872 km^2); *Smallest*—Australia Mainland (Area 76,17,930 km^2)

Desert, *Largest*—Sahara (N. Africa; maximum length 5,150 km EW; maximum width 3,200 km NS)

Dome, *Largest*—Singapore National Stadium (310 m)

Fish, *Largest fresh water*—Plabeuk (China, Laos and Thailand); *Most abundant*—Bristle mouth; *Most venomous*—Stone Fish (Indo-Pacific Waters)

Fountain, *Tallest* King Fahd's Fountain (Jeddah Saudi Arabia)

Gulf, *Largest*—Gulf of Mexico (1,544,000 sq. km)

Island, *Biggest*—Greenland (now known as Kalaatdlit Nunaat---2,175,000 sq km)

Lake, *Largest*—Caspian Sea (Azerbaijan, Russia, Iran border: 37.18 lakh km^2); *Deepest*—Baikal (Siberia); *Largest (fresh water)*—Superior Lake (USA---Canada border: 82,350 km^2)

Mountain, *Highest peak*—Mt. Everest (8848 m; Nepal); *Highest range*—Himalayas, Asia (upto 4200 m); *Greatest mountain range*—Himalaya-Karakoram (96 out of 109 peaks over 7315 m are here)

Museum, *Largest*—American Museum of Natural History, New York

Ocean, *Largest and Deepest*—The Pacific (Area: 166,240,000 km^2; Depth: 10,924 m)

Platform, *Longest (rail)*—Shri Siddharoodha Swamiji Railway Station, Hubballi (Karnataka; India, 1507 m. long)

Railway Station, *Largest*—Grand Central Terminal (New York City; 19 hc); *Highest*—Condor (Bolivia; 4786 m)

Rivers, *Longest*—(i) Nile (6650 km) (ii) Amazon (6437 km)

Sea, *Largest*—South China Sea (2,974,600 sq. km); *Largest (inland)*—Mediterranean

Star, *Brightest*—Sirius A (also called Dog Star)

Temple, *Largest*—Angkor Vat (Cambodia: 402 acres)

Train, *Fastest*—Japan's magnetically levitated (magler) train (Speed over 500 km/hr)

Tunnel, *Longest (railway)*—Gotthard Base Rail Tunnel (Switzerland; 57.1 km); *Largest (road)*—Laerdal, Norway (24.51 km)

FIRST IN INDIA

Governor General of Independent India — Lord Mountbatten

Cosmonaut — Sq. Ldr. Rakesh Sharma

Field Marshal — S.H.F.J. Manekshaw

Indian Governor General of Indian Union — C. Rajagopalachari

Indian I.C.S. Officer — Satyendra Nath Tagore

Indian to swim across English Channel — Mihir Sen

Indian Women to swim across English Channel — Miss Arti Saha

Man to climb Mount Everest — Tenzing Norgay

Man to climb Mount Everest without Oxygen — Phu Dorjee

Man to climb Mount Everest twice — Nwang Gombu

Nobel Prize Winner — Rabindra Nath Tagore

President of Indian National Congress — W.C. Banerjee

President of Indian Republic — Dr. Rajendra Prasad

Talkie Film — Alam Ara (1931)

Test Tube Baby (Documented) — Indira

Viceroy of India — Lord Canning

Woman Minister of Indian Union — Rajkumari Amrit Kaur

Woman Governor — Mrs. Sarojini Naidu

Woman President of Indian National Congress — Dr. Annie Besant

Woman Prime Minister — Mrs. Indira Gandhi

Woman Speaker of a State Assembly — Mrs. Shanno Devi

Prime Minister of India — Pt. Jawaharlal Nehru

Muslim President of Indian Union — Dr. Zakir Hussain

Speaker of Lok Sabha — G.V. Mavlankar

Women to Climb Mount Everest — Bachhendri Pal

Woman Judge in Supreme Court — Mrs. Meera Sahib Fatima Biwi

Women Chief Justice of a High Court — Smt. Leela Seth

The First Indian Weightlifter to Win bronze medal in Olympics — Karnam Malleshwari (Sydney, in 2000)

Chief of Defence Staff (CDS) —General Bipin Rawat

World Chess Champion — Vishwanathan Anand

India's First Woman Merchant Navy Officer — Sonali Banerjee

The First Woman Air Vice-Marshal — P. Bandopadhyaya

The First Indian to be appointed as United Nations Civilian Police Advisor — Ms. Kiran Bedi

The First Women to be appointed Deputy Governor of Reserve Bank of India — K.J. Udeshi

The First Indian Lady to win a medal in World Athletic Championship — Anju Bobby George

The First Sikh Prime Minister of India — Dr. Manmohan Singh

IMPORTANT DAYS

15th January	—	Army Day
26th January	—	Republic Day
30th January	—	Leprosy Eradication Day/ Martyr's Day
28th February	—	National Science Day
8th march	—	International Women's Day
15th March	—	World Consumer's Day
21st March	—	World Disabled Day
5th April	—	National Marine Day
7th April	—	World Health Day
18th April	—	World Heritage Day
22nd April	—	International Earth Day
Ist May	—	Worker's Day
3rd May	—	International Sun Day
21st May	—	Anti-Terrorism Day
24th May	—	Commonwealth Day
31st May	—	World No Tobacco Day
5th June	—	World Environment Day
21st June	—	World Yoga Day
26th June	—	International Day against Drug Abuse
11th July	—	World Population Day
15th August	—	Independence Day
24th August	—	Sanskrit Day
5th September	—	Teacher's Day
8th September	—	World Literacy Day
27th September	—	World Tourism Day
1st October	—	World Elder's Day
4th October	—	World Animal Day
8th October	—	Air Force Day
10th October	—	National Solidarity Day
16th October	—	World Food Day
24th October	—	U.N. Day
14th November	—	World Diabetes Day
14th November	—	Children's Day
19th November	—	National Integration Day
26th November	—	Law Day
1st December	—	World AIDS Day
4th December	—	Navy Day
7th December	—	Flag Day
10th December	—	Human Rights Day

PARLIAMENTS OF IMPORTANT COUNTRIES

Afghanistan	—	Shora
Britain	—	Parliament House of Commons, House of Lords
Denmark	—	Folketing
The Netherlands	—	States General
India	—	Sansad
Israel	—	Knesset
Iran	—	Majlis
Ireland	—	Airetann
Iceland	—	Althing
Japan	—	Diet
Norway	—	Storting
Russia	—	Supreme Soviet
Spain	—	Cortes
Sweden	—	Riksdag
U.S.A.	—	Congress Senate
Germany	—	Bundestag

MINERAL RESOURCES OF THE WORLD

Mineral	Largest Producers
Iron Ore	China, Japan, Russia
Tin	China, Indonesia, Peru
Lead	China, Australia, U.S.A.
Zinc	China, Australia, Peru
Manganese	South Africa, Brazil, Australia
Aluminium	China, Russia, Canada
Petroleum	Saudi Arabia, Russia, USA
Silver	Peru, Mexico, China
Coal	China, USA, India

WORLD'S LARGEST PRODUCERS

Articles	Producers	Articles	Producers
Carpets	Iran	Cheese	USA
Cocoa	Cote d'Ivoire	Coffee	Brazil
Copper	Chile	Cotton	China
Diamonds	Russia	Jute	India
Rice	China	Rubber	Thailand
Silk	China	Steel	China
Sugar	Brazil	Tea	China
Tin	China	Wheat	China
Wool	Australia		

TEN LARGEST COUNTRIES BY AREAS

Rank by Area	Country	Area (sq. km.)
1.	Russia	17,075,400
2.	Canada	9,976,139
3.	China	9,561,000
4.	U.S.A.	9,363,123
5.	Brazil	8,511,965
6.	Australia	7,686,848
7.	India	3,287,263
8.	Argentina	2,776,889
9.	Kazakhstan	2,724,900
10.	Algeria	2,381,741

PRESIDENT OF INDIA

He is the constitutional head of the Republic but not the real executive.

Qualifications: (1) Indian citizen; (2) age not less than 35 years; (3) should have qualifications for election to Lok Sabha; (4) should not hold any office of profit; (5) should not be a Member of Parliament or State Legislature.

Election: He is elected by the elected Members of Parliament and State Legislative Assemblies in accordance with the system of proportional representation by means of single transferable vote.

Powers: He makes appointment to all the Constitutional posts. He can address either House of Parliament and send message to them. He can summon and prorogue either House of Parliament and dissolve Lok Sabha. All Bills passed by Parliament must receive his assent to become an Act. He issues Ordinance when Parliament is not in session. No money Bill can be introduced in Lok Sabha without his recommendation. He can grant pardon, reprieve or remit punishment and he can commute death sentences. He can declare national emergency, state emergency and financial emergency.

VICE-PRESIDENT OF INDIA

The Vice-President acts as the ex-officio Chairman of Rajya Sabha and acts as the President when the latter is unable to discharge his functions due to illness, absence or any other reason, or till the election of a new President when a vacancy is caused by the death, resignation or removal of the President.

The Vice-President is elected by an electoral college consisting of the members of both Houses of Parliament in accordance with the system of proportional representation by means of the single transferable vote. He must be a citizen of India, not less than 35 years of age, and should be eligible for election as a member of the Council of States.

PRIME MINISTER OF INDIA

The Prime Minister is the leader of the majority party in the Parliament and the President cannot exercise his discretion in the appointment of the Prime Minister. He stays in office till the majority of the members of Lok Sabha has confidence in him. He occupies an important posi-tion in relation to the council of Ministers. He recommends the names of the persons to be included in the Council of Ministers. He allocates portfolios among them and can ask any minister to tender resignation. He can drop a minister while reshuffling the ministry. He coordinates the administration of various departments. He is the chief link between the President and the Council. He is the leader of the majority party and so, he has a great influence on the Parliament and the party. The Prime Minister enjoys such extensive powers as have been described as the virtual ruler of the country.

THE SOLAR SYSTEM: SOME FACTS

Number of Planets: 8—Mercury, Venus, Earth, Mars, Jupiter, Saturn, Uranus and Neptune.

Largest most

Massive planet .... Jupiter
Brightest planet .... Venus
Brightest star .... Sirius
Fastest orbiting planet .... Mercury
Longest (Synodic) day .... Mercury
Planet with largest moon .... Jupiter
Greatest average density .... Jupiter
Tallest mountain .... Earth
Strongest magnetic fields .... Jupiter
Most circular orbit .... Venus
Shortest (synodic) day .... Jupiter
Hottest planet .... Venus
No moons .... Mercury, Venus
Planet with moon with most eccentric orbit .... Neptune
Lowest average density .... Saturn
Deepest Oceans .... Jupiter
Greatest amount of liquid on the surface .... Earth

THE EARTH: FACTS AND DATA

Composition of the Earth: Aluminium (0.4%), Sulphur (2.7%), Silicon (13%), Oxygen (28%), Calcium (1.2%), Nickel (2.7%), Magnesium (17%), Iron (35%)

Surface area	: 510100500 sq km
Land Surface (29.1%)	: 148950800 sq km
Ocean Surface (70.9%)	: 361149700 sq km
Type of water	: 97% salt, 3% fresh
Total area of water	: 382672000 sq km
Equatorial diameter	: 12753 km
Equatorial Circumference	: 40066 km
Polar Circumference	: 39992 km
Polar diameter	: 12710 km
Equatorial radius	: 6376 km
Polar radius	: 6335 km
Mass (estimated weight)	: 594×10^{19} metric tons
Mean distance from the Sun	: 149407000 km

Earth's orbit speed (around sun)	: 107320 kmph	Time of Rotation (on its axis)	: 23 hrs 56 min 4.09 seconds
Period of Revolution (round the sun)	: 365 days 5 hrs 48 min. 45.51 seconds	Inclination of the axis (to the plane of the ecliptic)	: 23°27'

PRINCIPAL MOUNTAIN PEAKS OF THE WORLD

Mountains	Height in Metres	Range	Date of First Ascent
1. Mount Everest	8,848	Himalayas	May 29, 1953
2. K-2 (Godwin Austen)	8,611	Karakoram	July 31, 1954
3. Kanchenjunga	8,597	Himalayas	May 25, 1955
4. Lhotse	8,511	Himalayas	May 18, 1956
5. Makalu I	8,481	Himalayas	May 15, 1955
6. Dhaulagiri I	8,167	Himalayas	May 13, 1960
7. Mansalu I	8,156	Himalayas	May 9, 1956
8. Chollyo	8,153	Himalayas	Oct. 19, 1954
9. Nanga Parbat	8,124	Himalayas	July 3, 1953
10. Annapurna I	8,091	Himalayas	June 3, 1950
11. Gasherbrum I	8,068	Karakoram	July 5, 1958
12. Broad Peak I	8,047	Karakoram	June 9, 1957
13. Gasherbrum II	8,034	Karakoram	July 7, 1956
14. Shisha Pangma (Gosainthan)	8,014	Himalayas	May 2, 1964
15. Gasherbrum III	7,952	Karakoram	Aug. 11, 1975

POPULAR NICK NAMES OF SOME FAMOUS PERSONALITIES

Andhra Kesari	T. Prakasam
Anna	C.N. Anna Durai
Bang Bandhu	Sheikh Mujibur Rehman
Bapu	Mahatma Gandhi
Bard of Avon	William Shakespeare
Chachaji	Jawaharlal Nehru
Desh Bandhu	C.R. Das
Frontier Gandhi	Khan Abdul Gaffar Khan
Fuhrer	Adolf Hitler
G.B.S.	George Bernard Shaw
Grand Old Man of India	Dadabhai Naoroji
Grand Old Man of Britain	Gladstone
Guru Dev	Rabindra Nath Tagore
Guruji	M.S. Golwalkar
Iron Man of India	Sardar Patel
Lok Nayak	Jayaprakash Narayan
Lady with the Lamp	Florence Nightingale
Lal, Bal, Pal	Lala Lajpat Rai, Bal Gangadhar Tilak, Bipin Chandra Pal
Little Corporal	Napoleon Bonaparte
Lokmanya	Bal Gangadhar Tilak
Mahamana	Pt. Madan Mohan Malaviya
Maid of Orleans	Joan of Arc
Maiden Queen	Queen Elizabeth I
Missile Man	A.P.J. Abdul Kalam
Man of Destiny	Napoleon Bonaparte
Netaji	Subhash Chandra Bose
Nightingale of India	Sarojini Naidu
Panditji	Jawaharlal Nehru
Punjab Kesari	Lala Lajpat Rai
Shastriji	Lal Bahadur Shastri
Uncle Ho	Ho Chi Minh
Wizard of the North	Walter Scott

FAMOUS INTERNATIONAL ORGANISATIONS, HEADQUARTERS

International Organisations	*Headquarters*
United Nations Organisations (U.N.O.)	New York
International Monetary Fund (I.M.F.)	Washington D.C.
World Health Organisation (W.H.O.)	Geneva
Food & Agricultural Organisation (FAO)	Rome
International Labour Organisation (ILO)	Geneva
UNESCO	Paris
International Court of Justice	The Hague
Universal Postal Union (UPU)	Berne
International Civil Aviation Organisation (ICAO)	Montreal
UNIDO	Vienna
International Atomic Energy Agency (IAEA)	Vienna
International Finance Corporation (IFC)	Washington
United Nations Development Programme (UNDP)	New York
UNICEF	New York
International Maritime Organisation (IMO)	London
World Meteorological Organisation (WMO)	Geneva
International Telecommunication Union (ITU)	Geneva
Arab League	Cairo
Commonwealth of Nations	London
World Trade Organisation (WTO)	Geneva
International Development Association (IDA)	Washington D.C.
International Bank for Reconstruction and Development (IBRD)	Washington D.C.
World Intellectual Property Organisation (WIPO)	Geneva
Organisation of Islamic Conference (OIC)	Jeddah (Saudi Arabia)
European Union	Brussels
Red Cross	Geneva
Interpol	Lyons (France)
Asian Development Bank (ADB)	Manila
North Atlantic Treaty Organisation (NATO)	Brussels
Association of South East Asian Nations (ASEAN)	Jakarta

BHARAT RATNA AWARD WINNERS

No.	Name	Year
1.	Dr. S. Radhakrishnan	1954
2.	C. Rajagopalachari	1954
3.	Dr. C.V. Raman	1954
4.	Dr. Bhagwan Das	1955
5.	Dr. M. Visvesvaraya	1955
6.	Jawaharlal Nehru	1955
7.	Govind Ballabh Pant	1957
8.	Dr. D.K. Karve	1958
9.	Dr. Bidhan Chandra Roy	1961
10.	Purushottam Das Tandon	1961
11.	Dr. Rajendra Prasad	1962
12.	Dr. Zakir Hussain	1963
13.	Dr. Pandurang Vaman Kane	1963
14.	Lal Bahadur Shastri*	1966
15.	Indira Gandhi	1971
16.	V.V. Giri	1975
17.	K. Kamraj*	1976
18.	Mother Teresa	1980
19.	Acharya Vinoba Bhave*	1983
20.	Khan Abdul Ghaffar Khan	1987
21.	M.G. Ramachandran*	1988
22.	Dr. B.R. Ambedkar*	1990
23.	Dr. Nelson R. Mandela	1990
24.	Rajiv Gandhi*	1991
25.	Sardar Vallabhbhai Patel*	1991
26.	Morarji R. Desai	1991
27.	Maulana Abdul Kalam Azad*	1992
28.	Jehangir Ratanji Dadabhai Tata	1992
29.	Satyajit Roy	1992
30.	Gulzari Lal Nanda	1997
31.	Mrs. Aruna Asaf Ali*	1997
32.	Dr. A.P.J. Abdul Kalam	1998
33.	M.S. Subbalakshmi	1998
34.	C. Subramaniam	1998
35.	Jaya Prakash Narayan*	1999
36.	Prof. Amartya Sen	1999
37.	Pt. Ravi Shankar	1999
38.	Gopinath Bardoloi	1999
39.	Lata Mangeshkar	2001
40.	Bismillah Khan	2001
41.	Bhimsen Joshi	2008
42.	C.N.R. Rao	2014
43.	Sachin Tendulkar	2014
44.	Madan Mohan Malaviya*	2015
45.	Atal Bihari Vajpayee	2015
46.	Nanaji Deshmukh*	2019
47.	Bhupen Hazarika*	2019
48.	Pranab Mukherjee	2019
49.	Karpoori Thakur*	2024
50.	Lal Krishna Advani	2024
51.	Charan Singh*	2024
52.	P.V. Narasimha Rao*	2024
53.	M.S. Swaminathan*	2024

* Posthumous

ART AND CULTURE

☞ Classical Dances

Dance	*State*	*Famous Artists*
Bharat Natyam	Tamil Nadu	Yamini Krishnamurthy, Rukmini Devi Arundale, Swapna Sundari, Sonal Mansingh, Vaijanti Mala, Mrinalini Sarabhai, Chandralekha, Indrani, Ram Gopal, Bal Saraswati
Kathakali	Kerala	Gopinath, K.K. Nayar, Kunju-Kurup, T.K. Chandu
Kuchipudi	Andhra Pradesh/ Telangana	Sapna Sundari, Raja Reddy, Shobha Nayar, Radha Reddy, Vedantam Satyanarayan, Vimpanti Chinna Satyam.
Kathak	North India	Birju Maharaj, Gopi Krishna, Shambhu Maharaj, Sitara Devi, Vishnu Sharma, Durga Lal, Shobhana Narayan
Odissi	Odisha	Kelucharan Mahapatra, Indrani Rehman, Madhavi Mudgal, Pratima Bedi, Samyukta Panigrahi, Sonal Mansingh, Debudas
Manipuri	Manipur	Uday Shankar, Bipin Singh, Suryamukhi, Darohra Jhaveri

☞ Famous Folk Dances

State/UT	*Folk Dance*	*State/UT*	*Folk Dance*
Andhra Pradesh/ Telangana	Dandari, Banjara	Kerala	Mohini Attam, Padayuni
Assam	Bihu, Keli Gopal, Sataria	Madhya Pradesh	Lota Nritya, Jawara
Bihar	Chhau, Magahi, Durga dance	Maharashtra	Tamasha, Dahi Handi, Gof, Deepak Dindi
W. Bengal	Kirtan, Kalatri, Asweabadh, Brita, Kalidance	Manipur	Dhol Cholam
Chhattisgarh	Saila, Karama, Bhagoria	Meghalaya	Nongakarem
Gujarat	Garba, Rasalila, Tippani, Dandia,	Nagaland	Bamboo dance
		Odisha	Chhau, Maya Shabari, Dalachai
Haryana	Damyal, Lahoor	Punjab	Gidda, Bhangra, Panihari
Himachal Pradesh	Dussehra dance, Hikat, Notio	Rajasthan	Thumar, Kathaputali, Tera Tali
		Tamil Nadu	Terukalathu, Kabalatam, Kargam, Pulivesham
Jammu & Kashmir	Dumhal	Tripura	Hazagiri
Jharkhand	Jhau, Ghumakudia, Jadur, Sarhul, Soharai, Karama, Vaima, Loojhari, Jat-Jatin, Vidayat	Uttar Pradesh	Rasalila, Nautanki, Thali, Dhurang, Jhumela, Huraka, Bol.
		Uttarakhand	Kajari, Karan
Karnataka	Yakshagan, Dolu Kunitha	Goa	Dhode Modini

MUSIC

Main Schools of Classical Music

- There are two main schools of classical music, namely, the Hindustani and the Carnatic. The Hindustani school of classical music is in vogue in north-western India, eastern India and northern parts of the South India.

Musical Instruments

- ***They are:*** Tabla, Mridangam, Pakhawaj, Chandai, Dholak, Veena, Sitar, Sarod, Gootuvadhyam, Sarangi, Flute, Nadaswaram, Shehnai, Shringi and Turahi.

FAMOUS INTERNATIONAL AIR SERVICES

Air Service	*Name of Country*	*Air Service*	*Name of Country*
Air India	India	Lufthansa Airlines	Germany
British Overseas Airways Corporation	Britain	Iraqi Airways	Iraq
		National Airlines	Iran
Trans World Airlines	America	Quantas Airlines	Australia
Russian Airlines	Russia	Hong-Kong Airlines	Hong-Kong
Japan Airlines	Japan	Egypt Airlines	Egypt
Pakistan International Airlines	Pakistan	Slovak Airlines	Slovakia
Malaysia Airlines	Malaysia	S.I.A.	Singapore
Royal Nepal Airlines	Nepal	Garuda Airways	Indonesia
Swiss Airways	Switzerland	Bangladesh Viman Sewa	Bangladesh
Air France	France	Air Lanka	Sri Lanka
Kuwait Airways	Kuwait	Elitalia Airlines	Italy
Pan American World Airways	America	Air Canada	Canada
K.L.M. Royal Airlines	The Netherlands (Holland)		

FAMOUS RELIGIONS, FOUNDERS, HOLY BOOKS & PLACES OF WORSHIP

Religion	*Founder*	*Holy Books*	*Place of Worship*
Hinduism	Hinduism has no one Founder. (This religion is based upon the religion of original Aryan Settlers)	Ramayan, Vedas, Puranas and Geeta	Temple
Sikh	Guru Nanak Dev	Guru Grantha Sahib	Gurdwara
Christianity	Jesus Christ	Bible	Church
Islam	Prophet Mohammed	Koran (Quran)	Mosque
Parsi	Zoroaster	Zend Avesta	Fire Temple
Jainism	Adinath Rishavdev	Jain Granth	Jain Temple
Buddhism	Gautam Buddha	Tripitaka	Buddha Temple
Jew	Moosa	Torah	Synagogue

INTELLIGENCE AGENCIES OF SOME PROMINENT COUNTRIES

Country	*Intelligence Agency*	*Country*	*Intelligence Agency*
India	Research & Analysis Wing (RAW), Intelligence Bureau (I.B.), Central Bureau of Investigation (C.B.I.)	Russia	K.G.B. (Komitel Gosudarstvennoy Bezopasnosty) (Committee for State Security)
Pakistan	Inter Service Intelligence (I.S.I.)	Canada	Security Intelligence Service
U.S.A.	Central Intelligence Agency, Federal Bureau of Investigation	S. Africa	Bureau of State Security
		Iran	Sabak
Britain	Military Intelligence (M.I.)-5 and 6, Special Branch, Ultra, Joint Intelligence Organisation	Iraq	Al-Mukhabarat
		Australia	Australian Security and Intelligence Organisation
Israel	Mosad	France	S.D.E.C.E.
Egypt	Mukhabarat	Spain	C.E.S.I.D.
Japan	Nicho	Cuba	D.G.I.

SOME PROMINENT RACES OF THE WORLD

Races	Country	Races	Country	Races	Country	Races	Country
Veddas	Sri Lanka	Pygmy	Congo Basin	Eskimo	Canada, Tundra Region	Bushman	Kalahari Desert
Somaid	West Siberia	Bantu	Central and South Africa				
Masai	East Africa			Lapps	European Tundra	Red Indian	North America
Muree	New Zealand	Tartars	Siberia				
Yakoot	Russian Tundra	Baddu	Arab's Desert	Hausa	Nigeria		
Papuans	New Guyana	Semang	Malaysia	Kirghiz	Steppes (Russia)		

FAMOUS STRAITS OF THE WORLD

Strait	Between	Country
Malacca Strait	Andaman Sea and South China Sea	Indonesia
Palk Strait	Mannar and Bay of Bengal	India-Sri Lanka
Magellan Strait	Pacific and South Atlantic Ocean	Chile
Dover Strait	English Channel and North Sea	England-France
Berring Strait	Berring Sea and Chukasi Sea	Alaska-Russia
Sugaroo Strait	Japan Sea and Pacific Ocean	Japan
Sunda Strait	Java and Indian Ocean	Indonesia
Gibralter Strait	Mediterranean Sea and Atlantic Ocean	Spain
Harmuj Strait	Persia and Bay of Oman	Oman-Iran
Hudson Strait	Bay of Hudson and Atlantic Ocean	Canada

FAMOUS NEWSPAPERS OF THE WORLD

Newspaper	Place of Publishing	Language
Daily News	New York (America)	English
Guardian	London (Britain)	English
Pravada	Moscow (Russia)	Russian
Al-Ahram	Cairo (Egypt)	Arabic
Merdeca	Jakarta (Indonesia)	Indonesian
Times	London (Britain)	English
People's Daily	Beijing (China)	Chinese
New Statesman	Britain	English
Daily Mirror	Britain	English

Newspaper	Place of Publishing	Language
Hindu, Hindustan, Times of India, Tribune, Statesman, Indian Express, Economic Times	India	English
Hindustan, Nav Bharat Times, Dainik Bhaskar, Dainik Jagaran, Punjab Kesari	India	Hindi

IMPORTANT BOUNDARY LINES

Boundary Line	Countries	Boundary Line	Countries
Durand Line	Pakistan and Afghanistan	17th Parallel	The line which defined the boundary between North Vietnam and South Vietnam before the two were united.
Hindenberg Line	Germany-Poland		
Maginot Line	France and Germany		
Mannerhein Line	Russia-Finland		
Mc Mahon Line	India-China		
Order Niesse Line	Germany-Poland		
Radcliff Line	India-Pakistan	38th Parallel	North Korea and South Korea
Seigfrid Line	Germany-France		
24th Parallel	India-Pakistan	49th Parallel	U.S.A. and Canada

SIGNALS/SIGNS AND MEANING

Signal/Sign	Meaning	Signal/Sign	Meaning
Red Triangle	Family Planning	White Flag	Treaty or Surrender
Red Cross	Medical Help	Yellow Flag	Vehicles with patients of contagious diseases
Red Light	Danger, 'Stop' for the movement of vehicles	Two Bones across with a Skull	Danger of electricity
Green Light	Go		
Olive Branch	Peace	Half mast flown Flag	National mourning
White Pigeon or Dove	Peace	Lotus and culture	Sign of civilization
Black Strip on Arm	(i) Opposition (ii) Sorrow	Wheel (Chakra)	Sign of Progress
Black Flag	Opposition	A blind folded woman with scale in hand	Sign of Justice
Red Flag	(i) Danger (ii) Revolution	Reversed flown	National calamity flag

NATIONAL EMBLEMS OF IMPORTANT COUNTRIES

Country	National Emblem	Country	National Emblem
America	Golden Rod	New Zealand	Kiwi, Fern Southern Cross
Australia	Kangaroo	Norway	Lion
Ireland	Shamrock	Nepal	Kukri
Italy	White Lily	Pakistan	Crescent
Israel	Candelabrum	Poland	Eagle
Iran	Rose	France	Lily
Canada	White Lily	Belgium	Lion
Great Britain	Rose	Bangladesh	Water Lily
Chile	Candor and Huemul	Mongolia	The Soyombo
Germany	Corn Flower	Russia	Double headed eagle
Japan	Chrysanthemum	Lebanon	Cedar Tree
Zimbabwe	Zimbabwe Bird	Sudan	Secretary Bird
Denmark	Beach	Syria	Eagle
Turkiye	Crescent and Star	India	Lioned Capital
The Netherlands	Lion		

THE CONTINENTS OF THE WORLD

Name	Population (2021) (In million)	Per cent of the world's population
Asia	4,584	59.1
Africa	1,375	17.4
Europe	747	9.8
North America	373	4.8
South America	651	8.4
Australia	41.66	0.5
Antarctica	NA	NA

COMPUTER

The computer is the system of that electronic device through which various informations are processed on the basis of a definite set of instructions called program and mathematical (numerical) and non-mathematical both types of informations are processed.

The first mechanical computer was composed or fabricated by Blaise Pascal in 1642 and it is called Pascalene. But in 1833, Charles Babbage first time conceived an automatic calculator or computer. Charles Babbage is called the father of modern computer. Herman made an electronic tabulating machine based on punch cards which operates automatically.

In 1937, first mechanical computer mark-I was fabricated by Howard Akeen. The most outstanding contribution in the development of modern computer goes to John Wan Newmaan who brought the 2nd revolution in the area of computer in 1951. He discovered EDVAC (Electronic Discrete Variable Automatic Computer) and utilised the stored program and the binary number system in the computer.

FUNCTIONS OF COMPUTER

1. Collection and composition (input) of datas;
2. Storage of datas.
3. Processing of datas.
4. Retrieval or output of the proccessed informations and datas.

UNITS OF COMPUTER

1. Input unit.
2. Central processing unit–CPU.
3. External Memory unit.
4. Output unit.

The CPU of the computer is called brain of the computer and sometimes CPU is also called Micro Processor of the computer. The data is entered through the input unit in the computer and through the central processing unit with the help of External Memory Unit datas are arranged and processed. Ultimately by the output unit these datas or informations are issued or released.

PARTS OF COMPUTER

- **Monitor :** The monitor of the computer is like a television in which the picture appears in the form of doted points on the screen and these are called pixcels.
- **Hard Disc and Floppy Disc :** The Hard Disc is the permanent disc in the computers while the Floppy Disc is the disc utilised when datas or informations are to be transferred from one computer to another.
- **Mouse :** The mouse of the computer is like the remote control of TV through which computer is directly regulated or controlled without utilising the key-board.
- **Printer :** The printer is a device which prints any documents or processed informations of the computer.

SOME HIGH LEVEL LANGUAGES

1. **FORTRAN :** This language was developed for solving the mathematical formulae very quickly and conveniently.
2. **COBOL :** This language was developed for the commerical purposes. For the processing of this language a group of sentences is selected called paragraph and all paragraphs composed are called a section, while all sections composed are called a division.
3. **BASIC :** In basic a definite part of the prescribed instruction is only inserted in the computer.
4. **ALGOL :** This was basically fabricated and designed for the complex algebraic calculations.
5. **PASCAL :** It is an amplified and modified form of ALGOL.
6. **COMAL :** This computer language is used for the students of secondary level.
7. **LOGO :** This language is used for children and kids for drawing Graphic line diagrams.
8. **PROLOG :** This language is developed in 1973 in France and this language is used for Artificial Intelligence which is capable and equivalent to the logical program.

9. **FORTH :** This language was invented by Charles Mure which is frequently used in all types of the works in the computer.

COMPUTER VIRUS

The computer virus is an electronic code which is used to abolish or erradicate the inclusive informations or programs of the computer. Some important computer viruses are Micheleanjalo, Dork Avangor, kilo, filip, Macmug, Scores, Casecade, Jeruslem, Date crime, Coloumbs crime, Internet virus, Pachcom, Pach EXE, COM-EXE, Marizuana, C-brain, bloody, Chenge Mungu and Desi etc.

COMPUTER NETWORKING

There are two types of networkings which are usually occur—Local Area Networking (LAN) and Wide Area Networking (WAN). By LAN all the computers of the same buildings are connected like the computers of university premises, computers of offices etc.

By WAN all the comptuers of a large area are connected like the computers of all the offices of a city or town etc. In India a very large computer network namely INDONET has been installing through which all the main towns and cities has to be interlinked.

COMPUTER TERMINOLOGY

- **Bit :** The bit is a unit of measurement of the electronic data. One bit is either 0 or 1 but not both. On composing 8 bits, 1 byte is formed.
- **Bug :** The Bug is the error in the computer program or system and its eradication is called Debug.
- **Byte :** Total eight bits compose a byte. Thus 8 bits = 1 byte.
- **CD-ROM :** A CD like of music CD in which data can be stored substantially called CD-ROM. In a CD with comparison to floppy extremely more datas can be stored but one problem in it is that one time recorded data can not be deleted or modified.
- **Chip :** It is a thin slice on which by a special mechanism a circuit is designed which is normally made from Silicon.
- **Memory System :** The place where computer data and program are temporarily kept is called Memory system. Usually memory is implied from RAM.
- **Modem :** The device which converts digital signals into analogue signals and vice-versa is called Modem.
- **RAM :** It is Random Access Memory (a place) where datas to be processed are kept temporarily and it is unstable memory.
- **ROM :** It is Read Only Memory and it is stable or Non-valatile memory which doesn't ended after power off.
- **Scanner :** It is a device through which graphic image is transformed to digital image and the scanners are of usually two types one desktop and another hand operating.

PROGRAMING

Computers perform phenomenal feats of calculation, but they do not do so in a complicated way. They actually carry out very simple operations, such as addition and subtraction. They achieve their fantastic computing power by carrying out these operations at incredible speed.

The programme, or set of instructions for operating the computer, is therefore written as a sequence of very simple steps. (See box below) Several computer languages have been developed for different applications, including BASIC, COBOL, FORTRAN and PASCAL. Writing programmes is very skilled and time-consuming work. But for most typical computer applications ready-written programmes are available, called "packages".

☞ How A Programme Works

Without a programme to tell it what to do and how to do it, a computer is unable to function. If, for example, you wanted to know how many times the word 'the' appears in this paragraph, or in the whole book, it would not be enough merely to put the text into a computer and then ask it how many times the word appears. For the computer to accomplish the calculations it has to be told what to do in simple steps. The instructions might be:

1. Scan the text until a space followed by 'T' or 't' is found.
2. If the next letter is not 'h', go back to step 1.
3. If the letter is 'h', is the next letter 'e'?
4. If not, go back to step 1. If it is, go to step 5.
5. If 'e' is followed by a space, add 1 to the total.
6. Go back to step 1.

A full computer programme for this operation would need to be broken down into even more simple steps, but a series of such programmes could enable a computer to analyse any amount of text in great detail.

DEFENCE

The Supreme Command of the Armed Forces is vested in the hands of the President of the Country. The responsibility for national defence, however, rests with the Cabinet. All important questions having a bearing on defence are decided by the Cabinet Committee on Political Affairs, which is presided over by the Prime Minister. The Defence Minister is responsible to Parliament for all matters concerning the Defence Services. All the administrative and operational control of Armed Forces are exercised by the Ministry of Defence. The three services – Army, Navy and Air Force function through their respective service headquarters headed by the chief of Staff.

COMMISSIONED RANKS IN DEFENCE SERVICES

Army	*Navy*	*Air Force*
General	Admiral	Air Chief Marshal
Lieutenant-General	Vice-Admiral	Air Marshal
Major-General	Rear-Admiral	Air Vice-Marshal
Brigadier	Commodor	Air Commodor
Colonel	Captain	Group Captain
Lieutenant-Colonel	Commander	Wing Commander
Major	Lt.Commander	Squadron Leader
Captain	Lieutenant	Flight Lieutenant
Lieutenant	Sub-Lieutenant	Flying Officer

INTERNAL SECURITY ORGANISATIONS OF INDIA

S. No	*Name of Organisation*	*Year of Creation*	*Headquarters*
1.	Assam Rifles (A.R.)	1835	Shillong
2.	Central Reserve Police Force (C.R.P.F.)	1939	New Delhi
3.	National Cadet Corps (N.C.C.)	1948	New Delhi
4.	Territorial Army	1948	In different States
5.	Indo-Tibetan Border Police	1962	New Delhi
6.	Home Guard	1962	In different States
7.	Coast Guard	1978	New Delhi
8.	Border Security Force (B.S.F.)	1965	New Delhi
9.	Central Industrial Security Force (C.I.S.F.)	1969	New Delhi
10.	National Security Guard	1984	New Delhi
11.	Police	—	In different States

COMMANDER-IN-CHIEFS OF INDIA

1. General Sir Rob Lockhart	Aug. 15, 1947 — Dec. 31, 1947
2. General Sir Roy Bucher	Jan. 1, 1948 — Jan. 14, 1949
3. General K. M. Kariappa	Jan. 15, 1949 — Jan. 14, 1953
4. General Maharaj Rajendra Sinhji	Jan. 15, 1953 — March 31, 1955

FIRST INDIAN CHIEFS OF STAFF OF INDIAN FORCES

1. General Maharaj Rajendra Sinhji (Army Staff)	April 1, 1955 — May 14, 1955
2. Vice Admiral R.D. Katari (Naval Staff)	April 22, 1958 — June 4, 1962
3. Air Marshal S. Mukherjee (Air Staff)	April 1, 1954 — Nov. 8, 1960

ARMY INSTITUTES

1. Sainik Schools upto +2 Level	33 places in India
2. Rashtriya Indian Military College (prepare for entrance to N.D.A)	Dehradun
3. National Defence Academy (three services)	Khadakwasla, Pune
4. Indian Military Academy (Army)	Dehradun
5. Officers Training Academy (3 services) Short Courses	Chennai
6. National Defence College	New Delhi
7. The College of Combat	Mhow
8. The College of Military Engineering	Kirkee
9. Military College of Telecommunication Engineering	Mhow
10. The armoured Corps Centre and School	Ahmed Nagar
11. The School Artillery	Deolali
12. The Infantry School	Mhow and Belgaum
13. College of Material Management	Jabalpur

AIR FORCE INSTITUTIONS

Air Force Academy	Hyderabad
Helicopter Training School	Hakimpet
Flying Instructors School	Tambaram, Chennai
The College of Air Warfare	Secunderabad
Air Force Administrative College	Coimbatore
Air Force Technical College	Jalahalli

DEFENCE PRODUCTION UNITS

1. Bharat Dynamites Ltd.	Hyderabad
2. Praga Tools	Hyderabad
3. Mishra Dattu Nigam	Hyderabad
4. Bharat Electronics Ltd.	Bangalore
5. Bharath Earthmovers Ltd.	Bangalore
6. Heavy Vehicles Ltd.	Avadi, Chennai
7. Garden Reach Ship Builders and Engineers Ltd.	Kolkata
8. Mazagaon Dock	Mumbai
9. Goa Shipyard	Marmugao
10. Hindustan Shipyard Ltd.	Vishakhapatnam
11. Hindustan Aeronautics Ltd.	Bangalore, Hyderabad, Nasik, Koraput, Kanpur, Lucknow

☞ Indian Army Commands

Command	HQ Location	Command	HQ Location
Eastern Command	Kolkata	Western Command	Chandigarh
Northern Command	Udhampur	Southern Command	Pune
Central Command	Lucknow	Training Command	Shimla
South-Western Command	Jaipur		

☞ Indian Air Force Commands

Command	HQ Location	Command	HQ Location
Western Air Command	New Delhi	South-Western Air Command	Gandhinagar
Central Air Command	Prayagraj	Eastern Air Command	Shillong
Southern Air Command	Thiruvananthapuram	Training Command	Bengaluru

☞ Indian Navy Commands

Command	HQ Location	Command	HQ Location
Eastern Naval Command	Vishakhapatnam	Western Naval Command	Mumbai
Southern Naval Command	Kochi		

☞ Missile and Other Weapons

Name	Class	Range
✶ Agni I	SRBM	850 km
✶ Agni II	MRBM	2500 km
✶ Agni III	IRBM	3500 km-5500 km
✶ Agni IV *or* Agni II Prime	IRBM	4000 km
✶ Agni V	ICBM	5000 km-6000 km
✶ Agni VI	ICBM	8000 km-10000 km
✶ Agni 3SL	ICBM	5200 km-11600 km
✶ Dhanush	SRBM	350 km
✶ Nirbhay	Subsonic Cruise Missile	1000 km

Name	Class	Range
✶ Brahmos	Supersonic Cruise Missile	290 km
✶ Brahmos 2	Hypersonic Cruise Missile	290 km
✶ Prithvi I	SRBM	150 km
✶ Prithvi III	SRBM	350 km
✶ Sagarika	SLBM	700 km-2200 km
✶ Shaurya	TBM	700 km-2200 km
✶ Astra	Air to Air Missile	80 km-100 km
✶ Barak-I	SRSAM	12 km
✶ Barak-8	SRSAM	90 km

☞ Chief of Defence Staff (CDS)

To bring in reform in higher defence management in the country, the post of Chief of Defence Staff (CDS) was created in the rank of a four-star General with salary and prerequisites equivalent to a Service Chief. The Chief of Defence Staff will also head the Department of Military Affairs (DMA), to be created within the Ministry of Defence and functions as its Secretary. Gen. Bipin Rawat was the first CDS of the country from January 1, 2020 to December 08, 2021. Gen. Anil Chauhan assumed the charge of the second CDS on September 30, 2022.

MULTIPLE CHOICE QUESTIONS

1. Match List-I with List-II and select the correct answer from the codes given below the lists:

List-I

(*a*) Napoleon Bonaparte
(*b*) Jean Jacques Rousseau
(*c*) Croce
(*d*) Madame Roland

List-II

1. 'A history is contemporary history'
2. 'Liberty what crimes are committed in thy name'
3. 'Man is born free but everywhere he is in chains.'
4. 'I am the Child of Revolution'

Codes :

	(*a*)	(*b*)	(*c*)	(*d*)
A.	1	2	3	4
B.	4	3	1	2
C.	3	4	2	1
D.	3	4	1	2

2. Abraham Lincon was elected the President of United States in:
A. 1862 B. 1860
C. 1875 D. 1855

3. Who was known as the 'Prince of Humanists'?
A. Francisco Petrarch B. Dante
C. Boccacio D. Erasmus

4. D-Day is the day when:
A. Germany declared war on Britain
B. US dropped the atom bomb on Hiroshima.
C. Allied Troops landed in Normandy
D. Germany surrendered to the allies

5. Whose teachings inspired the French Revolution?
A. Locke
B. Rousseau
C. Hegel
D. Plato

6. At a time when empires in Europe were crumbling before the might of Napoleon which one of the following Governor-Generals kept the British flag flying high in India?
A. Warren Hastings B. Lord Cornwallis
C. Lord Wellesley D. Lord Hastings

7. Which one of the following statements regarding Fascism in Italy is *not* true?
A. The Fascists came to power as a result of popular uprising
B. In 1926, all political parties except Mussolini's party were banned
C. The Fascists suppressed the Socialist movement
D. The Fascists were hostile to the Communists

8. The fall of Czar Nicholas-II is known as:
A. Bloody Sunday
B. Bolshevik Revolution
C. February Revolution
D. October Revolution

9. Industrial Revolution took place first in:
A. France B. Germany
C. United Kingdom D. Japan

10. The British Prime Minister at the outbreak of World War II was :
A. Churchill B. Baldwin
C. Attlee D. Chemberlain

11. The 'Great Depression' (1929) economic crisis was met by adopting the policy of
A. Stimulus B. Marshall Plan
C. New Deal D. Open Door

12. The slogan "No taxation without representation" was raised during the:
A. American War of Independence
B. Russian Revolution
C. French Revolution
D. Indian Freedom struggle

13. In the nineteenth century the people of Europe started moving from the villages to the cities due to the impact of :

A. Epidemics
B. War
C. Industrialisation
D. Population explosion in villages

14. The important cause of the Civil War in America was:

A. Abolition of slavery
B. Quest for freedom
C. Industrialisation
D. Rebellion by the native Americans

15. Industrial Revolution could not have come about without:

A. Merchant capitalism
B. The Enclosure Movement
C. The services of the proletariat class
D. An agricultural revolution

16. Consider the following statements :
The French Revolution came about mainly due to the :

1. Extreme poverty of the people
2. Impact of the works of great writers
3. Cruelty of the rulers
4. Impact of impulsive reaction

Which of the above statements are correct?

A. 1, 2 and 4 B. 2 and 3
C. 1, 3 and 4 D. 1, 2, 3 and 4

17. Asia's oldest and largest Buddhist monastery is situated in :

A. Tawang (Arunachal Pardesh)
B. Lhasa (Tibet)
C. Trincomallee (Sri Lanka)
D. Ulan Bator (Mongolia)

18. Who was the main architect of the Russian Revolution?

A. Karl Marx B. Lenin
C. Stalin D. Tolstoy

19. V.I. Lenin is associated with :

A. Russian Revolution of 1917
B. Chinese Revolution of 1949
C. German Revolution
D. French Revolution of 1789

20. Which one of the following statements is *not* correct?

A. Voltaire believed in Natural Religion
B. Rousseau wrote *Social Contract*
C. Montesquieu authored *The Spirit of Laws*
D. Necker believed in 'General Will'

21. 6th April, 1930 is well known in the history of India because this date is associated with..........

A. Dandi March by Mahatma Gandhi
B. Quit India Movement
C. Partition of Bengal
D. Partition of India

22. Which ruler enforced the system of 'Price Control' in India?

A. Mohammad Tughlak
B. Razia Begum
C. Alauddin Khilji
D. Sher Shah Suri

23. The concept of 'Din-e-Elahi' was founded by which king?

A. Dara Shikoh B. Akbar
C. Sher Shah Suri D. Shahjahan

24. Who are supposed to be the earliest inhabitants of India? Where did they come from?

A. Aryans from Central Asia
B. Dravidians from Mediterranean
C. Negroids from Africa
D. Bhils and the Santhals from West Asia

25. The one chief characteristic of temple architecture of the Gupta Age was :

A. Absence of dome
B. Huge size
C. Beautiful carvings
D. absence of a covered courtyard for the gathering of worshippers

26. The Rigveda consists of :

A. 1000 hymns B. 2028 hymns
C. 1028 hymns D. 1038 hymns

27. The central point in Ashoka's dharma was :

A. royalty to kings
B. peace and non-violence
C. respect to elders
D. religious tolerance

28. The social evil which was conspicuously absent during ancient India was :

A. *Sati*-System B. *Devadasi*-System
C. Polygamy D. *Purdah*-System

29. Which, among the following, can be accepted as a novelty introduced by Mughal emperors to their buildings?

A. Domes B. Minarets
C. Arches D. Attached gardens

30. The first ruler of India who defeated Muhammud of Ghur was :

A. Mularaja II of Gujarat
B. Prithviraja Chauhan of Delhi
C. Jayachand of Kannauj
D. Parmaldeva of Bundelkhand

31. What important event happened in India in 1911?

A. Bengal was partitioned
B. Non-Cooperation movement was launched
C. India's capital was shifted from Calcutta to Delhi
D. Mahatma Gandhi presided over the Congress session

32. The first phase of the Congress Party (1885-1905) was characterized by its efforts to secure:

A. limited independence
B. complete freedom
C. Indianization of services
D. constitutional reforms

33. The Muslim League demanded a separate homeland for the Indian Muslims openly for the first time at its annual session held in Lahore in the year :

A. 1931 A.D. B. 1936 A.D.
C. 1940 A.D. D. 1941 A.D.

34. Under whose governorship did the East India Company secure the Diwani Rights in Bengal, Bihar and Odisha from Emperor Shah Alam?

A. Lord Cornwallis
B. Lord William Bentinck
C. Lord Clive
D. Lord Wellesley

35. The Simon Commission was generally boycotted by the Indian political parties. What was the reason for this general non-cooperation?

A. the Commission aimed at dividing the people
B. it was an 'all white' Commission
C. it came after the Jallianwala Bagh carnage
D. it was an eye wash

36. Aligarh Muslim University was founded by :

A. Dr. Saifuddin Kitchlu
B. Mohammad Ali Jinnah
C. Sir Syed Ahmed Khan
D. Maulana Mohammad Ali

37. Ibn Batutah was an African traveller visiting India during the time of :

A. Alivardi Khan
B. Ala-ud-din Khalji
C. Iltutmish
D. Mohammad-bin-Tughlaq

38. The battle of Wandiawash was fought in :

A. 1726 B. 1760
C. 1818 D. 1857

39. The abolition of *Sati* by government regulation was at the time of :

A. Warren Hastings B. Lord Wellesley
C. Lord Bentinck D. Lord Ahmerst

40. Pick out the wrong combination :

A. Dilwara Temple : Mt. Abu
B. Pashupati Temple : Kathmandu
C. Padmanabh Temple : Bangalore
D. Minakshi Temple : Madurai

41. Match the following:

(*a*) Chanhudaro (*b*) Kalibangan
(*c*) Lothal (*d*) Surkotada

1. Alleged discovery of the skeleton of horse.
2. Bead making.
3. Traces of a dock and ship on seal.
4. Evidence of ploughing the fields.

The Correct code is :

	(*a*)	(*b*)	(*c*)	(*d*)
A.	2	4	3	1
B.	2	1	3	4
C.	1	2	3	4
D.	2	1	4	3

42. Match the Harappan settlements with the banks of rivers on which they were located :

(*a*) Harappa	1. Ravi
(*b*) Mohenjodaro	2. Indus
(*c*) Ropar	3. Sutlej
(*d*) Kalibangan	4. Ghaggar
(*e*) Lothal	5. Bhogava

Codes :

	(*a*)	(*b*)	(*c*)	(*d*)	(*e*)
A.	1	2	3	4	5
B.	1	2	3	5	4
C.	2	1	3	5	4
D.	2	1	4	3	5

43. The Goddess 'Kannagi' whose many temples were erected during the 'Sangam Age' was the goddess of :

A. Chastity B. Love
C. Prowess D. Wisdom

44. The Jain goal of life is to attain deliverance from the fetters of mudane existence, the way to which lies through three jewels. Which one of the following was not included among the 'three jewels' of Jainism?

A. Right faith B. Right action
C. Right knowledge D. Right conduct

45. The most striking feature of the Ashokan pillar is polish. Name the Ashokan pillar which is considered to be the most graceful of all Ashokan pillars.

A. Sarnath
B. Rampurva
C. Laurya-Nandangarh
D. Rummindei

46. Which are the correct statements?

1. The land grants, started in Satavahana period, paved the way for feudal developments in India.
2. Silk and spices were the Chief Indian export articles of Indo-Roman trade.
3. The Guptas issued the largest number of gold coins in ancient India.
4. The first memorial of a 'SATI' dated 510 A.D. is found at Eran in Madhya Pradesh.

A. 1 and 2 B. 1, 3, and 4
C. 1 and 4 D. 1, 2, 3 and 4

47. Who among the following patronised the 'Gandhara' (Indo-Greek style) School of Art?

A. Ashoka, the Great
B. Harsha Vardhana
C. Kanishka
D. Chandragupta Vikramaditya

48. The Sultanate of Delhi had five ruling dynasties. The dynasty having longest and shortest period were :

A. Ilbari and Khalji
B. Tughlaq and Khalji
C. Tughlaq and Sayyid
D. Ilbari and Lodis

49. Which one of the following events took place at the last during reign of Muhammad-bin-Tughlaq?

A. Introduction of token currency
B. Increase of land-revenue in Doab
C. Transfer of Capital from Delhi to Devagiri.
D. Conquest of Khurasan and Iraq

50. The most learned medieval Muslim ruler who was well versed in various branches of learning including astronomy, mathematics and medicine was :

A. Jalaluddin Khilji
B. Sikander Lodi
C. Ghiyasuddin Tughlaq
D. Muhammad-bin-Tughlaq

51. The 'Sufis' had 12 silsilas. They propounded the idea of Union with God through:

A. Love B. Rituals
C. Fasts D. Prayers

52. Match the following:

(*a*) Peshwa	1. Foreign affairs
(*b*) Panditrao	2. Audit and accounts
(*c*) Amatya	3. Providing grants to scholars
(*d*) Sumant	4. General supervision
	5. Military affairs

Select the correct code :

	(*a*)	(*b*)	(*c*)	(*d*)
A.	2	3	4	5
B.	4	1	2	3
C.	4	3	2	1
D.	3	1	4	2

53. The Regulating Act of 1773 can be regarded as the first measure to :
A. assert the right of British Parliament to legislate for India
B. separate the legislature from the executive
C. separate the judiciary from the executive
D. centralise law-making

54. What was the exact constitutional status of the Indian Republic on 26th January, 1950?
A. A Democratic Republic
B. A Sovereign, Democratic Republic
C. A Sovereign, Secular, Democratic Republic
D. A Sovereign, Socialist, Secular, Democratic Republic

55. When the British obtained the grant of Diwani of Bengal, Bihar and Odisha they acquired the right to :
A. maintain law and order in these territories
B. administer civil justice and collect revenue in these territories
C. collect revenue and establish revenue administration in these territories
D. militarily defend these territories

56. Which of the following were responsible for the growth of nationalism in India during the British rule?
1. Economic exploitation of India.
2. Impact of western education.
3. Role of the Press.
Select the correct answer using the codes given below :
Codes:
A. 1, 2 and 3 B. 1 and 2
C. 2 and 3 D. 1 and 3

57. Which one of the following nationalist leaders has been described as being radical in politics but conservative on social issues?
A. G.K. Gokhale
B. B.G. Tilak
C. Lala Lajpat Rai
D. Madan Mohan Malviya

58. Provincial Autonomy in British India was envisaged by the :
A. Act of 1909 B. Act of 1919
C. Act of 1935 D. Act of 1947

59. Dyarchy means :
A. double government
B. a government in which the centre is very powerful
C. a government based on division of power between centre and provinces
D. None of the above

60. The Indian National Congress observed 'Independence Day' for the first time on 26th January in :
A. 1920 B. 1925
C. 1930 D. 1947

61. ....is situated near the banks of Sabarmati River
A. Bhavnagar B. Aurangabad
C. Ahmedabad D. Rajkot

62. Sericulture is:
A. science of the various kinds of serum
B. artificial rearing of fish
C. art of silkworm breeding
D. study of various cultures of a community

63. The most abundant constituents of earth's crust are:
A. Igneous rocks
B. Sedimentary rocks
C. Metamorphic rocks
D. Granite

64. Indian Standard Time is based on:
A. 80°E longitude B. 82½°E longitude
C. 110°E longitude D. 25°E longitude

65. Tides in the oceans are caused by :
A. Gravitational pull of the moon on the earth's surface including sea water
B. Gravitational pull of the sun on the earth's surface only and not on the sea water
C. Gravitational pull of the moon and the sun on the earth's surface including the sea water
D. None of these

66. Nagarjunasagar Project is situated on the river:
A. Tungabhadra
B. Cauvery
C. Krishna
D. Godavari

67. The difference between the Indian Standard Time and the Greenwich Mean Time is:
A. – 3½ hours B. + 3½ hours
C. – 5½ hours D. + 5½ hours

68. Which of the following dams is not on Narmada river?
A. Indira-Sagar Project
B. Maheshwar Hydel Power Project
C. Jobat Project
D. Koyna Power Project

69. Which of the following statements is **not true** about the availability of water on the earth, the crisis for which is going to increase in the years to come?
A. About 97.5 per cent of the total volume of water available on the earth is salty
B. 80 per cent of the water available to us for use comes in bursts as monsoons
C. About 2.5 per cent of the total water available on the earth is polluted water and cannot be used for human activities
D. Possibility is that some big glaciers will melt in the coming ten-fifteen years and sea level will rise by 3-4 metres all over the earth

70. Which of the following is **not** a cash crop?
A. Jute B. Paddy
C. Cashewnut D. Sugarcane

71. Through which States does Cauvery River flow?
A. Gujarat, M.P., Tamil Nadu
B. Karnataka, Kerala, Tamil Nadu
C. Karnataka, Kerala, Andhra Pradesh
D. M.P., Maharashtra, Tamil Nadu

72. Indian Standard Time is the local time of 82½°E which passes through :
A. Guntur B. Delhi
C. Allahabad D. Kolkata

73. The 17th parallel defines the boundary between:
A. North and South Korea
B. USA and Canada
C. North and South Vietnam
D. China and Russia

74. During the period of south-west monsoon, Tamil Nadu remains dry because:
A. the winds do not reach this area
B. there are no mountains in this area
C. it lies in the rain shadow area
D. the temperature is too high to let the winds cool down

75. Which country does top in producing cocoa?
A. Cote d'Ivoire B. Brazil
C. Croatia D. Nigeria

76. The biggest reserves of thorium are in :
A. India B. China
C. The Soviet Union D. U.S.A.

77. The Girnar Hills are situated in which of the following states?
A. Gujarat B. Karnataka
C. Madhya Pradesh D. Maharashtra

78. During December 22nd the sun is vertically over:
A. Tropic of Cancer
B. Tropic of Capricorn
C. The Equator
D. None of the above

79. Photosphere is described as the :
A. Lower layer of atmosphere
B. Visible surface of the sun from which radiation emanates
C. Wavelength of solar spectrum
D. None of the above

80. Broadly, there are three layers of the earth of the crust, the mantle and the core. The crust forms what percentage of the volume of the earth?
A. 0.5% B. 2.5%
C. 7.5% D. 12.5%

81. The grassland of Argentina is known as :
A. Pampas B. Campos
C. Savanna D. None of the above

82. Different seasons are formed because :
A. Sun is moving around the earth
B. of revolution of the earth around the Sun on its orbit
C. of rotation of the earth around its axis
D. All of the above

83. Eskers and Drumlins are features formed by:
A. underground water
B. running water
C. the action of wind
D. glacial action

84. Match List-I and List-II and select the correct answer using the codes given below the Lists :

List-I *(Rivers)*	List-II *(Towns)*
(*a*) Ghaghara	1. Lucknow
(*b*) Brahmaputra	2. Hoshangabad
(*c*) Narmada	3. Ahmedabad
(*d*) Sabarmati	4. Guwahati
	5. Ayodhya

	(*a*)	(*b*)	(*c*)	(*d*)
A.	4	5	1	2
B.	5	4	2	3
C.	5	4	3	1
D.	3	5	2	1

85. Which of the statements as regards the consequences of the movement of the earth is not correct?
A. Revolution of the earth is the cause of the change of seasons.
B. Rotation of the earth is the cause of days and nights.
C. Rotation of the earth causes variation in the duration of days and nights.
D. Rotation of the earth effects the movement of winds and ocean currents.

86. The world is divided into :
A. 12 time zones
B. 20 time zones
C. 24 time zones
D. 36 time zones

87. The 'Kiel' canal links the :
A. Pacific and Atlantic Oceans
B. Mediterranean Sea and Red Sea
C. Mediterranean Sea and Black Sea
D. North Sea and Baltic Sea

88. Match the following :

List-I	List-II
(*a*) Himadri	1. Outer Himalayas
(*b*) Shivalik	2. Inner Himalayas
(*c*) Himanchal	3. Middle Himalayas
(*d*) Sahyadri	4. Western Ghats

Codes:

	(*a*)	(*b*)	(*c*)	(*d*)
A.	1	2	3	4
B.	4	2	3	1
C.	2	1	3	4
D.	1	2	3	4

89. The term 'Regur' refers to:
A. Laterite soils
B. Black Cotton soils
C. Red Soils
D. Deltaic Alluvial Soils

90. Location of sugar industry in India is shifting from north to south because of:
A. cheap labour
B. expanding regional market
C. cheap and abundant supply of power
D. high yield and high sugar content in sugarcane

91. Consider the following statements :
1. Ozone is found mostly in the Stratosphere.
2. Ozone layer lies 55-75 km above the surface of the earth.
3. Ozone absorbs ultraviolet radiation from the Sun.
4. Ozone layer has no significance for life on the earth.

Which of the above statements are correct?
A. 1 and 3 B. 2 and 4
C. 2 and 3 D. 1 and 4

92. Match List-I with List-II and select the correct answer using the codes given below the Lists :

List-I *(Crops)*	List-II *(Producer)*
(*a*) Banana	1. Brazil
(*b*) Cocoa	2. Cote d'Ivoire
(*c*) Coffee	3. India
(*d*) Tea	4. China

Codes :

	(*a*)	(*b*)	(*c*)	(*d*)
A.	2	3	1	4
B.	3	2	1	4
C.	3	2	4	1
D.	2	3	4	1

93. Darjeeling and Dharamsala would be the right places to visit if one wanted to get a clear view respectively of :
A. Kanchanjunga and Dhauladhar ranges
B. Nandadevi and Dhauladhar ranges
C. Kanchanjunga and Nandadevi ranges
D. Nandadevi and Nanga Parvat

94. Atmosphere exists because:
A. The Gravitational force of the Earth
B. Revolution of the Earth
C. Rotation of the Earth
D. Weight of the gases of atmosphere

95. Victoria lake is located in the continent:
A. Africa
B. Asia
C. North America
D. South America

96. The famous Lagoon Lake of India is :
A. Dal Lake B. Chilka Lake
C. Pulicat Lake D. Mansarover

97. Where are most of the earth's active volcanoes concentrated?
A. Indian Ocean B. Pacific Ocean
C. Aral Sea D. Atlantic Ocean

98. Through which of the following states does the river Chambal flow?
A. U.P., M.P., Rajasthan
B. M.P., Gujarat, U.P.
C. Rajasthan, M.P., Bihar
D. Gujarat, M.P., U.P.

99. Which country is called the sugar bowl of the world?
A. Cuba B. India
C. Argentina D. USA

100. The area covered by forest in India is about:
A. 46% B. 33%
C. 23% D. 21.71%

101. A closed economy is the one which :
A. does not permit emigration or immigration
B. permits emigration but no immigration
C. engages in no foreign trade
D. engages in no foreign and domestic trade or transit

102. In a developed economy the major share of employment originates in the :
A. primary sector B. tertiary sector
C. secondary sector D. any of the above

103. The Economic and Social Commission for Asia and Pacific (ESCAP) is located at :
A. Bangkok B. Kuala Lumpur
C. Manila D. Singapore

104. Commercial vehicles are not produced by which of the following companies in India?
A. TELCO B. Ashok Leyland
C. DCM Daewoo D. Birla Yamaha

105. In India, the Public Sector is most dominant in:
A. transport
B. steel production
C. commercial banking
D. organised term-lending financial institutions

106. The main argument advanced in favour of small scale and cottage industries in India is that:
A. cost of production is low
B. they require small capital investment
C. they advance the goal of equitable distribution of wealth
D. they generate a large volume of employment

107. The most serious economic problems of India are:
A. Poverty and unemployment
B. Stagnation, not poverty
C. Unemployment, not poverty
D. Underdevelopment, not poverty

108. Which of the following is not one of the three central problems of an economy?
A. What to produce
B. How to produce
C. When to produce
D. For whom to produce

109. If saving exceeds investment, the national income will:
A. fall B. rise
C. fluctuate D. remain constant

110. In which of the following industries in India are the maximum number of workers employed?

A. Sugar B. Jute

C. Textiles D. Iron and Steel

111. Terrace Cultivation is practiced mostly:

A. In urban areas

B. on slopes of mountains

C. on tops of hills

D. in undulating tracts

112. Which of the following is a Selective Credit Control method?

A. Bank Rate

B. RBI directives

C. Cash Reserve Ratio

D. Open market operations

113. Which of the following taxes is not shared by the Central Government with the States?

A. Union excise duties

B. Customs duty

C. Income tax

D. Estate duty

114. ICICI is the name of a:

A. Financial Institution

B. Chemical Industry

C. Cotton Industry

D. Chamber of Commerce and Industry

115. Structural Unemployment arises due to

A. Deflationary conditions

B. Heavy industry bias

C. Shortage of raw material

D. Inadequate productive capacity

116. Which Commission replaced the Planning Commission in 2015?

A. NIYAM Aayog

B. NAGRIK Aayog

C. NITI Aayog

D. Jan Aayog

117. The largest public sector bank in India is:

A. Central Bank of India

B. Punjab National Bank

C. State Bank of India

D. Indian Overseas Bank

118. Which of the following statements best explains the term contraband goods?

A. Goods produced only for exports

B. Goods produced in joint sector only

C. Goods for the trading of which licence is not required

D. Goods that are forbidden, from export, import or even possession, by law

119. Price in the market is fixed by:

A. Stock exchange rates

B. The demand and supply ruling in the market at a particular time

C. The Finance Minister

D. None of the above

120. Devaluation of currency helps to promote:

A. National Income

B. Savings

C. Imports at lower cost

D. Exports

121. Balanced economic growth can be achieved only if:

A. All the sectors of economy grow at the same rate

B. Population growth is arrested

C. All the inter dependent sectors grow in harmony

D. Basic and heavy industries are assigned highest priority

122. P.V. Sindhu is associated with which of the following sports?

A. Badminton

B. Weightlifting

C. Swimming

D. Tennis

123. 'MODVAT' stands for:

A. Modified Value Added Tax

B. Deduction of cost of inputs from the value of output

C. Reduction in import duties

D. Imposition of tax on professions

124. Who among the following is the first to receive 'Dada Saheb Phalke' award?

A. Shivaji Ganeson B. Devika Rani

C. Dr. Raj Kumar D. None of the above

125. The term 'devaluation' means:
A. Reducing the value of a currency in terms of another currency
B. Increasing the value of a currency
C. Revising the value of a currency
D. None of the above

126. Per capita net availability of pulses has shown a tendency of:
A. Increase over time
B. Decrease over time
C. Constant over time
D. First increase then decrease

127. National Income is the same as:
A. Net national product at market price
B. Net domestic product at market price
C. Net national product at factor cost
D. Net domestic product at factor cost

128. Which one of the following is not an example of indirect tax?
A. Sales tax B. Excise duty
C. Customs duty D. Expenditure tax

129. The major aim of devaluation is to:
A. encourage imports
B. encourage exports
C. encourage both exports and imports
D. discourage both exports and imports

130. Structural unemployment arises due to:
A. deflationary conditions
B. heavy industry bias
C. shortage of raw materials
D. inadequate productive capacity

131. When was the Family Planning Programme officially started in India?
A. 1950 B. 1952
C. 1956 D. 1962

132. When was the Reserve Bank of India nationalised?
A. 1947 B. 1949
C. 1950 D. 1951

133. Which of the following is *not* a feature of the Indian economy?
A. High rate of population growth
B. Disguised unemployment
C. Lowest rate of adult literacy
D. High rate of exports

134. The 'Relative Deprivation' approach for measuring poverty has been adopted by:
A. developing countries
B. developed countries
C. under-developed countries
D. None of the above

135. One of the main factors that led to rapid expansion of Indian exports is:
A. Imposition of import duties
B. Liberalisation of the economy
C. Recession in other countries
D. Diversification of exports

136. Sustainable economic development means an increase in the rate of growth of real:
A. total and per capita product
B. total and per capita product and level of literacy rate
C. total and per capita product and life expectancy at birth
D. total and per capita product, taking into account the cost of degradation of the quality of environment in this process

137. Functional unemployment occurs when:
A. unemployed have no qualification for job
B. people frequently change their job
C. people were thrown out from job due to recession
D. None of these

138. Which among the following does **not** have a 'free trade zone'?
A. Kandla B. Mumbai
C. Visakhapatnam D. Thiruvanantpuram

139. Sun Belt of USA is important for which one of the following industries?
A. Cotton textile
B. Petrochemicals
C. Hi-tech electronics
D. Food Processing

140. Commercial banking system in India is
A. unit banking B. branch banking
C. mixed banking D. None of the above

141. Who gives recognition to political parties in India?
A. Parliament

B. President
C. Supreme Court
D. Election Commission

142. The Quorum of the Legislative Council is :
A. one-fourth of its total membership
B. one-third of its membership
C. one-tenth of its membership
D. 25

143. The Indian Constitution is:
A. federal
B. unitary
C. a happy mixture of the federal and unitary
D. federal in normal times and unitary in times of emergency

144. Universal adult franchise implies a right to vote to all:
A. adult residents of the State
B. adult male citizens of the State
C. residents of the State
D. adult citizens of the State

145. When a resolution prefering a charge against the President has been passed by a specified majority in the House, it is sent to the other House for investigation. If, as a result of such an investigation, a resolution is passed through a specified majority by the other House, declaring that the charge has been sustained, the President shall leave his office. The specified special majority must not be less than :
A. two-third of the members present and voting
B. one-third of the members present and voting
C. three-fourth of the members present and voting and two-third of the total membership
D. two-third of the total membership

146. Which one of the following judicial powers of the President of India has been *wrongly* listed?
A. he appoints the Chief Justice and other judges of the Supreme Court
B. he can remove the judges of the Supreme Court on grounds of misconduct
C. he can consult the Supreme Court on any question of law or fact which is of public importance
D. he can grant pardon, reprieves and respites to persons punished under Union Law

147. The Vice-president of India can be removed from his office before the expiry of his term if :
A. the Rajya Sabha passes a resolution by a majority of its members and the Lok Sabha agrees with the resolution
B. if the Supreme Court of India recommends his removal
C. the President so desires
D. None of the above

148. The Chief Justice of a High Court in India is appointed by the :
A. Governor of the State
B. Prime Minister of India
C. Chief Justice of the Supreme Court
D. President of India

149. Which of the following statements is constitutionally not true about the passing of the Union Budgets, Railway Budgets and Finance Bill in India?
1. Under the law, Finance Bill should be adopted by both the Houses of the Parliament within 45 days of its introduction.
2. If the Finance Bill is not adopted within specified period, the government loses its authority to levy the taxes proposed in the budgets.
3. In the absence of full budget, a vote-on-account gives the power to the government to spend.
4. Government cannot raise revenues without a proper approval of the Finance Bill

A. Only 2   B. Only 3
C. Only 4   D. Only 1, 2 and 3

150. Normally, on whose advice the President's Rule is imposed in a State?
A. Chief Minister
B. Legislative Assembly
C. Governor
D. Chief Justice of High Court

151. Which Article of the Indian Constitution deals with Amendment procedure?
A. Article 368 B. Article 358
C. Article 367 D. All of these

152. Government is the agency through which the will of :
A. the state is expressed
B. the people is expressed
C. the head of the state is expressed
D. the majority is expressed

153. In a unitary system of government :
A. The centre is all powerful
B. The centre is weaker than the states
C. The centre and states stand at par
D. The states and centre are supreme in their respective spheres

154. In Cabinet System of Government the real executive authority rests with :
A. The Council of Ministers
B. The Prime Minister
C. The Constitution
D. The Parliament

155. The Head of the State under a parliamentary government:
A. is an elected representative
B. is a hereditary person
C. is a nominated person
D. may be any one of the above

156. In the event of a ministerial proposal being defeated on the floor of the legislature, under the parliamentary system :
A. the government waits for a general no-confidence motion
B. the minister concerned is taken to task by the Prime Minister
C. the minister is forced to resign
D. the whole Council of Ministers resign

157. The "due process of law" is an essential characteristic of the judicial system of:
A. UK B. France
C. USA D. India

158. Under the Constitution it is :
A. obligatory for the President to accept the advice of the Council of Ministers but is not obliged to follow it
B. obligatory for the President to accept the advice of the Council of Ministers
C. not obligatory for the President to seek or accept the advice of the Council of Ministers
D. obligatory for the President to seek the advice of the Council of Ministers if his own party is in power

159. Which one of the following statements is correct?
A. the Presiding Officer of Rajya Sabha is elected every year
B. the Presiding Officer of Rajya Sabha is elected for a term of two years at a time
C. the Presiding Officer of Rajya Sabha is elected for a term of six years
D. the Vice-President of India is the ex-officio Presiding Officer of Rajya Sabha

160. The introduction of "no confidence" motion in the Lok Sabha requires the support of at least:
A. 50 members B. 70 members
C. 60 members D. 80 members

161. The High Court comes under :
A. State List B. Union List
C. Concurrent List D. None of the above

162. Which one of the following has been wrongly listed as a Fundamental Duty of the Indian citizens?
A. to develop scientific temper, humanism and spirit of inquiry and reform
B. to work for raising the prestige of the country in the international sphere
C. to protect and improve the natural environment
D. to strive towards excellence in all spheres of individual and collective activity

163. Which one of the following is not a Fundamental Duty as outlined in Article 51A of the Constitution?
A. to abide by the Constitution and respect its ideals
B. to defend the country and render national service when called upon to do so

C. to work for the moral upliftment of the weaker sections of society
D. to preserve the rich heritage

164. The main characteristics of the Directive Principles of State Policy given in the Indian Constitution are :
A. not enforceable by any court
B. fundamental in the governance of the country
C. 'Like instruments, instructions, political manifesto and a code of moral precepts which have to guide governors of the country'
D. no law can be passed, which is opposed to these principles

165. Of the following which are true?
A. In a State, the Legislative Council is dominant with regard to non-financial bills and the Legislative Assembly with regard to financial (money) bills
B. Vidhan Parishad can virtually block legisla-tion even if the same is passed by the Vidhan Sabha
C. In case of a tie between the two Houses, the Governor is duty-bound to call a joint session of the two Houses to have the issue settled on a majority verdict
D. If a Bill is twice approved by the Vidhan Sabha, it becomes law even if rejected by the Vidhan Parishad

166. Which one of the following types of emergency can be declared by the President?
A. Emergency due to threat of war and external aggresion
B. Emergency due to break-down of constitu-tional machinery in a State
C. Financial emergency on account of threat to the financial credit of India
D. all the three emergencies

167. The chairman of which of the following parliamentary committees is invariably from the members of ruling party?
A. Committee on public undertakings
B. Public accounts committee
C. Estimates committee
D. Committee on delegated legislation

168. Which of the following is not a formally prescribed device available to the members of parliament?
A. Question hour
B. Zero hour
C. Half-an-hour discussion
D. Short duration discussion

169. Which of the following is not a tool of executive control over public administration?
A. Power of appointment and removal
B. Line agencies
C. Appeal to public opinion
D. Civil services code

170. If the Speaker of the State Legislative Assembly decides to resign, he should submit his resignation to the:
A. Judges of the High Court
B. Deputy Speaker
C. Chief Minister
D. Finance Minister

171. Who was the first Home Minister of Independent India?
A. Rajendra Prasad
B. Jawahar Lal Nehru
C. B.R. Ambedkar
D. Sardar Vallabh Bhai Patel

172. India is a Federal State because of:
A. dual judiciary
B. dual citizenship prevalent here
C. share of power between the Centre and the States
D. rigid Constitution

173. Residuary Subjects are those subjects which are:
A. contained in the State list
B. contained in the Union list
C. contained in the Concurrent list
D. not covered by any of the three lists

174. Which of the following writs can be issued, by the Supreme Court, to enforce Fundamental Rights?
A. Writ of Habeas Corpus
B. Writ of Mandamus
C. Writ of Quo Warranto
D. All of these

175. When the offices of both the President and the Vice-President of India are vacant, who will discharge their functions?
A. Prime Minister
B. Home Minister
C. Chief Justice of India
D. The Speaker

176. The Supreme Court tenders advice to the President of India on a matter of law or fact:
A. on its own
B. only when such advice is sought
C. only if the matter relates to some basic issue
D. only if the issue poses a threat to the unity and integrity of the country

177. Six months shall **not** intervene between two sessions of the Indian Parliament because :
A. it is the customary practice
B. it is the British convention followed in India
C. it is an obligation under the Constitution of India
D. None of the above

178. The States of the Indian Union can be recognised or their boundaries altered by:
A. the Union Parliament by a simple majority in the ordinary process of legislation
B. two-thirds majority of both the Houses of Parliament
C. two-thirds majority of both the Houses of Parliament and the consent of the legislatures of concerned States
D. an executive order of the Union government with the consent of the concerned State governments

179. The Basic Feature theory of the Constitution of India was propounded by the Supreme Court in the case of :
A. Minerva Mills Vs. Union of India
B. Golaknath Vs. State of Punjab
C. Maneka Gandhi Vs. Union of India
D. Keshavananda Vs. State of Kerala

180. Which one of the following writs is issued by a court in case of illegal detention of a person?
A. Habeas corpus B. Mandamus
C. Certiorari D. Quo-warranto

181. Name the instrument with the help of which a sailor in a submarine can see the objects on the surface of the sea.
A. Telescope B. Periscope
C. Gycroscope D. Stereoscope

182. 'HEMOPHILLIA' is the disease of ....
A. liver B. blood
C. brain D. bones

183. Vitamin A is abundantly found in ....
A. Brinjal B. Tomato
C. Carrot D. Cabbage

184. .... is not soluble in water.
A. Vitamin A B. Vitamin B
C. Vitamin C D. None of these

185. The blood vessels with the smallest diameter are called ....
A. capillaries B. arterioles
C. venules D. lymphatics

186. Out of the following .... has the greatest elasticity.
A. steel B. rubber
C. aluminium D. annealed copper

187. Cooking gas is a mixture of which of the following two gases?
A. Carbon Dioxide and Oxygen
B. Butane and Propane
C. Carbon Monoxide and Carbon Dioxide
D. Methane and Ethylene

188. The substance most commonly used as a food preservative is:
A. sodium carbonate B. tartaric acid
C. acetic acid D. benzoic acid

189. Normally, the substances that fight against diseases in human systems are known as:
A. dioxyribonucleic acids
B. carbohydrates
C. enzymes
D. antibodies

190. The SI unit of temperature is ....
A. Kelvin B. Celsius
C. Fahrenheit D. None of the above

191. One of the common fungal diseases of man is :
A. plague B. ringworm
C. cholera D. typhoid

192. A clear sky is blue because:
A. red light is scattered more than blue
B. ultraviolet light has been absorbed
C. blue light is scattered more than red
D. blue light has been absorbed

193. Jenner introduced the method of making people immune to :
A. small pox B. rabies
C. cholera D. polio

194. The largest cell in the human body is :
A. Nerve cell B. Live cell
C. Muscle cell D. Kidney cell

195. What is the device that steps up or steps down the voltage?
A. Dynamo B. Conductor
C. Inductor D. Transformer

196. The protein deficiency disease is known as :
A. Kwashiorker B. Cirrhosis
C. Eczema D. Clycoses

197. Iron deficiency causes :
A. rickets B. anaemia
C. cirrhosis D. goitre

198. Blood group of an individual is controlled by :
A. Haemoglobin B. Shape of RBC
C. Shape of WBC D. Genes

199. In a normal man the amount of blood pumped out by the heart per minute is about :
A. 1 litre B. 3 litres
C. 4 litres D. 5 litres

200. Red/green colour blindness in man is known as :
A. Protanopia
B. Deutetanopia
C. Both A and B above
D. Marfan's syndrome

201. The blue colour of the water in the sea is due to :
A. Reflection of the blue light by the impurities in sea water
B. Reflection of the blue sky by sea water and scattering of blue light by water molecules
C. Absorption of other colours by water molecules
D. None of the above

202. The image formed on the retina of the eye is:
A. upright and real
B. larger than the object
C. small and inverted
D. enlarged and real

203. Unit of loudness of sound is:
A. bel B. decibel
C. phon D. none of these

204. Oil rises up the wick in a lamp :
A. because oil is volatile
B. due to the capillary action phenomenon
C. due to the surface tension phenomenon
D. because oil is very light

205. The 'stones' formed in human kidney consist mostly of :
A. calcium oxalate
B. sodium acetate
C. magnesium sulphate
D. calcium

206. We hear the sound later, while the light is seen earlier:
A. because light's speed is more than that of sound
B. because lights travel in a straight direction while sound in a zigzag direction
C. because sound's frequency is lower than light
D. All of the above

207. Which part of an eye is transplanted?
A. Cornea B. Retina
C. Iris D. Sciera

208. The Universal donor group of blood is:
A. O B. A
C. B D. AB

209. The green colour of the leaf is due to :
A. Presence of Chloroplast
B. Presence of Chromium
C. Presence of Nicoplast
D. Presence of excess of oxygen

210. Voice of a child is more shrill than that of an elderly person because:
A. the pitch of the child's voice is higher than that of the person
B. the pitch is lower
C. the child is more energetic
D. None of the above

ANSWERS

1	2	3	4	5	6	7	8	9	10
B	C	D	C	B	C	A	C	C	D
11	12	13	14	15	16	17	18	19	20
C	A	C	A	A	D	A	B	A	D
21	22	23	24	25	26	27	28	29	30
A	C	B	C	D	C	B	D	D	B
31	32	33	34	35	36	37	38	39	40
C	D	C	C	B	C	D	B	C	C
41	42	43	44	45	46	47	48	49	50
A	A	A	B	C	D	C	B	B	D
51	52	53	54	55	56	57	58	59	60
A	C	A	B	B	A	B	C	A	C
61	62	63	64	65	66	67	68	69	70
C	C	B	B	C	C	D	D	D	B
71	72	73	74	75	76	77	78	79	80
B	C	C	C	A	A	A	B	B	A
81	82	83	84	85	86	87	88	89	90
A	B	D	B	C	C	D	C	B	D
91	92	93	94	95	96	97	98	99	100
A	B	A	A	A	B	B	A	A	D
101	102	103	104	105	106	107	108	109	110
C	B	A	D	D	D	A	C	D	C
111	112	113	114	115	116	117	118	119	120
B	B	B	A	D	C	C	D	B	D
121	122	123	124	125	126	127	128	129	130
C	A	A	B	A	D	C	D	B	D
131	132	133	134	135	136	137	138	139	140
B	B	D	A	B	D	B	D	D	C
141	142	143	144	145	146	147	148	149	150
D	C	D	D	D	B	A	D	C	C
151	152	153	154	155	156	157	158	159	160
A	B	A	A	A	D	C	B	D	A
161	162	163	164	165	166	167	168	169	170
B	B	C	B	D	D	C	B	B	B
171	172	173	174	175	176	177	178	179	180
D	C	D	D	C	B	C	A	D	A
181	182	183	184	185	186	187	188	189	190
B	B	C	A	A	A	B	D	D	A
191	192	193	194	195	196	197	198	199	200
B	C	A	A	D	A	B	D	D	A
201	202	203	204	205	206	207	208	209	210
B	B	B	B	A	A	A	A	A	A

English

1 Spelling Errors

The most common errors in English are of spellings of words. Even the most learned men are sometimes confused about the correct spellings of some words. One must keep and use a dictionary religiously. Never ignore and let pass a new word casually.

A number of question to test your knowledge of spellings are compiled here. Try to solve as many as you can.

Multiple Choice Questions

Directions: *Find the correctly spelt word out of the four options in each question.*

1. A. Accompalish B. Ackmplesh C. Acomplush D. Accomplish

2. A. Acommodation B. Acomodation C. Accomodation D. Accommodation

3. A. Astonished B. Astronished C. Astoneshed D. Asstonished

4. A. Benefeted B. Benefitted C. Benifited D. Benefited

5. A. Belligerent B. Beligirent C. Belligarant D. Belligerrent

6. A. Chancelery B. Chancellery C. Chancellary D. Chancelary

7. A. Discriminate B. Discremineta C. Discrimenate D. Discriminat

8. A. Damage B. Dammage C. Damaige D. Dammege

9. A. Efficiant B. Effecient C. Efficient D. Eficient

10. A. Extravagant B. Extreragent C. Extreregant D. Extravegent

11. A. Efflorascence B. Eflorescene C. Effllorescence D. Efflorescence

12. A. Equinimity B. Equanimmity C. Equannimity D. Equanimity

13. A. Farmament B. Farmement C. Fermament D. Fremament

14. A. Grieff B. Grief C. Grieef D. Grrief

15. A. Guarantee B. Garuntee C. Guaruntee D. Gaurantee

16. A. Hypocritical B. Hypocretical C. Hypocriticel D. Hypocirticel

17. A. Humurous B. Humorous C. Humoreus D. Humorrous

18. A. Itenerary B. Itinarery C. Itinarary D. Itinerary

19. A. Indipenseble B. Indispansible C. Indispensable D. Indipensable

20. A. Imprecticability B. Impracticebility
C. Impracticibility D. Impracticability

21. A. Incradulous B. Incredulous
C. Incridulous D. Incredalous

22. A. Juddicious B. Judiceous
C. Judicious D. Judiceus

23. A. Kleptomonia B. Kleptemonia
C. Kleptomania D. Klaptomania

24. A. Lackdaisical B. Lackadaisical
C. Lckadaisicle D. Lackadisical

25. A. Licentious B. Licontious
C. Licenttious D. Licientious

26. A. Meddicine B. Medicine
C. Medicene D. Medicinne

27. A. Meritricious B. Merefrecious
C. Meretricious D. Merritricious

28. A. Missunderstood B. Miesunderstood
C. Misunderstood D. Misunderstod

29. A. Occurad B. Occurred
C. Ocurred D. Occured

30. A. Osttentatious B. Ostentetious
C. Ostentatious D. Ostenttatious

31. A. Obnosious B. Obnoxeous
C. Obnoxious D. Obnoseous

32. A. Omenous B. Ominous
C. Ommineous D. Omineous

33. A. Pecification B. Pacification
C. Pecifacation D. Pecefication

34. A. Prograssive B. Progressive
C. Progresive D. Prograsive

35. A. Pasiveness B. Passiveness
C. Passeveniss D. Passivines

36. A. Polyendry B. Poliendry
C. Pollyendry D. Polyandry

37. A. Puerille B. Puerrile
C. Puerile D. Purrile

38. A. Pesanger B. Passenger
C. Pessenger D. Pasanger

39. A. Querrelsome B. Quarrelsame
C. Quarrelsome D. Querralsome

40. A. Rigourous B. Rigerous
C. Rigorous D. Regerous

41. A. Survellance B. Surveilance
C. Surveillance D. Survaillance

42. A. Schedule B. Schdule
C. Schedale D. Schedeule

43. A. Sepalchrle B. Sepalchral
C. Sepulchrle D. Sepulchral

44. A. Sympathetic B. Smypathetic
C. Sympothetic D. Sympethetic

45. A. Sincerely B. Sencerely
C. Sincerelly D. Sincerrely

46. A. Satellite B. Sattellite
C. Satelite D. Sattelite

47. A. Teracherous B. Treacherous
C. Treacheraus D. Treachereans

48. A. Uncivilized B. Uncevilized
C. Uncivillized D. Uncevelized

49. A. Vainglorious B. Vaniglorious
C. Vaniglerious D. Vaingloreus

50. A. Vulnarable B. Valnerable
C. Velnerable D. Vulnerable

ANSWERS

1	2	3	4	5	6	7	8	9	10
D	D	A	B	A	C	A	A	C	A
11	**12**	**13**	**14**	**15**	**16**	**17**	**18**	**19**	**20**
D	D	C	B	A	A	B	D	C	D
21	**22**	**23**	**24**	**25**	**26**	**27**	**28**	**29**	**30**
B	C	C	B	A	B	C	C	B	C
31	**32**	**33**	**34**	**35**	**36**	**37**	**38**	**39**	**40**
C	B	B	B	B	D	C	B	C	C
41	**42**	**43**	**44**	**45**	**46**	**47**	**48**	**49**	**50**
C	A	D	A	A	A	B	A	A	D

2 Spotting Errors

The most common errors in English are of spellings, grammar and usage of words. By regular practice, the errors can be easily spotted and minimised.

Common Errors with Nouns and Noun-Phrases

Incorrect	Correct
1. I have bought new *furnitures.*	I have bought new *furniture.*
2. The wages of sin *are* death.	The wages of sin *is* death.
3. She told these *news* to her mother.	She told her mother this *news.*
4. He took *troubles* to do his work.	He took *trouble* (or pains) over his work.
5. The *cattles* were grazing.	The *cattle* were grazing.
6. He showered *many abuses* on me.	He showered *much abuse* on me.
7. I spent the holidays with my *family members.*	I spent the holidays with my *family.*
8. There is no *place* in this compartment.	There is no *room* in this compartment.
9. Write this new *poetry* in your *copy.*	Write this new *poem* in your *note-book.*
10. He took *insult* at this.	He took *offence* at this.
11. Put your *sign* here.	Put your *signatures* here.
12. She is my *cousin sister.*	She is my *cousin.*
13. *Sunil's* my *neighbour's* house was burgled.	*Sunil* my *neighbour's* house was burgled.
14. I lost a *ten-rupees* note.	I lost *a ten-rupee* note.
15. Road closed for *repair.*	Road closed for *repairs.*
16. His house is out of *repairs.*	His house is out of *repair.*
17. What is the *reason* of an earthquake?	What is the *cause* of an earthquake?
18. This building is made of *stones.*	This building is made of *stone.*
19. I disapprove of *these kinds* of games.	I disapprove of *this kind* of games.
20. Veena's and Sheela's father is ill.	Veena and Sheela's father is ill.
21. His *son-in-laws* are doctors.	His *sons-in-law* are doctors.
22. *Alms* is given to the *poor.*	*Alms* are given to the poor.
23. He always keeps his words.	He always keeps his *word.*
24. I carried the *luggages.*	I carried the *luggage.*
25. *Two-third* of the work is left.	*Two-thirds* of the work is left.

Common Errors with Pronouns

Incorrect	Correct
1. Both did not go.	Neither went.
2. We all did not go.	None of us went.
3. Each of these boys play.	Each of these boys plays.
4. Whoever does best he will get a prize.	Whoever does best will get a prize.
5. One should not waste his time.	A man should not waste his time.
6. I and she are sisters.	She and I are sisters.
7. He is wiser than me.	He is wiser than I.
8. Between you and I, Anil is not to be trusted.	Between you and me, Anil is not to be trusted.
9. Nobody was there but I.	Nobody was there but me.
10. Who is there ? It is me.	Who is there ? It is I.
11. Only he and me can use this card.	Only he and I can use this card.
12. Let you and I go now.	Let you and me go now.
13. Everyone got one's pay.	Everyone got his pay.
14. Everyone is frightened when they see a tiger.	Everyone is frightened when he sees a tiger.
15. These two friends are fond of one another.	These two friends are fond of each other.
16. I did not like him coming at that hour.	I did not like his coming at that hour.
17. Who do you think I met?	Whom do you think I met?
18. You should avail this opportunity.	You should avail yourself this opportunity.
19. When you have read these books, please return the same to me.	When you have read the books, please return them to me.
20. They that are humble need fear no fall.	Those that are humble need fear no fall.

Common Errors with Adjectives

Incorrect	Correct
1. These all oranges are good.	All these oranges are good.
2. He held the book in the both hands.	He held the book in both hands.
3. Both men have not come.	Neither man has come.
4. That man should do some or other work.	That man should do some work or other.
5. He is elder than I.	He is older than I.
6. Shakespeare is greater than any other poets.	Shakespeare is greater than any other poet.
7. He is a coward man.	He is a cowardly man.
8. Many villagers cannot write his own name.	Many villagers cannot write their own name.
9. Each of us loves our home.	Each of us loves his home.
10. Much efforts bring their reward.	Much effort brings its reward.
11. He found hundred rupees.	He found a hundred rupees.
12. He had leave of four days.	He had four days leave.

Incorrect	Correct
13. This is a worth seeing sight.	This is a sight worth seeing.
14. He will spend his future life here.	He will spend the rest of his life here.
15. There is a best teacher in that class.	There is a very good teacher in that class.
16. Of the two plans this is the best.	Of the two plans this is the better.
17. He is becoming strong every day.	He is becoming stronger every day.
18. He is worst than I.	He is worse than I.
19. Jaipur is hot than Delhi.	Jaipur is hotter than Delhi.
20. In our library the number of books is less.	In our library the number of books is small.

Common Errors with Verbs

Incorrect	Correct
1. He asked had we taken our luggage.	He asked if we had taken our luggage.
2. She asked what are you doing.	She asked what we were doing.
3. Rama asked to Anil why he is angry.	Rama asked Anil why he was angry.
4. He does not care for his money.	He does not take care of his money.
5. He does not care for his work.	He takes no care over his work.
6. No one cared for him after his mother died.	No one took care of him after his mother died.
7. He got angry before I said a word.	He got angry before I had said a word.
8. I met a man who was my tutor 20 years ago.	I met a man who had been my tutor twenty years ago.
9. I had been for walking yesterday.	I went for a walk yesterday.
10. If I shall do this I shall be wrong.	If I do this I shall be wrong.
11. I have left trekking.	I have given up trekking.
12. I came to know as to how he did this.	I learnt how he did this.
13. I came to know why he was sad.	I found out why he was sad.
14. He knows to swim.	He knows how to swim.
15. The criminal's head was cut.	The criminal's head was cut off.
16. I said to him to go.	I told him to go.
17. I told the teacher to excuse me.	I asked the teacher to excuse me.
18. He is troubling me.	He is giving me trouble.
19. I have got a hurt on my leg.	I have hurt my leg.
20. She gave a speech.	She made a speech.

Common Errors in Subject-Verb Agreement

Incorrect	Correct
1. The owners of this factory *is* very rich.	The owners of this factory *are* very rich.
2. The pleasures of nature that one can experience at Shimla *is* beyond description.	The pleasures of nature that one can experience at Shimla *are* beyond description.

Incorrect	Correct
3. There *is* no street lights in our colony.	There *are* no street lights in our colony.
4. He and I *am* entrusted with the job.	He and I *are* entrusted with the job.
5. Rice and curry *are* his favourite dish.	Rice and curry *is* his favourite dish.
6. The honour and glory of our country *are* at stake.	The honour and glory of our country *is* at stake.
7. Time and tide *waits* for none.	Time and tide *wait* for none.
8. All the passengers with the driver *was* killed.	All the passengers, with the driver, *were* killed.
9. The teacher, with her students, *were* going out.	The teacher, with her students, *was* going out.
10. I as well as they *am* tired.	I as well as they *are* tired.
11. Not only the soldiers but their captain also *were* captured.	Not only the soldiers but their captain also *was* captured.
12. Neither you nor I *were* selected.	Neither you nor I *was* selected.
13. Either of these two applicants *are* fit for the job but neither want to accept it.	Either of these two applicants *is* fit for the job but neither wants to accept it.
14. One of these students are sure to stand first.	One of these students *is* sure to stand first.
15. Everyone of these workers want a raise.	Everyone of these workers wants a raise.
16. None of these letters has been answered so far.	None of these letters *have* been answered so far.
17. None of the girls were present at the party.	None of the girls *was* present at the party.
18. Many a battle were fought on Indian soil.	Many a battle *was* fought on Indian soil.
19. A lot of work remain to be done.	A lot of work *remains* to be done.
20. The majority of these girls likes music.	The majority of these girls *like* music.

Common Errors in the Use of Modals/Auxiliary Verbs

Incorrect	Correct
1. When I shall see him I shall tell him this.	When I *see* him, I shall tell him this.
2. If I should do wrong, he would punish me.	If I *did* wrong, he would punish me.
3. Until he will have confessed his fault, he will be kept in prison.	Until he *has* confessed his fault, he will be kept in prison.
4. She will obey me.	She *shall* obey me.
5. You would work hard.	You *should* work hard.
6. You shall find him in the garden.	You *will* find him in the garden.
7. He must have died of exposure, but we cannot be certain.	He *might* have died of exposure, but we cannot be certain.
8. You might not show disrespect to your elders.	You *must* not show disrespect to your elders.
9. You may take exercise in order to maintain good health.	You *must* take exercise in order to maintain good health.
10. He must be a crook for all we know.	He *may* be a crook for all we know.

Common Errors in the Use of Adverbs

Incorrect	Correct
1. He is very much angry.	He is *very* angry.
2. She was very good enough to help me.	She was *good enough* to help me.
3. She runs much fast.	She runs *very* fast.
4. She runs very faster than Seema.	She runs *much* faster than Seema.
5. It is bitter cold today.	It is *bitterly* cold today.
6. He is a much learned man.	He is a very learned man.
7. She is thinking very hardly.	She is thinking very hard.
8. To tell in brief the film was boring.	*In short* the film was boring.
9. He told the story in details.	He told the story *in detail.*
10. I did it anyhow.	I *managed to do* it somehow.
11. Aeroplanes reach Europe soon.	Aeroplanes reach Europe quickly.
12. Before long there were dinosaurs on the earth.	*Long ago,* there were dinosaurs on the earth.
13. This book is too interesting.	This book is *very* interesting.
14. He lives miserly.	He lives in *a miserly* way.
15. Just I had gone when she came.	I had just gone when she came.
16. He sings good.	He sings *well.*
17. He sings good than I.	He sings *better* than I.
18. Really speaking it is cold.	*As a matter of fact* it is cold.
19. He is enough tall to reach the ceiling.	He is *tall enough* to reach the ceiling.
20. He went directly to his college.	He went *direct* to his college.

Common Errors in the Use of Conjunctions

Incorrect	Correct
1. As he is fat so he runs slowly.	As he is fat *he* runs slowly.
2. If he is fat then he will run slowly.	If he is fat, he will run slowly.
3. Though he is fat still he runs fast.	Though he is fat, *he runs* fast.
4. *As* I pulled the trigger at the sametime he shook my arm.	As I pulled the trigger, he shook my arm.
5. No sooner I had spoken than he left.	No sooner *had* I spoken than he left.
6. Not only he will go, but also he will stay there.	Not only *will he* go, but he *will also* stay there.
7. Neither he comes nor he writes.	Neither *does he* come nor *does he* write.
8. Scarcely he entered the room than the telephone rang.	Scarcely *had* he entered the room *when the* telephone rang.
9. Hardly she had left the house than it began to rain.	Hardly *had she* left the house *when* it began to rain.
10. He is the fastest runner and he comes last.	He is the fastest runner *but* he comes last.
11. She is as innocent as if she looks.	She is as innocent as she looks.
12. Until he does not try he must be punished.	He must be punished unless he tries.
13. I want to know as to why you are late.	I want to know why you are late.

Incorrect	Correct
14. I am fond of Chinese food as for example sweet and sour prawns.	I am fond of Chinese food, for example, sweet and sour prawns.
15. He was angry therefore I ran away.	He was angry so I ran away.
16. I was trying to work, at that time he was disturbing me.	While I was trying to work, he was disturbing me.
17. Supposing if he is late, what will happen?	Supposing he is late (or if he is late) what will happen?
18. He asked me that why I was late.	He asked me why I was late.
19. Let us catch a taxi lest we should not get late.	Let us catch a taxi lest we should get late.
20. She dresses herself like the teacher does.	She dresses herself as the teacher does.
21. Wait while I come.	Wait *until* (or *till*) I come.
22. Until, there is corruption in India, there can be little progress.	*As long* as there is corruption in India there can be little progress.
23. I have never told a lie nor cheated anybody.	I have never told a lie *nor have I* cheated anybody.
24. Both Mohan as well as Arun are responsible for this action.	Both Mohan *and* Arun are responsible for this action.
25. Hindus and Muslims both are to blame for the riots.	*Both Hindus* and Muslims are to blame for the riots.

Common Errors in the Use of Prepositions

Incorrect	Correct
1. I will not listen him.	I will not listen *to* him.
2. Copy this word by word.	Copy this word *for* word.
3. He enquired from her where she lived.	He enquired *of* her where she lived.
4. Sign here with ink.	Sign here *in* ink.
5. Has she come in train or by foot?	Has she come *by* train or *on* foot?
6. She said this at his face.	She said this *to* his face.
7. Open the book on page one.	Open the book *at* page one.
8. I was invited for lunch.	I was *invited to* lunch.
9. I am ill since three months.	I have been *ill for* three months.
10. This paper is inferior than that.	This paper is inferior *to* that.
11. This resembles to that.	This *resembles* that.
12. My brother is superior than you in strength.	My brother is superior *to* you in strength.
13. He wrote me.	He wrote *to* me.
14. I shall explain them this.	I shall explain this *to* them.
15. Send this letter on my address.	Send this letter *to* my address.
16. He suggested me this.	He suggested this *to* me.
17. He goes *on his* work.	He goes *to his* work.
18. He *reached to* Nagpur.	He *reached* Nagpur.
19. He told *to me* to go.	He told *me* to go.
20. The term begins *from* July 1st.	The term begins *on* July 1st.

Miscellaneous Errors

Incorrect	Correct
1. Many *homes* are lying vacant.	Many *houses* are lying vacant.
2. It is cool in the *shadow* of the tree.	It is cool in the *shade* of the tree.
3. She *keeps* good health.	She *enjoys* good health.
4. My leg is *paining.*	*I am feeling pain* in my leg.
5. *See* this word in the dictionary.	*Look up* this word in the dictionary.
6. The train will arrive *just now.*	The train will arrive *shortly.*
7. They are *pulling* on well.	They are *getting* on well.
8. The river has *over flown* its bank.	The river has *over flown* its banks.
9. He was appointed *on* the post.	He was appointed *to* the post.
10. Last but not *the least,* we have to discuss the problem of over population.	Last but not *least,* we have to discuss the problem of over population.
11. *Cities* after *cities* fell.	*City* after *city* fell.
12. What is the use Munir going there?	What is the use of Munir going there?
13. He *did many mischief.*	He *made much mischief.*
14. It is exact five *in* my watch.	It is exact five *by* my watch.
15. I will dine with them on *next Sunday.*	I will dine with them *Sunday next.*
16. Misfortunes when faced bravely and *manly* become less troublesome.	Misfortunes when faced bravely and *manfully* become less troublesome.
17. I am *laid down* with fever.	I am *laid up* with fever.
18. Hc is habituated to smoking.	He is *addicted* to smoking.
19. *According to my opinion* he is right.	*In my opinion* (or according *to me)* he is right.
20. Could you please *open* this knot?	Could you please *untie* this knot?

Multiple Choice Questions

Directions: *In this section, each sentence has three parts, indicated by (A), (B) and (C). Read each sentence to find out whether there is an error. If you find an error in any one of the parts (A, B, C), indicate your response by marking the letter related to that part. If a sentence has no error, indicate this by marking '(D)' which stands for "No error". Errors may belong to grammar, usage or idiom. Ignore errors of punctuation, if any.*

1. (A) Beware of/(B) a fair-weather friend/(C) who is neither a friend in need nor a friend indeed/ (D) No error.

2. (A) Copernicus proved/(B) that Earth/(C) moves round the Sun./(D) No error.

3. (A) Seldom we have been treated/(B) in such a rude manner/(C) by the police personnel./(D) No error.

4. (A) Some men are born great,/(B) some achieve greatness/(C) and some had greatness thrust on them./(D) No error.

5. (A) The property/(B) was divided/(C) among the two brothers./(D) No error.

6. (A) I am quite certain/(B) that the lady is not only greedy/(C) but miserly./(D) No error.

7. (A) The aircraft overloaded/(B) there was something wrong of the battery/(C) and the engine was making a queer noise/(D) No error.

8. (A) A thorough inquiry of the misappropriation of funds/(B) is now imperative/(C) to bring the guilty to book/(D) No error.

9. (A) The brilliant success in the examination/(B) as well as his record in sports/(C) deserves high praise/(D) No error.

10. (A) While travelling by a train/(B) on a cold winter night/(C) an argument rose between two passengers in our compartment/(D) No error.

11. (A) I cannot find/(B) where has he gone/(C) though I have tried may best/(D) No error.

12. (A) If I was/(B) the Prime Minister of India/(C) I would work wonders/(D) No error.

13. (A) Amit's severe bout of flu/(B) debilitated him so much/(C) that he was too tired to do for work for a week./(D) No error.

14. (A) This is the crux of the entire problem;/(B) everything centres on/(C) it being resolved./(D) No error.

15. (A) One of the major aims of the Air Force/(B) was the complete demolition of all means of transportation/(C) by the bombing of rail lines and terminals./(D) No error.

16. (A) His strong voice cut over/(B) the hum of conversation/(C) like a knife through butter./(D) No error.

17. (A) Even though they weren't expecting us/(B) they managed to knock up/(C) a marvellous meal./(D) No error.

18. (A) The celebrated singer was/(B) surrounded by the usual crowd/(C) of lackeys and hanger-ons./(D) No error.

19. (A) If it weren't/(B) for you,/(C) I wouldn't be alive today./(D) No error.

20. (A) He looked like a lion/(B) baulked from/(C) its prey./(D) No error.

21. (A) Widespread flooding/(B) is effecting/(C) large areas of the villages./(D) No error.

22. (A) She regards/(B) negotiating prices with customers/(C) as her special preserve./(D) No error.

23. (A) Often in political campaigns, a point is reached at which/(B) the candidates take out their gloves./(C) and start slugging with bare fists./(D) No error.

24. (A) If we really set to/(B) we can get the whole house/(C) cleaned in an afternoon./(D) No error.

25. (A) Pieces of rock plummeted/(B) down the mountainside/(C) in the ground below./(D) No error.

26. (A) Since the two parties each won/(B) the same number of seats,/(C) the minority party holds the balance of power./(D) No error.

27. (A) It's arrogant for you/(B) to assume you'll/(C)win every time./(D) No error.

28. (A) We've paid for our travel and accommodation,/(B) so we need only to take/(C) some pocket-money with us./(D) No error.

29. (A) There's no evidence to show/(B) that information technology secrets are more/(C) vulnerable in India than Britain or the US./(D) No error.

30. (A) It is shameful that hunting/(B) is still considered sport/(C) by some unscrupulous people in the civilized world./(D) No error.

31. (A) The Prime Minister's good looks won him/(B)the election but he has still to prove/(C) that he's not a just pretty face./(D) No error.

32. (A) The two books are the same/(B) except for the fact that this/(C) has an answer in the back./(D) No error.

33. (A) He estimated his income tax bill/(B) by extrapolation over figures/(C) submitted in previous years./(D) No error.

34. (A) The modern office block/(B) sticks out like a sore thumb/(C) among the old buildings in the area./(D) No error.

35. (A) I will try to put over/(B) some feelers to gauge/(C) people's reactions to our proposal./(D) No error.

36. (A) A major contribution of Mathura sculptors/(B)of that period were the creation and popularization/(C) of the Buddha's image in human form./(D) No error.

37. (A) Amit has been deceiving Mona/(B) for many years but she/(C) has not still tumbled to it./(D) No error.

38. (A) Mahavira was an advocate of nonviolence and vegetarianism,/(B) who revived and reorganized the Jain doctrine/(C) and established rules for their monastic order. (D) No error.

39. (A) Microwaves are the principle carriers/(B) of television, telephone and data transmissions/ (C)between stations on earth and between the earth and satellites./(D) No error.

40. (A) An unit is an abstract idea,/(B) defined either by reference to/(C) a randomly chosen material standard or to a natural phenomenon./ (D) No error.

41. (A) With the crisis deepening,/(B) the critics sense an opportunity/(C) about putting in place a more radical strategy./(D) No error.

42. (A) The salesman gave us/(B) a big spiel about why/(C) we should buy his product./(D) No error.

43. (A) I will need several weeks/(B) to invent the lie of the land before/(C) I can make any decision about the future of the business./(D) No error.

44. (A) You should be cautious/(B) and make a few discrete enquiries about/(C) the firm before you sign anything./(D) No error.

45. (A) Your husband doesn't/(B) believe that you are older/(C) than I./(D) No error.

46. (A) We are meeting today afternoon/(B) to discuss the matter/(C) and reach a compromise./ (D) No error.

47. (A) Either Ram or/(B) you is responsible/(C) for this action./(D) No error.

48. (A) The student flatly denied/(B) that he had copied/(C) in the examination hall./(D) No error.

49. (A) By the time you arrive tomorrow/(B) I have finished/(C) my work./(D) No error.

50. (A) The speaker stressed repeatedly on/(B) the importance of improving/(C) the condition of the slums./(D) No error.

51. (A) The captain with the members of his team/ (B) are returning/(C) after a fortnight./(D) No error.

52. (A) After returning from/(B) an all-India tour/ (C) I had to describe about it/(D) No error.

53. (A) The teacher asked his students/(B) if they had gone through/(C) either of the three chapters included in the prescribed text./(D) No error.

54. (A) Although they are living in the country/ (B) since they were married/(C) they are now moving to the town./(D) No error.

55. (A) Do you know/(B) how old were you/(C) when you came here?/(D) No error.

ANSWERS

1	2	3	4	5	6	7	8	9	10
D	B	A	C	C	C	B	A	D	C
11	**12**	**13**	**14**	**15**	**16**	**17**	**18**	**19**	**20**
B	A	C	C	B	A	A	C	C	C
21	**22**	**23**	**24**	**25**	**26**	**27**	**28**	**29**	**30**
C	A	A	A	C	A	A	B	D	B
31	**32**	**33**	**34**	**35**	**36**	**37**	**38**	**39**	**40**
C	C	C	D	A	B	C	C	A	A
41	**42**	**43**	**44**	**45**	**46**	**47**	**48**	**49**	**50**
C	D	D	D	C	A	B	D	B	A
51	**52**	**53**	**54**	**55**					
B	C	C	B	D					

❑❑❑

3 Articles

Definite and Indefinite Articles

(*i*) 'A' and 'an' are Indefinite Articles.

(*ii*) 'The' is Definite Article.

(*iii*) 'A' and 'an' modify a noun in a general way.

(*iv*) 'The' particularises it. *e.g.*,

Mohan has **a pen.**

The pen which you gave me was expensive.

Vowel and Consonant Sounds

(*i*) 'A' is used before words starting with the sound of a consonant.

(*ii*) 'An' is used before a vowel sound (vowels a, e, i, o, u) *e.g.*,

a book, a cat, a useful thing, a European girl, a university,

but an FDR, an MA, an honest boy, an hour, an owl, an egg, an umbrella, etc.

Use of Articles 'A' and 'An'

A cat mews. (*i.e.,* every cat)

The cat of my neighbour mews day and night. (*i.e.,* a particular cat)

He gave me **an** egg. (Here 'an' means 'one')

Use of Article 'The'

1. 'The' is used before names of rivers, mountains, seas, oceans:

   The Himalayas, the Ganga, the Yamuna, the Bay of Bengal, the Indian Ocean, the Nile, the English Channel, *etc.*
2. Names of newspapers and magazines:

   The Times of India, the Tribune, The Sun, *etc.*
3. Names of the famous and holy books:
   The Guru Granth Sahib, The Gita, The Ramayana, *etc.*
4. Names of creations of nature:
   the sun, the earth, the moon, the sky, *etc.*
5. While using Adjectives as Nouns:
   The poor should be helped by **the rich.**
6. Sometimes with the Comparative Degree:
   The more you think, **the more** you worry.
7. With the Superlative Degree:
   She is **the most intelligent** girl in our school.
8. Before the imaginary lines and directions:
   The Latitude, The Equator, the east, the west, etc.
9. Before the names of musical instruments:
   the violin, the piano, the flute, etc.
10. While using a Proper Noun as a Common Noun:

    Mohan is **the Sachin** of our team.

Omission of Article 'The'

1. Before some Nouns used to convey general sense, articles are not used but are used to particularise them:
   Man is mortal.
2. Before Proper Nouns:
   Rakesh is an intelligent boy.
3. With Abstract Noun:
   Childhood is the prime time of one's life.
   The childhood of Sohan was full of sorrow.
4. With Material Nouns:
   Milk is an essential food.
   The milk of the cow is sweet.

5. Usually no article is used before names of diseases:
   Cancer is a fatal disease.
   However, when we talk about a disease figuratively, we use an article before its name, *e.g.* Corruption is a cancer.
6. Names of games and language:
   I like football.
   I can speak Punjabi, Hindi and English.
7. Gold is a precious metal.

   NOTE: As you must have noted above, the definite article 'the' has been used where a noun is particularised.

Double Use of Article 'The'

Read the following sentences carefully to understand this :

1. The poet and novelist has been honoured.
   (The same person is the poet as well as novelist)
2. The poet and the novelist have been honoured.
   (The poet and the novelist are two different persons).
3. I have a black and white dog.
   (that is, one dog)
4. I have a black and a white dog.
   (that is, two dogs)

Multiple Choice Questions

Directions : *Fill in the blanks with suitable articles. Mark 'D' if no article required.*

1. Do you know .... boy in white?
A. a B. an
C. the D. No article

2. She is .... girl I am looking for.
A. a B. an
C. the D. No article

3. Have you read .... Mahabharat?
A. a B. an
C. the D. No article

4. ....rich are not always happy.
A. A B. An
C. The D. No article

5. Oranges are sold by .... dozen.
A. a B. an
C. the D. No article

6. Milk is sold by .... litre.
A. a B. an
C. the D. No article

7. .... Amazon is the longest river in the world.
A. A B. An
C. The D. No article

8. .... higher you climb, the colder it gets.
A. A B. An
C. The D. No article

9. She is .... untidy girl.
A. a B. an
C. the D. No article

10. I am .... M.A. is English.
A. a B. an
C. the D. No article

11. I have already spent .... few rupees I had.
A. a B. an
C. the D. No article

12. .... English are very hard-working.
A. A B. An
C. The D. No article

13. April is the fourth month of .... year.
A. a B. an
C. the D. No article

14. Rice is sold by .... kilogram
A. a B. an
C. the D. No article

15. She is .... best of the three girls.
A. a B. an
C. the D. No article

16. .... man in the car is a friend of mine.
A. A B. An
C. The D. No article

17. Brevity is .... soul of wit.
A. a B. an
C. the D. No article

18. .... thing of beauty is a joy for ever.
A. A B. An
C. The D. No article

19. .... little learning is a dangerous thing.
A. A B. An
C. The D. No article

20. .... best sauce for food is hunger.
A. A B. An
C. The D. No article

21. Birds of .... feather flock together.
A. a B. an
C. the D. No article

22. He makes .... living by begging.
A. a B. an
C. the D. No article

23. It is .... pity that he died so young.
A. a B. an
C. the D. No article

24. What .... nuisance it is?
A. a B. an
C. the D. No article

25. Delhi is .... London of India.
A. a B. an
C. the D. No article

26. Where is .... will, there is a way.
A. a B. an
C. the D. No article

27. Her father is .... physician and surgeon.
A. a B. an
C. the D. No article

28. This will benefit .... poor.
A. a B. an
C. the D. No article

29. ....bird in hand is better than two in a bush.
A. A B. An
C. The D. No article

30. As he is hard-working, he will win .... prize.
A. a B. an
C. the D. No article

31. .... water of this well is dirty.
A. A B. An
C. The D. No article

32. Only .... wearer knows where the shoe pinches.
A. a B. an
C. the D. No article

33. .... action will be taken against you.
A. A B. An
C. The D. No article

34. .... sun rises in the east.
A. A B. An
C. The D. No article

35. She was promoted to .... highest post.
A. a B. an
C. the D. No article

36. Did you see .... Taj Mahal?
A. a B. an
C. the D. No article

37. He is .... one-eyed man.
A. a B. an
C. the D. No article

38. This is .... useful book.
A. a B. an
C. the D. No article

39. Cloth is sold by .... metre.
A. a B. an
C. the D. No article

40. The sun sets in .... west.
A. a B. an
C. the D. No article

41. Amar bought......umbrella yesterday.
A. a B. an
C. the D. No article

42. Surinder is ...... honest boy.
A. a B. an
C. the D. No article

43. She wrote ...... book in French.
A. a B. an
C. the D. No article

44. ...... lion roars.
A. A B. An
C. The D. No article

45. ..... apple a day keeps the doctor away.
A. A B. An
C. The D. No article

46. John bought ...... car yesterday.
A. a B. an
C. the D. No article

47. His father is ..... engineer in the U.S.A.
A. a B. an
C. the D. No article

48. It is hard for ..... owl to fly during the day times.
A. a B. an
C. the D. No article

49. She had ..... rimmed hat.
A. a B. an
C. the D. No article

50. My uncle is ..... heart specialist.
A. a B. an
C. the D. No article

51. He looks as foolish as .... ass.
A. a B. an
C. the D. No article

52. Did you go to .... prison to visit him?
A. a B. an
C. the D. No article

53. I found .... one-rupee note in the market.
A. a B. an
C. the D. No article

54. It is a pleasure to meet such .... efficient man.
A. a B. an
C. the D. No article

55. The Sanyasi lived in a cave in .... Himalayas.
A. a B. an
C. the D. No article

56. There is .... union in our factory.
A. a B. an
C. the D. No article

57. He hit his wife on the head with .... umbrella.
A. a B. an
C. the D. No article

58. I caught him by .... collar.
A. a B. an
C. the D. No article

59. Child is .... father of man.
A. a B. an
C. the D. No article

60. He gazed at .... moon for two hours.
A. a B. an
C. the D. No article

ANSWERS

1	2	3	4	5	6	7	8	9	10
C	C	C	C	C	C	C	C	B	B
11	**12**	**13**	**14**	**15**	**16**	**17**	**18**	**19**	**20**
C	C	C	C	C	C	C	A	A	C
21	**22**	**23**	**24**	**25**	**26**	**27**	**28**	**29**	**30**
A	A	A	A	C	A	A	C	A	A
31	**32**	**33**	**34**	**35**	**36**	**37**	**38**	**39**	**40**
C	C	B	C	C	C	A	A	C	C
41	**42**	**43**	**44**	**45**	**46**	**47**	**48**	**49**	**50**
B	B	A	A	B	A	B	B	A	A
51	**52**	**53**	**54**	**55**	**56**	**57**	**58**	**59**	**60**
B	C	A	B	C	A	B	C	C	C

4 Prepositions

A Preposition is a word that comes before a Pronoun or a Noun and expresses the relationship between Noun or Pronoun and some part of the remaining sentence.

(*a*) He is busy **with** his work.
(*b*) The boy jumped **into** the river.
(*c*) The birds are chirping **in** the trees.

In these sentences the words **with**, **into** and **in** show the relationship between the verbs **busy, jumped** and **chirping** with the nouns **work, river** and **trees** respectively.

Position of the Preposition

A. A Preposition usually precedes its object.
(*i*) He laughs **at** the poor.
(*ii*) He is angry **with** you.
(*iii*) She agrees **with** me.

B. In the case of Relative Pronouns it comes after the subject.
(*i*) This is the boy whom I was looking **for**.
(*ii*) That is the pen whose mention I was making **of**.

C. In the following cases, the Preposition comes after its object.
(*i*) Where is the boy you were complaining **against**?
(*ii*) What things are there you are looking **for**?
(*iii*) Who is there, you are waiting **for**?

Omission of the Prepositon

In many cases when the sentences contain Nouns of Time or Place, the Prepositions **from, in** and **for** are often omitted.

(*i*) He walked many kilometres.
(*ii*) He came to see me last year.
(*iii*) As I could not find my puppy anywhere, I looked here and there.

Prepositions are small words that show the relationship between one word and another. Prepositions in the following sentences show the position of the paper in relation to the desk, the book, hand and the door.

The paper is **on** the desk.
The paper is **under** the book.
The paper is **in** his hand.
The paper is **by** the door.

Common Prepositions

about	at	by
in	onto	toward
above	before	concerning
inside	out	under
across	behind	despite
into	over	until
after	below	down
like	since	up
against	beneath	during
near	through	upon
along	beside	except
of	throughout	with
amid	between	for
off	till	within
among	beyond	from
on	to	without

Multiple Choice Questions

Directions: *Select the most appropriate preposition from the given alternatives to fill in the blanks and make the sentence meaningfully complete.*

1. Don't try to be an advocate ..... these criminals.
   A. for B. with
   C. across D. in
2. The audience admired him ..... his sweet voice.
   A. to B. on
   C. for D. at
3. I want to check your bag ..... fake currency notes.
   A. to B. for
   C. upon D. on
4. The dew drops clung .... the blades of grass.
   A. for B. on
   C. to D. in
5. The thief was chased ..... by the police.
   A. on B. after
   C. into D. at
6. Please carry this bag ..... my room.
   A. on B. for
   C. to D. in
7. A lorry bumped ..... a car.
   A. on B. over
   C. into D. to
8. They were begging ..... food.
   A. for B. on
   C. to D. after
9. She always boasts ..... her wealth.
   A. of B. for
   C. on D. after
10. She banged ..... the door violently.
    A. for B. to
    C. on D. down
11. I applied ..... the post of a clerk.
    A. for B. on
    C. in D. to
12. I applied ..... the Principal for the post of a teacher.
    A. to B. on
    C. with D. for
13. I begged ..... him not to divulge the secret.
    A. for B. of
    C. with D. to
14. You had better borrow a pen ..... Rakesh.
    A. over B. into
    C. from D. by
15. I baked a cake ..... the guests.
    A. to B. for
    C. on D. of
16. She is confident ..... (her) success.
    A. with B. on
    C. of D. for
17. The doctor will cure you ..... malaria.
    A. of B. with
    C. for D. from
18. This law is common ..... all.
    A. to B. upon
    C. over D. at
19. She was condemned ..... her bad hand writing.
    A. on B. for
    C. into D. of
20. In summer there will be a great demand ..... desert cooler.
    A. on B. with
    C. for D. of
21. We shall wait ..... you.
    A. on B. for
    C. towards D. after
22. Tom displayed his injury ..... all his friends.
    A. for B. upon
    C. to D. at
23. She distributed the sweets ..... the two brothers.
    A. among B. between
    C. for D. in
24. Please distribute these apples ..... all.
    A. among B. to
    C. for D. at
25. It rarely happened that he defended ..... an innocent person.
    A. against B. for
    C. upon D. at
26. The parents were disappointed ..... the performance of their son.
    A. on B. with
    C. at D. of
27. Common salt dissolves ..... water.
    A. for B. in
    C. with D. by
28. This medicare is free ..... sugar.
    A. on B. to
    C. from D. of

29. The manager granted leave ..... the clerk.
A. to B. on
C. into D. for

30. The air was heavy ..... aroma of perfumes.
A. on B. with
C. into D. from

31. She had a quick glance ..... the magazine.
A. at B. from
C. into D. to

32. The climate of Kashmir is favourable ..... me.
A. with B. in
C. to D. for

33. They hate you ..... your poverty.
A. for B. on
C. in D. of

34. He is eligible ..... this post.
A. for B. to
C. with D. at

35. The smoke was emerging ..... down the foot of the hill.
A. on B. to
C. from D. at

36. The criminal managed to escape ..... the prison.
A. upon B. from
C. with D. of

37. You should educate your friends ..... the benefits of living in villages.
A. on B. towards
C. upon D. in

38. She made a lot of efforts ..... win the match.
A. for B. to
C. upon D. at

39. The new inspector will enquire ..... the murder case.
A. on B. for
C. into D. at

40. The retired soldiers were exempted ..... all taxes.
A. from B. to
C. on D. of

41. She was adept ..... journalism.
A. at B. on
C. with D. in

42. She is afraid ..... snakes.
A. on B. to
C. of D. with

43. I agree ..... your proposal.
A. for B. on
C. to D. with

44. The children were amazed ..... so big a python.
A. at B. on
C. in D. with

45. She was anxious ..... the final match.
A. about B. on
C. with D. for

46. He apologized ..... his being late.
A. towards B. for
C. on D. as

47. The children were amused ..... his jokes.
A. for B. to
C. at D. on

48. She is angry ..... you.
A. to B. with
C. on D. for

49. She is angry ..... your teasing remark.
A. at B. in
C. for D. with

50. A big patch of land was allocated ..... the refugees.
A. to B. for
C. in D. upon

ANSWERS

1	2	3	4	5	6	7	8	9	10
A	C	B	C	B	C	C	A	A	C
11	**12**	**13**	**14**	**15**	**16**	**17**	**18**	**19**	**20**
A	A	B	C	B	C	A	A	B	C
21	**22**	**23**	**24**	**25**	**26**	**27**	**28**	**29**	**30**
B	C	B	A	A	C	B	C	A	B
31	**32**	**33**	**34**	**35**	**36**	**37**	**38**	**39**	**40**
A	C	A	A	C	B	A	B	C	A
41	**42**	**43**	**44**	**45**	**46**	**47**	**48**	**49**	**50**
A	C	C	A	A	B	C	B	A	A

❑❑❑

5 Synonyms & Antonyms

There are thousands of words in English language. No one can remember their meanings easily but with regular practice one can memorise most of them. A number of words with their Synonyms and Antonyms are compiled here. Try to learn as many as you can and answer the questions thereafter.

Words	*Synonyms*	*Antonyms*
Abandon	Cease, Forsake	Continue
Abhor	Hate, Loathe, Detest	Like, Love
Abiding	Enduring, Durable	Fleeting
Able	Proficient, Competent	Incompetent, Unfit
Ability	Skill, Power	Disability, Inability
Abortive	Fruitless, Futile	Fruitful, Successful
Abolish	Destroy, Undo	Restore, Revive
Abridge	Shorten, Curtail	Lengthen, Expand
Absolve	Forgive, Pardon, Excuse	Condemn
Accelerate	Hasten	Retard
Accord	Agreement, Harmony	Discord, Disagreement
Accumulate	Collect, Store, Amass	Distribute, Scatter
Adamant	Hard, Inflexible	Flexible
Adversity	Misfortune, Distress	Prosperity
Adept	Expert, Skilful	Inexpert, Unskillful
Aggravate	Heighten, Intensify	Quell, Suppress
Agile	Nimble	Clumsy, Undeft
Alert	Vigilant	Heedless
Allay	Calm, Soothe, Assuage	Arouse
Ameliorate	Improve, Advance, Amend	Worsen, Deteriorate
Ambiguous	Vague, Unclear	Clear
Amiable	Lovable, Agreeable	Disagreeable
Annihilate	Destroy	Create
Arduous	Hard, Strenuous	Easy

Words	Synonyms	Antonyms
Attacks	Assault	Defend
Audacity	Boldness	Cowardice
Auspicious	Favourable, Propitious, Lucky	Ominous, Inauspicious, Unlucky
Austere	Harsh, Severe, Rigorous	Easy-going
Authentic	True, Genuine	Spurious, False
Avarice	Greed	Generosity
Averse	Unwilling, Loath, Disinclined	Willing, Inclined
Aversion	Hostility, Hatred	Affinity, Liking
Base	Low, Mean, Ignoble	Noble, Exalted
Boisterous	Noisy, Stormy	Calm, Quiet
Brave	Courageous, Daring, Bold, Plucky	Cowardly, Dastardly, Timid
Brief	Short, Concise, Laconic	Lengthy, Diffuse
Bright	Vivid, Radiant	Dull, Dark
Brutal	Savage, Cruel	Humane, Kindly
Callous	Hard, Cruel, Indifferent	Soft, Tender, Concerned
Cautious	Careful, Wary	Rash, Reckless, Foolhardy
Censure (*n*)	Blame, Condemnation	Praise
Censure (*vb*)	Blame, Condemn	Praise, Commend
Circumscribed	Restricted, Confined, Limited	Unconfined, Unrestricted
Civil	Polite, Courteous, Gracious, Urbane	Rude, Uncivil, Impolite, Ungracious
Coerce	Compel, Force	Volunteer
Compassionate	Pitiful, Sympathetic, Merciful	Unsympathetic, Merciless, Cruel
Compress	Condense, Abbreviate	Expand, Lengthen
Conspicuous	Noticeable, Manifest	Inconspicuous
Constant	Steady, Steadfast, Uniform	Inconstant, Variable
Cordial	Friendly, Warm, Hearty	Cold, Unfriendly
Covert	Hidden, Secret	Overt, Open
Cruel	Savage, Ruthless, Vicious	Kind, Gentle, Benevolent
Cursory	Rapid, Superficial	Thorough, Exhaustive, Intensive
Credible	Believable, Probable, Plausible	Incredible, Unbelievable, Fantastic
Crafty	Cunning, Sly	Artless, Simple, Ingenuous
Costly	Expensive, Dear	Cheap, Inexpensive
Confidence	Trust, Reliance	Distrust, Doubt
Death	Decease, Demise	Existence, Life
Dearth	Scarcity, Lack, Want, Paucity, Shortage	Plenty, Abundance
Decay	Dissolution, Decline, Decomposition, Disintegration	Regeneration

Words	Synonyms	Antonyms
Deference	Respect, Reverence	Disrespect, Irreverence
Deficient	Lacking, Inadequate	Complete, Sufficient
Desolate	Lonely, Deserted	Crowded, Occupied
Destitute	Wanting, Needy	Rich, Affluent
Diligence	Industry, Perseverance	Idleness
Disgrace	Dishonour, Discredit	Honour, Credit
Dwindle	Decrease, Shrink	Grow, Increase
Earthly	Terrestrial, Mundane	Celestial, Heavenly, Unearthly
Eligible	Qualified, Suitable	Ineligible, Unsuitable
Emancipate	Liberate, Free	Enslave
Excited	Impassioned, Stimulated	Composed, Cool, Impassive
Extraordinary	Uncommon, Remarkable, Marvellous	Commonplace, Ordinary
Extravagant	Lavish, Prodigal, Wastrel, Spendthrift	Thrifty, Economical, Frugal
Fabricate	Construct, Make	Destroy
Fabulous	Fictitious, Mythical	Actual, Real
False	Untrue, Mendacious	True, Genuine
Famous	Well-known, Renowned	Obscure, Unknown
Fantastic	Fanciful, Imaginative, Visionary	Practical, Down to earth
Fearful	Nervous, Anxious, Afraid, Scared	Fearless, Dauntless
Felicity	Happiness	Sorrow
Gaiety	Joyousness, Hilarity	Mourning, Dullness
Garrulous	Talkative, Loquacious	Taciturn, Silent, Reserved
Generous	Liberal, Magnanimous	Stingy, Miserly
Gigantic	Huge, Colossal	Minute, Small
Graphic	Vivid, Pictorial, Meaningful	Vague
Guest	Visitor	Host
Guile	Fraud, Trickery	Artlessness, Ingenuousness
Gratitude	Gratefulness	Ingratitude, Ungratefulness
Gratuitous	Voluntary, Spontaneous, Unwarranted	Involuntary, Forced
Hamper	Hinder, Obstruct	Facilitate, Ease
Haughty	Arrogant, Proud	Humble, Modest
Hazardous	Dangerous, Perilous	Safe, Secure Protected
Headstrong	Obstinate, Stubborn	Weak-willed, Flexible

Words	*Synonyms*	*Antonyms*
Hope	Belief, Conviction, Expectation	Despair, Hopelessness
Improvident	Prodigal, Carelessness	Provident, Economical
Incessant	Unceasing, Continuous	Discontinuous
Indolent	Slothful, Lethargic	Active, Energetic
Joy	Delight, Pleasure	Sadness, Gloom
Jolly	Jovial, Merry	Gloomy, Sad
Judicious	Discreet, Prudent	Indiscreet, Injudicious
Knowledge	Enlightenment, Learning	Ignorance, Stupidity
Laborious	Industrious, Assiduous	Slothful, Lazy
Laxity	Slackness, Looseness	Firmness
Lenient	Mild, Forbearing	Strict, Stern
Lethal	Deadly, Fatal, Mortal	Life-giving, Vital, Vivifying
Liberal	Generous, Tolerant	Intolerant, Illiberal
Liberty	Freedom, Independence	Slavery, Bondage
Lively	Animated, Active	Dull, Listless
Loyal	Faithful, Devoted	Treacherous, Disloyal, Unfaithful
Lucky	Fortunate	Unlucky, Unfortunate
Lucrative	Profitable	Unprofitable
Magnanimous	Generous, Largehearted	Ungenerous, Stingy
Malady	Illness, Ailment	Health
Manifest	Noticeable, Obvious	Obscure, Puzzling
Meagre	Small	Plentiful, Large
Mean	Low, Abject	Noble, Exalted
Mendacious	False, Untruthful	Truthful
Misery	Sorrow, Distress	Happiness, Joy
Morbid	Sick, Diseased	Healthy
Mournful	Sorrowful, Sad	Joyful, Happy
Negligent	Careless, Heedless	Careful
Notorious	Infamous, Disreputable	Reputable
Obedient	Submissive, Compliant, Docile	Disobedient, Recalcitrant, Wayward
Obsolete	Antiquated, Out-of-Date	Current, Modern
Opportune	Timely, Seasonable	Inopportune
Opulence	Wealth, Riches	Penury, Poverty
Onerous	Heavy, Burdensome	Light, Easy
Palatable	Tasty, Delicious	Unpalatable
Pathetic	Touching	Joyous, Cheery
Persuade	Urge, Induce	Dissuade
Praise (*vb*)	Applaud, Eulogise	Condemn

Words	*Synonyms*	*Antonyms*
Praise (*n*)	Applause, Eulogy	Condemnation
Precarious	Risky, Uncertain	Safe, Certain
Pretence	Pretext, Excuse	Candour, Frankness
Propagate	Breed, Circulate	Terminate, Restrict
Quaint	Odd, Singular	Usual, Ordinary
Quell	Suppress, Subdue	Agitate, Arouse
Rare	Uncommon, Scarce	Common, Ordinary
Refined	Polished, Elegant	Crude, Coarse
Remote	Distant	Near, Close
Renown	Fame, Reputation	Infamy, Notoriety
Rigid	Stiff, Unyielding	Flexible, Yielding
Remorseful	Regretful, Repentant	Unrepentant
Rebellion	Revolt, Mutiny, Insurgency	Loyalty
Scared	Holy, Consecrated	Profane, Unholy
Sane	Sensible, Sound	Insane
Scold	Chide, Rebuke	Praise
Serious	Grave, Earnest	Frivolous
Shy	Bashful	Bold, Impudent
Simple	Plain, Artless	Complex, Cunning, Shrewd
Solitary	Single, Lonely, Secluded	Numerous, Multitude
Shallow	Superficial	Deep
Solace	Comfort, Relief	Discomfort, Grief
Spurious	Sham, False	Genuine, Authentic
Stagnant	Still, Motionless	Moving
Surplus	Excess	Deficit, Shortage
Tame	Gentle, Mild, Domesticated	Savage, Wild
Teacher	Instructor, Educator	Student, Pupil
Tedious	Wearisome, Monotonous	Agreeable, Lively
Temporal	Worldly, Secular	Spiritual
Temperate	Moderate	Immoderate, Intemperate
Tortuous	Winding, Circuitous	Straight, Direct
Tough	Hard, Strong	Tender, Soft, Flexible
Transient	Temporary, Fleeting	Lasting, Durable, Permanent
Trusworthy	Reliable	Unreliable, Untrustworthy
Tranquil	Calm	Agitated
Ugly	Unsightly, Repulsive	Beautiful, Attractive
Useful	Advantageous, Serviceable	Useless
Vehemence	Passion, Force	Apathy, Indifference

Words	Synonyms	Antonyms
Vindictive	Revengeful	Forgiving
Wholesome	Healthy	Unwholesome, Morbid, Unhealthy, Diseased
Wicked	Evil, Impious	Pious, Good
Wise	Sagacious, Erudite	Foolish, Stupid
Wrath	Anger, Fury, Rage	Love, Peace, Calm
Wreck	Ruin, Destroy	Create, Construct
Yield	Surrender, Submit	Resist, Revolt
Yielding	Submissive, Supple	Inflexible, Intractable
Yoke	Oppression, Bondage	Freedom
Zeal	Passion, Fervour	Apathy, Indifference
Zest	Relish, Enthusiasm	Distaste, Disrelish

Multiple Choice Questions

Directions (Qs. 1 to 50): *In the following questions choose the word which best expresses the MEANING of the given word.*

1. TEPID
   A. Hot B. Warm
   C. Cold D. Boiling
2. MAYHEM
   A. Jubilation B. Havoc
   C. Excitement D. Defeat
3. TIMID
   A. Fast B. Slow
   C. Medium D. Shy
4. CANTANKEROUS
   A. Quarrelsome B. Rash
   C. Disrespectful D. Noisy
5. PRECARIOUS
   A. Cautious B. Critical
   C. Perilous D. Brittle
6. TACITURNITY
   A. Dumbness B. Changeableness
   C. Hesitation D. Reserve
7. INEBRIATE
   A. Dreamy B. Stupefied
   C. Unsteady D. Drunken
8. HARBINGER
   A. Massenger B. Steward
   C. Forerunner D. Pilot
9. INTIMIDATE
   A. To hint B. Frighten
   C. Bluff D. Harass
10. IRONIC
    A. Inflexible
    B. Bitter
    C. Good-natured
    D. Disguisedly sarcastic
11. STRINGENT
    A. Tense B. Stringy
    C. Strict D. Causing to shrink
12. ECSTATIC
    A. Animated B. Bewildered
    C. Enraptured D. Willful
13. COMMENSURATE
    A. Measurable B. Proportionate
    C. Beginning D. Appropriate
14. DESTITUTION
    A. Humility B. Moderation
    C. Poverty D. Beggary

15. ASCEND
A. Leap B. Grow
C. Deviate D. Mount

16. UNCOUTH
A. Ungraceful B. Rough
C. Slovenly D. Dirty

17. LYNCH
A. Hang B. Madden
C. Killed D. Shoot

18. LAUD
A. Lord B. Eulogy
C. Praise D. Extolled

19. CORRESPONDENCE
A. Agreements B. Contracts
C. Documents D. Letters

20. VENUE
A. Place B. Agenda
C. Time D. Duration

21. STERILE
A. Barren B. Arid
C. Childless D. Dry

22. SYNOPSIS
A. Index B. Mixture
C. Summary D. Puzzle

23. GERMANE
A. Responsible B. Logical
C. Possible D. Relevant

24. PONDER
A. Think B. Evaluate
C. Anticipate D. Increase

25. CANNY
A. Obstinate B. Handsome
C. Clever D. Stout

26. ABUNDANT
A. Ripe B. Cheap
C. Plenty D. Absent

27. CONSEQUENCES
A. Results B. Conclusions
C. Difficulties D. Applications

28. SHIVER
A. Shake B. Rock
C. Tremble D. Move

29. DILIGENT
A. Progressive B. Brilliant
C. Inventive D. Hard-working

30. DISTANT
A. Far B. Removed
C. Reserved D. Separate

31. FORAY
A. Excursion B. Contest
C. Ranger D. Intuition

32. FRUGALITY
A. Foolishness B. Extremity
C. Enthusiasm D. Economy

33. GARNISH
A. Paint B. Garner
C. Adorn D. Abuse

34. VIGOUR
A. Strength B. Boldness
C. Warmth D. Enthusiasm

35. CANDID
A. Apparent B. Explicit
C. Frank D. Bright

36. BRIEF
A. Limited B. Small
C. Little D. Short

37. GARRULITY
A. Credulity B. Senility
C. Loquaciousness D. Speciousness

38. FURORE
A. Excitement B. Worry
C. Flux D. Anteroom

39. NEUTRAL
A. Unbiased B. Non-aligned
C. Undecided D. Indifferent

40. LAMENT
A. Complain B. Comment
C. Condone D. Console

41. ADVERSITY
A. Failure B. Helplessness
C. Misfortune D. Crisis

42. TURN UP
A. Land up B. Show up
C. Crop up D. Come up

43. DEIFY
A. Flatter B. Challenge
C. Worship D. Face

44. ERROR
A. Misadventure B. Misgiving
C. Ambiguity D. Blunder

45. SHALLOW
A. Artificial B. Superficial
C. Foolish D. Worthless

46. MASSACRE
A. Murder B. Stab
C. Assassinate D. Slaughter

47. COMBAT
A. Conflict B. Quarrel
C. Feud D. Fight

48. VORACIOUS
A. Wild B. Hungry
C. Angry D. Quick

49. IMPROMPTU
A. Offhand B. Unimportant
C. Unreal D. Effective

50. RABBLE
A. Mob B. Noise
C. Roar D. Rubbish

Directions (Qs. 51 to 100): *In the following questions choose the word which is the exact OPPOSITE of the given words.*

51. STRINGENT
A. General B. Vehement
C. Lenient D. Magnanimous

52. FLIMSY
A. Frail B. Filthy
C. Firm D. Flippant

53. BUSY
A. Occupied B. Engrossed
C. Relaxed D. Engaged

54. ADAPTABLE
A. Adoptable B. Flexible
C. Yielding D. Rigid

55. LOVE
A. Villainy B. Hatred
C. Compulsion D. Force

56. BALANCE
A. Disbalance B. Misbalance
C. Debalance D. Imbalance

57. RELINQUISH
A. Abdicate B. Renounce
C. Possess D. Deny

58. MOUNTAIN
A. Plain B. Plateau
C. Precipice D. Valley

59. FICKLE
A. Courageous B. Sincere
C. Steadfast D. Humble

60. PERENNIAL
A. Frequent B. Regular
C. Lasting D. Rare

61. RARELY
A. Hardly B. Definitely
C. Frequently D. Periodically

62. STARTLED
A. Amused B. Relaxed
C. Endless D. Astonished

63. ADHERENT
A. Detractor B. Enemy
C. Alien D. Rival

64. QUIESCENT
A. Indifferent B. Troublesome
C. Weak D. Unconcerned

65. CONDENSE
A. Expand B. Distribute
C. Interpret D. Lengthen

66. BENIGN
A. Malevolent B. Soft
C. Friendly D. Unwise

67. OBSCURE
A. Implicit B. Obnoxious
C. Explicit D. Pedantic

68. HYPOCRITICAL
A. Gentle B. Sincere
C. Amiable D. Dependable

69. EVASIVE
A. Free B. Honest
C. Liberal D. Frank

70. INDUSTRIOUS
A. Indifferent B. Indolent
C. Casual D. Passive

71. EXTRICATE
A. Manifest B. Palpable
C. Release D. Entangle

72. LUCID
A. Glory B. Noisy
C. Obscure D. Distinct

73. INSIPID
A. Tasty B. Stupid
C. Discreet D. Feast

74. OBEYING
A. Ordering B. Following
C. Refusing D. Contradicting

75. VICTORIOUS
A. Defeated B. Annexed
C. Destroyed D. Vanquished

76. COMMISSIONED
A. Started B. Closed
C. Finished D. Terminated

77. VANITY
A. Pride B. Humility
C. Conceit D. Ostentious

78. ZENITH
A. Acme B. Top
C. Nadir D. Pinnacle

79. TANGIBLE
A. Ethereal B. Concrete
C. Actual D. Solid

80. REPRESS
A. Inhibit B. Liberate
C. Curb D. Quell

81. EPILOGUE
A. Dialogue B. Prelude
C. Post script D. Epigram

82. FRAUDULENT
A. Candid B. Direct
C. Forthright D. Genuine

83. LOQUACIOUS
A. Reticent B. Talkative
C. Garrulous D. Verbose

84. NIGGARDLY
A. Frugal B. Thrifty
C. Stingy D. Generous

85. PERTINENT
A. Irrational B. Irregular
C. Insistent D. Irrelevant

86. FAINT-HEARTED
A. Warm-hearted B. Full-blooded
C. Hot-blooded D. Stout-hearted

87. VIOLENT
A. Humble B. Harmless
C. Gentle D. Tame

88. STATIONARY
A. Active B. Mobile
C. Rapid D. Busy

89. HONORARY
A. Dishonourable B. Reputed
C. Paid D. Official

90. COMMON
A. Rare B. Small
C. Petty D. Poor

91. REPEL
A. Attend B. Concentrate
C. Continue D. Attract

92. ARTIFICIAL
A. Red B. Natural
C. Truthful D. Solid

93. CAPACIOUS
A. Limited B. Caring
C. Foolish D. Changeable

94. PROVOCATION
A. Vocation B. Pacification
C. Peace D. Destruction

95. METICULOUS
A. Mutual B. Shaggy
C. Meretricious D. Slovenly

96. ABLE
A. Disable B. Inable
C. Unable D. Enable

97. COMFORT
A. Uncomfort B. Miscomfort
C. Discomfort D. None of these

98. GAIN
A. Loose B. Fall
C. Lost D. Lose

99. SYNTHETIC
A. Affable B. Natural
C. Plastic D. Cosmetic

100. ACQUITTED
A. Freed B. Burdened
C. Convicted D. Entrusted

ANSWERS

1	2	3	4	5	6	7	8	9	10
B	B	D	A	B	D	D	C	B	D
11	**12**	**13**	**14**	**15**	**16**	**17**	**18**	**19**	**20**
C	C	B	C	D	A	C	C	D	A
21	**22**	**23**	**24**	**25**	**26**	**27**	**28**	**29**	**30**
A	C	D	A	C	C	A	C	D	A
31	**32**	**33**	**34**	**35**	**36**	**37**	**38**	**39**	**40**
A	D	C	A	C	D	C	A	A	A
41	**42**	**43**	**44**	**45**	**46**	**47**	**48**	**49**	**50**
C	B	C	D	B	D	D	B	A	A
51	**52**	**53**	**54**	**55**	**56**	**57**	**58**	**59**	**60**
C	C	C	D	B	D	C	D	C	D
61	**62**	**63**	**64**	**65**	**66**	**67**	**68**	**69**	**70**
D	B	B	A	C	A	C	B	B	B
71	**72**	**73**	**74**	**75**	**76**	**77**	**78**	**79**	**80**
D	C	A	A	A	D	B	C	A	B
81	**82**	**83**	**84**	**85**	**86**	**87**	**88**	**89**	**90**
B	D	B	D	D	D	C	B	C	A
91	**92**	**93**	**94**	**95**	**96**	**97**	**98**	**99**	**100**
D	B	A	B	D	C	C	D	B	C

❑❑❑

6 One Word Substitutions

There are many words in English language which can be perfectly used for a number of words. These words help in expressing ideas in a short and correct manner for the right occasion. Such words not only enhance the vocabulary but also enable you to economise in the use of words to a great extent. Try to learn as many as you can.

Denoting Numbers

- A collection of poems — *anthology*
- A number of merchant ships protected by warships (in war-time) — *convoy*
- A number of stars grouped together — *constellation*
- A number of hired applauders, *i.e.* persons paid to clap — *claque*
- A number of people at church — *congregation*
- A number of people gathered together for some common purpose — *gathering, assembly, society*
- A group of people who get together to work for some cause of common interest — *coterie*
- A number of workmen, prisoners, thieves — *gang*
- A number of sheep — *flock*
- A number of geese — *gaggle*
- A number of leopards — *leap*
- A number of lions, monkeys — *pride, troop*
- A number of herrings, mackerel — *shoal*
- A number of fish taken in a net — *catch, haul*
- A number of whales, porpoises — *school, gam*
- A number of oxen or horses (two or more) harnessed together — *team*
- A number of ships, cars, buses — *fleet*

Denoting Places

- A place where bees are kept — *apiary*
- A place where birds are kept — *aviary*
- A place where fishes are kept — *aquarium*
- A dwelling-place of an animal underground — *burrow*
- A squirrel's home — *drey*
- A nest of a bird of prey — *eyrie, aerie*

- A place where spirituous liquors are produced *distillery*
- A place where clothes are washed and ironed *laundry*
- A place where Government records are kept *archives*
- A place where treasures of art, curiosities, etc. are preserved or exhibited *museum*
- A place where fruit trees are grown *orchard*

Pertaining to the Literary Sphere

- A work whose writer is unknown *anonymous*
- A record of one's life written by oneself *autobiography*
- The history of the life of a person *biography*
- The heading or short description of a newspaper article, chapter of a book etc. *caption*
- A humorous play, having a happy ending *comedy*
- A list of books in a library *catalogue, bibliography*
- A book in which the events of each day are recorded *diary*
- A books containing the words of a language with their definitions, in alphabetical order *dictionary*
- A book of names and addresses *directory*
- A short speech by a player at the end of a play *epilogue*
- A brief summary of a book *epitome*
- A book containing information on all branches of knowledge *encyclopedia*
- To remove the offensive portions of a book *expurgate*
- A speech delivered without earlier preparation *extempore*
- A noisy or vehement speech intended to excite passions *harangue*
- A written account, usually in book form of the interesting and memorable experiences of one's life *memoirs*
- A note to help the memory *memorandum*
- A declaration of plans and promises put forward by a candidate for election, political party or a sovereign *manifesto*
- A short speech by a player at the beginning of a play *prologue*
- Literary theft, or passing off an author's original work as one's own *plagiarism*
- Speaking aloud to oneself *soliloquy*
- A play with a sad or tragic end *tragedy*

Pertaining to Religion

- One who believes that man can have no knowledge of God but only of natural phenomena *agnostic*
- One who renounces his religious vows or forsakes his religious principles *apostate*
- One who does not believe in existence of God *atheist*
- One intolerantly devoted to a particular creed *bigot*
- To utter profane language against God or anything holy *blaspheme*
- A breaker of church images *iconoclast*
- Worship of images or idols *idiolatory*

- One who believes in God — *theist*
- One who believes in only one God — *monotheist*
- One who believes in many Gods — *polytheist*

Pertaining to Government

- To give up a throne or other office of dignity — *abdicate*
- Absence of government — *anarchy*
- Government by Sovereign of uncontrolled authority — *autocracy, despotism*
- Government by departments of states — *bureaucracy*
- Government of the people, for the people and by the people — *democracy*
- Government by the nobility — *aristocracy*
- The right of self-government — *autonomy*
- Government by a few — *oligarchy*
- Government by the wealthy — *plutocracy*
- Government by divine guidance — *theocracy*
- To decide a political question by the direct vote of the whole electorate — *referendum*
- Sweeping governmental change — *revolution*
- The science of government — *politics*

Pertaining to Professions

- One who attends to the diseases of the eye — *oculist*
- One who tests eyesight and sells spectacles — *optician*
- One who attends to the teeth — *dentist*
- One skilled in the care of hands and feet — *chiropodist*
- A physician who assists women at child-birth — *obstetrician*
- One who drives a motorcar — *chauffeur*
- One who makes or sells candles — *chandler*
- One who preserves the skins of animals and mounts them so as to resemble the living animals — *taxidermist*
- One who compiles a dictionary — *lexicographer*
- One who writes books — *author*
- One skilled in the treatment of diseases of animals — *veterinarian*
- A tradesman who manages funerals — *undertaker*
- One who draws up contracts and lends money on interest — *scrivener*
- One who lends money and keeps goods as security — *pawnbroker*
- A teacher who travels from place to place to give instruction. — *peripatetic*
- One who travels from place to place selling miscellaneous articles — *hawker, pedlar*
- One who collects postage stamps — *philatelist*
- One who lends money at exorbitant interest — *usurer*
- One who takes care of a building — *janitor*
- One who sells sweets and pastries — *confectioner*
- One who works in a coalmine — *collier*
- One who flies an aeroplane — *pilot, aviator*

- One who studies rocks and soils — *geologist*
- One who shoes horses — *farrier*
- A professional rider in horses races — *jockey*
- One who deals in silks, cotton, woollen, and linen goods — *mercer*
- One who deals in wines — *vintner*
- One who deals in fish — *fishmonger*
- One who deals in iron and hardware — *ironmonger*
- One who sells fruits, vegetables, etc. from a barrow — *costermonger*
- One who sets type in a printing office — *compositor*

Pertaining to Medicine

- A substance which destroys or weakens germs — *antiseptic*
- Any medicine which produces insensibility — *anaesthetic*
- A medicine to counteract poison — *antidote*
- Want or poorness of blood — *anaemia*
- A medicine which alleviates pain — *anodyne*
- To cut off a person's body a part which is infected — *amputate*
- One who is recovering from illness — *convalescent*
- To be able to tell the nature of disease by its symptoms — *diagnose*
- A disease affecting many persons at the same place and time — *epidemic*
- A disease confined to a particular district or place — *endemic*
- To disinfect by smoke — *fumigate*
- Free or exempt from infection — *immune*
- A person who is sick — *invalid*
- A cure for all diseases — *panacea*
- A disease widely epidemic — *pandemic*
- Confinement to one place to avoid spread of infection — *quarantine*

Pertaining to Characteristics and Actions

- One who devotes his life to the welfare and interests of other people — *altruist*
- One who can use both hands with equal ease — *ambidexterous*
- One who fishes with a rod — *angler*
- One who kills secretly or by surprise — *assassin*
- A person who collects things belonging to ancient times — *antiquary*
- One who is always finding faults — *censorious*
- One living at the same time as another — *contemporary*
- One who sneers at the aims and beliefs of his fellowmen — *cynic*
- One who delights in speaking about oneself — *egotist*
- One who exalts his own opinion — *egoist*
- One who dies for a noble cause — *martyr*
- One who retires from society to live a solitary life — *recluse, hermit*
- One who maliciously sets fire to buildings — *incendiary*

- One who is banished from his home or his country *exile*
- One who takes refuge in a foreign country *refugee, alien*
- One who runs away from justice or the law *fugitive*
- One who walks in his sleep *somnambulist*
- One who looks on the bright side of things *optimist*
- One who looks on the dark side of things *pessimist*
- A hater of mankind *misanthropist*
- One who knows everything *omniscient*
- One who is all powerful *omnipotent*
- One who is present everywhere *omnipresent*
- One who devotes his service or wealth for the love of mankind *philanthropist*
- One new to anything *novice, tyro, neophyte*
- One who engages in any pursuit for the love of it, and not for gain *amateur*
- One who journeys to a holy place *pilgrim*
- A leader of the people who can sway his followers by his oratory *demagogue*
- One who has special skill in judging art, music, tastes, etc. *connoisseur*
- One whose reasoning is clever yet false *sophist*
- One who makes a display of his learning *pedant*
- One who is indifferent to pain or pleasure *stoic*
- One who loves his country and serves it devotedly *patriot*
- One devoted to the pleasures of eating and drinking *epicure*
- One who poses to be what he is not *hypocrite, impostor*
- One who foretells events *prophet*
- One who pretends to know a great deal about everything *mountebank, charlatan, quack*
- One versed in many languages *linguist*
- One who cannot pay one's debts *insolvent*
- One who takes over after another in office or employment *successor*
- One who has been before another in office or employment *predecessor*
- One who is opposed to intellectual progress *obscurant*
- One who abstains from alcoholic drinks *teetotaller*
- One who hides away on a ship to obtain a free passage *stowaway*
- One who spends very little *miser*
- One who spends too much *spendthrift*

Pertaining to War

- An unprovoked attack by an enemy *aggression*
- Shells, bombs, military stores *ammunition*
- A place where naval or military weapons are made or stored *ordnance*
- An agreement between belligerents to stop fighting *armistice*
- A general pardon of offenders *amnesty*
- To reduce to nothing *annihilate*
- Nations carrying on warfare *belligerents*

- To surround a place with the intention of capturing — *besiege*
- To camp in the open air without tents or covering — *bivouac*
- To seize for military use — *commandeer*
- A person who is forced by law to become a soldier — *conscript*
- An order prohibiting ships to leave the ports — *embargo*
- A number of firearms being discharged continuously — *fusillade*
- To make an examination or preliminary survey of enemy territory for military objectives — *reconnoitre*

Pertaining to Marriage and Children

- One who marries a second wife or husband while the legal spouse is alive — *bigamist*
- One vowed to a single or unmarried life — *celibate*
- One engaged to be married — *fiancé, fiancee*
- A child whose parents are dead — *orphan*
- A hater of marriage — *misogamist*
- One who has more than two wives at a time — *polygamist*

Pertaining to Death

- Dead and decaying flesh (esp. of animals) — *carrion*
- A monument set up for persons who are buried elsewhere — *cenotaph*
- To preserve a dead body from putrefaction — *embalm*
- Words inscribed on a tomb — *epitaph*
- An examination of dead body — *postmortem, autopsy*
- An account in the newspaper of the funeral of one deceased — *obituary*
- The property left to someone by a will — *legacy*
- Occurring after death — *posthumous*
- The act of killing a human being — *homicide*
- Murder of a new born child — *infanticide*
- Murder of a brother — *fratricide*
- Murder of a sister — *sororicide*
- Murder of a mother — *matricide*
- Murder of a father — *patricide*
- Murder of a parent — *parricide*
- Murder of a king — *regicide*

Pertaining to Sciences and Arts

- The study of all heavenly bodies and the earth in relation to them — *astronomy*
- The science of land management — *agronomics*
- The study of mankind — *anthropology*
- The study of physical life or living matter — *biology*
- The study of plants — *botany*
- The art of beautiful handwriting — *calligraphy*

- The science which deals with the varieties of human race *ethnology*
- The study of the origin and history of words *etymology*
- The study of coins *numismatics*
- The study of human face *physiognomy*
- The art of making fireworks *pyrotechnics*
- The study of birds *ornithology*
- The study of languages *philology*
- At home equally on land or in water *amphibious*
- The inside of a nut *kernel*
- The central or innermost part of fruit *core*
- The animals of a certain region *fauna*
- The plants and vegetation of a certain region *flora*
- Absence of rain for a long time *drought*
- To supply land with water by artificial means *irrigate*
- One who studies plant and animal life *naturalist*
- A cud-chewing animal, *e.g.* the cow *ruminant*
- A gnawing animal, *e.g.* the rat *rodent*
- A four-footed animal *quadruped*
- Animals which carry their young in a pouch, *e.g.* kangaroo *marsupials*
- Soil composed largely of decayed vegetable matter *humus*
- A preparation for killing insects *insecticide*
- A plant or animal growing on another *parasite*
- Living for many years *perennial*

Miscellaneous

- Loud enough to be heard *audible*
- Not distinct enough to be heard *inaudible*
- Fit for food *edible*
- Unfit for human consumption *inedible*
- Fit to be chosen or selected *eligible*
- Not having the qualities for being chosen *ineligible*
- Writing that is easy to read *legible*
- Writing that is difficult to decipher *illegible*
- Able to read *literate*
- Unable to read *illiterate*
- Born of married parents *legitimate*
- Born of unmarried parents *illegitimate*
- To send back a person to his own country *repatriate*
- To banish from one's country *expatriate*
- To move from one country to another *migrate*
- One who leaves his country to settle in another *emigrant*
- One who comes into a foreign country to settle there *immigrant*

- That which cannot be rubbed out or blotted out — *ineffaceable, indelible*
- Incapable of being redeemed from evil, *i.e.* beyond correction — *incorrigible*
- That which cannot be conquered — *invincible*
- Incapable of making errors — *infallible*
- That which cannot be avoided or prevented — *inevitable*
- Incapable of being burnt — *incombustible*
- That which easily catches fire — *inflammable, flammable*
- That which cannot be seen — *invisible*
- Living for ever — *immortal*
- Increase the gravity of an offence — *aggravate*
- Ordinary or commonplace remark — *platitude*
- That which cannot be satisfied — *insatiable*
- That which cannot be repaired — *irreparable*
- That which cannot be imitated — *inimitable*
- Persons (or efforts) that cannot be wearied — *indefatigable*
- One who eats too much — *glutton*
- To destroy completely — *annihilate*
- A statement open to more than one interpretation — *ambiguous*
- A round about way of speaking — *circumlocution*
- Cautious observation of events, etc. — *circumspection*
- That which cannot be hurt — *invulnerable*

Multiple Choice Questions

Directions: *Below are given some statements each of which is capable of being expressed by one word only. Each statement is followed by four such words of which only one is correct. Out of the given alternatives A, B, C and D choose the correct word which very closely fits each definition.*

1. A set of papers giving information about a person or event:
A. editorial B. agenda
C. dossier D. clippings

2. List and explanations of technical, difficult, etc. terms:
A. preface B. glossary
C. bibliography D. appendix

3. One who pays too much care to his clothes and personal appearance:
A. conscious B. dandy
C. cynosure D. leer

4. A child born after death of father:
A. effeminate B. immature
C. fatherless D. posthumous

5. A person who is hard to please:
A. insensible B. hypocrite
C. egoist D. fastidious

6. Complete failure in something attempted:
A. fiasco B. vain
C. falsies D. flop

7. A word which can be interpreted in any way:
A. confusing B. misnomer
C. ambiguous D. precise

8. A group of persons united by common interests:
A. society B. class
C. clique D. coterie

9. A person who is inexperienced and easily deceived:
A. fool B. immature
C. blackhorn D. greenhorn

10. Instruction by question and answer:
A. interrogatory B. catechism
C. bulletin D. alibi

11. Record of events by someone with first hand knowledge:
A. novice B. report
C. memoir D. itinerary

12. A mode of talk familiar to a particular group or profession:
A. jargon B. colloquial
C. slang D. abuses

13. Person who is crazy:
A. lackadaisical B. tarter
C. scrupulous D. loony

14. A person who readily believes others:
A. hasty B. immature
C. credulous D. credible

15. One who eats human flesh:
A. beast B. cannibal
C. maneater D. carnivorous

16. Intentional destruction of racial groups:
A. genocide B. homicide
C. fratricide D. communal riot

17. One with weakness of mind caused by old age:
A. dastard B. dotard
C. fop D. philanderer

18. Study of insects:
A. zoology B. philology
C. entomology D. etymology

19. A critical judge of any art particularly fine arts:
A. connoisseur B. veteran
C. philistine D. dilettante

20. One who introduces items of an entertainment:
A. consort B. compere
C. director D. introducer

21. A combination of business firms:
A. enterprise B. franchise
C. cartel D. autonomous

22. Freeing of suppressed emotions:
A. catastrophe B. catharsis
C. epilogue D. chagrin

23. One who believes in the power of fate:
A. optimist B. pessimist
C. fearful D. fatalist

24. The murder of brother:
A. genocide B. homicide
C. salvage D. fratricide

25. Additional to proper payment:
A. premium B. overtime
C. ex-gratia D. fringe

26. A person or thing used to tempt somebody into a position of danger:
A. decoy B. provocateur
C. jinx D. scapegoat

27. Custom of having more than one husband at the same time:
A. polygamy B. polyandry
C. bigamy D. sexagenary

28. A person of refined taste in food and drink:
A. emeritus B. epicure
C. glutton D. gourmand

29. A tombstone inscription:
A. epithet B. encomium
C. epistle D. epitaph

30. An office which has no work but high salary:
A. fortuitous B. gratuitous
C. sinecure D. ceremonial

31. One who is indifferent to pains and pleasure of life:
A. stoic B. metaphysical
C. pessimist D. sceptic

32. List of names of persons showing duties to be performed by each in turn:
A. notice B. bulletin
C. roster D. agenda

33. Long angry speech of criticism or accusation:
A. track record B. tirade
C. taut D. outburst

34. One who is in favour of never drinking alcoholic drinks:
A. idealist B. uxorious
C. teetotaller D. unalcoholic

35. Trying to win favour by flattery and charm:
A. smarmy B. shrewish
C. toady D. loquacious

36. A decision on which one cannot go back:
A. incorrigible B. irrevocable
C. rigid D. invulnerable

37. The science that studies the varieties of human race:
A. phrenology B. physiology
C. sociology D. ethnology

38. A person who hates women:
A. philogynist B. philatelist
C. misogamist D. misogynist

39. A group of people in a particular grade in an organisation:
A. colleague B. staff
C. echelon D. commission

40. Honourably discharged from service:
A. emeritus B. latitudinarian
C. infallible D. meritorious

41. One who does not believe in the existence of God:
A. atheist B. altruist
C. agnostic D. flippant

42. The large money paid for an early retirement:
A. goldmine B. golden handshake
C. gratuity D. lion's share

43. A hater of learning and knowledge:
A. misologist B. misogynist
C. philologist D. philanthropist

44. One who lives and acts for the welfare of others:
A. misanthrope B. credulous
C. altruist D. gregarious

45. Mental weariness for want of occupation:
A. desperate B. depression
C. fatigue D. ennui

46. That which makes it difficult to recognise the presence in real of somebody or something:
A. cover B. mask
C. make-up D. camouflage

47. To bear a hand in one's new business:
A. partnership B. interfere
C. assist D. join

48. One who renounces the world and practices self-discipline in order to attain salvation:
A. devotee B. ascetic
C. theist D. parsimonious

49. A place where gambling is practiced:
A. hotel B. motel
C. casino D. stadium

50. A sad song is a:
A. dirge B. elegy
C. ditty D. knell

ANSWERS

1	2	3	4	5	6	7	8	9	10
C	B	B	D	D	A	C	C	D	B
11	12	13	14	15	16	17	18	19	20
C	A	D	C	B	A	B	C	A	B
21	22	23	24	25	26	27	28	29	30
C	B	D	D	D	A	B	B	D	C
31	32	33	34	35	36	37	38	39	40
A	C	B	C	A	B	D	D	C	A
41	42	43	44	45	46	47	48	49	50
A	B	A	C	D	D	C	B	C	A

7 Idioms and Phrases

- An idiom is a group of words established by usage as having a meaning different from the individual words.
- A phrase is a small group of words standing together as an idiomatic expression.

Learn and practise as may as you can.

Idioms and Idiomatic Phrases

✦ **ABC** (basic principles)
She does not know the ABC of photography.

✦ **At one's beck and call** (ready to obey)
He had a dozen men at his beck and call.

✦ **At sixes and sevens** (in disorder)
The drawing room articles were lying at sixes and sevens on the floor.

✦ **A wet blanket** (a discouraging person)
Don't allow Rakesh to accompany you to the hunting trip because he is a wet blanket.

✦ **A big gun** (an important person)
Mr Smith is a big gun in our city.

✦ **At a stone's throw** (at a short distance from)
My school is at a stone's throw from my house.

✦ **A man of word** (a person who keeps his promise)
Mr Sharma is a man of word.

✦ **A man of a few words** (a remarkable person)
Gandhiji was a man of a few words.

✦ **At arm's length** (to keep away)
We should always keep bad boys at arm's length

✦ **A bolt from the blue** (a sudden and unexpected event)
The news of my friend's death came to me like a bolt from the blue.

✦ **A man of letters** (a scholar)
Radha Krishnan was a man of letters.

✦ **A hard nut to crack.** (a puzzling problem)
To get a win over American basket ball team is a hard nut to crack for India.

✦ **A yeoman's service** (service which is beneficial to the human beings)
He did yeoman's service through his life.

✦ **A snake in the grass** (a hidden foe)
Beware of him because he seems to be a snake in the grass.

✦ **Acid test** (hard test)
The election will be an acid test for the ruling party.

✦ **A wolf in sheep's clothing** (a hypocrite)
You should not keep company with him because he is a wolf in sheep's clothing.

✦ **At the eleventh hour** (at the last moment)
The war was about to start but fortunately at the eleventh hour a messenger came to the PM with a message of peace.

✦ **A great card** (an important person)
Mr Sood is a great card in the ministry of finance.

✦ **A fool of the first water** (one completely foolish)
Being a fool of the first water he could not solve even the simplest sum.

✦ **A bone of contention** (to be the cause of quarrel)
Kashmir is the bone of contention between India and Pakistan.

✦ **A green hand** (not very much experienced)
We shall pay a little to a green hand.

✦ **All in all** (completely)
Rajesh is all in all in this office.

✦ **A bed of roses** (a comfort)
Life is not a bed of roses.

✦ **An apple of discord** (to be the cause of)
Kashmir is an apple of discord between India and Pakistan.

✦ **A white elephant** (of no use)
This sort of glib talker always proves a white elephant in the end.

✦ **A red letter day** (An important day)
15th August is a red letter day for the Indians.

✦ **By hook or by crook** (by any means fair or foul)

✦ **Black sheep** (a traitor)
Later on Mr XYZ proved a black sheep.

✦ **By dint of** (by means of)
By dint of hard work, she earned a lot of money.

✦ **Break ones back** (to work hard to get something)
He broke his back to earn his livelihood.

✦ **Break the back of** (accomplish the hardest part of a certain job)
There is nothing to be worried about as we've already broken the back of the problem.

✦ **Beat about the bush** (to go on talking on some worthless topic)
Stop this beating about the bush, come to the main task.

✦ **Beyond one's means** (beyond one's budget)
He is living beyond his means, therefore, he is sure to get ruined.

✦ **Cut loose** (Keep away)
India should cut loose from bad politics.

✦ **Chips of the same block** (having the same taste)
They are the chips of the same block.

✦ **Cut-throat competition** (a stiff competition)
There is a cut-throat competition among the publishers in the market.

✦ **Come what may** (no matter what happens)
I'll do it come what may.

✦ **Drop someone a line** (send a letter, etc.)
Please drop me a line of your well-being.

✦ **Dull the edge of** (reduce the intensity of)
Take this pill and it will dull the edge of pain.

✦ **From hand to mouth** (without any saving)
The poor factory worker is living from hand to mouth.

✦ **Fair and square** (clean)
One must be fair and square in one's dealing.

✦ **Hard of hearing** (somewhat deaf)
She is a bit hard of hearing.

✦ **In the good books of** (be good in one's mind)
Jack is in the good books of his teachers.

✦ **In black and white** (in written)
Don't give him anything in black and white.

✦ **In cold blood** (mercilessly)
The old woman was murdered in cold blood.

✦ **In a crack** (all of a sudden or rapidly)
The thief left the place in a crack.

✦ **In full swing** (in full force)
The studies of the students are going on in full swing.

✦ **In the twinkling of an eye** (quickly)
The monkey ate up grams in the twinkling of an eye.

✦ **Keep the ball rolling** (to maintain the progress of some activity)
After the death of his father he had to take the charge of his office to keep the ball rolling.

✦ **Neck and neck** (even)
There is a neck and neck fight between the two boxers.

✦ **Once in a blue moon** (seldom)
She visits her brother once in a blue moon.

✦ **Slow and steady** (slowly but continually)
Slow and steady wins the race.

✦ **To cut a sorry figure** (present oneself in a bad way)
She cut a sorry figure on the stage.

✦ **To give a red carpet reception** (to give a warm welcome)
The PM was given a red carpet reception in America.

✦ **To dance one's tune** (to follow someone submissively)
He always dances to his brother's tune.

✦ **To turn a deaf ear to** (to disregard)
She turned a deaf ear to her parents' advice.

- **To call a spade a spade** (to speak the truth)
Gandhiji always called a spade a spade.
- **To bring to book** (to scold)
The naughty boy was brought to book by the teacher.
- **To cut short** (to reduce)
Smoking will cut short your life.
He wants to get money by hook or by crook.
- **To grease the palm of** (to bribe)
Rohit greased the palm of the clerk and got the file moved.
- **Through thick and thin.** (under all circumstances)
We'll stand by you through thick and thin.
- **To die by inches** (to die a painful death)
The old man died by inches.
- **To eat one's words** (to retract one's statement)
You'll have to eat your words because you have spoken without thinking.
- **To burn the midnight oil** (to work hard)
You'll have to burn the midnight oil if you want to get good marks.
- **To poke one's nose into** (to meddle with)
It is bad to poke your nose into others' affair.
- **To fall flat** (to have no effect)
His father's advice fell flat on him.
- **To make a clean breast of** (to confess)
He made a clean breast of his involvement in the bomb blast.
- **To get the better of** (overcome)
Anger got the better of him.
- **To break somebody's back** (to give too much work to him to do)
She broke his back by giving him so much hard work to do.
- **Throw cold water on** (to discourage)
She tried to throw cold water on his plan but he was well-determined.
- **The long and short of** (in brief)
The long and short of his lecture is that we should live like brothers.
- **To burn one's fingers** (to get oneself in trouble)
You have burnt your fingers by speaking against him.
- **To turn over a new leaf** (to change the course of life)
He has turned over a new leaf in his life.
- **To have one's own axe to grind** (to have vested interest)
He has his own axe to grind in this matter.
- **To take to one's heels** (to run away)
The thief took to his heels as soon as he saw the policeman.
- **To move heaven and earth** (to make too much effort)
The young man moved heaven and earth to find a job.
- **To be caught red handed** (to be caught at the time of committing a crime)
The clerk was caught red handed when he was accepting bribe from Mr ABC.
- **To receive with open arms** (to give a warm welcome)
The new president of the club was received with open arms by the members.
- **To be born with a silver spoon in one's mouth** (to be born in a rich family)
Mr. J. L. Nehru was born with a silver spoon in his mouth.
- **To come to light** (to be known)
A new disease has recently come to light.
- **To be the apple of one's eye** (be very dear)
He is the apple of his parent's eye.
- **To make fun of** (laugh at)
The children made fun of the waiter in the hotel.
- **To let the cat out of the bag** (to divulge secret)
It was Sohan who let the cat out of the bag by telling the real matter.
- **To open a new chapter** (to start some habit, etc.
By drinking, you've opened a new chapter in your life.
- **To make the flesh creep** (to terrify)
The story made my flesh creep.
- **To lose ground** (to retreat)
After fighting for some time the Pakistani army began to lose ground.

✦ **To bring to book** (to punish)
The student was brought to book by the teacher.

✦ **To show a clean pair of heels** (to run away)
The thief showed a clean pair of heels as soon as he saw the policeman approaching.

✦ **To gain ground** (to be established)
He gained ground in India in a few years.

✦ **To get wind of** (to get information)
I got wind of his secret plans.

✦ **Under a cloud** (be in trouble or in a state of disgrace or suspicion)
His company seemed to be under a cloud as it had no funds to pay the wages to the workers.

Verbal Phrases

✦ **Act upon** (to follow)
I acted upon my father's advice.

✦ **Act upto** (to perform within limits)
He acted upto his conscience.

✦ **Act beyond** (to perform crossing limits)
We should not act beyond our capacity.

✦ **Act for** (to perform in place of someone else)
The vice principal acted for the principal.

✦ **Back up** (to make a queue)
The vehicles began to back up.

✦ **Back down** (withdraw claim in the presence of opposition)
The leader backed down from his previous statement.

✦ **Back off** (draw back some plan or action)
They backed off from building a flyover.

✦ **Back out** (withdraw from a promise, etc.)
The government backed out of its promise.

✦ **Break down** (stop working) My car broke down on the highway.

✦ **Break into** (enter in certain premises by breaking the door, etc.)
Last night a thief broke into my neighbour's.

✦ **Break off** (stop all of a sudden)
She broke off and began to think over about her/his hand.

✦ **Break out** (spread)
Cholera has broken out in the town.

✦ **Break out of** (escape from)
A prisoner broke out of the prison last night.

✦ **Break up** (disperse)
The cloud of fog began to break up as the sun rose.

✦ **Break something up** (Cause something to break into small pieces)
She broke up the chocolate to distribute it among the girls.

✦ **Break with** (Cut off connection after quarrelling with someone)
He has broken with his brother.

✦ **Call on** (pay a visit to somebody)
I'll call on Mohan's today.

✦ **Call out** (to start)
The workers have called out a strike.

✦ **Call off** (to stop the strike etc.)
The workers have called off the strike.

✦ **Call at** (to visit someone's house)
I called at his house yesterday.

✦ **Call in** (send for)
Please call in the doctor.

✦ **Carry on** (continue)
Please carry on your work.

✦ **Carry something out** (perform a task)
Our company is carrying out a big deal with a foreign company.

✦ **Carry something over** (postpone)
The fancy dress competition had to be carried over till Monday)

✦ **Carry someone off** (kill somebody)
Cancer carried her off on the day of her 20th birthday.

✦ **Come of age** (get established)
As our company has come of age, so, there is no problem in selling our goods.

✦ **Come of** (belong to)
She comes of a royal family.

✦ **Come over** (surmount)
We at last came over all our problems.

✦ **Come off** (to take place)
The marriage of my brother comes off in the next month.

✦ **Come round** (agree)
At last he came round to my views.

✦ **Come under** (fall in the category of)
All these animals come under the same species.

✦ **Come down with** (suffer from)
She came down with whopping cough.

✦ **Come from** (be the nature of)
She came from London.

✦ **Come about** (happen)
The explosion came about when the worker struck the match to light a cigarette.

✦ **Cut off** (die)
The princess was cut off in the prime of her life.

✦ **Cut down** (reduce)
The prices of consumer goods should be cut down.

✦ **Cut someone out** (exclude someone)
His father cut him out of his will.

✦ **Fall in**
She fell in love with the prince.

✦ **Fall down** (fail)
The deal fell down for lack of transparency.

✦ **Fall out** (quarrel)
She fell out with his elder brother.

✦ **Fall through** (fail)
The project fell through for lack of funds.

✦ **Get away** (escape)
She got away with her life.

✦ **Get by** (to accomplish something with great difficulty)
She is not rich. She has just enough to get by.

✦ **Get on** (perform)
How are you getting on with your studies?

✦ **Get out** (become known)
The news got out that the PM was paying a visit to Russia.

✦ **Get over** (overcome)
At last I got over all obstacles.

✦ **Get up** (rise)
When do you get up in the morning?

✦ **Give up** (stop)
He gave up smoking.

✦ **Give out** (emit)
Garlic gives out a pungent smell.

✦ **Give in** (collapse)
The bridge gave in under the heavy load.

✦ **Give away** (distribute)
The Principal gave away the prizes.

✦ **Give out** (announce)
It was given out that the President of India would visit the place soon.

✦ **Go off** (explode)
The gun went off suddenly.

✦ **Go on** (continue)
She went on about how she flew the aeroplane.

✦ **Go through** (examine)
I'll go through this book later on.

✦ **Go up** (be built)
The construction of the house is going up.

✦ **Grind on** (continue for a long time in a tedious way)
The discussion over political issues ground on.

✦ **Grind something out** (produce something a tedious way)
She will grind some more short stories.

✦ **Look out** (be careful)
Look out! there is a snake.

✦ **Look down upon** (hate)
We should not look down upon the poor.

✦ **Look at** (watch)
Look at the blackboard.

✦ **Look after** (take care of)
We ought to look after our old parents.

✦ **Look into** (investigate)
The new police inspector will look into the matter.

✦ **Look up** (rise)
The prices of consumer goods are looking up.

✦ **Look back** (think of the past)
It made her feel disolate when she looked back on things of the past.

✦ **Make up** (to fulfil)
I'll make up my deficiency in Mathematics.

✦ **Make out** (understand)
I could not make out what she said.

✦ **Make up one' mind** (to resolve)
I have made up my mind to settle in the USA.

✦ **Make off** (leave hurriedly)
She made off without informing anybody.

✦ **Make something over** (transfer)
She should make her property over to her sons.

✦ **Make over** (hand over)
He made over the charge of the file to Mr Robert.

✦ **Pull back** (retreat)
The government has pulled back from its previous policy.

✦ **Pull something down** (demolish)
The authorities concerned pulled down a few building which were illegally built on government land.

✦ **Pull out** (pluck)
The child pulled out a few petals of the flower.

✦ **Pull through** (recover)
The patient will pull through.

✦ **Push on** (continue a journey)
It was getting darker but we pushed on.

✦ **Push at** (exert force)
He pushed at the bell, but it did not ring.

✦ **Push for** (demand persistently)
The workers have been pushing for the installation of new machines for five years.

✦ **Put out** (extinguish)
She put out the light.

✦ **Put on** (wear)
He put on an overcoat.

✦ **Put off** (postpone)
The plan had to be put off.

✦ **Put by** (spare something for future)
We must put by some money for future.

✦ **Put up with** (stay)
Your aunt is out of town for a couple of days, you may put up with us till she comes.

✦ **Put something down** (record something)
She put a new idea down on the paper.

✦ **Take after** (resemble)
He takes after his father.

✦ **Take off** (remove)
He took off his shoes.

✦ **Take something out** (obtain)
You may take out some money from Rohit if you want to purchase this car.

✦ **Take to** (fall into the habit of)
He took to gambling.

✦ **Turn something down** (reject something)
The judge turned down his appeal.

✦ **Turn on** (attack)
The thief turned on him with a knife.

Multiple Choice Questions

Directions: *Some idioms/phrases are given below with their probable meanings. Select the options with their correct meanings.*

1. Carry out
A. To take from one place to another
B. To continue
C. To obey
D. To make efforts

2. In the same boat
A. A worn out choice
B. Indifferent
C. In identical circumstances
D. Carry off

3. In one's good book
A. A costly book
B. A priceless treasure

C. In one's favour
D. An enchanting beauty

4. Keep a straight face
A. To do make up
B. To change clothes
C. Assume responsibility
D. To remain serious

5. To be above board
A. To have a good height
B. To be honest in any business deal
C. To have no debts
D. To try to be beautiful

6. On the face of it
A. To agree
B. From an action
C. More than enough
D. Apparently

7. Let the bygones be bygones
A. In one's favour
B. To pretend
C. To forget the past
D. Other choice

8. To split hairs
A. Major distinctions
B. Hair with two ends
C. To make minute distinction
D. Without distinction

9. Bread and butter
A. Both bread and butter
B. Something essential
C. Livelihood
D. Relevant things

10. To bell the cat
A. To catch a cat and tie a bell round its neck
B. To make an effort
C. To be quick
D. To face a risk

11. Hard and fast
A. Strict
B. Solid
C. Fast moving
D. Some hard surface

12. Part and parcel
A. The part of a parcel
B. An essential part
C. A missing parcel
D. Some part of a machine sent by parcel

13. Null and void
A. Something invalid
B. Something that can be avoided
C. Something that can be nullified
D. Something evil

14. To make clean breast of
A. To gain prominence
B. To praise oneself
C. To confess without reserve
D. To destroy before it blooms

15. Trump card
A. A powerful means of achieving an object
B. Resourcefulness
C. The best gamble to attain success
D. None of these

16. Tall talk
A. A discussion continued for a long time
B. A high sounding talk
C. A meaningful talk
D. A useless talk

17. Small talk
A. Gossip
B. A discussion carried on for a long time
C. A brief discussion
D. None of these

18. Throw out of gear
A. To replace
B. Hinder, disturb
C. To decide
D. Take up tune

19. To and fro
A. Back and forth
B. Puzzled
C. Amazed
D. Reprove

20. To bell the cat
A. To do an easy job
B. To be indifferent to
C. To undertake a difficult job
D. To clarify

21. To be under cloud
A. Puzzle
B. Enjoy the favour
C. Talk thoughtlessly
D. To be under suspicion

22. A labour of love
A. A tragic end
B. A funny thing
C. Not fruitful
D. Work done without payment

23. Follow suit
A. Follow an example B. Wear a new dress
C. Irrelevant D. A gay person

24. Foul play
A. Bad intentions
B. A play not well acted
C. A play not liked by the audience
D. None of these

25. To pick holes
A. To find some reason to quarrel
B. To destroy something
C. To criticise someone
D. To cut some part of an item

26. To smell a rat
A. To see signs of plague epidemic
B. To get bad smell of a dead rat
C. To suspect foul dealings
D. To be in a bad mood

27. To put a spoke in one's wheel
A. To encourage
B. Act without restraint
C. Risk something
D. To obstruct one's progress

28. To pull one's leg
A. To give up B. Take care of
C. To befool D. To know

29. To play with fire
A. Grasp the truth
B. To handle something dangerous
C. To ridicule
D. To flee away

30. To reckon with
A. Take up time
B. Make an inventory
C. To deal with
D. Submit to punishment

31. To run short
A. Talk until one is tired at
B. Apply to oneself
C. To get rid of
D. To have or be too little

32. A man of letters
A. A postman B. A learned man
C. A hypocrite D. An ignorant man

33. A maiden speech
A. A speech made in the parliament
B. A speech made before unmarried girls
C. A speech made by a political leader
D. A speech made for the first time

34. Order of the day
A. An order passed on a particular day
B. A current law
C. Something common or general
D. None of these

35. To end in smoke
A. To make completely understand
B. To ruin oneself
C. To excite great applause
D. None of these

36. To give vent to
A. To allow to flow forth
B. To prove a failure
C. To amass wealth
D. To evade

37. To eat humble pie
A. To apologise or confess
B. To order
C. To flatter
D. To get rid of

38. A black sheep
A. An unlucky person
B. A negro
C. An ugly person
D. None of these

39. To catch a tartar
A. To trap wanted criminal with great difficulty
B. To catch a dangerous person
C. To meet with disaster
D. To deal with a person who is more than one's watch

40. Sit on fence
A. To remain neutral
B. To show contempt
C. To enjoy the surroundings
D. To become fond of

41. Pay off old scores
A. To repay the debt
B. To have revenge
C. To invite
D. Secretly

42. Turn turtle

A. To cheat
B. To be lopsided
C. To frustrate
D. To dance to the tune

43. Wash one's hands of

A. To refuse   B. To assist
C. To abuse   D. To refuse to be

44. Under duress

A. Under compulsion
B. Willing
C. To elicit information
D. To demand

45. To turn the tables

A. To ruin someone
B. To turn the situation to one's own side
C. To reverse the situation
D. To move from one point to another

46. On the cards

A. Possibly   B. Probably
C. Openly   D. Likely

47. To leave someone in the lurch

A. To come to compromise with someone
B. Constant source of annoyance to someone
C. To put someone at ease
D. To desert someone in his difficulties

48. To play second fiddle

A. To be happy, cheerful and healthy
B. To reduce importance of one's senior
C. To support the role and view of another person
D. To do back seat driving

49. To yearn for

A. To weep for
B. To remember
C. To admire
D. To long for intensely

50. Call off

A. To finish   B. To withdraw
C. To postpone   D. To cry

ANSWERS

1	2	3	4	5	6	7	8	9	10
C	C	C	D	B	D	C	C	C	D
11	**12**	**13**	**14**	**15**	**16**	**17**	**18**	**19**	**20**
A	B	A	C	C	B	A	B	A	C
21	**22**	**23**	**24**	**25**	**26**	**27**	**28**	**29**	**30**
D	D	A	A	C	C	D	C	B	C
31	**32**	**33**	**34**	**35**	**36**	**37**	**38**	**39**	**40**
D	B	D	C	D	A	A	D	B	A
41	**42**	**43**	**44**	**45**	**46**	**47**	**48**	**49**	**50**
B	B	D	A	C	D	D	C	D	B

❑❑❑

8 Narration

Direct and Indirect Narration/Speech

The exact words spoken by the speaker are known as Direct Speech.

The words spoken by somebody and expressed by someone else with some modification are known as Indirect Speech.

(*a*) Ram says to me, "You do not help me."

(*b*) Ram tells me that I do not help him.

The sentence (*a*) shows the words spoken by Ram. So, it is a sentence of Direct Speech.

The sentence (*b*) shows the words spoken by Ram and expressed by someone else with certain modification. So, it is a sentence of Indirect Speech.

The following points should be noted while changing Direct Speech into Indirect speech:

1. The verb outside the inverted commas is called the Reporting Verb.
2. The verb or sentence inside the inverted commas is called the Reported Speech.
3. If the Reporting verb is in the Present or Future Tense, there is no change in the tense in the Reported Speech.
4. If the Reporting Verb is in the Past Tense, the Tense in the Reported Speech is changed.
5. The Reporting verb may be in any Tense, in it the Pronouns are changed as under:
   (*i*) First Person according to Subject
   (*ii*) Second Person according to Object
   (*iii*) Third Person, No change.
6. If the Reporting verb is in the Past Tense the Adverb will change as under in the Indirect Speech.

Direct	***Indirect***
now	then
here	there
after	before
today	that day
yesterday	the previous day
these	those
tomorrow	the next day
last week	the previous week
this	that

7. Adjectives/Determiners are changed as under:

Direct	***Indirect***
this	that
these	those

Rules for Change of Tense

Reporting Verb	Reporting Speech	Change of Tense
Present Tense	Any Tense	No change
Future Tense	Any Tense	No change
Past Tense	Present/Future Tense	Change into corresponding Past Tense
Past Tense	Past Indefinite Tense	Change into Past Perfect Tense
Past Tense	Past Continuous Tense	Change into Past Perfect Continuous Tense
Past Tense	Past Perfect/Perfect Continuous Tense	No change
Past Tense	Universal Truth	No change
Past Tense	Proverb	No change

Transformation of Speech Based on Special Rules

1. Rule Related to Interrogative Sentence

- If the answer of an interrogative sentence is possible in yes-no manner.

Illustration.

Dhoni said to Sachin, "Will you help me?"
Dhoni asked Sachin whether he would help him.
(**Note :** The answer of R.S. is possible in yes-no manner)

Rule of Transformation from Direct to Indirect speech

Step I : Change R.V. into ask.
Step II : In place of comma use 'if/whether'.
Step III : Change interrogative sentence into assertive sentence.

- If the answer of an interrogative sentence is not possible in yes-no manner.

Illustration:

Sachin said to Dhoni, "What do you want?"
Sachin asked Dhoni what he wanted.
(**Note :** Only in Step II, you have to avoid comma and inverted comma and rest will be same as mentioned above).

2. Rule related to Imperative Sentence

- Imperative sentence is a sentence which shows Order/Advice/Request

Illustration:

My teacher said to me, "Go there".
My teacher ordered me to go there.

Rule of Transformation from Direct to Indirect Speech

Step I : Change R.V. as per meaning/sense of R.S. into order/request/advise.
Step II : In place of comma, use 'to'.
Step III : Rest portion will be same.

3. Rule related to Optative Sentence

- Optative sentence is a sentence which expresses the feeling of bless/curse/pray/wish.

Illustration:

Mother said to me, "May you live long!"
Mother blessed me that I might live long.

Rule of Transformation from Direct to Indirect Speech

Step I : Change R.V. as per meaning/sense of R.S. into bless/curse/pray/wish.
Step II : In place of comma, use 'that'.
Step III : Change optative sentence into assertive sentence.

4. Rule related to Exclamatory Sentence

- Exclamatory sentence is a sentence which takes note of exclamatory (!) mark in that sentence showing inner feeling.

Illustration:

She said, "Alas! I am ruined".
She exclaimed with sorrow that she was ruined.

Rule of Transformation from Direct to Indirect Speech

Step I : Change R.V. as per meaning/sense of R.S. into exclaim/exclaims/exclaimed/will or shall exclaim + joy/sorrow/anger/surprise/applause/contempt.
Step II : Change comma into that.
Step III : Change note of exclamation (!) into full stop (.)
Step IV : Change exclamatory sentence into assertive sentence.

Universal, Historical truth, etc.

If the Reported Speech expresses a Universal or Historical or Habitual truth, its Tense will not change.

1. The teacher said to the students, "The sun rises in the east."
   The teacher told the students that the sun rises in the east.
2. My father said to me, "The First Battle of Panipat was fought in 1526."
   My father told me that the First Battle of Panipat was fought in 1526.

Multiple Choice Questions

Directions (Qs. 1 to 13): *Select the correct Indirect Speech for the following sentences:*

1. I said to him, "I shall help you."
A. I told him that I can help him.
B. I told him that I would help him.
C. I told him that I will help him.
D. I told him that I shall be helping him.

2. My Teacher said to me, "The earth revolves round the sun."
A. My teacher told me that the earth revolves round the sun.
B. My teacher told me that the earth revolve round the sun.
C. My teacher told me that the earth had been revolving round the sun.
D. My teacher told me that the earth has been revolving round the sun.

3. I said to my friend, "My father daily goes for a walk."
A. I told my friend that my father daily goes for a walk.
B. I told my friend that my father daily went for a walk.
C. I told my friend that my father has to go for a walk.
D. I told my friend that my father had gone for a walk.

4. He said to me, "May God bless you!"
A. He requested that God can bless me.
B. He prayed that God can bless me.
C. He prayed that God might bless me.
D. He prayed that God will bless me.

5. The patient said, "Thank you, doctor."
A. The patient thanked the doctor.
B. The patient requested the doctor with thanks.
C. The patient told the doctor thanks.
D. The patient suggested the doctor thanks.

6. Satish said, "No, I shall not talk to him."
A. Satish told that he should not talk to him.
B. Satish suggested that he would not have talked to him.
C. Satish exclaimed with sorrow that he would not talk with him.
D. Satish refused to talk to him.

7. The child said, "What a lovely place!"
A. The child exclaimed with sorrow that it was a lovely place.
B. The child thought that the place was lovely.
C. The child exclaimed with joy that the place was very lovely.
D. The child suggested that the place was lovely.

8. He said, "What a fool I have been!"
A. He told himself with sorrow that he was a fool.
B. He confessed with regret that he had been a great fool.
C. He said himself a fool.
D. He suggested that he could be a fool.

9. He said, "Alas! I am ruined."
A. He told me that he had been ruined.
B. He exclaimed with joy that he had been ruined.
C. He exclaimed with sorrow that he was ruined.
D. He told me that he should not be ruined.

10. The accused said, "I am not guilty."
A. The accused exclaimed with sorrow that I am not guilty.
B. The accused exclaimed with joy that he was not guilty.
C. The accused stated that he was not guilty.
D. The accused told me that he has not been guilty.

11. My teacher said, "The earth is round".
A. My teacher said that the earth was round.
B. My teacher says that the earth is round.
C. My teacher said that the earth is round.
D. My teacher ordered that the earth is round.

12. He said, "What a place it is!"

A. He said that it was a very fine place.
B. He said that is a very fine place.
C. He said that the place is fine.
D. He exclaimed with joy/surprise that it was a very fine place.

13. Ria said, "Shall I thread the needle?"

A. Ria asked if she should thread the needle.
B. Ria asked if she shall thread the needle.
C. Ria ordered if she should thread the needle.
D. Ria says that if she would thread the needle.

Directions (Qs. 14 to 33): *Pick out the correct alternative that completes the incomplete sentence which is changed into Indirect Narration.*

14. She said to me, "I shall see you as soon as I get time."
She told me:

A. that she will see me as soon as she will get time.
B. that she would see me as soon as she would get time.
C. she would see me whenever she got time.
D. that she would see me whenever she gets time.

15. My secretary said to me, "Your plane will leave if you do not go at once."
My secretary told me that:

A. her plane would leave if she did not go at that time.
B. her plane would leave if I do not go at once.
C. my plane would leave if I did not go at that very time.
D. my plane will leave if I did not go at that time.

16. My mother said to me, "Don't quarrel among yourselves".
My mother:

A. forbade me to quarrel among ourselves.
B. asked me not to quarrel among ourselves.
C. asked me that not to quarrel among ourselves.
D. asked me to quarrel not among ourselves.

17. Her father said to her mother, "Excuse the daughter."
Her father:

A. requested her mother to excuse the daughter.
B. asked her mother to excuse the daughter.
C. asked her mother to have excused the daughter.
D. asked her mother to have been excused.

18. He said to his friend, "Wait here till father comes."
He requested his friend:

A. to wait here till father had come.
B. that to wait there till his friend came.
C. to wait there till father came.
D. to wait here until his friend came.

19. She said to her maid, "Run and catch the thief."
She ordered her maid:

A. ran and catch the thief.
B. that to run and to catch the thief.
C. ran and caught the thief.
D. to run and catch the thief.

20. Anita said to Sunita, "What are you doing?"
Anita asked Sunita:

A. what she will be doing.
B. that what she is doing.
C. that what she was doing.
D. what she was doing.

21. She said to me, "Are you meeting me today?"
She enquired of me:

A. whether I am meeting her that day.
B. whether I was meeting her today.
C. whether I was meeting her that day.
D. I was meeting her that day.

22. Nitish said to me, "When did you buy this pen?"
Nitish asked me:

A. when I was to buy that pen.
B. when I would buy that pen.
C. when I had bought that pen.
D. when I was buying that pen.

23. She said to me, "Are you going to market?"
She enquired of me:
A. I am going to market.
B. I was going to market.
C. if I was going to market.
D. if I had been going to the market.

24. Damini said, "Why did not you change your clothes?"
Damini asked me:
A. why I had not changed my clothes.
B. why I did not change my clothes.
C. why I would not change my clothes.
D. why I have not been changing my clothes.

25. Umesh said to me, "Have you read that novel?"
Umesh asked me:
A. if he was reading that novel.
B. if he had read that novel.
C. if I had read that novel.
D. if I was reading that novel.

26. She said to me, "I shall forgive you."
She told me:
A. that she will forgive me.
B. that she was going to forgive me.
C. that she will not forgive me.
D. that she would forgive me.

27. I said to her, "It was very hot last night."
I told her:
A. that it had been very hot the previous night.
B. that it was very hot the previous night.
C. that it has been very hot the last night.
D. that it had been very hot this night.

28. She said to me, "I thank you for the help you have given."
She:
A. told me that she thanked me for the help I had given.
B. thanked me for the help I have given.
C. thanked to me for the help I have given.
D. thanked me for the help I had given.

29. Mohini said to me, "Trust in God."
Mohini advised me:
A. that I should trust in God.
B. should trust in God.
C. trusted in God.
D. to trust in God.

30. I said to him, "Let us go to school."
I told him:
A. we would go to school.
B. we shall go to school.
C. that we would go to school.
D. that we should go to school.

31. Rajni said, "May God bless you?"
Rajni:
A. exclaimed with wish that God might bless me.
B. expressed a wish that God might bless me.
C. asked God to bless me.
D. shouted with joy to bless me.

32. My mother said me, "Do not have so many friends."
My mother forbade me:
A. to have so many friends.
B. not to have so many friends.
C. to have been so many friends.
D. to possess so many friends.

33. Ram said, "Pay attention to me."
Ram asked:
A. pay attention to him.
B. paid attention to him.
C. having paid attention to him.
D. to pay attention to him.

Directions (Qs. 34 to 50): *In questions below, the sentences have been given in Direct/Indirect Speech. Out of the four alternatives suggested select the one which best expresses the given sentence in Indirect/Direct Speech.*

34. She said that her brother was getting married
A. She said, "Her brother is getting married."
B. She told, "My brother is getting married"
C. She said, "My brother is getting married".
D. She said, "My brother was married".

35. "Please don't go away", she said.
A. She said to please her and not go away.
B. She told me to go away.
C. She begged me not to go away.
D. She begged that I not go away.

36. "If you don't keep quiet I shall shoot you", he said to her in a calm voice.

A. He warned her to shoot if she didn't keep quiet calmly.

B. He said calmly that I shall shoot you if you don't be quiet.

C. He warned her calmly that he would shoot her if she didn't keep quiet.

D. Calmly he warned her that be quiet or else he will have to shoot her.

37. I told him that he was not working hard.

A. I said to him, "You are not working hard."

B. I told him, "You are not working hard."

C. I said, "You are not working hard."

D. I said to him, "He is not working hard."

38. She said that she would finish the work the next day.

A. She said, "I will finish the work the next day."

B. She said, "I will finish the work tomorrow."

C. She said, "You will finish the work tomorrow."

D. She said, "I finished the work."

39. She said to him, "Why don't you go today?"

A. She asked him why he did not go that day.

B. She said to him that why he don't go today.

C. She asked him not to go today.

D. She asked him why he did not go today.

40. "Are you alone, my son?" asked a soft voice close behind me.

A. A soft voice asked that what I was doing there alone.

B. A soft voice said to me are you alone son.

C. A soft voice from my back asked if I was alone.

D. A soft voice behind me asked if I was alone.

41. My cousin said, "My room-mate had snored throughout the night."

A. My cousin said that her room-mate snored throughout the night.

B. My cousin told me that her room-mate snored throughout the night.

C. My cousin complained to me that her room-mate is snoring throughout the night.

D. My cousin felt that her room-mate may be snoring throughout the night.

42. He asked Rama if he needed his help then.

A. He said to Rama, "Do you need my help?"

B. He told Rama, "Tell me if you need help."

C. He asked Rama, "Do I need your help?"

D. He said to Rama, "Do you need my help now?"

43. Nita ordered her servant to bring her a cup of tea.

A. Nita told her servant, "Bring a cup of tea."

B. Nita said, "Bring me a cup of tea."

C. Nita said to her servant, "Bring me a cup of tea."

D. Nita said to her servant, "Bring her that cup of tea."

44. He exclaimed with joy that India had won the Sahara Cup.

A. He said, "India has won the Sahara Cup."

B. He said, "India won the Sahara Cup."

C. He said, "How! India will win the Sahara Cup."

D. He said, "Hurrah! India has won the Sahara Cup."

45. The boy said, "Who dare call you a thief?"

A. The boy enquired who dared call him a thief.

B. The boy asked who called him a thief.

C. The boy told that who dared call him a thief.

D. The boy wondered who dared call a thief.

46. The little girl said to her mother, "Did the sun rise in the East?

A. The little girl said to her mother that the sun rose in the East.

B. The little girl asked her mother if the sun rose in the East.

C. The little girl said to her mother if the sun rises in the East.

D. The little girl asked her mother if the sun is in the East.

47. Dhruv said that he was sick and tired of working for that Company.

A. Dhruv said, "I am sick and tired of working for this Company."

B. Dhruv said, "He was tired of that Company."

C. Dhruv said to me, "I am sick and tired of working for this Company."

D. Dhruv said, "I will be tired of working for that Company."

48. He said to his father, "Please increase my pocket-money."

A. He told his father, please increase the pocket-money.

B. He pleaded his father to please increase my pocket-money.

C. He requested his father to increase his pocket-money.

D. He asked his father increase his pocket-money.

49. She said to her friend, "I know where is everyone."

A. She told that she knew where was everyone.

B. She told her friend that she knew where was everyone.

C. She told her friend she knew where is everyone

D. She told her friend that she knows where was everyone.

50. His father ordered him to go to his room and study.

A. His father said, "Go to your room and study."

B. His father said to him, "Go and study in your room."

C. His father shouted, "Go right now to your study room."

D. His father said firmly, "Go and study in your room."

ANSWERS

1	2	3	4	5	6	7	8	9	10
B	A	A	C	A	D	C	B	C	C
11	**12**	**13**	**14**	**15**	**16**	**17**	**18**	**19**	**20**
C	D	A	B	C	A	B	C	D	D
21	**22**	**23**	**24**	**25**	**26**	**27**	**28**	**29**	**30**
C	C	C	A	C	D	A	A	A	D
31	**32**	**33**	**34**	**35**	**36**	**37**	**38**	**39**	**40**
B	A	D	C	C	C	A	B	A	D
41	**42**	**43**	**44**	**45**	**46**	**47**	**48**	**49**	**50**
A	D	C	B	A	B	A	C	B	A

❑❑❑

9 Voice

A sentence in active voice focuses on the person or thing doing the action. A sentence in passive voice focuses on the person or thing affected by the action. *e.g.,*

The idol was built. (Active voice)
Someone built the idol. (Passive voice)

Transformation of Voice

- Voice and Tense are closely associated with each other.
- Tense plays an important role while transforming the voice.

On the basis of following points, voice can be transformed from active to passive voice.

The Present Indefinite Tense

Active voice: Subject + V_1 + Object
Passive voice: Subject + is, am, are + V_3 + by + Object

1. **Active voice:** He sings sweet songs.
   Passive voice: Sweet songs are sung by him.
2. **Active voice:** She does not cause any hindrance in my work.
   Passive voice: No hindrance in my work is caused by her.
3. **Active voice:** Do they love their country?
   Passive voice: Is their country loved by them?

The Present Continuous Tense

Active voice: Subject + is/am/are + V_1 + ing + Object.
Passive voice: Subject + is/am/are + being + V_3 + by + Object.

1. **Active voice:** She is cooking food.
   Passive voice: Food is being cooked by her.
2. **Active voice:** Rita is not knitting a sweater.
   Passive voice: A sweater is not being knitted by Rita.
3. **Active voice:** Is Meena baking a cake?
   Passive voice: Is a cake being baked by Meena?

The Present Perfect Tense

Active voice: Subject + has/have + V_3 + Object.
Passive voice: Subject + has/have + been + V_3 + by + Object.

1. **Active voice:** I have written an essay.
   Passive voice: An essay has been written by me.
2. **Active voice:** They have not whitewashed the fence.
   Passive voice: The fence has not been whitewashed by them.
3. **Active voice:** Have you cut the cake?
   Passive voice: Has the cake been cut by you?

The Past Indefinite Tense

Active voice: Subject + V_2 + Object
Passive voice: Subject + was/were + V_3 + by + Object

1. **Active voice:** He composed a new song.
   Passive voice: A new song was composed by him.
2. **Active voice:** He did not operate the computer.
   Passive voice: The computer was not operated by him.
3. **Active voice:** Did she catch a fish?
   Passive voice: Was a fish caught by her?

The Past Continuous Tense

Active voice: Subject + was/were + V_1 + ing + Object

Passive voice: Subject + was/were + being + V_3 + by + Object

1. **Active voice:** The farmers were ploughing the fields.
   Passive voice: The fields were being ploughed by the farmers.
2. **Active voice:** He was not administering the new drug to the patient.
   Passive voice: The new drug was not being administered to the patient by him.
3. **Active voice:** Was she sewing a dress?
   Passive voice: Was a dress being sewn by her?

The Past Perfect Tense

Active voice: Subject + had + V_3 + Object.

Passive voice: Subject + had + been + V_3 + by + Object

1. **Active voice:** He had issued me an import licence.
   Passive voice: I had been issued an import licence.
2. **Active voice:** We had not visited the Taj.
   Passive voice: The Taj had not been visited by us.
3. **Active voice:** Who had taught you English?
   Passive voice: By whom had you been taught English?

The Future Indefinite Tense

Active voice: Subject + will/shall + V_1 + Object.

Passive voice: Subject + will/shall + be + V_3 + by + Object.

1. **Active voice:** He will remove the dust from the shelf.
   Passive voice: The dust from the shelf will be removed by him.
2. **Active voice:** He will not open the main gate.
   Passive voice: The main gate will not be opened by him.
3. **Active voice:** Will you help us?
   Passive voice: Shall we be helped by you?

The Future Perfect Tense

Active voice: Subject + will/shall + have + V_3 + Object.

Passive voice: Subject + will/shall + have + been + V_3 + by + Object.

1. **Active voice:** They will have sold their house by then.
   Passive voice: Their house will have been sold by them by then.
2. **Active voice:** He will not have informed the police about it.
   Passive voice: The police will not have been informed about it by him.
3. **Active voice:** Will they have accepted the deal?
   Passive voice: Will the deal have been accepted by them?

Imperative Sentences

1. **Active voice:** Open the window.
   Passive voice: You are ordered to open the window.

   Or

   Let the window be opened.
2. **Active voice:** Please/kindly open the window.
   Passive voice: You are requested to open the window.
3. **Active voice:** Never make a noise.
   Passive voice: A noise should never be made.

Infinitives

1. **Active voice:** It is time to open the shop.
   Passive voice: It is time for the shop to be opened.
2. **Active voice:** He begged the officer to forgive him.
   Passive voice: He begged the officer to be forgiven.
3. **Active voice:** He has to break the door.
   Passive voice: The door has to be broken by him.

Prepositional Verb

1. **Active voice:** She laughed at the beggar.
   Passive voice: The beggar was laughed at by her.
2. **Active voice:** He listened to the news.
   Passive voice: The news was listened to by him.
3. **Active voice:** They called in the doctor.
   Passive voice: The doctor was called in by them.

Double Object

1. **Active voice:** He gave me a pen.
   Passive voice: A pen was given to me by him.

   Or

   I was given a pen by him.
2. **Active voice:** She told us a story.
   Passive voice: A story was told (to) us by her.

   Or

   We were told a story by her.

Use of Preposition other than 'by'

1. **Active voice:** The jug contains juice.
   Passive voice: Juice is contained in the jug.
2. **Active voice:** The audience thronged the hall.
   Passive voice: The hall was thronged with the audience.
3. **Active voice:** I know her.
   Passive voice: She is known to me.

Quasi Passive Verbs

1. **Active voice:** Quinine tastes bitter.
   Passive voice: Quinine is bitter when tasted.

   Or

   Quinine is bitter when it is tasted.
2. **Active voice:** Sugar is sweet (to taste).
   Passive voice: Sugar is sweet when tasted.

   Or

   Sugar is sweet when it is tasted.

Implied Sentences

1. **Active voice:** The driver drove the bus.
   Passive voice: The bus was driven.
2. **Active voice:** Someone read the news.
   Passive voice: The news was read.
3. **Active voice:** They say work is worship.
   Passive voice: It is said that work is worship.

Multiple Choice Questions

Directions (Qs. 1 to 20): *In the following questions, a sentence has been given in Active/Passive Voice. Out of the four alternatives suggested, select the one that Best Expresses the same sentence in Passive/Active Voice.*

1. Circumstances will oblige me to go.
- A. I will oblige the circumstances and go.
- B. I shall be obliged to go by the circumstances.
- C. Under the circumstances, I should go.
- D. I shall be obliged by the circumstances to go.

2. We waste much time on trifles.
- A. Much time was wasted on trifles.
- B. Much time will be wasted on trifles.
- C. Much time is wasted by us on trifles.
- D. Much time is wasted on trifles.

3. Mohan gave the beggar an old shirt.
- A. An old shirt was given to Mohan by the beggar.
- B. An old shirt was given to the beggar by Mohan
- C. The begger was gave an old shirt by Mohan.
- D. An old shirt was gave to the beggar by Mohan.

4. They have made him a king.
- A. A king has been made by him.
- B. He was made a king by them.
- C. They have been made kings by him.
- D. He has been made a king by them.

5. Who taught you English?
A. By whom English was taught to you?
B. By whom you were taught English?
C. By whom was English taught to you?
D. By whom are you taught English?

6. Was he knocking at the door?
A. Was the door being knocked at by him?
B. Was the door being knocked by him?
C. Was the door knocked by him?
D. Was the door knocking at him?

7. What was Rani doing?
A. What was done by Rani?
B. What was Rani being done?
C. What was being done by Rani?
D. What was being doing Rani?

8. Why were you wasting your time?
A. Why was your time being wasted?
B. Why was your time being wasted by you?
C. Why was your time wasted by you?
D. Why was your time wasted?

9. She has laid out a small garden.
A. A small garden has been laid by her.
B. A small garden has laid her.
C. A small garden being laid by her.
D. A small garden has been laid out by her.

10. She had already solved all the sums.
A. All the sums had already been solved by her.
B. All the sums have already been solved by her.
C. All the sums have been solved by her.
D. All the sums are solved by her.

11. He will have posted the letter.
A. The letter has been posted by him.
B. The letter will be posted by him.
C. The letter will have been posted by him.
D. The letter is posted by him.

12. They will have sold all the books by 4 P.M.
A. All the books will be sold by 4 P.M.
B. All the books will have been sold by 4 P.M.
C. All the books were being sold by 4 P.M.
D. All the books must be sold by 4 P.M.

13. Do you speak English?
A. Is English spoken by you?
B. Does English spoken by you?
C. Is English being spoken by you?
D. Does English being spoken by you?

14. Had they seen me before?
A. Had myself been seen by them before?
B. Had me being seen by them before?
C. Had I been seen by them before?
D. Had I being seen by them before?

15. May I take this pen?
A. May this pen will be taken by me?
B. May this pen shall be taken by me?
C. May this pen should be taken by me?
D. May this pen be taken by me?

16. Can we send it by air?
A. Can this be sent by air?
B. Can it be sent by air?
C. Can it go by air?
D. Can it be send by air?

17. Who wrote this book?
A. By whom was this book written?
B. By whom is this book written?
C. By whom was this book being written?
D. By whom is this book being written?

18. What did you buy?
A. What is bought by you?
B. What is being bought by you?
C. What was bought by you?
D. What was being bought by you?

19. Whom do you want?
A. Who is wanted by you?
B. Who is being wanted by you?
C. You are wanted by whom?
D. You are being wanted by whom?

20. When will you raise this question?
A. When this question will be raised by you?
B. When will this question be raised by you?
C. When this question is being raised by you?
D. When is this question being raised by you?

Directions (Qs. 21 to 35): *In each of the following questions, a sentence is given in Active Voice. Below it are given four alternatives suggesting the Passive Voice form of the above sentence. Choose the correct alternative.*

21. Who did this?
A. This was done by whom?
B. By whom was this done?
C. Who has done this?
D. By whom this was done?

22. One should keep ones promises.
A. Promises should be kept.
B. Ones promises should be kept by one.
C. Promises must be kept.
D. Ones promises one should keep.

23. Give the order.
A. Order given.
B. Order be given.
C. Let the order be given.
D. Order may be given by you.

24. You will have to do it.
A. It will be done by you.
B. It will have to be done by you.
C. It has to be done by you.
D. It would have to be done by you.

25. Keep to the left.
A. You are ordered to keep to the left.
B. You ought to keep to the left.
C. You are advised to keep to the left.
D. You must keep to the left.

26. They will arrange a party.
A. A party will have to be arranged by them.
B. A party they will have to arrange.
C. A party will be arranged by them.
D. A party by them will be arranged.

27. Someone has picked my pocket.
A. My pocket is picked.
B. My pocket has picked.
C. My pocket has been picked.
D. My pocket was picked.

28. He kept me waiting.
A. I kept waiting for him.
B. I kept waiting by him.
C. I was waiting for him.
D. I was kept waiting by him.

29. Why do you tell a lie?
A. Why is a lie told by you?
B. Why is told a lie by you?
C. Why is told by you a lie?
D. Why has a lie been told by you?

30. I have written a letter.
A. A letter is written by me.
B. A letter has been written by me.
C. A letter was written by me.
D. A letter had been written by me.

31. They will have helped you.
A. You will have helped by them.
B. You will have been helped by them.
C. You will be helped by them.
D. You will be helped by them.

32. Open the door.
A. Door may be opened.
B. Let the door be open.
C. Let the door be opened.
D. Door be opened.

33. I am reading a book.
A. A book is read by me.
B. A book is being read by me.
C. A book has been read by me.
D. A book in been read by me.

34. Why did your brother write such a letter?
A. Why your brother wrote such a letter?
B. Why was by brother written such a letter?
C. Why was such a letter written by your brother?
D. Why was written such a letter by your brother?

35. Did you run a great risk?
A. Was a great risk run by you?
B. Was run a great risk by you?
C. Was by you run a great risk?
D. Had you run a great risk?

Directions (Qs. 36 to 45): *In each of the following questions, a sentence is given in Passive Voice. Below it are given four alternatives suggesting the Active Voice form of the above sentence. Choose the correct alternative.*

36. He was made king.
- A. He became king.
- B. They made him king.
- C. They had made him king.
- D. He has been made king.

37. Good news is expected by us.
- A. We are expecting good news.
- B. We have been expecting good news.
- C. We had expected good news.
- D. We expect good news.

38. The child must be looked after.
- A. The child you must look after.
- B. You must look after the child.
- C. You must look the child after.
- D. You may look after the child.

39. What is wanted by you?
- A. What you want?
- B. What did you want?
- C. What do you want?
- D. What you do want?

40. Your father is known to me.
- A. I am known to your father.
- B. I know your father.
- C. I have known your father.
- D. I knew your father.

41. She may be told the story by you.
- A. The story may be told by you to her.
- B. You may tell the story to her.
- C. You may tell her the story.
- D. You may tell to her the story.

42. Duty ought to be done.
- A. Let duty be done.
- B. One ought to do one's duty.
- C. One should do his duty.
- D. Do you duty.

43. Is English spoken by you?
- A. Did you speak English?
- B. Do you speak English?
- C. Have you spoken English?
- D. Do you know how to speak English?

44. Gold coins are contained in this box.
- A. This box contains gold coins.
- B. This box has contained gold coins.
- C. This box is containing gold coins.
- D. This box has gold coins.

45. Character is revealed by manners.
- A. Manners revealed character.
- B. Manners reveal character.
- C. Manners have revealed character.
- D. Manners do reveal character.

ANSWERS

1	2	3	4	5	6	7	8	9	10
D	C	B	D	C	A	C	B	D	A
11	**12**	**13**	**14**	**15**	**16**	**17**	**18**	**19**	**20**
C	B	A	C	D	B	A	C	A	B
21	**22**	**23**	**24**	**25**	**26**	**27**	**28**	**29**	**30**
B	A	C	B	C	C	C	D	A	B
31	**32**	**33**	**34**	**35**	**36**	**37**	**38**	**39**	**40**
B	C	B	C	A	B	D	B	C	B
41	**42**	**43**	**44**	**45**					
C	B	B	A	B					

❑❑❑

10 Sentence Completion

Filling the blanks is such an exercise that starts with the primary schools and continues at the highest level of competitive examinations. One must practise it regularly to score well.

Multiple Choice Questions

Directions: *Pick out the most effective word(s) from the given words to fill in the blanks and make the sentence meaningfully complete.*

1. One requires great .... to teach and handle little children who are restless.
A. patience B. attitude
C. determination D. knowledge

2. The researchers will .... some of the causes of increasing poverty in the state.
A. fund B. investigate
C. promote D. circulate

3. I usually perform .... when nobody is watching me.
A. alone B. good
C. better D. hard

4. It was .... to everyone that the minister had been drinking.
A. observed B. known
C. discovered D. realised

5. I would rather stay indoors .... the rain stops.
A. so B. waiting
C. until D. usually

6. The process should be completed as far as possible within a week, ... which the matter should be brought to notice of the officer concerned.
A. following B. failing
C. realizing D. referring

7. The officers are ..... to regular transfers.
A. free B. open
C. subject D. available

8. All letters received from Government should ..... be acknowledged.
A. suddenly
B. obviously
C. immediately
D. occasionally

9. Mumbai office ..... a meeting of senior officials to discuss the high incidence of frauds.
A. attended B. convened
C. reported D. registered

10. The note should be ..... to all the concerned departments for their consideration.
A. regulated B. requested
C. carried D. forwarded

11. Your present statement does not .... what you said last week.
A. accord to B. accord in
C. accord with D. accord for

12. I had a vague .... that the lady originally belonged to Scotland.

A. notion B. expression
C. imagination D. theory

13. The prisoner showed no .... for his crimes.

A. hatred B. obstinacy
C. remorse D. anger

14. It is inconceivable that in many schools children are subjected to physical .... in the name of discipline.

A. violation B. exercise
C. violence D. security

15. We have not yet fully realised the .... consequences of the war.

A. happy B. pleasing
C. grim D. exciting

16. Happiness consists in being .... what we have.

A. contented to B. contented with
C. contented for D. contented in

17. His rude behaviour is a .... his organization.

A. disgrace for
B. disgrace on
C. disgrace upon
D. disgrace to

18. No child is .... understanding. One has to wait and provide proper guidance.

A. dull to B. dull in
C. dull of D. dull for

19. I am fully .... the problems facing the industry.

A. alive with B. alive to
C. alive for D. alive on

20. The Romans were .... science.

A. bad in B. bad to
C. bad for D. bad at

21. Although I was .... of his plans, I encouraged him, because there was no one else who was willing to help.

A. sceptical B. remorseful
C. fearful D. excited

22. You have no business to .... pain on a weak and poor person.

A. inflict B. put
C. direct D. force

23. Her uncle died in a car accident. He was quite rich. She suddenly .... all her uncle's money.

A. succeeded B. caught
C. gave D. inherited

24. There was a major accident. The plane crashed. The pilot .... did not see the tower.

A. likely B. probably
C. scarcely D. hurriedly

25. The car we were travelling in .... a mile from home.

A. broke off B. broke down
C. broke into D. broke up

26. What are you .... in the kitchen cupboard?

A. looking in B. looking on
C. looking to D. looking for

27. I did not see the point of .... waiting for them, so I went home.

A. hanging around B. hang on
C. hang together D. hanging up

28. He lost confidence and .... of the deal at the last minute.

A. backed out B. backed on
C. backed down D. backed onto

29. To the dismay of all the students, the class monitor was ..... berated by the principal at a school assembly.

A. critically B. ignominiously
C. prudently D. fortuitously

30. All attempts to revive the fishing industry were ..... failure.

A. foredoomed to B. heading at
C. predicted for D. estimated to

31. There are ..... parked outside than yesterday.

A. fewer cars
B. few cars
C. less cars
D. a small number of cars

32. The minister had to ..... some awkward questions from reporters.

A. fend B. fend at
C. fend out D. fend off

33. The ..... of evidence was on the side of the plaintiff since all but one of the witnesses testified that his story was correct.

A. propensity B. force
C. preponderance D. brunt

34. Attention to detail is ..... of a fine craftsman.

A. hallmark B. stamp
C. seal of authority D. authenticity

35. Behaving in a .... and serious way, even in a .... situation, makes people respect you.

A. calm, difficult
B. steady, angry
C. flamboyant, tricky
D. cool astounding

36. Along with a sharp rise in ...., a recession would eventually result in more men, women, and children living in ....

A. crime, apathy
B. fatalities, poor
C. deaths, slums
D. unemployment, poverty

37. The government has .... to provide financial aid to the ones .... by severe floods in the city.

A. desired, troubled B. promised, havoc
C. failed, affected D. wanted, struck

38. An airplane with .... passengers on board made an unscheduled .... as the airport to which it was heading was covered with thick fog.

A. imitable, slip B. faulty, stop
C. variety, halt D. numerous, landing

39. Deemed universities .... huge fees, but have not been successful in providing .... education to our students.

A. collect, maintaining
B. pay, better
C. ask, good
D. charge, quality

40. If the banks desire to .... profit, they should get rid of .... measures.

A. lose, concentrate
B. increase, populist
C. earn, unhealthy
D. maximise, traditional

41. Leadership defines what the future should look like and ...... people with that vision.

A. aligns B. develops
C. trains D. encourages

42. We upset ourselves by responding in an ...... manner to someone else's actions.

A. unabashed B. irrational
C. arduous D. arguable

43. All the people involved in that issue feel a great ...... to his suggestion.

A. contradiction B. adherence
C. indifference D. repugnance

44. These elections will be remembered as much for its anti-incumbency mood as for its ...... mandate.

A. invincible B. rational
C. unprecedented D. deliberate

45. How do you expect us to stay in such a ...... building even if it can be hired on a nominal rent?

A. scruffy B. disperate
C. fragmented D. robust

46. ...... efforts from all concerned are required to raise the social and economic conditions of our countrymen.

A. Perpetual B. Dynamic
C. Massive D. Exploring

47. Many companies see technology as a ...... for a whole host of business problems.

A. consideration B. preference
C. linking D. panacea

48. Known as devout and serious person, she also has ...... sense of humour.

A. better B. plentiful
C. quick D. good

49. The matter would have become serious if ...... action had not been taken.
A. hasty B. fast
C. timely D. unusual

50. The ...... with which he is able to yield the paint brush is really remarkable.
A. ease B. practice
C. majesty D. sweep

51. You must ensure the correctness of the information before ....
A. drawing B. enabling
C. learning D. jumping

52. The rocket .... the target and did not cause any casualty.
A. sensed B. reached
C. missed D. exploded

53. It is desirable to take .... in any business if you want to make profit.
A. advice B. risk
C. loan D. recourse

54. They wasted all the money on purchase of some .... items.
A. excellent B. important
C. significant D. trivial

55. When he found the wallet his face glowed but soon it faded as the wallet was ....
A. empty B. vacant
C. recovered D. stolen

56. He has served the country by .... many significant positions.
A. appointing
B. creating
C. developing
D. holding

57. The frequent errors are a result of the student's ....
A. talent B. smartness
C. carelessness D. perception

58. The robbers eventually .... in breaking into the house.
A. succeeded B. decided
C. caught D. trained

59. I finally .... her to stay another day.
A. advised B. persuaded
C. suggested D. called

60. Most of the people who .... the book exhibition were teachers.
A. witnessed B. presented
C. conducted D. attended

ANSWERS

1	2	3	4	5	6	7	8	9	10
A	B	C	A	C	B	C	C	B	D
11	**12**	**13**	**14**	**15**	**16**	**17**	**18**	**19**	**20**
C	A	C	C	C	B	D	B	B	D
21	**22**	**23**	**24**	**25**	**26**	**27**	**28**	**29**	**30**
B	C	C	B	C	C	D	A	B	A
31	**32**	**33**	**34**	**35**	**36**	**37**	**38**	**39**	**40**
A	D	D	A	A	D	C	D	C	B
41	**42**	**43**	**44**	**45**	**46**	**47**	**48**	**49**	**50**
A	A	D	C	A	A	D	D	C	A
51	**52**	**53**	**54**	**55**	**56**	**57**	**58**	**59**	**60**
A	C	B	D	A	D	C	A	B	D

11 Sentence Improvement

One may use the same words in many ways but the best way is only one that makes the perfect usage of the words and conveys the proper meaning of the expression. Try it yourself in the following questions.

Multiple Choice Questions

Directions: *In these questions, a part of the sentence is bold. Below are given alternatives to the bold part at A, B and C which may improve the sentence. Choose the correct alternative. In case no improvement is needed, your answer is 'D'.*

1. Discreet salience **is extremely important** to create that 'irresistible-yet-unattainable' image for brands that want to take India seriously

A. was extremely important
B. is mainly important
C. was important extremely
D. No Improvement

2. This, over a designer outfit that he wanted for a friend's party and **that his sensitive** parents refused him.

A. which his sensitive
B. which his insensitive
C. that his insensitive
D. No Improvement

3. Goa was full of non-Goa property hunters **rushing about buying up the place** like tomorrow was an expired lease.

A. rushing in buying up the place
B. rushed about buying up the place
C. rushing about to buy up the place
D. No Improvement

4. Property hunting is a **tired and hungry** making business.

A. is a tiresome and hungry
B. is a tiring and hungry
C. is a tiring and waste
D. No Improvement

5. Cultural differences aside, **till luxury need speaks** in a manner that befits.

A. luxury still needs to speak
B. luxury still need to speak
C. luxury till need to speak
D. No Improvement

6. Indian food—the culinary avatar of the subcontinent's social history presented on a platter—**is without doubt the best food** in the world.

A. is undoubtedly the greatest food
B. is without doubt greatest food
C. is best food without doubt
D. No Improvement

7. It must retain the language of poetry. **It needed to create** stories, and not statements.
A. It needed creating
B. It needs creating
C. It needs to create
D. No Improvement

8. This year, Asia-Pacific has become the first region **to reach aggregate profiting** in biotech.
A. to reach aggregated profitability
B. to reach aggregate profitability
C. to reach aggregate of profit
D. No Improvement

9. India is deviating to embrace the West. If Western luxury brands deviate a little, **albeit selectively**, they will find rich Indian arms open far and wide.
A. though selectively
B. however selectively
C. albeit selectedly
D. No Improvement

10. China and India continued to attract attention and deals, motivated by the desire to increase access to these **largest and growing** drug markets and by the need to lower the costs of drug development.
A. larger and growing
B. large and growing
C. larger and grown
D. No Improvement

11. Luxury brands are **still above of the** clover curve here, with their elite (small) audiences.
A. still ahead of the
B. still in the
C. still far of the
D. No Improvement

12. Agencies **hence needed to be** sure of returns before investing, say admen.
A. hence needs to be
B. so needs to be
C. hence need to be
D. No Improvement

13. India is still a nascent market and that's the spirit everyone's **looking at it**.
A. looking for it B. looking in it
C. looking with it D. No Improvement

14. Questioning the state's move to allow women to serve liquor but not dance in bars **of the ground that** dancing aroused physical lust.
A. on the grounds that
B. of the grounds that
C. over the grounds that
D. No Improvement

15. For England the positives from their crushing series lose come in the shape of James Anderson and Kevin Pietersen, **both of which** have made significant strides up the rankings.
A. both of which B. both of whom
C. both of who D. No Improvement

16. International campaigns can work well for luxury here, **but context cannot be** ignored.
A. so context cannot be
B. but context cannot
C. but context couldn't
D. No Improvement

17. For one, the Indian luxury context, **while evolved rapidly**, still has its own meaning, and its own implications.
A. while evolved rapid
B. which evolving rapidly
C. while evolving rapidly
D. No Improvement

18. But too much of availability can compromise a luxury brand or **made it lose** its lustre.
A. make her lose B. make him lose
C. make it lose D. No Improvement

19. Still, it's under-the-upper **layers themselves who** are aspiring for slivers of luxury.
A. layers themselves which
B. layer itself who
C. layers themself which
D. No Improvement

20. It is like saying Hindi movies, with skimpily dressed dancers, would **effect public** order.
A. effect your B. affect public
C. affected public D. No Improvement

21. The court held that a few women being involved in prostitution was no **justice to deny other** bar girls the right to livelihood.
A. justification to declare other
B. justification to deny other
C. justice to let other
D. No Improvement

22. All-rounder cricketer has also made some progress **over the** player rankings.
A. above the B. at the
C. up the D. No Improvement

23. Former minister on Sunday **joined hands** with a suspended Lok Sabha member to float a new political outfit.
A. folded hands
B. walked hand in hand
C. shaked hands
D. No Improvement

24. Pakistan's former ministers will meet in London on Monday **to ask** a strategy to return home from exile.
A. to chalk out
B. to negotiate
C. to create
D. No Improvement

25. It's a family potboiler, medical thriller and political drama **all in one**—except that it's all too real and all too grim.
A. all 3 in one
B. all coupled into one
C. all rolled into one
D. No Improvement

26. India's efforts to get international support for its civil nuclear energy programme got **a go ahead on** Sunday as Germany indicated it would not come in the way of the India-US nuclear deal.
A. a life in B. a boost on
C. a boost at D. No Improvement

27. Is it time for old bungalows to **bite the dust**?
A. go down B. get down
C. come down D. No Improvement

28. The bungalows was an outward manifestation of a certain **way in life**, and with that era gone.
A. way for life B. way of life
C. way at life D. No Improvement

29. The builder Mittals will reportedly **raise their money**-raking high-rise behind it.
A. highten their money
B. rise their money
C. raise there money
D. No Improvement

30. The impatient present has usually demolished **more of the** past before we wake up to the irretrievable loss.
A. much of B. much of their
C. much of the D. No Improvement

31. Preservation is a romantic notion; demolition **quiet** more practical reasons.
A. has many, B. had many,
C. have many, D. No Improvement

32. You must get back to your **charming self** and impress the audience with your social skills.
A. own self B. main self
C. own uniqueness D. No Improvement

33. Stay focused on your goals and don't **get disturbed by** non-materialistic possessions.
A. get involved by
B. get betrayed by
C. get distracted by
D. No Improvement

34. You may appear more optimistic than your detractors **may want it to be**.
A. want you to be
B. wish yourself to be
C. seek you be
D. No Improvement

35. There are a number of mineral springs in the Czech territory, which **has been used** for medicinal purposes since the early 15th century.
A. have been used B. had been used
C. has being used D. No Improvement

36. The picturesque mountains **offers** excellent bungee jumping spots.
A. shows B. provides
C. offer D. No Improvement

37. Begin your **meal with** traditional faves like potato soup, beef soup with liver dumplings or dill soup made from sour milk.
A. meals with B. meal in
C. meals of D. No Improvement

38. You can also **go to the** National Museum building and the famous Prague State Opera.
A. went to B. visit the
C. saw D. No Improvement

39. If they close the Gulf for a **length of time** to shipping, then certainly we could look at $150, probably higher.
A. larger amount of time
B. larger duration of time
C. larger amount of hours
D. No Improvement

40. **More of them** are owned by the state and even the privately-owned ones are open to the public.
A. Most of which B. Most of them
C. Most of all D. No Improvement

41. Constructed in the ninth century by the Prince Booivoj, the castle has transformed **oneself** from a wooden fortress surrounded by earthen bulwarks to the imposing form it has today.
A. himself B. herself
C. itself D. No Improvement

42. Apart from frequent art exhibitions, **their are also** permanent collections devoted to archaeology, anthropology, mineralogy, natural history and numismatics.
A. there is also B. there are also
C. their are also D. No Improvement

43. You can visit the Czech Museum of Fine Arts, **at a** permanent exhibition on Czech Kubism.
A. with a
B. for a
C. in a
D. No Improvement

44. Tensions **above** Iran come at a time of strong demand for energy.
A. under B. inside
C. over D. No Improvement

45. Because its shores line the narrow Straits of Hormuz, Iran **could quickly hit** both military and commercial shipping.
A. will quickly hit
B. shall quickly hit
C. will be quick hitting
D. No Improvement

46. For most people who exercise **at the** morning, there is no getting around the question: Eat and run? Or run and eat later?
A. in the
B. in
C. at the time of
D. No Improvement

47. Are ad agencies even attempting to peer into the keyhole of this indulgence sanctum to garner consumer insights **ahead of** the curve?
A. above
B. over
C. within
D. No Improvement

48. Too many people rush into the world of credit and don't stop to think about how **their actions could affect their** credit score and ability to qualify for credit in the future.
A. their actions may affect their
B. their actions might affect their
C. their actions will affect their
D. No Improvement

49. According to the report, **number of deal with** vaccines were energized by concerns around avian flu, SARS, and biodefence products, while looming patent expirations led to more deals in generics.
A. number of deals in
B. number of deal in
C. number of deals with
D. No Improvement

50. This is how the Bombay High Court responded to the state government's purported **moral stand which** dance bars were causing grave harm to society.

A. moral stand in
B. moral stand at
C. moral stand that D. No Improvement

51. If you have a high credit limit, use **at least a** third of it.

A. atleast a
B. at last a
C. utmost a
D. No Improvement

52. Fitness experts will say that **first eating provides** fuel for a proper workout.

A. eating in the beginning provides
B. first eat provides
C. eating first provides
D. No Improvement

53. One study that examined the claim directly in 1995 found that a group of people did **burned much calories from fat on days** when they exercised on an empty stomach than on days when they had a small breakfast first.

A. burn more calories from fat on days
B. burn more calorie from fat on days
C. burnt more calories from fat on days
D. No Improvement

54. Carefree children spent their afternoons **to run about barefoot**, their clothes dusty, and telltale twigs of the neighbour's mango tree in their hair.

A. running barefoot in the sun
B. run about barefoot in the sun
C. running about barefoot in the sun
D. No Improvement

55. A year ago, a 13-year-old girl attempted suicide because her mother **refuses to pay his** mobile bills.

A. refuses to pay her
B. refused to pay her
C. refused to pay his
D. No Improvement

ANSWERS

1	2	3	4	5	6	7	8	9	10
D	C	D	B	A	D	C	C	D	B
11	**12**	**13**	**14**	**15**	**16**	**17**	**18**	**19**	**20**
C	C	D	A	C	D	C	C	C	C
21	**22**	**23**	**24**	**25**	**26**	**27**	**28**	**29**	**30**
B	C	C	A	C	B	D	B	D	C
31	**32**	**33**	**34**	**35**	**36**	**37**	**38**	**39**	**40**
A	D	C	A	D	C	A	B	D	B
41	**42**	**43**	**44**	**45**	**46**	**47**	**48**	**49**	**50**
C	B	A	C	D	A	D	C	A	C
51	**52**	**53**	**54**	**55**					
C	C	A	C	B					

❑❑❑

12 Reordering Words & Sentences

Different words form a sentence and convey their meaning only when arranged in a proper order. A Paragraph is formed from sentences, it will convey its true meaning and purpose only when the sentences are arranged in a proper manner. Try and practise it in this exercise.

Multiple Choice Questions

Directions (Qs. 1 to 20): *In the following questions, some parts of the sentence have been jumbled up. You are required to rearrange these parts which are labelled P, Q, R and S to produce the correct sentence. Choose the option with proper sequence.*

1. We are doing
P : to the people
Q : to give relief
R : all we can
S : but more funds are needed
The correct sequence should be
A. P Q R S B. R Q P S
C. Q P R S D. S P Q R

2. The man
P : when he was
Q : in the office last evening
R : could not finish
S : all his work
The correct sequence should be
A. P Q R S B. Q R S P
C. R Q P S D. R S P Q

3. The people decided
P : they were going
Q : how much
R : to spend
S : on the construction of the school building
The correct sequence should be
A. Q P R S B. P Q R S
C. P R Q S D. S Q P R

4. The man said that
P : those workers
Q : would be given a raise
R : who did not go on
S : strike last month
The correct sequence should be
A. P Q R S B. P R S Q
C. Q P R S D. R S P Q

5. I think
P : the members
Q : are basically in agreement
R : of the group
S : on the following points
The correct sequence should be
A. R Q P S B. S Q R P
C. P R Q S D. P Q S R

6. While it was true that
P : I had
Q : to invest in industry
R : some lands and houses
S : I did not have ready cash

The correct sequence should be
A. P Q R S B. P R S Q
C. S Q P R D. Q P R S

7. P : But for your help
Q : to finish this work
R : it would not have been possible
S : in time
The correct sequence should be
A. P R Q S B. S P Q R
C. R P Q S D. P Q R S

8. The boy
P : in the competition
Q : who was wearing spectacles
R : won many prizes
S : held in our college
The correct sequence should be
A. P Q R S B. R P S Q
C. Q R P S D. Q P S R

9. About 200 years ago,
P : in the south of India
Q : an old king
R : ruled over a kingdom
S : called Rajavarman
The correct sequence should be
A. Q S R P B. P Q R S
C. Q P S R D. Q S P R

10. P : his land
Q : a wooden plough
R : the Indian peasant still uses
S : to cultivate
The correct sequence should be
A. R Q P S B. Q P S R
C. S R Q P D. R Q S P

11. He was a man,
P : even if he had to starve
Q : who would not beg
R : borrow or steal
S : from anyone
The correct sequence should be
A. P Q R S B. P R Q S
C. Q R S P D. Q P R S

12. P : in the progress of
Q : universities play a crucial role
R : our civilization
S : in the present age
The correct sequence should be
A. S Q P R B. Q R S P
C. Q R P S D. S Q R P

13. P : far out into the sea
Q : for the next two weeks there were further explosions
R : which hurled
S : ashes and debris
The correct sequence should be
A. Q R P S B. R S P Q
C. Q R S P D. S R P Q

14. William Shakespeare,
P : in his lifetime
Q : the great English dramatist
R : wrote thirty-five plays
S : and several poems
The correct sequence should be
A. P Q R S B. R S P Q
C. Q S R P D. Q R S P

15. Whenever I am,
P : with an old friend of mine
Q : in New Delhi
R : to have dinner
S : I always try
The correct sequence should be
A. S Q P R B. Q S R P
C. R P S Q D. P R Q S

16. P : I don't know
Q : must have thought
R : what people sitting next to me
S : but I came away
The correct sequence should be
A. R S Q P B. R Q S P
C. P Q R S D. P R Q S

17. P : in estimating the size of the earth
Q : but they were hampered by the lack of instruments of precision
R : ancient astronomers
S : used methods which were theoretically valid
The correct sequence should be
A. R P Q S B. P R Q S
C. R S Q P D. R P S Q

18. P : It is a pity that
Q : by offering a handsome dowry
R : a number of parents think that
S : they will be able to ensure the happiness of their daughters
The correct sequence should be
A. S Q R P B. P R S Q
C. P S R Q D. P R Q S

19. The common man
P : in nurturing
Q : a more active role
R : communal harmony
S : should play
The correct sequence should be
A. P R S Q B. S Q P R
C. S Q R P D. P R Q S

20. The doctor
P : able to find out
Q : what has caused
R : the food poisoning
S : has not been
The correct sequence should be
A. S P R Q B. P R Q S
C. P R S Q D. S P Q R

Directions (Qs. 21 to 40): *A number of sentences are given below which when properly sequenced form a coherent paragraph. Each sentence is labelled as abcdef...... Choose the most logical order of sentences from among the given choices to construct a coherent paragraph:*

21. (a) Parts of northern region were pounded by heavy rains today,
(b) Vehicular traffic came to a near halt.
(c) As mid and high altitude areas of Himachal Pradesh were in grip of severe cold wave with snow lashing the tribal areas and mid ranges receiving showers.
(d) As the sky remained heavily overcast with dark clouds reducing the visibility considerably.
(e) A large number of tourists were forced to buy heavy woollens and stay indoors due to inclement weather.
A. ecabd B. adecb
C. edabc D. acbde

22. (a) The idea is that students should be able to find employment for themselves after the course.
(b) The Central Board of Secondary Education is planning a revamp of its vocational courses.
(c) For this it is necessary to tie up with the industry as well as mobilise schools for their support.
(d) While others will be made less academic and more in tune with the needs of the industry.
(e) A number of courses have been identified as 'deadwood' and will be done away with.
A. bedac B. abcde
C. acebd D. baced

23. (a) Clearly, age is not a deterrent in one's choice of learning.
(b) Perhaps, it was because of her childhood desire.
(c) When Rachna came to Delhi eight years back, she had not anticipated a career in the field of art.
(d) She has been successful in the various exhibitions that she has been part of in terms of business.
(e) She had got into expressing her thoughts with the help of a brush and colours only because her daughter refused to get initiated into it.
(f) She feels that her use of colour appeals to people.
A. aedcbf B. cdefba
C. cebadf D. aedebf

24. (a) The rehabilitation record has been dismal.
(b) It has been two years years since the earthquake rudely rattled the people of Gujarat.
(c) And since then, life has been a constant struggle.
(d) The quake set Gujarat's clock back by 10 years.
(e) Things changed forever.

A. bedca B. bcade
C. dbace D. edcba

25. (a) In fact, success in exams depended on rote learning from old notes.
(b) when he was studying civil engineering in a college in Gujarat.
(c) He was detained for lack of attendance.
(d) Lectures were soporific, classes rarely worth attending and 80 per cent attendance compulsory.
(e) The college became a trap he hated.
(f) His is a plight many engineers across India would identify with.
(g) He found the going tough.
A. abcdgef B. bgdacef
C. fabcdge D. abcdefg

26. (a) In a country that has close to 600 recognised engineering colleges, there are only seven IITs.
(b) Barring a few exeptions, the academic atmosphere in these is moribund.
(c) The very best students usually get there.
(d) many waste themselves in frustration.
(e) Most of those who get into engineering are good students.
(f) but about 1.25 lakh others and up in the remaining colleges.
A. aecfbd B. abecdf
C. abcdef D. acfbed

27. (a) Whatever the job market, common wisdom says that IIT graduates will find jobs where others have failed.
(b) The IIT brand name is a ticket to success.
(c) When recruiters go headhunting, the IITs are still top of their list.
(d) Its possessor is understood to have an excellent academic record and the will to succeed.
(e) In the job market, that counts.
A. bdeac B. abcde
C. abdce D. dbace

28. (a) It will pave the way ....
(b) signalling a new beginning in strategic ties......
(c) for a tangible Indian economic presence in Iran and Central Asia.
(d) Iran has offered India valuable road linkages to central Asia ......
(e) aimed at promoting peace and economic cooperation in the region.
A. dbeac B. debca
C. acebd D. abced

29. (a) A good college is essential for a successful career and admissions are based on marks.
(b) The marks-based system followed by all the boards in the country recognises only a small percentage of students as successful.
(c) The marks one scores in the crucial board exams dictate the path his life takes.
(d) Anyone scoring below a certain percentage is automatically branded a 'failure'.
(d) So if you cannot make it into the best college, your career is over even before it has started.
A. abcde B. bcdea
C. bdcae D. abdec

30. (a) The project has already started on an experimental basis in the west district.
(b) A website is soon going to be launched where application forms can be downloaded and submitted.
(c) Standing in a queue at a government office to submit application form will be a thing of the past.
(d) A unique code will be alloted while submitting the form which will help in finding the status of the application.
A. abcd B. dabc
C. cbda D. badc

31. (a) To curb bio-terrorism is a difficult task.
(b) To check these attacks and lessen their impact, we need an impartial team of sincere, strong and dedicated men.
(c) The media can play a strong role in stopping this unnecessary spread of panic.
(d) Since bio-terrorism is not visible or easily detectable, it can be used often.
(e) Men who honour the lives of their fellow countrymen before their own.

A. abcde B. dabce
C. adbec D. acbed

32. (a) He was dying.
(b) No one was ready to touch him as even shifting him from one place to another would lead to profuse bleeding.
(c) He was a five-day old infant, premature and bleeding profusely.
(d) Even if injected one small needle, blood would ooze out and continue to flow for an hour at a stretch.
(e) This small being had haematoma, a thick blood clot in his brain.
A. edbca B. cabde
C. eacdb D. cedba

33. (a) The day I don't treat a patient, I feel ....
(b) I have enough to eat, I crave for blessings now.
(c) But if a financially weak patient gives me only ₹ 50, I don't mind.
(d) Each month I do three to four operations free of cost.
(e) I have lost something in life.
(f) My consultation fee is ₹ 300.
A. fcdeab B. dfcbae
C. fcabde D. bdfcea

34. (a) When he was rushed to the nearby Primary Health Centre after his fall, the doctor referred him to a hospital.
(b) This worsened his injury.
(c) Had a little precaution been exercised after the accident, Tarun would have continued with his gymnastic classes.
(d) He was paralysed from waist downwards when he fell from the vaulting horse while doing gymnastics.
(e) However, the doctor forgot to tell Tarun's parents to take him on a stretcher as he had suffered spinal injuries.
(f) Tarun is wheelchair bound for two years.
A. fdeabc B. abcdef
C. fdcaeb D. fdbcae

35. (a) As the temperature rises, staying hydrated can become a greater challenge for people exercising both indoors and out.
(b) Several things can influence this process, including age, gender, physical conditioning. humidity and a lack of sufficient fluids.
(c) In hot weather, individuals can lose as much as two quarts of sweat per hour.
(d) As we age, we have a lower perceived level of thirst in response to fluid loss and early stages of dehydration.
(e) If not replenished, this can lead to dehydration, heat exhaustion and even heatstroke.
A. abcde B. dbcae
C. cbdea D. acebd

36. (a) The leopard was discovered in the servant quarters of a farmhouse.
(b) The injuries appeared to have been caused by the paws of the leopard, and were not teeth wounds.
(c) It took the wild life officials, Delhi Police and Delhi zoo vets eight hours to capture the leopard that had wandered into a factory in south Delhi.
(d) The leopard then jumped into the factory where the workers managed to lock it in a small generator room before calling in the police.
(e) Before its capture, the leopard attacked two women and a man in the farmhouse.
A. aebdc B. bdaec
C. eadbc D. adbec

37. (a) Police suspect a carpenter working at John's house as he has not reported for work since the day the boy went missing.
(b) John did not return home in the afternoon.
(c) John's mother had herself put the boy on the vehicle in the morning.
(d) John smiled at him and was last seen walking up to him.
(e) His parents called the school and were told John had not been to school at all and had been marked absent.
(f) He was about to enter the school when someone called out his name.

A. cfdbea B. debfca
C. bfdaec D. abcdef

38. (a) However, the mayhem over the last few months is deeply shocking.
(b) Yet I do not agree with the prophets of doom who see nothing but disaster ahead.
(c) When I came back to my motherland India after a stay in Switzerland, I felt I was trading a hotbed of intense religious and political violence for peace and quiet.
(d) I think our nation is searching for an identity.
(e) And a new vision of the future will emerge from this.
A. abcde B. cabde
C. cebad D. bedca

39. (a) An integrated and combined approach was required to reveal the mystery of the brain —its structure, composition and function.
(b) Since the early 80's, scientists were clear that the brain would be the final frontier to conquer.
(c) The initiative was flagged off and came to be known as the Human Brain Project.
(d) But that wasn't easy because understanding the brain involved completely integrating information from the level of the gene to the level of behaviour.
(e) To fulfill this requirement a group of American scientists from various disciplines decided to work together.
A. acbed B. bdaec
C. abdec D. badec

40. (a) A product is something that is made in a factory, a brand is something that is bought by a consumer.
(b) The trick therefore, lies in the brand positioning.
(c) For a consumer, the satisfaction of becoming associated with a name that is the 'best' and the 'leader' is far more important and at times makes him ignore the price factor.
(d) Brands come and go.
(e) Still there are those who manage to stay and develop an affinity with consumers.
A. aebcd B. debac
C. decab D. aecdb

ANSWERS

1	2	3	4	5	6	7	8	9	10
B	D	A	B	C	C	A	C	A	D
11	**12**	**13**	**14**	**15**	**16**	**17**	**18**	**19**	**20**
C	A	C	D	B	D	C	B	B	D
21	**22**	**23**	**24**	**25**	**26**	**27**	**28**	**29**	**30**
D	A	C	A	B	D	A	A	C	C
31	**32**	**33**	**34**	**35**	**36**	**37**	**38**	**39**	**40**
C	D	B	C	D	A	A	B	B	B

❑❑❑

13 Comprehension Passages

PASSAGES

Directions: *Read the following passages and answer the questions given below each.*

PASSAGE-1

In the Roman times, defected enemies were generally put to death as criminals for having offended the emperor of Rome. In the middle ages, however, the practice of ransoming of returning prisoners in exchange for money became common. Though some saw this custom as a step towards a most humane society, the primary reasons behind it were economic rather than humanitarian.

In those times, rulers had only a limited ability to raise taxes. They could neither force their subject to fight nor pay them to do so. The promise of material compensation in the form of goods and ransom was therefore the only way of inducing combatants to participate in a war. In the middle ages, the predominant incentive for the individual soldiers was the expectation of spoils. Although collecting ransom clearly brought financial gain, keeping a prisoner and arranging for his exchange had its cost. Consequently, procedures were devised to reduce transaction costs.

One such device was a rule asserting that the prisoner had to assess his own value. This compelled the prisoner to establish a value *without too much distortion;* indicating too low a value would increase, the captive's chances of being killed, while indicating too high a value would either ruin him financially or create a prohibitively expensive ransom that would also result in death.

1. It can be inferred from the passage that a medieval soldier

A. was less likely to kill captured members of opposing armies than was a soldier of the Roman Empire

B. was similar to a 20th century terrorist in that he operated on a basically independent level and was motivated solely by economic incentives

C. had few economic options and chose to fight because it was the only way to earn an adequate living

D. was motivated to spare prisoners' lives by humanitarian rather than economic ideals

2. Which of the following best describes the change in policy from executing prisoners in Roman times to ransoming prisoners in the middle ages?

A. The emperors of Rome demanded more respect than did medieval rulers and thus Roman subjects went to greater lengths to defend their nation

B. It was a reflection of the lesser degree of direct control medieval ruler had over subjects

C. It became a show of strength and honour warrior of the middles ages to be able to capture and return their enemies

D. Medieval soldiers were not as humanitarian as their ransoming practices might have indicated

3. The primary purpose of the passage is to
   A. discuss the economic basis of the medieval practice of exchanging prisoners for ransom
   B. examine the history of the treatment of prisoner of war
   C. emphasize the importance of a warrior's code of honour during the middle ages
   D. explore a way of reducing the cost of ransom

4. The author uses the phrase *"without too much distortion"* in order to
   A. indicate that prisoners would fairly assess their worth
   B. emphasize the important role medieval prisoners played in determining whether they should be ransomed
   C. explain how prisoners often paid more than an appropriate ransom in order to increase their chances for survival
   D. suggest that captors and captives often had understanding relationships

PASSAGE-2

The world dismisses curiosity by calling it idle or mere idle curiosity—even though curious persons are seldom idle. Parents do their best to extinguish curiosity in their children because it makes life difficult to be faced everyday with a string of unanswerable questions about what makes fire hot or why grass grows. Children whose curiosity survives parental discipline are invited to join our university. With the university, they go on asking their questions and trying to find the answers. In the eyes of a scholar, that is what a university is for. Some of the questions which the scholars ask, seem to the world to be scarcely worth asking, let alone answering. They asked questions too minute specialised for you and me to understand without years of explanation. If the world inquires of one of them why he wants to know the answer to a particular question he may say especially if he is a scientist, that the answer will in some obscure way make possible a new machine or weapon or gadget. He talks that way because he knows that the world understands and respects utility.

But to you who are now part of the university, he will say that he wants to know the answer simply because he does not know it, the way the mountain climber wants to climb a mountain, simply because it is there. Similarly a historian asked by an outsider why he studies history may come out with the argument that he has learnt to repeat on such occasions, something about knowledge of the past making it possible to understand the present and mould the future. But if you really want to know why a historian studies the past, the answer is much simpler, something happened and he would like to know what. All this does not mean that the answers which scholars find to their questions have no consequences. They may have enormous consequences but these seldom form the reason for asking the questions or pursuing the answers. It is true that scholars can be put to work answering questions for the sake of the consequences as thousands are working, now, for example, in search of a cure for cancer. But this is not the primary function of the scholars. For the consequences are usually subordinate to the satisfaction of curiosity.

1. According to the passage, the children make life difficult for their parents
   A. by their ceaseless curiosity
   B. by unceasing bombardment of questions
   C. by asking irrelevant questions
   D. by posing profound questions

2. The common people consider some of the questions that the scholars ask unimportant
   A. as they are too lazy and idle
   B. as they are too modest
   C. as it's beyond their comprehension
   D. as it is considered a waste of time

3. A historian really studies the past
   A. to comprehend the present and to reconstruct the future
   B. to explain the present and plan the future
   C. to understand the present and make fortune
   D. to understand the present and mould the future

4. Children whose curiosity survives parental discipline means
   A. children retaining their curiosity in spite of being discouraged by their parents
   B. children pursuing their mental curiosity
   C. children's curiosity subdued due to parents' intervention
   D. children being disciplined by their parents
5. According to the passage, parents do their best to discourage curiosity in their children
   A. because they have no time
   B. because they have no patience to answer them
   C. because they feel that their children ask stupid questions continuously
   D. because they are unable to answer all their questions

PASSAGE-3

The factor of geographical distribution is equally, possibly even more, significant that English is spoken as first or native language in at least four continents of the world, Russian in two, Chinese and the Indian languages in one. English is without question the closest approach to a world language today. It goes without saying that no two persons ever have an identical command of their common language. Certainly, they have not precisely the same vocabulary. There are at least minor differences in pronunciation, indeed the same individual will not pronounce his vowels and consonants in absolutely identical fashion everytime he utters them. Everyone possesses, in addition, certain individual traits of grammatical form and syntactical order, constituting that peculiar and personal quality of language which we term as style. All of this is implicit in the well-known phrase, 'Style is the man.' No men are identical, no two styles are the same. If this be true of but two persons, the potential of differences resident in a language spoken by more than 200 million truly staggers imagination.

1. The author argues that English is the closest approach to a world language because
   A. there are more native speakers of English than of any other language
   B. English has less number of mutually unintelligible dialects
   C. the geographical distribution of English covers a much greater area
   D. other languages are much too complex to be world languages
2. The fact that the same individual will not pronounce his vowels and consonants identically everytime shows that
   A. literary style varies from person to person
   B. mutual intelligibility is a myth
   C. vocabulary varies from individual to individual
   D. no two persons speak the same language exactly the same way
3. It is evident from the passage that style is
   A. a strange type of language
   B. a language where one does not have to be particular about correctness and grammar
   C. language used in a particular way by an individual
   D. a question of grammatical and syntactic correctness
4. According to some authorities
   A. more people speak Chinese dialect than English
   B. more people speak English as an auxiliary language than as a first language
   C. more people speak English in the UK than in England
   D. about one-fourth of the world's population speaks English
5. The overall implication of the passage is that
   A. to suppose that 230 million people speak English as a native language would certainly be an underestimate
   B. the 55 million inhabitants of the British Isles speak like the 30 million inhabitants of the dominions and colonies
   C. a little less than half the native English speakers in the world live in the US

D. about one-tenth of the total English-speaking world population lives in British dominions and colonies

PASSAGE-4

What is the future which awaits our children? The underlying assumption of the question, that Indian children have a common future, is itself dubious. It can legitimately be asked whether a student who is well-fed, attending a boarding school in the salubrious climate of the hills and learning to use computers has any future in common with a malnourished child who goes to a school with no blackboards, if indeed he does go to school. The latter may have no worthwhile future at all. And it might be worthwhile to analyse the significance of this marginalisation of more than 75 per cent of the children of this country.

The failure to provide an infrastructure for primary education in the villages of India more than 40 years after independence is in sharp contrast with the sophisticated institutions, for technical institutes of higher education are funded by the government, which essentially means that the money to support them comes from taxes. And, since indirect taxation forms a substantial part of the taxes collected by the government, the financial burden is borne by all the people. L.K. Jha put it graphically when he observed that 25 paise of every rupee spent on educating an IIT student comes from the pockets of men and women whose children may never enter a proper classroom.

1. The author is trying to highlight which of the following?

A. Faulty system of direct taxes

B. The greatness of L.K. Jha

C. Need of sophisticated education for rural poor

D. Need to have common future for Indian children

2. Which of the following pairs have been termed as 'sharp contrast' by the author?

(*i*) Infrastructure for technical education

(*ii*) Lack of infrastructure for rural primary schools

(*iii*) 25 paise of every rupee earned by Government is spent on education

(*iv*) The financial burden of higher technical education is borne by all people

(*v*) 75% of children have limited opportunities

A. (*ii*) and (*iv*) B. (*ii*) and (*iii*)

C. (*iii*) and (*iv*) D. (*i*) and (*ii*)

3. Which of the following statements is not true?

(*i*) The author welcomes Govt.'s initiative on primary education

(*ii*) 75% of the children have a bright future

(*iii*) 25% cost of educating a technocrat comes from poor people

A. Only (*i*) B. Only (*ii*)

C. Only (*iii*) D. Only (*i*) and (*ii*)

4. According to the author, who among the following does not have a hopeful and prosperous future?

(*i*) All students from technical institutes

(*ii*) All students financially supported by the Government

A. Only (*i*) B. Only (*ii*)

C. Both (*i*) and (*ii*) D. Neither (*i*) nor (*ii*)

5. What seems to be the likely answer of the author to the question posed by him in the first sentence of the passage?

(*i*) There is no common future for the Indian children

(*ii*) The future is worthwhile for majority of Indian children

(*iii*) The majority may never enter a proper classroom

A. Only (*i*) B. Only (*ii*)

C. Only (*iii*) D. Both (*i*) and (*ii*)

6. What seems to be the purpose of the author in writing this passage?

A. Setting goals for children of upper middle class

B. Questioning the legitimacy of public schools

C. Highlighting lack of infrastructural facilities for primary education

D. Focusing on inequality in educational opportunities

PASSAGE-5

Cyber crime is the branded stigma defacing the culture and magnanimity of computer technology. It is upkeeping the flag with indomitable triumph against developing computer technology worldwide.

Modern age is striding with marching steps of technology revolution beating the past decade of ancestral belief with ultimate care. Computer invention has unfolded the mystery of quick access with the objective of minimum manpower and cutting the time consumption parameters.

As each coin has dual face of its portrait, likewise computer technology is sick of creeping virus. Synthetic man-made dilemma of site hackers activation is causing setback to the expanding anchor of revolutionary device with great loss of time, economy and data profile as suffered by consumers. A recent report from Internet security firm Websense estimates that 85.6 per cent of all the unwanted e-mails contained links to spam sites. The company's data suggests that the number of malicious sites grew 233 per cent in the last six months and saw 671 per cent growth in the number of malicious sites during the last year. In June alone, the total number of e-mails detected as containing viruses increased by 600 per cent compared to May.

Chat rooms, blogs and message-boards where the users post comments have been identified as the top targets of hackers and spammers due to the high traffic these attract. According to Websense, 95 per cent of user-generated comments to blogs, chat rooms and message-boards during the first half of the year were malicious.

It is advisable not to click on spurious links and stay away from keying in passwords at unknown sites as they are most likely to be spammed. Hackers can steal your passwords and log in to your account and access critical information like account numbers and contact details among other things.

1. The above passage is:
   A. an advisory for the computer users.
   B. an advisory for the Internet users.
   C. a warning against possible threat to the Internet users.
   D. related to chat rooms, blogs and message boards.
2. People who use chat rooms and blogs,
   A. are safe and have no threats from spam.
   B. are more prone to malicious e-mails.
   C. create virus and hack the accounts of others.
   D. are unsafe.
3. According to the writer, it is not safe to:
   A. log on to spurious links.
   B. access one's own account frequently.
   C. have essential information stored in a computer.
   D. include data-stealing code.
4. Hackers and spammers, according to the writer, are:
   A. a new threat to the Internet users and the economy.
   B. only pranksters and not serious threat to the system.
   C. trained, professional technocrats who are an asset.
   D. not expert professionals.
5. Which word in the passage is synonym of *weblog*?
   A. blog B. password
   C. site D. e-mail
6. Which agency has assessed the data record with spam sites?
   A. Microsoft
   B. Internet security from Google
   C. Websense
   D. Spammers
7. Which month dominates the e-mails detection data record?
   A. May B. June
   C. Last six months D. Last year

PASSAGE-6

Progress in life depends a good deal on crossing one threshold after another. Some time ago, a man watched his little nephew try to write his name. It was hard work, very hard work. The little boy had arrived at an effort threshold. Today he writes his name with comparative ease. No new threshold confronts him. This is the way with all of us. As soon as we cross one threshold, as soon as we conquer one difficulty, a new difficulty appears, or should appear. Some people make the mistake of steering clear of thresholds. Anything that requires genuine thinking and use of energy, they avoid. They prefer to stay in a rut where thresholds are not met. Probably, they have been at their job a number of years. Things are easy for them. They make no effort to seek out new obstacles to overcome. Real progress stops under such circumstances.

Some middle-aged and elderly people greatly enrich their lives by continuing to cross thresholds. One man went into an entirely new business when he was past middle life and made success of it, De Morgan didn't start to write novels until he was past sixty. Psychologists have discovered that man can continue to learn throughout his life. And it is undoubtedly better to try and fail than not to try at all. There one can be placed in the category of the Swiss mountaineer of whom it was said, *"He died climbing"*. When a new difficulty arises to obstruct your path, do not complain. Accept the challenge. Determine to cross this threshold as you have crossed numerous other thresholds in your past. In the words of a poet, do not rest but strive *to pass from dream to grander dream.*

1. What obstructs real progress in life?
   A. Remaining at one and the same post
   B. Avoiding the thinking and energy
   C. Shunning every work
   D. Stopping education

2. What does progress in life depend upon?
   A. Good habits
   B. Hardwork
   C. Overcoming one difficulty after another
   D. Spirit of service and cooperation

3. What does *'He died climbing'* signify?
   A. He died when he was climbing the hill
   B. He died before getting at the top
   C. He strove hard till the last moment of life
   D. He climbed the hill and then died

4. What does *'to pass from dream to grander dream'* mean?
   A. Always having greater and greater aspiration in life
   B. Seeing one good dream and then greater aspiration in life
   C. Making plan after plan
   D. Seeing one dream after the other

5. What did the man entering a new business past middle life do of his business?
   A. He miserably failed in it
   B. He achieved partial success
   C. He dropped the business after some time
   D. He achieved good success in it

6. How can you accomplish the most difficult tasks?
   A. By mobilizing all possible resources
   B. By avoiding all obstacles
   C. By sticking to hardwork
   D. By doing it bit by bit and persisting in the effort

7. What does De Morgan's life teach?
   A. That it is futile to learn many things
   B. That one is never old in case he has vigour
   C. That it is never too late to learn
   D. That creative writing can be made even late in life

8. How do middle-aged and elderly people add brilliance to their lives?
   A. By overcoming difficulty one after another
   B. By getting sycophants to surround them
   C. By making fine speeches
   D. By acquiring resourcefulness

9. What should we do when a new difficulty obstructs our path?
   A. Run away from it
   B. Be bold and face it
   C. Manoeuvre to get it removed
   D. Enlist other people's help to get it over

10. When did De Morgan start to write novels?
   A. When he was sixty years old
   B. When he was below sixty
   C. When he studied psychology
   D. None of these

PASSAGE-7

It is *heartening* to know that if one had not had any heart attack earlier and he stops smoking, his chances of having a heart attack *drop* to that of a non-smoker in about six months' time. Stopping of smoking is also the single most effective means of secondary prevention (recurrence of a heart attack) in heart patients.

Smoking leads to pain and stiffness in the legs while walking. No amount of drugs can help. The only remedy is to give up smoking. If women smoke during pregnancy, there is an increased risk of death of the baby in the womb or soon after birth. Even where the baby survives, there is likelihood of delayed physical and intellectual development of the baby till it reaches 11 years of age.

Still worse the fact about smoking is that passive smoking is equally dangerous. Passive smokers are those who do not smoke but being in the company of smokers have to inhale smoke exhaled by the smokers They are equally prone to heart diseases, lung cancer and bronchitis, for no fault of theirs. It is seen that the incidence of these diseases is greater among women whose husbands are *heavy* smokers As such, every non-smoker has a fundamental right to safeguard himself against the danger of passive smoking. "Your smoking is injurious to my health and I have a right to stop you from smoking" could be the slogan against passive smoking. It is a great threat to the health of the individual, the family and the society. In fact one has to choose between health and smoking including passive smoking. *One cannot have both.*

Another matter of *grave concern* about smoking is the long time interval between the start of smoking habit and the manifestation of deadly diseases like cancer, chronic bronchitis and heart attack. People are generally not aware of the link between smoking and the misery they have to undergo years later and younger people often fall victim to this menacing habit under the wrong impression that they are *immune* to its disastrous effects, not realising that they are *heading* towards catastrophe. The prolonged incubation period of many tobacco-related diseases has prevented recognition of the size of the threat and the *grim* picture of chronic and life-threatening diseases.

1. What is "passive smoking"?

A. Giving up the habit of smoking abruptly
B. Exhaling smoke by a non-smoker
C. Unintended intake of smoke exhaled by smokers
D. Smoking cigarettes which are harmless in nature

2. The effects of passive smoking are more and more prominently observed among

A. the children
B. the smokers
C. the wives of smokers
D. the non-smokers

3. Which of the following is a heartening thing, according to the author?

A. People who have had a heart attack stop smoking
B. It takes only six months for any person to quit smoking
C. The smoker carries the risk of heart attack for six months
D. None of these

4. Which of the following statements is/are false in the context of the passage?

(*i*) Passive smokers are not free from risk of heart diseases
(*ii*) Intake of certain medicines helps recover pain and stiffness in legs caused by smoking
(*iii*) Younger people are immune to the disastrous effects if their regular smoking is under control

A. (*i*) and (*ii*) only B. (*ii*) and (*iii*) only
C. (*ii*) only D. (*iii*) only

5. Which of the following is not mentioned in the passage as a likely result of smoking by women during pregnancy?

A. Death of baby before birth
B. Death of baby after birth
C. Survival of baby with some abnormality
D. Abnormal delay in the childbirth

6. Which of the following is considered by the author as a matter of "grave concern"?
 A. Inordinate delay in appearance of symptoms of hazards of smoking
 B. Long time required for giving up the habit of smoking
 C. Manifestation of deadly diseases like cancer, bronchitis, etc.
 D. Lack of awareness of people regarding the hazards of smoking

7. The youth feel that they are immune to the hazardous effects of smoking because
 A. these effects of smoking are not visible within a short time span
 B. they do not realise that they are heading towards disaster
 C. they feel a great thrill in acquiring the habit of smoking
 D. the link between smoking and its disastrous effects cannot be established

8. Which factor prevents people from realising the extent of threat of smoking hazards?
 A. Their lack of awareness of civic responsibilities
 B. Their firm belief that they are not immune to these hazards
 C. The less disastrous effects of tobacco-related diseases
 D. None of these

9. The last sentence of the third para *"One cannot have both"* means
 A. active smoking and passive smoking
 B. smoking and risk of heart diseases
 C. threat to the individual and also to the family
 D. None of these

Directions (Qs. 10 to 12): *Choose the word which is most nearly the **SAME** in meaning as the word given in bold capitals as used in the passage.*

10. HEADING

A. crowning	B. marching
C. adorning	D. title

11. HEAVY

A. excessive	B. bulky
C. large	D. thick

12. DROP

A. roll	B. escape
C. remove	D. reduce

Directions (Qs. 13 to 15): *Choose the word which is most nearly the **OPPOSITE** in meaning of the word given in bold capitals as used in the passage.*

13. GRIM

A. dim	B. dark
C. presentable	D. pleasant

14. IMMUNE

A. free	B. vulnerable
C. powerful	D. weak

15. HEARTENING

A. cheerful	B. miserable
C. frightening	D. dangerous

PASSAGE-8

The happy man is the man who lives objectively, who has free affections and wide interests, who secures his happiness through these interests and affections and through the fact that they, in turn, make him an object of interest and affection to many others. To be the recipient of affection is a potent cause of happiness, but the man who demands affection is not the man upon whom it is *bestowed.* The man who receives affection is, speaking broadly, the man who gives it. But it is useless to attempt to give it as a calculation, in the way in which one might lend money at interest, for a calculated affection is not genuine and is not felt to be so by the recipient.

What then can a man do who is unhappy because he is encased in self? So long as he continues to think about the causes of his unhappiness, he continues to be self-centred and therefore does not get outside the vicious circle, if he is to get outside it, it must be genuine interests, not by simulated interests adopted merely as a medicine. Although this difficulty is real, there is nevertheless much that he can do if he has rightly diagnosed his trouble. If, for example, his trouble is due to a sense of sin, conscious or unconscious, he can first persuade his conscious mind that he has, no reason to feel sinful and then proceed, to plant his rational conviction in his unconscious mind, concerning himself meanwhile with some more or less neutral activity. If he succeeds in *dispelling* the sense of sin, it is possible that genuine objective interests will arise spontaneously. If his trouble is self-pity, he can deal with it in the same manner after first persuading himself that there is nothing extraordinarily unfortunate in his circumstances.

If fear is his trouble, let him practise exercises designed to give courage. Courage has been recognised from time immemorial as an important virtue, and a great part of training of boys and young men has been devoted to producing a type of character capable of fearlessness in battle. But moral courage and intellectual courage have been much less studied, they also, however, have their technique. Admit to yourself everyday at least one painful truth, you will find this quite useful. Teach yourself to feel that life still be worth living even if you were not, as of course you are, immeasurably superior to all your friends in virtue and in intelligence. Exercises of this sort prolonged through several years will at last enable you to admit facts *without flinching* and will, in so doing, free you from the empire of fear over a very large field.

1. Who according to the passage is the happy man?
A. who is encased in self
B. who has free affection and wide interests
C. who is free from worldly passions
D. who has externally centre passions

2. According to the passage, calculated affection
A. appears to be false and fabricated
B. makes other pen-on to love you
C. turns into permanent affection over a period of time
D. leads to self-pity

3. Which of the following virtues, according to the passage, has been recognised for long as an important virtue?
A. Patriotism B. Sacrifice
C. Courage D. Self-consciousness

4. Which of the following, according to the passage, has not been studied much?
A. Feeling of guilt and self-pity
B. The state of mind of an unhappy man
C. How to get absorbed in other interests
D. Moral and intellectual courage

5. If a man is suffering from a sense of sin
A. he should invite opinion of others
B. he should admit his sin at once
C. he should consciously realize that he has no reason to feel sinful
D. he should develop a fearless character

6. What happens to a man who demands affection?
A. His feelings are reciprocated by others
B. He tends to take a calculated risk
C. He becomes a victim of a viscious circle
D. None of these

7. What should a man do who is suffering from the feeling of self-pity?
A. He should control his passions and emotions
B. He should persuade himself that everything is alright in his circumstances
C. He should seek affection from others
D. He should develop a feeling of fearlessness

8. How to get out of the viscious circle mentioned in the passage?
A. By practicing skills of concentration
B. By inculcating the habits of self-absorption
C. Being true to others and one's internal circumstances
D. None of these

9. Which of the following statements is not *true* in the context of the passage?
A. Happy man has wide interests
B. Courage has been recognized as an important virtue
C. Unhappy man is encased in self

D. Issue of intellectual courage has been extensively studied

10. Which of the following words is ***SIMILAR*** in meaning of the word **'bestowed'** as used in the passage?

A. Conferred B. Accommodated
C. Trusted D. Withdrawn

11. Which of the following statements is *true* in the context of the passage?

A. All passions stem from unhappiness
B. The happy man lives in subjectively
C. Any virtue has a dark side, also
D. One feels happy if one receives affection

12. Which of the following words is ***SIMILAR*** in meaning to the word **'flinching'** as used in the passage?

A. Wincing B. Convincing
C. Explaining D. Debating

13. What happens when you think about cause of your unhappiness?

A. You try to introspect and look critically at yourself
B. You realize that the life can be lived in different ways
C. You try to practice exercise designed to give courage
D. You remain a self-centred person

14. What according to the passage is the real cause of happiness?

A. Material rewards and incentives received
B. Critical analysis of the happy state of mind
C. Affection received from others
D. Calculated risks taken

15. Which of the following words is ***OPPOSITE*** in meaning of the word **'dispelling'** as used in the passage?

A. Giving B. Accumulating
C. Projecting D. Scattering

PASSAGE-9

Education, particularly higher education, is the obvious but crucially important instrument for nation building. As Confucious has said:

"If you are thinking of one year, plant rice. If you are thinking of a decade, plant trees. If you are thinking of a century, educate the people."

When we set about the task of higher education, we should be absolutely clear in our perception of the goals of education in the specific context of our nation's development. No *doubt,* one of the important aims of education would be to create the required range and nature of trained manpower assessed to be needed by different sectors of national growth. The entire educational apparatus must be geared progressively to fulfill the requirements of different phases of our growth in every sector—primary, secondary and *tertiary.* The aim must be to ensure that our country does not experience either *paucity,* or a *surfeit* of trained manpower in any specific segment of our economy. The requirements of our country, as a free, democratic, secular, socialist, nation, *aspiring* for rapid development, *entail* a specific recipe for our educational institutions. Today's educational institutions must therefore be developed accordingly and must regulate themselves to give the country the precise nature and quantum of trained manpower as projected by the requirements of our planned economy.

1. The author has quoted thoughts of Confucious to stress

A. importance of planting trees for human beings
B. the worthless efforts in planting rice
C. the benefits of investing in education
D. the need for assessing manpower requirement

2. Which statement cannot be made on the basis of the passage?

A. Higher education should keep in view the requirements of national economy
B. Higher education has not been employed for nation building
C. All levels of education have a role to play in nation's growth
D. In our country we need to have a specially planned educational system

3. The writer believes that
   A. there are no problems related to higher education
   B. investment in education is of long-range
   C. higher education should be used to assess manpower needs
   D. aims of higher education in India are absolutely clear
4. The author's expectations from higher education, are essentially
   A. unrealistic B. confusing
   C. critical D. vague
5. The writer indicates that
   A. higher education did not play any role in national growth
   B. primary education did not play any role in national growth
   C. our nation experiences paucity of trained manpower in many sectors
   D. today's higher education has no precise goals to achieve
6. Author has used the word 'apparatus' to indicate the
   A. scientific nature of education
   B. complicated organization demanded by education
   C. readily visible benefits of education
   D. entire equipment of education to perform particular function
7. Which of the following has not been conveyed by the passage?
   A. Education at any level can contribute in nation building
   B. Manpower needs in many areas can be fulfilled through higher education
   C. Rapid development of our nation is possible through higher education
   D. Present higher education does not ensure surfeit of trained manpower
8. This passage is likely to be addressed to
   A. politicians only
   B. scientists only
   C. students only
   D. cannot be said
9. Choose a suitable title to the passage:
   A. Manpower Planning in India
   B. Importance of Higher Education
   C. Demands of Higher Education
   D. Role of Higher Education in India

Directions (Qs.10 to 12): *Choose the word which is most nearly the* ***SAME*** *in meaning as the word given in bold capitals as used in the passage.*

10. **DOUBT**
    A. suspicion B. certain
    C. definite D. sure
11. **TERTIARY**
    A. last B. important
    C. third D. terminal
12. **ASPIRING**
    A. inquiring B. awaiting
    C. involving D. striving

Directions (Qs.13 to 15): *Choose the word which is most* ***OPPOSITE*** *in meaning as the word given in bold capitals as used in the passage.*

13. **PAUCITY**
    A. moderate B. enormity
    C. mediocrity D. littleness
14. **SURFEIT**
    A. abundance B. redundancy
    C. repletion D. lack
15. **ENTAIL**
    A. entitled B. ensure
    C. dismiss D. retain

PASSAGE-10

Books are a great treasurehouse of knowledge. They are the living examples of man's *march* on the path to higher and higher civilisation. The great men who died long ago, live in their books. We feel their very personality and existence when we read their books. We feel as if they were conversing with us.

Books not only store civilization but also carry it forward. All coming generations get the light of knowledge from the books written by their ancestors and try to improve upon that knowledge. Civilization cannot make much *headway* in a country where there are not many *great* books. We get through books the latest knowledge in the fields of arts, science, commerce, etc. This knowledge is helpful to us and *enables* us to achieve success in the field of our choice.

Books are never failing friends. They never *desert* us, not even when all fair-weather friends have deserted us. They dispel the dark clouds of gloom from our minds and increase our happiness if we are already happy. Through the ages, the scriptures and other great books have provided immeasurable *solace* to the wounded and strife-torn humanity.

There may be books prescribed for some course or profession, but then there are books for general study. The books of literature—poetry, drama, novel, short stories, etc., are generally highly thrilling and inspiring if they are written by a good author. There may be tragic, comical or humorous books. The question is that of an individual's choice.

To be a lover of books, though not to be bookworm, is a sign of good luck. A voracious reader gets much *more pleasure* from reading books than a miser gets in hoarding money. The knowledge embedded in books is valueless; so is pleasure obtained from reading them. A good book absorbs the whole spirit of man; the reader's pleasure is indescribable.

1. Which of the following, according to the passage, is not true about books?
   A. They are source of inspiration
   B. They are source of knowledge
   C. They are source of happiness
   D. They are means of livelihood

2. How do the books help in progress of civilization?
   A. Based on the earlier books new knowledge is obtained
   B. The books provide solution to many problems
   C. The books inspire the scientists
   D. Not mentioned in the passage

3. How do the books make people more happy?
   A. They help the reader to overcome the shadows of uncertainty
   B. They help bring in joy by amusing the reader through their content
   C. They help the reader to understand the darker side of life
   D. Not mentioned in the passage

4. Which of the following is the author's view about the knowledge and pleasure derived from books?
   (*i*) We get more of knowledge and less of pleasure
   (*ii*) We get more of pleasure and less of knowledge
   (*iii*) We get knowledge and pleasure in equal measure
   A. only (*i*)   B. only (*ii*)
   C. either (*i*) or (*ii*)   D. only (*iii*)

5. The high quality of books produced by a country indicates:
   A. it has a high rate of literacy
   B. it has a progressive civilization
   C. it is not an industrialised nation
   D. it has learned ancestors

6. Why are the books, according to the passage, called never-failing friends?
   A. Books do not betray individuals
   B. Books are inanimate
   C. Books always give companionship to the reader
   D. Books are available in the market anytime unlike others

7. How do the books help in bringing peace in the minds of people?
   A. Books provide information about the past civilization
   B. Books help people learn to take correct steps with the help of the recorded information
   C. Books act as a window to the minds of the great men
   D. Not mentioned in the passage

8. Which of the following has been described as a sign of good luck?
- A. Being a miser
- B. Having lot of money
- C. Advancing the culture
- D. A passion for books

Directions (Qs. 9 to 12): *Choose the word which is most nearly the **SAME** in meaning as the word given in bold capitals as used in the passage.*

9. SOLACE
- A. peace B. tranquillity
- C. calmness D. console

10. ENABLES
- A. helps B. succeeds
- C. promotes D. stops

11. HEADWAY
- A. higher B. forge
- C. movement D. improve

12. MARCH
- A. move B. progress
- C. pass D. register

Directions (Qs. 13 to 15): *Choose the word which is most **OPPOSITE** in meaning of the word given in bold capitals as used in the passage.*

13. GREAT
- A. small B. thin
- C. short D. ordinary

14. PLEASURE
- A. displeasure B. pain
- C. happiness D. hardship

15. DESERT
- A. waterhole B. bitter
- C. accompany D. propel

ANSWERS

PASSAGE-1

1	2	3	4
A	B	A	A

PASSAGE-2

1	2	3	4	5
A	C	D	A	D

PASSAGE-3

1	2	3	4	5
A	D	C	D	A

PASSAGE-4

1	2	3	4	5	6
D	A	D	A	A	D

PASSAGE-5

1	2	3	4	5	6	7
A	D	A	A	A	C	B

PASSAGE-6

1	2	3	4	5
A	C	C	A	D
6	**7**	**8**	**9**	**10**
D	B	A	B	D

PASSAGE-7

1	2	3	4	5
C	C	D	B	D
6	**7**	**8**	**9**	**10**
A	A	D	D	B
11	**12**	**13**	**14**	**15**
A	D	D	B	C

PASSAGE-8

1	2	3	4	5
B	A	C	D	C
6	**7**	**8**	**9**	**10**
D	B	D	D	A
11	**12**	**13**	**14**	**15**
D	D	D	C	B

PASSAGE-9

1	2	3	4	5
D	D	C	D	D
6	**7**	**8**	**9**	**10**
D	A	D	B	A
11	**12**	**13**	**14**	**15**
C	D	B	D	C

PASSAGE-10

1	2	3	4	5
D	A	D	D	B
6	**7**	**8**	**9**	**10**
A	D	D	D	A
11	**12**	**13**	**14**	**15**
D	B	D	B	C

❑❑❑

14 Cloze Test

A cloze test is a procedure in which a person is asked to supply words that have been removed from a passage as a test of his ability to comprehend text. Practise it regularly to score well.

PASSAGES

Directions: *In each of the following passages some numbered blank spaces are given. For each numbered blank space four answer choices are given. Pick out the one which is the most appropriate for that blank space, keeping the trend of the passage in mind.*

Passage-1

Mankind's most ....(1).... treasure of thoughts is carefully preserved in the golden casket of books. The ....(2).... of books is as vast as the universe, for there is no corner of it which they have left ....(3).... . There is no ....(4).... of books on any topic, be it as simple as the composition of sodium nitrate or as ....(5).... as the mechanism of a spacecraft rocketing towards Mars. The ....(6).... of books is not only most easily available but is enlightened, dependable and lifelong. In times of distress they make us stoically ....(7).... of the object that causes uneasiness and we learn to ....(8).... with the sting of adversity.

Questions

1. A. costly B. important C. valuable D. vast

2. A. area B. scope C. storage D. kingdom

3. A. unexplored B. unseen C. untouched D. unapproached

4. A. lack B. dearth C. shortage D. insufficiency

5. A. extricate B. intricate C. intrinsic D. internecine

6. A. company B. assistance C. friendship D. companionship

7. A. defiant B. defendant C. defensible D. delusive

8. A. adapt B. adopt C. exist D. co-exist

Passage-2

Though the government has tried to ....(1).... Naxalism with all its might, much more needs to be done to totally root out the ....(2).... of Naxalism. The roots of Naxalism ....(3).... economic backwardness and social exploitation of the peasants and the weaker classes. Thus, the best way to ....(4).... Naxalism is to bring the naxals ....(5).... the mainstream. ....(6).... policies and schemes should be implemented effectively ....(7).... the Naxals economically stable. They should be ....(8).... to participate in democratic processes. The government has to ....(9).... the social upliftment of the Naxals. Use of force in ....(10).... Naxalism will yield little success.

Questions

1. A. crush B. handle
   C. tackle D. suppress
2. A. menace B. whole
   C. gamut D. stems
3. A. lies in B. are in
   C. abound in D. exist in
4. A. crash B. crush
   C. break D. defy
5. A. in B. on
   C. into D. within
6. A. Current B. Latest
   C. Occurring D. Existing
7. A. so that B. so as to make
   C. such that D. to make
8. A. insisted B. brought
   C. encouraged D. forced
9. A. assure B. insure
   C. guarantee D. ensure
10. A. countering B. defying
    C. banishing D. desecrating

Passage-3

We are living in very exciting ....(1).... . The ....(2).... change is dizzying and the impact this progress is having on our present and — more importantly — on our future is difficult to ....(3).... in its ...(4).... . This is the age of ....(5).... micro-processors, sophisticated software, new hardware technology and high bandwidth, high-speed networks. The PC gave us a new way to work, play and ....(6).... . In fact, it brought ....(7).... our desktops computing power, which until a few years ....(8).... had only been available to corporates. With the ....(9).... of the internet, the PC ....(10).... us the most convenient and flexible way to head on to the Net.

Questions

1. A. periods B. days
   C. phase D. times
2. A. phase B. pace
   C. sphere D. drastic
3. A. guess B. forecast
   C. comprehend D. approximate
4. A. whole B. entirety
   C. fruition D. fullness
5. A. strong B. changing
   C. powerful D. sonorous
6. A. convey B. communicate
   C. entertain D. enjoy
7. A. onto B. to
   C. on D. at
8. A. back B. earlier
   C. behind D. before
9. A. addendum B. adherence
   C. afoot D. advent
10. A. allowed B. privileged
    C. brought D. offered

Passage-4

What is required today in our country is ....(1).... of a new political culture based on full respect for human liberty, on pluralism and on a better social deal for all. The major ....(2).... facing us today is to carry out democratic transformation in all the ....(3)...., social, cultural, economic and political. The events of the 20th century ....(4).... one thing absolutely clear that human ....(5)...., everywhere, specially in countries whose political structures were ....(6).... to reflect the revolutionary aspirations of the people ....(7).... not only under stress and strain but are ....(8).... vast upheavals because of the ....(9).... of democracy. At the same time it has also to be understood that democracy cannot be ....(10).... into a static mould.

Questions

1. A. growing B. developing
   C. creating D. creation
2. A. development B. crisis
   C. challenge D. drawback
3. A. corners B. context
   C. realm D. spheres
4. A. have made B. has made
   C. had made D. made

5. A. travails B. traverse
   C. traps D. transverse

6. A. supposed B. meant
   C. caused D. forced

7. A. were B. was
   C. are D. have been

8. A. developing B. evolving
   C. experiencing D. faced with

9. A. denial B. rebuff
   C. rebuttal D. absence

10. A. shaped B. flex
    C. frozen D. caused

Passage-5

For centuries, women not only in India but all over the world ....(1).... treated as ....(2).... secondary position to men. ....(3).... human history men ....(4).... far greater power then women to name, classify, and order the worlds in which they both live. ....(5).... studies in various parts of the world point out to a wide ....(6).... in male and female roles ....(7).... cultures and demonstrate the possibility of change in these sex-determined roles. The 20th century in particular ....(8).... the cause of gender justice by internationalizing struggles for equality ....(9).... women and other oppressed people. Women's struggles against their ....(10).... were intertwined in ....(11).... degrees with ideologies and movements based on the values of freedom, self-determination, equality, democracy and justice.

Questions

1. A. has been B. have been
   C. had been D. were

2. A. occupying B. taking
   C. possessing D. serving

3. A. All through B. Throughout
   C. Since D. From

4. A. have B. had
   C. have had D. enjoy

5. A. Sociological B. Anthropological
   C. General D. Practical

6. A. concord B. repulsion
   C. disagreement D. variation

7. A. among B. across
   C. between D. of

8. A. developed B. evolved
   C. promoted D. entertained

9. A. for B. to
   C. among D. by

10. A. subsidiary B. subsequent
    C. subservience D. subordination

11. A. various B. varying
    C changing D. differing

Passage-6

Visualisation is a strong ....(1).... to memory. Those persons who ......(2)..... a powerful memory cannot do so without taking the help of visualisation. Such persons have developed the sk[illegible] visualisation even in such ....(4).... tas[illegible] remembering names and numbers. These persons have the names and numbers ....(5).... in their brain even after hearing those names and figures only once. On the other hand those who take the help of revising to memorise ....(6).... to forget it once they have ....(7).... the practice of revising ....(8).... the ones who have applied visualisation to memorise. Psychologists ....(9).... in visualisation a powerful tool for personality development. The more you visualise, the more you are ....(10).... your attitude and behaviour to the blue prints of your vision and ....(11).... more you are inching towards success.

Questions

1. A. way B. path
   C. aid D. symptom

2. A. command B. master
   C. rule D. enjoy

3. A. use B. apply
   C. put D. place

4. A. trivial B. difficult
   C. mundane D. unscrupulous

5. A. impress B. imprinted
   C. impinge D. store

6. A. bent B. incline
   C. prone d. tend

7. A. dropped B. left
C. gave up D. given up

8. A. unlike B. opposite
C. contrary D. not like

9. A. found B. have found
C. sees D. finds

10. A. shaping B. moulding
C. making D. attuning

11. A. actually B. factually
C. subsequently D. consequently

Passage-7

The development of an area depends on the resources ....(1).... in the area, the needs and ....(2).... of the people living there and the technological skill ....(3).... by them. Humans play an important and [illegible] ....(4).... of development of an [illegible] choose the ....(5).... of resources which could be developed to our ....(6).... . The natural ....(7).... available in an area ....(8).... value as a resource only when people find a use for them. There are ....(9).... where large potential resources are available, but they ....(10).... developed for economic reasons. Lack of capital for investments, roads and railway lines, and other ....(11).... facilities may stand in the way of resource development.

Questions

1. A. present B. prevalent
C. available D. exist

2. A. inspirations B. aspirations
C. ambitions D. curiosity

3. A. handled B. practised
C. availed D. possessed

4. A. system B. design
C. pattern D. style

5. A. class B. group
C. variety D. types

6. A. good B. advantage
C. approach D. favour

7. A. secrets B. phenomenon
C. products D. endowments

8. A. get B. acquire
C. possess D. takes

9. A. instances B. events
C. circumstances D. happenings

10. A. have not yet been
B. haven't been
C. are not yet
D. yet have not been

11. A. common B. general
C. infrastructural D. structural

Passage-8

The Naxal problem in India is basically socio-economic in ....(1).... . The main reasons ....(2).... the Naxal movement in India are the ....(3).... of peasants and their weak social and economic position. ....(4).... of the peasants are landless labourers whose lands have been ....(5).... occupied by the landlords. Moreover, the landlords give ....(6).... wages to the peasants. Their ....(7).... suffering at the hands of the landlords thus encourage many peasants to take law ....(8).... their own hands. Due to their poor economic condition the peasants easily ....(9).... the trap of the naxal leaders who have their ....(10).... interests. Illiteracy, unemployment, police excesses, corruption and ....(11).... administration further ....(12).... this complex problem.

Questions

1. A. form B. shape
C. behaviour D. nature

2. A. for B. of
C. in D. behind

3. A. complaisance B. exploitation
C. domination D. exculpation

4. A. Many B. Much
C. Most D. All

5. A. imperiously B. imperatively
C. forcefully D. forcibly

6. A. improper B. small
C. inadequate D. insufficient

7. A. long B. brutal
C. pathetic D. great

8. A. in B. into
C. on D. by

9. A. fall into B. fall in
C. fell in D. fell into

10. A. selfish B. vested
C. vicious D. vindictive

11. A. failed B. improper
C. inefficient D. bureaucratic

12. A. heighten B. deepen
C. add D. worsen

Passage-9

No doubt various ....(1).... and Acts are there to eliminate the ....(2).... practice of child labour. But the ....(3).... is that, these are not being implemented in both letter and spirit, for which the ....(4).... of the problem remains as it was. Therefore a judicious, pragmatic, integrated and time-bound ....(5).... supplemented by ....(6).... follow-up action is essential to ....(7).... the problem that ....(8).... deep root in our Society. It is true that child labour can't be ....(9)... with a magic wand. If we ....(10).... time-bound goals and follow, of course, with the ....(11).... assistance of ILO and UNICEF, it is possible to eliminate the problem of child labour. With strong political will power and people's backing nothing is ....(12).... . Rather ....(13).... the bud we should let it blossom and spread its fragrance all around. ....(14).... lies the progress and prosperity of the society.

Questions

1. A. means B. methods
C. source D. provisions

2. A. unjust B. inhuman
C. mal D. illegal

3. A. anxiety B. abrasion
C. tragedy D. conclusion

4. A. magnitude B. depth
C. gravity D. soaring

5. A. approach B. analysis
C. survey D. scheme

6. A. continuous B. thorough
C. throughout D. regular

7. A. outroot B. uproot
C. downroot D. grassroot

8. A. have B. has
C. had D. has taken

9. A. wipe out B. wipe off
C. wipe up D. wiped

10. A. keep B. put
C. put up D. set

11. A. ongoing B. continuing
C. unending D. frequent

12. A. insurmountable B. intangible
C. inscrutable D. incorrigible

13. A. killing B. hurting
C. destroying D. nipping

14. A. Here B. There
C. Therein D. Herein

Passage-10

Every action we perform ....(1).... a result. And, naturally, we lay claim ....(2).... the results or fruits ....(3).... from that action in the ....(4).... that it is we who perform the action. This is .....(5).... ignorance because ....(6).... is it the Lord who ....(7).... the result of any action, it is by His will ....(8).... that even the action is accomplished. The will of the Lord ....(9).... whether we cooperate with His will or strive ....(10).... . If God wills that an action takes place, he arranges for the ....(11).... for it to happen. It is ....(12).... experience that sometimes despite our best efforts we ....(13).... achieve the results we desire, and at other times the seemingly most ....(14).... situations mysteriously get ....(15).... . ....(16).... way man chooses to act, both the act and the outcome of the cost are dependent ....(17).... on the will of the Lord.

Questions

1. A. produce B. produces
C. causes D. undergoes

2. A. on B. at
C. to D. for

3. A. occurring B. obtaining
C. deriving D. falling

4. A. belief B. hope
C. fantasy D. folly

5. A. sheen B. keen
C. sheer D. sheathe

6. A. alone B. only that
C. not only D. for only

7. A. declares B. decides
C. ordains D. ornate

8. A. completely B. entirely
C. only D. alone

9. A. prevails always
B. prevails everywhere
C. is prevalent
D. always prevails

10. A. alone B. always
C. constantly D. independently

11. A. wherewithal B. whereabouts
C. whatsoever D. wherefore

12. A. usual B. general
C. universal D. common

13. A. does not B. may not
C. do not D. might not

14. A. intractable B. intangible
C. internecine D. intricate

15. A. subsided B. resolved
C. solved D. converted

16. A. Whatever B. All the
C. All those D. Whichever

17. A. mainly B. actually
C. entirely D. generally

ANSWERS

PASSAGE-1

1	2	3	4	5	6
C	D	A	B	B	D
7	8				
A	D				

PASSAGE-2

1	2	3	4	5	6
C	A	A	B	C	D
7	8	9	10		
B	C	D	A		

PASSAGE-3

1	2	3	4	5	6
D	B	C	B	C	B
7	8	9	10		
A	D	D	D		

PASSAGE-4

1	2	3	4	5	6
D	C	D	A	A	B
7	8	9	10		
C	C	A	C		

PASSAGE-5

1	2	3	4	5	6
B	A	B	C	B	D
7	8	9	10	11	
B	C	D	D	B	

PASSAGE-6

1	2	3	4	5	6
C	A	B	C	B	D
7	8	9	10	11	
A	A	B	D	D	

PASSAGE-7

1	2	3	4	5	6
C	B	D	C	D	B
7	8	9	10	11	
D	B	A	A	C	

PASSAGE-8

1	2	3	4	5	6
D	A	B	C	D	C
7	8	9	10	11	12
A	B	A	B	C	D

PASSAGE-9

1	2	3	4	5	6
D	B	C	A	A	D
7	8	9	10	11	12
B	D	B	D	B	A
13	14				
D	C				

PASSAGE-10

1	2	3	4	5	6
B	C	B	A	C	C
7	8	9	10	11	12
C	D	D	D	A	D
13	14	15	16	17	
C	A	B	D	C	

❑❑❑